Brit Cult

an a-z of British pop culture

ANDREW CALCUTT

PRION

First published 2000 by
Prion Books Limited
Imperial Works, Perren Street
London NW5 3ED

Text copyright © 2000 Andrew Calcutt
Compilation and design copyright © 2000 Prion Books

ISBN 1-85375-321-1

A catalogue record of this book can be obtained from the British Library

Jacket design by Jamie Keenan

Printed by Kyodo, Singapore

Picture Acknowledgments

p.27, 113, 126 courtesy of British Film Institute, p.130 Vin Mag Archive Ltd, p.172, 197 courtesy
of British Film Institute, p.201 © Allsport/Stu Forester, p.204 courtesy of British Film Institute,
p.207 Kobal collection, p. 256, 269, 298, 345 courtesy of British Film Institute, p.365 ©
Redferns/S&G Press Agency, p.371 courtesy of Jonathan Cape/Nick Vaccaro, p.378 courtesy of
Chatto & Windus/Kate Simon, p. 387 courtesy of British Film Institute, p.426 © Redferns/Ebet
Roberts, p.441 Redferns/Michael Ochs Archive, p. 421 courtesy of British Film Institute.

CONTENTS

Introduction
Ab Fab
Acid jazz
The Adam & Joe Show
Keith Allen
Alternative comedy
Ambient
Martin Amis
Lindsay Anderson
The Angry Young Men
Art school
Asian sounds
The Avengers
David Bailey
JG Ballard
Iain Banks
Syd Barrett
John Barry
Basement Jaxx
The Beatles
Alan Bennett
Steven Berkoff
Jeffrey Bernard

George Best
Bhangra
Bigbeat
Tony Blair
Alan Bleasdale
Blur
Ozwald Boateng
Marc Bolan
James Bond
Leigh Bowery
David Bowie
Danny Boyle
Billy Bragg
Kenneth Branagh
Richard Branson
The Bristol sound
BritArt
Britpop
Neville Brody
Julie Burchill
Michael Caine
Camden Town
Naomi Campbell

Robert Carlyle
Carry On
Michael Clark
Alan Clarke
Julian Clary
Clement and LaFrenais
Clubs
Jarvis Cocker
Coldcut
The Colony Room
The Comic Strip
Terence Conran
Steve Coogan
Peter Cook
John Cooper Clarke
Julian Cope
Patrick Cox
Croft and Perry
Cult TV
Cult Crime TV
Culture Club
Ian Curtis
Richard Curtis

Elizabeth David
Dexy's Midnight Runners
Doctor Martens
The dole
Dressing down
Drum'n'bass
Ian Dury
E-type Jaguar
Ealing Films
Eco-warriors
Ecstasy
Edinburgh Festival
Ben Elton
Harry Enfield
Brian Eno
Chris Evans
The Face
The Fall
Festivals
Feuds Corner
Football
Ford Sierra Cosworth
Norman Foster
Stephen Frears
The Full Monty
John Galliano

Galton & Simpson
Gangster chic
Paul Gascoigne
Gilbert and George
Glam
Goodness Gracious Me Goth
Peter Greenaway
Germaine Greer
The Hacienda
Katharine Hamnett
Happy Mondays
David Hare
Tony Harrison
Lenny Henry
David Hockney
Jools Holland
Nick Hornby
Ted Hughes
Ibiza
Indie
Eddie Izzard
The Jam
Derek Jarman
Elton John
James Kelman
The Kinks

Kitchen sink
KLF
The Krays
Hanif Kureishi
Ladettes
Mike Leigh
Mark Leonard
Ken Livingstone
Ken Loach
Loaded
John Lydon
Colin MacInnes
Madchester
Manic Street Preachers
Patrick Marber
Alan McGee
Ewan McGregor
Malcolm McLaren
Alexander McQueen
George Melly
Spike Milligan
Martin Millar
The Mini
Mods
Monty Python
Morecambe and Wise

Chris Morris	Rastafarian	Rod Stewart
Morrissey	Rave	St Luke's
Kate Moss	Reeves & Mortimer	Stone Roses
New Age travellers	Bridget Riley	Suede
New Order	Bruce Robinson	The *Sun*
New Romantic	Rolling Stones	Chris Tarrant
Jeff Noon	Tim Roth	Peter Tatchell
Northern Soul	The Royal family	Julien Temple
Oasis	The Royle family	Terry-Thomas
Gary Oldman	Salman Rushdie	Mark Thomas
Old school ties	The Saatchis	Emma Thompson
Joe Orton	Satire	Two-Tone
Tony Parsons	Jon Savage	The underclass
Jeremy Paxman	Scooters	*Wallpaper*
John Peel	ScotLit	Weird TV
Reginald Perrin	Will Self	Fay Weldon
Pet Shop Boys	Peter Sellers	Irvine Welsh
Harold Pinter	Skinheads	Vivienne Westwood
Pirate radio	Slade	Marco Pierre White
Planet 24	The Small Faces	Paul Whitehouse
Dennis Potter	Paul Smith	Richard Whiteley
Powell & Pressburger	Soaps	The Who
Primal Scream	Soho	Robbie Williams
The Prisoner	Soul II Soul	Tony Wilson
Prodigy	Johnny Speight	Barbara Windsor
Progressive rock	Spice Girls	Jeanette Winterson
Queen	Dusty Springfield	Peter York

Introduction

British culture in flux

'What does British mean now? Is there even such a thing as British?' Malcolm McLaren, the man who created the Sex Pistols and made his name by trashing traditional British institutions, recently found cause to wonder whether the British tradition was still identifiable as such. His fellow iconoclast Irvine Welsh, 'poet laureate of the E generation', agreed that British identity was in 'terminal decline'. McLaren and Welsh were flagging up the end of British culture in the context of devolution and the alleged break-up of the Union. But in the summer of 1999, at the very moment when the Scottish and Welsh assemblies were holding their first debates, two national airlines raced to claim the Union Jack for their livery. Having previously abandoned it in favour of tail fins painted with African jackals and Chinese calligraphy, British Airways rebranded its rebranding programme by reintroducing the Union Jack, only hours before Virgin unveiled its own Union Jack logos. Despite reports of the death of British culture, the company strategists who opted to 'fly the flag' must have felt that 'British' is still an identifiable label – a label, furthermore, that they themselves wanted to be identified with.

    It's British culture, Jim, but not as we knew it. The ponderous, all-white monoculture beloved of Enoch Powell and Alf Garnett is no longer sustainable, even as myth. Powell (intellectual offspring of Birmingham's most famous Conservative, Joseph Chamberlain) and Garnett (fictional creation of Cockney comedy scriptwriter Johnny Speight) were mid-twentieth-century inheritors of a history of Britain which had been developed in the late nineteenth century to provide a sense of continuity in a world where the first industrialised nation was already coming under pressure from newly established competitors. The notion of 'the island race', protected from alien influence by 'the senior service' (the Royal Navy) suggested that Britain and her institutions were naturally separate and superior to the rest of the world. Even while maintaining a position of superiority, however, 'the maritime nation' took in as many messages as it sent out: in recent times the sea has been more a channel of two-way communication than a watery wall guaranteeing immunity from outside influence. Thus the British ruled India but absorbed and were themselves altered by aspects of Indian culture. The island race was never really isolated (in purdah), but always a mongrel nation, socially and culturally modified by successive waves of immigration from Romans to Romanies to refugees from Romania.

Previously, images of Britishness and its components were socially constructed but held to be natural (the wearing of the tartan, for example, probably has more to do with Sir Walter Scott than with the real lives of pre-modern Scottish Highlanders, but it became embedded in the national imagination as an essential part of an allegedly organic tradition). Nowadays the idea of a fixed, natural British identity (singular) has been replaced by a complex of complementary British identities (plural), together with an understanding that these identities are subject to constant change and, as a result, increasingly difficult to define.

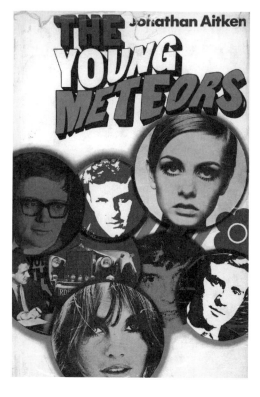

In an article entitled 'Real Britannia: what does it mean to be British?', the *Independent*'s Suzanne Moore noted that TS Eliot's list of essential British items (Derby Day, the Henley Regatta, Cowes, the dartboard, a Cup Final, beetroot in vinegar, boiled cabbage cut into sections, Gothic churches) would have to be heavily amended. 'But as what?', she asked, before hesitantly suggesting another list that might include 'the Notting Hill carnival, EastEnders, a lottery ticket, a themed pub, a take-away pizza cut into sections, a shopping centre of the kind from which James Bulger was abducted, a holiday in the sun, a chill and cook meal, a protester at Twyford Down up a tree?'

Moore's new list, and her own lack of certainty about it, shows how British culture is in flux. *Brit Cult* aims to distil this moving picture, to provide a necessarily static snapshot that nevertheless shows awareness of where we have come from and offers insights into where we are going.

Brit Cult consists of separate entries on more than 200 key players in current British culture. Each entry provides biographical details, analysis, observation and opinion. These are stand-alone essays on various individual items – people, products and phenomena; but, taken together, they add up to a composite picture of British culture as a whole. By deconstructing particular icons and identifying who or what they are, what they represent to us, and why we identify with them, *Brit Cult* builds up a broad reflection of identifiably British culture. While readily admitting that the list of entries is not absolutely definitive (one person's crucial icon is bound to be someone else's irrelevance, and *vice versa*), we hope that it is comprehensive enough to provide a definite picture of the current cultural stream and its antecedents.

Innovations (1): the coming of culture

British culture has never flowed so fast. Since 1997 we have lived through Cool Britannia, New Britain and the 'End of Britain?'. These labels came in and out of circulation so quickly that it is tempting to dismiss them as pure PR – admen's slogos for changes that are not really happening. But, though exaggerated, each of them represents real developments in the way we live now.

Initially welcomed as a signal of cultural change, Cool Britannia was later dismissed as a media opportunity manipulated by the incoming New Labour government. Having at first read great significance into the rebranding of Britain (from Rule to Cool, the-country-that-ruled-the-world to the-country-that's-cooler-than-the-rest), commentators soon rushed to declare that Tony Blair tippling with Noel Gallagher was as superficial as Harold Wilson's photocall with The Beatles – dressing up an old man's government in the guise of youth. But, unlike Blair, Wilson never played in a rock'n'roll band. In the 40s, the popular music of Wilson's youth was merely a soundtrack to the conduct of the Second World War and the establishment of the welfare state. By contrast, Tony and most of his cronies grew up inside pop music and its attendant attitudes. Pop culture was their formative experience, and their entry into government signifies a reformulation of British life. For the first time, the common currency of British politics is not ideology and economics

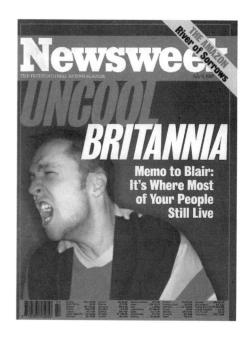

but lifestyle and emotion. The shared experience of culture is no longer the secondary element in what constitutes Britishness. With the collapse of Empire, the demise of British manufacturing and the end of ideology (no fascists to fight or commies to combat), Britain *is* British culture, no more and no less.

Despite its obvious shortcomings – people who declare themselves 'cool' necessarily aren't – as a summation of this new context, Cool Britannia was bang on target: it is the label that accurately reflected the coming of culture as the primary definition of what Britain is today. Of course British culture has always been a political football, but now – and only now – is it the only game in town.

In the first part of the twentieth century, images of enduring British culture were used to counterpose national continuity to the nerve-wracking changes wrought by economic developments and class conflict. Thus in 1924, during the period of social instability following the First World War, the Conservative prime minister Stanley Baldwin waxed lyrical about the unbroken and unbreakable tradition of 'the tinkle of the hammer on the anvil in the country smithy, the corncrake on a dewy morning, the sound of the scythe against the whetstone, the sight of a plough team coming over the hill'.

In films like *In Which We Serve* (1942), wartime propagandists offered images of a culture in which hierarchy (officers above ratings) and consensus (the war effort) were complementary rather than contradictory. By showing that he was acquainted with pop culture, Labour's Harold Wilson made a cursory attempt to reacquaint the younger generation with the world of post-war, consensus politics. Wilson and his Tory counterparts were succeeded by the anti-consensus politics of Margaret Thatcher, whose term of office was contemporaneous with the heyday of the 'heritage industry' and the revisiting of earlier forms of Imperial British culture. Thatcher's successor, John Major, borrowed from left-wing writer George Orwell in his back-to-basics evocation of British culture: 'long shadows on country grounds, warm beer, invincible green suburbs and old maids cycling to holy communion through the morning mist'. Blair, by contrast, offered *Britain: the young country* – the title of a promotional video produced by Spectrum Communications for the Commonwealth Conference of 1999.

Whereas Wilson's bit of business with The Beatles was mere back-up to the bigger project of 'the white heat of the technological revolution', in Blair's case British culture is the one and only project in a heavily depleted armoury. From being an occasional plaything of politicians, culture now holds sway over politics.

Innovations (2): New Britain?

Further developments in British culture were summed up in the notion of New Britain, coined by New Labour spin doctors in 1996 ('New Labour, New Britain') but brought into focus following the death of Princess Diana in September 1997. In the *Guardian*, Jonathan Freedland thought he saw a sea change in national character. 'In the New Dianised Britain,' Freedland claimed, 'hugs have replaced the stiff upper lip as the physical gesture of choice'. The New Britain would be 'less formal and deferential, more open and personal, more tolerant and optimistic, less macho and miserable, more diverse – less straight, more black – and less centralised'. On the same wavelength, Suzanne Moore, borrowing a phrase from Raymond Williams, described a new 'structure of feeling' and suggested that the reaction to Diana's death represented the 'replacing of the irrelevant old Establishment with the new'. By the time of the first anniversary of Diana's demise, however, many commentators had drawn back from the extravagance of their earlier prognoses, and some insisted that the 'mourning sickness' of September 1997 was just a moment of lost control, followed by the return of 'business as usual' Britain. But, as with the backlash against Cool Britannia, this over-reaction to the excesses associated with the New Britain label, loses sight of the deep-seated developments the label partially describes. A society in which even the army presents itself as a collection of post-Diana aid workers is by no means the same as the bullish nation that sought to regain a reputation for military prowess and geopolitical power through the Falklands War of 1982. The naked ladies of the Women's Institute (in 1999, members of the Rylstone and District Women's Institute reversed centuries of Protestant prudery by posing nude for a charity calendar) are another case in point.

Innovations (3): not the end of Britain

Of the triptych of labels, the 'End of Britain?' thesis is the most specious – but even this had some sort of basis in reality. In the spring of 1999, commentators pointed to the BBC's newly issued instruction booklet for journalists, *Within The Changing UK*, with its pluralist emphasis on 'the nations of England, Scotland and Wales' in preference to a singular Britain, and concluded, erroneously, that 'British' had been banned by its own broadcasters. Others noticed football supporters sporting the cross of St George, the exclusively English patron saint, and prophesied an English, as opposed to a British, revival in response to the particularism of Scottish and Welsh nationalism. But despite the best efforts of Simon Heffer, author of *Nor Shall My Sword: the reinvention of England*, and *Observer* columnist Andrew Marr ('the English are stumbling back into history'), the popular tide of Englishness is nowhere to be seen. The partial adoption of symbols like the cross of St George represents not a close identification with Englishness but the desire to disengage from the old-fashioned aspects of Britishness. It is motivated by the same factors that prompted Cool Britannia as an antidote to the dotage of Rule Britannia. In any case it is matched by an equally powerful nostalgia for traditional British symbols. The Union Jack, as we have seen, has not gone away; although nowadays it is more likely to connote the Who and the swinging 60s than Empire and the Battle of Omdurman (more I Was Lord Kitchener's Valet than Kitchener himself).

Continuities: history repeating

Despite the frantic pace of cultural development, British culture is characterised by continuity as well as change. Traditionally, there has been a stand-off between old and new (Rockers vs Mods, bitter vs lager, Laura Ashley vs Habitat), but more recently the two poles have been brought together in nostalgia for futures past. New products are frequently framed and legitimated in reference to their predecessors. In the compulsive snacking of 'history-lite' (historical artefacts with no context and little content), any decade is grist to the mill, but the 60s are the junk-food of choice. This is because the 60s are associated with innovation yet belong safely in the past. Thus Britpop was packaged as a rerun of the British Beat Boom of the 60s. The Blur vs Oasis feud was billed as a return to the days of when their respective record companies (EMI and Decca) put The Beatles head to head against the Rolling Stones. The cultural kudos of the 60s was confirmed in August 1999 when Channel 4 ran a season of programmes pointing out how much the 90s had borrowed from 'the summer of love'. Writing about the TV advert for the S-type Jaguar, Richard Williams observed how it was not alone in selling the new by evoking an illustrious predecessor: 'Film of the mid-60s car [the E-type] is intercut with footage of the new one, leaving no prospective purchaser in any doubt that the S-type incarnates the louche hedonism of a bygone age, much as – no, make that exactly as – *Lock, Stock and Two Smoking Barrels* updated the mood of *Get Carter.*'

These are just a few examples of retro-sampling: lifting from the past in order to give a lift to the present. It is a recurring feature of British culture today, which prompts Richard Williams to suggest that 'Britain is unable to put all its faith in the present and the future, but must rely on the crutch of the past.' On the face of it, this seems at odds with the celebration of innovation associated with Cool Britannia and the declaration of New Britain.

Can any national culture be simultaneously obsessed with the new and preoccupied with the old? In Britain today, this duality is not only possible; it may even be a necessary consequence of recent British history.

Recycling is one feature of British culture; embracing the rejected is another. Some of the highest rungs in the ladder (and there is a ladder, even though the distinctions between high and low culture are said to have been erased) are reserved for those who were once excluded from the canon. From film-makers such as The Archers and Derek Jarman, to pop/rock performers such as Jarvis Cocker and Blur, the experience of having once been panned by the critics serves as extra evidence of excellence. Many of those who qualify as quintessentially British today were previously vilified for being anti-British. This is partly a consequence of the British tradition of siding with the underdog; partly a result of retro-sampling – if a decade (the 70s are the classic instance) have been put down for long enough, their time is bound to come again soon; partly to do with the formation of a new order by rejection of the old (as in New Labour, New Britain) – hence the indiscriminate embrace of those whom the old order rejected; and partly to do with British disdain for success. In the days of the old British establishment, the trappings of success were regarded as 'bad form'. Nowadays, they are associated with the odious 80s and seen as politically incorrect. This aspect of British etiquette is still going strong, but by another name.

Neophilia and neophobia

The peculiar combination of fetishising the past and the future simultaneously arises from the British experience of the American century. Throughout the last hundred years, Britain has been engaged in a long and gradual process of decline, especially in relation to the United States. The British habit of searching for certainty in the past is widely understood as a response to the single, all-embracing fact that Britain will never again be the dominant power it once was. A much healthier response, you might think, is to explore what Britain could be in the future, particularly in the realm of culture. After 40 years of exploration, however, Britain seems even less certain of itself than ever before. Moreover, critics maintain that Britain's cultural probes are chiefly characterised by two negative aspects. The first is old-fashioned chauvinism transposed to a new arena, with royalties for recorded music replacing revenues from iron and steel in the league table of competing national economies. In this light, Britpop and Cool Britannia are interpreted as defensive declarations by a nation that still feels under pressure from American culture (the American-born journalist Cosmo Landesman holds that anti-Americanism has always been the defining element of British youth culture), and newly threatened by an increasingly global economy.

The other mainstay in the negative critique is that Britain's love affair with newness is not symptomatic of wholesale reconstruction, but more indicative of a cult of the new, in which near-mystical invocations of successive New Britains take the place of rational policy or progressive developments, and the short-lived, adrenaline rush of rebranding is a substitute for fundamental social improvement. The founding father of this approach is Christopher Booker, whose book *The Neophiliacs* (1969) claimed that 'neophilia' (love of the new) was a British disease rather than the sign of a healthy body politic. More recently, some critics have likened Cool Britannia in London in the 1990s to the cult of youth in Vienna in the 1890s (Vienna being the capital of the senile Austro-Hungarian Empire). If Booker and co are correct, then the continuing babble about New Britains may also be an attempt to escape the contemporary experience of national decline, just as much as the well-worn nostalgia for Old Britain. Through the discussion and evocation of British culture old and new, it seems that this country is both burrowing in the past and gnawing nervously at the future.

Britain is living in what the Chinese would call 'interesting times': never before has so much national self-interest been riding on British culture; and British culture has never been so interesting. *Brit Cult* details what is important in British culture, and documents the importance we ascribe to its various manifestations.

Many thanks are due to Andrew Goodfellow at Prion Books, an inspirational editor whose creative input to this book has been at least as considerable as my own. All errors, however, are entirely of my making.

Andrew Calcutt, 2000
East London

Absolutely Fabulous
Ladies of uncertain age

Written by Jennifer Saunders (**The Comic Strip**, *Girls on Top*, French and Saunders), *Absolutely Fabulous* follows the trials and tribulations of PR/fashion person Edina Monsoon (Saunders, in a role allegedly based on PR guru Lynne Franks), who is less mature than her teenage daughter Saffron and tends to regress with partner-in-crime Patsy (Joanna Lumley, radically reinventing herself), an ex-model who lives on champagne ('Bolly'), vodka ('Stolly') and cigarettes. Lumley's profile as a siren of the 70s – Purdy in *The New Avengers* – made her ideal to play Patsy. Probably the most successful sitcom of the 90s (1992–96: three series and a two-part special), *Ab Fab* was the first mainstream TV programme to look at the generation of fortysomethings who had refused to grow up – subsequently dubbed 'adultescents' and 'SWATs' (Still Waiting for Adulthood at Thirty-plus). Saunders took an affectionate swipe at medialand's schmoozeoisie, career women and their pretensions, and cocked a snook at the idea of British trendiness that anticipated Cool Britannia and the backlash against it. The show was so popular with the very people it ridiculed that they were queuing up to do cameos, often as themselves: Britt Ekland, **Naomi Campbell**, **Germaine Greer**. Roseanne Barr bought the rights to make a US version but called it all off when censors refused to allow her to get away with some of the things featured in the original. American audiences had to be content with the British version which, fortunately, they thought was truly fabulous – so much so that there are even two muppets on *Sesame Street* modelled on Edina and Patsy who run around saying 'Sweetie!' and 'Darling!'.

PARENTS Lynne Franks, *The Liver Birds*, *Take Three Girls*
CHILDREN media luvvies everywhere

Acid jazz
The rebirth of cool

'You gotta hear Blue Note to dig Def Jam' (1992): for US hip-hopper Gangstarr, this line was an endorsement of black heritage. The same goes for US3, who also delved into the Blue Note catalogue at around the same time (since the release of the anthology *Blue Beat Breaks Vol 1*, Blue Note now advertises itself as 'the world's most sampled label'). On the British side of the Atlantic, mixing cool jazz with funky dance beats was not so much an exercise in black consciousness raising, more of a return to **Mod**.

The inspiration for the Acid Jazz and Talkin' Loud labels came from a mixture of clubs such as Dingwalls (Sunday Afternoon) in Camden, the UK's young jazz scene (Courtney Pine, Steve Williamson, Cleveland Watkiss, Jazz Warriors) and a passion for the jazz funk experimentations of the early 70s by the likes of Donald

Byrd, Roy Ayers and Miles Davis. Acid jazz combined the fluidity of modern jazz improvisation with the open-ended flow of the E experience, and underpinned these rhythms with dance elements derived from **Northern Soul**, 70s rare groove and 80s jazz-funk all-niters. The result was a cohort of 'goatee devotees' who mixed and matched jazzmen's beards with the combat trousers and trainers associated with **rave** and hip-hop (these aspects were brought together by the Covent Garden designer label and shop, Duffer of St George). In musical terms, this sometimes translated into a modernist, organ-based sound (the James Taylor Quartet); more often than not it resulted in a Green-tinged psychedelic funk philosophy as espoused by Galliano, The Young Disciples and Jamiroquai.

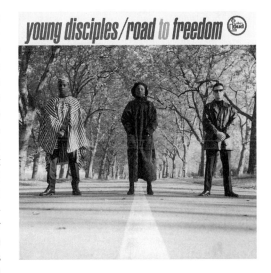

But the various elements in acid jazz never really gelled consistently: the 'acid' and the 'jazz' (of which there was not all that much) kept separating out. Maybe it was a case of young musicians looking for a template of 'cool' and finding that, although you can go back, the effect is never the same. The nebulous and increasingly eclectic definition that is the very charm of acid jazz has meant that the movement has never had the strong rallying cry of some other musical genres.

Acid jazz was regularly featured in *Straight No Chaser*, a magazine with broad parameters (its title was taken from a Thelonious Monk tune and it was subtitled 'the magazine of world jazz jive'). Founded in 1987 by Neil Spencer (former *NME* editor and anchorman of the Labour Party's 1987 general election roadshow, Red Wedge) and editor Paul Bradshaw (who wrote about reggae in the 70s before moving on to jazz dance and thence to acid jazz), it was designed by Ian Swift, who produced artwork for Talkin' Loud (see below) and, latterly, James Lavelle's Mo'Wax label.

The initial print run was a modest 1,000, and Bradshaw half expected the magazine to fail: 'there was the ironic side that if we only did one, that would be it, you know – straight, no chaser'. But there was a demand (limited yet sustainable) for a music magazine that was not cynical (Bradshaw: 'there's a strand of music writing in Britain that is really negative and cynical and I don't want anything to do with that') and yet passionately believed in a broad cultural mix encompassing dubmaster Lee 'Scratch' Perry and radical Nigerian patriarch

Fela Kuti alongside younger musicians such as **Talvin Singh**. If the acid jazz tag never developed into anything tangible, the continued minor success of *Straight No Chaser* proves that there is a place in British culture for the spacey, open-ended aesthetic which 'acid jazz' was meant to conjure up.

The Acid Jazz label was set up in 1987 with a policy of 'no house music'. Although co-founders Ed Piller and Gilles Peterson claimed their initiative was 'a tongue-in-cheek response to the Acid House explosion', they did harbour heartfelt preferences for pre-disco 70s funk, Philly, Motown and jazz – music that was cooler and more controlled than the gay abandon associated with house. The Mod in Piller and Peterson may have been at odds with the pagan primitivism of the emerging British rave scene.

Describing himself as 'a face of the late 70s', Piller edited a Mod fanzine, *Extraordinary Sensations*, and DJ'ed at Northern Soul all-niters. In the early 80s, after establishing his own reissue label, Re-Elect The President, he was employed by Stiff's David Robinson to run the Countdown imprint, where he signed The Prisoners (an early incarnation of the James Taylor Quartet). In 1994 he acquired the Blue Note club (formerly the jazz-orientated Bass Clef) in Hoxton Square, which hosted legendary club nights such as Talvin Singh's Anokha, **Goldie**'s Metalheadz and Andrew Weatherall's Blood Sugar. The Blue Note was an important factor in the gentrification of Hoxton (the new 'East Village' of London as its residents would have you believe), but it was forced to relocate because of local licensing problems.

Peterson was a programme presenter at BBC Radio London. He went on to work for Jazz FM, but was sacked in spring 1991 after expressing anti-Gulf War sentiments on air. By this time he had already parted company with Piller, setting up the Talkin' Loud label within the Polygram Group (1989). In the late 80s and early 90s he was promoter of The Fez, the jazz-dance club held weekly in Paddington's Great Western Hotel.

In its early days Acid Jazz released records by Galliano (the first Acid Jazz single was Galliano's *Fredrick Lies Still*, an almost tongue-in-cheek cover of Curtis Mayfield's *Freddie's Dead* from the film *Superfly*), the Brand New Heavies, Jamiroquai, the James Taylor Quartet, D-Influence and Corduroy. Although there is considerable variety in this roster, there is also a mellow groove running through all these acts, in keeping with the co-founders' roots in rare groove and their original intention of being a cool counterpoint to the all-out rush of house and rave. Since then the label has adopted 'a musical policy that allows anything', and diversified into various imprints: Focus (**indie**); All Seeing Eye (**drum'n'bass**); Acid Jazz Roots (reggae). In 1999, Piller was pleased to announce that two seminal 70s albums by the Watts Prophets would be re-released on his label.

PARENTS Blue Note, 70s jazz-funksters Roy Ayers and Donald Byrd
KEY WORKS *The Rebirth of Cool* and *Totally Wired* compilation series, The Young Disciples' *Road to Freedom*

Keith Allen
Lust for life

Comic, actor, writer, director Keith Allen has driven through life at a rate which makes Stirling Moss seem like Miss Marple.

Born in 1953, Llanelli, Wales. Attended one of the first comprehensive schools in the country. (Replacing the British educational system which divided pupils between grammar schools for the best 11-year-olds and secondary-modern schools for the rest, comprehensives were introduced by the Labour government which was elected in 1964.) Won scholarship to Brentwood Naval (father in Navy) College (previous luminaries: Douglas 'Hitch-hiker' Adams and Noel 'House Party' Edmonds). Expelled. Sent back to the same comprehensive. Expelled. Ran away. During the riotous summer of 1968 toured France with a group of communists. Roadie for soul bands Jimmy Jones and the Vagabonds and Geno Washington and the Ram Jam Band. Petty crime. Sent to detention centre and then borstal; taken on as a trainee by Community Service Volunteers, helped run a children's home in Bethnal Green and took the kids out thieving paving stones and cement to build a playground. Went to drama college ('for the women'). Played **football** for the University of Wales, apprenticed to Southampton FC. Came up to London. Squatted in a mansion in Eaton Square with two ballrooms. Worked as stage manager at the Institute of Contemporary Arts. Put on fringe theatre and punk bands (the Sex Pistols, Subway Sect, The

Nips featuring the young Shane McGowan). Sacked. Printed posters for The Clash. Joined radical troupe Crystal Theatre of the Saint. As a stagehand at a Max Bygraves concert, was so fed up with the performance he walked out on stage naked. Formed a band, the Atoms, which only played at talent contests. Attracted a following among QPR supporters who wrecked the pub when Allen's band did not win. The Atoms split after releasing one record, 'Max Bygraves Killed My Mother'. One of the first performers at the Comedy Store, which opened in 1979 and soon established itself as the home of subversive, non-showbiz humour. Too established for Allen's liking: he moved into even more dangerous territory. Billed as 'the punk comic' in the early 80s, would go out on stage with a row of glass bottles and refer to them as his ad libs if anyone got lippy. A regular attender of Glastonbury **festivals** (18 years in a row), in those days Allen sold beer from the back of his van at £1 a can and a free snort of amyl nitrate. On election night 1983 Allen appeared in his own TV show as a raving security guard – a role that prefigured the authoritarianism of the Thatcher years and the intense antagonisms of the decade. In 1984 he wrote and starred in *The Bullshitters*, a TV parody of the TV series *The Professionals*. Followed up in 1988 with *The Yob*, a parody of *The Fly* in which yuppie Patrick Church (Allen) turns into a football hooligan. Wrote the lyrics to the England World Cup/Italia 90 anthem, 'World In Motion', recorded by Mancunians **New Order**, which contains the Magritte-style line 'this is not a football song' – spoken by John Barnes. In 1998, as half of the duo Fat

The Adam and Joe Show British slackers

Adam Buxton and Joe Cornish are fans of American culture. Although they have sold a section of their TV show to Stateside channel VH-1, they are resigned to the fact that US TV won't buy the whole package because the in-jokes are too British to travel across the Atlantic.

Adam and Joe are media-savvy slackers. 'Professional skivers' at school, they borrowed the cameras that Adam's dad (who was, at that time the *Daily Telegraph*'s travel editor) was asked to try out, and 'used to practically live in the Trocadero' (a slightly tacky entertainment complex in London's Piccadilly). Joe went to film school in Bournemouth, Adam lasted a term at Warwick University but left because he did not like the nearby city of Coventry (people who were born there don't like it either). Joe later worked in the video section of Tower Records (also in Piccadilly) while Adam became a barman at an American theme bar in the Trocadero.

After Adam failed an audition for *The Word*, the two of them replied to an advert in the *NME* asking for someone to host a TV series compiled from viewers' own videos. They got the job with Takeover TV, and then took it over to such an extent that they were offered their own late-night/early-morning slot on Channel 4.

Now moved upwards and onwards from this graveyard slot, *The Adam and Joe Show* is a pick'n'mix combination of spoofs (such as the skit on BBC consumer programme *Watchdog*), recreations of classic films and fondly remembered TV shows using toys instead of actors, and ironic pseudo-investigations such as Vinyl Justice, in which Adam and Joe dress up as police officers and giggle at the record collections of pop personalities. It also features Adam's father, Nigel Buxton, in the role of Bad Dad – a plummy accented raconteur who both reproduces and gently mocks the image of the British gent. Their programme has been described both as 'post-youth TV' – that is, youth TV for people who are not so young – and as a 'telezine' (a fanzine on TV).

Adam and Joe's shows are entirely self-made: besides writing and acting, they rig the lighting, build the sets, operate the cameras and edit the film. They have brought the DIY tradition of classic British fanzines like *Sniffin' Glue* in to the zoo-TV age. A series of six 25-minute shows takes them about six months to complete. This is the other side of the slacker mentality: apart from lack of interest in traditional career paths and family values, slackers often show attention to detail that verges on the obsessional. Brit-slackers Adam and Joe are no exception.

PARENTS fanzines, Richard Linklater, Mark Perry, children's TV
CHILDREN webzines

Les (the other half being artist and fellow piss-artist **Damien Hirst**), released 'Vindaloo' – an alternative to the official England World Cup record.

Meanwhile, Allen had also made a name for himself as a presenter (on Channel 4's first yoof TV programme *Whatever You Want*), a video director – New Order's 'Ruined In A Day' (1993), **Blur**'s 'Country House' (1995) and a mini-film for UB40 – and as a straight actor appearing in **Stephen Frears**' harrowing drama *Walter* (broadcast on Channel 4's first night), Steven Soderbergh's *Kafka*, as Jonas in the BBC production of Charles Dickens' *Martin Chuzzlewit*, in TV crime series such as *Inspector Morse* and *Between The Lines*, in *Shallow Grave* – the film that, along with *Four Weddings and a Funeral*, prompted the British movie renaissance of the 90s, and as a bestial serial killer in the controversial film *Beyond Bedlam*. He has also appeared in an advert for Listerine mouthwash and, in 1999, starred in the television series *Jack of Hearts*.

Along the way Allen fathered five children from four different relationships (he supports them financially but does not live with any of them; his advice to his own children is 'don't waste time – have a great time') and acquired a reputation as a 'difficult' person to work with (he admits to having deliberately spoiled the performances of people he did not like), a king-size boozer (in 1985 he was jailed after smashing up the Zanzibar Club when refused service), a debauchee (aided by his propensity for stripping off in public) and drug-user (abetted by his appearance on Channel 4's infamous late-night chat show *After Dark* in a T-shirt bearing the slogan 'I love cocaine').

Allen's appetite for mind-altering substances is legendary. But he is equally well known for his integrity. He worked with the **Comic Strip** team but would not allow his output to become fully incorporated into that brand and almost certainly lost out as a result. His criticisms of alternative comedy and the Comedy Store for having sold out within a year (he has described his peers as 'the living dead') prompted *The Modern Review* to label him 'a doggedly right-on performer'. But Allen was not just attitudinising. He sincerely believes that 'you can do anything you like, anything, as long as you have some kind of integrity about yourself,' adding 'what defines you as an actor is … what you're doing when you're not on stage and not in front of the camera'. One of the defining aspects of Allen is his refusal to be tied down either to a single-track career or to a single relationship. In his mind's eye, his restless questing is one and the same thing as his integrity; and this is why he does not own a car or house and 'cannot trust' himself with a credit card or even a cheque book.

Allen is one of only ten people allowed credit at the Groucho Club in Soho. He eats and drinks there, running up a tab until money from one of his many gigs comes in, at which point he pays off his bills. Only Allen could make having a tab at Groucho's sound like the mark of a true, free spirit. Then again, his sense of integrity is widely admired. Asked why New Order had chosen to work with Allen, Peter Hook replied, 'because we love him'. Allen himself fondly remembers a group of football fans (he'd gone over to ask them for a light) who told him that he is the only one who speaks for them in the media.

Allen is a contrary customer (he would say 'cunt') who once admitted that, 'If the world was full of bank clerks I'd be a bank robber; if the world was full of bank robbers I'd be a bank clerk.' Among the targets of his belligerence are Britain and Britishness, yet the England football team is one of his passions. He once told the late Gavin Hills of *The Face* that 'there is a malaise in the country' which is 'full of stupid fucking people who save all their poxy money to buy shithole houses'. But, unwitting or not, there seems to be as much love in him for Britain as there is hate. Although he remembers being 'a fish out of water' at Brentwood Naval College, his lustful attitude to life would surely qualify him as one of Admiral Lord Nelson's 'hearties'. His restlessness is perhaps only an exaggerated version of the social mobility facilitated by the Labour-led British welfare state. Looking back at the British institution of borstal he remembers it as being 'fabulous'. He even has a good word for National Service, describing it as 'one big fucking joke' which nevertheless inspired a host of 'comic geniuses' which in turn were the inspiration for some of his own work. When he says it should be brought back, he's only half-joking. Like George Orwell, Allen is critical of Britain but Britishness is deeply embedded in him, which is why Hills' portrait of Allen in *The Face* was entitled 'A very British gentleman'.

Hills went on to describe Allen as neither a lion nor a pussycat but 'a British gent; a Taoist trouble-maker ... a unicorn, a wild horse of fantasy with a horn so strong it occasionally pricks the bubble of hypocrisy'. He also observed that, even if Keith Allen spends all his time playing the part of Keith Allen, it is still 'a class act'.

PARENTS Neal Cassady, Jackson Pollock, William Brown

Alternative comedy
There is no alternative

When London's Comedy Store (modelled on the Comedy Store in LA) opened below a Soho strip club in May 1979 (the same year Margaret Thatcher was elected prime minister), it served as base camp for a new generation of comics who used the stage as an instrument of social criticism. Performers such as compere and gongmeister Alexei Sayle, Ade Edmonson and Rik Mayall (the Dangerous Brothers), and Nigel Planer and Peter Richardson (the Outer Limits), followed a year later by **Ben Elton**, were anarchic, belligerent and anti-establishment. They were snipers shooting at the hierarchy of entertainment as well as the high-ups in politics and public life: 'Thatch' was Elton's prime target, but 'straight' comedians such as Max Bygraves, Bernard Manning and Bob Monkhouse were almost as high on the alternatives' hit-list. Also, by foregrounding women (French and Saunders, Jenny Eclair) as comics (not 'comediennes'), alternative comedy set out to be different from the 'patriarchy' of showbiz.

Alternative comedians (the term 'alternative cabaret' was coined by comedian and occasional club promoter Tony Allen) also represented a challenge to the Oxbridge Footlights domination of the upmarket end of British comedy broadcasting. Since the satire boom of the 60s, Oxbridge types had been allowed to say cheeky things about the social order, but this privilege had rarely been extended to comics from the lower echelons, or even from redbrick universities like Manchester (Elton, Edmondson).

By the mid-80s, the Comedy Store and its alumni had become models for a growing comedy scene (live venues mushroomed all over London and in other major cities), which was also making its presence felt on TV (*The Young Ones*, *Saturday Night Live*). Within the space of a few years, the 'alternative' brand of anti-racist, anti-sexist humour became ubiquitous – and increasingly predictable. Existing, mainstream comedians followed the trend and turned politically correct, so that, in the 90s, 'alternative' comedy came to be pretty much mainstream and the few incorrigibles such as Bernard Manning were transformed into the new outsiders.

Much has been made of the left-wing character of alternative comedy. It did represent a radicalisation of humour; but it was also in keeping with a decade in which most people grew increasingly sceptical about the possibility of large-scale social and political change. In an age when, as Thatcher said, 'there is no alternative', getting an audience to laugh at the apparently invincible Tories seemed as much as anyone could aim for.

The uniqueness of alternative comedy is also overstated. In the early 60s, **Peter Cook** and his associates opened a comedy club little more than a stone's throw from the site of the original Comedy Store. Mockingly entitled The Establishment, Cook's venue was a platform for anti-establishment mavericks such as American satirist Lenny Bruce (replayed by **Eddie Izzard** in a West End stage show nearly 40 years later).

By the late 80s the radical sentiments associated with alternative comedy were losing ground to an epidemic of irony – what *The Modern Review* referred to as 'irony in the soul' (a pun on the title of Jean-Paul's Sartre's philosophical novel *Iron in the Soul*). In this context the much-hated 'straight' comedians came to be rehabilitated as camp artefacts. The first ones to be interpreted in this way were camp to start with (Frankie Howerd and the **Carry On** team, for example). But, by the mid-90s, even smooth operators like Bob Monkhouse were getting the revisionist treatment, culminating in the TV conversation piece between Ben Elton (now the beneficiary of multi-million-pound publishing deals) and Monkhouse, which in effect ratified the peace treaty between the previously warring worlds of British comedy. This *entente cordiale* was further extended in 1999 when Oxford man Angus Deayton introduced a major TV documentary series on alternative comedy, now fully integrated with the Oxbridge set.

The Comedy Store is the Balliol of alternative comedy, and its graduates now occupy a dominant position on the British broadcasting scene. Apart from the founding fellows mentioned above, its alumni include: **Julian Clary**, Jack Dee, Lee Evans,

Harry Enfield, Harry Hill, Lee Hurst, Mark Lamarr, Paul Merton, Frank Skinner, Arthur Smith and **Mark Thomas**. Appearing on the Comedy Store stage is a rite of passage akin to the public school play and the Footlights revue.

PARENTS Bertolt Brecht, **Johnny Speight**, Vivian Stanshall, Lenny Bruce
READ ON *Didn't You Kill My Mother In Law?* by Rosie Wilmot and Peter Rosengard

Ambient
Unbeatable

'A classic definition of ambient is music with no beats at all; it's just floaty,' says guitarist and synthesiser player Steve Hillage (a veteran of Gong in the 70s, resurrected by rave in the 90s). By his definition, the first British ambient musicians would be the Third Ear Band, a quasi-medieval, acoustic, hippie troupe led by cellist Paul Buckmaster.

An electro-instrumental version of ambient was developed in the early 70s by Terry Riley (*Rainbow in Curved Air*) and **Brian Eno** (*Here Come The Warm Jets*). For Eno, 'ambient' meant plugging into the ambience of a particular location: the musician began by listening to an environment before reproducing it in music, producing sounds that would then enhance the environment – improve the ambience – of the consumer.

Ambient remained on the margins until the late 80s when it gained a new role as the 'floaty' musical counterpoint to the relentless beats of house and techno. In the 20-plus years between Eno's first ambient album and its take-up by the British club scene, the music lived on in Italy, Austria and southern Germany where, according to Mixmaster Morris (joint organiser of Telepathic Fish, the first London club devoted to ambient), 'people would trip out' while listening to the psychedelic sounds they preferred to call 'Cosmic music'. When ambient became an accessory to British **rave** culture at the end of the 80s, its definition was stretched. As clubs began to provide 'chill-out rooms' where the frenetic activity of dancing was mirrored by intense immobility, so any music that got played in these laid-back spaces came to be known as ambient.

The first chill-out space was the White Room (VIPs only) in Paul Oakenfold's acid house Land of Oz (a club night held at Heaven, underneath the arches at Charing Cross), where in 1989 DJ Dr Alex Paterson (ex-roadie for post-punks Killing Joke) started playing records by Eno, Pink Floyd and Mike Oldfield. With a recording engineer called Thrash, Paterson formed The Orb, whose track 'A Huge Ever Growing Pulsating Brain That Rules From The Centre Of The Ultraworld' became one of the early classics of ambient, alongside the **KLF**'s tongue-in-cheek *Chill Out* LP and *Selected Ambient Works 1985–92* by the Aphex Twin, aka Cornish misfit Richard James.

In its early 90s incarnation, ambient was produced using the same technology as house and often incorporated snatches of house beats. But it also absorbed many elements from a hippie-

Arcadian-Green tradition, while simultaneously sending them up with, for instance, jokey references to Pink Floyd albums. On the one hand ambient reflected a desire to become 'timeless' ('Our music doesn't reflect the times,' said Paterson, 'it ignores them'), but even this desire was of its time: in the early 90s Terence McKenna was getting a big hearing for his 'archaic revival', but mysticism was unpalatable unless it came with an ironic escape chute. In this context, ambient, with its cartoon version of Gaia, arose as a kind of balm for sceptical souls which also allowed the soul to retain its scepticism.

As the rave scene fragmented, the suffix 'ambient' was applied in turn to each new musical sub-genre. This simply means that, for each beat-driven form of music, there is a more laid-back version in which the beats are implicit rather than explicit. Big band singers used to perform ballads as well as 'up tempo' tunes; rock bands always broke up the boogie with a couple of slow numbers in their sets. Nowadays, producers don't say 'slow', they call it 'ambient', but the effect is much the same.

PARENTS Third Ear Band, Brian Eno, Terry Riley, John Cage, Debussy, church bells
READ ON *Ocean of Sound* by David Toop

Martin Amis
The transatlantic Englishman

Novelist **Will Self** has said that every British man under the the age of 45 wants to be Martin Amis (b. 1949). After gaining a first from Oxford, Amis had a hit with his first novel, *The Rachel Papers* (1973), published when he was 24. He has been in the limelight ever since, producing a wealth of fiction (*Success, Dead Babies, Other People, Money, London Fields, Time's Arrow, The Information, Night Train*) and developing a second career as a journalist and essayist ('writing with my left hand', as he calls it).

Amis' parents were divorced when he was 12. Following the death of his father, novelist Sir Kingsley Amis, in 1995, he divorced his first wife in 1996, married an American, Isabel Fonesca, and is known to have spent much more on getting his teeth done than on their wedding. He also divorced himself from literary agent Pat Kavanagh, wife of snooker chum and novelist Julian Barnes, to take up with the predatory Andrew Wylie who secured him a £500,000 advance from HarperCollins for a novel that did not sell well (*The Information*). Amis has since returned to his original publisher, Jonathan Cape, but even a stupendous advance cannot compensate for failing to win the Booker Prize: he came closest in 1989 with *London Fields* but two of the judges are thought to have been turned off by the allegedly misogynistic treatment of 'murderee' Nicola Six.

Amis used to write in Ladbroke Grove, the setting

for much of *London Fields*. He now lives and works in Primrose Hill; but the less funky, more clean-cut atmosphere of his new surroundings has yet to figure in his writing. A complaint against the Amis œuvre is that we are 'barely able to see the ointment for the flies'. He is accused of 'Hobbesian cynicism' and 'sterility', and criticised for being a proponent of 'satirical disgust' who lacks the 'redemptive mysticism' of his American friend and mentor Saul Bellow. In short, a tennis-playing toff with an addiction for unhealthy roll-ups and degraded low-life.

Amis speaks in a modern British upper-class accent, but his speech patterns are Americanised. The same dual identity figures in his writing: a character like John Self in *Money* (subtitle: 'a suicide note') is a very British failure, wallowing in self-doubt in a way that is truly un-American; but the phrasing and timing of his self-expression are as dependent on the Americanese of Hemingway and Hammett as they are on the traditional English language.

Some critics have accused Martin Amis of being too much his father's son. Kingsley Amis came to prominence in the mid-50s as the author of *Lucky Jim*, a comic novel about social change in a provincial British university. Although dubbed an 'AYM' (**Angry Young Man**) and thought of as a radical, he soon became known as a crusty, conservative misanthrope. Journalist and former *Independent* editor Andrew Marr lumps Amis Snr and Jnr together as 'the worst of England'.

Amis Jnr is a supreme stylist, prompting complaints that he puts style over content. In an essay on Amis entitled 'Venus Envy', Adam Mars-Jones complained that 'his very method is overkill'; others call it brilliance. Mars-Jones also suggested that Amis himself is always the real protagonist of his books. But the tendency to write about oneself is a staple of modern literary fiction, as Tom Wolfe noted in his clarion call for contemporary writers to regain their relevance by becoming reporters and realists in the manner of a Dickens or Zola.

Despite the many criticisms levelled against Amis, there is no getting away from the fact that his highly mannered evocations of low life have been hugely influential, while his combination of British satire with various transatlanticisms have helped to provide a new lease of life for the English novel.

PARENTS Kingsley Amis, Dashiel Hammett, Saul Bellow, Evelyn Waugh, Henry Fielding
CHILDREN Will Self

Lindsay Anderson
The revolt of the elites

Born in Bangalore, India in 1923 (the late afternoon of the British Raj), Lindsay Anderson went to Cheltenham college, where he befriended novelist-to-be Gavin Lambert, and from there to Oxford University. On coming down he started a cinema magazine, *Sequence*, with Lambert as his assistant, and was then offered the job of publications director at the British Film Institute (BFI). Anderson was also a founder member of Free Cinema, a short-lived group of young, radical film-makers who made documentaries about the changes in British society and London life (it folded in 1961). Following in the British documentary tradition founded by John Grierson (*Drifters*) and developed by visionaries such as Humphrey Jennings (*Timothy's Britain*), Free Cinema held that documentary films should be true to the real lives of working people and a reflection of their potential. For Anderson, Free Cinema was also a way of addressing the apathy and depoliticisation of Britain which he observed in response to Suez (delusions of imperial grandeur) and Hungary (Stalinist-dominated left fails to challenge the Soviet occupation of Budapest). In the autumn 1956 edition of the BFI magazine *Sight and Sound*, Anderson published his call to arms, 'Stand Up, Stand Up' ('Why are so many young voices resentful and defeatist rather than pugnacious and affirming?'); and in *Declaration*, an influential anthology published the following year, his politically committed contribution (along with that of Doris Lessing) stood out against the alienated existentialism and DIY spirituality of other participants such as Colin Wilson.

Anderson was a theatre director of note (Royal Court, National Theatre) who also dabbled in TV (five episodes of the *Robin Hood* series) and advertising. But he is best known for his feature films. These show the influence of the French New Wave; they also showcase Anderson's radical left politics: from David Storey's novel, *This Sporting Life* (1963), depicts a working-class hero disorientated

Malcolm McDowell in *If* (1968)

by the commercialism of professional Rugby League; *If* (1968) is a story of mutiny among gun-toting public schoolboys, with obvious references to Jean Vigo's *Zero de Conduite* (1933); *O Lucky Man!* (1972) shows the Common Man losing out to an avaricious, bureaucratised world; and *Britannia Hospital* (1981) is a parable of Britain's decay seen through the apocalyptic prism of a near-collapsing NHS.

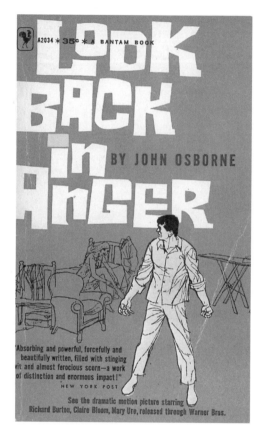

all regimented, hierarchical institutions. In *Britannia Hospital*, satirical allegory heavily out-weighs character and the film is poorer as a result.

In the mid-50s Anderson noted that, 'It's over ten years now since we [the junior officers] nailed a red flag to the roof of the mess ... to celebrate the glorious news from home (I mean, of course, the result of the 1945 election).' Like many of his generation, he rejected the ruling elite into which he was born, and believed that the 1945 Labour government would be a stepping stone to a socialist society. But Anderson's socialist Britain never materialised, and he spent most of his life frowning and grappling with the consumption-led, depoliticised country that did emerge from the post-war boom.

PARENTS John Grierson, Humphrey Jennings, François Truffaut, Jean Vigo
READ ON *Hon. Rebels* by Jessica Mitford; *The Revolt of the Elites* by Christopher Lasch

The Angry Young Men

In May 1956 the Royal Court Theatre staged a play by an unemployed 26-year-old actor called John Osborne, whose previous claim to fame was his brief appearance as the prefect Wingate in the tele-visation of Frank Richards' Billy Bunter stories. Stuck for a phrase with which to sum up the play, the Royal Court publicist told a journalist that it was written by 'a very angry young man'.

Three weeks later Gollancz published a book,

Throughout his career, Anderson walked a fine line between the real and the allegorical: *This Sporting Life* is a portrait of intimate relationships interspersed with Rugby League sequences which serve as a metaphor for the rat race that envelops them; *If* demonstrates the real energy of youth while the public school functions as an allegory for

Richard Burton's Jimmy Porter (1959)

*The Outside*r, by an unknown from Leicester called Colin Wilson. Its account of alienation and spiritual yearning caught the mood of the moment, and Wilson was hailed overnight as 'the coffee bar philosopher' and the British equivalent of the French existentialists.

On *Panorama* in July 1956, Malcolm Muggeridge asked John Osborne if he was an angry young man, and in the *Daily Mail* freelance journalist Daniel Farson hailed Osborne and Wilson, along with novelist Kingsley Amis and playwright Michael Hastings, as the writers of 'the post-war generation'. Two weeks later in the *Daily Express*, John Barber took the same quartet of writers and, noting their hostility to gentlemanly culture and comparing them, erroneously, to George Bernard Shaw, proclaimed them 'Angry Young Men'. The AYM was born.

Of the original quartet, Hastings failed to maintain his place and soon disappeared into obscurity. Wilson's second book (*Religion and the Rebel*, 1957) was as great a failure as his first was a spectacular success; after an unsavoury incident involving an angry father and a horsewhip, he left London and has lived in Cornwall ever since, writing a raft of books full of eccentricity and occasional insight. Osborne and Amis remained centre stage. Although neither of them liked being tagged as AYMs (Osborne liked it even less than Amis), their early work seems to merit the label.

'DON'T LET THE BASTARDS GRIND YOU DOWN'

From the grim working-class realists of the provinces to angry young middle-class men rejecting the traditions of their fore-fathers, here's a checklist of the gritty post-war fiction that attempted to map out a different Britain to that seen in the tra-ditional English novel (many of them providing ready material for the new British '**kitchen sink**' cinema of the 60s). Though many of these accounts (both the novels and their films) are now accused by some critics of being patronising and naive middle-class renditions of working-class or outsider culture, they are nevertheless still authentic documents from a time when Britain's class and social structure was going through a painful labour into modernity. While all their protagonists rail against society's binds, ultimately they are rebels without a cause and the novels largely view any hope of escape or improvement as an illusion.

Hurry On Down (1953) **John Wain** A picaresque tale of a roguish middle-class drop-out who exchanges the shackles of uni-versity life for the freedom of window cleaning, drug running and sleeping rough, Wain's first novel (published three years before the premiere of *Look Back in Anger*) has, posthumously, been viewed as the opening salvo from the soon to be Angry Young Men.

Lucky Jim (1954) **Kingsley Amis** Although eventually a grand old man of English literature, Amis' first novel was seen as a radical departure. Set in a provincial backwater university, its anti-hero, the disgruntled and dislikeable Jim Dixon, is a lec-turer on probation who runs amok with complete disregard for traditional deference and good manners. At the time, Somerset Maugham described Dixon in *The Sunday Times* as 'scum'.

Saturday Night and Sunday Morning (1958) **Alan Sillitoe** Though critically well received on publication, its five-million-plus sales didn't take off until the release of Karel Reisz's film two years later starring Albert Finney. Arthur Seaton, the angry young Nottingham factory worker with a lust for life, looks to sex and drink – without caring about the consequences – as a means of escape from the grim horizons of his working-class world. Finally, a reluctant marriage traps him in the com-munity he has raged against where everyone is 'dead from the neck up'.

Billy Liar (1959) **Keith Waterhouse** A kind of English take on Thurber's daydreaming Walter Mitty, the eponymous 'hero' com-ically explores the aspirations and frustrations of northern working-class youth. Ultimately its defeatist ending portrays escape from the daily grind in the provinces as illusory. The John Schlesinger film (1963) scripted by Waterhouse starred Tom Courtenay and Julie Christie.

The Loneliness of the Long Distance Runner (1959) **Alan Sillitoe** The story of a rebellious borstal boy and his private battle of wills against the governor. Smith (played in Tony Richardson's film version by Tom Courtenay) has been entered for a race by the governor like a 'prize racehorse' and decides he will very publicly lose it on purpose.

PAN books G505

THE LONELINESS OF THE LONG DISTANCE RUNNER

ALAN SILLITOE

author of
SATURDAY NIGHT AND
SUNDAY MORNING

Brilliant and
biting tales of
working class
life and morals

The title story
is now a Woodfall Film
presented by Bryanston
starring
MICHAEL REDGRAVE
and introducing
TOM COURTENAY

Absolute Beginners (1959) **Colin MacInnes** Rather than looking to the provinces or the working classes for the heroes of a New Britain, MacInnes looked to the first teenagers and the marginalised black communities of London. He saw in both a creative authenticity that refused to toe the line laid down by mainstream culture.

This Sporting Life (1960) **David Storey** Arthur Machin uses professional rugby as an escape from the daily grind and lack of money he would face working as a miner. But he soon realises that, despite the money and fame, he can never be more than a pawn of his club's owners. Memorably filmed by Lindsay Anderson in 1963.

A Kind of Loving (1960) **Stan Barstow** A tragi-comic vision of life and love in the north of England. Vic Brown, the son of a miner, is forced into an unhappy marriage when his girlfriend falls pregnant. The film version (John Schlesinger, 1962) starred Alan Bates.

Alfie (1963) **Bill Naughton** First a play and then a novel, *Alfie* comically follows the misogynistic sexual adventures of a Cockney Lothario and proto-lad who roams wild before being sobered to a certain maturity by near tragedy. The role shot Michael Caine to stardom in the 1966 film version.

A Kestrel for a Knave (1968) **Barry Hines** The story of Billy Casper (filmed in 1969 by Ken Loach as *Kes*), an unloved misfit from a north-east council estate who shelters from his grim present and lack of prospects in his relationship with a kestrel. Ultimately the novel portrays a bleak environment where trust and any hope of escape are punished.

Osborne's first play centres on the figure of Jimmy Porter, trumpet player, layabout and enemy-of-the-bourgeoisie – and that includes his wife (and colonel's daughter) Alison. Published two years earlier in 1954, Amis' first novel was *Lucky Jim*, a comic tale of young, provincial university lecturer Jim Dixon and his struggle to survive the dead weight of academic life. Both works brought a new kind of protagonist to the fore: the lower-middle-class male, educated enough to make an entrance into the bourgeois world but unwilling to do so.

When *Look Back in Anger* was televised during the Suez Crisis of autumn 1956 (Britain and France made an abortive invasion of Egypt but backed off when the USA failed to support them in their imperial adventure), Jimmy Porter's disillusionment with the British upper classes seemed entirely appropriate. But there was no recourse to the left either, given that the Soviet Union had just invaded Hungary and discredited communism in the eyes of many young westerners. Written before Hungary or Suez, Porter's declaration that 'there are no brave causes left' struck a chord with Britain's young when it was broadcast in October 1956.

The term 'angry young men' had come into circulation a decade or so earlier to describe politicised people who were angry with the social system operating in Britain. The distinctive aspect of Porter/Dixon's disaffection was its lack of political character (see Amis' 'The Labour Party and the Intellectuals', explaining why he couldn't bring himself to join even after Suez).

In the decades that followed, the mantle of the AYM was worn mainly by pop stars – from John Lennon to Johnny Rotten (**John Lydon**) and the Gallaghers (see **Oasis**). But in the mid-90s the tag was resurrected and applied to a new crop of writers. The *Observer* saw the 'return of the Angry Young Men' in the 'raw novels that are "better than books" to the **Britpop** generation'; the angriest man was **Irvine Welsh**, closely followed by Alan Warner (*Morvern Callar*) and John King (*Football Factory*). In *The Sunday Times*, however, Cosmo Landesman was sceptical. While recognising the fashion for being 'prolier than thou', he thought it was a contrived exercise in nostalgia: 'I suspect that, central to the appeal of the AYM, is the fact that, for many, he represents the defiant radicalism that has all but disappeared from political and intellectual debate.' The problem for today's AYMs, it would seem, is the lack of anything tangible to rebel against.

PARENTS The Beats, Orwell's Gordon Comstock
CHILDREN John Lennon, Irvine Welsh
READ ON *Success Stories – literature and the media in England* by Harry Ritchie

Art school
The dance has been going on forever

Described by sociologist and Mercury Music Prize judge Simon Frith as the place where young people could 'live out, however briefly, a fantasy of cultural freedom', for nearly half a century art schools have been the premier primer for Britain's pop culture.

BBC *Arena*'s Top 20 of twentieth-century British art and design

1 Glasgow School of Art – Charles Rennie Mackintosh
2 *Three Studies for Figures at the Base of a Crucifixion* – Francis Bacon
3 *Madonna and Child* – Henry Moore
4 *Angel of the North* – Antony Gormley
5 *Mr & Mrs Clark and Percy* – David Hockney
6 The Lloyd's Building – Richard Rogers
7 Sandham Memorial Chapel at Burghclere – Stanley Spencer
8 Concorde
9 *House* – Rachel Whiteread
10 London Underground Map – Harry Beck
11 *20/50* – Richard Wilson
12 *Crest* – Bridget Riley
13 Sleeve for *Sgt Pepper's Lonely Hearts Club Band* – Peter Blake and Jann Haworth
14 *Torso in Metal* – Jacob Epstein
15 Little Sparta sculpture garden – Ian Hamilton Finlay
16 The Mini – Sir Alec Issigonis
17 *Early One Morning* – Anthony Caro
18 De La Warr Pavilion – Erich Mendelsohn and Serge Chermayeff
19 *Pharmacy* – Damien Hirst
20 *Propped* – Jenny Saville

But it's a two-way street: as well as the legions of art students who have gone on to become pop personalities, since the setting up of the Americanophile Independent Group at the Institute of Contemporary Arts on the cusp of the 50s, many British artists and art school teachers have been in love with the idea of pop culture. Richard Hamilton's *Swinging London* (1967), a painting developed from a newspaper photo of Mick Jagger and art dealer Robert Fraser, handcuffed after a drugs bust, is a case in point.

In the 50s, art schools thrived on a diet of Bauhaus and The Beats, with trad jazz, duffle coats and CND thrown into the mix alongside American-style abstract expressionism. Trad jazz was soon replaced by r&b: those were the days when John Lennon, Paul McCartney and **The Beatles**' first bass player Stuart Sutcliffe attended the Liverpool art school in Hope Street, while future **Rolling Stones** Keith Richards and Brian Jones dabbled in art at colleges in Cheltenham and Dartford. Before being admitted to the Royal College of Art, singer and East End bloke **Ian Dury** went to art school in Walthamstow where one of his tutors was Peter Blake, who later painted the cover of The Beatles' *Sgt Pepper* album. In the 60s, painters such as **Bridget Riley** were labelled 'pop art', and the **Who**, featuring ex-art student Pete Townshend, were billed as 'the first pop art band' (the Who's destructive stage act was influenced by the idea of 'auto-destructive/auto-creative' art as taught to Townshend by Gustav Metzger, a refugee from Nazi Germany who became an art lecturer at Ealing College). Nicholas Ferguson, the designer of the seminal 60s pop show *Ready, Steady, Go!* with its Frank Stella-esque lines, was inspired by artist Derek Boshier who was in the same year as **David Hockney** at the Royal College of Art; Boshier, who was sometimes to be seen among the dancing crowd on *Ready, Steady, Go!*, later produced work for The Clash, who dressed like Jackson Pollock after a hard day's action painting and were managed by Situationist ex-art student Bernie Rhodes. **Queen**'s Freddie Mercury enrolled at Ealing the year after Townshend left. Meanwhile **Syd Barrett** studied art at Camberwell before going on the road with the Pink Floyd (the other band members were architecture students) and a light show put together by students from Hornsey College of Art (site of a student revolt in 1968). Formed by Viv Stanshall and Legs Larry Smith who were students at the Central School of Art, the Bonzo Dog Dooh Dah Band took their name from the Dada anti-art movement of the years following the First World War; the band also included Neil Innes (Royal College of Art) who wore a costume with John Constable's *Haywain* painted on it. South of the river, **Malcolm McLaren** was an art student at **Goldsmith's**. While studying fine art under Richard Hamilton at Newcastle University (1964–68), Bryan Ferry developed a taste for Americana which came to fruition in Roxy Music's debut single 'Virginia Plain'. The band's 'non-musician' **Brian Eno** has referred to art schools as 'the cradles of experimental music':

he attended two of them, in Ipswich and Winchester. The Specials' Jerry Dammers studied fine art at the Lanchester Polytechnic in Coventry where an animated cartoon about a boxing bout was the main item in his final degree show. Adam Ant (then known as Stuart Goddard) studied at Middlesex Polytechnic where he was taught by Allen Jones, whose paintings have been condemned by feminists as pornographic. He also attended a series of lectures on Erotic Arts given by Hockney's biographer Peter Webb. Two members of the Gang of Four studied Fine Art at Leeds University under left-wing artist Terry Atkinson and feminist critic Griselda Pollock. Down the road at Leeds Polytechnic ('a haven for oddballs and lunatics'), Marc Almond and David Ball were combining cabaret and expressionism in an experiment that became gay pop duo Soft Cell. Meanwhile, former Manchester art students Kevin Godley and Lol Creme had moved on from Wayne Fontana and the Mindbenders and from their own rock-pop-art band 10cc (first album: *Art for Art's Sake*, 1975) to become Britain's leading pop video makers of the 80s, directing influential promos for the likes of **Culture Club**, Duran Duran, Frankie Goes To Hollywood and Visage.

Colleges of art were originally sponsored by the Victorians as a means of systematising creativity, just as museums were sponsored in order to generalise the appreciation of excellence. By the 1960s there were 56 local art schools and 29 major art colleges in Britain, one third of them in the London area. In the 70s the art schools were rationalised, and the local institutions all but disappeared (some of them were closed, others were incorporated into polytechnics). Throughout this period, art schools and colleges served as places where middle- and working-class students could rub up against each other (they were in part designed for working-class youth who were gifted but not academic).

These establishments fostered a mentality that was rebellious without being overtly political or intellectual. Art school lecturers developed student-centred curricula (sometimes they were spurred on in this direction by student pressure, as in the case of Hornsey) in which experimentation and self-exploration were encouraged. As a result, art school students tended to be funkier and more streetwise than their university counterparts. In many respects they were more in tune with the burgeoning social and cultural mix which has since been suffused throughout Britain.

John Walker, author of a history of the connections between pop and art schools, provides a list of ex-art student pop stars which includes: David Allen (early Soft Machine, Gong), Marc Almond (Soft Cell), Adam Ant, Syd Barrett, Jeff Beck (The Yardbirds), **David Bowie**, Eric Burdon (The Animals), Jerry Dammers (The Specials), Ray Davies (**The Kinks**), Ian Dury, Brian Eno, Bryan Ferry, John Foxx (Ultravox), Kevin Godley (10cc), Mick Karn (Japan), John Lennon, Malcolm McLaren, Freddie Mercury, Jimmy Page (Led Zeppelin), Keith Richards, Sade, Viv Stanshall (Bonzo Dog Dooh Dah Band), Tommy Steele and Pete Townshend.

READ ON *Cross-Over* by John Walker

Asian sounds

It only started in 1997 but by the end of the decade it had used up a whole family of names: New Asian Cool, Asian Undergound, Asian Fusion, Eurasian Sound, Asian Nu Skool and Future Asian Beatz. Beneath the various labels the idea is the same: take dance rhythms and lay some Indian influences (classical, film music, **Bhangra**) on top. As a media phenomenon, it quickly caught on with the British music press and the trendiest London clubbers who made **Talvin Singh**'s Anokha and Nithin Sawhney's **Outcaste** the hottest nights of the 90s. But the disappointing sales of Singh's first solo album *OK* (1998) suggested that Asian Fusion has not yet come together with the British mass market.

Champions of Asian Fusion often talk about its potential appeal to a worldwide audience. But it has yet to overcome the divisions between British audiences for various types of Asian music. At the premier of Zindagi, a club night in **Camden** that opened in 1999, Tarsame Jamail of **Sub Dub** Records (aka Taz of Swami, aka Johnny Zee of Stereo Nation) talked about closing the gap between the Bhangra-based 'Brasians' (British Asians) in the north and the post-**rave**, I-never-listen-to-Bhangra London scene. Pervaiz Khan, who provides digital images for Zindagi, explained that there are musical differences even among Brasians with a preference for western music. In London, he said, they lean towards **drum'n'bass** and a style of music-making that relies on mixing and sampling, whereas in Birmingham they are rooted in soul and reggae, and they tend to write songs instead of producing

Cornershop Open for remixes

Hailing from Leicester, Cornershop pre-date the late 90s interest in Asian cool. Since their debut album *Hold On It Hurts*, they have combined pop with Punjabi influences. Their origins lie in the radical wing of the **indie** scene (in an early incarnation they were best known for burning pictures of **Morrissey**), but bandleader Tjinder Singh became more interested in dance music and DJ'ing. In 1997 Cornershop's 'Brimful of Asha' (a homage to Bollywood actress/singer Asha Bhosle) was remixed and speeded up by Norman Cook (Fatboy Slim), producer, DJ and former bass player in left-wing 80s band The Housemartins. In its original indie form, the single peaked at No 65; but the dance track reached No 1 and became the surprise hit of the year. Cornershop's 1997 album *When I Was Born For The 7th Time* was widely regarded as the soundtrack to the new diversity of British culture ('if UK multiculturalism has a sound, this is it' – *Select*), but Singh's refusal to produce a follow-up in the same vein, concentrating instead on a funky sideline called Clinton, may mean that he has missed his moment.

PARENTS Indo-jazz fusions, Bally Sagoo, Norman Cook, Family, Bollywood

tracks. Jamail's colleague Diamond Duggal introduced yet another distinction. He complained that the press had concentrated on the music of 'Bengali kids' from East London: 'fair play to them, but most Asians in Britain are Punjabi and they want something they can relate to'.

Then there are further differences between Brasians and their counterparts in the Indian subcontinent. On the one hand, British Asians are revered because the standing of the British pop scene is high. But whereas young Indians are relatively unconcerned about their identity and do not need confirmation of it from, say, snatches of Indian classical music, Brasians tend to be more hung up about who they are, and often look for confirmation of their Asian roots in the music they listen to. For them, there is pleasure in recognising a sample from their parents' favourite record. For young people in India, the same sample simply reproduces the status quo.

Since the days of Debussy, westerners have looked to the East in the hope of finding relief for their sense of alienation. In the late 90s, 40 years after their grandparents arrived in Britain with the aim of losing their traditional identity, third-generation British Asians are looking for the *je ne sais quoi* that cannot be found in western culture. Like their white counterparts, their Orientalism is now a response to what seems to be missing in the West.

The fact that today's young British Asians are concerned with questions of identity is something of an advance. It shows that, unlike previous generations, they do not have to be constantly focused on racist attacks and how to survive them. Furthermore, there has been a distinct blurring of the stereotypical roles (shopkeepers and junior civil servants) which, thanks to the British Empire, Indians and Pakistanis were traditionally associated with. For many Brasians, this is a period of greater social mobility which allows them to put some distance between themselves and the uncool image of Asians.

Only a few years ago, Asians were so unfashionable that Apache Indian had to be marketed as quasi-African-Caribbean. Although there are still plenty of young Asians who pretend to be American blacks ('wiggas', as Pervaiz Khan describes them; see the 'Bhangramuffins' on **Goodness Gracious Me**), being ostentatiously Asian is increasingly acceptable – especially at a time when Janet Jackson and Demi Moore wear bindis, and Prince and Madonna have been painted with mehndi henna tattoo patterns.

If there is more space today for Brasians to express themselves, there is also greater scope for talking at cross-purposes. Brasians want to be identifiably Asian, but they do not want to be confined to the cultural ghetto called 'exotic' – hence their ambition to be global as well as local. But for young whites in search of authenticity, the (to them) exotic aspect of Asian music is one of the main reasons for buying it. The relationship is not as black and white as it used to be, in the days when 'white negroes' bought music made by blacks because it was considered alien to the British way of life, and therefore served as an appropriate emblem through which to express their alienation from society. In Britain today the dividing lines between white and non-white are not as sharp; which means there are fewer prohibitions on the spread of Asian music; but, on the other hand, it is not invested with the illicit aspect traditionally ascribed to black music.

In today's British culture, brown cannot be the new black. At a time when no one is sure of their identity, neither black nor brown, nor white, are the colours they once were.

PARENTS: Bhangra, **bigbeat**, drum'n'bass

Talvin Singh
Asian overground

Born in Leytonstone, East London, in 1960 (parents part of the exodus from Uganda prompted by Idi Amin), studied in India under drumming master Pandit Lashman Singh, Talvin Singh is the star tabla player – prodigy of the drum rolls known as 'thtkthths' – who has produced Bjork, played for both Sun Ra ('the original underground artist') and Madonna, and supported first **Massive Attack** and then **David Bowie**, besides producing the groundbreaking compilation Soundz From The Asian Underground (1997), hosting the hot club night Anokha (Urdu for 'unique'; he killed it off when it got too commercial, in the hope of 'resisting the commodification of everything'), and releasing his own album OK (recorded in London, New York, Madras and Okinawaa).

As a youth Talvin Singh would go to Southall to buy classical Indian records: he learnt the tabla parts by playing them at a slower speed. But he showed little interest in **Bhangra**, the Anglo-Asian pop music of the time: 'I was never really into British Bhangra beat. I thought it combined the worst of Indian and western music.' He is similarly unimpressed by the idea of musical fusion. For Singh, creativity means more than juxtaposing various elements that do not really go together. 'I'm not fusing styles,' he insists, 'I'm finding a map and showing how they connect.' He is keen on **drum'n'bass** because it is open to further development and experimentation, like 'twenty-first century jazz'; and he likes the Internet and the prospect of selling his sounds online, especially in the Indian subcontinent where existing distribution systems are complicated and music piracy widespread.

When Singh won the Mercury Music Prize ahead of **Blur** and the **Manic Street Preachers** in 1999 it was the biggest thing to ever happen to Asian music in Britain.

Outcaste
Asian in-crowd

Before **Talvin Singh**'s Anokha there was Outcaste, the club night and label set up by music PR man Shabs Jobanputra (clients include Jamiroquai, the Fugees, Finley Quaye and Apache Indian). But it was not until the late 90s, partly as a result of the involvement of DJ Nitin Sawhney, that Outcaste became an 'in' name in the music press. Other Outcastes include Bombay-born virtuoso bass player Shrikanth Sriram (Sri), DJ and programming whizz Badmarsh (born in Yemen, grew up in Hackney) and tabla player Aref Durvesh. Early Outcaste releases usually featured vocals by Tina Grace, but more recently the label has also issued records fronted by other DJs and 'new breed' artists. Jobanputra promises to make 'great pop records that reflect our own culture and experiences. Yes, they may be universal experiences like love, but they're given an Asian perspective.'

In February 1998 Jobanputra signed a profit-share deal whereby the seminal American hip-hop label Tommy Boy would market and distribute Outcaste product throughout the USA and the rest of the world. When Tommy Boy first considered the Asian market they were considering a spoken-word record by Hollywood guru Deepak Chropra. But Brasian fusion now seems a better bet.

Sub Dub Records
Outsiders from Birmingham

Sub Dub is largely the creation of Birmingham-based brothers Simon and Diamond Duggal – songwriters, musicians and producers who have previously worked with Boyzone, Erasure, Maxi Priest and Janet Kaye. The Duggals were the original co-producers and songwriters for their cousin, Apache Indian, who left them behind when he signed a major record deal. Their relationship with

Stereo Nation has been more productive: singer Johnny Zee has joined Sub Dub's DJ collective Swami (under the name of Taz), and he also acts as A&R man for the label.

Whereas **Talvin Singh** does not want to be associated with **Bhangra**, Sub Dub seeks to bring Bhangra fans together with those who are coming to Asian Fusion from a background in **drum'n'bass**. Kam, the tabla player with Swami, says that, 'anyone from the progressive Asian scene who doesn't see the importance of Bhangra, is a fool'. As Midlanders, the Sub Dubbers are conscious of London's domination of Asian Fusion (at least in the eyes of the media), and their club night Zinadgi was set up as a self-conscious exercise in 'taking coals to Newcastle'. They hope that Birmingham will turn out to be 'the new Bristol'.

The Avengers
Exaggerated Englishness

'If Steed is not identifiably English – an English icon, in fact – then what is he?' Interviewed in the *Daily Telegraph*, actor Patrick McNee (a long-term resident of Palm Springs) was talking about his role as the bowler-hatted John Steed in *The Avengers*, the TV series which combined old-style *sang-froid* with the new sexuality of the 60s.

The role was created in 1960 by Canadian director Sydney Newman (he also invented *Dr Who*); but McNee brought to it his own experience as a

wartime naval officer, combined with memories of a commanding officer who used to come on deck wearing a carnation, recollections of his father – a racehorse trainer with a liking for brocade waistcoats – and echoes of a couple of early role models: Leslie Howard as the Scarlet Pimpernel and Ralph Richardson in *Q Planes*. The result was an elegant self-caricature of Britishness, and an engaging character who tackled his enemies with nothing more than umbrellas and raised eyebrows. Not that he always beat them; the fact that the ever-charming Steed was more often captive than captor seemed to indicate that the British were learning how to lose gracefully.

If Steed was a self-consciously exaggerated representation of the traditional aspects of Britishness, in the world of *The Avengers* the future was personified by the female leads: first the leather-clad Honor Blackman as Mrs Catherine Gale; followed by the catsuited Diana Rigg as Mrs Peel; and rounded off by another leather-lover, Linda Thorson as Ms Tara King. All powerful women hinting at psycho-sexual role reversal.

Of this trio, Rigg's Mrs Peel is generally regarded as the supreme specimen. In the *New Statesman* (1998), Maria Alvarez wrote that 'the Peel appeal lay in her maturity … the combination of athleticism, ruthlessness and cool intellect' reflected in her 'blue Lotus – feline and phallic, leather catsuit and kinky boots'; all of which made her 'often Steed's rescuer' rather than a mere damsel in distress.

Rigg (now Dame Diana), who came down from Leeds to London in the days when proper girls still

Diana Rigg as Emma Peel

wore girdles, and was nearly thrown out of the Royal Academy for Dramatic Arts (RADA) at the end of her first year, was the ideal standard-bearer for a changing Britain in which women would play more demanding roles.

It was during the Rigg–McNee partnership that *The Avengers* took off in the USA, becoming the first British TV series to be networked and nominated for the Emmys. In response, producer/writer Brian Clemens exaggerated *The Avengers'* Englishness

still further and took the series into the realm of high camp. This proved a difficult altitude to maintain, and the series was halted in 1969. In 1976 there was a revival: 26 episodes of *The New Avengers* were made featuring Joanna Lumley as Purdy.

A much more expensive revival came 22 years later, with the Time-Warner film version of *The Avengers* (US$36 million to produce, US$30 million to promote), starring British actor Ralph Fiennes and US actress Uma Thurman (and a small role for

Shaun Ryder of the **Happy Mondays**). But Fiennes in a bowler hat resembled Freddie 'parrot-face' Davies more than John Steed! Perhaps he could not 'do' a bowler hat like McNee because the traditional uniforms of the British gent are now museum pieces (worn only by out-of-favour Orangemen), whereas in McNee's 60s prime they were still widespread and entirely relevant. Repeats of the original TV series, from the days when traditional Britishness was extant rather than extinct, are shown frequently on satellite channels.

PARENTS Noël Coward, Raffles, Modesty Blaise
CHILDREN **Ozwald Boateng**, Jonathan Ross

David Bailey
'I feel unBrit, slightly foreign'

Although he has spent his professional life behind the camera, for many people David Bailey is the face of fashion. His career spans the lifetime of Modern Britain. *Models Close Up*, his documentary series about modelling, was first broadcast on Channel 4 in autumn 1998, more than 40 years after Jonathan Aitken in his book about 60s swingers, *The Young Meteors*, described Bailey as the author of the 'Debrett of the new aristocracy'.

Aitken was referring to Bailey's *Box of Pin-Ups* (1965), 'a book of photographic portraits featuring contemporary characters on the London scene, ranging from two well-known gangsters [**the Krays**,

with their pet snakes Gerrard and Nipper] to Lord Snowdon'. These black-and-white photos captured the 'ephemeral glamour' of a new Britain. The 'new aristocracy' also included two actors, eight pop stars, a pop artist, three more photographers, two graphic designers, two pop group managers, a film producer, three models, a hat maker, an advertising exec, two gangsters and a club manager – a list of job descriptions whose time had come. In Bailey's lens the people playing these roles were depicted as 'isolated, vulnerable, lost'. His *Box of Pin-Ups* is still the template for British style, hence the title of the Bailey retrospective at the Barbican in London in 1999: 'birth of the cool'.

Born in 1938, Bailey grew up near the Mile End Road in London's East End, within spitting distance of Terence Donovan and Brian Duffy, two more working-class boys who used photography as their springboard to success. Bailey first tried to be a trumpet player like Chet Baker ('if you were from the East End, there are only three things you could become – a boxer, a musician or a car thief'), but his horn was stolen and, inspired by Henri Cartier-Bresson, he bought a camera in 1957 while in Singapore doing National Service. After demob, he was apprenticed to leading fashion photographer John French, and shot to fame when the *Daily Express* started using him for a weekly fashion page. In 1960, aged 22, he moved from the *Daily Express* to *Vogue*, and to vicar's daughter Jean 'the Shrimp' Shrimpton, the model whom he made famous and then lived with for three years (his first wife cited Shrimpton in divorce proceedings) before leaving her for French actress Catherine Deneuve.

In the mid-60s Bailey was a one-man mythology, a legend of social mobility (East End boy done so good he owned a canary-yellow Rolls-Royce) and groovy, sexy (headline: 'David Bailey makes love daily') classlessness. **George Melly** described him as 'uneducated but sophisticated, elegant but a bit grubby'. Cecil Beaton observed that before Bailey 'a photographer had no social position at all … now photographers can go anywhere'. He was the epitome of the new Britain of the 60s, but 30 years later Bailey remarked that he has never really associated himself with British (capital 'B') culture: 'I hate that kind of comfortable, cosy Brit attitude. It makes me ill, actually. I feel unBrit, slightly foreign.'

Widely known as a connoisseur of models (during and after the photo shoot), he himself was said to be the model for the photographer played by David Hemmings in Michelangelo Antonioni's *Blow Up* (1966), a film about reality and illusion in Swinging London which is as stylish as it is unsettling. Bailey was considered so successful that by 1965 the *Daily Mirror* was asking whether down was the only way for him to go.

In 1967 Bailey told Aitken he was bored with fashion photography and wanted to move into film directing. But he continued to live in the fashion world (his third wife was model Marie Helvin). Until 1988 when he stopped taking fashion shots for magazines, Bailey worked consistently for all three editions of *Vogue* (American, British and Italian), while also making around 500 TV commercials, including the famous one for Olympus with the punchline 'Who do you think you are, David Bailey?'.

According to *Guardian* editor Eamon McCabe,

Bailey 'proved that British photographers were worthy of the title "world class". His inventive, powerful black-and-white style inspired a thousand imitators who have come nowhere close to achieving, as he has, a body of work that can hold its own against the best the Americans can put up, Avedon included.' For McCabe, the secret of Bailey's success is his responsiveness to the sitter: he always 'cared mainly about emotion in a photograph, the composition came second. … Fashion photography today is all to do with clothes, but when Bailey was flying, it was all to do with photography.' Perhaps it was also to do with giving a sense of the sitter as a fluid subject, a moving human being – even in the medium of still photography. As Bailey puts it: 'I'm interested in the person. Photography is secondary.'

Bailey is most famous for his high-contrast, black-and-whites – possibly influenced by French New Wave cinema. In his early days he often used a 35mm SLR camera, which facilitated the spontaneity and informality of his work, in contrast to the formal, fashion style of the 50s. Bailey rarely took pictures of models in motion, rather he put them in poses that looked dynamic as well as elegant. For the epochal *Box of Pin-Ups* he preferred a plain white backdrop, on the grounds that 'you've got nothing to interfere with the person'. The effect was incisive but non-judgmental – a new way of approaching the subject. Bailey claims to be 'styleless', but as the Barbican catalogue pointed out, 'crisp tonality and a direct, generally frontal viewpoint have remained dominant and consistent characteristics of his portraits, resulting in a readily identifiable signature style'.

Bailey the rogue reckons he has slept with 500 female models (not bad for a man who once described himself as a homosexual – at the time he was taking nude pics of Deneuve for *Playboy* and he wanted to make her relax). But he says he has not enjoyed the 'new lad' fad as symbolised by **Loaded**. He also says he has no time for acting up the idea of being working class – what he once described as 'that working-class **Gary Oldman** thing'. Looking back at his days as a young-man-about-town, Bailey recalled that 'we were working class, but very well mannered – bourgeois almost'.

Some critics have looked back at the swinging 60s and declared that it was all a myth. Jonathon Green, for example, claims that 'Looking back, one can see Swinging London as a mass delusion, a world of endlessly self-aggrandising mythologies. If there was novelty, it was not in the much acclaimed but barely supportable "classlessness", but in the creation of a massively successful media myth, a mix of pop sociology and the propagandist's chestnut: the big lie.' But myths, though they exaggerate, have to be based on a kernel of reality; and Bailey's photos demonstrate that there really was something unprecedented going on in 60s Britain.

PARENTS John French, Chet Baker, Jean-Luc Godard's *A Bout de Souffle* (1959)
READ ON *Box of Pin-Ups* (1965), *David Bailey's Rock'n'Roll Heroes* (1998), *Blow Up* (1966, directed by Michelangelo Antonioni)

JG Ballard
Reworking reality

James Graham Ballard (b. 1930) is the son of a British businessman who ran a textile firm in Shanghai. After the invasion of China by Japan, Ballard and his family were interned in a civilian prison camp for nearly three years – an experience that is central not only to his account of this period (*Empire of the Sun*, published in 1984 and subsequently filmed by Stephen Spielberg) but also to much of his other writing.

The Ballards moved back to England when they were released, and James went on to read medicine at Cambridge. He did not qualify as a doctor but turned to writing instead, encouraged by sci-fi and fantasy writer Michael Moorcock who edited the magazine *New Worlds* in which Ballard was published for the first time. In 1962 his first novel appeared, *The Drowned World*, which turned out to be the first part of a dystopian trilogy. For many years Ballard's work was labelled 'science fiction', even though his future worlds were really 'external equivalents of the inner world of the psyche'. He says that the Surrealists were his biggest influence because 'they anticipated by 50 years that external existence can be remade by the mind'.

Recalling the 60s at the launch of *The Kindness of Women* (the second instalment of his autobiography, 1991), Ballard said that 'they were an important catalyst for me: the death of Kennedy and the creation of the media landscape. Fiction became reality and reality became fiction. Polarities were reversed.' Ballard is convinced that we have come to live in the shadow of the media: 'In the world we inhabit now, reality is virtually a complete fiction. Now the image of a hamburger is more real than a real hamburger. What happened is that the media landscape wrapped itself around this planet and redefined reality as itself, and the amazing thing is we all went along with it.'

In the late 60s he began experimenting with sex and violence. Of *Crash*, which was first an exhibition at the Arts Lab (1969; subtitled 'The Atrocity Exhibition' – which prompted a song by Joy Division), then a book (1973) and subsequently (1997) a film by Canadian director David Cronenberg, he says: 'this was a serious undertaking to test whether violence and sexuality and technology were making a nightmare marriage. I had these huge cars [three wrecks bought in an East End scrapyard] lifted on to the ground floor and left there as sculpture. I threw a party, the demi-monde of the 60s was there, and I had a topless girl to interview guests on closed circuit TV.' This woman, who claimed she was nearly raped in the back of one of the cars, then wrote an article entitled 'Ballard crashes' for an underground magazine.

Ballard as he is now – professorial, paunchy and plummy voiced – seems alien to the counter-culture. But perhaps he was an outsider even in that community of outsiders. He lives the life of a recluse in Shepperton (a suburb on the west side of London, associated with film-making), in a house which he has inhabited for three decades. Alienated by his Britishness from the land where he was born (China), Ballard's years in China and in a Japanese prison camp also separate him from his British-born contemporaries. At times, Ballard seems hyper-British, at other times he really is a stranger in a strange land.

Comparing his recent work to his earlier books, Ballard says that, '*Empire of the Sun* is like a prequel but written after the rest of the stuff. My childhood fed itself into my fiction, but I postponed facing it fairly and squarely. The science fiction books are a disguised version of what I finally got around to writing in the past few years.' He may finally have faced his past, but he will always be an alien who, as he himself puts it, 'fell to earth in Shepperton 30 years ago'.

PARENTS Michael Moorcock, HG Wells, Salvador Dali, Daniel Boorstin's *The Image*
READ ON *High Rise*, *Crash*, *Empire of the Sun*

Iain Banks
Feersum Eemadjinayshun

Iain Banks (literary novelist) and Iain M Banks (sci-fi hack) are one and the same. Born (1954) in Dumfermline in the lowlands of Scotland, Banks went north to read English at Stirling University, where he dallied with rock music and wrote a number of songs that remained unperformed until 1998 when they featured in a 'rockumentary' radio presentation of his novel *Espedair Street* (1985).

Banks without the 'M' came to prominence with

The Wasp Factory (1984), a Gothic tale of a sexually ambiguous child, Frank, who murders other children and then retires to his 'factory' to torture animals. Published in the year that the Video Recordings Act became law, in the wake of a moral panic about screen violence, *The Wasp Factory* was accused of being the literary equivalent of a 'video nasty' – an unusual occurrence given that, in Britain, books are generally safe from moral outrage on the basis that they are read only by the educated middle classes and not by the allegedly incapable oiks who go to the cinema.

Throughout his other novels he has continued to unsettle readers with a mixture of cunning stylistic devices and cruel violence. *Walking On Glass* (1985) dealt with incest and prompted questions as to whether any of it was autobiographical. 'Being an only child I didn't have much opportunity for it,' Banks replied, 'and I didn't fancy my mother or father.' *The Crow Road* (1992), critically acclaimed when televised by BBC2, is also a family melodrama laced with murder. The plotline of *Complicity* (1993) centres on a serial murderer with a penchant for knocking off establishment figures. 'I'm against the death penalty,' Banks explained, 'but at the same time it was very cathartic for me to write about somebody doing all these horrible things to those, you know, bastards.'

The combination of high fantasy and low realism is a hallmark of Banks' writing. He has pointed out that *Espedair Street*, set in the 70s when he was a student but not conceived as a book until the mid-80s, 'is a fantasy novel set in reality, at a time when people who are young enough to still have outrageous fantasies get their hands on enough money to fulfil them'. *A Song Of Stone* (1997), described as 'a *Mad Max* set in the Scottish highlands', is a 'post-apocalyptic novel with incest as a subtext'.

The sci-fi output of Iain M Banks includes *Consider Phlebas* (1987), *The State of the Art* (1989) and *Against A Dark Background* (1993). In 1994 Banks produced *Feersum Endjinn*, phonetically written and probably the most extravagant sci-fi story of the decade, using overlapping multi-narratives to 'keep people interested'. *Inversions* (1998) tells two stories, one about a king's physician and the other focusing on a bodyguard who shields a regicide from drug-fuelled assassins. Reminiscent of the sword-and-sorcery genre, it sits oddly with the other work of Iain M Banks, described by the *NME* as 'poetic, humorous, baffling, terrifying, sexy' and recommended by the *Guardian* for its 'dazzled melding of cinematic adventure, technological creativity and left-wing politics'. While his style and subject matter keep him somewhat removed from the new wave of Scottish writers, he is similarly radical about his Scottishness: he was renowned for wearing a T-shirt saying 'Fuck the Tories'.

If Banks had been born a generation later, there would have been no need for him to publish under two (slightly) different names. Nowadays genre fiction and literary fiction are closely interwoven. Sticking to the traditional but outdated divide between high and low culture shows that Banks is something of an old stager; on the other hand, in his rejection of party politics in favour of personal polemic, he is entirely in sync with today's Britain.

PARENTS Artaud's Theatre of Cruelty,
William S Burroughs, Angela Carter, JG Ballard
READ ON *The Wasp Factory, Feersum Endjinn,
The Business*

Syd Barrett
The cult of casualty

Roger 'Syd' Barrett grew up in Cambridge alongside Roger Waters and the man who would eventually replace him in Pink Floyd, Dave Gilmour. By 1964 a 19-year-old Barrett was studying art at Camberwell College and sharing a flat with Waters, an architecture undergraduate at Regent Street Polytechnic. They messed around with rhythm and blues, although they were not very proficient at it, and formed a band, Pink Floyd, whose name was taken from two bluesmen (Pink Anderson and Floyd Council). They played their first gig towards the end of 1965.

Backed by a light show provided by students from Hornsey College of Art, Pink Floyd became the house band at multimedia events such as UFO and the Spontaneous Underground. This was the moment when, in partial imitation of the San Francisco scene, an acid-influenced swinging London switched on to flower power. Pop started to become rock, and the Floyd became the first of the third generation of musicians, superseding **The Beatles**' cohort in the same way that the latter had succeeded Elvis and Co. In this context, it did not

matter too much whether they were proficient blues imitators: right from the start, their music was primarily English art, even though they borrowed from West Coast luminaries such as Love's Arthur Lee.

The first Floyd single came out early in 1967, prefiguring the 'summer of love'. Written and sung by Barrett, 'Arnold Layne' featured a poppy organ and lyrics about a youth stealing women's clothes from washing lines. It was banned by the BBC. Their record company, EMI, also looked askance and insisted that the band must work with Norman Smith, a reliable engineer and producer then known as 'Normal' (under the name of 'Hurricane' Smith he had hits of his own in the mid-70s). In Abbey Road studios, where engineers wore white coats and behaved like scientists, Pink Floyd recorded their first album, *Piper At The Gates of Dawn* – the sound of British psychedelia. (Drummer Nick Mason later said that 'none of us were tripping except for Syd. We surfed on the psychedelic movement.')

Barrett wrote eight out of the eleven songs on *Piper*, only one on the second album, *Saucerful of Secrets*. The rest of the band were edging him out, but he himself was already out of it. Legend has it that Barrett had been taking LSD almost daily for more than three years. When Pink Floyd embarked on a package tour (headlined by Jimi Hendrix) early in 1968, Barrett went on stage in clothes from Granny Takes A Trip, playing a Fender Telecaster decorated with mirrors that reflected the light show, with a mixture of drugs and Brylcreem mashed up in his Hendrix-style perm. He never made it to the end of the tour.

In her autobiographical novel *Groupie*, Jenny Fabian described her relationship with Ben (Syd) from the Satin (Floyd). The chapter ends as follows: 'This time he made no bones about his problem, nor the effect it was having on him. He went on stage, silent, pale and sweaty again, and just sat on the floor with his guitar in his lap. He stayed like that for the whole set. It was the last time he played for the Satin, and the last time I saw him. He left for some Spanish monastery to find himself. The Satin got themselves a new lead guitarist. They were established and could do without Ben. For me, the Satin's magic went with him.'

Barrett's first recordings as a solo artist took place in May 1968 under the direction of Floyd manager Peter Jenner. But Barrett could not finish the job. A year later he went back into the studio, and *The Madcap Laughs* was released in January 1970 with a cover showing Barrett crouched in an empty room and an inside pic of a baby lost in the clouds. The most notable song was 'Terrapin', a pared-down, acoustic love song. The follow-up, simply entitled *Barrett*, was something of a throwaway.

After that, Barrett did the thing that has made him famous: he disappeared. In 1975 he made a surprise visit to his former colleagues in Pink Floyd: a much chubbier Barrett ('I've been eating a lot of pork chops') turned up during the recording of *Wish You Were Here*, prompting his old group to come up with 'Shine On You Crazy Diamond'. Then he went to ground again and has hardly been seen since. His brother-in-law Paul Breen told biographer Pete Anderson that Syd is a 'balding, rather heavyset figure who … doesn't really see anyone apart from his sister … but certainly gives the impression that he is comfortable and settled into his way of life'.

Barrett made a significant contribution to British pop. By taking the title of the Floyd's first album from a chapter of Kenneth Grahame's *Wind In The Willows*, he connected pop with pastoralism and conjured a whimsical idea of an acid-based Arcady (as discussed by Michael Bracewell in his book, *England is Mine*). His adopted name, Syd, connotes the English tradition associated with names like 'Sydney' and tampers with it – an instance of subverting but also restating Britishness which provides the pattern for much of recent British culture.

Finding a new take on Britishness made Barrett influential, but losing it has made him even more so. The notion of Barrett as an idiot savant, who has gone too far and seen too much to be able to do anything as trivial as pop music, continues to exercise the imagination of those who know there should be more to life than the record industry. The song by post-punk band the TV Personalities, 'I Know Where Syd Barrett Lives', won't be the last to be written about him.

PARENTS Aldous Huxley, Arthur Lee, William Blake, Samuel Taylor Coleridge
CHILDREN Robyn Hitchcock, Julian Cope
READ ON *Groupie* by Jenny Fabian; *Kaleidoscope Eyes* by Jim DeRogatis

John Barry
Sounds of the 60s

Yorkshireman John Barry has never been formally credited for the **James Bond** theme (he says he wrote it even though East Ender Monty Norman gets the royalties), but he is acknowledged as the composer for a host of Bond films as well as *The Ipcress File* (widely regarded as a strong influence on **Portishead**), *Born Free*, *Midnight Cowboy* and *The Persuaders!*.

Born in York in 1933 to a cinema owner and a classical musician, John Barry Prendergast was trained as a concert pianist but says he did not have the memory for solo concerts. Although he disliked performing, he formed a pop group (The John Barry Seven), orchestrated Adam Faith records, and was commissioned to write the score for the film *Beat Girl* when Faith was signed up as the star. Barry was a man of the swinging 60s (**Michael Caine** slept in his spare bedroom after being thrown out of his flat) who worked at a prolific rate (he wrote his first Bond score in less than five days and dashed off memorable tunes like the theme for BBC's *Juke Box Jury*), and enjoyed a pop star's lifestyle. Three decades later, his smooth but slightly melancholy music (often in a minor key) has brought him five Oscars, three Grammies, and countless accolades from younger musicians and celebrities. TV presenter Jonathan Ross thinks Barry 'is god'.

Shaken and Stirred, the 1998 compilation produced by David Arnold which reworked some of

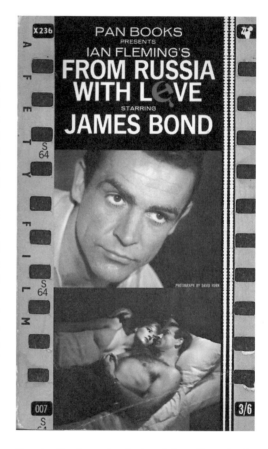

Barry's Bond music, featured Iggy Pop, **Jarvis Cocker**, Chrissie Hynde, Shara Nelson, Leftfield, LTJ Bukem and a collaboration between Shirley Bassey and the Propellerheads. Barry says he particularly likes Iggy Pop's version of *All The Time In The World* (originally sung by Louis Armstrong), and the Heads' bigbeat retake of the theme to *On

Basement Jaxx 'Two English white dweeby guys'

Basement Jaxx (vicar's son Felix Buxton and ex-squatter Simon Ratcliffe) used to be in awe of American house ('American music traditionally has a class to it that British music hasn't had ... when we started Masters At Work were like gods. ... We were two English white dweeby guys and the Americans were phoning us telling what we were doing was cool'). Their first EP as Basement Jaxx ('EP1', 1994) was a New York soundalike which they shrink-wrapped to make it look like an import. But between 1994 and the 1999 release of their debut album *Remedy* (on XL, the same label as Prodigy), they turned their backs on 'sleek American garage' and learnt to love their Englishness.

'There is a kind of crappiness in English music that's very appealing,' explains Ratcliffe, 'it's the punk thing in a way: "fuck off, in yer face, so what?" Americans don't really have that sense of ridiculousness. They're very uncomfortable with things that aren't cool.' Buxton agrees: 'We're not trying to make Chicago ghetto music. We enjoy being English. Punk, Carry On ... they're all part of it'. Instead of the Windy City, Ratcliffe waxes lyrical about Camberwell (the location of their studio) and its atmosphere: 'There's a charming ugliness to it that is very English and I think some of that has gone on to the album.'

Basement Jaxx divide dance music into two categories: 'shiny' (corporate, commercial) or 'raw' (authentic, underground), with a loud preference for the latter. Along with Aussie ironist Baz Lehrman (part-time record producer and director of *Strictly Ballroom*), their motto is 'a life lived in fear is a life half-lived'. Reacting against the apprehensive mood in Britain at the end of the 90s, Buxton and Ratcliffe developed a 'big-hearted' attitude that 'was not scared to be daft'.

Her Majesty's Secret Service. But now that lots of performers cite him as a seminal influence, and music journalists are liberally applying the label 'Barryesque' to the likes of Orbital and the Boo Radleys, he admits to being nonplussed: 'record companies keep sending me stuff that's supposed to sound like me but I can't hear it myself'.

Perhaps the aspect of Barry's work that makes so many recording artists want to sound like him (even if they don't) is his ability to combine a pop sensibility with lush orchestration derived from his clas-sical training. His music was the soundtrack to an instant when Britain was modern, cool and optimistic; internationally cosmopolitan (influenced by Hollywood and Europe) and yet distinctively British. What the likes of the Boo Radleys and Portishead take from his sound is not just great music but the nostalgia for the lost cool of 60s Britain.

PARENTS Bruckner, Dave Brubeck, **The Beatles**, Hollywood

CHILDREN Nineties easy listening and ambient

The Beatles

World changers

In *The Times* William Mann declared Lennon and McCartney 'the greatest songwriters since Schubert'. In *The Listener* Fritz Spiegl complained that The Beatles had done more damage to music than anyone else. On a more positive note, musicologist Peter Wicke agrees that their influence is unprecedented: 'Nothing has changed … the music culture of the twentieth century more fundamentally than the meteoric rise to fame of The Beatles.' So what makes The Beatles world-changers as well as best-sellers?

For former *NME* assistant editor Ian MacDonald, 'The Beatles' lives and works are perfect models of post-Christian "nowness".' They are the exemplars of what MacDonald calls the 'revolution in the head', whereby awareness and consciousness of the present moment ('simultaneity'), rather than ideas of material progress and historical advancement, have come to be the criteria through which we both evaluate, and indeed live, our lives. The new consciousness was ostensibly apolitical, but its effect has been to disrupt traditional politics and the accompanying social order. If MacDonald is right then The Beatles were playing the soundtrack to the end of history long before the Berlin Wall came down in 1989. Maybe their songs had the same effect as Joshua's trumpets on the walls of Jericho.

In January 1960 Liverpool art student Stuart Sutcliffe (bass) joined a three-piece skiffle group called the Quarrymen (John Lennon, Paul McCartney and George Harrison). Changing their name to The Beatles, then the Silver Beetles, they backed Larry Parnes' protégé Johnny Gentle before leaving for Hamburg where they played like human jukeboxes (seven nights a week, six hours a night at weekends) in various waterfront clubs. Out of hours they befriended the local existentialists ('exis') such as Astrid Kirchher (credited with persuading them to comb their DA hair forwards in the style of upper-class German schoolboys).

Sutcliffe stayed in Hamburg but was soon to die of a brain haemorrhage. The others struggled back to the UK, and gained a following in Liverpool before returning to Hamburg for another dockside stint. With Pete Best on drums, they were playing raucous rock'n'roll with a Scouse twist – raw but witty.

In 1961, record shop manager Brian Epstein came to hear The Beatles play a lunchtime set at the Cavern. In December he became their manager, and replaced their black leather jackets with ties and collarless suits (suits for urban sophistication; collarless for non-conformism). Epstein arranged an audition with Decca, who turned The Beatles down, perhaps because they did not think that a Liverpool group could capture a nationwide audience. Undeterred, Epstein made overtures to George Martin, a house producer at Parlophone (the EMI subsidiary previously associated with novelty records: Martin had been Spike Milligan's producer). He was impressed more by The Beatles' wit than their musicianship, and in May 1962 they were offered a contract. Their first single was 'Love

Me Do' (recorded in September and released the following month), written four years earlier by a 16-year-old McCartney playing truant from the Liverpool Institute. The Beatles also gained a new drummer in Ringo Starr.

With its simple chord structure and unpretentious harmonica, 'Love Me Do' located The Beatles within the (then) fashion for northern grit and neo-realism (see also films such as *Saturday Night, Sunday Morning* and *A Taste of Honey*). But the range of The Beatles' early work soon outstripped such narrow typecasting: chord sequences derived from Buddy Holly; harmonies taken from the Everly Brothers, with faint echoes of barbershop quartets; r&b influences translated into proto-metal tracks such as the cover of Berry Gordy's 'Money'; the rock'n'roll of 'I Saw Her Standing There'; and the distinctly English innovations in 'I Want To Hold Your Hand', probably the first British pop record to be imitated on the American side of the Atlantic.

In the UK, 'I Want To Hold Your Hand' was top of the hit parade for five weeks, prompting *The Times* to tag Lennon and McCartney as 'the outstanding English composers of 1963'. In the USA in February 1964, The Beatles' performance on the *Ed Sullivan Show* was broadcast to an audience of more than 70 million – a historic event credited with lifting the nation's gloom following the assassination of President Kennedy in November 1963. After 'I Want To Hold Your Hand' topped the US charts, each of The Beatles' previous issues was re-released in the States, and each one went to No 1. This was the height of 'Beatlemania'.

With the opening chord to ' A Hard Day's Night' (G eleventh suspended fourth), The Beatles announced their middle period, a three-year burst of intense creativity characterised by increasing sophistication and experimentation. Recorded in February 1964, the song became the title track for their first film, directed by Richard Lester. The move into films signalled the end of their days as a live band. Lennon wrote books (*In His Own Write, A Spaniard In The Works*), read poetry on TV and was feted at literary luncheons. In June 1965, during a break between filming and recording *Help!*, the Fab Four received MBEs from the Queen, prompting some medal-holders to send theirs back in disgust (The Beatles later returned the compliment). In March 1966, the *London Evening Standard* published an interview with Lennon in which he declared that The Beatles were 'bigger than Jesus'.

In August 1966 The Beatles released *Revolver*, an album that reflected the increasing diversity of their individual tastes. According to MacDonald, 'while Harrison was devoting himself to Indian music and McCartney to classical, Lennon had become interested in exploring his mental "inner space" with LSD'. Of the tracks on *Revolver*, 'Tomorrow Never Knows' is the clearest rendition of Lennon's psychedelic vision. With its heavily echoed drum pattern, tape loops, Mellotron, sitar and 'fade-out Goons-style piano', MacDonald describes it as 'a production which, in terms of textural innovation, is to pop what Berlioz's Symphonie Fantastique was to nineteenth-century orchestral music'.

Their touring days behind them, The Beatles needed something to hold them together. With

Richard Lester

Although born in Philadelphia, Richard Lester, director of The Beatles movies, qualifies as an honorary Brit. The wacky humour (he loved the Goons), trickery, rapid editing and kinetic exuberance of his classic period – *A Hard Day's Night* (1964), *Help!* and *The Knack and How to Get it* (1965) – influenced the whole visual style of the swinging 60s on film (and eventually came to influence the modern pop video). On film, everyone in pop tried to emulate the same irreverence and youthful energy – from the Dave Clarke Five to the Monkees and *Ready, Steady Go!* (and eventually even Austin Powers). To viewers who weren't around in the 60s, it seems like the whole era was shot at high speed in vertiginous zooming and spinning angles – a youthful Britain literally on the move.

McCartney as group liaison officer, they combined a wide variety of elements in the making of probably their most famous album, *Sergeant Pepper's Lonely Hearts Club Band* (1967). The first track to be recorded was 'When I'm 64', McCartney's affectionate tribute to music hall, George Formby and the lost lives of their parents' generation. It contrasts with 'A Day In The Life' (banned by the BBC on account of 'drug references'), Lennon's mystic but sardonic meditation on the self-induced death of socialite and counter-culturist Tara Browne (the sustained E major chord at the end of the track is sometimes referred to as the coda to The Beatles' most creative period). The two styles are brought together in the album's title song, described by MacDonald as 'a shrewd fusion of Edwardian variety orchestra and contemporary "heavy rock"'.

In June 1967, The Beatles' performance of 'All You Need Is Love' was the main attraction in the BBC's *One World* broadcast, watched by an estimated audience of 400 million. But the house band

to the new global village had already embarked on the road to self-destruction, a route that became more clearly signposted after the death (from an overdose of tranquillisers) of manager Brian Epstein at the end of August 1967. Lennon and McCartney were always competitors as well as collaborators, but now the gap between McCartney's narrative songs and Lennon's self-portraits was becoming unbridgeable. The establishment of Apple Corps (with its offices in Savile Row) and the launch of the Apple boutique in Swinging London's Baker Street were displays of unity, but the fall-out was intensified when Lennon found a new partner in Japanese concept artist Yoko Ono.

In January 1969 The Beatles gave a concert on the roof of Apple HQ in London, but this short event could not compensate for the long and winding rows and recriminations which occurred during the recording of *Let It Be* (1969/70). Tensions were exacerbated in February 1969 when Lennon, Harrison and Starr asked hard-headed businessman Allen Klein to rescue their financial affairs, while McCartney appointed his future father-in-law John Eastman. The hippieish hopes that had accompanied the launch of Apple (designs by Dutch artists, The Fool; electronic sounds by 'Magic Alex'; the Apple Foundation for the Arts) foundered when the boutique became a shoplifters' paradise. Musically The Beatles resorted to back-to-basics ('Lady Madonna'; 'Back In The USSR'; 'Get Back') and pastiche ('Obla-di, Obla-da'; 'Rocky Racoon'). 'Come Together' topped the US charts for one week towards the end of 1969 (in the UK it stalled at No 4), but by the beginning of 1970 both Lennon and McCartney were recording under separate names. On 10 April, McCartney announced that The Beatles were a thing of the past.

Three decades later (ten years longer than the original life of the band), they are still with us. Not just because of artificial attempts to prolong their existence (such as additions by the other three to the late John Lennon's vocal track 'Free As A Bird', released as a single in 1995), but because their influence continues to pervade British, and indeed global, culture.

The Penguin Encyclopedia of Popular Music holds that The Beatles 'invented nothing'. Instead they 'combined Tin Pan Alley chord patterns, a rhythm and blues framework and folk harmonies; later they experimented with electronics and sound collage, which Cage and Stockhausen had done before them. ... The Beatles were no more or less than a deeply loved pop group who made people feel good and whose original, essentially English tunes contained a large element of seaside post-card and music hall.'

The references to an English cultural tradition are pertinent, but this summation under-estimates the inventiveness and audacity it took to bring together such a variety of elements. Now that pick'n'mix and mix'n'match are central to our mode of existence, The Beatles' ability to integrate the incongruous may seem unexceptional. At the time it was unprecedented (high and low culture were worlds apart when they started out); and the very fact that it now appears ordinary means we are living through their legacy, eight days a week. In the *Q* magazine poll of the Top 100 pop stars of all time, John Lennon and Paul McCartney were voted No 1 and No 2 respectively; Ringo Starr and George Harrison came in at No 26 and No 36.

PARENTS classical, Indian, blues, folk, music hall
CHILDREN everybody else
READ ON *Revolution In The Head* by
Ian MacDonald

Alan Bennett
Fogeyman

Born in Leeds in 1934, playwright and comic performer Alan Bennett is only now old enough to be the fogey he has always pretended to be. From the early days of *Beyond The Fringe*, he has dealt with the decline of the 'Old Country' and the phoney words, authentically spoken, that Britons use both to describe and to hide from our degenerative national condition.

Educated at Leeds Modern School and Exeter College, Oxford, Bennett did his National Service at the Cambridge-based Joint Services College for Linguists. He might have become a don (junior lecturer in history, 1960–62), were it not for the success of *Beyond The Fringe*, the satirical review he co-wrote and in which he performed. The *Beyond The Fringe* sketch most frequently associated with Bennett is 'Aftermyth', a skit on the Blitz and its mythical role in post-war Britain. Writing has been Bennett's priority during the rest of his career, although he takes occasional acting roles and is a popular TV raconteur.

Forty Years On (1968) is a comic allegory of England which takes the form of a play-within-a-play. The headmaster of Albion School oversees the annual review performed by staff and students. The review includes parodic portraits of leading figures in national life and literature, such as TE Lawrence (of Arabia) and Virginia Woolf. Bennett suggests that we Brits use language as a comforter, but that it cannot protect us from the realities of decline.

In *Getting On* (1971), a fortysomething Labour MP craves order, in language as in life. 'Words fail me,' he finally admits. The central character of *Habeas Corpus* (1973) is a lecherous doctor living on the south coast. The play is an elegy to the decline of England in the form of a farce (the two elements are not always entirely compatible). *The Old Country* (1977), which prefigures the themes of the television play *An Englishman Abroad* (1983), is set in a house outside Moscow where a British defector, Hilary, has tried to recreate the country he left behind. His brother arrives with an invitation to return to a nation he would no longer recognise. Unsure whether he should stay or go, Hilary retreats into ironic wordplay, recognising all the time that this is no solution: 'Irony is inescapable. We're conceived in irony. We float in it from the womb. It's the amniotic fluid. It's the silver sea. It's the waters at their priestlike task washing away guilt and purpose and responsibility. Joking but not joking. Caring but not caring. Serious but not serious.' The British, Bennett suggests, have an inordinate need of irony that both protects and imprisons us.

In the television plays *Doris and Doreen* and *A Visit From Miss Prothero* (1978), and the stage play *Enoy* (1980), Bennett translates similar concerns into lower class territory. The past is disappearing, reclaimable only as spurious heritage. Faced with futility, people play with words, but, as in *Beyond The Fringe*, 'when we play language games, we do so rather in order to find out what game it is we are playing'.

There is added irony in the fact that the satire boom of the early 60s, which Bennett helped to set off, was meant to be Britain's ticket out of 'the stagnant society'. Perhaps Bennett always knew it would not work. When *Beyond The Fringe* went on tour to the USA, he wore the same modernist suits as the others in the team. But while the rest of London went **Mod** in the mid-60s, Bennett started to dress and talk in as old-fashioned a manner as his fictional characters. He is both public chronicler and personal witness to the persistent promise and recurring failure of Young Britain.

In 1987 Bennett wrote *Talking Heads*, a series of six monologues for TV. Well observed, much praised and oft repeated, these pieces are redolent with melancholy and loneliness. Unlike Bennett's more analytical work, they also tend towards the sentimental. In recent years he has narrated Kenneth Grahame's *Wind in the Willows* (the classic piece of early twentieth-century English Arcadia) on Radio 4 and adapted it for the National Theatre. He also wrote the script for the award-winning film *The Madness of King George*, a tragicomic account of George III's alienation from the machinations of his court (the lead role played by Nigel Hawthorne of *Yes, Minister*).

PARENTS EM Forster, JB Priestley, Robert Graves, Alistair Sim
CHILDREN Russell Harty, Morrissey, **Jarvis Cocker**
READ ON *Writing Home* by Alan Bennett

Steven Berkoff
The Euro Cockney

As an actor-manager, writer and director, Steven Berkoff has staged a lifelong one-man show against the conservative and insular tendencies within British theatre. He is, however, probably better known as Hollywood's idea of British villainy – a handsomely paid gig that subsidises his experimental work.

Born in Aldgate, London E1, within earshot of Petticoat Lane street market, young Berkoff went swimming in the Thames near Tower Bridge while his father made zoot suits at £12 a time for a mainly black clientele. Recalling his Jewish home life in comparison to that of his English contemporaries, Berkoff wrote that 'our heritage was rather more continental. It was talk, talk and more talk that governed our lives.'

As a youth he frequented Mecca dance halls and other dens of iniquity such as the Stamford Hill Boys' Club. At 15 he was sentenced to three months in borstal (youth prison) for stealing a bicycle. Having an ulcer saved him from National Service. He became a salesman for Sanderson's (furnishings) and then sold suits for John Michael at his boutique in the King's Road, Chelsea. In 1958 Berkoff enrolled at the Webber-Douglas Academy of Dramatic Art, returning there to teach in 1967. For many years he soldiered on as an actor in provincial repertory theatres (Coventry, Liverpool, Nottingham), his career briefly illuminated by minor film roles (*A Clockwork Orange*, 1971; *Barry Lyndon*, 1975; *Joseph Andrews*, 1977) and working with Joan Littlewood at her Stratford East theatre (he was so nervous on the first night of Edward Albee's *Zoo Story* he took a large dose of librium). Berkoff has described this period as his 'years in purgatory': he did not find his metier until he started writing and directing himself.

Based on his experience as an East End boy but drawing on dramatic and literary traditions that encompass Europe (Greek tragedy, Antonin Artaud's Theatre of Cruelty), England

(Shakespeare) and America (counter-cultural experiments like Julian Beck's Living Theater), Berkoff wrote and directed a series of plays (*East*, 1977; *West*, 1980; *Greek*, 1980; *Decadence*, 1981) which combine blank verse with Cockney slang. He also acquired a reputation for dramatising and radically reworking the texts of other authors (Kafka's *Metamorphosis*, Poe's *The Fall of the House of Usher*, Wilde's *Salome*). His productions rely heavily on ensemble work, which Berkoff says 'is a tricky concept for the Brits, since it really comes from countries where people like and love each other'.

Berkoff is a sworn enemy of tight-arsed Britishness, always ill at ease with the traditional British theatre. He did not identify with the **Angry Young Men** of the 50s: in his memoirs he says he felt closer to Josef K than Jimmy Porter. Nor did he get on with left-wingers from the Royal Court Theatre in upmarket Sloane Square. Instead he has carved out an Artaudian ('since I started with Artaud I have never flirted with anyone else'), visceral form of theatre in which even the words (musical as well as meaningful) have a physical impact. Berkoff applies these techniques to political issues as well as personal concerns. Written in blank verse, *Sink The Belgrano!* (1986) offers a George Grosz-style depiction of Thatcher (Maggot). *Decadence* (1981) was a theatrical assault on Britain's ruling class, and comic monologues (complete with sick-eating British bulldog) such as *Harry's Christmas* (1986) are equally vehement.

Berkoff's creative independence has been financially underwritten by a series of profitable film roles. In *McVicar* (1978), the film about reformed murderer John McVicar (played by Roger Daltrey), he based his character on real-life East End gangster Charlie Richardson. Other 'heavy' roles include General Orloff in the **Bond** film *Octopussy* (1980) and assorted British bad guys in various big-budget movies such as *Beverley Hills Cop* (1984) and *Rambo: First Blood, Part II* (1985). Berkoff's Hollywood villainy is what gets him recognised by London taxi drivers. Given the distance he keeps from British traditions, it is ironic that Hollywood regards him as the epitome of Britishness, and that this is what bankrolls his anti-British theatre.

There are those who think that Berkoff's drama is overdone. *Time* magazine once described his work as 'the theatre of too much'. Reviewing his 1998 one-man show *Shakespeare's Villains* (billed as 'a masterclass in evil'), the *Observer*'s Susannah Clapp reported that 'he creates a hologram of himself – a vision of Berkoff that comes between the audience and the part he performs'. Also in 1998, Berkoff entered into a highly public argument with Neil Norman of the *London Evening Standard*. Norman described Berkoff's criticisms of British theatre as 'a rant too far'. In reply, Berkoff reiterated his complaint that theatre 'has become a little musty … the theatre is not putting out enough voltage in performance or acting power'. His own performances are always highly charged.

PARENTS George Grosz, Antonin Artaud, Oscar Wilde
CHILDREN **Keith Allen**, Alexei Sayle
READ ON *Free Association* by Steven Berkoff

Jeffrey Bernard

Britain is unwell

Born in 1932, Jeffrey Bernard was not widely known until late middle age. In 1970 he began writing a column for *The Sporting Life*: 'the punters identified with it because I took the piss out of racing people. They're terribly self-important.' He was sacked after a number of incidents including throwing up on the Queen Mother's feet at Ascot and whipping out his penis in front of the editor and saying 'beat that!'. In 1978 he began writing his politically incorrect Low Life column in the right-of-centre magazine *The Spectator* (he was originally given the TV column but refused to watch TV). Like old man Steptoe given a column, he ranted about his problems (drink: too little, too much, his pancreas, the taxman, his ex-wives) and railed against the steady decline in the British way of life (favourite targets included feminists, fast food and **football** hooligans), bemoaning the relentless encroachment of political correctness on all that was of worth. Yet somehow through all his mean invective he still managed to cut a charming and sympathetic figure.

John Osborne called him the 'Tony Hancock of journalism' while the *Mirror* described his column as 'a suicide note in weekly instalments'. His former editor Alexander Chancellor described him as 'a nightmare to work with. He used to ring me at three in the morning and shout: "You fucking cunt, I hate you".' He was sometimes so drunk or ill from the effects of drink, or both, that he could not deliver

> 'I was a prince when I first came to Soho aged 15, got kissed and was turned into a toad. It takes all my muscle to refrain from croaking now. But if you think it is a wonderful life propping up bars surrounded by people who used to be something or who were never going to be anything, plus listening to Norman's mum telling you how her grandfather opened the first umbrella shop in Gower Street in 1867 and on top of that backing horses like Framlington Court which came in 19th, then you are the only woman in the world not in touch with reality.'
>
> *Low Life* by Jeffrey Bernard

his column in time. In which case the editor would put in a line: 'Jeffrey Bernard is unwell'. This line was picked up and used by Keith Waterhouse as the title of a stage play about Bernard and his wasted life as a drinker and womaniser in bohemian Soho. Played by Peter O'Toole, another larger-than-life personality whose creative talents and talent for boozing are inextricably linked, the stage role brought a new level of notoriety to the real Bernard. On stage and in reality, the decayed ('My face now reminds me of a crumpled shroud … tough tit') yet intelligently stoical figure of Jeffrey Bernard seemed to reflect the experience of Britain's decline, symbolising the loss of power on the part of a country that knows it is losing it. Bernard seemed to reap a perverse pleasure from his slow decline and was most comfortable when on the ropes. He talked

Jeffrey Bernard

about 'the agony of victory and the thrill of defeat'. Equally British was his ability to go down with a sense of humour – 'like a man making jokes being carried away from a bad accident'.

Bernard himself once said: 'I'm quite good on the subject of loss.' He could have been referring to his leg (amputated as a result of complications arising from his alcohol intake), his wives, or his whole life which seemed to have slipped away while he had one more for the road. Towards the end, he even lost interest in drinking, saying 'I've become almost bored with drinking, which is a strange thing for an addict to say about his addiction.'

Bernard may have become preoccupied with being inside pubs because as a child he was often left outside in his pram by his parents. By the time he finished school he was a chain smoker (Player's) obsessed with Hollywood film star Veronica Lake. In 1946 he visited Soho for the first time and it was said that 'from that point on he never looked forward'. Bernard later said that he only started drinking in Soho pubs and clubs 'because I was desperate to be grown up'. But drinking (preferably vodka) and Soho soon became the north and south poles of his adult life.

His many drinking buddies included novelist and

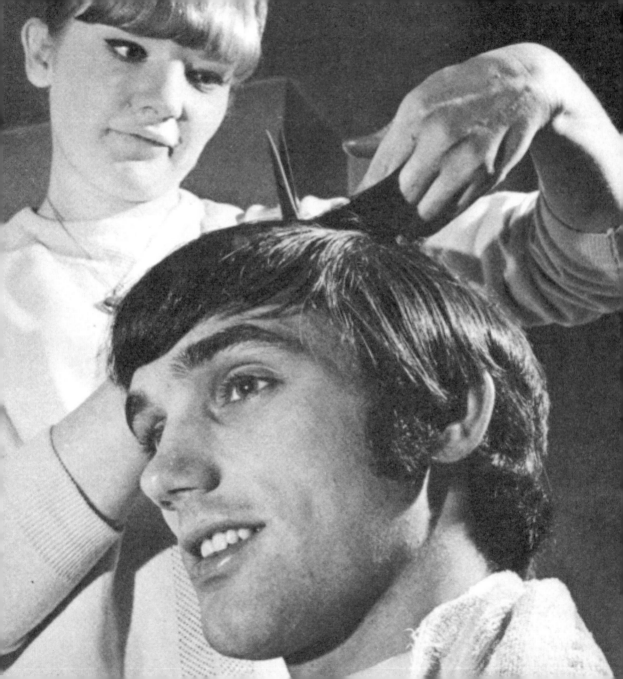

journalist Graham Greene and painters Lucian Freud and Francis Bacon. Early photos of Jeff show a stylish young man who could easily have walked out of today's drinking clubs like Black's or Groucho's. In recent years Bernard was admired partly as someone who represented the Absolute Beginning of modern British bohemia. He was also revered as the plummy-voiced old man who'd done it all (years of drinking in the Coach and Horses run by Norman Balon, four wives, over 500 lovers, including many of his best friends' wives, and countless hours in the bookie's) and was now paying the price – but with grace and without moaning.

Not long before he died in 1997, Bernard put a personal ad in *The Spectator* which read: 'alcoholic, diabetic amputee seeks sympathy fuck'. If they had known it was Jeff, there would have been plenty of takers.

PARENTS Malcolm Lowry, Patrick Hamilton
CHILDREN **Keith Allen**
READ ON *Low Life* by Jeffrey Bernard

George Best
Bested only by himself

Belfast-born George Best showed more skill, courage, speed, flair and finish than any other footballer of his generation. Manchester United fans remember him fondly as the height of 'Red Devilry'. To a wider public, 'he was the first footballer to take advantage of the mass media age and demonstrate … that **football** could be an art as well as a sport'. To his youthful contemporaries, Best was a modern stylist and iconoclast who symbolised the end of deference. According to sports commentator and TV interviewer Michael Parkinson, he was also 'a mini-series waiting to be written … the man who could beat everyone, except himself'.

From the age of 15 months, young George was always chasing after a ball. As a child he could usually be found playing football in the field at the end of his street, a Protestant living in the Catholic Craigie estate. Spotted by talent scout Bob Bishop he agreed to go for a fortnight's trial at Old Trafford. Homesick, he went back to Belfast after 24 hours. But in February 1961 he tried again. In digs with the maternal Mrs Fulloway, he found his feet.

Manager Matt Busby was still trying to rebuild his team after the Munich air disaster of 1958. Best was able to make his debut for the Manchester United first team at the age of 17 – in the same week that **The Beatles** first entered the charts. Busby described him as 'better than Pele'; journalists took one look at Best's long hair (for those days) and dubbed him 'the fifth Beatle'.

It was not only his haircut that made commentators bracket Best with pop culture. His looks, his casual air and his playfulness on the field were all in accordance with the new mentality primarily associated with pop music and its young audience. Besides being dressed *à la mode*, Best was soon opening his own boutiques, and this only confirmed the impression that he was 'tailor-made for the 60s'.

The fashionable accoutrements would have

meant little, however, if Best had not been a virtuoso on the pitch. Manchester United won the FA cup in 1963, not least because Best bested so many defenders (Busby said he had 'never seen another player who could beat a man in so many ways'), most of whom seemed hell-bent on chopping his legs from under him. Paddy Crerand, a team-mate at Old Trafford, has said that Best could make the opposition feel like 'twisted blood'. Capped for Ireland, his side won a rare victory against Scotland in what appeared to be a one-man show. 'It looks like the ball is tied to his feet,' said one commentator. In 1966 when Manchester United beat Benfica 5-1 in the quarter final of the European Cup, Best played the key role and also took the lion's share of the ensuing publicity. In newspapers across Europe he was pictured in a sombrero with the caption 'El Beatle'. Of course he went on to play a starring role in United's European Cup-winning team of 1968 but, off the pitch, the strains of stardom were taking their toll.

By this time Best was drinking hard and pulling plenty. He moved out of Mrs Fulloway's and built himself a futurist dream home in the Cheshire suburb of Bramhall. In a series of deals arranged by agent Ken Stanley, Best's sideburned face was used to endorse all kinds of products from crisps to Fore aftershave and Stylo boots. Perhaps he was getting too big for his. For some time now he had hardly bothered to listen to the boss Busby's team talk. A couple of days before his 26th birthday he announced he was giving up football. Although he retracted the statement soon afterwards, the Old Trafford hierarchy insisted that Best must stop playing the playboy and move in with rock-solid Crerand and his young family.

It worked, but only for a short time. In 1972 Best was placed on the transfer list, and he again announced his retirement. Less than a year later he was back at Old Trafford under new manager Tommy Docherty. But on the day of an FA Cup tie with lowly Plymouth Argyll, he turned up 'in no condition to play'; and was never seen again by Docherty. Here began Best's long years in the wilderness. He signed for Dunstable, Fulham and the Los Angeles Aztecs. In the city of angels he co-owned a bar and married Essex girl Angie (personal trainer to Cher). They had a son, Calum, but soon afterwards his wife kicked George out saying 'I can't look after two babies – the big one has to go.' Back in Britain he fell in love with Miss World and, at 37, signed for Bournemouth. A year later, in 1984, he was stopped for drunken driving in the vicinity of Buckingham Palace, failed to turn up in court to answer the charge and was arrested by a squad of police in his Chelsea flat. Best was convicted of assaulting a police officer, while he accused them of beating him up in the van and hurling anti-Irish insults at him. He was sentenced to three months in jail; he served seven weeks in Pentonville and Ford open prison.

In 1990 a bearded and besotted Best appeared on Terry Wogan's early evening TV chat show. It was a disaster ('Terry, I like screwing' was typical of George's small-talk), which in the annals of media moments is as legendary as inebriated Oliver Reed's high jinks with Michael Aspel. But the sheer awfulness of Best's worst TV moment somehow replanted him in the public imagination. How could a player of such finesse have become so boorish and boring, we wanted to know. Meanwhile Best himself benefited from the care and attention of his second wife Alex. For some years now he has been regarded as the wastrel who finally learnt the error of his ways (too late to redeem his career but not too late for Best-the-man). In that respect he is the template for a raft of soap operas 'waiting to happen': **Paul Gascoigne**, Paul Merson, Tony Adams …

PARENTS Pele, The Beatles, Matt Busby
CHILDREN Gazza
READ ON *The Good, the Bad and the Bubbly* by George Best

Bhangra
Missed the boat

Bhangra is a traditional form of music from the Punjab, associated with peasants harvesting crops and played on big drums and a plucked instrument with only one string. In the late 70s and 80s, musicians from Asian families living in England brought the drums and rhythms associated with Bhangra together with guitars and synthesisers. Starting out from the music shops in Southall, to the west of London, a Bhangra circuit soon grew up, and Indian parents were relieved to be able to send their teenagers to Bhangra dances where their culture was represented, albeit in a modified form.

In the late 80s Bhangra was remodelled: instead of incorporating guitars it took its cue from the burgeoning club scene and adapted to the new sound of house. In the early 90s Bhangra evolved again, incorporating aspects of hip-hop as adapted by artists such as Sheila Chandra and Apache Indian. More recently, Bhangra has gone pop with Bally Sagoo, the Punjabi-speaking singer from Birmingham who is signed to Sony.

Although Sagoo's records have made it to the Radio 1 playlist, it is by no means certain that Bhangra will make it into the mainstream. Asian culture became fashionable in Britain in the late 90s. But for today's young Anglo-Asians, Bhangra is old-fashioned without being properly authentic. They prefer music that combines Eastern elements with **drum'n'bass**, in the style of **Talvin Singh**.

Then again, Bhangra may already be in the mainstream of British cultures. Most Bhangra records are sold not in the designated shops that feature in chart returns, but in high-street grocery stores frequented mainly by Asians. Many Bhangra acts claim that the only reason they don't appear in the charts is because their recordings are sold largely through such unlisted outlets. In this respect their popularity may be as hidden as the US market for black American writers like Donald Goines, whose crime novels were traditionally sold in local shops rather than bookstores.

READ ON *Dis-Orienting Rhythms: the politics of the New Asian Dance Music* by Sanjay Sharma, John Mutnyk and Ashwani Sharma

Bigbeat

Indie cuts some shapes

Bigbeat is the musical equivalent of lad mags: on the one hand it is muscular and ostentatiously 'big' – music to be played in the locker room (appropriately, **Norman Cook**'s 1999 battle with American DJ Armand Van Helden was advertised as a boxing bout); on the other hand, this pantomime muscularity only half-hides a sense of vulnerability and not-quite-adulthood. Hence Cook's stage name is Fat*boy* Slim. Likewise, the **Chemical Brothers** combine a huge sound – as heard on their hugely successful third album, *Surrender* – with endearingly boyish characteristics.

Norman Cook

Born in 1964, Norman Cook was working as a funk DJ in suburban Surrey when singer Paul Heaton asked him to be the bass player in The Housemartins, the Hull-based, left-wing, late 80s, guitar band. When The 'Martins broke up (Heaton went on to front The Beautiful South), Cook went back to dance music and released a spate of records under a series of pseudonyms: Beats International (with former *Grange Hill* actress Lindy Layton), Pizzaman, The Mighty Dub Kats and Freakpower (with Ashley Slater). As Fatboy Slim, he is renowned for a series of bigbeat singles such as 'Praise You', 'Gangster Trippin', 'Right Here Right Now' and 'The Rockafeller Skank' (snippets of

which have formed the soundtrack for both Adidas and Nike adverts). But his standing as a remixer is equally high: Cook was the man who spliced a Kool and the Gang riff with Eric B and Rakim's 'I Know You Got Soul'; he also speeded up **Cornershop**'s 'Brimful of Asha' and added the breakbeats, taking it from an **indie** cult record that reached No 65 in the charts to the No 1 spot and the kudos of being the most talked-about British record of 1997.

Wary of becoming known as a record-doctor, Cook turned down subsequent remix offers from U2 and Madonna: 'I don't want to remix rock or old records any more. I've turned down tons of tracks I really like. I don't want to churn them out. It's like shooting fish in a barrel. I mean, I got offered a remix of Noël Coward's "Mad Dogs and Englishmen". What's that all about?'

The job of the remixer is to add a twist to the original track: an element which is incongruous yet latent, contradictory but waiting to happen. The remixer is therefore a kind of ironist – a role entirely in keeping with the bigbeat sub-genre with which Cook is primarily associated. Commenting on his 'Rockafeller Skank', Cook described it as a combination of 'tough production' and a twee hook line: 'There's that bit in the middle where there's that really extreme whining noise and then the whole song deconstructs. I like hearing that on Radio 1, driving along, seeing people wincing like their radios have gone wrong. As long as you're breaking new ground with the production, I think you can get away with using hook lines your auntie taps her feet to.'

Recognising that irony is the essence of bigbeat is the only way to make sense of Cook's previous gig in the caring, sharing Housemartins: whereas Heaton's Beautiful South went on to make an even more feminised music, Cook produced an ironic take on masculinity. Put another way, it was the ironist in Cook that rejected the old-fashioned first name his parents gave him (Quentin), replaced it first with the even more antiquated 'Norman', and then with the consciously contradictory 'Fatboy Slim'.

The Chemical Brothers

After 'an idyllic childhood' in Henley-on-Thames thanks to his 'groovy parents', Tom Rowlands met Ed Simons (absent father, barrister mother, public school, 'I used to get hit a lot') at Manchester University where they bonded around Eastern Bloc record shop. Still at college they set up their own club night, Naked Under Leather, as an alternative to the house-dominated **Madchester** clubs. In 1992 they made 'Song to the Siren', a 'hip-hop headfuck track' which was played repeatedly by top-flight DJ Andy Weatherall. By 1995 the Chemical Brothers (name changed from the Dust Brothers after threat of litigation by an American act with the same name) were playing at London's Sunday Social nightspot (punters' drug of choice: cigarettes dipped in amyl nitrate. Later described by promoter Robin Turner as full of 'people who were slightly past it, trying to relive their youth'), where they got together with Tim Burgess of the Charlatans. Soon they were in the remix business (**Primal Scream**, **Manic Street Preachers**, the Sandals, the Charlatans and **Prodigy**), *The Face* associated them

with reinventing 'the notion of "indie dance"', their debut album *Exit Planet Dust* was selling 200,000 copies in the UK alone and top-ranking director Spike Jones was shooting their first promotional video starring the daughter of John Ford Coppola. Two years later (1997), during which time they were 'thrown off the decks' at **Ibiza** and their single 'Setting Sun' went straight into the British charts at No 1, the Chemicals' follow-up album, *Dig Your Own Hole* (title taken from graffiti near their studio) boasted an eclectic list of guest appearances from **Oasis**' Noel Gallagher, Grand Wizard Theodore – the man who taught Grandmaster Flash how to scratch, US **indie** band Mercury Rev and Beth Orton. In *The Face*, Sylvia Patterson described it as 'a collusion of psychedelic hip-hop trance-melt space-bombed electro-techno rock'n'roll with extra superfly funk. And a bit of guitar. And a sitar. And the siren which signifies the end of the world. An LP by a band at its creative pinnacle rather than a groove by the graphic equaliser.'

In their enjoyably over-the-top manner, the Chemical Brothers took dance tracks towards rock-'n'roll: they met Primal Scream coming the other way and carried the resulting combination to the top of the US and UK charts ('Surrender' was No 1 in the summer of 1999). Despite their name, they are not particularly into drugs (especially not amyl nitrate). Their official line on illegal substances is: just say 'yo'.

Previously thought of as rivals, although Cook always acknowledged the influence of the younger Brothers, Fatboy Slim and the Chemical Brothers toured the USA together in 1999.

Tony Blair
Post-politician

Elected leader of the opposition in 1994 and appointed prime minister after the landslide general election of 1997, Tony Blair is the first head of government to present himself as a man defined more by lifestyle than political ideology.

Tony is the son of former Tory councillor Leo Blair (working-class Glasgow background made good; army major in the Second World War, called to the bar afterwards). Leo lectured in Australia when Tony was a toddler and suffered a stroke when the boy reached the age of ten (he has since recovered and has become a Labour Party member). The Durham-based Blair family scrimped to send Tony to Fettes, one of the top public schools in Scotland. At St John's, Oxford, he read law and, along with erstwhile *Smash Hits* editor and *Q* publisher Mark Ellen, played in a band called Ugly Rumours (named after a track on the Grateful Dead's *Live At The Mars Hotel*). After Oxford Blair talked his way into pupillage in the chambers of Labour barrister Derry Irvine (his future Lord Chancellor), where the rising star was his future wife Cherie Booth, daughter of TV actor (the 'Scouse git' in *Till Death Us Do Part*) Tony Booth. Blair's career as a barrister specialising in employment law was successful but unremarkable.

It was Derry Irvine who introduced Blair to John Smith MP, who in turn was instrumental in getting Blair a seat in parliament. After standing in Beaconsfield and losing his deposit, Blair was selected for the safe Labour seat of Sedgefield in County Durham, and was duly elected in 1983. He shared an office in the Palace of Westminster with another new MP, Militant's Dave Nellist.

Questions have been asked about the strength of Blair's political convictions. Schoolteacher Eric Anderson remembers that young Blair 'took very little interest in politics'. He only ever attended two political demonstrations (both against neo-fascists), and joined the Labour Party in his final year at Oxford (a career move?). Michael Foot, the Labour leader vilified for wearing a donkey jacket to the Remembrance Day parade and who fronted the radical general election manifesto (1983) which became known as 'the longest suicide note in history', thought him 'a real left-winger, just the thing'. But Blair reckons his formative political experience was an impromptu confrontation with left-wingers at a local party meeting in Newcastle in 1982, two years before the Labour Party annual conference at which Neil Kinnock dished out the same treatment to Militant's Derek Hatton.

Under the leadership of John Smith (Kinnock stood down after failing to win office in 1992), Blair (shadow home secretary) was known to be dissatisfied with the pace of modernisation: he wanted shot of 'outdated and misguided ideological baggage'. When Smith died suddenly of a heart attack, Blair pipped Gordon Brown to the leader's chair and seized the opportunity to speed up the pace of change. He also acquired a reputation as a Christian socialist who paid close attention to the work of a communitarian priest called Peter

Thompson, a mature student at Oxford during Blair's time there.

Blair may have a chequered ideological past, but this is hardly relevant. He has left ideology behind to become the first successful, post-ideological politician in Britain. Left-wing opponents believe that Blair's abandonment of the party's socialist roots must make him a Tory. But he is as hostile to Tory philosophy as he is to traditional socialism. Blair's New Labour is new because it is distanced not just from Old Labour, but from everything that 'old' politics used to consist of, including the battle of ideas, competing worldviews and coherent programmes.

Other critics have complained that Blair is all image and no substance. After the Cool Britannia /New Labour bandwagon (the future PM plays a Stratocaster and presents a Brit award to **David Bowie** – wow!), there was an anti-Blair backlash in which the glitterati lambasted him as a shallow poseur (a copper-bottomed case of the pot calling the kettle African-American). Likewise, *Times* columnist Matthew Parris has compared Blair to a surfer, skating over the surface of things. This is true, not only of Blair but of the whole new way of politics which he has helped to develop. In this new context, practising headers with Kevin Keegan, clinking glasses with **Oasis**' Noel Gallagher and sharing a sofa with Richard and Judy are not only photo opportunities but also heartfelt statements of who Blair is and what he is about. He is committed to generating a sense of shared national experience, and nowadays – so the new post-political theory goes – our shared experiences derive from lifestyle and consumption, not from political ideologies, metanarratives and the outdated desire to change the world.

There are times, however, when Blair's readiness to pounce on anything that might generate a shared experience seems like a bathetic form of ambulance chasing – the deaths of Princess Diana and Frank Sinatra ('I grew up with Frank Sinatra,' he claimed, although there is no record of the infant Blair's sojourn in Little Italy), England's exit from the World Cup, Glen Hoddle's foolish remarks about reincarnation, the Internet, etc, etc. Furthermore, Blair's look of wide-eyed expectancy (the look which says, I'm as excited about this as you are – the Bambi expression which has prompted comparisons with **Blur**'s Damon Albarn) is matched by a new mode of emotional authoritarianism (never mind the autonomy of the individual, you will feel grief when I tell you to). In both instances the electorate are treated like permanent adolescents who will never be mature enough to see beyond pop culture and **football**. Whereas in the first instance Blair claims to share in our childlike naivety, in the second he comes on as Super-Nanny, knowing what's good for us because we'll never be able to work it out for ourselves. Apparently contradictory, these two sides of Blair are both based on new ideas of the electorate as pre-adult cultural consumers, unlike traditional political ideologies in which adult voters were formally respected as the agents of history.

PARENTS JFK, Bill Clinton, Derry Irvine
READ ON *Labour Camp* by Stephen Bayley

Alan Bleasdale
Liverpool lament

Scouse writer Alan Bleasdale came to fame in the early 80s with *Boys from the Blackstuff* (1982), a hard-hitting TV series about a group of construction workers from Liverpool (a city hit so hard by recession it no longer had a rush hour). 'Gizzajob', the constantly repeated demand of desperate psycho-dolie Yosser Hughes (played by Bernard Hill), became one of the catchphrases of the decade – the other side of the coin to Gordon Gekko's 'greed is good' (*Wall Street*, 1988).

Born in 1946, Bleasdale was a child of the post-war consensus who grew up in a city that reflected the opportunities of the period (the Mersey Sound, the Liverpool Poets, the art college scene in Liverpool 8, the Catholic cathedral, Shankly's Anfield) and its limitations (the Port of Liverpool was in slow decline throughout the twentieth century, and state-backed strategies to industrialise the surrounding area were never wholly successful). The British economy stagnated in the 70s, and Merseyside became increasingly reliant on the welfare state. When the Tories came into office in 1979 with a mission to replace the mixed economy with market forces, the people of Liverpool felt the pinch more than most.

Bleasdale is the supreme chronicler of this context. Born a Catholic, trained as a teacher, he taught in secondary schools for the best part of a decade before becoming resident playwright at the Liverpool Playhouse. In early plays such as *Fat Harold and the Last* (1975) and *The Party's Over* (1975) he mined much the same seams (comedy plus social realism) as London's **Johnny Speight** and local writer Alun Owen. With the novel *Scully* (1977), Bleasdale wrote about Liverpool's council estate youth ('scallies') and their entrance into a largely hostile world. Translated first into a stage play, then a one-off television play, and finally a TV series in the mid-80s (with title music by Elvis Costello) and a second book *Scully and Mooey* (1984), Scully may turn out to be more influential than *Boys From The Blackstuff*.

Although the latter is best remembered for its representation of social decay, there was more to it than reportage. Bleasdale wrote sharp comedy, while at the same time debunking the myth of the ever-saucy scouser: 'if you don't laugh you'll cry – I've heard it for years – this stupid, soddin' city's full of it'. He clearly respected the tradition of working-class solidarity, while questioning whether tradition alone would be sufficient defence against the new age of 'management's right to manage' (the defeat of the miners' strike in 1985, reliant on the conventions of British trade unionism, indicates the prescience of this question).

Bleasdale posed the right questions but could provide no answers – for the working class or for himself. Through the rest of the decade his work lurched between romantic radicalism (*The Monocled Mutineer*, 1986, adapted from the book by William Allison and John Fairley, following the career of First World War conscript, mutineer and style warrior Percy Toplis) and sardonic fatalism (*No Surrender*, 1987, subtitled 'a deadpan farce', it straddles Liverpool's sectarian divide and ends in an almighty fist-fight).

By the early 90s Bleasdale had moved on. He scripted the TV series *GBH*, a proto-New Labour parable in which a Kinnockite socialist played by Michael Palin went to war with a manipulative left-winger apparently based on the Militant Tendency's Derek Hatton, the sharp-suited councillor (and modern-day Percy Toplis) who took Liverpool to the brink of chaos during 1984–86 in the hope of squeezing more funds from the Tory government. The part of the Militant councillor was played by Robert Lindsay in a straight-faced reprise of his earlier comic role as 70s revolutionary Wolfie ('Citizen') Smith, leader of the Tooting Popular Front.

In *GBH*, there was no doubt that Bleasdale's loyalties lay with Palin's schoolmaster, whose family always looked as wholesome as an Oxo advert. If in the 80s he attacked Thatcher more effectively than the Labour Party managed to do, in the 90s he participated in Labour's amputation of its own left-wing.

From Benn to **Blair**, Bleasdale's political trajectory is in keeping with that of many of his generation. In the 80s he also provided the model for local writing with left-wing leanings: after watching *Boys From The Blackstuff*, in cities across Britain unemployed workers set up writers' groups, partly to describe what had happened to their own lives, and partly to see if they could get a TV series out of it. Funded by councils and arts boards, local writing lives on – but without the socialist politics that used to inform it.

PARENTS Johnny Speight, **Ken Loach**
CHILDREN Jimmy McGovern, Phil Redmond
READ ON *Scully* by Alan Bleasdale,
Liverpool On The Brink by Michael Parkinson

Blur
True Brits, false grits

Blur succeeded in recapturing an idea of British pop but lost out to **Oasis** when it came to representing gritty 'working-class' experience. Blur's frontman Damon Albarn was born in March 1968, the year of student marches. His mother was a set designer at Stratford East, home of Joan Littlewood's radical Theatre Workshop (which staged the seaside concert party pastiche *Oh, What A Lovely War!*, later a film with John Lennon), while his father, having been manager of the Soft Machine and the first person to put on a Yoko Ono show in London, was by then running a hippie shop in the West End. They all lived together in a silver-painted house in Leytonstone (well-built Victorian houses, cheap in those days; also the birthplace of **Talvin Singh**).

When Damon was ten his father was invited to run the North Essex School of Art and the family moved to the garrison town of Colchester. There he met guitarist Graham Coxon (they were both into **Two-Tone**) whose father was a bandsman in the RAF. The two of them stood out against an environment which suited neither one. 'The moment I was

(influenced by **Madchester**) and was compared to **The Stone Roses** and My Bloody Valentine. Seymour signed to the Food label and became Blur, described by the *Daily Mirror* as 'Britain's brainiest band'.

Blur's first pose could easily have been struck in opposition to the '68-style radicalism of Damon's parents. Damon: 'There's a whole generation of bands that understand that every musical movement has failed to change anything, so we're deliberately shallow in order to avoid the embarrassment of it all.' Blur's first album *Leisure* (which reached No 7 in the charts) was nearly called *Irony* in the UK. Yet 'Badgeman Brown', the B-side of their single 'Popscene', has been described as 'straight out of the '68 handbook' – so close to **Syd Barrett** ('a Syd-U-Like storyboard') that Pink Floyd's album designer Storm Thorgerson of Hypgnosis suggested that Blur possessed the original spirit of Barrett-vintage Floyd. Thorgerson was later to work with the band on a long-form video set in provincial England.

During a lacklustre tour of the USA, Blur discovered their defining element: anti-Americanism. They shared a hatred of 'mall culture' (Damon said: 'I get physically ill when I go there, I just come over with this depressed American malady') and a determination to 'make English music important again on a world basis'. Interviewed in *Select* magazine, Damon said: 'Life for many Americans exists within these huge sheds … these huge bubbles. And that really made us look at England and see how much of American culture had been absorbed into a very innocent England.' He set about ingesting all things

shoved into right-wing Essex it all went wrong,' Damon recalled in 1994. 'We've traded community for a disenfranchised life of Barratt homes and neuroses.'

Although he thought about being a social worker, Damon went from secondary school to acting college – the E15 school in (East End) Stratford, home of the company of actors working with theatre and film director **Mike Leigh** – where he refused to learn anything as outdated as tap dancing, although he later described himself as 'part of a music hall-clown-entertainer tradition'. Along with bassist Coxon, Alex James and drummer Dave Rowntree, he formed a band, Seymour, which was baggy-ish

71

English, from London pop bands like **The Kinks**, especially their 1969 single 'Waterloo Sunset', to London writers like the left-wing, 30s and 40s novelist Patrick Hamilton, who wrote famously about drinking and not being able to stop (*Hangover Square*). **Martin Amis** was another favourite. Of Amis' *London Fields*, Albarn said 'it saved me', although he seems to have identified with the prole protagonist more than the author intended: 'Keith Talent was so English and I wanted to be him.'

Blur's next album, eventually entitled *Modern Life Is Rubbish*, was nearly called *England versus America*, or *British Image 1*. Released in May 1993 at the height of the influence of Seattle-based grunge, it has been described as a 'soundtrack for a fantasy London', invoking Saturday markets, Sunday roasts, sugary tea and *Songs of Praise*. 'We killed baggy with our first album. This one will kill grunge,' boasted Damon. Influences include **Bowie**, Madness, **The Smiths** and above all The Kinks. *Select* reviewed the album under the heading 'Rule Britannia'.

Around this time, Blur were feuding with **Suede** as to which of them should be considered the ambassadors of what came to be known as **Britpop**. There was a personal element too: Damon's partner Justine Frischmann of Elastica had been the girlfriend of Brett Anderson (Suede lead singer) as well as being the rhythm guitarist in the original line-up of Suede (she says she thought of the name). It all got a bit fraught when Suede guitarist Bernard Butler entered the fray by telling the *NME* that the lyrics to Blur's song 'Bang' were the worst he had ever heard.

The theme of Englishness was amplified in Blur's next album, *Parklife* – complete with front cover photo taken at Walthamstow dog track and voiceover from Phil Daniels, star of *Scum* (**Alan Clarke**'s pivotal 70s film about borstal boys, based on the TV play and novelisation by Roy Minton) and *Quadrophenia* (1979 film of the **Who**'s 1974 album which revisited the spirit of 60s **Mod**). In *The Sunday Times* Robert Sandall recommended Blur as 'leaders of the Cockney rock revival', likening them to XTC (post-punk electro-experimentation and British eccentricity, fronted by Andy Partridge), Syd Barrett, **The Small Faces**' Steve Marriott and The Kinks. Barrett's 'Arnold Layne' and Ray Davies' 'The Village Green Preservation Society' seem to have been particularly inspirational. But by this time Damon was saying that his songs 'criticise this country' as well as celebrating it and defending it from American domination.

In 1994 Blur had seen off Suede and conquered Americanism (if not America). *En passant* they killed off what in the mid-90s was briefly touted as the next big thing, namely the New Wave of New Wave. Then, in a hyped-up confrontation that was meant to recall the rivalry between **The Beatles** and the **Rolling Stones** in the 60s, they locked horns with Oasis – and lost.

Blur seemed to be in the lead. It was Damon who deliberately rescheduled the release of 'Country House' to coincide with the release of 'Roll With It', and this ruse seemed to pay dividends when the Blur single went to No 1 while Oasis were held at No 2. But album sales tell a different story: *(What's The Story?) Morning Glory* sold more than five

Damon Albarn

million worldwide, trumping the two million sales of Blur's *The Great Escape*. The record-buying public seemed to have decided that northern working-class boys were the real thing.

Blur had always played with their identity. They knew they were Mockney rather than true Cockney ('I feel caught between the cultures. I don't know if I'm art school or Essex man'), and their readings of working-class Britain were always literate rather than authentic – but then such artificiality is in the nature of the authentic pop tradition. Oasis, in a presentational mode which in fact recalls the middle-class Rolling Stones rather than the working-class Beatles, acted out the role of proletarian hooligans. Noel Gallagher bragged that Oasis are 'working-class heroes' whereas 'Blur are a bunch of middle-class wankers'. Suddenly it was clear not only that the pictures of Blur at Walthamstow dog track were a pose, but that the local youth would laugh at them just like Oasis did. (This is exactly what happened when Cliff Jones of *The Face* accompanied Blur to the dog track. 'As the group leave the stadium,' he reported, 'two small boys dressed in shell suits hoot with laughter. "Look at you lot!", they shout. "I bet you get your clothes at Oxfam".'.)

Not all Walthamstow residents are yer aktual East Enders. The area has been gentrified, house prices in 'the village' are comparable with those of West London, and the punters at 'the dogs' are more likely to be graphic designers than barrow boys. But prolier than thou Gallagher had taken the high ground, and Blur could only reply, somewhat lamely, that his band should be called 'Oasis Quo' (on the dubious grounds that 'Roll With It' sounded like 'Rockin' All Over The World'). Recalling the feud a year later in the *Guardian*, Damon claimed he had not been taken seriously because 'I'm not working class and I've got a pretty face.'

In the 60s Blur might have won. Back then, Mod was described as 'Jean-Paul Sartre and John Lee Hooker on speed', and the exaggerated anti-bookishness of the Gallaghers would have been characteristic only of antediluvian Rockers. But in the 90s it seems that even working-class boys from Burnage are ready to act out a middle-class fantasy of what working-class youth are really like.

1997–98 were quiet years for Blur. They released an eponymous album – often the sign of a band that wants to get back to basics but does not know how. Albarn and guitarist Graham Coxon dabbled with psychedelic sounds at **John Peel**'s Meltdown festival on the South Bank; and William Orbit

remixed some of their earlier material for release in Japan. Early in 1999 Blur issued *13*, hailed by *The Face* as their best yet, sometimes described as their 'divorce album' – a reference to the material derived from Albarn's break-up with Justine Frischmann. Its songs were less to do with Englishness and more about personal pain. Like many other performers at the end of the twentieth century, Blur went into the confessional. Even the carousing bassist and absinthe tippler Alex James (also one-third of comedy recording trio Fat Les, along with **Keith Allen** and **Damien Hirst**) looked back at the antics of his 20s and pledged that 'it will never be that ridiculous again'. Blur also turned their back on anti-Americanism with a hit single, 'Tender Is The Night', which seemed to be a respectful reference to F Scott Fitzgerald's jazz-age novel.

PARENTS XTC, The Kinks, Colchester Art College
READ ON *Blur – the whole story* by Martin Roach, *3862 Days* by Stuart Maconie

Ozwald Boateng
Rags for the rich

Born in 1959, Anglo-Ghanaian Ozwald Boateng's standing as a tailor is as high as his 6ft 4in frame. Although his fortunes took a dive early in 1998 (end of seven-year marriage to French model Pascale, theft of collection, closure of his Savile Row store, companies in receivership after cancellation of £1.2 million foreign contracts for off-the-peg suits), Boateng raised capital from his friends, did a deal with Debenhams department store, bought back his own name from the receivers, and opened 'the first men's bespoke couture shop' in Wimpole Street, London W1 (he lives above the shop). Boateng later insisted 'the whole experience opened me up as a creative person'.

Boateng's client list already included Mick Jagger, Peter Mandelson, Chris Smith (who says he buys Boateng ties 'because I cannot afford his suits'), Jonathan Ross, Seal, **Goldie** and **Robbie Williams**. Brought up in Muswell Hill, he was taught tailoring by a girlfriend, started selling clothes to West End shops when he was 16, opened a shop in the Portobello Road in 1991 and another in Vigo Street, central London in 1995. By then he had already become the first British tailor to show his wares on a Paris catwalk (Men's Fashion Week, 1994). In Paris two years later he won the best male designer award at the Trophées de la Mode. Boateng also supplied suits for Hollywood's *Tomorrow Never Dies* and for the East End gangster flick *Lock, Stock and Two Smoking Barrels* (1998).

After the publicity surrounding his fall and rise, Boateng made it on to the list of *Tatler*'s most-wanted party guests. He was also invited to be a panellist on BBC1's *Question Time*. Producer Nick Pisani said he regarded Boateng as 'a face of modern Britain'. Boateng, who says he was first motivated by Thatcherite ideas of entrepreneurship, also accepted an invitation to join the **Blair**ite Creative Britain committee.

'I believed in the concept and the traditions of Savile Row,' says Boateng, 'it's the birthplace of the suit and I respected that. My view was to modernise it and bring it into the new millennium because the tailoring tradition was dying.' He is associated with angled pockets, concealed buttons, tapered trousers and blindingly bright linings. At their best, Boateng's suits are colourful and classy, recalling the innovations of the 60s – he acknowledges the inspiration of **The Avengers** and *The Italian Job*. But what was innovative then is fairly predictable now. Peter Howarth, editor of the UK edition of men's magazine *Esquire*, described Boateng's '1960s edge' as a conservative approach. On the other hand, the narrator of *DeadMeat*, the mid-90s, club culture novel written by a black Londoner known only as Q, clearly believes that Boateng's style makes for a powerful combination of the classic and the contemporary:'The clothes weren't boring, they screamed of sex. They were pucker, not for suckers … definitely the sort of garments that would do something for me, make me more approachable, give me an elegant look. … I just had to put one on then I could walk strong and feel like a don.'

PARENTS Beau Brummell, John Stephen, Miles Davis ('the man in the green shirt'), John Steed

Marc Bolan

Electric elf

Born Mark Feld into an East End Jewish family, Marc Bolan grew up with the crew-cutted, cigar-chomping, future footballers' agent Eric Hall and by the age of 12 was being quoted by journalists as the youngest and sharpest of the **Mods**. Bolan's first venture into the pop world was with John's Children, an art/pop group who released one single of note ('Desdemona Lift Up Your Skirts And Fly'), supported the **Who** on a European tour and were looked after by the Who's management team of Chris Stamp (brother of actor and heartthrob Terence) and Kit Lambert (son of composer Constant). When the music of Indian sitar player Ravi Shankar became fashionable – around the same time that the fairy stories of JRR Tolkien came back into vogue, Bolan left John's Children to form a duo consisting of himself (acoustic guitar, whimsical lyrics and drone-like vocals) and Steve Peregrine-Took (bongos – the poor man's tablas). The two of them sat cross-legged on the floor (Bolan looking like 'a little prophet') and went out under the near-impossible name of Tyrannosaurus Rex. Promoted by DJ **John Peel** (who used to get letters complaining about the singer who sounded like Larry the Lamb), Tyrannosaurus Rex released an album which became popular in hippie-ish circles (*My People Were Fair And Had Sky In Their Hair*), and Bolan published a collection of poems, *Warlock of Love*.

At that time Bolan did not take drugs, saying he was 'already afraid of my head': unlike Peregrine-Took, who lived up to the second half of his name. Took soon got taken out of the band (did he leave or was he pushed?). Bolan brought in Mickey Finn as percussionist, stood up on stage, shortened the name of the band to T Rex, and switched from acoustic back to electric guitar. While **The Beatles** reverted to their roots with 'Lady Madonna', Bolan went back to Eddie Cochran's 'C'Mon Everybody' and started to synthesise his fairytale singing voice with sexy rock'n'roll. It all came together in the single 'Ride A White Swan' which was played repeatedly at the 1970 Isle of Wight festival by DJ Jeff Dexter, and slowly crossed over into a wider market.

'Ride A White Swan' took three months to get to the top of the charts, and even then it was held at No 2 by Clive Dunn's 'Grandad'. But Bolan had made it into the mass market. He was a hot pin-up in *Jackie*, the magazine for pubescent girls, and his next single, 'Hot Love', went all the way to No 1; it was also one of the first records to be released with an accompanying film (video was not yet widespread) to be shown on the (then) highly influential BBC show *Top of the Pops*). Bolan modified his image as well as his music. He kept his cherubic curls but added some glitter (at the suggestion of his PA Chelita Secunda) to the velvet and satin he already wore. The result was elf-like and camp (he liked wearing women's shoes), but bursting with testosterone.

For a couple of years Bolan was in the ascendant. Based on simple blues progressions, layered with rock'n'roll and topped off with the elfin element, a series of hits ('Get It On', which ex-patron

Peel openly disliked; 'Jeepster'; 'Telegram Sam'; 'Metal Guru') came naturally to him ('I just get them out of the air') and went straight to the top of the charts. In Britain at least Bolan was briefly considered to be bigger than The Beatles. The release of his movie *Born To Boogie* led to extravagant headlines such as 'T Rextasy'.

But then Bolan started to believe his own publicity; and his drug use began to interfere with his judgement. According to veteran rock writer Charles Shaar Murray, this was 'the point where hubris and cocaine became interchangeable'. Interviewed by hippie-ish magazine *Zigzag* about what it was like to be a sex symbol, Bolan summed up his attitude to jealous boyfriends saying 'maybe I'm a better lay than you are'. His stage act became overblown: people giggled when he entered attached to a hydraulic star. His figure also went over the top: the satin suits were filling with fat and there were snide comments about 'the porky pixie' and 'the glittering chipolata'. Another lapse of taste occurred when Bolan duetted on TV with Cilla Black, the epitome of middle of the road entertainment. On tour in the USA, he made some headway in the urban, coastal states; but Middle America just laughed and headliners Three Dog Night made him the butt of their jokes.

To his credit, Bolan worked himself back into shape, and caught up with the mood of the moment. Hosting his own TV show for British teenyboppers, he introduced them to various punk performers and duetted with **David Bowie** in what turned out to be his last screen appearance. Aged 30, he was killed when the **Mini** driven by his part-

ner Gloria Jones hit a tree on Barnes Common in south-west London. He died on the same day as opera singer Maria Callas, 16 September 1977, but it was Bolan who got the front page in most of the British papers.

The trend towards gender-bending had been discernible in pop culture since Jimmy Dean, but by combining the macho aspects of rock'n'roll with softer – some would say effeminate – elements, Bolan took it a notch or two further. The young **Morrissey** was spellbound by Bolan's concert at Manchester's Belle Vue. Holly Johnson, soon to be frontman for Frankie Goes To Hollywood, recalls being 'obsessed with Marc Bolan for four years'. Bolan's publicist BP Fallon believes that 'he opened the door for David Bowie'. Bolan set the pattern for many who followed. He was also one of the last pop performers to combine the avant-garde with teenybopper appeal: these two areas soon separated out into distinct market segments.

PARENTS Elvis Presley, James Dean, JRR Tolkien
CHILDREN **Suede**

From Russia With Love (1963)

James Bond

The fiction of British supremacy

James Bond appeals to a wide audience from all corners of the globe. The Bond films are the longest-running series of movies in cinema history (by 1999 18 films had been made over a 36-year period), estimated to have been seen by more than two billion people. But Bond has also been the subject of a two-day conference at Britain's elite cultural institution, the Institute of Contemporary Arts,

and the focus of a lavish book, *Dressed To Kill: Bond as suited hero*, produced by art publishers Flammarion. Bond the icon suggests that there is no longer a gulf between high and low culture in Britain.

There is no doubt about the high-class origins of James Bond, however: he was created a bona fide British toff. Schooled at Eton and the army officers' college at Sandhurst, Ian Lancaster Fleming was a banker, a stockbroker and a correspondent for Reuters news agency before enlisting for war service and rising to the rank of commander in British

Naval Intelligence. As a serving officer he was assigned to work with US intelligence agencies, and was received by J Edgar Hoover, the infamous autocrat at the head of the FBI. After the Second World War Fleming worked as foreign manager at *The Sunday Times*. He used his experience of high places and powerful people in the writing of 12 novels (beginning with *Casino Royale* in 1953 and ending with *The Man With The Golden Gun* in 1965) and seven stories featuring Commander Bond (aka 007, licensed to kill; in the words of his creator, 'that cardboard booby').

Fleming once said he invented Bond in a moment of intense boredom, and he soon got bored with his invention. He wrote like a journeyman (2,000 words a day) and would have ended the Bond series with *Diamonds Are Forever* (1955) if Raymond Chandler had not persuaded him to continue.

The multi-million-selling Bond books are partly drawn from Fleming's own experience, but they are also an exercise in wishful thinking. Fleming was brought up to think that the British Empire was the nearest thing to heaven on earth; but by the time he reached adulthood Pax Britannica was being superseded by Pax Americana, and the secular seat of world power was shifting from London to Washington. After the Second World War this process continued apace. By the time of the Suez Crisis of 1956, when Britain and France invaded Colonel Nasser's Egypt and then had to back off because the USA failed to support them, British supremacy was already a thing of the past. Anthony Eden, the failed British prime minister, left the UK in disgrace and holed up for a few weeks in

Bond in the USA

Although Bond was a fictitious statement of British supremacy, he was loved by Americans. US novelist Jay MacInerney recalls reading the Bond books by torchlight under the bedclothes in 1963. As a boy, he hero-worshipped first Davy Crockett and then James Bond. Agent 007 was even endorsed by President Kennedy, who listed *From Russia With Love* among his Top 10 novels of 1961. For MacInerney, urbane sophistication was Bond-like, British and 'almost un-American'. He suggests that the *Man From UNCLE* (and you can add to that Dean Martin's Matt Helm and James Coburn's Derek Flint) was an American attempt to combine Bond with The Beatles, and maintains that 'killing with a quip' is a Bond legacy discernible in Hollywood movies through to *Indiana Jones* and *Die Hard*.

In the summer of 1999, Americans went mad for Bond-like special agent Austin Powers. Created by Anglophile Canadian Mike Myers (the man behind *Wayne's World*), Powers parodies Bond – the joke is that Bond-like capers have no place in the 90s. With bad teeth and specs, Powers enjoys Bond's self-confidence but without any of the qualities (good looks, physique, intelligence) to back it up. He is a latter-day Malvolio whose greatness has been thrust upon him. In June 1999 *Austin Powers: The Spy Who Shagged Me* eclipsed the box office returns for the *Star Wars* prequel.

Fleming's Jamaican estate, Goldeneye. As if to compensate for the indignities suffered by Britain on the international stage, Fleming pumped out books in which Johnny Foreigner always gets his comeuppance (for example, the Asian villain Dr No is dispatched under tons of stinking guano), and not even the Americans can match the *sang froid* of a British hero who conquers all with consummate style. Unlike the Yanks, Bond always knows what to wear and what drink to ask for. As the *London Evening Standard*'s 'ginger fop' Nick Foulkes once said, in an age of change and increasing uncertainty 'it's comforting to have these immutable things'.

Fleming's books were nasty, brutal and short. Produced by Albert 'Cubby' Broccoli (like Sean Connery, the first actor to play Bond, Broccoli had once been an undertaker) and Harry Saltzman (famous for having discovered **Michael Caine**, by the time Saltzman got together with Broccoli his only asset was a soon-to-expire option on the Bond books), the long-running film series played up Bond's good taste and his gadgets (this was the new age of technology and consumerism). They also made Bond more accessible by introducing a self-deprecating, humorous element which is hardly there in Fleming's books. As the series wore on, and Roger Moore and his cocked eyebrow replaced Connery ('the walking aphrodisiac'), this aspect became the *raison d'être* of Bond films. Audiences laughed with Agent 007 but later they came to laugh at him too.

True Brit with tongue in cheek, up until this point you knew where you were with Bond – but at the

ICA conference held in October 1997, the *Guardian*'s Robin Hunt pointed out that in the 90s Pierce Brosnan's Bond is less readily identifiable, perhaps because nowadays 'we don't know what we want from Bond'. In the era of safe sex does Bond wear a condom? When somebody popped this question to screenwriter Bruce Feirstein, he could only dodge it by saying that Bond's traditional 'protection' is a Walther PPK.

PARENTS Raffles, Bulldog Drummond, the Scarlet Pimpernel
CHILDREN Philip McAlpine, UNCLE, Derek Flint, Matt Helm, Austin Powers
READ ON *Dressed To Kill – Bond as suited hero*, edited by Colin Woodhead; *A Life of Ian Fleming* by John Pearson

Leigh Bowery
Bumming with style

Born in Australia on 26 March 1961 to parents who were in the Salvation Army, Leigh Bowery realised he was gay when he was 12. In October 1980 he hid his accent and came to England with a suitcase, a sewing machine and dreams of getting in with the **New Romantics** and the St Martin's art college crowd. Instead he worked in Burger King in the Strand, stealing from the National Gallery bookshop and fan-worshipping Divine (the transvestite star of John Waters' films).

Bowery made his entry on to the London scene via the Club for Heroes run by New Romantic Steve Strange. He started making clothes for friends, first in the style of the Hard Times look but swiftly moving on to a more glamorous approach. Bowery's first media appearance occurred in ex-*Vogue* art editor Terry Jones' *i-D* magazine in September 1984. The quote beneath his picture said 'I am very spiritual. The cosmic and I are one'. Later that year he was interviewed by Paula Yates on *The Tube*, Channel 4's early-Friday-evening music show. His notoriety increased dramatically when he masturbated on stage at *i-D*'s fifth birthday party at the ICA in 1985; also when at the Pink Panther club in Soho's Wardour Street he shat on a poster of one-hit wonders Kajagoogoo and said it was art.

As co-promoter of the club night Taboo, Bowery made his mark. The door policy was implemented by a man who held up a mirror to doubtful punters and asked, 'Would you let yourself in?' The bouncer was the gay, skinhead, neo-fascist Nicky Crane. Bowery wore a different outfit each week: a typical ensemble consisted of a short, pleated skirt and a glittery denim Chanel-shaped jacket topped off with a policeman's helmet. This was the 80s reaction to the overbearing social conscience associated with punk and its aftermath: pure pleasure was a taboo and Bowery was out to break it. His art was himself; his œuvre consisted of the myriad creatures he turned himself into. 'Every time I go out it turns into a performance,' he said.

Bowery once described one of his new looks as 'a cross between polka dots and skin rash … simulating infection and disease'. Publicised for free by Lynne Franks (allegedly the real-life role model for Jennifer Saunders' character in **Absolutely Fabulous**), he came up with the Paki From Outer Space look. Asked to customise a jacket for style magazine *Blitz*, he covered it in hair grips. He was the fashion stylist for Boy George's *Generation of Love* video in 1990. On one occasion he appeared in a knitted dress that unravelled to reveal a naked Leigh Bowery. As a guest lecturer at the Architectural Association he instructed students to make a costume in the style of their favourite building. He painted **Damien Hirst**'s genitals and his short-lived band, Minty, was banned by Westminster City Council.

Reviewing a lifetime of performance Bowery said, 'I'm interested in a jarring aesthetic and the tensions between contradictions – the idea that something can be frightening and heroic and pathetic all at the same time.' On the other hand, maybe it was a case of an overgrown kid who just couldn't stop dressing up.

Leigh Bowery was once described as 'the Warhol of London', but he was never as fey as pale Andy. In fact he was a big man who could break the lights above a bar if he decided to do a high-stepping kick. As a nude model for painter Lucian Freud, he stands revealed as a corpulent, heavy-framed bruiser. But he was vulnerable to AIDS all the same. Diagnosed HIV positive in November 1988, Bowery died on New Year's Eve 1994. Somebody said he made 'a glorious corpse'.

David Bowie began the trend for artists to make themselves into their art; but he started out as a musician, and had to work gradually towards his new subject – himself. Bowery short-circuited this process. Right from the outset, his changing appearance was his metier. In this respect he represented two contradictory trends in British culture: his identities were all provisional, lasting only as long as the costumes on which they were based; on the other hand, the turn to the body as canvas is in line with ancient, unchanging ritual. The ancient and the modern in British culture were both represented by Bowery.

PARENTS David Bowie, Jordan, Steve Strange
READ ON *Leigh Bowery – the life and times of an icon* by Sue Tilley

David Bowie

The chameleon

Surveying the **glam** era of the 70s and comparing it to the Todd Haynes film *Velvet Goldmine* (1998), cultural critic **Peter York** described David Bowie as 'arguably the most significant and influential postwar British artist in any medium'.

Born in inner-city Brixton and brought up in the suburbs, David (Jones) Bowie learnt the saxophone, formed an r&b band and a society to stop the persecution of men with long hair, made a cheeky Cockney novelty record ('The Laughing Gnome'), studied mime and Japanese kabuki theatre with far-out, gay performance artist Lindsay Kemp, was turned down by **The Beatles'** Apple

Record Co in 1968, hit the charts the following summer as Major Tom in the eerily futuristic 'Space Oddity', made a fairly poor album for Deram, and ran an equally unsuccessful arts lab in Beckenham before picking up speed again with a couple of records which hinted, visually, at androgyny and bisexuality while sounding almost folk-ish (*Hunky Dory* and *The Man Who Sold The World*, both of which were compared to the work of **Syd Barrett**). From the beginnings of his career, then, Bowie combined innovation with tradition, both homegrown and exotic.

The watershed in Bowie's life and career was *The Rise and Fall of Ziggy Stardust and the Spiders from Mars*, released in 1972. For this album and the accompanying tour, Bowie created a semi-fictitious role for himself as a glam pop star/creature from outer space. While others claimed to be authentic and natural, he constructed an image that was ostentatiously self-conscious and premeditated.

The Ziggy Stardust character was an Anglicisation of the deliberate decadence of New York bohemianism and its luminaries such as Andy Warhol and Lou Reed. York suggests that 'Bowie took those New York people, completely sucked their skulls and used them to make high drama for the high street. He repackaged them for people like me, who didn't know their work.'

Urban sophisticates like York were not the only ones affected. Throughout Britain and across the spectrum of social class, daring young people struggled to catch up with the complex self-image that Bowie had manufactured: gay-ish, garish, sexy, cool – reinforced by his famously 'lazy eye' – and cerebral. York points out that this 'Bowie constituency' was also the 'original punk constituency': that is, punk would have been impossible without Bowie preceding it, and Johnny Rotten's role as anti-Christ was partly dependent on Bowie's prior performance as 'the leper messiah'.

According to cultural commentator Michael Bracewell, 'the trappings of transvestism, thanks to Bowie, were granted the broadest currency of street fashionability'. Gay became the new black and the high street was never the same again. Queens like **Elton John** and Freddie Mercury might still be in the closet if Bowie had not broken new ground by declaring himself bisexual.

Just as the masses were catching up, he moved on. Ziggy Stardust was killed off and Bowie reappeared as A Lad Insane (*Aladdin Sane*) with a tortured psyche and an increasing interest in soul music (coming right to the fore in 'Young Americans'). In 1974 he was the subject of *Cracked Actor* (BBC2), a seminal TV documentary made by Alan Yentob. Bowie was portrayed as a performer on the brink of mental collapse, experimenting lyrically with Burroughs-style cut-ups while coming close to cutting himself off from the rest of humanity. This portrait of alienation may have persuaded director Nicholas Roeg to cast Bowie in the lead role in *The Man Who Fell To Earth* (1986).

The subsequent roles that Bowie pursued (including the lead in the New York stage production of *The Elephant Man*, Baal in **Alan Clarke**'s televisation of the first play by Bertolt Brecht, a British PoW in Oshima's *Merry Christmas, Mr*

Lawrence and a dying vampire in Tony Scott's *The Hunger*) continued, much like his musical *personae*, to be alienated outsiders. Yet as an actor he has a reputation for being wooden – odd for a pop artist whose ability to flow from one persona to another (from Ziggy to Aladdin to the Thin White Duke, etc) has been likened to a chameleon.

Having suckled on black American soul ('Young Americans'), in the second half of the 70s Bowie moved back across the Atlantic in search of a new teat. Working with **Brian Eno** in Berlin, he produced a series of synthesiser-based albums (*Low, Sound and Vision, Heroes*) which influenced a new generation of bands such as the Human League. Now relabelled the Thin White Duke, he returned in glory to Britain, and at Victoria station – with (Boy) George O'Dowd among the hundreds of fans in attendance – he indulged in a piece of theatre which for some people came too close to a fascist rally.

After all this time, Bowie still hadn't cracked the USA. He failed to become a fully fledged stadium rocker until the *Let's Dance* tour of 1983. Although Bowie is now known as the gender-bender who broke into the Midwest, he only got into Middle America by holding back on the exotic and presenting himself as the epitome/parody of a white heterosexual soul boy.

Bowie has never stopped reinventing himself, but his sampling of new blood (**Goldie**, A Guy Called Gerald) now seems greedy rather than innovative. When he invited Howie B to produce a recent album, there were complaints that Bowie was leeching on jungle. With his Somali wife, his sponsorship of art publishers Booth-Clibborn and support for the London-Asian music of tabla-player and producer **Talvin Singh**, his liking for Japanese art and his proselytising for the Internet (with 'Bowienet' he established himself as an Internet Service Provider) and cyberculture (he provided the music for the world's first Buddhist computer game; in *Omikron – the Nomad Soul*, produced by **Lara Croft** creators Eidos, you never die but are reincarnated instead), Bowie seems almost too hip to be true.

Even Peter York felt compelled to describe him as 'the Rip Van Withit of western culture'; and **Irvine Welsh**'s *Trainspotting* contains a debate between two stoned characters about how Bowie blew it. Answer (in my book): it's a toss-up between the relentless noise of Bowie's band Metal Machine and his acceptance at the Brits 1996 of a special award for services to British music presented by (then) opposition leader **Tony Blair**. The wearing of stilettoes, a dangly earring and a goatee was not enough to redeem him. Hence in the *Q* magazine poll to decide the Top 100 pop stars of all time, Bowie ranked sixth – four or five places down from where he might have been ranked 20 years ago.

PARENTS Lindsay Kemp, Bob Dylan, Lou Reed, Andy Warhol
CHILDREN punk, **New Romantic**
READ ON *Style Wars* by Peter York

Danny Boyle
anti-realist

Together with producer Andrew Macdonald (grandson of Emeric Pressburger) and medic-turned-scriptwriter John Hodge, director Danny Boyle is one of the triumvirate credited with revitalising British cinema in the 90s. Their work includes *Shallow Grave* (1994), *Trainspotting* (1996) and *A Life Less Ordinary* (1997). All three movies starred **Ewan McGregor,** but Boyle's latest film, an adaptation of Alex Garland's debut novel *The Beach* (1999), features Hollywood's Leonardo di Caprio in the lead role.

Born in Manchester, Boyle was brought up in a working-class household. Grammar school was his ticket out, first into the theatre (deputy director of the Royal Court), and then television (BBC Belfast, followed by the director's chair for some episodes of *Inspector Morse* and the mini-series *Mr Wroe's Virgins*). Keen to direct a feature film, he endeared himself to fellow first-timers Macdonald and Hodge by comparing the latter's script for *Shallow Grave* (three Scottish yuppies in Edinburgh's stylish New Town take on a new flatmate who dies leaving a bagful of money; the flatmates fall out over it and how to dispose of the body) to the Coen Brothers' *Blood Simple*. All three shared an affection for American independent film-makers (hailed as the first offspring of the British film renaissance, *Shallow Grave* was originally conceived with an American cast and setting) and a preference for British glamour and style (**Powell and Pressburger**) over arthouse experimentation (**Peter Greenaway**) or '**kitchen sink**' seriousness (**Ken Loach**). 'Here was a script that didn't have all the moral baggage that British films carry around all the time,' Boyle later said. '*Shallow Grave* is not about class or society or people being crushed by forces they can't control. Everybody takes responsibility for their decisions. We didn't want this film to be soaked in British social realism.'

In the introduction to the published screenplay of *Shallow Grave*, Hodge describes Boyle as 'a man of sensitivity and endless patience but with a thuggish streak of low, animal cunning. In short, a man who could work with actors.' In order to establish a working relationship, Boyle rented a flat and moved in for a week with his three leading players (McGregor, Kerry Fox and Christopher Eccleston). As a result, the teamwork of the behind-the-camera trio was matched by the camaraderie of the three leading actors in front of it. *Shallow Grave* has a taut quality which has prompted comparisons with Hitchcock. Like the work of Hitchcock, the film has a cruel streak. 'I suppose the film is cruel,' Boyle conceded, 'but then life can be cruel and cold. There are other sides of life, of culture, but *Shallow Grave* doesn't choose to look at them.'

Boyle's next film was also informed by dislike of worthy British social realism. Producer Andrew Macdonald was drawn to **Irvine Welsh**'s novel of heroin-based Edinburgh lowlife because of 'the surrealistic style of it, the way it refuses to conform to social realism, which as a genre is one of my pet hates'. For his part, Welsh was equally determined that his bleakly humorous stories should not

become celluloid moral tracts. He had refused previous offers for the film rights because 'I could see they wanted to turn it into some dull and worthy bit of social realism.' In consultation with Welsh and Macdonald, Hodge worked through four drafts before arriving at a version that combined 'looseness and urgency … playful fringes and harrowing interiors' – a highly innovative package, and experimental, which clocked in only a few seconds adrift from the standard length (90 minutes) for mainstream films.

Boyle's sources for *Trainspotting* included the paintings of Edward Hopper, Francis Bacon, Francisco Goya and Egon Schiele, and the recovering addicts of Edinburgh's Calton Athletic Club, who tutored his actors in the technicalities of shooting up. The results, according to Xan Brooks, 'swung between gritty naturalism and surreal flamboyance, between chic style-piece and gruelling exposé, and yet all the while maintained a wholeness and integrity.'

In the run-up to the UK release of *Trainspotting* in February 1996, there were rumours that the cast had dabbled with heroin ('total bollocks' retorted Jonny Lee Miller/Sick Boy), and complaints that the film glamorised addiction ('heroin chic'). Veteran critic Alexander Walker voiced his opposition: 'In style, structure and subversive imagination, it recalls Stanley Kubrick's *A Clockwork Orange*. Kubrick's film made one think. Boyle's film, overall a clever pastiche of the senior director's style, makes one puke.' Ken Loach believed that it presented 'a distorted view' of life in Britain, and objected to its American style. 'It is aggressively young and Tarantino-esque,' he explained, 'with a lot of violence and what the Americans call in that horrible phrase which I loathe: "in-your-face". That's not true of the way we live in Britain.' But Boyle refuted all accusations of irresponsibility or lack of integrity, while once again rejecting the British tradition of social-realist sermonising: 'Our guiding aim was always to try to be honest about heroin. So, yes, the beginning of *Trainspotting* is completely seductive. The dilemma was that we wanted to make an entertaining film about something that is potentially lethal, something that people may find unacceptable.'

Despite the deliberate distance between *Trainspotting* and traditional British cinema, Boyle's film gained a government seal of approval. Tory minister Virginia Bottomley (secretary of state for National Heritage) welcomed it as 'a harrowing film that leaves you in no doubt as to the ravages of drug addiction.' By the end of 1996, *Trainspotting* had achieved something else that endeared it to the friends of the free market: from an original outlay of US$3. 5 million, it grossed a respectable US$72 million, making it the most profitable film of the year.

Originally set in Scotland and France, Hodge's script for *A Life Less Ordinary* (1997) was relocated to the USA. Combining gangster violence with Hollywood romanticism, vintage screwball comedy, and homage to Powell and Pressburger's *A Matter of Life and Death, A Life Less Ordinary* is an extraordinary package which even the Boyle-Macdonald-Hodge troika cannot quite carry off. Although the ostensible romance is between a Scot and an American, there is also a love element between the British film-makers and the landscape of the American Midwest.

British critics accused Boyle and Co of 'narcissistic self-regard'. Released two months after the **Oasis** album *Be Here Now*, their film received a similar critical drubbing. In the UK edition of *Premiere*, Ryan Gilbey described one as a 'cocaine movie', the other as a 'cocaine album.' The media darlings of 1995–96 were deemed to have over-indulged themselves in 1997. As Ewan McGregor subsequently pointed out, the British backlash tradition came into full swing against *A Life Less Ordinary*.

Along with Macdonald, Hodge and McGregor, Boyle has made film as much a part of British culture as pop music. Since **The Beatles**, every other medium had taken second place, but pop's pole position is no longer guaranteed. Boyle's champions would claim that the rise in the relative cultural weight of 'Reel Britannia' is largely due to his combination of artistic integrity and entertainment value, which means that, after many years, cinema audiences can once again enjoy art and entertainment at the same time. Others would say that the improved status of British cinema is down to the declining significance of indigenous pop rather than any great improvement in its own intrinsic merit.

PARENTS Coen Brothers, Alfred Hitchcock, Powell and Pressburger
READ ON *Choose Life – Ewan Mcgregor and the British film revival* by Xan Brooks

Billy Bragg
Wiley Woody

Bragg by name, not by nature. His backing band are called The Blokes, and 'bloke' is also the best description of their frontman: a Cockney bloke (born in Barking in 1957), a working-class bloke (father a warehouse chargehand), and a straightforward bloke who has never hidden his left-wing leanings. In Billy Bragg's socialist-realist songs, the wit and wisdom of American hobo hero Woody Guthrie meets British film-maker Lindsay Anderson and novelist Gerald Kersh (*Night and the City, Fowler's End*) in a paean to ordinary working folk.

Bragg was already a leftie when he joined the army in 1981 (possibly the only recruit ever to have been given 'Call Up' by The Clash as a going-away present). He later explained that, at the hottest moment of the Second Cold War, he felt he'd 'rather be in a tank than an armchair'. In the Irish Hussars he did drive a tank but refused to go to Northern Ireland (Protestants in his regiment were not sent there anyway). Perhaps he thought he was joining a people's

Billy Bragg

army, a continuation of the Popular Front fighting force sometimes represented in British war films (years later he wrote an article in *The Independent* recalling and reclaiming the radical populism of the Diggers, a seditious offshoot of Cromwell's New Model Army). Instead he found himself committed to an institution more like the American military depicted in Stanley Kubrick's *Full Metal Jacket* (shot in Beckton, East London, next door to Bragg's Barking home). When Bob Marley died and nobody around him noticed, Bragg realised how alienated he was from the squaddie's world – and got out as quick as he could. Ten years after signing on, he was singing at the Anti-Gulf War Rally in Hyde Park.

Bragg's first band Riff-Raff played the lower end of the London pub rock circuit (free entrance at Hammersmith's Red Cow, poor relation to The Nashville in West Kensington). His first solo album, *Life's A Riot*, was released at the beginning of 1984, shortly before the start of the marathon miners' strike. With his plaintive voice, strumming guitar and punk-ish delivery, Bragg's sardonic songs of working-class love and life could have been the soundtrack for the events of 1984–85. Three years later, in the run-up to the general election of 1987, Bragg was a mainstay of the Red Wedge tour designed to drum up young voters' support for the Labour Party. His songs of political anger and boyish angst ('How can you lie there and think of England when you don't even know who's in the team') became the sing-a-long favourites of a generation of unhappy socialists living through the Thatcher years.

For more than a decade, in which he twice became a father, Bragg chugged along in his blokeish way. He next came to prominence in 1998 when, backed by American 'alt country' band Wilco, he released *Mermaid Avenue*, an album of Woody Guthrie songs named after the street where Woody lived with his wife after the Second World War. Bragg narrated a TV documentary about making the LP, which was shortlisted for a Grammy (Lucinda Williams was the eventual winner). The *Observer* announced that 'Billy Bragg is hip again', not realising that he had never before been cool.

Bragg is so uncool he must be authentic. He might be wearing a leather jacket or top hat and tails but he will always sound like he's dressed in a donkey jacket. The man himself is genuine enough, but what of his new trendiness? Could the fad for Bragg represent a real return to his socialist values? Or, as seems much more likely, a nostalgia for the days of the 80s when 'flying pickets' meant more than a novelty band and the name of the trade unionists' pub in Liverpool? As with **John Peel**, it seems that even the most uncompromising and rebellious talents are if not entirely diffused then at least domesticated and welcomed into the fold at a certain age as a 'national treasure' that was secretly loved all along by mainstream culture. In 1999 Bragg even had a *Brookside*-style close named after him in his native Barking, proving that, even in the eyes of the civic elders, the boy done good.

PARENTS Woody Guthrie, punk
READ ON *Billy Bragg* by Andrew Collins

Kenneth Branagh
Over-exposed

Writer, producer, director, manager, actor, narrator – Kenneth Branagh is the man who's done it all. He did so much so young that the British public became sceptical of his considerable achievements.

Born (1960) in Belfast, Kenneth Charles Branagh (father in business, mother a teacher) grew up in Reading. At 15 he appeared in a local production of *Toad of Toad Hall*. At London's Royal Academy of Dramatic Art (RADA) he won the Bancroft Gold Medal. By 1984 he was playing the title part in the Royal Shakespeare Company's *Henry V*; five years later, he adapted, directed and starred in his own film version. That same year (1989), Branagh published *Beginning*, an autobiographical account of his first 29 years (an example of self-confidence surpassed only by writer and broadcaster Beverley Nichols' *21*).

Henry was Branagh's third film part, preceded by the roles of Rick Lamb in *High Season* (1986, about the effects of tourism on a Greek village) and First World War casualty James Moon in *A Month In The Country* (1987). He followed it with two acting parts in the Hitchcockian thriller *Dead Again* (1991), and two roles (acting and directing) in *Peter's Friends* (1992). His role in *Much Ado About Nothing* was three-fold (male lead, screenplay, director), a feat of multi-skilling he repeated for the widely acclaimed *Hamlet* (1996).

On television and in theatre the Branagh profile was equally high: (TV) lead role in the *Billy* trilogy of plays, DH Lawrence in *Coming Through* (1985), Oswald Alving in Ibsen's *Ghosts* (1986), Guy Pringle in *The Fortunes of War* series (1987), one of the most talked-about TV drama series of the 80s, and Jimmy Porter in John Osborne's *Look Back In Anger* (1989). In April 1987 he formed his own theatre group, the Renaissance Theatre Company (RTC). The first RTC production was a play written by Branagh himself, *Public Enemy* (this was his second play; the first, *Tell Me Honestly*, was written in 1985). Subsequent productions included *Twelfth Night*, *King Lear*, *Uncle Vanya* and *Coriolanus*. The RTC was formed with the expressed intention of facilitating collaboration between writer, director and actor. But since Branagh played all these roles at some point, there can be no doubt that he (the Renaissance Man implied in the company's chosen title?) was really carrying on the British actor-manager tradition associated with Henry Irving and Donald Wolfitt. Branagh also found time to be narrator for a host of important projects, including a four-part television series on European cinema, a top-flight documentary series on the Cold War, the Disney production *Anne Frank Remembered* (1995), for which he won an Oscar (his only Academy Award to date), and the BBC's *Walking With Dinosaurs* (1999).

On the set of *The Fortunes of War*, Branagh met left-wing actress **Emma Thompson**, daughter of *Magic Roundabout* author Eric Thompson. They were married three years later. After a brief sojourn as the golden couple of British stage and screen they separated in 1995. 'Our work,' they explained in a joint statement, 'has inevitably led to our spending long periods of time away from each other and, as a result, we have drifted apart.' By contrast, Branagh's relationship with the viewing public may have suffered from too much proximity. In the early to mid-90s it seemed as if there was no escape from Branagh and his côterie. At the end of the decade, after a brief period in which he, wisely, kept out of the limelight, Branagh made a further flurry of feature films: *The Theory of Flight, The Gingerbread Man, Tempting Fate* and *Celebrity*, a comedy directed by Woody Allen in which Branagh played the familiar Allen *persona*. In the late 80s and early 90s Branagh was synonymous with British film: the natural choice for narrator of the aforementioned major documentary series about European cinema including a programme on the lost opportunity of British movie-making. It was widely understood that, with Branagh, that lost opportunity had been found again. Less than a decade later, however, Branagh was playing a role associated with an American auteur and working under his direction.

In response to an Internet question about Branagh as both actor and director, his assistant Tamar Thomas replied, ominously: 'Although Kenneth has promised not to do both jobs at the same time in the future, I doubt whether he will be able to resist the temptation should someone offer him a very exciting film.' He was back on song in 2000 with his film of Shakespeare's *Love's Labours Lost* done as a musical set between the wars.

PARENTS Henry Irving, Laurence Olivier, Donald Wolfitt

Richard Branson
More than hot air

Born into a prosperous middle-class background in 1950, Richard Branson is most famous for failing (so far) to circumvent the world in a hot air balloon. He is also a big businessman, a role model for a cohort within the current generation of post-Thatcherite under-25s – Branson says he wrote his autobiography *Losing My Virginity* (1998) 'so that young people might be inspired' – and as boss of the less-than-perfect Virgin Trains service, something of a hate figure.

As a youth Branson founded *Student*, a magazine for school-leavers. Then he started a mail-order record retailing operation called Virgin. Out of this grew a chain of record shops with a hippie ambience (you could hang out in a Virgin shop and headphones were provided for you to listen to as many records as you liked) and a record label that released both the Sex Pistols' *Never Mind The Bollocks* and the multi-million-selling post-hippie muzak of *Tubular Bells* by Mike Oldfield. Along the way Branson lost his first wife Kirsten (divorced after a wife-swapping evening involving spaced-out singer Kevin Ayers). After a dodgy moment when charged with irregularities concerning the import/export of records, he gained enough capital to build an empire (still no corporate headquarters) involving 200 companies with annual sales in the region of £2.5 billion.

Having sold his radio station to **Chris Evans**, Branson's interests now include airlines (established in 1984 against City recommendations), railways, hotels, records, banking, soft drinks, software, cinemas and high-street retailing, with potential developments in health clubs and helicopters. The empire is ruled by a goateed Branson who looks nothing like the traditional image of imperiousness: never wears a tie, often in jeans, gives money to beggars, is known as 'the king of casj [casual]'. Quizzed by a colleague as to why he hadn't put on a suit and tie for an important business meeting with Coutts, he replied that, if he had, 'they'd know we were desperate and refuse the loan'. Officially he has quit smoking, but has also been known to cadge fags – a bit rich from a man with a mansion in fashionable Holland Park and a private island in the Caribbean.

Branson is the acceptable face of capitalism. He symbolises business acumen without sharp practice (he reckons that sleaze denied him the chance to run the National Lottery), accountancy with attitude, a principal with principles. But his own financial arrangements are a little less straightforward than his reputation might suggest. Branson's empire depends on a complicated set-up involving various holding companies in the British Virgin Islands. This allows him to keep the show on the road, even though according to the *Economist* in February 1998, among all the offshoots of Virgin only Virgin Atlantic was making money consistently.

Branson has his critics. After travelling with Virgin Trains, *Guardian* columnist Linda Grant noted that the king of casj is anything but casual about the dress code of his staff: 'tattoos out, piercing out, no jumpers under jackets; for women, short nails, neutral make-up and black shoes'. Reviewing Branson's career in 'hippie capitalism', Grant suggested that 'Virgin is a paradigm of what everything is tending towards – the triumph of form over substance.' She added: 'If Virgin has been revolutionary, it is in its 30-year project of framing the blueprint for New Labour.'

READ ON *Losing My Virginity* by Richard Branson

The Bristol sound
Slow-motion city

Built on shipping, slavery (streetnames include Whiteladies Road and Blackboy Hill), tobacco, sherry, chocolate and aerospace, Bristol is a big city with a village feel to it. Perhaps because it is the gateway to the cider-drinking West Country, or because of the grandeur of its setting (between the Cotswolds and the Mendips, next to the Avon Gorge straddled by Brunel's suspension bridge), or its elegant architecture (the best that slavers' money could buy), or even because of its proximity to the travellers' festival trail, Bristol has acquired a laid-back reputation. It could have been as glorious as Rome, one commentator suggested, except that Bristolians could not be bothered. Others have dubbed it Britain's San Francisco. Appropriate, then, that the 'Bristol sound' of the 90s was a slowed-down, relaxed form of dance-derived music commonly called 'trip-hop' (a term disliked by most of those supposedly involved in it, many of whom denied there was 'a Bristol sound' at all).

Bristol missed the credit boom of the 80s. Its financial services sector has grown but not to the point of remoulding the city in its own image, as occurred in London during the yuppie years. On the other hand, Bristol was the seminal 80s 'inner city', in that it was here, in April 1980, outside the Black and White cafe in the district of St Paul's, that rioting broke out in Britain for the first time since the 30s. Black youth, with some assistance from white post-punks, fought the police in the first of a spate of riots which spread to Liverpool, Handsworth in Birmingham, Brixton, and later Broadwater Farm in London.

Although Bristol marked the Thatcher years by getting rid of its left-wing Labour MP Tony Benn, the city's music scene was not transformed by a new aesthetic of conspicuous consumption. It continued to combine punk, funk, jazz and reggae in a radical, left-leaning mix. With the addition of hip-hop, scratch'n'mix DJ'ing (the US movie *Wild Style* was a big influence), graffiti and other aspects of street style, all the various elements of the Bristol sound were in place before the end of the 80s. After a false start with the collapse of the Wild Bunch (Miles Johnson went to Japan and then New York, Nellee Hooper joined **Soul II Soul** and Robert Del Naja went into hibernation before forming **Massive Attack**), Bristol came on to the musical map in the first half of the 90s (previously, its best-known musician was pianist Russ Conway).

Much has been written about Bristol's multiculturalism. But, as documented in Kenneth Pryce's

Endless Pressure, in the 70s black people in Bristol were as marginalised as anywhere else. Local drum and bassman **Roni Size** remembers Bristol as being 'pretty tough for a lot of people', and prefers to describe the city as 'a hotbed of frustration' rather than a 'hotbed of musical talent'. But there were a couple of venues where musical and cultural crossover took place: Revolver record store, with an extensive stock of black music but close enough to the middle-class district of Clifton for bohemian white boys to feel at home there; and the Dug Out, a club on Park Row within a stone's throw of the university where students and straights mixed with pimps and people from the margins. The Dug Out was the main conduit between reggae sound systems, hip-hop posses and the Clifton-based bohemian punk and funk bands (**The Pop Group**, Rip, Rig and Panic, Maximum Joy, Glaxo Babies). In its scuzzy atmosphere, the elements that go to make up the Bristol sound came together for the first time. After 20 years of cultural cross-fertilisation, this combination has, according to Ekow Eshun of *Arena* magazine, produced 'a generation of people who grew up with the idea that complexity and random possibilities are to be welcomed'.

Massive Attack
'Non-specific music'

Massive Attack consists of three Bristol-based musicians (not one of them is a traditional singer or instrumentalist) whose output is small (three albums in nearly ten years: *Blue Lines*, 1991; *Protection*, 1994; and *Mezzanine*, 1998) but highly significant. In the *Daily Telegraph*, music writer Neil McCormick suggested that the work of Massive Attack 'reflects the musical language of modern Britain more than anything by such celebrated pop luminaries as **Oasis** or the **Spice Girls**'.

Robert Del Naja aka 3-D, Grant Marshall aka Daddy G and Andrew Voles aka Mushroom trained as rappers, graffiti artists, DJs and producers. Throughout the 90s they were at the forefront of a new generation of digital recording artists whose primary role is to manipulate sounds rather than write songs on piano or acoustic guitar. Their method of working is to build up a data bank of riffs, figures, breaks and phrases to which other elements, such as samples from DJ Grant Marshall's extensive record collection, can then be added. They also incorporate the work of traditional music-makers into their production process. Vocalists Tracey Thorn (Everything But The Girl) and Liz Fraser from the **indie** scene, veteran Jamaican reggae singer Horace Andy, and soul diva Shara Nelson, have all featured on their albums (in early TV appearances attention was focused largely on Nelson). They have also used the instrumental output of local duo The Insects. *Blue Lines* and *Protection* featured slow-motion raps from **Tricky** (in the early days he was known as Massive Attack's 'YTS member' because he was kept on a retainer of £25 a week). Combining elements from reggae, film scores, hip-hop, soul and rock, Massive Attack's Grant Marshall describes their work as 'non-specific music'. With roots in

sound systems, Massive Attack make dance-derived music that you don't dance to.

They also have a reputation for attitude. When Sarah Ferguson, ex-wife of HRH Prince Andrew, tried to present them with the 1998 MTV award for best video, Del Naja responded by saying, live on stage, 'Someone's having a fucking laugh.' Communications between band members can be almost as abrasive. According to Marshall, 'We don't actually see eye to eye, and in a way that's our weakness and our strength.'

Tricky
Difficult

Born Adrian Thaws in the Hartcliffe district of Bristol in 1958, and brought up in nearby Knowle West, Tricky acquired his moniker after he failed to meet a friend in the city centre as arranged; instead he disappeared to Manchester for a month and a half, and when he returned to Bristol and walked through the city centre his friend happened to be standing in the place where they had agreed to meet six weeks earlier. 'You tricky bastard,' said the friend. It's a description that Thaws has lived up to ever since (notably when he turned down an invitation to produce Madonna, and repeatedly denied any connection to award-winning reggae star Finley Quaye who is understood to be his maternal uncle).

While still a virtual apprentice with **Massive Attack**, Tricky made a menacing solo debut with 'Nothing's Clear', a track produced by Geoff Barrow

Tricky

(also the tape operator on *Blue Lines* and subsequently the 'boss' of **Portishead**) which appeared on a local charity album, *The Hard Sell*. He demonstrated his talents on another slow rap (the privately pressed 'Aftermath') before releasing the highly acclaimed *Maxinequaye* in 1995 (*NME* album of the year, named after his late mother and featuring the ethereal vocals of Martina Topley-Bird), a remarkable combination of rage and reserve which was confirmed by a stage act in which Tricky appeared as a boxer. Two subsequent albums (*Pre-*

Millennial Tension and *Angels With Dirty Faces*, which reflects Tricky's move to New York) were influential but possibly less successful. Yet Tricky has managed to break the dance-music mould of the traditional black performer. Variously described as 'a black **Bowie**' and 'Nick Cave with street cred', he has entered areas of self-expression and self-exploration that have previously been barred to most black musicians.

Tricky's work is rooted in his mixed race ('we're mongrels') background (his great-grandmother was the first person of mixed race to live in Knowle West, probably the hardest area in Bristol; various relatives had a reputation as local toughs). His output is also locked into the difficulties he experienced as a child suffering from asthma and eczema. His epileptic mother committed suicide when he was three. At nine he was caught stealing a bar of chocolate. In his teens he tried housebreaking and small-scale drug dealing. His Uncle Michael was murdered (stabbed in a dispute about paying a £1 entrance fee to a club), and on the day he was buried, nephew Adrian was arrested for passing forged £50 notes. Tricky has explained that he would have been a villain except that he was no good at it; so to make money he had to make music instead.

Although he objects to being typecast as 'a mass murderer', as in early publicity shots in which he looked psychopathic, the aura of criminality remains part of Tricky's image. When a **Face** writer expressed doubts about Tricky's commitment to his daughter by Martina, he told *Time Out* he wanted to waste him. His record label Durban Poison takes its name from a type of marijuana (talking about weed, he once said 'I need it, I have to have it, it's an addiction'); in 1998 he put together an album (*Products of the Environment*) with ex-gangsters such as Mad Frankie Fraser (the proceeds went to charity); and when interviewed by Chris Heath for *The Sunday Times* he talked about real-life violence imitating screen violence ('People hold their guns in a fashionable way now – they turn them on their side when they shoot. We follow films.'), insisting that 'we're a violent, violent culture'. Kung Fu star Bruce Lee has always been a hero.

But Tricky is not just another clichéd bad boy. As a teenager he paid a girl to steal a dress for him, and he says he's worn dresses on and off ever since. His feelings about England are not straightforward either. He told Chris Heath that the problem with England is 'It gives me time to think. And I don't like thinking. I don't like feeling.' One-time collaborator Terry Hall (The Specials singer idolised by a young Adrian Thaws) confirms that Tricky's attention span is notably short, but insists that this adds to the immediacy of his music. Tricky moved to New York because the pace of life there 'doesn't give me time to think'. Yet this is also a man with a penchant for Rowntree's Fruit Pastilles who complains that in the Big Apple 'you can't even get a good biscuit to dip in a cup of tea'.

Roni Size
Drum'n'bass matters

When the Mercury Music Prize was awarded to Roni Size and the Bristol collective Reprazent for their 1997 album *New Forms*, **drum'n'bass** came in from the margins to become the most-talked about British music of the late 90s; and Roni Size, with his dreadlocks, fine features and Bristolian accent, was cast in the role of a British Bob Marley.

It is often said that drum'n'bass is as distinctively British as hip-hop is black American. According to some commentators its emergence has taken black people in Britain beyond 'the Black Atlantic' – they no longer feel the need to look to black

America as their model. But Size is the first to admit that he has drawn on a wide range of musical sources from the USA, Jamaica and Europe. The idea of this 'crossover music' was to get a wide range of people interested. Set against rhythms running at the rate of approx 160bpm, with dub-style basslines at half that speed, sieved through a sampler, broken down and reconstructed by means of digital technology, all these influences are metamorphosised into a new British sound held together by an MC and anointed with luscious vocals. The result, according to Size is 'music of the future' (hence the album title *New Forms*) which incorporates the avant-garde into the realm of pop music. Ekow Eshun, editor of *Arena*, believes that the Reprazent version of drum'n'bass is as rich and diverse as contemporary city life. He has described their work as 'a crystallisation of urban experience' which ranges from 'silence' to 'freneticism'.

Now in his late 20s, Size is softly spoken; but as a raucous youth he was chucked out of school for throwing a chair at a teacher. He found his metier at the Basement Project, a local youth centre where he learnt basic studio techniques and subsequently became a teacher (the Basement Project was the eventual recipient of the £25,000 prize that went with the Mercury award). Another learning experience for Size was the Glastonbury **festival** nearby, which 'set it all off' by teaching him that heavy bass and drums could be brought together with the experimental techniques associated with digital technology. Despite international acclaim, he is still rooted in the city where he grew up.

Portishead
Angst with muffled beats

Named after the outlying town where the band's main man Geoff Barrow spent his teenage years, Portishead are a reclusive duo (Barrow and publicity-shy singer Beth Gibbons are signatories to Portishead contracts, supported by engineer Dave McDonald and jazz guitarist Adrian Utley). Their million-and-a-half-selling first album, *Dummy* (1994, winner of the 1995 Mercury Music Prize), combined Gibbons' **indie**-angst vocals (she learnt her trade singing Janis Joplin songs in Devon pubs) with Barrow's beats (he recalls that at 16 and 17 he stayed in listening to hip-hop and reading Teletext), combined with a twangy guitar sound (Utley) that recalls 60s films and TV themes, all at a surreally slow pace. It sounded like the accompanying music for the ultimate existential B-movie, transposed to British post-**rave** culture (Portishead wrote and starred in a *Breathless*-style promotional film, *To Kill A Dead Man*, which obtained limited release in cinemas when their debut album started to get noticed, and it was subsequently shown on Channel 4).

Nearly four years later, Portishead offered more of the same in the shape of their eponymous second album. But they may have already crossed over into the territory of high-quality muzak: one of their tracks was used as the theme music for *The Vice* (1999), a dour and depressing ITV police drama series about sexual abuse and prostitution, and another appeared in an advert for *Red*, the women's magazine aimed at 'adultescents' (those chronologically old enough to be adults but mentally young enough to be into lifestyle and music). Although their sound is bleak and alienated, in the late 90s Portishead were the preferred dinner-party music of a large cohort of middle-class thirtysomethings.

The Pop Group
The daddies of diversity

The diversity and experimentalism associated with 90s Bristol were prefigured in the late 70s and early 80s by The Pop Group, who, as their name suggests, attempted to bring a new level of self-consciousness and radicalism (their debut single was 'We are all prostitutes'; 'capitalism is the most barbaric of all religions,' they claimed) to the process of making music. Dressed in kilts and kitsch military jackets, the five serious white boys in The Pop Group mixed dub reggae with avant-garde jazz and combined Mark Stewart's politicised post-punk screams with riffs that could have come from George Clinton's Funkadelic. Their first album *Y* (1979) was produced by British reggae star Dennis Bovell, but it failed to sell beyond the radical ghetto. After an uneven second album (*For How Much Longer Do We Tolerate Mass Murder?*), The Pop Group broke up in 1981. But in its finest moment it had set a precedent for funky experimentalism that was still discernible in the **Bristol sound** of the 90s.

Besides appearing occasionally as frontman for

The Mafia, Mark Stewart brought the Sugarhill Gang's rhythm section over to Britain and combined them with local hard man Gary Clail. He was also a mentor to **Tricky** and is still regarded as a legendary figure in Bristol although he has long since moved to **Ibiza**. Gareth Sager formed Rip, Rig and Panic – the band that launched Neneh Cherry who was subsequently influential in making London contacts for the Wild Bunch and **Massive Attack**.

READ ON *Straight Outta Bristol* by Phil Johnson; *To Ride The Storm – the 1980 Bristol 'riot' and the state* by Harris Joshua and Tina Wallace

BritArt
But is it art?

The significance of Young British Artists (**YBAs**) is still being debated: is this a real British renaissance, or a case of effective marketing by adman, art buyer and head honcho of the new art establishment, **Charles Saatchi**?

Sensation

The BritArt controversy came to a head in September 1997 with the opening of Sensation, a Royal Academy exhibition of work by 42 Young British Artists from the Saatchi collection. The show included 'offensive' mutant child/adult figures by the **Chapman Brothers**, and **Marcus Harvey**'s *Myra*, an image of Moors Murderer Myra Hindley constructed from the handprints of children. This work was defaced twice. It also attracted the attention of the Vice Squad, and prompted protests from Winnie Johnson, the mother of one of Hindley's victims. At one point it was going to be de-selected from the show, but the decision was reversed on the grounds that the catalogue was already at the printer's.

That the show was hosted by the Royal Academy, the most venerable institution on the British art scene, made it all the more sensational although, after viewing it, pop singer and painter **Ian Dury** said, he 'didn't know why it was called Sensation because sensation for me is about sex and pleasure'.

In marketing terms, however, Sensation was certainly the appropriate title for the Saatchi show. It was the talking-point of the decade for British art, and even the spin-offs prompted headlines and turned a profit: badges showing a detail from Mona Hatoum's *Rectum* sold at 95p; genitalia fridge magnets were also on sale, while the Chapman Brothers signed 1,000 £5 BT phonecards retailing at £19.95 apiece.

Charles Saatchi

In December 1998 Charles Saatchi put 130 of his pieces up for auction at Christies, including works by **Damien Hirs**t and the **Chapman Brothers**. He used the money from the sale to establish bursaries at four London art schools. This sounds like the action of a genuine philanthropist, but Saatchi is

sometimes portrayed not as a 'Maecenas of modern art' but as a heartless broker who uses the art market as a substitute for the stock exchange, without care or concern for the artists he makes and breaks along the way.

An art collector for more than 20 years, Saatchi buys in bulk – up to a dozen paintings or even a whole show at a time. He says he 'buy[s] for the sheer pleasure of mounting interesting shows', and denies that his purchases are primarily for investment purposes ('90 per cent of the art I buy will probably be worthless in ten years' time to anyone else but me'). There is a constant turnover within his collection, but he insists there is no financial motive: buying and selling is necessary to 'keep the collection on some kind of cutting edge'.

Saatchi may one day be added to the list of philanthropic entrepreneurs such as Samuel Courtauld (benefactor of London's Courtauld Institute), the Scottish shipping mogul Sir William Burrell, retailer Robert Sainsbury, and radio manufacturer Ted Power, who gave generously to the Tate. But his detractors insist that he is a businessman on the make, adding that his 'adman's eye' gives unwarranted value to second-rate art which is instant but ultimately superficial.

Goldsmith's

Many of the best-known **YBAs** were students at Goldsmith's College in New Cross, South London (**Damien Hirst**, Julian Opie, **Gary Hume**, **Sarah Lucas**, Fiona Rae and Ian Davenport, for example). A key person on the staff is artist Michael Craig-Martin, who has been teaching there for more than 25 years. Asked for the secret of Goldsmith's success, Craig-Martin explained that, 'You were left alone to figure things out without constraints. … We wanted to find a way of teaching that was consistent with our sense of ourselves.' Goldsmith's evolved methods of student-centred learning which facilitated what Craig-Martin refers to as 'resplendence in diversity' (odd then, that so many of Goldsmith's successful students seem fixated with the single subject of death). He also believes that the current generation of YBAs are reaping benefits from the work of successive generations of students and teachers since the Second World War: 'We have [had] 40 years of art schools, produced thousands of art graduates and there has been a cycle of them going into schools to teach. … [This is] the third generation of that phenomenon. That is how it has happened.'

YBAs

Rachel Billingham

Rachel Billingham is known for photographs of her family home in Birmingham, including intimate shots of her father drinking.

The Chapman Brothers

After growing up in an 'autistic not artistic' family background, brothers Jake and Dinos Chapman went to the Royal College of Art ('the teaching was crap. It's just a nice little place for people who aren't prepared to get dirty in the real world'), graduated in 1990, and became assistants to **Gilbert and George**. Their most infamous work, *Zygotic acceleration …*, consists of a circle of naked figures joined into a single entity. The figures are childlike except for the adult penises that germinate from unexpected places and for the vaginas in place of mouths. *Ubermensch '95*, their portrait of the wheelchair-bound physicist Stephen Hawking, is almost as controversial.

Dinos Chapman explains that their work is 'about presenting ideas and being as adversarial as possible'. After failing to see eye to eye with them during protracted interview sessions, celebrity journalist Lynn Barber reckons they are just rude and controversial for the sake of being rude and controversial – and not very original at it either ('the Chapmans seem committed to going down the old Ken Russell route').

Tracey Emin

Best known for her rumpled and soiled *Bed* (shortlisted for the Turner prize in 1999), and for drunken, four-letter-word outbursts during a live Channel 4 talk show about the 1997 Turner Prize, Emin has described herself as 'the slag from Margate with big tits and a gold chain'. Born in 1963 she was brought up in a Margate hotel, raped at 13, became promiscuous at 15, and then gave up sex for dancing until she was slow-handclapped off a local dancefloor by a group of boys chanting 'slag'. Having dropped out of school she was accepted by the Royal College of Art. Her work is highly personal, as in *Everyone I Have Ever Slept With 1963–95*, an appliquéd tent containing relics of everybody she has shared a bed with, including two of her own aborted foetuses.

Only two years after graduating, Emin's first solo show was entitled My Major Retrospective: one of the items in it was the Benson & Hedges packet held by her uncle at the moment his head was chopped off in a car accident. In 1995 she opened the Tracey Emin Museum in a former minicab office near Waterloo station. 'I really want everyone to be their own institution,' Emin explained, 'everyone's got a story. Everyone's famous.' Of her method of work, she has said that 'I start with myself but end up with the universe.' Critic Matthew Collings seems to agree. He describes Emin as 'a blast of warm humanism in an art world that had got used to cool cerebralism as the norm'. Her critics complain that Emin's work is not about humanity, but merely concerned with herself, to which she replies: 'Of course, how can you be an artist and not be? It comes with the territory?' She has said she is going to stop being an artist in 2003, when she turns 40.

Anthony Gormley

Turner Prize-winner Anthony Gormley is famous for being the sculptor of *The Angel of the North*, the enormous winged construction which stands on the side of the A1 overlooking Newcastle upon Tyne. A British junior climbing champion was reprimanded for scaling it, and Toon fans covered part of it with a Shearer shirt. 'Football is where life and spirit meet,' says Gormley. In the summer of 1998 the courtyard of the Royal Academy was populated by his work *Critical Mass*, 60 lifesize cast-iron figures all of which were moulded from the naked body of the artist. The effect was like entering a town where everyone had been put to sleep. Gormley said: 'I hope it will shock … People will wonder about the disaster of these bodies lying there …'.

Marcus Harvey

Marcus Harvey graduated from **Goldsmith's** in 1986. Apart from the controversial *Myra*, he is known for 'cool conceptualism and lush, painterly abstraction'. His usual subject is the female body, treated in a manner that combines porn magazines with the style of US pop artists Andy Warhol and Roy Lichtenstein.

Damien Hirst

Critic Andrew Graham-Dixon maintains that 'Hirst has been almost single-handedly responsible for the recent, enormous, worldwide rise in the status of contemporary British art.' On the other hand, plummy-voiced critic Brian Sewell believes that after a moment of high creative ambition, Hirst has now lowered his own tone. Sewell is said to have nicknamed him 'Darren' Hirst.

Born in Leeds in 1965, Hirst's dad left when he was 12, but he later discovered that the absentee parent was not his natural father. As a youth in Leeds, Hirst painted Levi jackets with heavy metal

Damien Hirst

motifs, but recalls that 'there were a couple of other guys, who were using airbrushes, who did them better'. He all but failed art A-level (E grade) yet was admitted to **Goldsmith's** where he teamed up with aspiring art dealer Jay Jopling (son of one-time Tory agriculture minister Michael Jopling). He put on the first Freeze exhibition in 1988. Held in the empty Port of London building in Docklands, the show featured his own work and that of 15 fellow students. He curated two subsequent shows (Modern Medicine and Gambler) in the spring and autumn of 1990.

Hirst was the first Brit artist to be bought by **Charles Saatchi**, who hitherto had been buying only Americans. *The Physical Impossibility of Death in the Mind of Someone Living* (1991), aka the shark in formaldehyde, was commissioned by Saatchi.

Hirst has said: 'you kill things to look at them'. In 1994 *Esquire* magazine ran a six-page spread of Hirst's images of a pig's head cut in two with a chainsaw. He won the Turner Prize in 1995 for *Mother and Child Divided* (pickled cow and calf carcasses sliced in half). In 1997 Booth-Clibborn published Hirst's £59.95 picture book, *I Want To Spend The Rest Of My Life, Everywhere, With Everyone, One To One, Always, Forever, Now*, containing, among other things, lots of photos of dead bodies ('they're like cookery books'). In 1998 he designed a special edition of *Snowblind*, a book about cocaine smuggling in the 70s. One thousand copies were printed, each including a credit card and a US$100 bill, retailing at £1,000 apiece. Hirst says: 'the art world's about money but art is about life'.

As part of Fat Les, Hirst makes spoof pop records with comedian **Keith Allen** and Alex James from **Blur**. He opened a restaurant, Pharmacy, in Notting Hill which was subject to litigation (the Royal College of Pharmacists believed that people might think it was a chemist's). He also reopened Quo Vadis restaurant in partnership with Marco Pierre White (his sculptures were removed in 1999 after a disagreement with White).

Hirst says that having a kid is 'infinitely better than any art you could ever make'. He also told **Jeremy Paxman** that 'if God walked in here now, if he existed, I'd just punch his lights out'.

In recent years Hirst has been spending more time away from London and its revelries, preferring to live in his country house in Devon (on the landing there is a framed letter from the Groucho: 'Dear Damien, how would you like it if one of us came round to your house and pissed in the sink?' In 1998 he sold £1-million worth of art; in early 1999 he refused a £1-million offer to produce another 30 medicine cabinets. According to *Observer* feature writer William Leith, Hirst is in Devon because 'he wants to be Damien Hirst, an artist who keeps having new ideas, rather than Damien Hirst, the man who put a shark in a tank and made sculptures from medical supplies'.

Gordon Burn described Hirst as the artist of 'the post-object, neo-swinging, postmodern world'. Sister Wendy Beckett thinks his work is 'pathetic … one-look art'. He says his method is: 'ask a stupid question; keep asking it'.

Gary Hume

Gary Hume is the self-styled 'beauty terrorist' who participated in the seminal Freeze show (1988) organised by **Hirst**. Shortlisted for the Turner Prize in 1996, he declares that 'the surface is all you get of me'.

Sarah Lucas

Sarah Lucas graduated from **Goldsmith's** in 1987 and six years later, along with **Tracey Emin**, opened a gallery in an old shop on the Bethnal Green Road in London's East End. 'Androgynous' Lucas explores the depiction of the female nude. *Sod You Gits* (1990) is a polemic against the tabloids. In *Two Fried Eggs and a Kebab* (1992), she substituted food for breasts and female genitalia in a parody of porno painter Allen Jones. Lucas says 'I use sexist attitudes because they are there to be used. I get strength from them.'

Cathy de Moncheaux

Shortlisted for the 1998 Turner Prize, Cathy de Moncheaux produces sexually fetishistic sculptures which have been described as 'bordello chic'.

Steve McQueen

A film and video artist, born in 1969, Steve McQueen studied at Chelsea, Goldsmith's and the Tisch school in New York and came to prominence winning the 1999 Turner Prize. His work, known for its repetition and enigma and evoking a sense of both movement and dislocation, includes *Bear* (1993) featuring a confrontation between two naked men and *Deadpan* (1997), the reinactment of a Buster Keaton stunt where a house falls down around him. His work, shot mainly black and white, is peppered with references to Sergei Eisenstein and Orson Welles.

Chris Ofili

Chris Ofili (30) is the Nigerian/Mancunian who won the 1998 Turner Prize for work including *No Woman No Cry*, a tribute to Stephen Lawrence in which the face of the murdered black teenager appears in the tears cried by a black woman. But Ofili is more widely known for having attached large lumps of elephant dung to some of his canvases. One of the Turner judges described his work as 'very much bordering on the edge of the permissible'.

Marc Quinn

Marc Quinn is known for sculptures of exploding bodies, and for *Self*, a model of his own head in nine pints of his own blood, shown in **Saatchi**'s **YBA** II (1993).

Jenny Saville

Jenny Saville hails from Glasgow and paints fleshy, female nudes. She says dieting is 'like an epidemic'. Her enormous canvases dominate galleries, empowering her warts-and-all subjects with iconic status.

Sam Taylor-Wood

Born 1967 and married to art dealer Jay Jopling, photo and video artist Sam Taylor-Wood studied at Hastings with Jake Chapman, North East London Polytechnic and then at **Goldsmith's**. Art college was her place of escape from a dysfunctional family. After college she worked at the Royal Opera House and made video projections for West End shows and for the **Pet Shop Boys**.

Taylor-Wood's remake of the *Last Supper* features a topless woman in place of Jesus. An early work consists of herself dancing to the sound of a machine gun. *Atlantic* and *Travesty of a Mockery* depict a violent argument. These pieces are like extensions of film sequences. Taylor-Wood says she is 'fascinated by the cinema, but often when I see something in a film – like an argument – I want to see more of it. Rather than a 30-second edit, I want to see it really thrashed out.' In 1998 Taylor-Wood recovered from cancer of the colon.

Gavin Turk

Gavin Turk failed his degree show but was taken up by Jay Jopling and then by **Saatchi**. When he did eventually graduate he mounted a blue plaque in his own studio (a spoof on the English Heritage blue plaques that mark the homes and workplaces of important cultural figures). Saatchi bought the plaque. Turk does not over-exert himself. *Stool* (1990) is the paint-splattered stool from his studio. For the 1995 Saatchi show he contributed *Pop* (1993), a waxwork of himself as Sid Vicious.

Gillian Wearing

Gillian Wearing's work is concerned with 'individuals, their secrets, the small dramas of the city'. She made her name with *Signs* (1992). To make this piece, she approached people in the street, asking them to write a message of their own choosing on a piece of paper and be photographed holding it. She complained, but did not sue, when an advert for Volkswagen was based on the same process. She complained again in 1999 when **Charles Saatchi**'s agency (M&C Saatchi) produced an ad for BSkyB that resembled her piece *10–16*, in which adults are shown addressing the camera but their voices have been overdubbed with those of children. Winner of the Turner Prize in 1997, she works in video, photography and text.

Rachel Whiteread

When Rachel Whiteread won the 1993 Turner Prize for *House*, a concrete cast of a house in Bow, east London, the local Liberal Democrat council voted to knock it down (the vote was cast on the very same night that the prize was awarded to her). Meanwhile, pranksters the K Foundation nominated Whiteread as the worst of the four shortlisted artists and awarded her double the Tate prize money. She gave it away. A graduate of the Slade School of Art, like **Hirst** she is attracted to the subject of death. In 1999 she produced a Holocaust Memorial sculpture sited in Judenplatz, the epicentre of the Jewish quarter in Vienna.

BritCrits

Critics of **BritArt** are legion. In *Art Review*, Brian Ashbee declared that artists, critics and institutions are all playing the same superficial game:'Since the 1960s, we have witnessed the complete institutionalisation of the avant-garde. Our major institutions are devoted to cutting-edge art. Most of this has been in the areas of conceptual art, photography, video and installation. This is the work that people in power in public institutions deem to be significant. It gets written about, funded and shown. It is the official art of our time.'

Despite the grandiose terminology applied to such work, much of it is worthless: 'There is a vast quantity of writing ... loosely based on the misunderstood and ill-applied work of French philosophers, used as a smokescreen to hide the poverty of the intellects which support the work, and the poverty of much of the work itself' (*Art Review*).

Brian Sewell is not quite so dismissive of **Damien Hirst**. Distinguishing between Hirst the serious artist (his prison cells and bleak laboratories from 1991–92), Hirst the superficial, repetitive artist (all those animals in formaldehyde) and Hirst the showman ('man-about-town in the stews of London and Berlin'), he suggests that, having turned away from his potential as an artist, the latter role may now be the only one open to him.

Sewell identifies the American roots of Hirst's early work ('Warhol's electric chair ... the rooms devised by Edward Keinholz'), and locates him within a tradition of conceptual art and effrontery dating back to Marcel Duchamp's urinal in 1917:

'those who accept it as art are damned as dupes, and those who object are damned as reactionary fogies'. While others have claimed that the **YBAs**' concern for the corporeal is a characteristic of British art that goes back to the animal portraits of George Stubbs, Sewell doubts whether this is art: 'is it enough to present, dead or alive, with not the smallest aesthetic intervention, a creature that induces fear? Is this not the purpose of a natural history?'

YBAs seem to be a continuation of two already existing schools – the Conceptual and the Abject, both of which are mainly American. What, then, is characteristically British about them? Noting that it would be highly unusual for a genuinely great movement to have only one collector (**Saatchi**), Berlin art critic Nicola Kuhn suggests that the branding of YBAs stems largely from the fact that they all know each other: 'like soap opera, their work and personal lives criss-cross in bizarre convoluted ways'. They may be ungentlemanly but YBAs are highly clubbable. Meanwhile the British media have been keen to present BritArt as a club that everyone wants to get into. The trouble is that, beyond Britain, the rest of the world is disinterested.

Perhaps it says something about Britain today that so many people were so determined to believe that BritArt really mattered. But, by the end of the 90s, the bubble had burst, so even the true believers could not bring themselves to maintain their belief for very long. The subject matter of BritArt is equally under-confident. Noting the preoccupation with death and human failure that frames so much of it, *LM* editor Mick Hume suggested that BritArt reflected not Cool Britannia but 'Ghoul Britannia' –

a perverse country where frailty and morbidity are fashionable and modish.

The Controversy Repeats Itself

The BritArt controversy came round again in 1999 with the reaction to **Charles Saatchi**'s discovery of New Neurotic Realism, a movement (or is it?) that includes Nicky Hoberman ('shocking' paintings of little girls), ex-**Goldsmith's** student Martin Maloney (deliberately 'slapdash' paintings), Tomoko Takahashi (collages of rubbish), Tom Hunter (photographs), Jason Brooks (photorealist paintings), **Paul Smith** (quasi-documentary photos in which he plays every role), Steven Gontarski ('repellent' models) and Brian Griffiths, whose Planet Yesterday is a Heath Robinson-meets-*Blue Peter* installation in which 'epic is reduced to domestic and science fiction becomes an egg whisk'. The manifesto Saatchi issued to coincide with the opening of the Neurotic Realism show at his gallery in January 1999 declared that these artists all shared a distinctive interest in strange psychology and the real. In the *Guardian* Jonathan Jones complained that this could be said of almost any artist working today; and that, far from constituting a real-ism, by announcing this arbitrary collection as a new art movement, Saatchi was debasing the revolutionary effect of real art movements throughout the twentieth century. In the *Observer*, while denying that he and his fellow artists were a movement, if 'a movement is five Italian artists sitting down and writing a manifesto, rather naive and sweet, tomor-

row starts here', Neurotic Realist Martin Maloney maintained that they represented a movement in society nonetheless: 'I'd say there is a new look, a new spirit abroad. It's less ironic and more celebratory. The 80s were about perfection and ease, money, *Dynasty* and *Dallas*, life sucks. 90s art is full of confession, the admission of inadequacy, quirkiness, dreaminess, the fallibility of us all.' Maloney described his own work as 'clumsy, messy, full of emotional gush. Definitely not cool.'

READ ON *Blimey!* by Matthew Collings

Britpop

Popped

In the early 90s when the influence of grunge bands like Nirvana seemed to indicate that the USA was going to dominate even **indie** (traditionally associated with guitars, personal pain and British-led middle-class rebellion), the UK hit back with Britpop, a neat marketing tag which identified a crop of new-ish bands as a continuation of the British pop tradition originating in the swinging 60s (**Blur**, **Suede**, Supergrass and **Oasis** were linked with **The Kinks**, **The Beatles** and **The Small Faces**).

Possibly at the behest of Camden-based music publicists Savage and Best, the magazine *Select* premiered the idea of Britpop in April 1993 with a feature headed 'Yanks Go Home'. A year later in *The Sunday Times*, music critic Robert Sandall sought to distance Blur from the already-banal 'Brit-pack', and, comparing lead singer Damon Albarn to English icons **Syd Barrett** ('feyness') and Steve Marriott ('blokeish'), identified 'the leaders of the Cockney rock revival' as keepers of a long-burning flame: 'Ever since the mid-1960s, when The Kinks started writing songs about Carnaby Street fashion victims, indolent squires and courting couples on Waterloo station, many of the best-loved British rock bands have tried to do their bit for the old country. Every decade, in fact, seems to bring forth a crop of aspirant social observers who seek to relocate rock music in a context about 3,000 miles West [sic] of Route 66. The Kinks were soon joined by authentic Cockneys with attitude, The

Small Faces, and then by The Beatles, whose most celebrated album, *Sgt Pepper's Lonely Hearts Club Band*, was also their most dedicated exploration of a fading English culture of northern brass bands, vaudeville entertainers and travelling circuses.' ('Blur of new voices', *The Sunday Times*, 8 May 1994)

Sandall went on to include **Bowie**'s *Ziggy Stardust*, the tattered and snarling version of Blighty offered by the punks, and the charm of Neil Tennant (**Pet Shop Boys**) and **Morrissey**, in the canon of self-consciously British pop culture.

If the British pop of the 60s sometimes evoked home-grown traditions, back then 'beat music' was a relatively new form and the echoes of Britain's past were therefore presented in a new setting. By contrast, the 90s Britpoppers were looking back both to a previous Britain and to a (by then) long-established format (well-crafted pop songs played by intelligent, guitar-driven bands – 'rock masquerading as pop, basically', as Sandall described it) with only slight modifications. Recognising its predominantly retro character, in the art magazine *Frieze* Simon Reynolds observed that 'Britpop's nostalgia denied it the quality of modernism that was required to justify its label as the "new **Mod**".'

Britpop never really undermined US domination of the global music industry. But while retaining many reassuringly familiar elements, it seemed to offer a new template for what British society could become. Three years after *Select*'s 'Yanks Go Home' feature, writing in the *Observer* former *NME* editor Neil Spencer trumpeted 'Britpop's morning glory' and announced that 'pop now earns the UK as much abroad as the steel industry'. Given the steep decline of the British steel industry over the previous 15 years, this didn't mean a great deal. Nevertheless Spencer was articulating a real hope that tired, old British industry could be remade in the image of young, energetic pop music. Not long afterwards, in a special feature in the *Independent on Sunday* ('The cool economy', 15 February 1998), Britpop had become generalised into 'Cool Britannia', and Peter Koenig declared that: 'Cool Britannia could be a form of post-industrial capitalism that combines hard-nosed profits with a fuller recognition of the human creativity on which they hinge.' From its origins as a publicists' tag, Britpop had developed into a full-blown theory of political economy.

Perhaps '*over*-blown' would be a better description. Only four months later, the *NME* declared 'the Great Rock'n'Roll Dwindle' and **Alan McGee** (Oasis manager and boss of Creation Records) foretold the disappearance of the British music industry as we know it: 'Technology is overriding the development of music and we should be asking ourselves, are there actually going to be any record companies in ten years' time? I don't think so.' McGee went on to report that pop music was no longer inherently subversive, unlike the Internet: 'People say: it's a dilution of a dilution. The other criticism is that music doesn't have an ideological point of view any more so it's not central to people's existence the way that punk or acid house were ... but if you're 15 years old and you buy a laptop, your mum doesn't even know how to turn it on, man! That's rock'n'roll.'

McGee's pronouncements about the demise of the music industry were exaggerated (and the concurrent launch of the Creation Records website was surely no coincidence); but the enthusiasm with which the industry and then the rest of society latched on to something as retro as Britpop suggests that British culture is clinging to the past, even when it is desperate to innovate. While Britpop – invented, played, written about and bought by white middle-class males – was being done to death, the eminently more progressive and ethnically diverse sounds of British club culture went relatively ignored.

PARENTS Swinging London, the heritage industry

Neville Brody
Design matters

Through his work on **The Face**, Neville Brody became known as the most important British graphic artist of the 80s. In the 90s his focus moved from magazines towards the Internet, where he sought to create 'the visual language we're going to be using in the electronic communication world'.

Born in Scotland in 1957, Brody was brought up in a north-London suburb. He always wanted to be an artist, and in 1975 enrolled for his foundation year at Hornsey College of Art which had gained a reputation for experimentation and debate since the student occupation of 1968. At Hornsey, Brody was confronted by conflicting trends within fine arts and applied (commercial) art. He found the fine artists elitist, and enrolled the following year on a BA course in graphic design at the London College of Printing. But the tramlines of this course were too narrow, and Brody went out into the world determined to take a painterly and emotional approach to the arena of graphic design, which had previously been ruled by a functionalist ethos. Looking back at his early ambitions, he recalls 'feeling that within mass communication, the human had been lost completely. I wanted to understand everyday images that were around me at that time and the process of manipulation particularly within commercial art. By understanding the mechanisms at ground level, I hoped to produce the opposite effect by turning them on their head.'

Borrowing from Russian Constructivism and the Dutch school of De Stijl, Brody's first commercial work was for independent record companies such as Stiff and Fetish. In 1981 he was invited by publisher Nick Logan to redesign *The Face*, billed as 'the world's best-dressed magazine' and, under Brody's art direction, soon to become the bible of style for a whole generation. Working on a shoestring budget and at a frenetic pace in a cramped studio on the Tottenham Court Road, Brody turned *The Face* into a design-led publication. He insisted that its potential readership would not identify with a traditional, text-dominated layout; but would gravitate towards a publication that imbued its own appearance with 'emotional weight'. The success of *The Face*, voted magazine of the year in 1983 and billed by adman's paper *Campaign* as 'the barometer of pop style', proved him right.

Brody used graphic design as a lead instrument, which often took precedence over both photos and body copy. This is an approach with which we are all familiar now, but only 20 years ago it was an almost unprecedented reversal of the standard pecking order of the printed page (previous experiments had been carried out by upmarket American magazines and the underground press). Brody's techniques implied the rejection of linearity, and his approach has since been amplified and developed on the famously non-linear World Wide Web. Brody, in other words, designed the Net on the printed page, before anyone knew it existed.

In 1984 Brody redesigned *The Face* again in order to take account of corporate logos and other new forms for presenting information. The following year, the Photographers' Gallery hosted a retrospective exhibition on *The Face*. Brody himself was subsequently the subject of a show at the prestigious Victoria and Albert Museum. In 1986 he designed the magazine *New Socialist*, which became a temporary forum for leftist cultural politics.

Brody was never on the staff of *The Face*, preferring to work for Logan as a freelancer. In 1998 he left Logan altogether, and has subsequently worked for Nike, Swatch and the New York Museum of Modern Art, among others. In 1990 Brody cofounded Fontworks, a typographical design company geared for the digital age. When Brody was born in the 50s, typography was limited by the technical aspects of printing – everything on the printed page was an impression taken from pieces of metal, cut out and arranged in order. Nowadays there is less need for printing or paper and the possibilities of digital development are virtually endless. Brody is an innovator for new times, but he is also grounded in the traditions of pure and applied art – a rule-breaker who knows what rules he is breaking.

PARENTS *Vanity Fair*, *Oz*, *Black Dwarf*, Paul Cézanne
READ ON *The Art of Neville Brody*, Vols 1 and 2, by Jon Wozencroft

Julie Burchill
Ambition

Squeaky-voiced Julie Burchill was born in Bristol in 1960, and could hardly wait to leave home. In 1976 she answered an advert for 'two young gunslingers' to work on top pop paper the *New Musical Express*, the editor of which had just decided to go with punk rather than pub rock and was looking for some young blood. Burchill got the job (thousands applied, hundreds of their letters were never opened) along with her husband-to-be **Tony Parsons** (sampling Wordsworth, she later declared: 'it was bliss to be young in the second half of 1976, but to be young and working at the *NME* was like dying and going to heaven'). Together they terrorised ageing music journalists in the same way that the Sex Pistols scared the hell out of tired old pop stars. Apart from a host of high-speed articles for the *NME*, they also wrote *The Boy Looked At*

Johnny (1978), a history of punk and a coruscating attack on the smug self-regard of the pop-rock tradition.

But speed kills, and Burchill and Parsons soon broke up. Moving on from the *NME* and her husband (she described the early 80s as a period of careerism and 'cultural freefall' which 'would have losers as well as winners, and for the first time the losers looked highly likely to be white and male'), Burchill wrote for *The Sunday Times*, the *Mail on Sunday* and the *Express* (salary £130,000) as well as *Tatler*, *Elle*, **The Face**, *Cosmopolitan*, *Arena* and *Sky*. Projecting an image of herself as a shopgirl-turned-media-star ('daughter of two factory hands who had given up school as a bad job at 15 and flounced off to sell scent in swinging London'), whose cutting-edge writing derived from her working-class roots and desire for self-betterment, she soon acquired a reputation as a Thatcherite populist (her criticisms of feminism, homosexualism and the 60s went down well with right-wing philosopher Roger Scruton).

Responding to the accusation that she had sold out, Burchill said that the only people who don't are the ones with nothing to sell. She herself began to live up to the literal meaning of a cynic: a creature that barks all the time. The idea that superbitch Burchill might actually like someone became as unlikely as the prospect of the Rev Ian Paisley kissing the Pope.

In the 80s Burchill published three books of criticism, *Love It or Shove It*, *Damaged Gods* and *Girls On Film*, all of which displayed brilliant insights combined with increasingly predictable misanthropy. Her first novel, *Ambition* (1989), was the best-selling tale of a hard-headed female journalist. During this period Burchill was a regular at the Russell Hotel bar (near the flat in Holborn where she lived) and Soho's Groucho club. She married Cosmo Landesman, *Sunday Times* columnist and son of American bohemian Jay Landesman. They have since divorced. Her autobiography, *I Knew I Was Right*, appeared in 1998 – the fact that it was remaindered a few months later suggests that she isn't quite infallible. In 1999 she published *Married Alive*, not a kiss-and-tell account of her unsuccessful marriages, but a novel about a thirtysomething woman who invites her grandma to live with her in a one-bedroom Docklands flat.

In the 90s Burchill contributed financially and in an editorial capacity to *The Modern Review* (the pages of which documented her personal feud with Camille Paglia – a case of verbal wrestling between two strong women who were both opposed to mainstream feminism). Subtitled 'low culture for highbrows' (Burchill envisaged it as *Smash Hits* edited by FR Leavis), this short-lived magazine wanted to take pop culture seriously … but not too seriously. It was also heavily ironic, while polemicising against the over-use of irony. With assistance from Cosmo Landesman, *The Modern Review* was edited by Toby Young – son of the author of the 1945 Labour manifesto, Michael (later Lord) Young, founder of the Open University – until Burchill left Landesman and took up with Charlotte Raven, prompting Young to flee to New York, protesting that the two women were trying to turn his magazine into a feminist tract. With Burchill's backing, Raven revived *The Modern Review* a couple of years later. But within 12 months it had foundered again.

In the 90s Burchill finally (she had dallied briefly with Take That) found someone to praise: Princess Diana. Having identified Diana early on 'as the pop princess', Burchill went into emotional overdrive when the (by now) ex-wife of Prince Charles was killed in a car accident in the late summer of 1997. Her eponymous book about Diana (1998) was more hagiography than biography. Some of it was so syrupy it could have been written by romantic novelist and sentimentalist Barbara Cartland. After two decades as a young gunslinger, Burchill was finally smitten by the Princess of Wails.

PARENTS Dorothy Parker, Jean Rook
CHILDREN Suzanne Moore, Charlotte Raven, Decca Aitkenhead
READ ON *Damaged Gods, Ambition, I Knew I Was Right*

Michael Caine
In the money

The Sun says that, 'Despite his flaws Michael Caine has a lasting place in the affections of the British public.' We love him for the cynical characters he has portrayed and, in real life, as a man who makes no bones about being calculating as well as charming.

As a young man (son of a Billingsgate fish porter, suffered as a child from rickets and a nervous tic) Michael Caine (born Maurice Joseph Mickelwhite in Camberwell, 1933; chose his stage name after seeing *The Caine Mutiny*) made a pact with himself that either he would make it as an actor by the age of 30, or he would give it up and get a day job. As the deadline approached, he had been a messenger for the Rank Organisation, played the lead (a young thug) in a **Johnny Speight** drama, and 'made it' lots of times in 'the ultimate bachelor pad' which he shared with another struggling actor by the name of Terence Stamp (Caine recalled their technique as 'men behaving shrewdly … we did everything that would please a lady'). None of these achievements matched his ambitions. After 11 years of trying to get a major role in the movies – he'd done smaller parts in films such as *Hell in Korea* (1956) – and with only hours to go before he turned 30, he was offered the plum part of an officer in the film *Zulu* (1964). He substituted a cut-glass accent for his Cockney vowels, clasped his hands behind his back in the manner of HRH Prince Philip, and a star was born.

Not long afterwards Caine met producer Harry Saltzman in a restaurant – a meeting that led to him being offered the part of Harry Palmer in the film of Len Deighton's *The Ipcress File* (1965). Deighton, ex-RAF, had created a character who was quick-witted but full of what film critic Alexander Walker dubbed 'dumb insolence' towards officers. In his glasses and raincoat, and in his enjoyment of gourmet food, Caine's Harry Palmer typified a new social mobility and embodied the beginning of the end of British deference.

Looking back at his career in 1999, Caine claimed that in his early days as an actor, he was on a mission to correct the patronising image of working-class people in British films: 'I started out in this business with two humble ambitions – to make a living that would make me almost as much as I could get in a factory, and to portray working-class people as they really were rather than how I had seen them on screen during the 40s and 50s. We were always grovelling, cap-doffing prats in British movies. All the lads where I came from around Elephant and Castle used to get very angry to see us portrayed as snivelling, grovelling twits who could not fight. We were always seen as not very intelligent either. Yet I was with a gang of guys who were brilliant mentally but the education was not there for them. That's what I tried to do in British films until I fell to the lure of Hollywood.'

His early efforts are summed up in one critic's observation that 'Caine made ordinariness look sexy.'

'Michael Caine IS Alfie.' The publicity blurb surrounding Lewis Gilbert's film *Alfie* (1966, from Bill Naughton's novel) suggested that Caine and the title role (upwardly mobile working-class Lothario finally realises that, for all the women in it, his life is empty) were really one and the same person. In the public imagination Caine was closely associated with the character of Alfie for many years (although in *Candid Caine*, a documentary made for LWT in 1969, he complained that he never had time to 'get the girls'). The catchphrase forever associated with Caine/Alfie, 'not a lot of people know that', was coined as a joke by **Peter Sellers**.

Alfie made Caine a household name and bankrolled his flat in Grosvenor Square, SW1. He topped it by playing a stylish British villain in the comedy crime movie *The Italian Job* (1969) and then moved on to a picture that made crime look anything but a caper. With its ultra-violent storyline of revenge among pornographers, *Get Carter* (1971, directed by Mike Hodges from the book by Ted Lewis, re-released in 1999) is one of the grittiest British films ever made.

Having married Shakira Baksh, the former Miss Guyana who appeared in a Maxwell House coffee advert (Caine saw the ad on TV, found out she was living in London and pursued her all the way to the altar), he starred opposite Sean Connery in *The Man Who Would Be King* (1971), the story of two Indian Army deserters who con some villagers into believing that one of them is a god. Taken from a story by Rudyard Kipling, John Huston's film is now regarded as a classic. But at the time of its release it was not so favourably received.

After the failure of *The Man Who Would Be King*, Caine the consummate craftsman turned into a journeyman actor whose main concern, according to the satirists of *Spitting Image* – and, later, on his own admission – was whether the price was right. Tax-exiled in Los Angeles, he starred in second- and third-rate films such as *The Swarm* ('to buy my mother a house'), *Jaws – The Revenge*, *Beyond The Poseidon Adventure* and *The Muppet Christmas Carol*. 'I never thought I'd be a success,' says Caine, 'so I accepted whatever crap they sent me.' Later he altered this account, saying 'Contrary to what some people believe, I never went into a movie assuming it would be crap. Some were special-effects movies where the effects weren't that special.'

Caine redeemed himself with performances in Woody Allen's *Hannah And Her Sisters* and, back in Britain, in *Educating Rita* (lecturer loves working-class lass), and as a gangster in *Mona Lisa*. In 1982 he even moved back to Britain. In 1999 Caine received a Golden Globe award for his role in *Little Voice* as Ray Say, a seedy agent who latches on to a young and talented performer (Jane Horrocks).

Well past retirement age, until recently Caine continued to make two films a year. He invests in restaurants (he once said of his first restaurant partner Peter Langan that it was possible to have 'a more interesting conversation with a cabbage'), and grows his own potatoes. Canny Caine is almost as calculating as the anti-heroes he has portrayed. During a recent TV documentary he explained his outlook on life: 'You've got to make the day count, and once it gets to evening, start thinking about how to make tomorrow count.'

PARENTS Captain Hooper in Evelyn Waugh's *Brideshead Revisited*
CHILDREN everyone in black-framed rectangular specs
READ ON *The Ipcress File* by Len Deighton; *Alfie* by Bill Naughton, *Get Carter* by Ted Lewis

Camden Town

'Camden Town for the rough lie down'(trad.)

The market in Camden Town is said to attract more visitors than any other London monument. The 'market' is not a market as such – more like a rag-bag of shops and stalls stretching parallel to the railway line along Camden High Street over the canal bridge towards Chalk Farm tube station. There are more stalls inside old warehouses (built first for the canal, then for the railway) and in the open spaces surrounding them. What's on sale – mainly clothes, music, lifestyle paraphernalia and fast food – is not all that special (although established pitches are combined with 'casual spots' which anyone can rent for a day if they get up early enough, which means that budding entrepreneurs and designers often make their first sales here); but people (Londoners and tourists alike) come here (rather than to other markets such as Greenwich) in droves (at times the place is so packed that the tube station is shut down) partly because Camden is so accessible (five minutes from Euston or King's Cross) and partly because it is ingrained with more than 50 years of cultural experimentation and hard living. Somehow a second-hand jacket from Camden seems more authentic than it would do from anywhere else.

In the mid-90s Camden was closely associated with **Britpop**. The office of **Blur**'s Food Records is in Camden Parkway (just yards from legendary Good Mixer pub), in the same building as Britpop's chief publicists and press agents (Phill) Savage and (John) Best (originally known as Best in the Press), whose client list includes **Suede**, Elastica, Echobelly and Menswear. Legend has it that Britpop was born after Savage phoned the editor of *Select* and suggested that Suede and their contemporaries were part of a recognisably British reaction to American grunge. *Select* printed the famous front cover with the Union Jack on it and, ironically, Suede got left off the ensuing bandwagon.

Camden's previous incarnation was 'groovy grunge', combining guitar thrash with a tinge of dance rhythms. Centred on the Vertigo club at the Falcon pub, the core constituency of this early 90s phenomenon consisted of dreadlocked crusties supping Tennent's Extra. The *NME* coined the phrase 'Camden lurchers' to describe their distinctive dancing style.

On the cusp of the 90s Camden's Dingwalls was one of the main venues for a jazz-based dance scene which never quite made it to the mainstream, although the Jazz Cafe in Camden Parkway continues to draw good crowds. In the mid-80s Camden had been home to a club scene that did make a wider impression, albeit in a modified form. In 1983 Steve Strange (self-styled 'King of the **New Romantics**') and his partner Rusty Egan took over the Music Machine opposite Mornington Crescent tube station and renamed it the Camden Palace. Strange referred to it as 'the People's Palace – a place for all the trendy young things to call their own'. The 'trendy' people he was talking about were a select group heavily into posing in highly elaborate costumes they had designed and made for each other (the British equivalent of what was known as 'voguing' on the New York gay scene). There were not enough of them to fill a huge club every night of the week; so on most evenings the Palace was just an ordinary disco, but on some nights it would be turned into a kind of garish music hall featuring the likes of **Leigh Bowery** and Frankie Goes To Hollywood. The club was full of primadonnas but did not always take itself too seriously. One night, when comedian **Peter Cook** gave a mocking rendition of the Palace posers and their exotic dancing, he received a thunderous round of applause. Apart from launching the careers of Bowery (later a prominent club promoter and a model for Lucian Freud) and DJ 'Fatboy' Tony (then a precocious 15 year old), the Camden Palace premiered a highly theatrical take on lifestyle which has now become almost commonplace. In the Britain of the coming decade, the influence of the Palace scene will be in evidence even on an ordinary disco night in a provincial town.

The Palace was certainly Camp if not always Gay. Around the same time, other venues in Camden were hosting a much straighter scene based on guitar bands such as The Three Johns (managed by the future boss of Creation Records and sometime **Tony Blair** supporter, **Alan McGee**). This was a difficult age for musicians who took themselves in any way seriously. They were not sure whether to be politically radical (but how?) or whether to live simply for kicks (but how to justify this?). Their dilemma is articulated in *Faithless* (1997), a novel set in early 80s Camden by John L Williams, who worked locally as a musician and in a record shop.

In the late 70s the ska-based band Madness learnt their chops playing Camden venues such as the Dublin Castle. Two decades later, ex-Madness frontman Suggs is still highly regarded as a Camden Town character. Madness were originally connected to the record label **Two-Tone**, initiated by The Specials who came from Coventry but used to rehearse in a Camden warehouse run by Bernie Rhodes, manager of The Clash. Like Sex Pistols manager **Malcolm McLaren**, Rhodes was a radical-turned-entrepreneur whose formative years were the 60s. One of the landmarks of the 60s counter-culture is the Roundhouse, a disused railway engine shed at the north end of Camden, which was the venue for a series of 'happenings' and for one of the keynote cultural/political events of the decade, a conference entitled 'The Dialectics of Liberation' which featured black power leader Eldridge Cleaver alongside 'anti-psychiatrist' Dr RD Laing. This was the period in which the radical London Film Makers' Co-operative set up shop in Camden (the area also boasted two arthouse cinemas, now closed); and literary appetites were served by Compendium Books (they still are), one of the first places in Britain where the American Beats could be bought.

Counter-cultural types were attracted to Camden, as were the artists of the 30s known as the Camden School, because of the availability of spacious (Victorian) premises (housing and commercial) which were relatively cheap. Camden was cheap because of the significant Irish presence in the area. Irish immigrants and their offspring had an undesirable reputation for drunkenness and wild behaviour; and the saying 'Camden Town for the rough lie down' is a reference to the Irish people said to be lying in the street after the pubs closed and the fighting stopped. But what reduced the market value of Camden property also raised the reputation of the area in the eyes of the original bohemians and their latter-day counterparts. They wanted to live and work in an area that was a bit rough and ready, in order to distance themselves from the buttoned-up, tied-down aspects of the traditional British Way of Life. In the 90s the grit in the eye of Camden (the exteriors of many of the buildings have not been cleaned since they were built in the 1850s) is still part of its attraction. The non-Britishness of the Irish element, and the vague anti-traditional-Britishness of the counter-cultural tradition are key elements that make Camden Town the uncrowned capital of today's BritCult.

PARENTS: Irish immigration, the railways, the Roundhouse, gentrification
CHILDREN: Brixton, Greenwich, Spitalfields

Naomi Campbell
Swaning around

'I don't have big tits, I don't have wide hips. I seem to fit every outfit that's put on me.' Known as 'the perfect body', Naomi Campbell is also known as a superbitch among supermodels. Sacked in 1993 by Elite chairman John Casablancas because 'no amount of money or prestige could further justify the abuse that she has imposed on our staff and clients', months later she was welcomed back by him.

Born (1970) in south London to a Jamaican, Valerie Campbell, and a mixed-race father whom she has never known, Naomi was an Italia Conti stage school student out shopping for tap shoes in Covent Garden when she was spotted by talent scout Beth Boldt, former head of Synchro. By April 1986 she was cover girl for *Elle*. In August 1988 she became the first black model to appear on the front cover of *Vogue* (French edition). Her early campaigns were for Lee Jeans, Olympus, Jazz, Ralph Lauren and, most famously, Versace.

Tall and muscular, to her many admirers Campbell is unsurpassed as a model. As soon as Campbell hit the catwalks she was associated with 'haughtiness, untouchability and unwavering confidence in her own beauty'. Throughout the first half of the 90s, British tabloids loved to hate her, and they had a field day when she finally tripped over and fell on the runway. Campbell's critics were almost as gleeful when, months after appearing in an anti-fur poster for People for the Ethical Treatment of Animals (PETA), she was sacked by the organisation after wearing a fur coat for Fendi in Milan.

In 1996 Campbell complained to journalist Ian Katz that the British begrudged her success: 'I don't feel accepted in England at all. The only way they have accepted me is that Madame Tussaud's just did a waxwork of me.' Based by then in New York, and a regular at the ex-patriot haunt Tea and

Sympathy, Campbell maintained that English hostility towards her 'doesn't bother me any more. At one point it did, but not any more.' She seemed more concerned with the diversification of her career: absentee restaurateur, absentee novelist (of her debut *The Swan* she said, 'I had it written by someone else but all the characters and plot were from me'), actress (appearing in Spike Lee's *Girl Six*) and singer (LP *Babywoman*, 1995).

Even perfect bodies must submit to the indignities of ageing and, in 1999, Campbell was sacked by Versace for allegedly asking twice the market rate and because, at 28, she was no longer considered a suitable model for young women's clothes. Dressed, pointedly, in an Armani suit, Campbell told the press it was she who had made herself unavailable for Versace's winter previews.

PARENTS Shirley Bassey, Josephine Baker, Violet Elizabeth
READ ON *The Swan* by Naomi Campbell

Robert Carlyle
The British De Niro

'I've never set out to be a star or, heaven forbid, a celebrity. That would be a bit daft.' Robert Carlyle has little time for showbiz glitter – this is the man who shouted 'shite' when **Kenneth Branagh** was awarded the gong for best actor at the 1990 European Film Awards. But at 38 he was awarded

a gong of his own. Throughout Britain and beyond, Robert Carlyle OBE is known as an unlikely sex symbol and as a method actor of extreme dedication.

Born (1961) in Maryhill, Glasgow, and brought up in various communes by a roving father, Carlyle is a former painter and decorator who took up acting aged 21, started his own left-wing, experimental theatre company (Raindog, named after the Tom Waits LP) after drama school, and since then has played a series of working-class roles in memorable movies such as **Ken Loach**'s *Riff Raff*, **Danny Boyle**'s version of **Irvine Welsh**'s *Trainspotting* (Begbie), and *The Full Monty* (Gaz), the highly profitable tale of redundant Sheffield steel men who pull down their pants and take up stripping. In Antonia Bird's *Priest*, he played the spurned gay lover of Linus Roache's curate. Other notable roles include the scouse psychopath Abbie in Jimmy McGovern's award-winning *Cracker*, the dope-smoking Scottish policeman *Hamish Macbeth*, and Ray, the robber-on-the-run in *Face*. Carlyle co-starred in *Plunkett & Macleane* (1999), an amiable eighteenth-century romp, and has followed the Christopher Walken/Robert Shaw path by taking on the role of a '**Bond** baddie'. In the summer of 1999 he also formed his own production company, 4WayUp Pictures, with Antonia Bird and Mark Cousins, former director of the Edinburgh Film Festival. Among their first projects is *Benny Lynch*, the biopic of a Scottish boxer who was a world champion in the 30s.

Carlyle is known for the De Niro-style rigour with which he approaches his roles. His preparation has included the acquisition of a passenger vehicle driving licence in order to qualify for the part of a bus driver (*Carla's Song*, directed by Ken Loach), and living in cardboard city before tackling the role of a homeless man (in *Safe*, directed by Antonia Bird). Rare among British thespians, this scale of preparation is more often associated with actors from the USA, where Lee Strasberg's method school has been fashionable since the 50s. It can be a high-risk approach, as Carlyle explained to *Observer* interviewer Andrew Smith. For the role of Abbie, the sociopathic Hillsborough survivor, he spoke in a scouse accent for three months continually, until:'I found it difficult not to. It was easy to get immersed in something like that. I looked back at the tabloid reports of Hillsborough, and it didn't take long to get angry. I sunk quite deep into that one. Part of it was the good professional actor, but partly it just felt easier to keep going like that. ... The line between fiction and reality can get blurred.'

Carlyle maintains that the role is everything, and the actor next to nothing: 'What I'm trying to be is an actor who makes people believe that I'm somebody else. This façade here, the one sitting in front of you, is irrelevant.' But this is patently untrue. For a start there is his sex appeal, possibly derived from the way he 'gives off the notion that there is a darkness there, another aspect to him that you never get to grips with'. There is also the fact that he is Scottish, and therefore outside the mainstream English acting milieu. In Scotland too he is an outsider, who ran out on middle-class drama school after a couple of months and still does not know how he was persuaded to go back.

'But then things started to change,' Carlyle observes, 'suddenly, the outsiders were the ones that were getting the work – because we were different from them.' The rise of Robert Carlyle, and others like him, seems to indicate that, nowadays, even the people holding the purse strings are keen to distance themselves from old formulae and include outsiders in new versions of British culture.

PARENTS: Robert De Niro, Bob Hoskins, Tom Waits, Ken Loach

Laid bare

Carlyle on the experience of doing a full strip in front of 300 women for the final scene in *The Full Monty*: 'There is nothing you can do to prepare yourself downstairs, to make sure you don't let yourself down – you're wearing a fuckin' red leather thong which I've described before as anal dental floss. It's disgusting. I don't think anyone believes me but I was pissed for that scene. I couldn't fuckin' handle it ... As it happens I don't think I let myself down. He was all right. Yes, the young chap was OK.'

Carry On

Unstoppable

The Carry On films were made on a shoestring (as opposed to a G-string) as popular entertainment. More than 40 years on, they have become a debating point for the intelligentsia.

Based on a play about National Servicemen by RF Delderfield, *Carry On Sergeant* was a minor success in 1958. It turned out to be the first in a series of 31 low-budget film comedies which depended on execrable puns ('Infamy, infamy – they've all got it in for me'), double entendres and a recognisable company of actors including Kenneth Williams, Charles Hawtrey, Hattie Jacques, Joan Sims and the rubber-faced Sid James. The visual comedy of the Carry Ons often involved flying bras and splitting pants. The overall effect was like a series of Donald McGill naughty postcards come to life.

The repertory-style company gave the Carry Ons the feel of pantomime. Each member of the team represented a characteristic British type and the bawdy drama of their interaction was ritually played out again and again across the changing backdrop of each movie – wild west, hospital, camp site, Roman Egypt, Empire India, you name it. Kenneth Williams with his flaring nostril was the prudish face of middle-management authority, Charles Hawtrey (Private Widdle in *Carry On Up the Kyber*, 1968) was the harmless, madly camp, upper-class twit. Sid James (Sir Sidney Rough Diamond in *Kyber* and the Rumpo Kid in *Cowboy*, 1965), the lusty and resourceful man of the people, and Bernard

Bresslaw his less resourceful sidekick. Joan Sims and Hatty Jacques (Miss Haggard in *Camping*, 1969) played the battleaxe wives they always ran from, while **Barbara Windsor** played the bit-of-alright they always ran straight for. A simple pageant that resembled, more than anything else, the role-play of the medieval carnival.

The semi-official history of the Carry Ons has it that they were based on the complementary aspects of prudery and naughtiness: relevant enough in a decade of repression such as the 50s; but when Britain underwent something like a sexual revolution in the 60s and 70s, the Carry Ons, so the story goes, were undermined by social change they could not keep pace with. Thus in 1992 when *Carry On Columbus* revisited the old formula, which had been allowed to lapse since the late 70s, even an intake of new talent (**Keith Allen**, Alexei Sayle, Rik Mayall and **Julian Clary**) could not revive it. But this scenario, summed up in a favourable *Sunday Times* article by Bryan Appleyard, cannot explain how the heyday of the Carry Ons – the 60s – was also a period of accelerated social change. Robert Ross, author of *The Carry On Companion*, reckons that the films documented the changes in British society – unwittingly, he says, but all the more accurately for it.

Another possibility is that the Carry Ons were appealing precisely because they always were out of step with the times. When *Carry On Sergeant* was released, the end of National Service had already been announced. Nor were the Carry Ons eclipsed by the new comedy of the 60s: in 1969, the year of **Monty Python**, the two most successful British

Censored   A 'What's Not On' guide to British cultural life

Eisenstein's *Battleship Potemkin* (1926) remained banned in Britain until 1954.

In the 1930s, *Church Times* editor Sidney Dark warned that foreign films would corrupt the national stock: 'This vast army of the least intelligent and least morally equipped members of society were allowed to have all kinds of intellectual and moral poison pumped into them without any kind of interference. … In this complex age it was race suicide to allow foreigners to impregnate falsehood into the lifeblood of this nation.'

The full edition of J D Salinger's *Catcher in the Rye* was not published in Britain until 1994.

'Having regard to the present widespread concern about juvenile crime', the British authorities refused to certificate *The Wild One* (1953). Resubmitted in 1964, the film was again rejected following the Mods vs Rockers ructions in Clacton. In 1968, during the peace-loving hippie era, it finally received its British premiere.

From 1960, even wives and servants were allowed to read the unexpurgated version of DH Lawrence's *Lady Chatterley's Lover*, following the failed prosecution of Penguin Books.

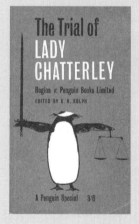

Roger Daltrey's vocal on the Who's 'Substitute' (1964) was judged 'detrimental to stutterers' and banned by the BBC.

Ever since the Licensing Act of 1737, all theatrical scripts had to be vetted by the Lord Chamberlain. Alterations required of John Osborne's *The Entertainer* (1957) included: 'page 21 omit "balls" … page 43 omit "rogered" (twice)'. The Lord Chamberlain's powers were abolished in 1968 – one of the last plays to be affected was Edward Bond's *Early Morning*, which features scenes of fictional violence among the British Royal Family.

In 1971 the three editors of *Oz* were jailed for publishing the *School Kids' Issue*.

The sound of Jodie Foster unzipping Robert De Niro was pulled out of *Taxi Driver* (1976).

In 1976 when COUM Transmissions (Genesis P Orridge and Cosey Fanny Tutti) mounted an exhibition (featuring a used tampon) at the Institute of Contemporary Arts, it was closed down following four days of parliamentary questions.

Despite official denials and a rigged system of chart returns, the Sex Pistols' 'God Save The Queen' held the No 1 spot in the week of the Queen's Silver Jubilee (1977).

In 1989 artist Rick Gibson was fined £500 for exhibiting a pair of earrings made from freeze-dried human foetuses.

Records banned by the BBC during the Gulf War (1991) included John Lennon's 'Give Peace A Chance' and Lulu's Eurovision entry 'Boom Bang A Bang'.

Westminster Council made itself look foolish when it banned David Cronenberg's *Crash* (1996) from London's West End.

In 1983 when the ICA exhibited *Rosie*, the Robert Mapplethorpe photo of a three-year-old girl with no knickers, no one gave it a second thought. In 1996, it was labelled 'child pornography' by ChildLine chair Esther Rantzen, and the Hayward Gallery declined to include it in a Mapplethorpe retrospective.

More than 25 years after its cinema release, and coinciding with the retirement of long-standing chief film censor James Ferman, in 1999 *The Exorcist* (1973) finally became available on video in Britain.

READ ON *Censored – the story of film censorship in Britain* by Tom Dewe Mathews; *The Trial of Lady Chatterley* edited by CH Rolph; *The Trials of Oz* by Tony Palmer; *Mrs Grundy – studies in English prudery* by Peter Fryer comedies were Carry On films. Right from the start, the Carry Ons may have been an exercise in incipient nostalgia. A familiar counterpoint to the unknown quantities of the swinging 60s, perhaps they represented a world of working-class vulgarity which may never have existed but was already perceived to be disappearing even then.

Film critic Andy Medhurst once declared that, even in an age of retro-rehabilitation, there was no way that the Carry On films could be recovered on behalf of high culture. But Roland Barthes had already set the tone with a Carry On article in *Sight and Sound*. In 1998 Channel 4 scheduled a Carry On night, including a documentary on the personal trauma underlying the cosiness of the Carry Ons (for instance, how repressed homosexual Kenneth Williams overdosed on barbiturates having written in his journal 'Oh what's the bloody point?'). In the winter of 1998–99, London's Museum of the Moving Image mounted an exhibition in honour of the Carry Ons, and the prestigious National Film Theatre ran a whole season of Carry On films. Novelist and literary theorist Malcolm Bradbury welcomed them as 'a broad expression of English vulgarity'. Phillip Dodd, director of the Institute of Contemporary Arts, compared the Carry On series to the way that composers such as Bach wrote variations on a theme. Former queen of youth TV Janet Street-Porter acknowledged that 'you can't call them art,' adding 'but to me they are popular art'. Film director Ken Russell was outspoken: 'Why don't we stand up and say it's crap, and then forget it.'

PARENTS music hall, Donald McGill postcards, the experience of the Second World War
READ ON *The Carry On Companion* by Robert Ross

Michael Clark
'The Gazza of dance'

When Michael Clark returned to the London stage after a four-year absence, the *Evening Standard* likened his rehabilitation to that of footballer Paul Gascoigne.

Born in 1962, Michael Clark grew up in Kinmore, a fishing village on the north-east coast of Scotland. He remembers dancing from the age of four: 'it was the only way I could get something out'. At school in Aberdeen, Clark was bullied: the biggest bully died at 16 – he was driving a manure truck when it blew up.

Aged 13, Clark came south to the Royal Ballet School and soon afterwards began leading 'a Jekyll and Hyde existence' that included ballet training by day and, by night, going out to see punk bands like the all-girl Slits. While still in his teens he began writing his own ballets 'because I thought the two lives – dance and punk – could feed off each other'. After a short spell as lead dancer with the Ballet Rambert (traditional avant-garde), at 22 Clark left to form his own small company. Depicted in the Sunday supplements in tutu and **Doc Martens**, he worked with Mark E Smith and **The Fall** and **Leigh**

Bowery, put Stravinsky next to Public Image Ltd and staged a show at the Anthony D'Offay Gallery (Heterospective) which began with Clark and his boyfriend Steven having sex 'as much as we could'. Clark claimed that 'our audience is much broader than the usual dance audience' (he also claimed that the ideal spot to do one of his shows would be during the interval in an Old Firm football match between Celtic and Rangers), and saw himself as someone who was too street-level to fit in with either the traditional dance scene or its modern counterpart: 'I dislike the dance establishment and they dislike me. I don't fit in with the "new dance" crowd either. My work deliberately pokes fun at most dance, which I see as quite ridiculous, as most people do.' Clark also maintained that there was 'too much dance about dance'.

In one sense Clark was really street-level: since 1988 he had been using heroin. In 1994 a combination of knee injury and drug addiction prompted him to retire to Kinmore where his mother 'fed him up on stovies, mince and tatties and cullen skink [fish] soup'; and 'he slept a lot'. After a four-year 'sabbatical' Clark returned to London with a new company but with 'no lurid sets or wild costumes'. The *Evening Standard* noted that 'the prince of punk has turned into the prince of purity'. Excess; reorientation; moderation – the Michael Clark story is a parable of pop culture people in the 90s (see also music journalists Nick Kent and Ian Penman, guitarist Peter Green, and a host of prodigal footballers).

Alan Clarke
The walking wounded

Born in Liverpool in 1935, the son of a bricklayer, after a varied career (labourer, insurance salesman) Alan Clarke started making films in the late 60s. He made around 40 features for TV (including a production of Brecht's *Baal* starring **David Bowie**) but only three cinema releases (*Scum, Billy the Kid and the Green Baize Vampire* and *Rita, Sue and Bob Too*). Although he rarely wrote his own scenarios he judiciously chose scripts that shared his angry sentiments about Britain. He was most at home focusing on the hopelessness of the disenfranchised lower classes and, understandably, came into his own during the upheavals of the Thatcher era.

Though no visual stylist, his work is recognisable in the way it unflinchingly shows, without comment, the ravages and realities of the demonised and forgotten in British life. Without trying to moralise or become sentimental, Clarke shows the violent not as faceless scum but as characters with an intelligence who have made decisions on how to live contingent upon their environment.

Scum (1977) – which was originally commissioned and then banned by the BBC – follows the violent power struggle in a borstal, with Ray Winstone in the central role. *Made in Britain* (1983), written by David Leland, follows the nihilistic trail of destruction left by Trevor (a nazi skinhead played by **Tim Roth**) without attempting to explain his actions. Though intent on a life of crime and

125

racism, what is unnerving is that behind the raw rage Trevor is clearly smart. *Contact* (1985) and *Elephant* (1989) are both set in the conflict in Northern Ireland and largely dispensed with dialogue altogether. *Elephant* (written by Clarke), using a handheld camera, shows a series of murders without emotion or offering a context.

Rita, Sue and Bob Too (1986, from Andrea Dunbar's play), probably his most accessible, humorous and personable film, and *Road* (1987, from Jim Cartwright's play and starring Jane Horrocks) are both set amid trapped lives on harsh housing estates in the north of England. *Billy the Kid and the Green Baize Vampire* (1985) is definitely his least typical: an eccentric rock musical starring Phil Daniels and set in a strangely nightmarish world of seedy pool halls.

Perhaps his lasting legacy (he died in 1990) will be his final film, *The Firm*. Following a gang of football hooligans it does away with the myth of the mindless bovver boy and showed the truth that, in the 80s, the hooligan was a well-organised, lower-middle-class, fully paid-up member of Thatcher's society. **Gary Oldman** plays the ringleader Bex: an estate agent with a loving family who seeks the tribal 'buzz' of violence like a drug.

Critic David Thomson identifies Clarke's 'central metaphor of cramped existence' in the angry walking many of his characters do, calling them 'beasts who pace and measure the limits of their cage': the cage being a Britain not fit to live in.

PARENTS **Ken Loach**, **Lindsay Anderson**
CHILDREN Tim Roth, Gary Oldman, John King

Julian Clary
Naughty but nice

Provider of what he refers to as 'a camp comedy service', Julian Clary plays on his gayness in a manner that used to be outrageous but now seems merely mildly amusing. No wonder he hosted the revived 'classic hit TV game show' *Mr and Mrs*.

Born to a policeman father and a probation officer mother, and brought up in the suburban town of Teddington to the west of London, Julian Clary attended a good Catholic day school (St Benedict's). He might have been a bank manager or a priest; but from the age of seven he had enjoyed playing with his mother's make-up, and when he grew up he became the gay man in the rubber dress and chainmail who called himself the Joan Collins Fan Club (in homage to the superbitch character played by 60s British starlet Joan Collins in the US television melodrama *Dynasty*), and seemed to be on a mission to shock British humour out of its conventional straitjacket (the other performer in the Joan Collins Fan Club was a mongrel dog called Fanny). Since the mid-80s, as a quiz show host and panellist as well as a stand-up comedian, Clary has continued to tease live audiences and TV viewers with his faux bitchiness, although he insists he is 'never cruel to anyone'.

But what can a gay boy do when he hits 40 (b. 1959) and feels the need to stop clubbing and grow up? In 1997 Clary thought about fathering a child, but then had second thoughts. His chances of a mature, long-term relationship were blighted in

1991 when his boyfriend died of an AIDS-related illness, and his love life was subsequently described as 'turbulent'. Clary's stage presence has settled down, however. In 1996 he gave up the fancy costumes, which 'were starting to feel undignified' and opted for a kind of camp casual look with lots of velvet and more than a smidgeon of mascara. The result is the kind of of gay man that you could take home to meet your mother.

In today's Britain, Clary is as respectable as the **Queen**. Things were different when he started out: the mid-80s was the period of anti-gay legislation such as Clause 28, fuelled by queer-bashing remarks from senior figures such as Manchester's chief constable James Anderton. But British society has now adopted a less hostile approach to homosexuality, and making a play of being gay no longer makes for cutting-edge comedy. Major US television companies still hesitate, however, before taking on the new ethos (in 1998, Warner Bros ditched the pilot for a show starring Clary only two days before it was due to be broadcast), but in Britain, the last time Clary caught the whiff of controversy was in 1993 when he made a feisty remark about Tory cabinet minister Norman Lamont during a live television show. More recently he has been as safe as houses (as opposed to bath houses). Wisely perhaps, in 1998 Clary said he did not expect to be doing comedy in ten years' time, but hoped to be writing books 'about myself'.

PARENTS Kenneth Williams, Frankie Howerd, Joan Collins

CHILDREN Lily Savage, Graham Norton

Clement and LaFrenais
Men only

Along with **Galton and Simpson** and **Croft and Perry**, Dick Clement and Ian LaFrenais (both north-easterners born in 1937) make up the British triumvirate of classic post-war sitcom writing duos. Their particular areas of expertise are the all-male relationship, the all-male environment and an uncanny ability to plug into the prevailing zeitgeist of British male identity.

The cultural shift into modernity that took place in the late 60s and early 70s was explored in *Whatever Happened To The Likely Lads?* (1973–74) – a sequel to their already successful 60s series *The Likely Lads*: the adventures of two Tyneside proto-lads Terry Collier (James Bolam) and Bob Ferris (Rodney Bewes). Bob is the straight man, doing his best to get on and better himself, while Terry plays the rogue, continually getting the pair of them into hot water. At the end of *The Likely Lads*, Terry heads off for a five-year stint in the army. So at the beginning of *Whatever Happened To …?* he returns to a changed Britain of lager and flares that he barely recognises. A luddite and a misanthrope (in the mould of old-man Steptoe) Terry sets about decrying everything new that Bob has taken to heart. The whole thing is epitomised by Terry's reactions when Bob takes him to a men's hair salon rather than his old barbers to get his hair cut. The theme tune ('What Happened To You?'), a minor hit in 1974, was co-written by Ian LaFrenais and Mike Hugg (ex-Manfred Mann).

The duo's success continued with *Porridge* (1973–77) set in the ultimate all-male environment of prison. Norman Stanley Fletcher (Ronnie Barker) is the habitual jailbird – sharing a cell with young Lennie Godber (Richard Beckinsale) in Slade Prison – whose man-of-the-people street nous allows him to keep one step ahead of prison officers Mr Barrowclough (wet liberal) and Mr Mackay (bootcamp authoritarian).

With *Auf Wiedersehen Pet* (1983–86) Clement and LaFrenais switched from Aunty to ITV and yet again picked up the prevailing zeitgeist. The series followed a ramshackle group of Tyneside brickies, stripped of work, washed up in the **dole** queues of Thatcher's Britain and forced to look abroad to find dignity in labour. Working in an alien Germany (with their wives and girlfriends at home), the group find out just who they are as both men and Britons. The two series struck a chord with the nation and became a star vehicle for several of the actors involved: Kevin Whately (Neville), Jimmy Nail (Oz) and Timothy Spall (Barry).

Not content with their television creations Clement and LaFrenais have also been successful scenarists for the big screen – from *The Jokers* (1966) to *The Commitments* (1991) and *Still Crazy* (1999). They now enjoy the Hollywood ex-pat lifestyle (see Evelyn Waugh's *The Loved One*) as respected screenwriters and producers for film and television (producing, amongst other things, Emmy award-winning Brit Tracey Ullman).

129

Jarvis Cocker

Jarvis Cocker

Geek chic

When *GQ* magazine published its Great British Issue back in 1996, the man the editor chose to put on the front cover was Jarvis Cocker, because 'we think his brand of sartorial nous and social satire is defiantly and definingly British'. But Jarvis does not consider himself a patriot: 'I'm not really in the habit of eulogising this place we call the UK – jingoism and flag-waving make me sick … intolerance to difference is one of the sides of the British character that I find very unappealing.' He went on to say that, in spite of themselves, the stultifying aspects of traditional British life have acted as a spur to creativity: 'it's the unpleasant things about Britain that force people to create the good things … the key to Britain's musical prowess is boredom'.

Spectacle-wearing, Silk Cut-smoking (before he gave them up on New Year's Day 1999), rake-thin (*The Times* said he 'resembles an erotic coathanger') Jarvis Cocker was born in 1963 in Sheffield and brought up by his mother (father skipped the country when he was seven) whom he describes as 'the nearest Sheffield gets to a bohemian' (not very near: she sent him to school in *lederhosen* and later became a Conservative parish councillor). He has been in bands since the age of 13, and spent years on the **dole** after forming Pulp, who only became successful after more than a decade together. But Jarvis always acted the part: 'even when I was only a pop star in my head, I considered it my duty to be like that all the time. I don't own any casual clothes. You never know who you'll bump into.' After years of practice, Jarvis became a geek with chic. His nerdishness seems to be a selling-point rather than a flaw. Almost alone among critics, **Will Self** warned of Pulp's 'wimp pop music' to match the 'wimp fiction' of **Nick Hornby** and Helen Fielding. He threw one of Cocker's lines back in his face: 'If you stopped being so feeble you could have so much more.'

Jarvis did not get into Oxford University, possibly because at interview he was caught out about a book he falsely claimed to have read. Instead he attended St Martin's School of Art in London (film studies), and in his songwriting he has repeatedly returned to the experience of being a boy from the provinces who is both awed and angered by the rich art school types whom he encountered there.

Jarvis once jumped/fell 30 feet from a window ledge in order to impress a girl. For some time afterwards he went on stage in a wheelchair. After years of being ignored **indie** also-rans, the album *His'n'Hers* started to get Pulp noticed. But their 1993 compilation *Intro* was a collection of non-hits and, in 1994, Jarvis was best known for having got every question right in the quickfire round of *Pop Quiz*. Then, in 1995, the album *Different Class* (artwork showing the influence of one of Jarvis's most prized collections: a set of the ground-breaking 60s magazine *Nova*) was released, including the influential single 'Common People'. Pulp made a triumphant appearance at the Glastonbury **Festival** and when they won the coveted Mercury Music Prize, Jarvis forced the assembled industry bigwigs to sit through his recitation of the entire lyrics of the

Clubs new and old

The new media clubs and the old institutions they're superseding

The Athenaeum   bishops and dons
Brooks's   liberal establishment
The Carlton   Tory grandees
The Garrick   actors, lawyers, publishers
The Marlborough   exclusive
MCC   the cricket set
The Turf (Cairo)   ex-pats
White's   Dukes, Earls, Etonians
Cavalry and Guards   MI6 and generals
Reform Club   civil servants and left-wing MPs

The Groucho (£250 joining fee, £325 per annum, waiting list 30 months)
Soho House (£100 joining fee, £300 per annum, waiting list 18 months)
Home House (£1,500 joining fee, £1,500 per annum, by invitation)
The Met Bar (free, by invitation)
Momo (£50 per annum, by invitation)
China White (£500 per annum)
Teatro (£150 to join, £300 per annum)
Two Bridges (£300 per annum)
K Bar (£250 per annum)
Kabaret (free, by invitation)

over-blown 70s anthem 'Music' by John Miles. At the Brit Awards of 1996 Jarvis invaded the stage during the performance of another over-blown anthem – Michael Jackson's 'Earth Song'. He dropped his trousers and waggled his bare bottom before being hustled off stage by security and interviewed by the police. The music press regarded this stunt as a gesture of British defiance against American domination, and rallied to his defence. For the rest of the year Jarvis' star was as high as it could be. He was even represented on *Stars In Your Eyes*.

At the end of 1996 Jarvis took stock and started to wonder whether he had anything left to say. This stock-taking involved a great deal of party-going, to the point where he reached the No 1 spot in *The Sun*'s league of liggers. After a couple of years he took stock of his ligging and called a halt to it. He has been in demand as a social/cultural commentator, especially in relation to BritArt and the surrounding controversy. In early 1999 he hosted a TV series on *Outsider Art* – work by eccentrics outside the art world.

It was not until the end of 1997 that Pulp returned with a new single and album (by which time one member had left, amicably). Released in late autumn, 'Help The Aged' is a song about growing old, in line with Jarvis' realisation that he himself was not getting any younger, either physically or psychologically. Only a few months previously he had been proud to call himself 'imma' (immature) but now he was trying to find a way to grow up: in interviews he started talking about Radio 2 and the BBC World Service. The single was widely seen as a sensitive and thoughtful meditation on a difficult subject. It was favourably received.

Not so the album, *This Is Hardcore*. The front cover, consisting of a staged photograph of a naked woman who might have been the victim of a sexual assault, was widely criticised. One broadsheet newspaper published an editorial advising its readers not to buy such an offensive record. Yet the songs on the album are entirely in accordance with 90s notions of humility and integrity. Jarvis (all Pulp's lyrics are his: other band members contribute to the music and the royalties are shared equally) writes about the hollow character of fame, the futility of the rock'n'roll lifestyle and the superior status of the ordinary.

At the *NME* awards early in 1999 Jarvis spoke out against New Labour's 'cocaine socialism' and **Tony Blair**: 'Sometimes I think New Labour is OK. Then I heard the other day that Tony Blair had said we are all middle class now, and that horrified me. Being middle class is having two Sunday newspapers in your house and a Dyson vacuum cleaner. It is a certain materialistic way of furnishing your own coffin as comfortably as possible, a terrible blandness. Nobody should aspire to that.'

In these comments Jarvis displayed his customary, contradictory attitude towards the majority of the population: on the one hand he identifies with the masses, and even sees himself as their representative ('Common People'); on the other hand, he sometimes looks down on the common people and the mistakes we supposedly make ('Sorted for Es and Whizz').

What about Jarvis himself? Does he now take two Sunday papers and vacuum with a Dyson? After refusing to buy a house for many years, he finally settled on a five-storey home in the newly fashionable district of Hoxton (original home of the Blue Note Club and the Lux cinema, known as 'Silicon Alley' because of the proliferation of digital design companies in this formerly run-down area). His legendary Hillman Imp car has also been replaced. But don't expect him to turn into a smoothie – at least, not of the old school. The glasses, the suits, the combination of camp voice and deadpan Sheffield accent, the theatrical energy of his mannered stage presence – these elements are already woven into one of the smoothest performances in contemporary pop.

PARENTS Mark E Smith, Harry Worth, **David Hockney**, Andy Warhol

Coldcut
From DJ to VJ

'Don't hate the media, be the media.' With this slogan Coldcut announced the release of their video-sequencing software program VJamm, which retails at around £30. VJamm cuts out the fussy, messy business of tape splicing and allows video consumers to manipulate visual material and become TV producers, just as the sampler and the sequencer enabled DJs to turn themselves into record producers. If it sounds like cyberbabble, remember that this is the duo, comprised of ex-art teacher Jonathan More and computer programmer Matt Black, which back in 1987 constructed 'Say Kids What Time Is It?', the first UK record to be built entirely from samples. They were at the forefront of one breakthrough in DIY culture, and they might just be right about the next one.

After their ground-breaking debut, Coldcut hotted up with a remix of Eric B and Rakim's 'Paid In Full' (with vocals by Ofra Haza), hit the charts with 'Doctorin' The House' and 'The Only Way Is Up' and branched out into club nights, radio shows and live appearances. They produced *Jockey Slut* magazine's all-time No 1 remix compilation album, *Journeys By DJs*, and established the influential Ninja Tune label, featuring jazz-tinged hip-hopster The Herbalizer and ambient producer Mixmaster Morris.

With the CD-Rom *Let Us Play* (1996) Coldcut went beyond music into multimedia. They believe that digital sound and imaging is the new art form, at least as important as what goes on in galleries. When *Tomorrow's World* (BBC1) wanted to show how music could be made online with contributions from various performers in different parts of the world, they chose Coldcut to produce a track featuring Sinead O'Connor, Brinsley Forde and Thomas Dolby, among others.

In 1999 Coldcut released a remix CD-Rom/album, *Let Us Replay*, which also included a demo version of VJamm. If cultural critic John Peralez is correct and music is already shaped by TV, then Coldcut may be the model and VJamm could be the means to turn the wheel full circle by

empowering music-orientated people to make their own TV.

PARENTS Gustav Metzger, Grandmaster Flash, Emergency Broadcast Network

The Colony Room
The nursery of British bohemia

Groucho's is more widely known but the Soho haunt with the most kudos is the Colony Room, a drinking club halfway down Dean Street. Opened by the domineering Muriel Belcher on 15 December 1948 (when Britain was still in the grip of post-war rationing), the honour roll of Colony Room-mates includes singer and Surrealist **George Melly** and the louche Labour MP Tom Driberg. It is probably true to say that more artists have made an exhibition of themselves in the Colony Room than anywhere else in London.

In the early days, the young Francis Bacon was taken to Muriel's by aesthete Brian Howard (Evelyn Waugh's model for Anthony Blanche in *Brideshead Revisited*). Muriel recognised that Bacon had talent and offered him £10 a week and free drinks if he brought enough big spenders into the club. As his fame and fortune increased, Bacon became a big spender himself. His favourite toast was 'champagne for my real friends and real pain for my sham friends'.

Muriel Belcher was a Portuguese-Jewish lesbian

who used a high camp argot in which, for example, the führer of the Third Reich would always be referred to as 'Miss Hitler'. She was impatient with punters who were not spending enough. If Muriel thought someone was being tight (in the monetary sense), she would shout 'Open your beanbag, Lottie' and bully the unfortunate soul into buying a round for everyone in the room.

Belcher and Bacon have passed on, and the Colony Room is frequented by a new crop of hard-drinking artists including **Damien Hirst**. But nowadays there is no need to hustle for punters; the waiting list is as long as Bacon's drinks bill.

The Comic Strip Presents
Genre can be fun

Robbie Coltrane described The Comic Strip Presents … as 'halfway between **Carry On** and a Joe Orton play'. Like the Carry On films, The Comic Strip Presents … featured a recognisable company of actors (including, apart from Coltrane, Adrian Edmonson, **Keith Allen**, Dawn French, Rik Mayall, Nigel Planer, Daniel Peacock and Jennifer Saunders) and a handful of writers (including Edmonson, Peter Richardson, Peter Richens and Roland Rivron) in a long-running strand (30 shows throughout the 80s, a one-off revival in 1998). Unlike the Carry On series, The Comic Strip Presents … was made for TV (Channel 4) rather than the cinema, and the humour was reliant not so

much on tits and bums but on the liberties taken with dramatic formats such as the western, the children's adventure story and the serious documentary. The joke was in the genre and the undermining of it, just as Joe Orton undermined the well-made play in his iconoclastic sex comedies.

Broadcast on Channel 4's opening night in November 1982, the first Comic Strip Presents … was *Five Go Mad In Dorset*, a spoof on Enid Blyton's Famous Five stories (followed in the second series by *Five Go Mad On Mescalin*). This was followed by *War* – a spoof on Cold War intrigue, *The Beat Generation* – a take-off of cool cat movies such as *The Subterraneans*, *Susie* – a parody of small-town melodrama and, pre-empting *Spinal Tap*, Adrian Edmonson's fake rockumentary *Bad News Tour*. Highlights of the second series included: *Geno,* a satire on the relationship between crime and the media (15 years before *Natural Born Killers* and Ben Elton's *Popcorn*); *A Fistful of Travellers' Cheques*, featuring two Spanish-sounding Englishmen with a yen for the Old West; and *Eddie Monsoon* – a life, a spoof documentary about a failed TV personality starring former BBC2 film pundit Tony Bilbow. Other memorable shows included *Slags*, written by French and Saunders (formerly billed as Kitsch'n'Tile, they went on to star in their own TV show, and in 1999 wrote and appeared with Alison Steadman in *Let Them Eat Cake*, a busty parody of Marie Antoinette and the French revolution) and *The Yob*, a take-off of *The Fly* (as remade by David Cronenberg in 1987) featuring Keith Allen.

Punning and parody is a long-established aspect

DEFENDERS OF THE FAITH Great British comedy misanthropes

Many of the great British comic creations are tragic misanthropes: small men caught out of time, distrustful of the new and entrenched in the received prejudices and snobberies of the crumbling old world.

Tony Hancock   *Hancock's Half Hour* (1954–59)
Anthony Aloysius St John Hancock, of 23 Railway Cuttings, East Cheam, the original outspoken champion of the Little Englishman, setting the nation to rights.

Albert Steptoe   *Steptoe and Son* (1962–74)
Galton and Simpson's second great work. Determined to keep him tied to the apron strings, Albert Steptoe (Wilfrid Brambell) continually frustrates and undermines his son Harold's (Harry H Corbett) ambitions to self-improve and embrace the modern liberal culture of a changing Britain with his vile old-world ways.

Alf Garnett   *Till Death Us Do Part* (1966–75)
Johnny Speight's East End bigot who ranted for a decade about the state of the nation. He has opinions about everything (lefties, poofs, blacks, Jews, women) and is not afraid to let you know them.

Terry Collier   *Whatever Happened To The Likely Lads?* (1973–74)
After five years in the army, Terry (James Bolam) comes home and doesn't like the changes he finds. Hard to please, a classic conversation he has with Bob about his dislikes starts on the other side of the world with the Chinese and ends up with the confession that he's not too keen on the people next door or even his own family.

Rupert Rigsby   *Rising Damp* (1974–78)
Eric Chappell's Rigsby (Leonard Rossiter), a lodgings landlord, is a picture of desperation. Single, ageing and distinctly ineligible, he hangs on to the remnants of an Empire sensibility as he fears the new world is leaving him behind. Alan (young) and Philip (young, black and intelligent) provide adversaries to rant against, while Miss Jones represents his last chance to get the leg-over he believes all but himself are enjoying.

Basil Fawlty *Fawlty Towers* (1975–79)

John Cleese wrote and played the rudest hotelier in Britain. Obsequious and ingratiating with his betters and vicious with those he deems his lessers ('riff-raff' and foreigners), the hotel is halfway between a prison camp and a mental institution.

Arkwright *Open All Hours* (1976–85)

Roy Clarke's stuttering, miserly Arkwright (played by Ronnie Barker) is a man out of time. He keeps his northern cornershop open all hours ostensibly to make money, but in reality because he fears what he'll find if he ever leaves its confines.

Harry Truscott *Fairly Secret Army* (1984–86)

David Nobbs' second and 'fairly secret' creation, a retired Major (played by Geoffrey Palmer) who, finding it hard to adjust to the rigours of civilian life, sets up a quasi-military organisation to defend Britain from the forces of anarchy. 'Amen, at ease.'

Victor Meldrew *One Foot in the Grave* (1990–97)

Forced into retirement at 60 when he is replaced in his job by a 'box'. In frustrated and bad-tempered old Victor Meldrew, David Renwick created a Charles Pooter for the 90s and absurdity worthy of Samuel Beckett.

Alan Partridge *Knowing Me, Knowing You*

Talentless media megalomania and the voice of middle England's small-minded prejudices made frighteningly real. 'And on that bombshell … '.

Jim Royle *The Royle Family*

Ricky Tomlinson in his finest rendition yet of a Northern slob, playing the Caroline Aherne and Craig Cash created Jim Royle – tinpot patriarch of the eponymous TV-watching Manchester family. Like Alf Garnet meets Homer Simpson, he has strong opinions about everything (he's never happier than when he's got his mouth open) but rarely leaves the comforting security of his armchair. 'Misanthrope, my arse.'

of British culture, traceable back to Shakespeare and beyond. Until recently, however, this aspect was usually a sideline – an aside to the audience. In the 80s, playing with existing formats became the point of many an exercise – The Comic Strip Presents ... included – prompting Toby Young and Ed Barrett to refer to the twenty- and thirtysomethings of the period as the 'Quotation Generation'.

PARENTS Carry On, Joe Orton, Baudrillard

Terence Conran
Tastemaker

'He's made a more useful contribution than anybody else to the quality of life in Britain since the war.' So says Stephen Bayley of his former mentor, Sir Terence Conran.

Born in 1931, Conran was sent away to school at the age of six. He was expelled from Bryanston and did not finish his course at art college, opting to spend a year in Paris working as a cook. His paternal grandparents lost their money in the stockmarket crash of 1929, but Terence has more than made up for it. In his early 20s he opened a no-frills restaurant in Covent Garden called The Soup Kitchen (at a time when the very word 'restaurant' meant frilly tablecloths and traditional etiquette); and in 1964 he opened the first Habitat store on the up-and-coming Fulham Road (a byword for trendiness in the early 60s, just as Clerkenwell was

in the 90s) in south-west London. The declared aim of Habitat was 'to make simple good taste affordable' – for the first time in Britain, your house could be as stylised and modern as the Bauhaus.

While their younger brothers and sisters got high on drugs and pop music, Britain's middle-class late-twentysomethings OD'ed on Habitat furnishings: strong colours, bold checks; modernity and authenticity combined in a new environment that sent a message Ikea was still repeating 35 years later in its slogan 'chuck out the chintz'. This was a novel and indeed brave stance to take in a country where lace antimacassars still hung on every armchair (to stop the Brylcreem soiling them). At Habitat, even the method of purchase was different: while most shops might have been modelled on the Grace Brothers department store in the TV sitcom **Are You Being Served?**, Habitat was self-service. With its clean lines and direct approach, and an ethos which said that the domestic environment should be a reflection of individuality rather than conformity (*Wallpaper* magazine is covering the same ground in the 90s), Conran's Habitat is said to have 're-invented British attitudes to interior design'.

In the decades that followed, Conran's commercial empire expanded just as his tastes seemed to spread throughout British society. By the end of the 80s he was running a £1.5-billion business which included Habitat shops, Heal's, Richard's Shops, Mothercare and BHS (evoking wartime and rationing, the traditional name 'British Home Stores' was too old-fashioned), all under the corporate flag of Storehouse. But in 1991, when Conran was 60, he left the business. Now worth millions, he says he wears frayed shirts and resoles his shoes.

In the 90s Conran set up the Design Museum (in the shadow of Tower Bridge, halfway between the City and Docklands) and concentrated on his restaurants. Quaglino's in Green Park (round the corner from the Ritz) brought large-scale New York-style dining to London – a little bit too reminiscent of power-dressing and the 80s to be quite the height of fashion after the early 90s. His other eateries include Mezzo's in Soho, the Butler's Wharf Chop House, the Blueprint cafe (next to the Design Museum), Bibendum in Fulham, the Coq D'Argent above Bank tube station in the heart of the City and the Bluebird Gastrodome in Chelsea. He has also opened restaurants in New York and Paris. Conran enjoys choosing dishes for his various restaurants and says that his 'primary purpose' as a restaurateur is to 'have a good time'.

Conran's three marriages have included bad times as well as good. The first Mrs Conran (designer Brenda Davison) went back to an ex-boyfriend after less than a year. His marriage to Shirley Conran (author of *Superwoman* and a succession of sex-and-shopping novels) ended in 1959. Caroline, his third wife, lasted 34 years until 1995. She sued him for a £10.5-million settlement, and won. After an affair with Sunita Russell (nearly 40 years his junior), Conran has found a new partner in Vicki Davis. In 1997 he told *Daily Mail* journalist Lynda Lee-Potter: 'I think I've had my ration of pretty girls.'

According to Bayley, the loves of Conran's life are 'women, drink, food, cigars, buildings, art'. Today, this list looks traditional and even conservative: the man whose tastes were well ahead in the 60s is now a monument to his times.

PARENTS Bauhaus, Elizabeth David
CHILDREN Jasper Conran, Habitat, Ikea

Steve Coogan
Which one is he?

Born (1967) into a 'Catholic socialist' family in Manchester, as a youth Steve Coogan learnt **Monty Python** sketches off by heart. Rejected by the Royal Academy of Dramatic Art (RADA), he studied drama at Manchester Polytechnic and made a name for himself doing impressions of famous people in unlikely situations. During the 80s he provided the voices of both Margaret Thatcher and Labour leader Neil Kinnock for *Spitting Image*. Light entertainment beckoned: he was soon doing £1,000-a-night stand-up and corporate functions; and at 22 he had already made it to the London Palladium. But Coogan did not want to be 'like all those disposable, cut-price' comics. He started to develop original characters and leapt at the chance when left-field performer **Patrick Marber** (soon to be a successful playwright) offered to work with him.

Within ten years, Coogan's stable of characters became an established part of the British comedy repertoire: Paul and Pauline Calf – the dregs from

the council estate; Latin singer Tony Ferrino; handyman Ernest Moss; salesman Gareth Cheeseman; and, most of all, Alan Partridge, who came to life when co-writer Armando Ianucci asked for 'a sports reporter who sounds like all the sports reporters you've ever heard'.

Paul Calf, keenly observed from the streets of Coogan's home town (besides Marber, he collaborates with another Manchester comedian, Henry Normal), is a badly dressed, lager-drinking, kebab-eating, foul-mouthed fuck-up whose only goal in life is the next shag, fag and pint. Though he sees himself as a sage of the streets (most of his philosophy is garnered from Chuck Norris videos), he is deeply suspicious of and threatened by anything beyond his immediate realm. Hence his most number one prey, the 'poncy' middle-class student.

Coogan's greatest achievement, though, is

undoubtedly Alan Partridge. For Allison Pearson, Partridge is 'up there' among the greatest comic characters such as Captain Mainwaring (*Dad's Army*) and Basil Fawlty. In his work, she adds, Coogan 'absorbs a range of British prejudices and habits to form a new social type'. A talentless TV and radio presenter, Partridge gives the cultural void of middlebrow, Middle England a voice on the hotseat of fame. A reminder that the saloon-driving, Chris Rea-listening, 'hanging's-too-good-for-them' ill-informed constituents of our island are alive and well in weekend driving gloves and colourful v-necks. Like Paul Calf he is sure of his own small-minded opinions and unable to tolerate anyone that threatens his worldview (women, foreigners, experts and so on): in the final series, he tells two Irish TV executives that the potato famine is the price the Irish paid for being 'fussy eaters'. His bigotry makes for patronising and insulting exchanges with anyone that crosses him, both in front of and behind the camera, and inevitably excruciating self-humiliation. Perhaps his most endearing legacy is his ability to invest the mundane artefacts and manners of everyday life in Middle England – from owl sanctuaries and motorway service stations to a Terry's Chocolate Orange – with an ironic deified charm. In his desire to retain his sinking stardom, the series just got darker and darker. His desperation finally resembled that of Scorsese's Rupert Pupkin in *The King of Comedy*.

Allison Pearson has compared the Partridge/Coogan coupling to that of Dame Edna and her creator Barry Humphries. Besides solo shows, his credits range from *On The Hour*, the spoof radio news show that also featured **Chris Morris** (*Brass Eye*), *The Day Today* – the TV version of *On The Hour*, to *The Fix*, a straight television drama, set in the early 60s, in which he played a news reporter investigating rigged football matches.

In the mid-90s Coogan visited a psychotherapist: the combination of cocaine and performing on an empty stomach at the **Edinburgh Festival** (he won the Perrier Award there in 1992) may have induced his panic attacks. He was briefly known in the tabloids as a 'love cheat' after he left his girlfriend, and mother of his daughter, Anna Cole.

In 1998 Coogan did a sell-out season as *The Man Who Thinks He's It*, a spoof on the suave, smooth male of yesteryear. Although the show mocked masculine arrogance, Coogan seems to have quite a high opinion of himself. When *Guardian* reviewer Phil Daoust published a luke-warm review of Coogan's performance and criticised him for not taking risks, *The Man Who Thinks He's It* not only fumed about it but included his response in the video of his show.

After nearly 20 years of performing, the British public is none the wiser as to the 'real' Steve Coogan. Some 20 years ago, the indefinite personality of impressionist Mike Yarwood was ultimately his downfall: it seemed that there was no one there to relate to. But in these pick'n'mix times, now that we are used to the idea of playing different roles in various social situations (like Zelig in Woody Allen's eponymous film), perhaps we do not need Coogan to show us who he 'really' is.

PARENTS Mike Yarwood, David Coleman

Peter Cook

The man who never found his voice

According to Ian Hislop, current editor of the late Peter Cook's co-creation *Private Eye*, the problem with Cook was that he suffered from 'existential boredom from an early age'. Among his contemporaries, the verdict is that this was a man who was profligate with his considerable comic talents and never learnt to apply himself consistently. But perhaps Cook's comedy and his lack of direction were both derived from the same source: his languorous and sometimes affectionate disdain for the British tradition and the character types associated with it.

Cook was born in 1937 in the upmarket seaside town of Torquay. His father was a diplomat who spent most of his working life in Africa, and Peter's first male role model was the gardener. At 13 he went to public school (Radleigh) and he found ways of getting into the school sick bay on the days when the Goon Show could be heard on radio. At Radleigh, where he was labelled 'unclassifiable', Cook developed his first comic character, based on a waiter in the school dining hall. The slightly snobbish tone of Cook's comedy, which was anti-establishment without necessarily being egalitarian, would re-emerge in the 70s with the creation of Derek and Clive. Perhaps his considerable height encouraged him to look down on people.

At Cambridge, Cook read modern languages with a view to joining the Foreign Office. In 1960 he was elected president of Footlights, the university revue group. David Frost remembers Cook as 'the most amazing ad-libber' who embodied 'the spirit of Cambridge' at the time; Cook was 'seminal to everyone's sense of humour'. His reputation came to the attention of Jonathan Miller, who mentioned Cook to the producer of *Beyond The Fringe* – a satirical show staged at the official **Edinburgh Festival** which subsequently toured the UK and the USA, and which made the names of Jonathan Miller, David Frost, **Alan Bennett** and the latecomer among the group, Peter Cook.

Christopher Booker, founder member of the team that started the satirical magazine *Private Eye*, believes that Cook was 'the first to pick up on the change of mood that was the onset of the 60s'. The *Eye*'s first editor Richard Ingrams was impressed by Cook's impersonation of Harold Macmillan: 'It was the first time anyone had got up in public and ridiculed the prime minister'. With the money he made from *Beyond The Fringe*, Cook set up a comedy club, The Establishment (members only, therefore no censorship), which featured new acts like recently arrived Australian Barry Humphries and the infamous American iconoclast Lenny Bruce. A few months later he bought a controlling interest in *Private Eye* and inaugurated a weekly, boozy lunch for the staff of his club and his magazine.

In the early 60s, after years of deference and observance of tradition, British society gorged itself on satire. But suddenly there was a glut of it and, in 1963–4, the satire boom crashed. Forced to find a new role for himself, Cook forged a partnership with Dudley Moore who in the resulting TV show *Not Only … But Also*, played the puzzled proletarian to Cook's patrician absolutist. This coupling was

Cooking: the new rock'n'roll, sex, black etc.

Although Elizabeth David laid the foundations for our gastronomic return from the wilderness to rediscover our national taste-buds, it was not until the mid-80s that cooking really took off as the new rock 'n' roll, eventually becoming a national obsession.

By the late 60s and early 70s restaurants had discovered the continental touch. It was the era of the bistro: all checked tablecloths and phallic pepper mills, but the food was by-and-large still showy and aspirational rather than truly tasty. Chefs and punters were still finding their feet and were in the awed grip of Escoffier and his ilk, whose cruel and distant gospel was not to be questioned by anyone this side of the Channel. Chefs clung to dire standards like coq au vin, coquilles st jacques, boeuf bourguignon (washed down with Beaujolais Nouveau) and murderously anglicised them into our own bland canon. Indeed, in the wilds of Britain, there are hotels still peddling this fayre.

In a crucial two year period, starting in 1986, a new type of restaurant and chef began to appear: Sally Clarke (Clarke's), Alistair Little (Alistair Little's), Simon Hopkinson (Bibendum), Rowley Leigh (Kensington Place), Marco Pierre White (Harvey's). Old-fashioned, long and intimidating menus were replaced by short, daily-changing menus and a style of cooking that fused far-flung tastes in exciting new combinations. According to Little, they were 'outside the restaurant establishment because, not only had most of us never trained professionally, we were also literate.' Add to that media-literate: they were enthusiastic, iconoclastic and in many cases outspoken in their views. Perfect material to create that new breed: the celebrity chef. This new breed wasted no time in boiling over into caricature: artistic tantrums and expelling ingratiates from their gastro-palaces became standards on the menu. They were superstars to be snapped by the paparazzi alongside supermodels, footballers and film stars. The 80s excess of violent tantrums soon largely disappeared (if you discount Gordon Ramsay) and the new breed of chefs concentrated on the food.

The rest is history. Once the super chef's star potential had been realised on TV, the country went steadily food barmy until you couldn't move for cookery programmes (and even channels) and tie-in books. Delia Smith, the nation's tried-and-trusted cook, became bigger than ever and a plethora of new faces – Nigel Slatter, Gary Rhodes, Ainsley Harriot – arrived to make our lives and tables better. The range of goods that supermarkets stock has rocketed in the 90s to accommodate the new tastes British households were willing to try, while refurbished gastro-pubs have replaced smokey old dives on every high street as the place to eat and socialise for the young and hip. Eating, for a certain section of the nation, has moved on from refuelling in private to become a 'lifestyle' statement and London, rather than New York or Paris, is now seen by many as the culinary capital of the world.

especially effective at a time when Britain's patricians (the kind of people who ran the Foreign Office) were feeling increasingly compromised and insecure. The Pete/Dud combination was regarded as the most intelligent comedy on TV and sometimes compared to the Theatre of the Absurd (Beckett, Ionesco, Albee).

After making a film with Moore (*Bedazzled*, 1967), Cook tried to make it in comic roles in the movies (*A Dandy In Aspic*, 1968; *The Rise and Rise of Michael Rimmer*, 1970). But the fluent, original improviser seemed awkward when learning other people's lines. Cook retreated to the bottle. On an afternoon TV chatshow in 1973 he admitted 'I tend to drink too much' and tried to pass it off as 'a symptom of boredom'. His next foray was another partnership with Moore: together they developed a duo of stupid, belligerent bigots named Derek and Clive – unattractive characters who might be said to personify Cook's rejection of his own intelligence. After all, if there's nothing to be done with it one might as well be stupid; and if you aren't not stupid already, you can always come closer to your ambition by having another drink.

As Derek and Clive, Pete and Dud made three successful LPs, followed by a disastrous remake of *The Hound of the Baskervilles*. Ironically, it was Moore who was asked to go to Hollywood as a comedy lead, and Cook was left at a loose end. Briefly on the wagon, he wrote a shortlived column for the *Daily Mail*. In 1978 he hosted Mike Mansfield's Saturday-night music show *Revolver*, but the audience did not know what to make of him and he did not know how to handle them either. In 1980 he made *Cook & Co*, a special for ITV; but its reception was lukewarm. In 1981 he played an English butler in an American sitcom, but it was chopped after one series. His BBC chatshow was taken off air after just three programmes.

For a time Cook gave up. According to Ingrams 'he just didn't want to see anyone, he would sit at home drinking, watching TV and reading'. Then, late at night, he took to calling Clive Bull's phone-in show on LBC and pretending to be a Scandinavian called Sven. Occasionally he would come into the *Eye* office after six months or a year of not being seen and behave as if he'd been there all the time. There were occasional flashes of the past glory: an appearance on *Clive Anderson Talks Back* in 1993, a stage show with Eleanor Bron. But despite the love and care of his wife Lin, Cook never got back on track. He died of internal haemorrhaging in January 1995.

'I have never attempted to achieve my potential,' Cook once declared. According to Alan Bennett, 'the only regret he voiced was that he'd saved David Frost from drowning' (in Connecticut back in the 60s when *Beyond The Fringe* was playing in the States). Of course it is a pity that Cook could not save himself from drowning; but surely his humour and his talent lay in not being able to swim with the traditional British tide.

PARENTS Lenny Bruce, Alistair Sim
CHILDREN Alternative comedy, Monty Python

John Cooper Clarke

The one that got away

Dressed in the 'essential uniform of the paranoid urbanite', comprising Dylan hair and shades ('National Health jobs sprayed with the stuff used for tinting taxi windows'), pointy shoes, three-piece pinstripe, cokespoon earring, Salford poet ('I talk in tune') John Cooper Clarke was at the crest of the new wave in 1978. While many of his contemporaries went on to enjoy global status, Cooper Clarke 'stopped being famous' and now lives a quiet life in Colchester, Essex, interspersed with occasional readings in small clubs. But his influence on poetry, comedy and the British *persona* remains considerable.

Born in 1950, Cooper Clarke attended a Catholic secondary-modern school and wrote his first poem about a parish priest who farted. After a series of jobs (window cleaner, apprentice motor mechanic, assistant to an insurance company photographer who took pictures of wounds), he became a technician ('all I did was hand out chisels') at Salford College. After playing bass in unknown psychedelic bands in the late 60s, he lost interest in 70s music (moronic metal, fey pop and pomp rock) but felt inspired by the imaginative and emotional range of punk. 'It's the nearest thing that there's ever been,' he told the *NME* in 1978, 'to the working classes going into areas like Surrealism and Dada.'

Punk wasn't all about intellectual stimulation, and the Salford poet had a hard time from those punters who only came to gob and pogo. But his

records (*Snap, Crackle and Bop*, 1980; *Zip Style Method*, 1982; both with backing music from Martin Hannett's Invisible Girls) and books (*Ten Years In An Open-necked Shirt*) sold respectably. He might have been on the brink of the big time, but a heroin habit intervened (for many years he shared a flat with Nico, formerly of the Velvet Undergound). Together with Cooper Clarke's distaste for the business side of music, this took him from centre stage down to obscure poetry cellars. During the late 80s his biggest exposure came from an acting role as the sidekick to the Honey Monster in Sugar Puffs adverts.

In the late 70s Cooper Clarke set a new tone of muted anger and throwaway rebellion. Ostensibly deadpan, his delivery was knowingly transparent: you were meant to see through to the emotion and frustration beneath, as in the poem 'Beasley Street': 'Where the action isn't/That's where it is/State your position/Vacancies exist/In an X-certificate exercise/Ex-servicemen explete/Keith Joseph smiles and a baby dies/In a box on Beasley Street.' Ostentatiously provincial, with an Albert Tatlock-accent so thick you could wrap chips and gravy in it, Cooper Clarke's voice became a template for both performance poetry and alternative comedy. Those in his debt include Craig Charles, Jack Dee, John Hegley and Murray Lachlan Young. The demeanour which he introduced now constitutes a recognised type – northern phlegm meets cool cat – in the cast list of British life.

Having missed his own bandwagon, Cooper Clarke retreated into heroin and its poetry. While living in a candle-lit flat in Salford, he wrote prose and poems in the tradition of Coleridge, De Quincey and Baudelaire. Now entering his 50s, he still looks like 'Keith Richards meets eighteenth-century courtier', but has become a father and a cleaned-up 'citizen above suspicion'.

PARENTS John Betjeman, Philip Larkin, Samuel Coleridge, Nico, the Sex Pistols
CHILDREN Craig Charles, Jack Dee, Murray Lachlan Young
READ ON *England Is Mine – pop life in Albion from Wilde to Goldie* by Michael Bracewell

Julian Cope
Exploding antiquarian

Q magazine dubbed Julian Cope 'the Andrew Lloyd Webber of garage rock'. 'Britain's premier pop nutter' is how Andrew Smith of *The Sunday Times* described him to his face. Cope did not welcome the description, but continues to live up to his reputation as a serious eccentric in his new role as chronicler of neolithic Britain.

Born (1957) in Wales, Cope grew up in Liverpool and participated in the scene around Brady's/Eric's, the local club featuring **Bowie**/Roxy Music/punk. In 1978 he was part (bass player) of the short-lived Crucial Three (full title: Arthur Hostile & The Crucial Three), the other two being Ian McCulloch (soon to be the kingpin in Echo and the Bunnymen) and Pete Wylie (frontman for

Wah!). Cope played briefly in Nova Mob and A Shallow Madness, then formed The Teardrop Explodes (name taken from a caption in a *Marvel* comic), who made their live debut (at the end of 1978) at Eric's along with Echo and the Bunnymen, released a couple of singles on the local Zoo label (Zoo's co-director Dave Balfe played keyboards and contributed to the band's West Coast 60s sound), before signing with Mercury and producing two albums (*Kilimanjaro*, 1980; *Wilder*, 1981) described by Smith as 'quirky classics of the post-punk era'. Since 1984 Cope has been a solo artist (solo debut characteristically entitled 'World Shut Your Mouth'), releasing an album a year on average: he now sells his own records by mail order.

Cope used to be famous for doing a lot of acid. His song 'Out of My Mind On Dope and Speed' is entirely true to his own life. He has lacerated his chest, appeared naked except for a turtle shell (on stage and on the cover of *Fried*, 1985) and declared that he is a building. Cope was creative as well as crazy. Absorbing the passion and melodrama of his idol Scott Walker, combining melody, psychedelia and wry humour, his songs were in turn exuberant, egotistical, menacing and relentless. Performing was another form of high for him, but when The Teardrop Explodes finished their farewell tour in 1983, it seemed that Cope might have gone too high to come back. *Q* writer Gavin Martin notes that people 'wondered if the abyss that had swallowed previous lysergic loons like Rocky Erikson was now beckoning JC – a guy whose very initials seemed to have cursed him with a messianic/crucifixion complex'.

Despite this prognosis, Cope survived, and gave up drugs some years ago. His new visions are from a different and altogether more ancient source. Now living in the converted stables of a manor house overlooking Silbury Hill in Wiltshire, Cope is author of *The Modern Antiquarian* (1998), the result of an eight-year odyssey around the monuments of neolithic Britain (for Cope, Stonehenge is not ancient enough). The book is part-essay, part-travel guide, part-poetry ('On Knapp Hill I eat my snot/For 'tis the only food I've got'). Some reviewers have marvelled at its breadth of vision, others have questioned Cope's knowledge of Welsh and his criticisms of traditional scholars.

'Not only is there nothing like this in general circles,' boasts Cope, 'there's nothing like this in scholarly circles or head circles.' He struggled to come up with 'something entirely alternative but entirely complete'. Cope had already published two books: *Krautrocksampler*, an account of German electronic music; and *Head On*, memoirs of his time on the Liverpool scene. Both were favourably received, but neither was acclaimed like *The Modern Antiquarian*.

As it turns out, *The Modern Antiquarian* is less about the old world and more to do with current preoccupations. When Cope says 'visiting and studying the temples of the neolithic peoples is in itself a highly nourishing and healing act, for it reveals the ancients to be just as stubborn and over-achieving as ourselves', you can be fairly sure that he is transposing his own concerns on to prehistoric Britain and finding that, surprise surprise, 'this is all so close'. Indigenous opposition to Roman imperialism (the dictatorship of 'straight lines') sounds very much like a backwards-projection of today's widespread hostility towards road building, social regimentation and philosophical linearity. (A hostility shared by Cope and expounded on solo works such as *Peggy Suicide* (1991) which lyrically championed the political activism of the streets, and green ethics.) In truth Cope's book is not an archaeology of the ancients but an expression of Britain's modern-day psychology.

The ex-post-punk-pop star now lives in the English countryside with his American wife and two children of primary-school age. He keeps the kids out of scripture lessons at school, but everything else about Cope seems to fit in fairly well with the remade, remodelled version of rural Middle England. Most recently, he published a second volume of autobiography, *Repossessed*, chronicling his brain-frying post Teardrops years.

PARENTS Scott Walker, Arthur Lee, **Spike Milligan**
READ ON *Head On*, *The Modern Antiquarian*

Patrick Cox
British sole

Shoemaker to the stars (even '**underclass**' luminaries like Shaun Ryder enjoy stepping out in Cox's high-class footwear), Patrick Cox is a Canadian (b. 1963) who at 20 left his native Alberta for Cordwainer's College in London. As a student he designed footwear for **Vivienne Westwood**'s Clint Eastwood collection. Graduating in 1985, he worked with fashion designers **John Galliano**, John Rocha and **Katharine Hamnett**. He produced his first independent collection in 1986, and set up his own shop five years later. Cox won the title of Accessory Designer of the Year at the British Fashion Awards in 1994 and 1995. In 1998 the Victoria and Albert Museum exhibited a pair of his Eiffel Tower sandals.

Cox was soon established in couture circles, but he is more widely known for his mid-price shoes, first dubbed Wannabe and now simply labelled the Patrick Cox Collection. He reinvented the loafer (incredibly, in the 80s loafers could be worn with white socks), surpassing the design of the classic Bass Weejun. In the 90s asymmetrical heels and toes were his trademark. He now produces a wide range of footwear for men and women, from lace-ups to mules to sneakers. Cox – who has shops in Sloane Street ('the interior is as cool and confident as **James Bond** or Emma Peel'), in the Club Building in Manchester, and in Paris, New York and the Far East – also lends his name to a range of clothing (spaghetti-strap slip dresses, zip-front jackets and draped-neck tunics were among his 1999 collection). But his loafers, sometimes with a Union Jack on the insole, remain the epitome of the modern British classic – especially in the eyes of Americans.

PARENTS Church's, Bass Weejuns

Croft and Perry
Happy at war

The continuing success of the TV comedy *Dad's Army*, conceived more than 30 years ago and set among the Home Guard in the small seaside town of Walmington-on-Sea, shows how rerunning the Second World War is a deadly serious business for Britain. Apart from the World Cup in 1966, it was the last time a British team won.

First shown in 1968, *Dad's Army* was co-written by BBC producer David Croft and Jimmy Perry (who also wrote the 40s-style theme tune 'Who do you think you are kidding, Mr Hitler?'), a veteran of the Home Guard (local defence volunteers, known first as LDVs, who were meant to be Britain's last line of defence against invasion; wartime comedians nicknamed them 'Look, Duck and Vanish'; 1.5 million enrolled). The programme ran for nine years (a total of 80 episodes). It was said to be the Queen's favourite, and won the Bafta award for Best Comedy in 1970. The last episode was shown for the first time on Remembrance Sunday 1977, but the whole series has been repeated many times since – and remains a national favourite to this day. Through their roles in *Dad's Army*, many actors in the Home Guard company became household names (Arthur Lowe as Captain Mainwaring, John Le Mesurier as Sergeant Wilson, Clive Dunn as Corporal Jones).

Dad's Army is nostalgic (when first broadcast, the majority of its audience had lived through the Second World War; more than 30 years later, most viewers are nostalgic about an experience they never had), but its comic portraits are also sharp and pointed. Mainwaring is a tinpot dictator who has been waiting all his life to get out of a bank manager's suit and into a military uniform. Like Mr Pooter in George and Weedon Grossmith's *Diary of a Nobody* (1892), he is a bore who thinks he is charismatic. Jones is a lick-spittle who will do anything to please the officer class. Only the world-weary Wilson – so urbane and sophisticated one can only wonder how he ended up in a hick town on the south coast – emerges with dignity. Yet though these characters are pompous, incompetent and craven, they are drawn with sympathy and affection. The effect is to invoke Englishness and laugh at it (underpowered, overblown) at the same time.

Croft and Perry's next comedy pursued the same formula. *It Ain't Half Hot Mum* (1974–81) was set in the only place more English than Walmington-on-Sea: Empire India. Set amid a Second World War concert party in the Burmese jungle, it has fun with the same petty pecking order of class rank witnessed in *Dad's Army*, as the platoon of twittish officers and misfit squaddies (armed with music hall songs rather than guns) constantly find themselves in situations they are ill-equipped to deal with.

Croft and Perry then went on to write *Hi-De-Hi*, another long-running comedy series, this time set in one of the holiday camps that were landmarks in British culture after the Second World War. In their original incarnation, holiday camps were a peace-time continuation of the Blitz Spirit (nowadays they have been reformatted to resemble shopping malls rather than army bases), and Croft and Perry's

scripts showed continuities with wartime (regimentation) and developments associated with unprecedented post-war austerity (the effect of rock'n'roll).

The Second World War still looms large in the British psyche. It was a moment of common purpose which in this age of fragmentation stands out as an oddly attractive proposition. Whereas heroic war films are a bit too heroic for today's understated style, Croft and Perry's creations are as cosy and comforting as boiled egg and soldiers.

PARENTS The Navy Lark, The Army Game
The Men from the Ministry

Are You Being Served?

David Croft also co-wrote *Are You Being Served?* (1973–75): the sub-Carry On sitcom set in the clothing departments of Grace Brothers' department store. Awash with cheap sexual innuendo (Mrs Slocombe: 'Sorry I'm late Captain Peacock, I trapped my pussy in the door') and everyone desperate for a leg-over (from the sex-mad octagenerian director 'Young' Mr Grace to the overtly gay, inside leg-measuring Mr Humphries), its three series would have been largely forgotten had it not generated such a cult following in the States in the 90s. Whether it's the camp factor (John Inman is a camp icon over there) or the longing for a pre-AIDS politically incorrect attitude to sex that makes the show so popular is unclear. But popular it remains.

Cult TV
Pay per re-view

One of the main attractions of cable and satellite TV is the number of channels devoted to repeats. Millions of viewers are happy to pay to see what they have already seen. Terrestrial broadcasters have got in on the act also, recognising that 'rpt' need not be a dirty word if the programme in question can be presented as a 'golden oldie'.

It's not just old people wanting to relive their life through TV programmes; there is also a new audience for old TV. 60s cop show *The Mod Squad* was reshown in 1999 as part of late-night programming for a mainly young audience. This is just one example of how TV shows are frequently reintroduced not for strength of plot or depth of characterisation, but because their period style appeals to the appetite among young and old for Pop Culture Past.

In summer 1999 Channel 4 started repeating *The Word*, the Friday-night music and talk show first broadcast in the early 90s. By the end of the decade in which it was produced, *The Word* had already entered 'the Loop' – the unofficial but unavoidable list of recurring artefacts from the recent past. The Loop is like the conveyor belt with prizes on it at the end of Bruce Forsyth's *Generation Game*. The aim of the game was to identify and appropriate the various items, not in any particular order; likewise it is less useful nowadays to talk about the orderly 'revival' of a particular decade. The schedules for Bravo and numerous other channels show that every decade is now available simultaneously, a riot of nostalgia to be tapped into and logged out of according to the whim of the viewer.

Not that anyone really relives the complexities of the historical period which they are dipping into. Our retro-sampling tends to be simplistic and banal (the 60s = drugs and pop; the 70s = sex and disco): not history, but history-lite.

READ ON 'The Age of Plunder' by Jon Savage in *The Face*, July 1983

Cult Crime TV
Irony in the soul

Many crime-related TV programmes from the 70s now attract a tongue-in-cheek audience. But the original viewers and makers of these programmes were no strangers to camp either. So what happens when 70s camp is added to by a further level of critical distance on the part of today's viewers? Do the camps cancel each other out, or are such shows now subjected to a self-replicating chain of ironic reinterpretation?

Budgie

Starring early 60s pop singer Adam Faith as a hapless young criminal (the character was a good ten years younger than the actor) caught between the police and his employer, Soho pornbroker Charlie

Endell (named after a street in nearby Covent Garden, played by Ian Cuthbertson), the hour-long episodes of *Budgie* were made by London Weekend Television and broadcast nationally in 1971–72. Among boys in approved schools (a form of punitive care that was scrapped not long afterwards) *Budgie* was essential Friday-night viewing: despite his misfortunes, in his bomber jacket and with a haircut, in the words of music journalist Ian Penman, like a 'throttled collie', he was still a role model to them.

Jason King

'Jason King – author, private investigator and off-shoot of Department 'S' – was the personification of 70s man. Sporting a ludicrous moustache, flamboyant shirts, velvet catsuits and the largest of medallions, he leapt from bed to bed, purring catchphrases like "whenever I feel the need for exercise I lie down until it passes". It's now the most popular show on Bravo, so turn on, tune in and dust off those flares' (*Radio Times*, October 1995).

The catsuited Jason King emerged from the ATV series Department 'S' (a section of Interpol set up to solve unaccountable events, see also *The X Files*) in 1971. Played by Anglo-French actor Peter Wyngarde, King was an amateur sleuth and professional crime writer who strongly identified with Mark Caine, the protagonist of his own books. A fop who was traumatised when burglars violated his clothes, a wit who could not stop quoting from Oscar Wilde, and a womaniser who also displayed a misogynistic streak, King was ultimately a narcissist: 'I am my own favourite subject.' Critic Andy Medhurst has interpreted King's popularity as 'conclusive proof' that 'camp had stopped being primarily a subcultural guerrilla code and [had become] big business'.

The Persuaders!

Another ATV production (1971–72), this time starring world-renowned film stars Tony Curtis and Roger Moore, *The Persuaders!* featured the escapades of two playboys, one American (Curtis) and one British (Moore). The title sequence is a recap of their different backgrounds (rags to riches, Curtis; born with a sliver spoon, Moore) and most of the subsequent episodes play on their different, but ultimately complementary, ways of solving crimes and bedding women – just as the two strands of the split-screen title sequence finally converge in a panorama of girls and gambling in casinos. Moore had previously raised his famous eyebrow as Simon Templar in the TV series *The Saint*, and he went on to raise it still higher as **James Bond**, beginning with Guy Hamilton's *Live and Let Die* (1973).

The Sweeney

As in 'Sweeney Todd' (the demon barber of Fleet Street), rhyming slang for Flying Squad, *The Sweeney* was a 70s Cockney cop show starring John Thaw (later to star as Inspector Morse) and

Denis Waterman (later to co-star with George Cole's Arthur Daley in *Minder*) as hard-drinking, hard-driving, rule-bending detectives. Made by Thames TV in the early 70s, the Sweeney was cast and scripted against a background of news stories and inquiries into police violence and corruption.

The Sweeney was the *NYPD Blue* of its day; nowadays it is viewed for its period charm (big Fords, wide collars and everybody smokes). Even the violence and grittiness has a 70s label on it. What once was hard-hitting is now part of our insatiable appetite for snacking on old times. Even the heavies from Scotland Yard have been absorbed into our low-calorie, insubstantial version of history.

Culture Club
Queer Queen Mum and Co

Culture Club might have been so named because the individual members of the band brought together their various musical tastes and formed a kind of club out of their cultural differences. Nearly 20 years on, they have become 'like an English institution'. Commenting on their 1998 reunion tour, drummer Jon Moss went on to compare the band to a well-loved series of British comedy films: 'George is Barbara Windsor, he'll say I'm Kenneth Williams, probably. It's **Carry On** Culture Club, let's face it.'

Bass player Mikey Craig had been keen on the Monkees as a kid but his playing style was more influenced by the dub reggae sound systems that accompanied his parents' blues parties. Guitarist Roy Hay was an Essex Man with roots in jazz-funk. Drummer Jon Moss was the adoptive son of rich Jewish parents (father owned a chain of gents' clothes shops) who brought business acumen and a background in punk (he had done short stints as the drummer in The Clash and The Damned). Vocalist George O'Dowd (Boy George) embodied 'council estate glamour' (he was brought up in Eltham, south-east London, near where black schoolboy Stephen Lawrence was later murdered), developed during his years as a **Bowie** fan (George was there at Victoria station when the Thin White Duke seemed to enjoy a fascist-style homecoming) and latterly as a post-punk/**New Romantic** (he was the cloakroom attendant at the Heroes club nights which were put together at Blitz in Covent Garden by Steve Strange and Rusty Egan; and briefly a singer with **Malcolm McLaren**'s Bow Wow Wow).

The behind-the-scenes element in the make-up of Culture Club was the love affair (boy meets boy who looks more like a girl) between Jon and George. Front-of-camera, Boy George became famous as the gay guy that teenage girls adored.

After the seriousness of punk, New Romantics just wanted to revel in being themselves. With Boy George, celebratory selfhood was turned into marketable pop product; although Mikey and Roy may have resented it (especially when they were pushed out of the way by photographers rushing to snap George and Jon), the band was really there to frame him and back him up. Meanwhile the profits were split four ways under a business arrangement

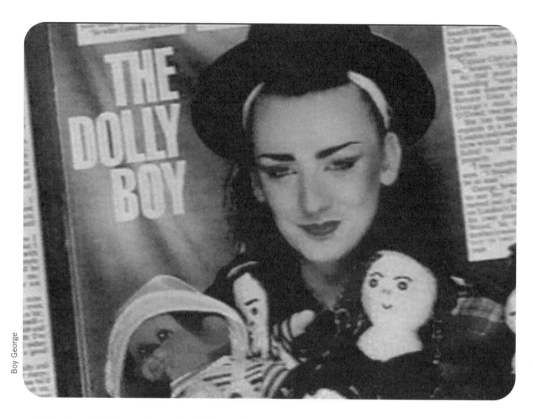

Boy George

put into place by Moss, who realised that varying percentages can be highly corrosive (as was the case with **The Smiths**).

Boy George was an unlikely pop product. If not officially Out (to the annoyance of some gay lobbyists), he was clearly not a traditional male role model. Starting out with make-up and dreadlocks topped by a Hasidic hat, his costumes became more outrageous as the band's budget increased.

Yet even in the decade of anti-gay legislation such as Clause 28 Boy George did not, generally speaking, provoke an angry response: more like an affectionate tut-tutting accompanied by loyalty and devotion – on the part of parents as well as their kids. Described by Malcolm McLaren as the 'teddy bear of soul music', Boy George was billed by the tabloids as 'a gender-bender' and 'the Dolly Boy'. But even when journalists knew about the

George/Jon relationship, they were not wont to shoot down the goose that lays the golden egg (as **The Sun**'s former columnist Rick Sky has explained), especially at a time when pop stars like Boy George were becoming the standard currency of the tabloids alongside royalty and television personalities.

For a couple of years Culture Club rode the crest of the British wave. With Annie Lennox (Eurythmics), Boy George appeared on the front cover of *Newsweek*. His 'English camperie' also graced the cover of *Rolling Stone*. In both the Midwest and Middle England he was the first pop star to make gender-bending lovable and miraculously acceptable in the eyes of your grandparents. In the summer of 1983 there were 18 British singles in the US Top 40, and Culture Club were the subject of an early day motion in the House of Commons congratulating them (and the Police and Duran Duran) for 'their success in the Grammy awards'. Their second album *Colour By Numbers* spawned five hit singles, of which 'Karma Chameleon' (September 1983) is probably the best known. Boy George and his crew proved that they were masters of 'plunder and pastiche', with traces of Motown and the Sigma Studio sound from Philadelphia (sweet soul such as the O'Jays and Harold Melvin and the Bluenotes) alongside rock guitar and reggae basslines. This was perfect postmodern pop which fitted right in with the new mood in a music industry that was acting, as author Dave Rimmer has explained, 'like punk never happened'. The record-buying public was equally enthusiastic: in 1983 they made Culture Club the biggest-selling band in the world.

But in 1984 the perfect mix began to get mixed up, mainly due to personal problems between George and Jon. As the band started to unravel, Boy George began to take drugs (he had always been known for his anti-drug stance), moving swiftly from marijuana to heroin and a conviction for possession (fined £250). Then an American musician friend died at his London home and another friend was hospitalised after an overdose. George had shaved off his locks and for a while it looked as if his consummate charm had been chopped off as well.

By this time the band had split up. Boy George succeeded in reformulating himself as a club DJ, which kept him busy for 12 years.

The members of Culture Club did not part company on friendly terms. But after more than a decade of hardly speaking to each other, they got together for a reunion tour in 1998 (the package also included ABC and The Human League). Culture Club always were self-conscious about their role as a 'pop group': right from the start they were playing a part. In their reformulation for the late 90s, they took this process on another step: they were playing the part of a 'pop group' that was already acting out the role of being a 'pop group'.

PARENTS David Bowie, Stevie Wonder, Trojan Records, the Sigma Sound of Philadelphia
READ ON *Like Punk Never Happened* by Dave Rimmer

Ian Curtis
Lost control

Ian Curtis was an epileptic whose fits became more severe as the popularity of his band, Joy Division, increased. He hanged himself in 1980 and has been revered ever since as a tortured artist who could not cope with this twisted world.

Born (1956) and brought up (son of a Transport Police officer who wrote plays) in Macclesfield, a dormitory town just south of Manchester, the young Curtis ingested James Dean, MC5, Roxy Music, Mott the Hoople, **David Bowie** and Jacques Brel's *My Death* (echoed years later in his own *Dead Souls*). He moved to Manchester to study for A-levels at further-education college, but quit after a couple of weeks. Girlfriend Deborah gave up her studies to fund their marriage (they wed in August 1975); meanwhile Ian became a low-grade civil servant. Inspired by the Sex Pistols in July 1976, the Curtises journeyed to the south of France for the punk festival at Mont de Marson, but Ian's skin reacted badly to the hot sun.

Ian became lead singer of punk band Warsaw who played a support slot for visiting US pre-punk Johnny Thunders (ex-New York Dolls) and were featured in Paul Morley's fanzine *Out There*. In July 1977 they were included in the piece on Manchester that Morley wrote for the *NME*. Following complaints from the London band Warsaw Pact, they changed their name to Joy Division (the term applied to female prisoners used by the Nazis for sex; adopted by the band via the

pulp novel *House of Dolls*, set in a concentration camp). Curtis was acquiring a reputation for self-destruction on stage: with his frightened eyes, edgy stance and windmill arms, he always looked like hurting himself. Unlike other performers, Curtis held nothing back. He dared or felt compelled to reveal himself totally in the volatile, unprotected surroundings of small, crowded clubs.

Borrowing £400 from the bank, Joy Division put out an EP, 'Ideal for Living', complete with Hitler Youth-style sleeve. At a battle of the bands at local club Rafters, hosted by the earliest independent record labels Stiff and Chiswick, they came to the attention of **Tony Wilson**, presenter of local TV news programme *Granada Reports* and host of TV show *The Other Side of Midnight*. He signed them to his new label, Factory.

Curtis experienced his first epileptic fit after Joy Division's debut gig in London at the Hope and Anchor in Upper Street, Islington. His dancing on stage became more like a parody of his offstage seizures. Meanwhile in January 1979 he overcame his resistance to press interviews and appeared on the front cover of the *NME* (in long overcoat and wearing the alienated expression that came to be associated with Manchester musicians). Soon afterwards the band recorded their first session for the **John Peel** show on Radio 1, displaying what has been described as 'a dark, cold, terrible centre which exists in no other rock band'. In April that year they went into Strawberry Studios to record their first album, *Unknown Pleasures* (Factory), with Martin 'Zero' Hannett (previously their agent) in the producer's chair. The punk days of Warsaw were long gone; this was still an aggressive sound, but with occasional Northern Soul influences (such as NF Porter's 'Keep On Keeping On') and distant echoes of Kraftwerk, Giorgio Moroder and the 'motorik' beat developed by producer David Bowie for Iggy Pop's *The Idiot* (1978). Echoed in the original name of The Specials – the [Coventry] Automatics – the automatic aspect of this kind of rhythm expressed intense alienation from British society (it said: I am going through life on automatic pilot; the mechanised world has turned human beings into machines). Furthermore the externalised anger associated with punk seemed to have turned inwards. **Jon Savage** suggests that Curtis was a creature of 'De Quincey's Manchester', a city of closure and 'an environment systematically degraded by industrial revolution, confined by lowering moors, with oblivion as the only escape'. Wilson later explained that Joy Division were dealing with the question of 'I'm fucked'. In *Sounds* (weekly music paper; ceased publication), the album was described as 'death disco' that 'would push you over the edge'.

It was a prophetic insight. Curtis' moods became 'increasingly erratic' and in her book about her late husband, *Touching from a Distance*, Deborah Curtis reports that 'all Ian's time was spent reading and thinking about human suffering'. Ian was in psychological pain but perhaps also at the peak of his creativity. He dominated an edition of the new TV show *Something Else* with an over-the-edge performance of 'She's Lost Control'. In March 1980 Joy Division recorded their trademark single, 'Love Will Tear Us Apart', the chorus a haunting refrain based

around a simple chord sequence and set against a sparse and relentless drumbeat. They also completed their second album, *Closer* (like **Patrick Marber**'s play of the same name, written nearly 20 years later, an account of the alienated trying, and failing, to connect). On stage, Curtis' fits became almost indistinguishable from his stage act – some people thought the myth of Romantic self-destruction was what Wilson wanted from him. It certainly added to the band's marketability.

After taking an overdose Curtis went to Wilson's Gloucestershire cottage to recuperate. In May 1980 he returned to the family home in Macclesfield. Hours before Joy Division were due to leave for an American tour, he committed suicide by hanging himself in the kitchen. To Curtis' corpse Wilson said: 'You daft bugger.' He later said that the suicide was 'altruistic'.

Chris Bohn has summed up Joy Division as a record of 'the corrosive effect on the individual of a time squeezed between the collapse into impotence of traditional Labour humanism and the impending cynical victory of Conservatism'. But the mythic status of Joy Division has outlasted the moment of social change they originally described; and the idea that 'altruistic' Curtis died for all of us ('this man died for you' – Dave McCullough) is an essential part of their ongoing appeal (the same idea is confirmed in Bono's description of his voice as 'holy').

Ever since the Beats defined themselves as 'beatific' by virtue of being 'beaten', the counter-culture, following the Romantic model, has made icons of individuals who seem too sensitive to the world and too tortured by it to survive. Ian Curtis, even if he did always vote Conservative, was beatified in death and is now a patron saint of alienated angst. Even though his look and sound were minimalist and industrial, the extravagance of his alienation had an effect on London's New Romantics and the long-running **Goth** genre.

PARENTS Thomas Chatterton, Jim Morrison
CHILDREN Sarah Kane
READ ON *Touching from a Distance* by Deborah Curtis

Richard Curtis
The real Hugh Grant

At the end of the original draft of *Four* [originally *Five*] *Weddings and a Funeral*, Charles (Hugh Grant) got wed; but when comedy writer Richard Curtis and his partner, the broadcaster Emma Freud, decided not to make it legal, Charles did not make it to the altar either. This is not the only point of similarity between the real-life Curtis (self-deprecating ex-public school charmer) and the Charles character he created.

Son of a Czech immigrant who adopted the name Tony Curtis (no relation) and became a top exec for Unilever, Richard Curtis was brought up in New Zealand, Manila, Stockholm, Folkestone and Warrington. As head of his house at Harrow he banned fagging (it was reinstated as soon as he left). At Oxford, where he gained a first, he wanted to be an actor but realised 'I was not good at all. I would always be cast as Fabian in *Twelfth Night*.' Teaming up with fellow student Rowan Atkinson he became his scriptwriter and straight man. After a stint at the **Edinburgh Festival**, Curtis started writing for the new satirical sketch show *Not The Nine O'Clock News* (which featured Rowan Atkinson, Pamela Stephenson, Mel Smith and Griff Rhys Jones). It was he who wrote the Bee Gees spoof 'Meaningless Songs in Very High Voices' (years later he said it should have been called 'Fantastic, Long-Lasting Songs By the Best Partnership Since The Beatles').

Together with Atkinson, Curtis developed the silent comedy *Mr Bean* ('something we used to do on stage') about a lonely, hapless man who is always trying out crazy schemes: a nerd who never gives up. The show became ITV's most popular comedy, eventually pulling in domestic audiences of 18 million (1990) and it has been sold on to 94 countries.

While *Mr Bean* is widely regarded as a down-market comedy (one commentator once pondered whether it was a form of slumming), *Blackadder*, in which Atkinson stars as a nobleman who is as cynical as he is accident-prone, is generally thought to be upmarket. According to Atkinson, some people find *Bean*'s visual comedy too accessible, preferring the relative exclusivity of *Blackadder*'s 'wit and verbal dexterity'.

The four series of *Blackadder*, set successively in a fifteenth-century castle, Queen Elizabeth's court, 'mad' King George's palace and the trenches of the

First World War, look upon English history as a pantomime of eccentricity. Blackadder is forced to use all his guile and wit to navigate a path through the borderline-certifiable figures that have always run Britain (from mad kings to insane upper-class generals). A classic comedy of social class, national empathy with Blackadder (and his feckless servant Baldrick) reached a high point with the last-ever episode ('grave and realistic' – Curtis), set during the First World War, in which the main protagonists go over the top in a scene reminiscent of *Butch Cassidy and the Sundance Kid*.

Although *Blackadder* became a popular favourite, the first series was no great success: Curtis still has the letter from the BBC saying that the show would not be recommissioned. For the second series (and those that followed) he worked with **Ben Elton** (they collaborate by swapping computer disks and improving each other's drafts) who insisted that shooting must take place before a studio audience. A Bafta award was in the bag soon after.

Curtis went on to script Hollywood's *The Tall Guy* (edited by his friend Helen Fielding, author of *Bridget Jones' Diary*), the BBC sitcom *The Vicar of Dibley* in which a female priest (Curtis says he is 'passionate' about the ordination of women) wrestles with the backwardness of a country parish and *The Thin Blue Line* (co-written with Ben Elton, starring Atkinson) about the police. But his most famous script is the one for *Four Weddings and a Funeral*, the highly successful film about the lives and loves of a group of British young professionals (post-yuppie, too well off to be slackers). Prominent

among these is Charles, the lacksadaisical young British gent who is backward about coming forward. Played by Hugh Grant, Charles is widely understood to be a projection of Curtis' own character. The latter confesses that in his 20s 'I went to a lot of weddings and I was always late'; and that when 'left on my own I turn into a pathetic 23-year-old bachelor'. He is fulsome in praise of Grant, the 'one in a hundred' who could do the part with 'heightened realism' and without becoming 'parodic'. In his admission that he must be 'a very bad writer if only one in a hundred can get it right', Curtis is just as self-deprecating as we would expect Charles to be.

Four Weddings and a Funeral was not expected to succeed. According to Curtis, Polygram had forecast that it would 'make US$0'. Instead it became one of the biggest-grossing British films of all time. In the USA it was interpreted as a reflection of British life and culture; and in Britain it was welcomed as a representation of how we would like British life and culture to be. The term 'feelgood film' could have been invented for it. In fact *Four Weddings* is derived from the lifestyles of a privileged minority of youngish Brits: Curtis says that he writes for his (Oxbridge) friends and compares successful comedy to 'the good mood at the end of a dinner party'. Although Britain is not yet a nation of dinner-party goers, *Four Weddings*, as well as *Mr Bean* and *Blackadder*, enjoyed wide appeal. It seems that comedy about the class war (*Blackadder*) need not be the cause of it; and comedy set among the upper middle classes can prompt the sympathy as well as the mirth of

Britain's lower orders. *Notting Hill* (1999) in which Grant plays a divorced bookseller whose life is lacklustre until Julia Roberts walks into his shop, pushes some of the same buttons.

Curtis has never known poverty or prejudice ('from my perfect parents to my perfect children, I have had a life that's rolled easy'), but he is actively sympathetic towards those less fortunate than himself. He founded Comic Relief, the showbiz-led charity whose annual calendar culminates in Red Nose Day and a fundraising 'telethon'. Curtis says that his motivation 'might be to do with Manila' where, locked inside a compound with servants to cater for his every need, even as a child he became aware of 'the simultaneous presence of poverty and luxury'. Looking back at more than a decade of involvement with Comic Relief, he observed that 'it gives you some security that you have done something to help'.

Curtis has lived out his life according to pop records. The Beatles have always been his greatest 'passion' and he reckons he received his 'emotional education' from women singers such as Joan Armatrading and Chrissie Hynde. He uses pop music to help him write, and his life and work show how Britishness has been able to take in pop and other aspects of American culture and reinvent itself accordingly.

PARENTS *Brideshead Revisited*, Billy Bunter, **The Beatles**

Elizabeth David
Cooking comes out of the closet

Britain, the first industrial nation, lost the love of food along with its peasantry. From the seventeenth century onwards, the Protestant work ethic helped make Britain tasteless as well as prudish. But by the 1960s, British people were gaining a feeling for good food, thanks mainly to an increase in holidays abroad and the cookery books of Elizabeth David.

Born (1913) in the closing moments of pre-First Wold War Britain, Elizabeth was one of four daughters of a Conservative MP, Rupert Gwynne. After a failed career on the stage, at 26 she sailed away on a yacht with her pacifist lover, but they were shipwrecked on the coast of France just as the Second World War began. She escaped to a Greek island and from there to Egypt where she became a librarian for the Ministry of Information, mixing with a crowd of literary ex-pats which included Lawrence Durrell and Olivia Manning. She returned to Britain via India, entered into an unsuccessful marriage, and started to write cookery books as a reaction to the hardships of rationing (which extended well into the 50s) and the meagre diet of her Edwardian childhood. David's mission to rid the British kitchen of its dowdiness chimed in with the modernising mood of the moment.

The first tourist airfares were made available in 1952. By the end of the decade about two million Britons each year were enjoying what *Observer* columnist Katharine Whitehorn later described as 'the instant whiff of garlic' as soon as they touched down on the Continent. Cookery writer Prue Leith recalls that by holidaying in Europe 'ordinary people' discovered 'sun and sex and food' simultaneously.

Having enjoyed 'a good table' in France or Italy, how could returning British tourists prevent their new-found taste in food from fading as fast as their suntan? Their saviour was Elizabeth David, whose series of cookery books had the effect of importing the Continental spirit into British kitchens. 'She completely opened up the insularity of British cooking,' says Whitehorn.

In a series of books (*A Book of Mediterranean Food*, *Italian Cooking*, *French Country Cooking*, *Summer Cooking*), David offered recipes for key Continental dishes (plenty of roasted peppers, tomatoes and garlic). Her descriptions of European peasant food, written in measured English prose, became the last word in metropolitan elegance. Although David presented cooking as a country pursuit, her books became the bible for urban sophisticates.

David's style is clearly discernible in her observations upon an omelette: 'As for the omelette itself, it seems to me to be a confection that demands the most straightforward approach. It should not be a busy, important urban dish, but something gentle and pastoral, with the clean scent of the dairy, the kitchen garden or basket of early morning mushroom, or the sharp tang of freshly picked herbs – sorrel, chives, tarragon.' The irony is that her readers *were* 'busy, important, urban' people who came to her to renew the experience of rustic authenticity enjoyed during their holiday.

Whenever David returned to Britain from the South of France she brought with her earthenware crocs and other kitchen utensils. Soon she opened a shop – the only place in Britain where such items could be purchased, until **Terence Conran** developed the idea of 'an urban dream of farmhouse living' and made it the basis for his Habitat (1964).

David has been heralded as the 'Lenin of the cooking revolution'. Thanks to her, 'cooking came out of the closet'. A chore best left to servants was recast as a kind of sensual pleasure: foreplay for foodies. This form of sensual activity could even be enjoyed by men. In 1965, Len Deighton published *Où Est Le Garlic?*, a compilation of recipes culled from his weekly culinary column in the *Observer*. As in the case of Deighton's fictional hero, gourmet spy Harry Palmer (played by **Michael Caine** in the film of *The Ipcress File*), expertise in the kitchen was presented as the natural accompaniment to know-how in the bedroom.

In British upper-class families, eating was traditionally a formal ritual to be endured rather than enjoyed. Among the hoi polloi, food was 'grub' – nourishing and necessary but not often pleasurable. But since the 50s, Britain has been in love with foreign food and its ambience: the cool chic of espresso bars, the romance of the trattoria, the American steakhouse as a temple to full-blooded appetites. Beginning with Elizabeth David, Britain's openness to foreign food has advanced to the point where curry has now replaced fish and chips as the first national dish. David was made an OBE in 1976 and a CBE in 1986. She was also a fellow of the Royal Society of Literature and a Chevalier du Mérite Agricole. She died in May 1992.

CHILDREN Prue Leith, Delia Smith, Nigel Slater
READ ON *Elizabeth David* by Lisa Chaney

Dexy's Midnight Runners
Intense emotions

Led by Wolverhampton-born (1953) Kevin Rowland, ex-The Killjoys, and a peripheral part of the post-punk **Mod** revival, Dexy's Midnight Runners (their name a reference to the up-all-night effects of dexedrine) were an eight-piece outfit from Birmingham who dressed like building workers (woolly hats and donkey jackets, the image was influenced by Martin Scorsese's *Mean Streets*) and had a huge hit with their second single, 'Geno' (1979), a tribute to 60s soul singer and Mod idol Geno Washington (and his Ram Jam Band). With prominent keyboards and horns (the first British pop record to include a trombone solo), the Northern Soul-inflected emotions of 'Geno' brought a challenge to the dominance of guitar-based post-punk.

The ensuing album, *Searching for the Young Soul Rebels* (1980), proclaimed 'soul' as an authentic rebellion against the marketplace and the cheapening of human life. The band that played together also trained together: they seemed to regard music as a kind of martial art in which those dedicated to the cultivation of the true soul, in both its aggressive and sensitive aspects, would also learn to defend themselves against the soulless-

ness of the surrounding environment. This was rock as politics (Dexy's wrote manifestos like a political party) and religion (Michael Bracewell describes them as 'Dominicans in donkey jackets').

After a row with Rowland, five of the original eight were ex-communicated. While they went on to form the Bureau, Rowland swapped the brass-based soul sound of *Searching* for the folksy violins of *Too-Rye-Ay* (1982), which included the stomping hit single 'Come On Eileen' (the highlight of this track is a difficult-to-accomplish speed-up, held together by the solid drumming of Seb Shelton, ex-Secret Affair). The sound was different, veering to violins from saxes and trombones, and the image was also altered, digressing from donkey jackets to faux-Celtic dungarees. But the aim was the same: to propagate the expression of the authentic soul. Hence the name of the Dexy's fan club: Intense Emotions Ltd.

Another album, another makeover: *Don't Stand Me Down* featured a yuppified Dexy's in business suits, and lyrics that included dismissive comments about left-wing politics. Released in 1985, the year of the miners' strike and probably the most highly politicised moment in British post-war history, the 'accountants' incarnation of Dexy's was regarded by the left-leaning music press as nothing short of treachery.

For the cover of his solo album *The Wanderer* (1988), Rowland dressed up as a moustachioed dandy. The Latin look complemented the lounge-lizard sound achieved by Brazilian producer Deodato. But Rowland did not release another album for 11 years (he admitted to *Q* magazine that he had been a drug addict from 1987 to 1996). In 1999 he advertised his album *My Beauty*, a covers collection released by **Alan McGee**'s Creation label, by appearing in skirt, suspenders and make-up. 'It's not a gay thing, it's not a transvestite thing, it's me as a man expressing my soft, sexy side,' he insisted.

On the surface, Rowland's latest look seems diametrically opposed to the hard-man image of the original Dexy's; but in another sense all his various incarnations have been an exploration of what it means to be a British male now that the traditional masculine types are all but extinct.

PARENTS Friedrich Nietzsche, Stax, Van Morrison

Dr Martens
Workwear chic

Some 40 years on from their humble beginnings as a work boot, English-made Dr Martens shoes have become a symbol of British style. Along the way, 'DMs' fell into the hands of **skinheads**, left-wing militants and Thatcher's post-political children. Black, cherry and 'black greasy', today they are a fashion evergreen, as trend-proof as the little black dress.

The combination of toughness, durability and comfort at work was the original selling-point of Dr Martens three-eyelet shoes and eight or fourteen-eyelet boots: lashed to the leather uppers with 'Goodyear welt strong stitching', the air-cushioned sole, incorporating 'honeycombed air compartments' (AirWair), was designed to support the foot and provide 'superb grip'. With the advertising slogan 'made like no other shoe on earth', the first DMs were industrial-strength shoes made for industrial workers.

Skinheads started wearing Dr Martens boots because of the context – the blue-collar workplace – in which they had previously been worn. Originating in the late 60s, skins were a working-class youth cult who tried to re-establish a traditional, white, working-class way of life. Disillusioned **Mods**, they mixed fashion consciousness with anti-fashion, and the DM combination of neatness and toughness fitted their inclinations exactly. DMs had the extra merit of being far removed from the clogs and sandals that middle-class kids were wearing. They also came in handy for a good kicking.

Skinheads were right-wing, racist and retro. They sometimes came into confrontation with organised left-wingers, many of whom shared their affection for the old-fashioned British working class. By the mid-70s, the demand for DMs had spread from skinhead 'boot boys' to left-wing militants, and via the latter to a a wider circle of leftish, arty types. Wearing DMs became a sign that, just because you were an art student, it didn't mean you had lost touch with the inner-city street and what goes on there.

By the end of the 70s, skinheads were on the wane, council estate kids would not be seen dead in workwear, but DMs were becoming commonplace among young, middle-class males. Another decade, and they were equally popular with young, middle-class women: black DM shoes for office work (to go with the uniform black tights of the late 80s); and big boots for weekends (the combination of skirts and dresses above boys' boots was pioneered by 70s all-girl punk bands such as The Slits and developed by riot grrrls and grunge babes such as Courtney Love).

In the early 80s DMs were customised by Wayne Hemingway, founder of the fashion house Red Or Dead. Starting in 1982 with a stall in **Camden** Market, Hemingway launched a range of DM-based designs including the Space Baby boot: DM soles with see-through uppers decorated with grinning babies' faces. Such clothes, claimed Hemingway, were 'too witty for most working-class people to understand'.

In the 90s Dr Martens diversified into clothing and accessories. The firm now sponsors non-League English football. Just as football has been taken out of the hands of the working class, so DMs have shifted to middle-class feet.

PARENTS: Levi's, customised army surplus, boiler suits
READ ON: *Streetstyle – from sidewalk to catwalk* by Ted Polhemus

The dole
Soul on the dole

The 'dole' (benefit money for the 'indolent') was originally something to be avoided at all costs; now it is recommended as a character-building, creative experience. In the days when Walter Greenwood's *Love On The Dole* was published (1933), most people assumed they had a right to a job. In the early 80s, Birmingham's UB40 sang about being unemployed as if they expected not to be. But in the 90s there is no such thing as a job for life, and England expects almost everyone to be on the dole for some time in their life – if not the time of their lives.

For the protagonists of Geoff Dyer's *Colour of Memory* (1991), a nostalgic recollection of life in bohemian Brixton in the early 80s, the dole was a way of life. Through the 90s, as 80s-style ambition became associated with 'sleaze', so slackerdom became more respectable. When the New Labour government introduced welfare-to-work schemes for the young unemployed, various **Britpop**pers complained, claiming that the dole had been a formative, creative experience for them (I wouldn't have got where I am today, etc, etc). Following **Alan McGee**'s (temporary) walkout from the government's Creative Industries Task Force, the employment ministry devised a set of measures whereby musicians who can persuade 'personal advisers' of their talent and commitment will be exempt from pressure to take any job or join any scheme that's offered to them. It brings a new dimension to the rhyming slang 'rock'n'roll'. McGee, who was himself a recipient of the Tories' Enterprise Allowance Scheme designed to kick-start new entrepreneurs in the mid-80s, sees this as a step forward.

Meanwhile the British government has revamped benefit offices, some of which have been turned into 'New Deal campuses' with T-shirted staff, swipe cards, adverts produced by the fashionable **St Luke's** agency, and new jargon in which claimants are known as 'candidates'.

The dole has been a central element in a spate of British films including *Trainspotting*, *24Seven*, *The Boxer*, *Nil By Mouth*, *Brassed Off*, and **The Full Monty**, the big earner about Sheffield steelmen-turned-strippers of which US magazine *Time* said: 'sounds as though it would make a better movie than a life'. From the mid-90s there has even been an anti-work magazine, *The Idler* (founding editor: Tom Hodgkinson), dedicated not to the dignity of labour but to the joy of leisure. It was a revival in the spirit of Jerome K Jerome's humorous magazine of the same name published in the 1890s and dedicated to the kind of indolent Victorian City clerks he wrote about in *Three Men in a Boat* (1889) who in truth would rather stay in bed and dream. Perhaps we're all doing so many part-time temporary jobs we could do with a rest; or perhaps our jobs are so high powered we dream of downshifting to a less stressful way of life. Either way, at a time when benefits are decreasing and so, generally speaking, are unemployment figures, the dole has acquired a relatively rosy image. Though there are differences. For a single parent in Sheffield who can't get a job it can be a lifesaver, to your *Notting Hill* trustafarian it's more a 'lifestyle' decision.

READ ON *The Idler's Companion*; *The Empty Raincoat* by Charles Handy

Dressing down
Radical chic revisited

In the 80s there was power dressing: broad pin-stripes, shoulder pads and double-breasted suits. It all added up to a body shape that spoke of sub-stance and authority. Those were the days when showing your wad was acceptable if not mandatory (people laughed at **Harry Enfield**'s Loadsamoney because he was true to life). But in the 90s the eti-quette changed. Posing with *The Big Issue* seller outside London's Met Bar became cool, while standing next to **Kate Moss** was not. The hate-figure of 1998–99 was socialite, big spender and *Sunday Times* columnist Meg Mathews (wife of **Oasis'** Noel Gallagher). Over-dressed, over-shopped and ostracised, Mathews gave up her *Sunday Times* column in March 1999, for fear, allegedly, of caus-ing further damage to hubbie's street-cred.

Pop culture's VIP enclosure is full of prodigal sons who have ostentatiously withdrawn from the high life. The Pulp album of 1998, *This is Hardcore*, dwelt on the 'shallowness' of celebrity and the 'guilt' of money. **Jarvis Cocker** has a line about doing the dishes instead of coke. The **Manic Street Preachers** also enjoyed a spell on London's party circuit, before returning to the valleys where life is more 'down to earth' and 'interesting'. Like

Jarvis, Nicky Wire now finds fulfilment in domestic chores, except that his preference is for hoovering. Perhaps he sings the Manics' ditty about domesticity, 'My Little Universe', while he does it.

Even erstwhile superbitch **Julie Burchill** admitted that she lost her soul during her days as queen of the Groucho. In 1998 she wrote: 'I've gone out of my way not to have famous friends, and to cultivate those people I have met who have jobs for which getting drunk isn't compulsory. There is something euphorically tranquillising about putting one weary foot back into the lukewarm footbath of everyday life'. In her *Guardian* column (there's 'everyday life' for you – we're all columnists now, aren't we?), Burchill names the rich and shames the famous ('I've never had a drearier time than I've had with famous people, so identified with the DJ Sasha who said recently that a night at Supernova Heights just felt seedy'). She exemplifies a new social type in British culture: the recovering celebrity. Other examples include Michael Barrymore, **Robbie Williams** and Paul Merson.

High fashion is also dressing down. Under the influence of British bands like Oasis, Gucci has been awash with combat trousers and cagoules. Not long ago, men were refused entry to posh places if they were not wearing a tie; nowadays punters are turned away from the trendiest bars and clubs (the Riki-Tik, for example) because they are wearing suits, not a pastiche of shopfloor overalls like Cahartt 'work pants'. Meanwhile cabinet members address each other by their first names; chancellor Gordon Brown went to a City dinner in a lounge suit; the most popular politician, Mo Mowlam, is the least glamorous; and the prime minister likes to be photographed in his shirt sleeves, preferably with a Fender Stratocaster in hand or a football at his feet.

Hailed as the new freedom from formality, is this perhaps a new etiquette of informality, as tyrannical and constraining as the last? If you want to fit in with today's Britain, don't go out in a dinner jacket unless you're wearing it with leather trousers and Doc Martens boots. As Noel Gallagher observed, 'In London, everybody wears street gear at all times, even at the poshest dos.'

PARENTS 70s radical chic, when middle-class whites dressed like street-corner blacks (who would have preferred to dress like middle-class whites)

Drum'n'bass
New horizons

Drum'n'bass is a musical hybrid containing elements from **rave**, reggae, hip-hop, techno, electro-pop and jazz. Its audience is equally mixed. According to *Arena* editor Ekow Eshun it is a 'music of volatility and dynamic tension' and the soundtrack to a culture where 'racial diversity is celebrated'.

The sampler is the key instrument in the creation of drum'n'bass tracks. Starting with a central beat, running at approximately 160bpm, the track is created by layering sampled sounds on top, sounds 'that could be anything,' says Bristol-based drum'n'bassman **Roni Size**.

These elements may then be mixed with live instruments and vocals. It is a mode of making music that is entirely different from songwriting, in which tune, chords and lyrics come as a basic package with instrumentation as value-added. Historically, the possibility of making music the drum'n'bass way comes about through a long-running process of breaking down the song (jazz and dub reggae onwards) and building up the riff (jazz and rock onwards). But with drum'n'bass the process reaches its logical conclusion: the music is no longer song plus mix – the music *is* the mix. The relationship is facilitated (but not determined) by new music technology such as the sampler and the sequencer.

Commenting on the *New Forms* album by Roni Size and the Reprazent collective (Mercury Prize winner, 1997), critic Simon Frith declared, 'this is what music is now about'. Ben Watt, the male half of **indie** duo Everything But The Girl, has said: 'you've got to stop saying it doesn't sound like **The Beatles**. The sampler is the new electric guitar, the sequencer is driving the sampling technology.' Size himself says 'it is about trying to look into the future'.

Digital music technology is not unique to drum'n'bass, however. The position it occupies in the dance music tradition is equally important in defining the genre. Drum'n'bass is one of the latest in a succession of attempts to keep the cutting edge of dance music, to retain its entertainment

value while avoiding cliché and self-parody. Hardcore (speeding up the breakbeats), darkcore (reflecting the pessimistic mood of the early 90s) and jungle (taking a negative term for black music and turning it around) are all previous episodes in the same narrative. Thus some of the original advocates of hardcore (Fabio and Grooverider, for example) are also regarded as the grandfathers of drum'n'bass, along with Manchester's seminal acid house producer A Guy Called Gerald. **Goldie** is another name that spanned a spate of dance-based sub-genres throughout the 90s.

Goldie

In the 'Future' issue of *i-D* magazine (1997), Goldie was described as 'a musician who is also an editor /creator/mutator/engineer'; and as someone whose output shows that in contemporary music-making, 'creative control over the studio is more important than the sounds you choose to manipulate'.

Born in 1965 of a Scottish mother and a Jamaican father who left the family home not long afterwards, Clifford 'Goldie' Price spent some years in care before knocking on the door of his mother's flat in Wolverhampton and moving back in. As a youth Goldie was involved in burglary, then break-dancing (his peers have said he was not a brilliant dancer but he had a great personality). In the early 80s he started doing grafitti on walls around Birmingham and Wolverhampton (he sprayed the Statue of Liberty on his mum's bedroom wall; Birmingham City Council once commissioned him to do a mural), and by 1984 he was featured on *Central News* as 'the king of the spray can'. Shortly afterwards he appeared in the documentary film *Bombin'* (1985).

In the mid-80s Goldie moved to Miami to be with his father. He designed T-shirts and set up a business fitting gold teeth (this was the period when he started wearing a lot of gold, including his trademark teeth; with the rings on his fingers and the chains on his neck, he reckons he wears £70,000 of 'status projection'). Returning to Britain at the request of his mother, Goldie shared a London flat and learnt a lot about art and design.

At Rage in 1991 he was blown away by Grooverider and Fabio, and soon started producing his own tracks. His first important release was *Terminator* (1993, described by *State of Bass* author Martin James as 'the most perfect slice of genuflected chaos'), followed by the album *Timeless* (1995) and the single of the same name. The success of these records ('Timeless' entered the Top 10) helped bring drum'n'bass from the margins to the mainstream; so did Metalheadz, Goldie's club night at the Blue Note in Hoxton.

Goldie's gigs are noted for their multicultural crowd. 'Anyway, who is British in Britain?', he asks. Goldie describes drum'n'bass as 'urban UK music' that 'cannot be pigeonholed' because it reflects the 'integrated city which is balanced, not black nor white'. In a similar vein, Ekow Eshun has hailed drum'n'bass as the work of a generation 'that sets few limits around its sense of self. You can be more than one thing at the same time … difference can be an enriching way to look at the world.' The

fusions and crossovers heard in drum'n'bass stand in stark contrast to the more rigid racial separation of musical genres in the USA, prompting Eshun and others to ask whether the age of the Black Atlantic, when blacks in Britain looked to the USA for a lead, is now passed.

For all its futurism, however, drum'n'bass contains some elements that are at least as old as the jazz-rock fusion of the 70s. Afficionados reckon that the intensity of the beats coupled with half-speed bass figures and the 'heart-stopping surge of the sub-bass', can induce a state of timelessness, just as more than a quarter of a century ago 'heads' used to say that the Mahavishnu Light Orchestra could take you 'out there'. Likewise, the breakneck drum patterns heard in drum'n'bass do not sound so very different from the furiously fast drumming of someone like Bill Bruford in Yes. Drum'n'bass may even turn out to be the new **prog rock**.

PARENTS jazz, reggae, hip-hop, Kraftwerk
READ ON *State of Bass* by Martin James

Ian Dury
Art, slang and Dickens

Aged 7, Ian Dury contracted polio (probably from the water in a swimming pool), which left him crippled for life. He was sent away from home (Upminster, East End overspill in Essex), and went from there to art school, first at Walthamstow where he sat next to future film director **Peter Greenaway**, and afterwards to the Royal College of Art. This was the period (late 50s/early 60s) in which colleges first admitted that 'art could be something that you liked rather than what you were supposed to', and Dury was excited by the cosmopolitan atmosphere he found there.

As an artist Dury says he was 'good enough to know that my limitations would never satisfy me'. He started writing song lyrics by chance: playing in a band was preferable to teaching as a means to subsidise his painting; and the band needed original songs and lyrics. From the start Dury used rhyming slang (frequently associated with Cockneys and scousers but said to have been invented by Irish navvies as a code that their bosses would not understand) as a way of saying things that might have been crude otherwise. Years later he said of rhyming slang 'it's a little bit like swearing, you've got to be careful how much you use'.

In the early to mid-70s Dury was frontman for Kilburn and the High Roads, who looked good (cool but eccentric) and deployed dark humour rather than the venom and spite punk introduced a couple of years later. The Kilburns are often held up as the precursors of punk but Dury is not particularly flattered by the association. He says he enjoyed the great visual flair of punk, and he speaks highly of the Sex Pistols and The Clash, but 'the rest of them? Stick it.'

In the latter half of the 70s Dury fronted his own outfit, the Blockheads, and developed a compelling stage persona: Richard III with a touch of Fagin, a slice of Max Miller (flashy and vulgar), a pinch of Max Wall (the veteran comedian returned the com-

plement by recording a version of Dury's 'England's Glory' – the brand-name of an old-style box of matches), and a whiff of Samuel Beckett (world-weary yet sympathetic). Dury was Dickensian and Dostoyevskian, with additional helpings of Elvis Presley, experimental jazz trumpeter Don Cherry and 'sweet' Gene Vincent – the original rock'n'roll leather boy with a limp. With the funky bass of Norman Watt-Roy and the melodious keyboards of Chaz Jankel prominent in the mix, a Blockheads gig was like the world of Hogarth with the warmth and humanity put back in. It was also a peculiarly British experience – an impression Dury reinforced when he had a union jack painted on his teeth.

After an exceptionally strong debut album (*New Boots and Panties*, 1977) and a series of hit singles ('Sex and Drugs and Rock'n'Roll', 'Hit Me With Your Rhythm Stick', 'What A Waste', 'Reasons To Be Cheerful' – recorded for Stiff with sleeve designs by **Neville Brody**), by 1979 Dury was feeling the pressures of fame ('I hated the restriction on my freedom') and he decided to disappear for a while. Instead of rehearsing, touring and recording he spent many hours swimming and getting fit, emerging briefly to record 'Spasticus Autisticus' as a 'war cry' for the Year of the Disabled in 1981.

In the 90s Dury was diagnosed as suffering from cancer of the colon, then cancer of the liver. Interviewed by Trevor Phillips for the *London Programme*, he described the experience as 'like being hit by a bus slowly'. In 1999 he recorded with long-time admirers madness.

PARENTS Max Miller, Max Wall, Don Cherry

169

The E-type Jaguar

Cool cat

Designed by aerodynamicist Malcolm Sayer, the E-type was unveiled at the Geneva motor show of 1961. A high-performance car at the relatively low cost of £2,197, it was an overnight sensation. Singer Adam Faith couldn't wait to get his hands on one. Footballer **George Best** said that nothing compared to it. Racing driver Jackie Stewart later praised the car for 'elegance and beauty as well as function' and recalled that 'I got the thrill of speed through the E-type better than anything else.' The E-type met with the approval of aristocrats too. Appearing in the BBC2 series *The Car's The Star*, photographer Lord Litchfield described it as 'an extraordinary flowing wave of a car'. Enzo Ferrari nominated it as the one car he wished he had made, but hadn't.

The small, Coventry-based firm of Jaguar could not make enough E-types to satisfy demand, which kept on rising despite poor brakes, cramped cockpit and 'imperfect gearbox'. In 1965 Jaguar launched an improved version, the E-type 4.2. But improvements were not always for the best, as car commentator Quentin Wilson explained. In further modifications designed to match the new requirements of American safety and pollution laws (the E-type earned £150 million in foreign currency), the line of the original design was lost and the car became a caricature of itself – the sort of vehicle that porn queen Fiona Richmond would drive with the personalised number plate FU2.

The last E-types were made in 1975. By the late 80s the E-type was back in high fashion, and people were paying £70,000 for an original model. Ten years later the asking price has come down to around £25,000, but the E-type has consolidated its reputation as the king of the classics. Jaguar is now a subsidiary of the Ford Motor Corporation of Detroit, USA.

PARENTS Malcolm Sayer
CHILDREN the Ford Capri

Ealing Studios
Not so cosy

Ever since film critic (and future novelist) Gavin Lambert compared them unfavourably to the poetic work of documentary film-maker Humphrey Jennings, the movies made at Ealing Studios have been written off as cosy comedies for a Little England audience. But this is to underestimate the sardonic and sometimes bleak humour that underlies the Ealing output. The films made there often entail a recapitulation of the sense of community that arose from the common experience of the Second World War. But this experience, and the rose-tinted perception of it, are subject to a quiet dissection that can be just as disturbing as the noisy rejection of Britishness. With hindsight, *Went the Day Well?* (1942, Alberto Cavalcanti's story of a clandestine German invasion force falling on fertile soil in the English countryside) is not just an effective piece of wartime propaganda; it is also a more subtle critique of our national character than ranting John Osborne's *Look Back In Anger*.

In *Kind Hearts and Coronets* (1949), which has been described as 'a brilliantly cynical film', Louis Mazzini (Dennis Price) kills eight snobbish relatives (all played by Alec Guinness) who have spurned him because of his lowly birth (aristocratic mother married an Italian organ grinder) and who stand between him and the Dukedom of Chalfont. Ealing boss Michael Balcon subsequently fell out with director and co-writer Robert Hamer over the 'darkness' of the latter's artistic vision.

The Man In The White Suit (1951) is the story of a young scientist (Alec Guinness) who invents a cloth that will not get dirty – an invention that picks up flak from both mill owners and workers. Directed by Alexander Mackendrick, who went to the USA to make The Sweet Smell of Success with Burt Lancaster and Tony Curtis (another brilliantly cynical film), The Man In The White Suit is a soft comedy that deals with hard issues: the impact of technology, the greed of big business, and narrow-minded resistance to innovation.

In Ealing comedies cosiness is usually undercut by criticism, as in the case of Passport To Pimlico (1949). True, sex and violence are noticeable by their absence from Ealing (what violence does occur is highly stylised). Their protagonists tend to be middle class and middle aged; and so, perhaps, was their target audience. But this does not mean that Ealing comedies are insipid; rather they are compatible with the brief moment of confidence when, having won the Second World War, the British middle classes thought they could overcome their own faults and win the peace.

Far from holding on to traditional social structures, Ealing aimed for modernity, and a low-key version of classlessness. The villains and fools of Ealing films tend to be either snobbish toffs or at the very bottom of the working class, the inference being that everyone else – the sensible sections of the upper class and working class, brought together by the all important middle classes – can work together and maintain a consensus in the national interest.

The grit in the eye of Ealing is traceable back to Michael Balcon, the studio boss. Schooled by John Grierson, the founding father of British documentary cinema, in 1951 Balcon declared that 'the feature carries on in the documentary tradition'. Through teamwork (weekly script meetings and a sense of 'social responsibility'), he sought to develop a liberal, humanist form of cinema – an ambition he strove for again in the 60s through his involvement in Bryanston, a production company that became the funding agency for Woodfall Films (*Look Back In Anger*, *Room At The Top* and most other '**kitchen sink**' dramas).

Critics have traditionally played on the differences between Ealing and Woodfall, with particular emphasis on the middle-class leanings of the former and the working-class focus of the latter. In fact they have common roots in the documentary wing of British cinema. Gavin Lambert may have felt frustrated by the coded character of British self-criticism, and the extent to which Ealing films

hedged around their targets. But the veil of Ealing puts a fine weave on British experience; it is not just a cosy way of hushing it all up.

PARENTS John Grierson, the Second World War
CHILDREN Woodfall Films, Dad's Army

Eco-warriors
A mission to decontaminate

In its original form, the counter-culture was more interested in good times than the environment. But towards the end of the 60s, it took on an ecological aspect. In the USA, Charles Reich referred to 'the Greening of America', British hippies turned rustic, and on both sides of the Atlantic more people started reading Rachel Carson's *The Silent Spring* (1961). By the end of the century Green concerns were commonplace, and eco-warriors enjoyed widespread, if passive, support from large sections of the British population. At a time when everyone agrees we should consume less, the militant expression of this sentiment tends to get a fairly good press.

The antecedents of eco-warriors did not always enjoy such a favourable reception. In the early 80s, when a group of women (Green-tinged, feminist CND-ers) camped out at Greenham Common in protest against the deployment there of Cruise (nuclear) missiles, they were frequently reviled. A few years later (1985) a caravan of post-hippie travellers (crusties) were attacked by the police at the so-called Battle of the Beanfield. The treatment they received from the media was only marginally more sympathetic. In 1992 the tone changed somewhat after the arrest of demonstrators trying to halt the construction of the M3 and the destruction of Twyford Down, a place of natural beauty ('just to shave a few minutes off the route from Southampton to London'). In 1993–94, anti-roads protesters congregated on the north-east side of London in an attempt to stop the demolition of houses and trees as part of the construction of the M11 link road. The anti-roads protesters established a colony and received a surprising level of support from local residents – East Enders were not hitherto enamoured of young people with matted hair, wearing combat gear and leading dogs on string. But with the battle for 'Wanstonia', eco-protesters stopped being mere riff-raff and became something akin to heroes in the eyes of the general public.

The following year (1995) was marked by a series of protests against the export of live animals for slaughter. The protests centred on the east-coast port of Brightlingsea and at Coventry Airport in the West Midlands, where a protester died during a demonstration. The memorial service for Jill Phipps in Coventry Cathedral was widely and sympathetically reported. In some respects it was a small-scale prototype for the national mourning that followed the death of Princess Diana.

By the mid-90s the militant environmentalists who began as folk devils had acquired the status of latter-day saints. In the long drawn-out McLibel case (the libel action brought by McDonald's against eco-activists who made contentious claims about its production methods) the public and the media looked favourably upon the two defendants. Swampy, who tunnelled underground in an effort to prevent the extension of Manchester Airport, was rewarded with a guest appearance on the topical quiz show *Have I Got News For You?* He smiled sweetly, said next to nothing and a legion of Middle Englanders wanted to mother him. Publicist Max Clifford expressed an interest in General Survival, an 11-year-old from Kingston who moved into a squatters' camp. A misguided but ultimately sympathetic eco-warrior (Kate Aldridge) appeared in Radio 4's long-running village soap *The Archers*; and, finally, in the form of a character called Spider, eco-warriors arrived in Salford's *Coronation Street*, the longest-running TV soap.

What accounts for the change of public attitudes towards eco-warriors? Their own media-friendliness is a factor. Pilloried by the mainstream media 20 years ago, Green activists established their own communications networks (DIY video footage distributed informally; information increasingly spread by means of the Internet). As the media became less actively hostile, eco-warriors swiftly learnt how to raise their own profile: don't just send out a press release, carry out stunts that will look good on camera; if TV companies can't afford to send cameras down to a site, send them an email or a fax offering broadcast-quality footage.

Apart from New Labour politicians, today's eco-warriors are probably more media savvy than anybody else in Britain. But even this is not a sufficient explanation for the wholesale change in their media fortunes. Another, and perhaps more important factor is the shift in wider opinion, possibly but not necessarily influenced by previous eco-campaigns, which means that what were once exclusively Green issues are now the common concern of the whole population.

When the Conservative Party was driven out of government in May 1997 and the New Labour administration announced drastic reductions in the new road building programme, it looked like the end of the line for anti-roads protesters. But by this time, with the advent of BSE and a host of food scares, car culture was not the only villain for eco-types to wage war against. Food manufacturing in general, and the development and manufacture of genetically modified (GM) food in particular, became the target of a new generation of eco-warriors. In March 1997 Jacklyn Sheedy, formerly of the anti-car campaign Reclaim The Streets, formed the Genetic Engineering Network. During the summer of 1998, newspapers started carrying pictures of white-suited protesters pulling up fields of genetically engineered crops. By the summer of 1999, 'crop crusaders' had already appeared in *The Archers*, and they made national headlines in July 1999 when Greenpeace chairman Lord Melchett was one of 30 people arrested for uprooting plants in a government-sponsored test site for GM foods. 'Crop crusaders' have also been in action against companies such as Monsanto, DuPont, Zeneca and Novartis.

Hunt saboteurs are a sub-set of eco-warriors who also looked like they might be short of a role when

New Labour promised to outlaw fox hunting. But the government has failed to take the bull by the horns, thereby granting 'hunt sabs' a new lease of life. Typically middle-class, hunt saboteurs frequently engage in scuffles and skirmishes with the aristocrats and *nouveaux riches* of the hunt. Just in case hunting is outlawed, some of them are now directing their efforts against angling.

In the early 90s when the crusties known as the Donga Tribe called themselves 'indigenous Englanders', they seemed a long way off from most people's idea of Englishness. But in Britain there has been always an anti-urban tradition of Arcadian art and anti-industrial culture. When Prince Charles declared against genetic modification on the grounds that it 'takes mankind into realms that belong to God and God alone', he showed that it is entirely feasible to be both a True Brit and an eco-warrior. The arrest of Lord Melchett provided further confirmation.

PARENTS vegetarians, Greenham women, Tom and Barbara in *The Good Life*

Ecstasy
'Penicillin for the soul'

3, 4 Methylene-dioxy-N-methyl-amphetamine aka MDMA aka Adam aka Empathy aka Ecstasy aka E was invented in Darmstadt by the German firm Merck in 1912 and tested in the 50s by the US military to see whether it would disorientate enemy troops. Its 'stepfather' is the American biochemist and psychoactive researcher Dr Alexander Shulgin who synthesised it in the mid-60s and returned to it in 1977. The drug is thought to have been brought to Britain by the orange-clothed followers of Indian guru Bhagwan Rajneesh when they moved out of their ashram in Oregon, USA. It reached these shores in the mid-80s at around the same time that it took off among young holiday-makers in **Ibiza**.

E went into circulation at unlicensed warehouse parties in London during 1987 (LSD was the previous drug of choice); it mixed well with house, the new brand of high-speed dance music imported from the gay and black clubs of Chicago and New York. The resulting combination – drugs, music and illegality – was a familiar one. But its contrast to the prevailing 80s ethos gave it an extra kick.

Noting its facility for inducing friendliness and a sense of togetherness, a psychotherapist described E as 'penicillin for the soul'. Simon Reynolds, author of *Energy Flash*, reports that in the late 80s E seemed to be 'the magic pill, a miraculous agent of individual and social transformation whose "loved up adherents" believed that house music and MDMA were set to change the world'. Previously known as Empathy, E was seen as a remedy for the aggression and pressures of the Thatcher years when greed was good, and also as an antidote to the coldness and reserve traditionally associated with the British way of life: 'Ecstasy's empathy and intimacy-inducing effects didn't just offer a timely corrective to Thatcher-sponsored

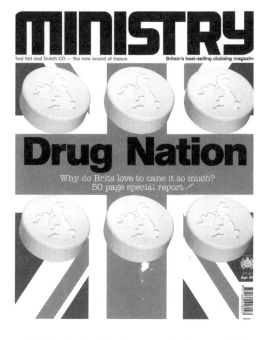

social atomisation; the drug was also the remedy for the English diseases of class-consciousness and emotional reserve.'

At the height of yuppiedom, says Reynolds, E 'catalysed an explosion of suppressed social energies'. It also brought out the sensual qualities of particular types of music, turning them into aural spaces which the user/listener could enter into and be enveloped by:'The drug seemed to fit the music like a glove. On E its repetitive rhythms induced a blissed trance rather than irritation. And because MDMA intensifies sensations to the brink of pre-hallucinogenic synaesthesia, house and techno's ultra-vivid textures become even more sensuously tactile; the music seemed to caress and surround you in an immersive environment.'

Embodied in the widespread adoption of the smiley logo (designed in 1969 by Frenchman Franklin Loufrani in an attempt to cheer up a nation riven by student rioting), by the early 90s the empathy effect of E+house was the defining experience of burgeoning British dance culture. The experience was no longer confined to the mainly middle-class coterie which had experimented with drugs in the 60s. Former **Face** editor Sheryl Garratt recalls 'how quickly it spread to small country villages. This really was every kid on the street'. She believes that club culture and the technologies that facilitated it (by which she means E as well as sound systems and digital images) were key factors in 'democratising pleasure' during the late 80s and 90s. Reynolds agrees that for millions of British people E is now 'normal, as banal and benign as a pint of lager … predictable, obvious, even slightly naff; in a word, "safe"'.

Not everyone agreed E was safe. When 18-year-old Leah Betts died in November 1994 after taking Ecstasy and drinking an excessive amount of water in an attempt to offset the effects of the drug, her parents became protagonists in a drugs panic. They made countless media appearances, where as 'secondary victims' they were invested with tremendous moral authority. But the E-controversy was never as sharp as the drugs debates of the 60s. Back then, opposing factions invoked absolutes and principles such as 'law and order' and 'experimentation'. In the 90s, pragmatism was paramount. Safety was the watchword on both sides, and the debate was about how to achieve this magical state. Drugs are dangerous, declared the moral guardians. But this one makes you feel safe, the E-heads said.

The late Nicholas Saunders (he died in a car accident in South Africa in 1996), a drop-out from Imperial College in the early 60s, author of the influential 70s book *Alternative London* and the owner of Neal's Yard in Covent Garden, published books and maintained a website that countered the moral panic. Saunders highlighted the anti-aggressive effects of E, particularly among men. In E culture, he pointed out, women felt less at risk from predatory males. The same could be said of bromide, but personal safety was at such a high premium in the 90s that merely to have pointed this out would have seemed dangerously macho.

Safety is an elusive quality, however: the more you chase it, the more it recedes from view. Thus in 1999 when Zane Monroe aka David Smith began offering risk-free 'E-hypnosis' – hypnotising punters into believing they had taken a pill, there was immediate concern about 'another problem like the date rape pill'. Generally speaking, the E-induced communal high of ten years ago seems to have turned into a collective, nervous hangover. In her book *Adventures in Wonderland* (1998), Garratt wrote of 'the sense of an era coming to a close' and reported that 'the Es are so bad that without any help from the law the cycle is burning itself out'. While the late Gavin Hills observed that E had become just another entertainment device like the video recorder ('the club structure is like the pub structure'), Reynolds concludes that it is now an instrument of confusion rather than clarity: 'E, the magic pill, has lost both its aura of enchantment and its status as the most favoured drug of the "chemical generation"; it is now just one more brain-blitzing weapon in the neurochemical arsenal. Because of this "polydrug" culture of mix-and-matching, the atmosphere in clubs has changed: instead of the clean, clear high of MDMA and the electric connection between total strangers, the vibe is bleary and untogether. Instead of getting "loved up", people talk of getting "merry".'

Reviewing *Human Traffic* (1999, billed as 'the decent movie about clubbing', others warned it would be the 90s equivalent of a 'Joe Brown film') *Ministry* magazine noted: 'the painful silence of the comedown is nicely illustrated here. The party's over, the fun has ended. The pain is in the post.' In similar vein, the most influential short film of the latter-day E scene is entitled *Coming Down* (1998).

PARENTS LSD, amphetamines, holy communion
READ ON *Once in a Lifetime* by Jane Bussman; *Altered State* by Matthew Collin; *Adventures in Wonderland* by Sheryl Garratt; *Heaven's Promise* by Paolo Hewitt; *Energy Flash* by Simon Reynolds; *Ecstasy and the Dance Culture* by Nicholas Saunders

The Edinburgh Festival
Antidote to austerity

Conceived as a summertime 'cosmopolitan extravaganza' that would offset some of the deprivations of wartime and the subsequent age of austerity, the first Edinburgh Festival took place in 1947. In the next half century the Festival developed into a three-limbed beast: the official Festival; the professional Fringe; and the amateur Fringe. In the closing decades of the twentieth century, events at the Festival started to subdivide into two further categories: those that remained within the original ethos of internationalism and those that gave particular expression to Scottish identity.

In its earliest days the Festival focused on music and theatre. Its first director was Austrian-born Sir Rudolf Bing, the former manager of Glyndebourne who left Edinburgh in 1949 to run the Metropolitan Opera House in New York. In 1947 Alec Guinness appeared as Shakespeare's *Richard II*, and the Film Festival was opened by the founding father of British documentary cinema, John Grierson. In 1948, Edinburgh hosted the premiere of TS Eliot's *The Cocktail Party* (soon to be lambasted as the embodiment of old-fashioned, formal drama as opposed to the youthful vitality of the **Angry Young Men**). That year the local paper reported that 'round the fringe of official drama there seems to be more enterprise than before'. Soon the 'enterprise' round the fringe of the Festival became known simply as the Fringe, which for many years has been a byword for experimentation of a vigorous but generally playful kind.

In 1952 the first late-night revue, *After The Show*, was staged by the New Drama Group. In 1960 perhaps the most famous revue ever, *Beyond The Fringe* (featuring David Frost, **Peter Cook**, Jonathan Miller, **Alan Bennett**) was mounted by the official Festival, partly as a response to the radicalism and risqué reputation which the Fringe had already acquired. In the early 60s there was more radicalism in the shape of the Edinburgh International Writers' Conference, organised by publisher John Calder and featuring contributions from Alexander Trocchi, William Burroughs and many more. In the official Festival, however, the main strand of programming remained fairly safe, with centrepiece events such as Sir Thomas Beecham conducting mass bands on Castle Esplanade (1950), Richard Burton as *Hamlet* (1953), the visit by diva Maria Callas (1957), and the British premiere of American playwright Eugene O'Neill's *Long Day's Journey Into Night*.

In 1966 Tom Stoppard's *Rosencrantz and Guildenstern Are Dead* followed a successful run at the Fringe with a sell-out season in the West End, thereby launching Stoppard's career and introducing British theatre audiences to a new kind of playfully absurd comedy. The eventful year of 1968 (riots and revolution on the Continent) brought contributions from Jerzy Grotowski's radical theatre in Poland, and the premiere of Harrison Birtwistle's first opera *Punch and Judy*. After the invasion of Alexander Dubcek's Czechoslovakia by Soviet tanks, protesters picketed the Edinburgh concerts of the USSR State Orchestra.

The year 1979, the first under the directorship of John Drummond, was the fiftieth anniversary of Diaghilev's death, and for the first time the centre stage of the Festival's programming was given over to ballet. Drummond's successor Frank Dunlop was associated with a populist approach and a slight preference for drama over music; but this was offset by Dunlop's successor Brian McMaster whose background was the opera.

In the 80s when **alternative comedy** was king, it became mandatory for comedians to play the Edinburgh Festival if they wanted to make an impact in London during the following season, or on TV the next year. When the influx of agents, producers and commissioning editors reached its peak in the 90s, comics started trying out their Edinburgh shows in London before they went up. By the end of the century, the smart ones were inviting all the important people to their London previews, thus avoiding the need for anyone to go to Edinburgh to see them.

Edinburgh is a city of contrasts: the old city is elegant, often picturesque, with a grandeur that matches that of any European capital, hence its traditional tag, 'the Athens of the North'. But the outlying districts contain areas of the deepest poverty, of a kind that corresponds to the worst that Glasgow can offer. In Edinburgh the cultural elite jostles for space with real-life equivalents of **Irvine Welsh** characters; and radical counter-culturalists rub shoulders with the straight-backed ladies of Morningside – the embodiment of strict Scottish puritanism.

The Festival is equally contradictory in its

simultaneous leanings towards Scottishness and cosmopolitanism. 'The cosmopolitan impulse the Festival embodies,' writes novelist AL Kennedy, 'sits beside an energetic, purely Scottish aesthetic which is especially forceful (and necessary) as it relates to language.' Kennedy supports the development of a 'purely' Scottish literature insofar as it represents a challenge to 'the imposition of a narrow linguistic orthodoxy', but writing in the summer of 1998, she also rejected the charge that the Edinburgh Festival might have become parochial: 'In celebrating the rest of the world at Edinburgh, Scotland will also be celebrating itself.'

PARENTS Henry Wood's season of promenade concerts, continental fiestas, the Festival of Britain

Ben Elton
The entertainer

Born in Catford (south-east London), moving to Guildford, Surrey, aged ten, when his father (a German–Jewish refugee from Frankfurt) was made a physics professor, Ben Elton's interest in theatre was encouraged by his mother. As a child he loved PG Wodehouse and wanted to be like Noël Coward. 'Half-getting' *The Outsider* by Albert Camus, he went to Manchester University where he read drama. Although as a student he worked on the obligatory plays by Bertolt Brecht, he now claims that his first love was always light entertainment.

Morecambe and Wise, he says, are like Vladimir and Estragon (in Samuel Beckett's fatalistic comedy *Waiting for Godot*), 'but funnier'. Elton insists that 'it's more difficult to be entertaining. It's simple to stuff a load of ideas in and be complex and Channel 4.'

In the 80s Elton was the man most associated with the idea that comedy could/should be political. On *Saturday Night Live*, the alternative TV variety show, he made searing attacks on 'Mrs Thatch'. As a stand-up comedian and compere, a sample sign-off line would be: 'My name's Ben Elton. Support the miners. Good night.' In retrospect Elton says he was never a revolutionary but always 'a welfare-state democrat'. He recalls that 'Mrs Thatch' was only a tiny aspect of his stand-up act, most of which referred to a small part of his anatomy ('my knob'). He insists that 'I've always only wanted to entertain.' Nowadays, as a stand-in for Terry Wogan, as a TV host with a spot in his show for veteran comedian Ronnie Corbett, and as compere of the Brit Awards and other ceremonies, he is close to filling the old-fashioned role of 'all-round family entertainer'. His refusal to do adverts or corporate functions is the last remnant of a radical past.

Dubbed 'the George Bernard Shaw of our times' by BBC2's *The Late Review*, Elton has admitted that he is limited as a performer but feels more committed to his writing. In 1980 he was the youngest scriptwriter ever appointed by the BBC. He contributed to *The Young Ones*, and wrote the second, third and fourth series of Rowan Atkinson's Blackadder with **Richard Curtis**. Also with Curtis (and again with Rowan Atkinson starring) he co-

Ben Elton

wrote the comedy police series *The Thin Blue Line* (Elton says his favourite among his own jokes was written for Inspector Grim: 'My arse is on the line and I don't want a cock-up'). In addition, Elton has published a series of satirical novels, two of which polemicise against pollution and car culture (*Stark* and *Gridlock*), and two more which are critical of Hollywood and the media (*This Other Eden* and *Popcorn*). Featuring a Quentin Tarantino/Oliver Stone-type film director (Elton made his own debut as a director in 1999) who becomes the victim of the violent culture he himself has helped to engender, *Popcorn* (a successful play as well as a novel) is partly a plea for artists to take more responsibility for their work ('you have to overcome your behaviour, y'know. That's what civilisation is'). Elton's

1998 novel *Blast From The Past* was sold to Transworld (publishers) for £1.1 million. It follows the relationship between an ex-army officer and a female former prisoner; and some critics have noticed its similarity to **David Hare**'s play *Skylight*.

Unlike most artists who cite some kind of traumatic experience as a turning point in their lives, Elton says he has had no crises and does not think he is angst-driven (in his 20s he suffered from psoriasis, the condition that crippled **Dennis Potter**; but fortunately it went into remission). Happily married to Sophie, a musician from Australia, they share one car (a Volkswagen Golf; Elton explains that 'the private car … has increased the quality of life, but it has damaged it too'), and he goes running to stay fit.

181

Elton sounds relaxed ('I only do one working period of four hours a day. My social life is as important, if not more so, than my work') and at peace with himself. But some would make war on him, including Victor Lewis-Smith, television critic for the *London Evening Standard*. Noting that Elton (who is the sole employee of his own company Stand Up Ltd, which *The Sunday Times* – erroneously, according to Elton – valued at £15 million in 1997) is rich enough to say 'escort me to my Rolls', but talks with an accent that suggests he rolls off in an Escort, Lewis-Smith has dubbed him 'king of the hippos' (hypocrites), who 'instead of spitting vitriol, gushes like a human grease gun'. Fiercely denying that his accent is anything but authentic ('Yeah, I affected it. When I was three I affected it'), Elton retaliated by calling Lewis-Smith 'a truly desperate man, a really desperate sort of wannabe'. Elton himself is not at all desperate, but he really does wannabe an entertainer.

PARENTS Lenny Bruce, Morecambe and Wise, George Bernard Shaw

Harry Enfield

Loadsacharacters

Harry Enfield (b. 1961) is the comic whose creations are as likely to feature in adverts as they are in TV programmes: Loadsamoney (Sekonda); Only Me (British Gas); Mr Cholmondeley-Warner (Mercury); DJ Nicey (Fab Ice Cream); and Frank Doberman (Hula Hoops).

Brought up in Billingshurst (Conservative commuter belt), educated at Worth (Roman Catholic public school) and York University, Enfield started out as half of the unsuccessful comedy double act Dusty and Dick before landing a job doing voices for Spitting Image, LWT's satirical puppet show (his father Edward found it cruel and coarse). Enfield was sharing a house in Hackney with **Paul Whitehouse** (writer and performer) and Charlie Higson (comic writer, novelist and leader of 80s band The Higsons) when, with some input from Whitehouse, he developed a character called Stavros based on the owner of their local kebab shop, Adam Athanassiou. Stavros was a modern-day Mrs Maloprop ('Mrs Thatcher, the ironing lady') who became a firm favourite on *Saturday Night Live* (Enfield was invited to do Stavros on the show after a talent scout saw the sketch on *Spitting Image* in which Prince Philip went to visit his Greek 'cousin', a kebab shop owner).

Enfield's next character also originated in a fortuitous coincidence: Whitehouse's habit of walking around saying 'you want to melt that down, mate', in the manner of a Cockney tradesman with an eye out for easy money; and a story told by a friend down from Newcastle of how, when Chelsea FC came up to play United, their southern supporters taunted the Toon crowd by taking rolls of notes out of their pockets, waving them in the air and shouting 'Never seen that before, that's loads of money'. This was the period of the 'north-south divide' (the de-industrialised, redundant north and the growing service sector in the buoyant south) and these occurrences were fused together in the character of Loadsamoney, the Tory-voting ('Mrs Thatcher's done a lot for the country, but you wouldn't want to shag it') southern worker-made-good, who announced himself on *Friday Night Live* saying, 'Shut your mouth and look at my wad.'

Overnight, Loadsamoney became a household name. Jokes about yuppies were commonplace but this was the first jibe at the working classes doing well out of the Lawson boom, and it struck a national chord. So resonant was the response that it sensitised Enfield to the possibility of Loadsamoney becoming another Alf Garnett – a working-class Tory intended as a figure of fun but adopted as a role model nonetheless. He quickly killed off Loadsamoney, briefly replacing him with beer-bellied Geordie, Bugger All Money. Apart from the Sekonda ads, Loadsamoney appeared on British television for less than 15 minutes in total, but that was enough to leave a lasting impression. Enfield's character became the template for Essex Man, the mythical figure used by psephologists and other commentators to denote the southern, working-class Tory voter. Nearly 20 years later, Loadsamoney is still widely used as shorthand for greedy southern workers.

Enfield left Loadsamoney behind, and together with TV producer Geoffrey Perkin, created the character of Sir Norbert Smith, veteran British thespian. The two of them holed up in **Ibiza**, stripped to their shorts and immersed themselves in Anna Neagle movies. From this osmosis of old-fashioned Englishness came the award-winning Sir Norbert,

and another character soon to feature on *The Harry Enfield Programme*, the pinstriped and Brylcreemed Mr Cholmondeley-Warner, who, in the patronising tone of pseudo-Public Information Film lecturers, provides answers to present-day problems in the entirely inappropriate manner of a civil servant of the post-war nanny state.

For his long-running TV programme, imaginatively entitled *Harry Enfield's Television Programme*, Enfield (supported by Whitehouse and Higson) has created a cast of characters he refers to as his 'football team'. He aims to include something for everybody, while recognising that if you get the kids interested the whole family will probably end up watching. His most popular characters include Kevin the teenager (catchphrase: 'I hate you'), and the two geriatric DJs, Smashy (played by Whitehouse, based on Noel Edmonds, Tony Blackburn and Simon Bates) and Nicey (played by Enfield, based on Alan Freeman and Dave Lee Travis, who was not amused). Kathy Burke, aka Waynetta Slob, believes that 'everybody recognises someone they know' in Enfield's characters, adding that 'they are actually quite lovable'. While just having fun, Enfield and Whitehouse have an uncanny ability to keep their fingers on the nation's cultural pulse, identifying social sub-types and breeds faster than any team of social analysts.

Enfield's versatility has prompted comparisons with Dick Emery, who starred in his own TV shows throughout the late 60s and 70s. But Enfield, although his work is mainstream, has come up through **alternative comedy** rather than variety. Comedy is no longer thought of as an alternative form of politics but, as one producer has pointed out, along with Whitehouse and Higson, Enfield is a highly intelligent writer who 'has a view of the world'. In the run-up to the 1997 general election Enfield's worldview prompted him to give money to New Labour, but he later asked for it back.

PARENTS old British movies,
young working-class lads
CHILDREN Edward Enfield, Harry's real-life father, became a TV personality after his son found fame; *The Fast Show*

Brian Eno
Ambient intuition

'I am: a mammal a father a European a heterosexual an artist a son an inventor an Anglo-Saxon an uncle a celebrity a masturbator a cook a gardener an improviser a husband a musician an employer a teacher a wine-lover a cyclist a non-driver a pragmatist a producer a writer a computer-user a Caucasian an interviewee a grumbler a "drifting clarifier".' That's how Brian Eno described himself on the back of his published diary/commentary, *A Year With Swollen Appendices* (1996). He didn't mention that one of his hobbies is developing his own perfumes.

Eno was born in 1948 in the Suffolk village of Woodbridge, where his father (a Belgian immigrant) was a postman. After grammar school, with

his ears full of music from USAF radio (from the local US air bases in East Anglia), he went to Ipswich Art School (run by the same man, Roy Ascott, who had taught Pete Townshend at Ealing) and then to Winchester School of Art. By 1969 he was in London, where he met up with saxophonist Andy McKay with whom he shared an interest in John Cage and Karlheinz Stockhausen, and played in improvisational bands such as Maxwell's Demon.

In the early 70s Eno was an integral part of Roxy Music (along with McKay), the art-rock band who knew how to be simultaneously glam-camp and hetero-sexy. In the original Roxy line-up he played the role of a mad professor and 'non-musician': his job was to 'treat' the sounds made by the others. He joined because he was attracted to the 'idiot energy' of rock.

On stage, Eno was fond of ostrich feathers: he looked halfway between an egghead with sex appeal and a half-bald Marlene Dietrich. He once said: 'I don't like masculine clothing. The western version of masculinity opposes rational man against intuitive woman. The part of my being that interests me has always been my intuition.' So much so that when his Moog synthesisers developed glitches Eno preferred their new-found unpredictability and refused to have them serviced. Around this time he also issued a set of 100 cards, titled *Oblique Strategies*, which contain dilemmas in the manner of the I-Ching.

Eno had been making solo albums since the *Here Come The Warm Jets* in 1973; and when Roxy Music became too much of a vehicle for singer Bryan Ferry, he left to concentrate on this area of work. Alongside Terry Riley, whose first album (*Rainbow In Curved Air*) was released a couple of years earlier, Eno is generally credited with the invention of **ambient** – repetitive music, usually electronic and reliant on tape loops, which is less intrusive than song or solo-based pop and rock. Eno followed up *Warm Jets* (a reference to urinating) with *Another Green World* (1975), *Discreet Music* (1975) and *Ambient 1: Music for Airports* (1978). For a while he played in another band, 801, with ex-Dulwich schoolboy and Roxy guitarist Phil Manzanera, but later said that 'for me, rock isn't capable of producing that spiritual quality any more'.

Rock journalists were highly critical of Eno and his ambient music. He later recalled that 'for four years the *NME* was … obscenely rude about it. Just because it wasn't some ballsy, flesh-and-blood testosterone rocker thing. Eno-esque was a term of abuse. … There were five of them [journalists], and I will never forget them. Two of them, I'm delighted to say, are dead, and I look forward to the day when I read the obituaries of the other three.'

By the early 90s ambient had become the height of fashion, not least because of the chart-topping CD *U.F.Orb* by The Orb, whom **Tony Parsons** described as 'ex-ravers who make Eno music for the dance crowd', and who 'freely admit that they would never have existed without the musical experiments conducted by Brain Eno'. In recent years Eno's *Discreet Music* has been heard in maternity wards, and the waiting halls of New York's La Guardia have echoed to the sound of his *Music for Airports*. Once confined to the margins,

his influence is now everywhere.

It is Eno's work as a record producer that gets the widest hearing. His first session in the producer's chair was for the Portsmouth Sinfonia. Created by Cornelius Cardew (Dadaist who turned Maoist before he was run over and killed), the Portsmouth Sinfonia was an orchestra made up of 'non-musicians' who could hardly play. Eno soon moved on to Midge Ure's pomp-electronic Ultravox, followed by Devo (American weirdos from 'rubber city' Akron) and New York bohos the Talking Heads (his sampling for Byrne and co's *My Life In The Bush of Ghosts* has been celebrated for its innovation and derided as 'cultural imperialism'). His mid-to-late-70s collaboration with **David Bowie** in Berlin (he worked on *Low*, *Station to Station* and *Heroes*) brought synthesised music to a new level of artistry. Bowie said of his collaborator that he played the recording studio 'like an instrument'.

Eno went on to produce U2, whose best-selling albums *Achtung Baby* and *Zooropa* are credited with having raised the level of media literacy in the USA. He has also found the time to produce exhibitions and installations (light, video, slides and sound), to write scores for **Derek Jarman** films, and to be a major contributor to the War Child charity project which aimed to help the children of Bosnia.

Eno epitomises the kind of eclectic creativity associated with the postmodern world where 'the curator is king'.

PARENTS Erik Satie, Hawkwind (first rock band to use electronic noise)
CHILDREN The Human League, The Orb

READ ON *A Year With Swollen Appendices* by Brian Eno

Chris Evans
Freak or unique?

Born in Warrington on 1 April 1966, Chris Evans is the carrot-top at the pinnacle of British broadcasting. He is also top of the list of men we love to hate: he once said that, after buying an eight-seater dining table, he realised he did not have seven friends.

Brought up on a council estate, Evans was academically gifted but flunked school and graduated to hospital radio, while helping out at Manchester's Piccadilly Radio (apprenticed to eccentric DJ Timmy Mallett), and working in a newsagent's, as a forklift truck driver, and as a pot-man in a city centre pub. He was deeply affected by his father's death (from cancer) in 1979. With his stand-out ginger hair, he had been bullied at school: one local tough even claims to have pissed on his head.

After a stint in his own right at Piccadilly (his relationship with Alison Ward, the mother of his daughter, Jade, ended during this period), Evans moved on to Greater London Radio and into television: *The Power Station* for Sky and *TV-Mayhem* which he co-produced and starred in for TV-AM. But the Evans assault on our screens was aborted by the termination of Bruce Gyngell's British broadcasting operation. When TV-AM went off air, replaced by GMTV, *TV-Mayhem* went with it.

Months later (1992) Evans was back as co-host of *The Big Breakfast*, Channel 4's self-consciously wacky breakfast show produced by Planet 24 and chosen by (then) network boss Michael Grade as a high-risk but innovative package. Evans subsequently applied his wacky-if-not-tacky style of presenting to *Don't Forget Your Toothbrush*, Channel 4's Saturday-night audience-participation/quiz show: it seemed highly improvised but was very tightly scripted.

In the mid-90s Evans could do little wrong. A popular broadcaster, he hosted major events such as the Brit Awards. *TFI Friday*, his Friday-evening (reminiscent of the halcyon days of *Ready Steady Go!* in the mid-60s) pop-and-chat show for Channel 4, was highly regarded; and BBC Radio 1 lured him (£1.4-million salary) on to the all-important breakfast slot in an attempt to raise the ratings and restore the station's faltering reputation.

Evans added more than 1 million to the listening figures, and media commentators were forced to take note. But by autumn 1996 it was all becoming too much. Evans asked Radio 1 controller Matthew Bannister if he could take Fridays off, and was refused. In November he told the viewers of *TFI Friday* that 'my bosses won't give me any time off, but I am mentally unwell'. A few weeks later he took his staff out on an all-day, all-night binge and (deliberately?) did not turn up for his breakfast show on the morning after. On 17 January 1997 he announced he was being forced off Radio 1 by Bannister's intransigence.

After Evans' exit, DJ and children's TV presenter Zoe Ball was offered the breakfast chair at Radio 1. Meanwhile Evans took on the breakfast slot at

Richard Branson's Virgin Radio in what was billed as a battle between 'the Crumpet and the Ginger Nut'.

While at the BBC Evans prompted more reprimands from the Broadcasting Standards Council (now renamed the Broadcasting Standards Commission, a regulatory body with a remit to monitor and maintain standards in taste and decency) than any other broadcaster. Fleet Street picked up on his stresses, strains and drinking habits, and made him the star, alongside **Paul Gascoigne** and Danny Baker, of what became known as 'the Yobocracy'.

For years Evans was admired by media people as a rebel, a non-conformist who did not listen to the corporate men in suits. But towards the end of the 90s his fellow professionals turned against him. Suddenly the talking-point about Evans was his lack of taste: he drives an 'obvious wealth' sports car, for instance.

'Chris Evans must be silenced,' declared Caitlin Moran in *The Times*, after the the ginger one committed the crime of appearing in a phone advert in which he said that John Lennon was the person he most wanted a one-to-one with. 'Lennon is cool,' continued Moran, 'because he was exactly the kind of person who would have loathed Chris Evans.' In the spirit of fantasy phone calls, Moran concluded by imagining what Lennon might have said about Evans: 'Just because we dislike you doesn't mean we don't understand you, Chris. It's never been a question of not understanding you, you charmless, over-exposed philistine. It's because we get you entirely, right down to the last act of your waxy, pea-sized heart, that we loathe you.'

Maybe Evans is self-indulgent; and perhaps there are too many items in his shows that are distastefully freakish (Steve Wright meets Howard Stern). Some commentators have suggested that this behaviour is rooted in his own ostracism as a ginger-haired kid. A more likely explanation for his ostracism is that he is just too successful. Not only does Evans host the breakfast show on Virgin (denigrated by its critics as an 'aural Big Mac'), he liked it so much he bought the company, beating established bidders like Capital Radio after securing a £40-million-plus loan from Banque Paribas.

Evans now heads the Ginger Media Group, comprising Virgin Radio and his TV company, Ginger Productions (makers of *Babes in the Wood* with Denise Van Outen). His £30-million deal with Channel 4 brings in £250,000 for each episode of *TFI Friday*, while his radio breakfast show is sponsored to the tune of £3 million by BSkyB, in a deal signed with personal friend Elizabeth Murdoch. In July 1999 Evans teamed up with Talk Radio's Kelvin Mackenzie (another hate figure) in a consortium that aims to be a big player in digital radio.

Not so much a freak, more uniquely successful (although critics are quick to point out that 'the Ginger Effect' will have its job cut out meeting the financial demands made by Apax, Evans' venture capitalist backers).

PARENTS Jeremy Beadle, Steve Wright, Kenny Everett, **Chris Tarrant**
READ ON *Freak or Unique? – the Chris Evans Story* by David Jones

The Face

Changing faces

Launched on a shoestring (publisher Nick Logan, b. 1947, ex-Ilford **Mod**, trainee on the *West Essex Gazette*, reporter then editor of *New Musical Express* and *Smash Hits*, put up his £4,000 savings and second-mortgaged his flat), the first issue of *The Face* came out in May 1980 with the grinning, gap-toothed, tonic-suited Jerry Dammers on the front cover. The early issues carried few adverts. According to Logan this was deliberate because 'at *NME* the awful shapes of ads often meant that you couldn't do what you wanted with the design'. Ad shortage meant minimal profits: 'I wear second-hand clothes and eat cheaply,' Logan 'cheerfully' told *Music Week*.

The debut issue of *The Face* was a halfway house: its standard layout and content (**Two-Tone**, The Clash) were not so very different from either *Smash Hits* or the *NME*; but the package (glossy magazine, issued monthly) indicated a new direction. The journey began in earnest when Logan brought in **Neville Brody** to do a redesign. Their combined efforts resulted in an entirely new product which was both luxurious and experimental – the same characteristics as the club culture which the likes of Steve Strange and Boy George were starting to develop around the same time. Almost overnight, *The Face* became the 'style bible' which framed the interests and concerns of this new generation ('the cult with no name'). Within months the magazine was picking up awards, advertisers were flocking to buy space in it, and jealous radical publishers were complaining that Logan had capitulated to the capitalist marketplace. (Describing himself as 'diffident, mortgaged, married and the father of three children,' Logan explained that 'the only reason I'm an entrepreneur, if I am, is because that's the only way you can have the freedom to follow your own instincts'.)

In *Hiding In The Light*, cultural critic Dick Hebdige cites *The Face* as the Ur-text of the 80s, and uses it to contrast the first world of print in which language is paramount and publishing is an activity derived from Enlightenment rationality, with the second world where magazines are meant for 'cruising' (the term comes from French semiotician Roland Barthes), image is privileged over text, and boundaries between politics and pastiche are continually blurred. He recalls an episode from John Berger's TV series *Ways of Seeing* (1974) in which the presenter flicked through *The Sunday Times* colour supplement and noticed the proximity and the absurd distance between a picture of starving refugees and an advert for bath salts. Berger had argued that 'there is such a gap, such a fissure that we can only say that the culture that produced these images is insane'. But Hebdige recognised this proximity as the space where young people live, and declared that '*The Face* is composed precisely on this fissure. It is the place of the nutty conjunction.'

Hebdige's location of *The Face* was apparently borne out by a photo-led feature in which guerrilla armies in the Middle East were shown and described in terms of their dress sense – as if they

THE FACE

MAY 1980
ISSUE No. 1

THE CLASH
MADNESS
PUBLIC IMAGE
DEXYS

JERRY DAMMERS PHOTOGRAPHED BY CHALKIE DAVIES

IAN DURY on
ELVIS PRESLEY

THE SPECIALS: 2-MUCH PRESSURE

too were dressing up as cod-revolutionaries in the manner of London style warriors. However, at a conference in London in the summer of 1986, frequent contributor Robert Elms denied that *The Face* turned everything, even terrorism and political radicalism, into mere style: its mission was to present interesting ideas and images in a form that was both radical and stylish. For Elms (who found Logan 'a joy to work for'), *The Face* was democratic and pluralist, a new shop window for the aspirations of 'ordinary people' – aspirations hitherto denied and obstructed by left-wing do-gooders who claimed to speak for the masses. (Some people disagreed with this, complaining that *The Face*'s embrace of Buffalo Ray Petri's gay iconography in preference to 'the momentous scally/casual culture of the early 80s' meant that it only ever represented a metropolitan mafia.)

When 80s enterprise culture was superseded by E-culture, *The Face* took on a new image and a new editor, Sheryl Garratt. Feminist ex-*City Limits* (left-leaning weekly London listings magazine), Garratt was enthused by what she saw as the community-enhancing, democratising effects of the music and culture surrounding dance-based clubs and E, and she moved the magazine away from being a 'style bible' towards these developments. Its circulation doubled in the process. Logan, meanwhile, sold a major share of his company, Wagadon, to long-established magazine publishers Conde Nast.

When Richard Benson (Leeds United supporter, son of a South Yorkshire pig farmer, read English and Theology at King's College, London, before signing up for a journalism course at City University) took over the editorship of *The Face* in 1995, doubts were already spreading about the E-experience and the magazine took these into account. Benson was more confident about the validity of the British contribution to global culture. In his first editor's letter, he prefigured what became known as Cool Britannia: 'Britain is riding the biggest wave of creativity for years and we're proud to be a swinging part of it.' Afterwards he recalled his determination to 'fight for British talent, we recognised it and tried to push a new agenda'. He has since criticised the New Labour government for riding the Creative Britain bandwagon; and in 1998 he expressed a desire to connect with the new mood among British people in the wake of the death of Princess Diana.

Having vacated *The Face* editor's chair in March 1998 to make way for Adam Higginbotham, formerly of lad-mag **Loaded**, Benson moved upstairs to become group editor for an expanding Wagadon roster including *Arena* (launched in 1986, the first British style magazine for men), *Arena Homme Plus* (a fashion spin-off from *Arena*), *Deluxe* (launched 1998, billed as 'post-Lad, pre-Dad'), and *Frank* – Wagadon for women. But all was not well in Logan-land. *Deluxe* foundered after a few issues; *Frank* hit financial difficulties and became a quarterly. Even *The Face* was not immune: circulation dipped by nearly 30 per cent, down to 70,000; the art department decamped to a rival publication, *Dazed & Confused*; and Higginbotham had to be eased out. In a letter to the *Guardian* headlined 'Face it, you're old', former contributor Phil

Thornton declared that *The Face* 'has come to look as tired and ridiculous as any other 40-year-old at an 18th-birthday bash'. Critics suggested that Logan should have done what he apparently thought about doing in 1988: quitting at issue number 100 when *The Face* was still ahead. Instead he bought back Conde Nast's share of Wagadon, explaining that 'we are now at a stage when it makes sense to have back full control, so enabling me to determine how that development will continue'. A few months later, he took the plunge and sold his company Wagadon to EMAP.

Benson, meanwhile, had been trying to find the pulse of the period. In a series of exploratory articles, he came up with suggested new social types such as SOFT (searching for ordinary fundamental truths) Lad, New Sensible (staying at home instead of clubbing), and the Flexi (the flexible executive who has replaced the yuppie). But the 90s were resistant to precise definition, and despite the best efforts of Benson and his successors, *The Face* no longer seems to know who it's looking at. Publishing director Rod Sopp has admitted that there is 'no great trend going on, unlike a few years ago when clubbing took off'.

Perhaps *The Face*'s current difficulties are derived from the same factors that gave rise to its initial success. As Hebdige pointed out, it was among the first to invite the reader to cruise between a range of different lifestyles; 20 years later, not only have we all learnt how to do this, but the cruising range of most media-literate consumers is far wider than any single magazine could hope to be. Making his debut as editor, Johnny

Davis noted that 'everybody's cool nowadays' and asked 'how do you find some cool to call your own when the answers – the lists of the right clubs, clothes, comedians – are everywhere?' Once *The Face* played the role of the Oracle in a stylised world, but now there is no demand for a bible, even of style.

PARENTS *NME*; *Vanity Fair*, *Details*, *Esquire* and *GQ* (American editions)
CHILDREN all broadsheet supplements bear the marks of *The Face*
READ ON: *Cultures of Consumption* by Frank Mort; *Hiding in the Light* by Dick Hebdige

The Fall
Professional outsider

The Fall (named after the novel by Albert Camus) are misanthropic Mark E Smith plus whoever he happens to be working with. Since 1977, when Salford-born Smith was inspired by punk but not of it, The Fall have been a constantly shifting fixture of the British music scene. Smith, who includes records by The Maytals, The Ramones and Arnold Schoenberg among his favourites, is a self-consciously 'working-class' singer and songwriter. He describes himself as 'white crap that talks back' and deliberately stands outside the confines of media-driven pop-land; yet pop-land has always found a (small) place for him, and the British music press has considerable regard for him as a belligerent old codger.

Dressed in anorak and pullover, Smith made the Buzzcocks and the other Manchester punk bands seem like fashion models. Since the release of The Fall's first album (*Live At The Witch Trials*, 1979), he has been a byword for anti-fashion. In 1999 he expressed admiration for Pete Waterman (Steps producer), avant-garde composer Karlheinz Stockhausen and nineteenth-century German chancellor Bismarck – not the kind of role models that would endear him to the cool and trendy.

Smith's stylised Mancunian drawl and whine, delivering his densely allusive, freely associative, cut-up lyrics, is The Fall's trademark sound. His belligerence is not just an act; he applies it offstage as well as on, even to the people he works with. On tour in the USA at the beginning of 1998, the rest of The Fall walked out on him (only keyboard player Julia Nagle made it to the 1999 album *The Marshall Suite*). In 1997 Smith had been working with Manchester-based electro-production team DOSE, who contributed to the album *Levitate*; but he says he 'had to fire them'.

Throughout the 20-year history of The Fall, backing musicians have constantly come and gone (a pattern that invites comparisons with Captain Beefheart and his Magic Band): their role is to provide a sometimes rough and ready version of rock/electro formats, which, combined with Smith's intelligent lyrics, have the effect of simultaneously recycling pop music and deconstructing it. Yes, for all his student-hating, media-baiting bile, Smith and the Fall are the artiest of them all.

In the 80s The Fall enjoyed a stable relationship with the major-minor record label Beggars Banquet, and Smith got married to a Californian guitarist named Laura Elise, better known as Brix. In the second half of the decade, The Fall's anti-pop looked like going commercial. *The Frenz Experiment* and *I Am Kurious Oranj* (both 1988) picked up favourable reviews and respectable sales. But Brix left in 1989, and Smith retreated into his own belligerence (*The Infotainment Scam*, 1993; *Middle Class Revolt*, 1994). Still feeling the loss of John Lennon, British culture was ripe for another, acerbic northern knocker; but the starring roles went instead to the Gallaghers and the relatively mild-mannered **Jarvis Cocker**. Meanwhile Smith plays on as the elder statesman of pop misanthropy. His recent work includes the aptly named album *Cerebral Caustic* (1995), and collaborations with Coldcut, Edwyn Collins and Inspiral Carpets.

PARENTS Albert Camus, Punk, Philip K. Dick

Festivals
All the fun of the fayre

Going to a music festival used to be like visiting another planet: being with thousands of other people who defined themselves through pop music and its rebel ethos was an extraordinary experience (in his song about Woodstock Ian Matthews noted with wonderment that there were half a million cothinkers there). Nowadays it is much less memorable; and although the summer months are still festooned with festivals (a couple were cancelled in 1998 due to poor ticket sales), not even Glastonbury has the same Kudos.

In the years 1956–59 there were small-scale jazz festivals at Beaulieu. In 1960 and 1961 the numbers grew larger and there were outbreaks of violence. Lord Montagu, who had inaugurated the festivals in order to augment the income of his stately home, announced that there would be no more such events at Beaulieu. In 1961 Harold Pendleton, owner of the Marquee Club in Soho, held a National Jazz Festival (loosely modelled on the Newport Jazz Festival in the USA) in the grounds of Richmond Athletic Club. Pendleton repeated the exercise the following year. In 1963, the **Rolling Stones** (who had been playing a residency at the Marquee) were on the bill, and the premises were besieged by their fans. The takeover of the festival by the Stones and their fans marked the advent of r&b/pop and the end of jazz as essential music for youthful rebels. The gig was renamed the National Jazz and Blues Festival, but after the 1965 event it was banned from Richmond. Pendleton took it first to Windsor (1966), where police moved in on 'immorality', and then on to Sunbury in 1968. But this event was eclipsed by the first ever festival on the Isle of Wight, attended by 8,000 people who came to hear The Move, Tyrannosaurus Rex and (from America) Jefferson Airplane.

British festivals in the early 70s were influenced by the good vibes of Woodstock and the negative associations of Altamont, both of which occurred in 1969 – the same year that the Rolling Stones played a free concert in Hyde Park attended by 250,000, policed by Hell's Angels and marked both by the public debut of **skinheads** and by Mick Jagger reading Shelley and releasing butterflies in commemoration of former Stones guitarist Brian Jones, who had drowned in his own swimming pool a few days before. While some festivals got bigger (the 2,000-watt PA system for the 1969 Isle of Wight festival – headlined by Bob Dylan and the **Who** – brought pop to the ears of reclusive monks who had not heard any music since the Second World War), better organised and more expensive, others (Windsor, Glastonbury Fayre, Harmony Farm) rejoiced in being small scale and (almost) free. With their handicraft stalls and ready supply of drugs, the free festivals sought to evoke a tradition of trading and pleasure-taking which is traceable back to medieval times.

By this time festivals had become a political issue: they symbolised the divide between the standard-bearers of family values and the champions of 'free love' and youthful, playful experimentation. After numerous questions in parliament and a succession of panicky press stories, the Isle of Wight Act (1971) and the Night Assemblies Act (1972) were passed. Repressive legislation had the effect of increasing the determination of free festival organisers; and this, in turn, confirmed the intransigence of those in authority. In 1974 police cleared the site of the third Windsor Free Festival. When Ubi Dwyer and Sid Rawle advertised the fourth festival (their smiley logo reappeared in the iconogra-

Feuds corner 5 cases of media handbags at dawn

Sewell vs Ross After a less-than-flattering profile in which Deborah Ross (*The Independent*) condemned art critic Brian Sewell for his 'pantomime dame' demeanour, he responded in the *London Evening Standard* by calling Ross a 'cacographer' (writer of crap).

Burchill vs Paglia An exchange of agitated faxes enlivened the pages and brought much-needed publicity to Toby Young's fledgling *Modern Review*; for example, Paglia to Burchill: 'Alas, your letters have done more damage to you than anything I could do' and Burchill to Paglia: 'Fuck off, you crazy old dyke.'

Winterson vs Gerrard When the *Observer*'s Nicci Gerrard described Jeanette Winterson as 'self-taught, self-improved, self-produced, self-invented and oh-so-self-confident', Winterson and her partner Margaret Reynolds turned up at Gerrard's door and, as Gerrard recalls, warned her to 'never come near me or my writing again, do you hear?'

Berkoff vs Iley In *The Sunday Times*, Chrissie Iley described Steven Berkoff as 'tantalisingly repulsive ... he is woman meets thug'. 'I was fed into a human incinerator,' replied Berkoff.

Paxman vs Rumbold Of the young Jeremy Paxman, the *Guardian*'s Judy Rumbold observed that 'what was above average ... was the lustrous pile of his velvet loon pants and the high number of refusals he received when replying for journalism traineeships'. Commenting on profile writers a few months later, Paxman noted that 'the trick they try to pull is to construct a piece to which the interviewee is incidental'.

phy of E-culture in the late 80s) in 1975, they were arrested. But in the second half of the 70s, the Labour government pursued a policy of informal regulation, mainly through the mediation of a newly established organisation called Festival Welfare Services.

In the late 70s there were clashes between punks and the older generation of festival goers: at Reading in 1978, **Jam** fans and Status Quo follow- ers did not get on (neither did Jam fans and Sham 69 supporters). During the early 80s, festivals came to reflect the segmentation of the British music market. Castle Donington in Leicestershire was established as the outdoor home of heavy metal. Directed by Peter Gabriel, the first Womad (1982) was a financial disaster but set a trend for World Music festivals attended by a Green-tinged, mainly middle-class clientele.

Towards the end of the decade, the revamped Reading Festival, dominated by Vince Power's Mean Fiddler organisation, took account of the growing connections between **indie**, dance, and hip-hop (**New Order** topped the bill in 1989, Sonic Youth in 1991, and in 1992 Public Enemy appeared alongside Kurt Cobain's Nirvana). Growing out of rave culture, the 1995 Tribal Gathering represented a merger of the commercial and counter-cultural aspects of British festivals. With the **Prodigy** as headliners, the event was a partnership between Universe, known for being campaigners against the Criminal Justice Bill, and Vince Power, widely regarded as the sharpest business operator on the London music scene. The two factions later fell out, resorting to legal action over ownership of the name 'Tribal Gathering'; but not before corporate and counter-culture had become wedded in the festival arena. Since the mid-90s festivals have become a prime site for corporate sponsorship (the list of sponsors includes Sony, Diesel, Casio, Marlboro, Ericsson and Virgin) and, according to *Select* magazine editor John Harris, 'now no one has any notion that sponsorship sullies the integrity of a festival'.

The history of 'Glasto' is indicative of the changing role of festivals in British culture. Throughout its 30-year history, the man who has made it possible is farmer Michael Eavis (recognisable by his Amish-style beard). Inspired by the Bath Festival of 1970 (which took place in Shepton Mallet, Somerset), Eavis allowed the Glastonbury Fayre to take place on his land (the £1 entrance fee included free milk from his cows) in September 1970 (1,500 people heard Tyrannosaurus Rex). In some circles, this made farmer Eavis a traitor to the British way of life (among *NME* readers he has always been considered a hero). But by 1997, Glastonbury was not only a major commercial operation; it had also become part of the fabric of British society, and when the rain came down heavily that year and turned the festival site into a mudbath, national broadsheets (even the *Daily Telegraph*) gave sympathetic coverage to the antics of the mudlarks.

Glastonbury is now as much a part of the British cultural calendar as the Last Night of the Proms. Some people believe that there is no longer any 'such thing as the Glastonbury Festival, only the Glastonbury Festival Experience', and complain that this represents the Disneyfication of what was once an important site for the British counter-culture. In the *London Evening Standard*, Glasto-veteran Hettie Judah (she's been coming for 15 years running) thought it was all too predictable: 'if people come to see mainstream bands, complain about the lavatories and return on Sunday afternoon in time for work, should they be at a festival in the first place?'

Festivals are rarely about freedom these days, but some things never change. Both the dubious character of festival sanitation and the intractable nature of the star system were demonstrated once again by the **Manic Street Preachers**' stipulation at Glasto 99 that they must have their own private lavatory.

PARENTS Nottingham's Goose Fair, Woodstock
READ ON *The Politics of Festivals* by Michael Clarke

Brit Film   The British Film Institute's top 10 'culturally British' movies for each decade

1940s   *The Third Man* (Carol Reed, 1949), *Brief Encounter* (David Lean, 1945), *Great Expectations* (David Lean, 1946), *Kind Hearts and Coronets* (Robert Hamer, 1949), *The Red Shoes* (Powell and Pressburger, 1948), *Brighton Rock* (John Boulting, 1947), *Henry V* (Laurence Olivier, 1944), *A Matter of Life and Death* (Powell and Pressburger, 1946), *Whisky Galore!* (Alexander MacKendrick, 1949), *Black Narcissus* (Powell and Pressburger, 1947)

1950s   *The Bridge on the River Kwai* (David Lean, 1957), *The Ladykillers* (Alexander MacKendrick, 1955), *The Lavender Hill Mob* (Charles Crichton, 1951), *Room at the Top* (Jack Clayton, 1958), *I'm All Right Jack* (John Boulting, 1959), *The Man In The White Suit* (Alexander MacKendrick, 1951), *The Dam Busters* (Michael Anderson, 1955), *The Cruel Sea* (Charles Ford, 1952), *Genevieve* (Henry Cornelius, 1953), *The Belles of St Trinians* (Frank Lauder, 1954)

1960s   *Lawrence of Arabia* (David Lean, 1962), *Kes* (Ken Loach, 1969), *If* (Lindsay Anderson, 1968), *Saturday Night and Sunday Morning* (Karel Reisz, 1960), *The Servant* (Joseph Losey, 1963), *Dr Zhivago* (David Lean, 1965), *Zulu* (Cy Endfield, 1964), *Alfie* (Lewis Gilbert, 1966), *The Italian Job* (Peter Collinson, 1969), *Dr No* (Terence Young, 1962)

1970s   *Don't Look Now* (Nicholas Roeg, 1973), *Get Carter* (Michael Hodges, 1971), *Monty Python's Life of Brian* (Terry Jones, 1979), *Performance* (Nicholas Roeg, 1970), *The Go-Between* (Joseph Losey, 1970), *Sunday, Bloody Sunday* (John Schelsinger, (1971), *The Railway Children* (Lionel Jeffries, 1970), *The Day of the Jackal* (Fred Zinnemann, 1973), *A Clockwork Orange* (Stanley Kubrick, 1971), *The Wicker Man* (Robin Hardy, 1973)

1980s   *Chariots of Fire* (High Hudson, 1987), *The Long Good Friday* (John McKenzie, 1980), *Withnail and I* (Bruce Robinson, 1987), *Gregory's Girl* (Bill Forsyth, 1980), *Gandhi* (Richard Attenborough, 1982), *Local Hero* (Bill Forsyth, 1983), *A Fish Called Wanda* (Charles Crichton, 1988), *My Beautiful Launderette* (Stephen Frears, 1985), *My Left Foot* (Jim Sheridan, 1989), *Brazil* (Terry Gilliam, 1985)

1990s   *Trainspotting* (Danny Boyle, 1996), *Four Weddings and a Funeral* (Mike Newell, 1994), *The Full Monty* (Peter Cattaneo, 1997), *The Crying Game* (Neil Jordan, 1992), *The Commitments* (Alan Parker, 1991), *Secrets and Lies* (Mike Leigh, 1995), *The Madness of King George* (Nicholas Hytner, 1994), *Shakespeare in Love* (John Madden, 1998), *The English Patient* (Anthony Minghella, 1996), *Sense and Sensibility* (Ang Lee 1995)

The Third Man (1949)

Football

More important than life or death

Football was born in the late-Victorian era when the working classes of the industrial north had their first taste of leisure time as half-day working on Saturdays became the norm. Once an unruly excuse for street rioting, the village game was taken up first by the public schools as a tool of 'muscular Christianity': a game with rules that could develop character, spirit and discipline, and thence on to the industrial north. Many of the Football Association's founding members, QPR, Barnsley, Bolton, Blackburn, were originally church clubs. As the game grew in the 1880s as a working-class spectator sport and money became involved, professionalism was recognised by the FA and clubs began to build their own stadiums. The game became an export of the Empire: the Corinthians toured Latin America, while Europe followed Britain's lead in the game (Juventus took their strip design from Notts County and Real Zaragosa from Sheffield United). Industrial philanthropists soon sought to sponsor the game and take control of its assets, wanting to wrest its prestige and to have a hand over the workers in play as well as at work.

Once playing and watching football were established as the nation's obsession, things changed very little until the modern era. It provided a sense of pride and escapism for the spectators from the daily drudge and for the few lucky professionals who played the game a way out of their working-class cul-de-sac.

Football has always walked a fine line between the civilising impulses of muscular Christianity and the more ancient traditions of all-out war with a ball. It always aroused high passion and violent rivalry, both on and off the pitch. Yet by the mid-1960s the media had begun to pick up on and define a new type: the football 'hooligan'. The stereotype in the 60s and 70s was an unruly working-class caricature, bovver-boy **skinheads** in boots and braces. It was mob violence and crowd mentality, ugly and unwanted but nothing more sinister. Yet by the turn of the next decade something more ominous was on the horizon. Hooligans weren't just oiks from the **underclass** mire, they were the bastard offspring of Thatcher's revolution: gangs of well off working-class and lower-middle-class males looking for the thrill of the match-day rumble. This was the birth of the football casual. Originating in Liverpool and Manchester in the late 70s they dressed in expensive designer 'casual' sports gear that proclaimed wealth and status – a streetstyle take on the money decade. (As with the US rap scene, its nearest counterpart, it was about conspicuous comsumption.) European games for both club and country (it was a time when British clubs dominated European competition) became an excuse for both guerrilla warfare against continental fans (proving who was cock of the walk) and shopping trips to pick up the latest designer sports labels.

Big-city casuals took pride in turning up at small-town fixtures looking like dandified aliens to the locals and then running riot. It was all about one-upmanship: Chelsea casuals would wave their wads of money in the air at Liverpool and

Manchester games, towns hit harder by the recession. Renowned 'firms' developed nationwide, every team had one, from Chelsea's Headhunters to West Ham's Inter-City Firm (named after the trains they used to travel to matches on – first class of course). Drink, which at one stage had been thought to be the cause of much of the trouble, was conspicuous by its absence. These hooligans had the cool, collected regime of the sportsmen themselves. They liked to have their wits about them. Organising rucks became a precision art, using mobile phones to outwit the police. Often it would kick off in a designated place far from the game itself. The firms used calling cards. Everything was sleek except for the violence itself which still made liberal use of the Stanley knife – the working man's weapon. Just as Britain gave the world football, it also gave it modern football violence. Soon the Dutch and Belgians sides and many other European football clubs had their own hooligans who idolised and emulated the so-called British disease.

It took several things to stop the escalation: the death toll at the Heysel stadium in 1985 which saw English teams (and their fans) banned from European competition; the Hillsborough disaster in 1989 which brought about the Taylor Report, the demise of the beloved terrace and the advent of all-seater stadiums. But potentially more liberating than any of this was the rise of **Ecstasy** in the late 80s. The terraces got loved up as youths went to see their teams after a Friday night of raving. As the city of Manchester went E mad City fans began taking hundreds of inflatable bananas into the stands

intent on continuing the party. Football was on one, and fighting was off the agenda.

Some say the violence never really went away though, it just went underground, biding its time. If anything it has become more parochial. You rarely see it on Sky's coverage as the worst violence is now in the lowly Conference league and at forgotten clubs like Millwall and Cardiff City. Crowds at England away games which still attract hooligans are often made up of these small teams' fans, the sort that don't get to flag-wave abroad unless they're on tour with the national team. More recently there has been the rumour that even when fighting occurs the media and the government don't like to give it the oxygen of publicity now that football is a matter of financial, cultural and national (England's 2006 World Cup bid) importance.

After the purges of the 80s, the 90s saw the commodification of football and the yuppification of its support. On the international stage **Gazza**'s tears during Italia 90 turned the nation back on to football as something to be proud of, and the ban on British clubs in Europe was lifted. The seats that now covered the terraces were taken up by families and middle-class males looking (like **Nick Hornby**) to find a sense of identity in the game. Hornby also made writing and talking about football something that could have respectable literary aspirations.

Meanwhile, Rupert Murdoch brought us Sky TV and football saturation and the nation has never looked back. (After the success of England's Euro 96 tournament, even the government has taken note and been careful to court the football vote. Tony Blair picks up a football almost as often as

Gazza Euro '96

Clinton reaches for his sax, and ministers enthuse at every opportunity about the teams they support.)

The revenue the Premiership took from Sky turned the league into a cosmopolitan circus of overpaid world stars, who in turn accelerated interest in the game. The city investors moved in, clubs went plc and football became as much about balance sheets as clean ones. Clubs now take more money through merchandising operations than turnstiles. Football and the cult of sport have become the true God of our postmodern national culture.

PARENTS Charles Alcock, Saturdays off, 1966, Gazza's tears
CHILDREN Andy Gray, replica kit wearers everywhere, Posh'n'Becks, fantasy football
READ ON *Fever Pitch* by Nick Hornby; *All Played Out* by Pete Davies; *Away Days* by Kevin Sampson

Ford Sierra Cosworth

Hijacked by the underclass

'We only use performance cars. The only Ford I would drive is this one – the Cosworth.' This was one endorsement that the Ford Motor Company had not asked for. Sitting in the Recarro raven leather driver's seat, the speaker was one of the 'hotters' who brought illicit thrills and spills to the Blackbird Leys estate, Oxford, in the summer of 1991. Crowds came out on hot summer nights to watch handbrake turns executed by daring young men in stolen vehicles, until the police moved in and occupied the area. A few months later, with sales affected by the early 90s recession and insurance costs at a prohibitive £14,000 per annum, Ford announced that the Cosworth 4x4 would not feature in the 1993 Sierra line-up. The last batch off the assembly line was in the showrooms by autumn 1992, and the car was immediately hailed as a 'future classic'.

The Ford Sierra Cosworth had been launched in July 1986 as a turbo-charged four-wheel-drive luxury saloon (max speed 150mph, 0–60mph in 6.6 seconds). Ford boasted about its race and rally-proven suspension, electronically controlled ABS brakes, hand-built YBG Cosworth engine, and 'sleek aerodynamic lines, emphasised by stylish and distinctive alloy wheels, a deep front air dam and rear spoiler'. The firm's PR department promised 'exhilaration' and 'a totally satisfying motor experience'. *Autocar and Motor* magazine described the traction as 'awesome', noting 'sharp steering response and terrific grip … stunningly competent chassis'. To get the full benefit, drivers were advised to 'find a tight corner and a low gear, get to the apex, floor the throttle' and expect to be 'hauled down the road, glued to your selected line'.

The Cosworth was billed as 'the executive express'. It was meant to provide 'performance and style' for men in red braces on their way home from the trading floor. But the 'Cossie' was hijacked by a different kind of (non-paying) clientele. Granby Street in Liverpool 8 became an unofficial drag strip for stolen Cossies, and 'twockers' (taking without owner's consent) in nearby Risley remand centre amused themselves by swapping Cossie stories while waiting for their cases to come up in court. The roads circling Lakeside shopping centre in Thurrock also became a racetrack for 'twocked' Cosworths. One police force even used a Cosworth as bait to catch car thieves, until somebody drove it away so fast that the plods could not keep up. Then, in 1991, the exploits of the Oxford hotters were splashed across the national newspapers. They succeeded in making the model their own, just as the Teddy Boys made off with the Edwardian-style coats designed for the young toffs of the 50s, and turned them into something their makers had not intended.

PARENTS Porsches, Dean Moriarty

Norman Foster
Dynamic monuments

Shaven-headed and softly spoken, Sir Norman Foster combines finesse with forcefulness. Spanning the world from Berlin to Hong Kong to Barcelona and London, the buildings of this leading British architect are monuments not to solid mass, stability and tradition, but to dynamism, movement and energy.

Born in Redditch in 1935, Foster grew up in Manchester, left school early to work as a clerk in the town hall, and studied architecture while moonlighting as a bouncer, baker and ice-cream man. After a scholarship to Yale (1961), he founded Team 4 Architects (1962) along with his first wife Wendy Cheeseman, who died of cancer in 1989, and Su and Richard (later Lord) Rogers. Their first building was a glass-roofed lookout in Cornwall. Team 4 disbanded in 1967, after designing the Reliance Controls factory in Swindon, one of the first workplaces to put management and production staff under the same roof. Team 4 also symbolised the transformation of British architects, from bow ties and tweed suits to black polo necks and fast cars.

Foster's career continued with a series of buildings in Britain: IBM head office (1970) and technical park (1979); Willis Faber Building, Ipswich (1975, already Grade 1 Listed); and the Sainsbury Centre for Visual Arts at the University of East Anglia (1977). He moved further afield to design the Hong Kong and Shanghai Bank (1986, the world's most expensive building), Tokyo's 170-storey Millennium Tower (1990, the world's tallest skyscraper), the telecommunications tower in Barcelona, Torre de Collserola (1992), Bilbao Metro station (1995), Chep Lap Kop Airport in Hong Kong (1998), and the rebuilt Reichstag in Berlin (1998). Back in Britain he also built Stansted Airport terminal (1991) and the award-winning American Air Force Museum in Cambridgeshire (1998). In 1998 he won the commission to reconstruct Wembley Stadium in time for the FA Cup Final in May 2002. His 'headlamp' design for the ten-storey offices of London's Lord Mayor has been heavily criticised, notably by Simon Jenkins who foresaw 'a Cycoplean eye glaring across at the City'. Other Foster projects that have come in for criticism include the Glasgow Conference Centre, the 'noisy' Cambridge Law Library and, years ago, the flat-roofed houses in Milton Keynes which eventually had to have pitched roofs planted on top. English Heritage refused to allow the 'erotic gherkin' which he designed to replace the Baltic Exchange, blown-up by the IRA in 1992. But Foster's revised design has been described as 'the most civilised skyscraper in the world'.

Although renowned as an ultra-modernist, Foster has always taken note of local traditions, from Palladian villas to Norwegian barns and Norfolk windmills. Jonathan Glancey observes that his 'genius, in later years, was to marry such traditional structures to sophisticated new materials and high technology, to create what are effectively barns of the aerospace age' (asked to nominate his favourite building for a TV series, Foster chose a

My Beautiful Laundrette (1986)

Boeing 747; he himself pilots a white Cessna Citation).

The firm of Foster and Partners (500 staff) operates from a glass-walled structure in Battersea. Sir Norman (Royal Gold Medal, 1983; knighted 1990, Royal Academy 1991, Order of Merit 1997) lives above the office in another glass box which recalls the lift he designed for the Royal Academy's Sackler Galleries. Glass is one Foster trademark, dynamism is another. Often prefabricated and then shifted on-site for assembly, his buildings are sweeping, spacious and energetic. The man himself verges on the frenetic, and his ambitions sometimes seem over-weaning. Even the German government made him rethink the Reichstag after his initial design proved too expensive. It's not only Britain that cannot always afford to fund full-on Foster and his exhilarating vision.

Foster's calculating character was crudely drawn in Philip Kerr's novel *Gridiron*, in which a cruel, cold protagonist designs a fully intelligent building. The man himself, though he lacks the networking superskills of friend and rival Lord Rogers, is much warmer than this cartoon of him, especially since his (third) marriage (1996) to psychiatrist Elena Ochoa, known as 'Dr Sex' for her former role as host of the Spanish TV programme *Let's Talk About Sex*.

PARENTS Buckminster Fuller, Mies van der Rohe, Frank Lloyd Wright, Alfred Waterhouse (architect of Manchester's neo-Gothic town hall)

Stephen Frears
Friendship under pressure

In the 60s Stephen Frears was an apprentice film-maker: he worked for veteran director Karel Reisz on *Morgan: a suitable case for treatment*, and assisted **Lindsay Anderson** on *If* (1969). Both films brought a liberal-left perspective to questions of class and social mobility in the new Britain of the period; it was in this atmosphere that Frears reached maturity.

Frears' first film was *The Burning*, a 30-minute short set in South Africa under apartheid. In 1971 he directed his first feature. Starring Albert Finney as a Liverpool bingo caller and would-be jazz musician who dreams of living a film-noir life and then finds himself involved in a real murder, *Gumshoe* combined hard-edged narrative drive with real affection for its characters and stylistic references.

Throughout the 70s and early 80s Frears worked mainly in television; not that he was impressed by the big shows of the period. He has said that *Jewel In The Crown* (mammoth series from Paul Scott's epic novels about the last days of the British Raj), *Upstairs Downstairs* (all's well in the class society) and *Brideshead Revisited* (transferring Evelyn Waugh's elitist nostalgia for a lost Britain into a popular format) together 'perpetrated an England that no longer exists while failing to illustrate British life as it is'.

Frears was far from happy with 'British life as it is'. He believed that 'Thatcher has divided the country between north and south, between employed and unemployed, between the rich and poor, between the people who've got and the people who haven't.' *My Beautiful Laundrette* (1986), the film he made from Hanif Kureishi's script, was partly a tongue-in-cheek salute to the Tories' much-vaunted enterprise culture, partly a depiction of the social conflicts that had been accelerated by Tory rule, and partly a declaration that love and friendship would succeed in crossing race, class and sexual orientation, albeit with difficulty. For its time it offered an audaciously leftfield, multi-cultural perspective.

Scripted by **Alan Bennett** from the biography of gay playwright **Joe Orton** (**Gary Oldman**) by John Lahr, *Prick Up Your Ears* (1987) tells the story of Orton's relationship with Kenneth Halliwell (Alfred Molina), the live-in lover who eventually killed him. As represented by Frears, the class-bound, sexually repressed England of the 50s and early 60s has been interpreted as 'a metaphor for Thatcher's 80s'.

With *Sammy and Rosie Get Laid* (1988), Frears tried to build on the achievements of his previous partnership with Kureishi. The film successfully shows the yearning for the past that was characteristic of Britain in the late 80s (the decade that invented the heritage industry), but is less compelling than *Laundrette*.

Both *Sammy* and *Laundrette* demonstrate what has been defined as 'hydridity' – the combination of different cultures that play distinctive but complementary roles in a person's chosen lifestyle. This was a new notion: previously it was assumed that society would tend towards cultural and racial integration (*e pluribus unum*) or violent conflict. The idea that people could pick'n'mix their differences (sharing a broad identity while emphasising particular aspects of it) has now become commonplace; but Frears was among the first to discover it.

Frears offered a 'comedy of cruelty' in *Dangerous Liaisons*. His *Grifters* (1991), from the Jim Thompson novel, proved that a Brit could do noir as darkly as any American. He switched ambience entirely for *The Snapper*, a film of Roddy Doyle's novel of sex, drink and pregnancy on the wrong side of Dublin. In *The Hi-Lo Country* (1999), a western, Frears told a traditional but intelligent story of male bonding. The tangible pleasure he takes in showing how people live, and the diversity of his output, have prompted comparisons with Hollywood greats such as Howard Hawks and John Huston.

PARENTS Karel Reisz, Lindsay Anderson

The Full Monty
Men without a man's job

The Full Monty (1997) is a comedy about the end of traditional masculinity and the human cost of de-industrialisation. Opening with newsreel footage from the 70s when Sheffield was known as the 'city of steel', the film follows five redundant steelmen and their transformation into a troupe of strippers (inspired by the Chippendales, the first high-profile group of male strippers in Britain): Gaz (**Robert Carlyle**) needs money to maintain his estranged wife and child; Dave (Mark Addy) does not realise how tubby he is; Horse (Paul Barber) can dance but he's not getting any younger; for Lomper (Steve Huison), stripping staves off suicide; Guy (Hugo Speer) has tremendous tackle. This quintet is choreographed by former steel mill foreman Gerald (Tom Wilkinson). Stripped of their traditional image (breadwinner/boozer) by the closure of the mills, their move into showbiz is as much about finding a new identity as earning a living.

The Full Monty presents an image of Britain as a battered country that's past its sell-by date, and it raises questions about the social role of working-class men following the demise of the hard-drinking, hard-working factory hand. Stripping is traditionally performed by women in order to entertain successful men. But in *The Full Monty* these roles are reversed: Gaz and friends must display themselves to women in order to earn their living and find a new form of masculinity. The movie reflects real changes (sometimes referred to as 'the feminisation of work') and the problems arising from them. But its downbeat side is outweighed by the representation of ordinary people trying, however desperately, to rise above their difficult situation. This makes *The Full Monty* a 'feelgood film', although following its huge success, some local residents felt unhappy about the spate of film-makers arriving in Sheffield in search of urban blight and cultural deprivation.

PARENTS the Chippendales, the steel strike of 1981 (defeated), *Boys from the Blackstuff*

John Galliano
The history man

A Gibraltar-born (1960) plumber's son, John Galliano was awarded a first for his degree show at St Martin's College of Art and Design (1983). Inspired by the French Revolution of 1789, the collection – Les Incroyables – was bought wholesale by Brown's, the London boutique. The following year Galliano launched his own label and, three years after that (1987), he was the first-ever winner of the British Designer of the Year award (he won it again in 1994 and 1995, and shared it with **Alexander McQueen** in 1997). In 1990 he began showing in Paris rather than London, eventually securing a sizeable order from the luxury goods corporation LVMH (Louis Vuitton Moët Hennessy).

In 1995 Galliano was the first British designer ever to be asked to head a French couture house – Givenchy. In 1996 he moved from Givenchy to Dior (both couture houses are owned by LVMH; McQueen replaced him at Givenchy), where he produces six collections a year besides his own-name range. Clients include Madonna, Tina Turner, Kylie Minogue and the Ballet Rambert.

Galliano, who dances the flamenco and looks like a pirate, is only a decade older than McQueen, but his sources and reference points are much more ancient. Whereas McQueen's work is usually ultra-modern, Galliano takes his inspiration from history. Like **Vivienne Westwood**, he rifles through the centuries picking out themes and images that can be transposed to today's context (for example, the flap-per from the 20s, the 'new look' from the 40s). The collection he unveiled in July 1999 took hunting as its theme, with pink jackets and Edwardian-style picture hats, designed by long-standing collaborator Stephen Jones and adorned with dead foxes, boars, pigeons and rabbits. In foreign eyes, Galliano is more readily recognisable as a British designer because of his associations with heritage and history.

PARENTS Vivienne Westwood, costume drama, Errol Flynn

Galton and Simpson
The midwives of sitcom

Ray Galton and Alan Simpson met in a TB sanatorium in south London during the Second World War. There was nothing much to do but sit around hoping to get better, so they decided to write material for the hospital radio. As Simpson subsequently said, 'neither of us were writers before we met'; but after four years practising they sent some sketches to the BBC and were taken on to write jokes for Derek Roy, star of the radio show *Happy Go Lucky*. After a few more years writing gags at five bob a time, Galton and Simpson started work on a new show. Based, in the traditional way, around a single comedian, it was novel in that it contained 'no jokes and no funny voices, just relying on caricature and situation humour'. The name of the show was *Hancock's Half-Hour*.

Hancock

Until then radio comedy had always included 'boom-boom gags, silly voices and a musical interlude': its origins in the world of variety and music hall were still prominent. By devising radio comedy based entirely on characterisation, Galton and Simpson brought it into the world of drama and virtually invented the dramatic genre of situation comedy. Not that the BBC let them do it all at once: the production hierarchy insisted on the continuation of the silly voice tradition by foisting a cameo appearance from Kenneth Williams on to their show. Maurice Gran, co-writer and producer of a succession of TV comedy hits from *Shine On Harvey Moon* to *Birds of A Feather*, suggests that in their early work 'narrative comedy is struggling to get out from under variety'.

The comic situation under development was that of Anthony Aloysius Hancock, resident of East Cheam and an unsuccessful social climber. The real-life Tony Hancock had already been a hit on comedy shows such as *Forces All Star Bill* and *Educating Archie*. Galton and Simpson invented a character that was a less intelligent, less sophisticated version of Hancock's own personality, so that he 'virtually played it as himself'.

Their characterisation is widely praised, but another, less widely known aspect of their work is its quasi-musical quality. As Galton says, 'one too many syllables in a line can render it unfunny'. They worked hard to make the rhythm right. In writing the script for *The Blood Donor*, for example, they spent a good quarter of an hour deciding whether a shocked Hancock should say that a pint of blood is 'nearly an armful' or 'very nearly an

armful', before opting for the latter.

Hancock's Half-Hour ran until 1959 on radio, by which time a TV version had already come out. Galton and Simpson then developed a new comedy specially for television. Starting from an idea about 'first rag and bone man' and 'second rag and bone man', they came up with the father and son team of Steptoe and Son, in which the younger man, Harold, represents the liberal-minded new Britain – ready to broaden his horizons and try new experiences – which was then emerging from underneath the old country of Empire and fuddy-duddy conservatism, symbolised by his dad, Albert. But the sting in the tail of the situation is that, although Harold always resents his father for holding him back, the real obstacle to his social advancement is his own unwillingness to leave the nest (scruffy though it may be) and strike out on his own. Thus Galton and Simpson distilled big themes arising from family life and the generation gap into 30-minute miniature dramas that have been compared to Chekhov, Pinter and others. If drama is the depiction of conflict, then, as Maurice Gran suggests, comedy in the Galton and Simpson vein is 'finding the funny side of the truth of conflict'.

With viewing figures of up to 25 million (almost half the population of Britain), *Steptoe and Son* was not just a comedy show but also a social phenomenon. It is said that the streets were empty at 8.30pm on a *Steptoe* night, and that Labour leader Harold Wilson asked the BBC to postpone the edition due to be broadcast on election night in October 1964, in case Labour supporters stayed in to watch it rather than going out to vote.

In 1978 the writing partnership of Galton and Simpson came to an end when Simpson decided first to take a year off, and then came to the realisation that he was 'horrified' by the idea of going back to it. Scriptwriting partnerships have been compared to a marriage, and after three decades of a particularly intense relationship (they say they missed the 60s because they were too busy writing), the creators of Hancock and the Steptoes were divorced.

PARENTS Anton Chekhov, Molière
CHILDREN **Johnny Speight**, Lawrence Marks and Maurice Gran

Frankie Fraser

Gangster chic
Crime does pay

In Britain, a certain breed of home-grown gangster has been strangely revered and mythologised as a 'working-class boy made good', whose brawn and brain has given him the wherewithal to escape his humble background and carve out a brighter future. Ever since **David Bailey** made the **Krays** 60s icons, the media and mainstream culture have been involved in an illicit romance with many of the more colourful figures of organised crime. The villains have responded in kind by tastefully dramatising their bloody actions to fit the audience. More recently, they have become so media-literate that they have their own PR set-ups to drum up and maximise potential publishing, TV and movie deals. Like ex-sports stars, retired gangsters, it seems, are now a sought-after cultural commodity as carnival culture returns to some areas of the media.

In the gangster icon hall of fame, close behind the Krays come the Great Train Robbers, the gang that, in 1963, stole £2.6 million – the equivalent of about £30 million at today's values – from a Royal Mail train. The members of the gang, whose heist was the subject of a movie (*Buster*, 1988), were all finally captured but Ronnie Biggs scaled the walls of a London jail and escaped in 1965 after serving only 15 months of his term. After having plastic surgery to change his appearance and hiding out in Australia, Biggs settled in Brazil, a popular haven for international fugitives because of its lack of extradition laws. Over the years he has infuriated the authorities by flaunting his freedom, appearing on television to promote his autobiography and living in an apartment with a giant British flag signed by his many visitors. In the 1970s he also had a brief flirtation with the Sex Pistols: featuring in their film *The Great Rock'n'Roll Swindle* and singing vocals on several songs, including 'No One is Innocent (a Punk Prayer by Ronnie Biggs)'.

According to the man in the street, the perception of Biggs is of someone who achieved early retirement in the sun through pure cunning 'and good luck to him too'. Each week to this day, like a far-flung wing of the heritage trail, Biggs, for £25 per curious traveller, will recount over barbecued sausages at his Rio villa the tale of his escape.

Recently the most keen self-publicist among media gangsters has been 'Mad' Frankie Fraser, a former altar boy dubbed the most dangerous man in Britain by two Home Secretaries. Now in his 70s, he has spent 42 years of his life behind bars. He admits to killing two people and has been certified insane three times. He was wooed by both the Krays and their East End rivals the Richardsons and eventually became Charles Richardson's enforcer. Frankie's nickname, 'The Dentist', came from the fact that when he could not extract money from his victims, he extracted teeth instead. Among his 15 convictions, he did seven years for slashing rival gang leader Jack 'Spot' Comer, five for leading a riot at Parkhurst Prison and ten for his part in the Richardson Torture Gang's reign of terror. Yet Fraser, who views himself as a romantic hero of the 'good old days' of gangland, talks of honour among thieves and making the East End safe for 'nice,

ordinary people'. Since writing his bestselling biography he has developed a website and has been looking for an investor to take an option on the film rights to his story.

The phenomenon reached its inevitable conclusion with the next generation: 40-year-old debt collector, extortionist and professional hard-man Dave Courtney, who was twice charged with murder, has managed nightclubs and famously provided the security for Ronnie Kray's funeral in 1995. Having been portrayed by Vinnie Jones in *Lock, Stock and Two Smoking Barrels*, his star has ascended with a bestselling autobiography and an album made with other gangster cronies (produced by Tricky) called *Products of the Environment*, not to mention a Channel 5 talkshow in the offing. He was even asked to address the Oxford Students' Union. At least he is refreshingly honest about his criminal past, 'secretly you love us because we do the unthinkable, what most people are scared of'. If gangsters are your passion, these days, you might stand a better chance of bumping into one clinching a deal in the Groucho Club in Soho than nursing his shooter in the Blind Beggar in Whitechapel.

PARENTS: Robin Hood, Bill Sykes, Cosa Nostra
CHILDREN: *Lock, Stock and Two Smoking Barrels*
READ ON: *Mad Frank And Friends* by Frankie Fraser; *Stop the Ride, I Want to Get Off* by Dave Courtney; *Odd Man Out* by Ronnie Biggs

Paul Gascoigne

Tears of a clown

In 'Gazza Agonistes', a brilliantly titled essay which recalls Milton's verse drama *Samson Agonistes*, biographer and critic Ian Hamilton sums up what Paul Gascoigne has come to represent: the flash but tacky life of the footballer (Gazza); and the painful loss of strength and ability (Agonistes). Gazza's story is not a matter of life and death: as a series of near misses and as a near-myth which reflects current expectations of British football, it is more important than that.

Born in Gateshead, Paul Gascoigne played first for his beloved Newcastle United where after three seasons and 22 goals in 126 games he acquired a reputation for courage, creativity, immaturity and Mars Bar consumption. This reputation was confirmed during his stint at Tottenham Hotspur, who paid £2 million for him and then sold him on to Lazio for £5.5 million (knocked down from £8 million after Gazza snapped an anterior cruciate ligament in an unwise challenge during the FA Cup final in 1991, and spent the next 12 months in physiotherapy). After an unsettled period in Italy (homesick for the Wednesday-night drinking session traditional among English clubs, Gazza complained that 'Italians … don't drink like we do'), he returned to Britain for a reasonably successful spell with the Scottish club Glasgow Rangers – although on arrival in 1995 he offended Catholic sentiments when pretending to play an Orangeman's flute after scoring his first goal at Ibrox Park. In 1997 he came back south of the border to Middlesbrough, under the watchful eye of manager Bryan Robson.

On and off the pitch, Gazza has captured the British imagination. TV personality Nick Hancock described him as 'a player who could take your breath away, who could dazzle and destroy, and who, best of all, gave the impression he'd wandered on to the pitch from the pub'. A famous photograph (1988) of Gascoigne and archetypal football hardman Vinnie Jones, shows Jones gripping Gazza's balls while the latter's face and posture display a mixture of pain, comedy and determination. In 1990 Gazza had his defining moment when he cried as England were knocked out of World Cup in Turin, and his crumpled face became an icon, a martyr to the national cult of heroic defeat and a symbol of what some observers described as the new emotionalism among British men. Five years later when coach Glenn Hoddle left Gazza out of the England team for the World Cup, this was seen as the culmination of a career that has repeatedly misfired, whether through injury, lack of fitness (Gazza tends to put on the lard), or through excesses off the field ('another doner and you're a goner').

Gazza has always liked a drink; and when pressure mounts he tends to like drinking even more. He missed the birth of his son while away on a 'mid-season rest and recreation break' with the Rangers team. During Euro 96 his birthday celebrations turned into the tabloids' idea of 'mayhem'. This was the time when Gazza and **Chris Evans** became known as 'the yobocracy'. His explosive relationship with girlfriend Sheryl has also made headlines: first because of his alleged violence towards her ('Black and Blue'); then because she agreed to marry him (Gazza wore a cream suit with matching hair); and finally because she divorced him and obtained a healthy financial settlement.

In his combination of clownishness (belching, wearing false boobs, telling a Norwegian camera crew to 'fuck off') and trauma, Gazza came to represent the current, confused condition of many British males. At times he has seemed so out of control that observers suggested he was suffering from a mild form of Tourette's syndrome (intermittent bulimia has also been rumoured). Maybe the real Paul Gascoigne is a traditional man who has simply failed to keep up with the times. In declaring that 'I don't like being on my own', he seemed to sum up his desire for the kind of traditional (and fast disappearing) life of the working-class male: nearly always in groups, whether at school, work or play; kids in gangs; men in a workforce; OAPs in a community. This is the collectivised way of life from which emerged the modern (late nineteenth-century) game of football. But it is not how we live now, and neither is it too fanciful to suggest that old-style gregarious Gazza (never happier than when drinking in the Dunston Excelsior working men's club with his mate Jimmy Five Bellies) has always been out of sync with the more atomised existence that society now requires us to lead – even within the world of team sports.

PARENTS Jimmy Greaves, **George Best**, the Phantom Flan-flinger

READ ON *Gazza Agonistes* by Ian Hamilton

Gilbert and George
The Eric and Ernie of the avant-garde

Gilbert (b. 1943 in the Italian Dolomites; apprentice wood carver; native tongue is the obscure Jewish language of Ladino; father a poor shoemaker) and George (b. 1942 in Plymouth, evacuated to Totnes; brought up by mother, 'a free spirit', and grandmother who were keen on 'betterment' – dressed him in shoes and white socks while other children wore boots) have been an item since they met at St Martin's School of Art in 1967 (although at some point George was married long enough to father two children).

At St Martin's, George, dressed in a dark suit and behaving 'like a doctor', acted as mentor to Gilbert, who could not speak English. Since the late 60s they have lived together in a tall, terraced house (built by Huguenots; they say their best friend is their cleaner) in Fournier Street, Spitalfields, London E1 (in the shadow of one of Nicholas Hawksmoor's churches; possibly the most cosmopolitan area in Britain – just about every ethnic group has passed through it).

Dressed (like the comedy duo of **Morecambe and Wise**) in identical suits (they say they never sweat), they eat breakfast and lunch in the same greasy spoon every day. At first the locals, especially the porters from the nearby fruit and veg market, looked at them askance; but Spitalfields market has now been replaced by an arts and crafts fair, and in any case crazy artists do not seem so crazy in today's Britain: Gilbert and George were even

Gilbert and George

included in the video compilation of British life and culture issued by the Foreign Office in 1998.

On leaving college, Gilbert and George had nowhere to show their work. They hit on the idea of *being* their work ('you just make yourself the object and then you are more complex than a piece of metal'; 'we wanted to make living sculpture like pop-star artists, just standing there with metallised faces'). While still at college they had produced a human face. Having arranged for photographs to be taken of themselves with the sculpture, it dawned on them that 'we were the sculpture'. They took the living sculpture idea to Labour Minister of Works Bob Mellish who, they claim, was masturbating under the table while he interviewed them.

Perhaps their most representative piece is *The Singing Sculpture* in which the two of them sing (the orchestral verse) and mime (the sung chorus) to Flanagan and Allen's Underneath the Arches, continuously, for a whole working day, like mechanical toys. 'We felt lost and homeless', says George, and so identified with two tramps trying to be cheerful.

In 1969 Gilbert and George experimented with face painting. Three years later **David Bowie** carried out similar experiments. Bowie and others brought

215

the idea that the artist *is* the artwork into the pop world; but it had already been developed in the art world by Gilbert and George. On the face of it they were not doing very much; but by proclaiming this as art they helped changed the course of British cultural history.

In the 70s Gilbert and George decided to 'take our art to the edge'. They issued a series of pictures based on piss, shit, tears and spunk. *Bum Hole*, claimed critic and Soho roué Daniel Farson, 'is the greatest self-portrait of the twentieth century'. In the 80s, when their work took on a monumental appearance (and *Men Behaving Badly* star Martin Clunes became their model), some people accused them of pandering to racism and fascism (immigration has long been a feature of life in the Spitalfields/Aldgate area of East London, but so too has racism; this was one of the few areas in which Britain's neo-fascists built a strong local base in the 70s and early 80s). Gilbert and George replied that they were showing things as they really are. Art critic Andrew Graham-Dixon has short-circuited the 'pseudo-debate' by saying 'I never thought there was enough content in their work to discern this [racism].'

Are they gay? In the 70s, when they 'first had money', Gilbert and George frequented early gay pubs such as the Vauxhall Tavern (within the space of a week each of them was arrested for being drunk and disorderly). But they dislike the term 'gay' on the grounds that 'it was stolen from female prostitutes in eighteenth-century London'; nor do they describe themselves as homosexual, 'a quasi-medical term from Denmark in the last century'.

Noting that the adopted personae of Gilbert and George resemble Magritte businessmen who 'have fallen out of the sky and come to life', Graham-Dixon recognises the social comedy in their work and praises their 'subtle perception of the melancholy of London' which is represented through the cultivation of their own 'pretty melancholy sensations'. Gilbert agrees that 'what we are doing [is] based on unhappiness'. Unless, of course, the rumour is true and Gilbert and George really go home at weekends to their cosy, suburban families. In which case they might not be so far removed from the punter in Barnstaple, Devon, who after seeing one of their shows, told the pair of them to 'Fuck off, you weird-looking twats.'

PARENTS Marcel Duchamp, Morecambe & Wise
CHILDREN **Jarvis Cocker**, David Bowie

Glam
'Hod carriers in bacofoil'

In the early 70s there was **progressive rock** (Colosseum, The Nice), folk (Fairport Convention, the Incredible String Band), soul (the silver sleeve of *Motown Chartbusters Vol 3* was a perfect match with bleached Levi's and Ben Sherman shirts) and teenybop (Tony Orlando and Dawn, Edison Lighthouse). And then came glam: rock without pomp; pop with rock guitar and a deliberately cheap form of glamour – as cheap and as sexy as

Gary Glitter

the lipstick and mascara that boys started to wear. Suddenly we were all tarts with a touch of art.

At the top end of the market were **David Bowie** ('leper messiah', 'the rent-boy who fell to earth') and Roxy Music ('a cabaret futura of decadent romance,' according to Michael Bracewell). Style critic and cultural commentator **Peter York** has set the record straight on the 70s by pointing out that 'no decade with Roxy in it can fairly be called the one that taste forgot'. Describing Roxy Music as 'English art school brought to life', he compares them to Noël Coward and praises their 'breathtaking cultural steals and slants', resulting in a package that was 'utterly ironic yet strangely moving'. Bowie and Roxy, says York, 'could obviously be consumed as *kultur*'.

At the other end of the marketplace there was 'low glam': performers like Sweet, Slade, Gary

Glitter and rock'n'roll revivalists Mud. These were mutton dressed as mutton and sprinkled with glitter. Brian Connolly, Sweet's lead singer, wore mascara and threatened to smack anyone who laughed at him. In Slade, formerly a **skinhead** band, lead guitarist Dave Hill camped about on stage while gravel-voiced singer Noddy Holder, his mutton-chop sideburns always threatening to close around his face and form a beard, bestrode the *Top of the Pops* studio like an outrageously butch Edwardian – to squeals of delight from not-so-naive pop fans. Gary Glitter, in his outrageous 'bacofoil outfit', was a simultaneously comic and aggressive parody of pop excess.

Pop had always been camp since the early days when the gyrating Elvis sent himself up. Ten years later Mick Jagger played coquettishly with his hair, and celibate **Mods** posed all night in front of the mirror. But glam took the game of hetero/homosexuality a few notches further, and produced an audience of 'brickies in mascara'. As Michael Bracewell has observed, 'that Bowie's glam rock could turn barrow boys into screaming queens was the greatest triumph, and irony, of its period. The trappings of transvestism, thanks to Bowie, were granted the broadest currency of street fashionability.'

For a few precious months between 1972 and 1974, barrow boys and public schoolboys converged on the common ground established by glam. Not that everyone welcomed this consensus. Radical sociologists Ian Taylor and David Wall complained that, with glam, the music industry had managed to suffocate youthful rebellion in glitter: 'The creators of the new "classless" product for consumption by a class appear to have successfully neutralised any liberating potential there might have been in the condition of youth in the 1960s.'

At the time, Bowie was widely criticised for replacing radicalism with the narcissism of the 'me' decade. In 1998, with the publication of Barney Hoskyns' *Glam* and the release of Todd Haynes' film *Velvet Goldmine*, there was a renewal of interest in the tacky splendours of the era. York went so far as to suggest that, in pop terms, glam represented the advent of the postmodernist agenda, with its emphasis on time travel, quotation, irony and consumption.

PARENTS Jean Genet, Danny La Rue
CHILDREN *Velvet Goldmine,* Heavy Metal excess
READ ON *Glam* by Barney Hoskyns; *England is Mine: pop life in Albion from Wilde to Goldie* by Michael Bracewell

Goth
A deathly lifestyle

In *Hex Files: the Goth Bible*, Mick Mercer lists more than 100 bands and 40 fanzines in the UK. Throughout the 20-plus years since Siouxsie Sioux used the word 'Goth' to describe the barbaric sound of the Banshees, and Factory boss **Tony Wilson** talked about the gothic, sonic architecture of Joy Division, Goth has been a recurring feature of British culture.

Mercer claims that Goth is 'constant … not just a transient fashion'. Adherents have always been identifiable by their combination of black leather, white make-up, dyed hair (preferably backcombed) and silver jewellery. Unlike other styles, Goth has not been fully assimilated by corporate culture, which has yet to find a way of marketing morbidity on a large scale.

Goth turns the living into the undead. It is an ostentatious reaction against the 'normal' attributes of youth. Instead of exaggerating their strength and comeliness, Goths seek to resemble death and decay. They are half-joking, of course – but this means that they are also half-serious. Goth is pantomime, but also a genuine renunciation – choosing not life but the iconography of death.

With roots in the alienated angst of punk, often combined with the dry ice and bombast of heavy metal, and topped off with some minor-chord melancholy, the first fully fledged Goth bands (Southern Death Cult, Bauhaus, Alien Sex Fiend, Sisters of Mercy, Flesh for Lulu) got going on the cusp of the 80s. Bauhaus had the first Goth single with 'Bela Lugosi's Dead' (1979), followed by The Cure's 'A Forest' and 'This Corrosion' by the Sisters of Mercy. But the initial stream of hits soon ran dry. Apart from The Cure, who are regarded by aficionados as Goth-lite, today's Goth bands rarely venture into the bright light of the pop charts. Seclusion is an essential part of the Goth style.

The combination of humour, seclusion and alienation is traceable all the way back to the birth of British Goth, traditionally linked to the publication of Horace Walpole's 'supernatural romance', *The*

Goodness Gracious Me
Anglicised Asians

Following a successful radio series, *Goodness Gracious Me* transferred to BBC2 and appeared on TV for the first time in 1998. Produced by Anil Gupta, it is a sketch-based comedy series written by and starring young British Asians. Much of the comedy relates to the generation gap as experienced by Asians in Britain, exploring the differences in attitude between Indian and Pakistani immigrants and their British-born children (Brasians).

Some of the most effective comedy characters in *Goodness Gracious Me* are based on Asians trying too hard to be British: Dennis and Charlotte Kapoor (pronounced Cooper) who cannot wait to get out of the multicultural inner-city to their heart-of-England home in Chigwell, Essex; and Check Please Bloke, the small-time businessman and would-be seducer whose role model is club owner Peter Stringfellow. Others are derived from British gullibility about the East: Guru Maharishi Yogi, whose divine words of wisdom are nicked from Dr Seuss books. But probably the best characters in the show are the Bhangramuffins (catchphrase: 'Kiss my chuddies'), the London-born Asian youth who want to be black boyz in the hood. Laughable, yes – but that's how Apache Indian started out.
PARENTS Faroukh Dhondy, Hanif Kureishi, Johnny Speight's *Curry and Chips*

Castle of Otranto (1764). During the eighteenth-century Age of Enlightenment, Gothic novels served as a kind of pornography of the intellect, deliberately dishonouring the faith in rationality and perfectibility that was characteristic of the period. Two and a half centuries later, today's Goth style expresses a similar distrust of human life – but now that lack of faith is the new orthodoxy, it no longer carries the same frisson.

Besides setting his novel in a fictional castle, Walpole built his own pseudo-fortress at Strawberry Hill near Twickenham (the premises are now part of St Mary's College). But the 'castle' was a fraud, made partly of papier mâché. Although the dignified atmosphere of Walpole's structure seems far removed from the noise of a Goth gig, they both delight in the dramatisation of the deathly.

PARENTS Gothic tradition, glam, punk, teen angst
READ ON *The Castle of Otranto* by Horace Walpole; *The Monk* by Matthew Lewis; *Hex Files – the Goth Bible* by Mick Mercer

Peter Greenaway
Painting on celluloid

'Contemporary cinema is extremely boring, moribund, dead … I'm very pessimistic now about cinema. There are no interesting film-makers any more. They have all gone to the new media.' So said Peter Greenaway (35 years a film-maker, 49 films and videos to his credit) at the opening of a retrospective exhibition of his paintings in Edinburgh. His work has consistently crossed over between film and painting (the film *Drowning By Numbers* had a pre-existence as a set of collages, *The Falls*, and an after-life as a book, *The Fear of Drowning*). Now Greenaway is expanding his range still further: his current project involves four feature films, a 16-part TV series, a clutch of CDs and a website.

Born in 1942, Greenaway attended Walthamstow College of Art (alongside **Ian Dury**), where he was told that his paintings were too literary. Accordingly, he moved towards cinema as an art form which would incorporate text (but not necessarily narrative) as well as images. After graduating he got a job as a doorkeeper at the British Film Institute, rising to 'third assistant editor on trial' before being taken on by the Central Office of Information (civil service). Greenaway spent 11 years as an editor at the Crown Film Unit (the home of British documentary).

In his early films Greenaway plays with genres: *Intervals* (1969) is more-than-a-tourist film about Venice; *House* is more-than-a-home movie depicting his wife and daughter messing about in a country house; *Vertical Features* (1978) is a spoof documentary.

In David Pascoe's *Museums and Moving Images*, Greenaway is quoted as saying that, 'I started my career as a painter and painting is still for me the supreme visual means of communication,' adding, 'cinema is a grossly conservative medium.' Perhaps Greenaway has tried to enliven cinema by making it more painterly. Pascoe holds that there is a clear line of descent between various painters and particular Greenaway films: *A Walk Through H*, he says, was influenced by Greenaway's own canvases; *The Draughtsman's Contract* (1982) shows the influence of Georges de La Tour; *A Zed and Two Noughts* looks something like Vermeer; *The Belly of An Architect* evokes Piero della Francesca; *Drowning by Numbers* connotes the pre-Raphaelites, *The Cook, The Thief, His Wife and Her Lover* corresponds with Frans Hals and Dutch still life; and *Prospero's Books* harks back to Titian, Giorgione and Botticelli.

But Greenaway is also interested in text: the proximity of fact and fiction, reality and artificiality. Textuality and sexuality are repeatedly brought together in his films. 'Perhaps it is a commendable ambition,' he says, 'to try to bring these two stimulations together, so close together in fact that they can be considered, at least for a time – perhaps for the length of a film – as inseparable.' His frequent concern with the flesh and its mortality is always emotionally cool, analytical and, some say, misanthropic.

Greenaway's films have their rarefied aspects: they are also visceral; often controversially so. *The Baby of Macon*, the story of a child-murderess who is condemned to be raped to death by the militia, was widely censured. *The Cook, The Thief, His Wife and Her Lover* (1989, towards the end of Margaret Thatcher's long period in office) was intended as 'a passionate, angry dissertation … on the rich, vulgarian Philistine anti-intellectual stance of the present cultural institutions in Great Britain'.

Greenaway's presentation at Cannes in 1999, the sado-masochistic study of sexual fantasies *Eight and a Half Women* prompted walk-outs and strong criticism.

Often backed by minimalist music from Michael Nyman, the films of Peter Greenaway are the work of an encyclopedic British eccentric with a continental taste for the beauty of ideas.

PARENTS Vermeer, pre-Raphaelites, Fellini, RB Kitaj
READ ON *Museums and Moving Images* by David Pascoe

Germaine Greer
Feminist seer

Born in Melbourne, Australia in 1939, Germaine Greer is one of a group of antipodeans (others include Clive James, Barry Humphries and Richard Neville) who came to Britain because they felt constrained by life in the ex-colony. But Greer found that the 'spittoon theory of womanhood' (women as vessels for men to empty their fluids into) was a national institution in Britain too. Nearly 40 years on, she is still trying to realise the maxim that 'women should do what they want, and want what they do'.

Denied affection by her distant father (see her memoirs *Daddy, We Hardly Knew You*), and alienated from the Aussie cult of sport, as a child Greer 'used to ride my bike to Port Melbourne and watch ships sailing away to Europe'. At 25 she got away, after a couple of years with The Push, Sydney's anarcho-libertarian commune. Arriving in Cambridge, Greer busied herself with her PhD (on Shakespearean comedy; during her career she has published more books on literature than on sexual politics). Her doctorate was awarded in 1968, and Dr Greer soon found a job as an English lecturer at the newly established University of Warwick. By this time she was also co-hosting Granada TV's *Nice Time* with Kenny Everett, and writing for Richard Neville's *Oz* (she edited a special edition, *Female Energy*). Eventually she set up her own underground sex magazine, *Suck* ('a counterpoint to *Screw*'), for which she posed nude.

Greer's career was made by her first book, *The Female Eunuch* (1970, reprinted 15 times in Britain during the 70s alone). Described by the *New York Times* as 'the best feminist book so far', it is still Greer's most influential publication. Part literary criticism, part history, part social observation, *The Female Eunuch* is a full-frontal attack on our repressive society and the medico-male mentality that assigns women to passive and menial roles. On the basis that 'wedlock is deadlock', Greer preached 'female sexuality as something that has its own agenda'.

Looking back at the early 70s, Greer describes her writing as 'an attempt to put the juice into the idea of women … not as an unsex that an actual sex locks into, but as a sex of their own'. In an introduction to the 21st-anniversary edition of *The Female Eunuch*, she wrote that, '20 years ago it was important to stress the right to sexual experimentation and far less important to underline a woman's right to reject male advances; now it is even more important to stress the right to penetration by the male member.'

Greer always insisted she would never write a follow-up to *The Female Eunuch*, but in the mid-90s she accepted a £500,000 advance to do just that. Published in 1999, *The Whole Woman* sticks to the once-innovative format of its illustrious predecessor (in the use of boxed quotes, for instance). But its conclusions are more pessimistic. Convinced that there has been no sexual liberation and that the position of women (either on their backs or with their feet in the doctor's stirrups) has not really changed ('the sexual liberation of the 60s which some people think was my fault, never really happened. What happened was that it became okay to market virtual sex, and the tide of virtual sex has overrun the world'), Greer now reckons that no sex is worse than bad sex and recommends that the two sexes should lead separate lives. ('Separation is better than humiliation,' she claims. 'Equality is a blind alley which renders women into imitations of men.') Once a swinger, she herself lives a solitary life nowadays.

Reviewing the original edition of *The Female Eunuch* in the *Observer*, Kenneth Tynan (the critic who helped launch previous generations of radicals such as the **Angry Young Men**) noted that Greer had 'converted me (in theory) to Women's Lib, as much by her bawdy sense of humour as by the bite of her polemic'. But from the TV documentary that followed her first lecture tour of America in 1971, to her recent appearances on BBC2's *The Late Review*, Greer has always been a polemicist, relishing the cut and thrust of debate and tackling opponents with aplomb. Not long ago she referred to the 'bird's-nest hair' and 'fuck-me shoes' of columnist Suzanne Moore. But her greatest polemical outing was the televised debate with misogynist US author Norman Mailer, described by Camille Paglia as 'one of the great moments in the history of women'. American author and editor Bill Buford remembers that Greer was 'sexy and obviously the most intelligent person at the table'. Other targets of her sharp tongue have included Mother Theresa, Tom Hanks ('a face like a King Edward potato') and the 'lifestyle feminism' of post-feminism.

Greer pulls no punches, but she's taken plenty of blows too. In the 70s she was reviled as a commie degenerate. The current received wisdom is that she used to be right-on and sexy (bra-less low-cut tops, no knickers and frizzed-out hair halfway between the Biba look and Angela Davis), but that nowadays she is slightly dotty. This impression was confirmed in *The Whole Woman* when Greer, who lives in a spacious country house, suggested that taking up residence on a park bench as 'an apple-cheeked bag lady', might be better than staying home and doing housework ('the only way to escape this tyranny is to abandon the house').

The loves of her life (**Martin Amis**, Julian Barnes, Warren Beatty) featured prominently in *Germaine Greer: Untamed Shrew* (1999). Biographer Christine Wallace seems to disapprove of her subject's chosen role as sexual 'predator'. Greer, observes Wallace, 'pursued male partners with a gusto unparalleled among her contemporaries … she seemed almost bent on a deliberate assault of her reproductive organs'. In fact Greer was assaulting the myth that women could not/should not enjoy sex in the same way that men do, as informed consumers. Some 30 years later the same theme was still being explored in the American-made TV series *Sex and the City*.

Greer and feminism are no longer synonymous. In a radio interview in 1999 she was asked whether her career since *The Female Eunuch* could be described as a kind of gradual role-reversal in which she has now come to attack the things she once set out to champion. Greer may have riled her sisters on many occasions (refusing to criticise the Third World practice of clitorectomy, for instance), but at a conference in Wolverhampton in 1998 (Coming Down Fast: reconsidering the radicalism of 1968), she praised American feminist pioneers such as Shulamith Firestone, renewed her polemic against the male-dominated medical profession, and mentioned only in passing that some academic feminism might have been self-defeating.

In 1999 *The Whole Woman* was serialised in the *Daily Telegraph*, aka the 'Torygraph'. This does not mean that Greer has become a conservative, but that even conservatives must now pay attention to the agenda she has helped to set. Britain has moved a long way since the early 70s when Greer and her monstrous regiment of women were denounced as dungaree-clad bra-burners who could not get a man.

PARENTS Mary Wollstonecraft, Mary Shelley

CHILDREN *Spare Rib*, *Cosmopolitan*
READ ON *The Female Eunuch* and *The Whole Woman* by Germaine Greer

The Haçienda
Britain's first superclub

Labelled 'the world's most famous nightclub' by *Time* magazine, the Haçienda was established in 1981 by **Tony Wilson** and his partners, the members of **New Order** (drummer Stephen Morris recalls having 'to pay to get in on the first night'). At a time when 'club' usually meant working men's, a low dive, or a room above a pub hired for one night a week, the Haçienda, aka Fac 51 (the 51st product made by Factory Records), was an upmarket, high-ceilinged ex-yachting warehouse (on Whitworth Street to the south of Manchester's city centre), open every night complete with balcony, downstairs bar and food bar. In the *NME* Wilson advertised free membership for the first 100 applicants, but the crowds stayed away in droves. In the first two years the Haçienda cost its owners £400,000; but, says Wilson, 'it looked good'. Local comedian Bernard Manning (his own Embassy Club is half a mile up the road) did not agree. 'I've played some right dumps in my time,' he quipped on opening night, 'but this is really something.'

Manning's professional life has been spent in overheated rooms decked out in red velour. He was hardly likely to appreciate the cold, functionalist, deliberately 'industrial' decor of the early Haçienda: painted airforce grey with occasional black and yellow hazard stripes; minimal furnishings – the look was an extension of the futurist, machine-loving sleeve designs produced for the Factory label by Peter Saville, who was himself influenced by 1920s typographer Jan Tschichold. Nor would Manning have approved of its left-wing ambience (the club's name was nicked from the Situationists). It remained half-empty and uncomfortably spartan until DJ Mike Pickering started his house nights, Bez and Co put the E in housE to make acid house, and suddenly the huge barn of a place was a swaying, grooving cathedral of sound. This was the moment when the Haçienda's double life came into focus as a single entity: on the one hand a dance club, on the other hand a live music venue hosting top local bands (The Smiths, James, New Order, **Happy Mondays**) and a venue on the international circuit (much-vaunted New York outfit Defunkt made their British debut there, so did Madonna). The Haçienda helped blur the line between studio-based dance and live-orientated listening-music.

The publicity surrounding **Madchester** brought a new type of tourist-clubber. People would fly in from Europe and the USA just to experience 'the Hac'. There was a downside too. In 1989 Claire Leighton became Britain's first E-casualty after a night at the Haçienda. In the territorial disputes between Manchester's drugs gangs, the Haçienda was highly desirable turf. In May 1990 the police closed the club for six months so that Wilson could sort out the drugs problems. A year later he closed it himself for six weeks following a firearms incident.

In the mid-90s there were financial difficulties. Peter Hook (bass player in New Order) remembers the kudos of being waved in by bouncers but reckons that the Hac was costing its owners £10,000 a week for the privilege. Stephen Morris recalls that they started staying away from their own club because every time they went 'you'd see something that needed doing'. Then the violence made a comeback: in 1997 a magistrate and police officers witnessed a clubber being attacked. After years walking a tightrope between pressures applied by criminals and restrictions enforced by police, Wilson decided to quit. The premises were sold to GM Morris Construction for £1.2 million. In 1998 the Haçienda closed for the last time, and the site was due to be levelled prior to the construction of new offices. 'I've hundreds of memories,' said Wilson, 'but it needed blowing up.' In a postscript with echoes of Wilson's Situationist background, in June 1999 the Okasional Cafe staged a party in the disused club before being expelled by the police.

The Haçienda is no more, but its influence is still strong (this is the place where **Alan McGee** first experienced acid house). In size and quality it set new standards for British clubs; and it did a lot to make 'clubbing' a popular and credible activity in its own right.

PARENTS the Twisted Wheel, the Marquee
CHILDREN the Ministry of Sound, Cream

Katharine Hamnett
Cross dresser

In 1984 Katharine Hamnett turned up to meet Margaret Thatcher in a T-shirt that said '58 per cent don't want Pershing' – a reference to Cruise missiles. Throughout the 80s her 'choose life' T-shirt slogans were the last word in left/Green protest chic: 'education not missiles'; 'stop acid rain'; 'clean up or die'; 'preserve the rainforest'; and 'passports for pets'. Some 15 years later, Hamnett issued a new line: 'no to the euro' and 'no to EMU'. After many years as a Labour Party member (in 1997 she said she could not vote for the Tories 'because I hate them'), in 1999 she crossed over to the Conservatives on account of New Labour's stance on Europe and the 'puke-making' Millennium Dome.

Hamnett (b. 1948) is a diplomat's daughter (her father committed suicide in 1976) who went to 11 schools including Cheltenham Ladies' College. After St Martin's School of Art and Design, she established a fashion business (Tuttabankem, 1969) in partnership with Anne Buck, setting up on her own a decade later. Apart from environmentally friendly fashion, Hamnett is known for combining parachute and padded silk with soft, tailored cotton, distressed denim and leather jackets. Despite occasional failures, like frock coats for men and condom pockets on boxer shorts, she was the darling of British fashion (Designer of the Year 1984) in the 80s. But at the end of the decade she slammed the British Fashion Council and shifted her business to Paris, then Milan. In 1995 she returned to Britain with a head-turning show at the Natural History Museum. Her collections have not been seen on the catwalks since 1997, however. With shops in Hong Kong, Japan and Taiwan as well as a flagship store in Sloane Street, Hamnett heads a fashion business with a turnover of £100 million; but most of this is derived from accessories and diffusion ranges, while her main-line collections are no longer seen as so important.

Hamnett is not a vegetarian, nor a Buddhist, although she has associated herself with both. She is widely known for her contrariness, and often plays up to it. Interviewed by Judy Rumbold for the *Sunday Telegraph*, Hamnett suggested she should be photographed standing on a concrete floor wearing sunglasses with diamante frames. 'Is that contradictory enough for you?', she quipped.

Her quirkiness masks a deep conviction that can even account for her recent change in political allegiance. Hamnett is totally serious about conservation: she gives a percentage of her profits to the Pesticides Trust, tries to reduce packaging in her shops, promotes natural materials and environmentally friendly fibres, such as Tencel, and avoids plastic (PVC is banned from her stores). But none of these policies are inimical to the Conservative Party and its historical tradition. Conservationism, as the term itself suggests, originated as a conservative doctrine. In the 80s, when the Tories briefly became modernisers, it found a home on the left. In the 90s Hamnett has simply gone back to her upper-class roots, bringing upper-class conservationism back with her into the Conservative fold.

226

PARENTS Winston Churchill, the National Trust, Caroline Coon, Coco Chanel
CHILDREN Stella McCartney

Happy Mondays
Happy go lucky

'We were all no-hopers with a bit of hope,' says Bez (Mark Berry), the dancer and occasional percussionist with the Happy Mondays. A gang of five mates from the dead-end estate of Little Holton in Salford, when they started (1981) the Mondays were 'clueless … no money, no songs, nothing'. But 'it was better than sitting on your arse all day,' recalls singer and frontman Shaun Ryder, a dyslexic who told his careers officer he wanted to be a journalist and then a porn star in Germany. Formed in the midst of recession, with no jobs to go to, the Mondays hit upon a version of enterprise culture (selling drugs not shares, making music not merchandising) that Thatcher and Co had not bargained for. For Bez, jerking frantically around the stage was also a way of kicking against the pricks: 'We all had the same desperate thoughts, desperate lives, same expectations – no one was going to get a job. Our band was that feeling of telling everyone to fuck off. I was doing a war dance, my fuck off to society, I'm a mental mad fuck, and what are you going to do about it? An act of desperation but also saying you're not going to control me.'

It was six years before Factory Records released

Shaun Ryder

their first album. By this time the Mondays were the vanguard of a youth-cult revolution. 'While I was giving staff speeches,' recalls Factory boss **Tony Wilson**, 'there was another youth revolution round the corner. One of our own groups is hanging out in our club selling small tablets and one of them is on stage waving his hands in the air – it's already happening.'

Produced by John Cale, Squirrel and G-Man *Twenty-Four Hour Party People Plastic Face Carnt Smile (White Out)* (1987) was hailed in the *NME* by Manchester music guru Dave Haslam as 'a bagful of honest, crazy energy'. As a debut album Haslam said it was as significant as Television's *Marquee Moon* (1977), which turned out to be almost an underestimation. With Martin Hannett at the controls, the Mondays went on to make *Bummed* (1988). James Brown, future founding editor of *Loaded*, then a cub reporter on the *NME*, observed 'the energy of acid and the awkward aggression of good, independent rock', and likened the Mondays to Dennis Hopper, Charles Bukowski and Johnny Rotten. For *Pills, Thrills and Bellyaches* (1990) they travelled to Los Angeles with producer and influential DJ Paul Oakenfold. The result was dancier, groovier but also good-quality pop. The *NME* described it as 'pan-cultural in a Tesco's shoplifted kind of way'. The location for *Yes, Please* (1992, produced by ex-Talking Heads Tina Weymouth and Chris Frantz) was the Bahamas, but by this time the Mondays were in a drug-addled, rock'n'roll world of their own. Ryder recalls 'rocks for breakfast, rocks for lunch, rocks for tea'. Tony Wilson thought about flying out there to sort out the mess, but didn't. Instead Factory ended up footing the bill for possibly the most expensive **indie** record ever made, described by the *NME* as 'a stream of nauseousness emission. It's horrible, but fascinating, of course.' The band broke up soon afterwards, only to reform six years (to the very day) later.

Looking back at the Mondays' first incarnation, Bez declared: 'I can't remember any of it.' Shaun Ryder's recollection was also incomplete: 'Throughout all the Mondays' big moments I was heavily sedated by smack.' He did remember that, 'I was right into sex, drugs and rock'n'roll but for me the rock'n'roll always came last.' The pecking order in which music came a low third actually made for some great music: heavily influenced by black records, the Happy Mondays were nonchalant white trash whose very name was a rejection of the working week, the sober, Protestant ethic and the seriousness of art. You would not have wanted them to be serious musicians and, according to Ryder, it was only at the end when the drugs got out of hand that the Mondays' self-importance got out of proportion too. Before that they were happy to take bits of other people's songs (recalling Nick

Lowe's adage that pop music is the art of knowing what to steal), strap them on to some original ditties ('I might be a honky but I'm hung like a donkey': it has been said that Ryder did for pop lyrics what Quentin Tarantino did for movie dialogue), and come up with a result that was fun to make, great to listen to and, as it happens, music of great originality. Their combination of indie and groovy was much commented on, but Shaun Ryder maintained there was nothing to it: 'We just wanted to make naughty, funky, sexy, pop music. With good beats.'

The professional career of the original Mondays lasted about as long as the shelf-life of the word '**underclass**'. From the second half of the 80s through to the early 90s, this term was used to describe the section of the working class that had allegedly fallen off the bottom of the social ladder and into a twilight world of **dole**, drugs and devil dogs. Sociologists and some politicians used it to suggest that a significant section of the population was too far gone to live by the rules. Parodying the exaggerated image of the underclass, the Happy Mondays came on like ignoramuses, while letting it be known that they knew the rules but were too smart to live by them. They made their reputation by representing 'sex, drugs and trouble' at a time when the New Right seemed to want to ban all three.

While Bez ran wild and free, Shaun Ryder was always the sharp one (although if his published interviews are anything to go by he seems to have been permanently on the brink of nodding off). Born in 1962, as a youth he was sexually precocious:

'When we were growing up a lot of their old men was in prison, so when we were 16 or 17 we got passed on through all these older ladies. We got well fucking beaten into shape. That's why me ears stick out.' He spent his early twenties 'Jimmy Corkhilling around' before heading off to Amsterdam in 1986 where 'I grew me hair and had me first E.' Asked if E changed his life spiritually, he quipped 'No, financially.' Bez describes him as 'a proper psycho bastard'. After years on smack, he took a cure. He used to own a 357 Magnum but doesn't any more. When asked to sum himself up he said 'Shaun William Ryder: he still smokes Embassy filter.' He could have said: 'Shaun William Ryder, still having fun playing the bad prole boy.'

The only time the Mondays' prole image rebounded on them was after they used some apparently homophobic language in an interview with right-on rock writer and sometime performance poet Steven 'Seething' Wells. A few years later Tony Wilson said he regretted not having immediately taken out a full-page advert showing Shaun kissing a bloke, but he understood that the Mondays were working-class boys who used street language without necessarily being anti-gay. The rest of the music press was not so understanding; and by the time the bad odour around the Mondays had started to clear, they were already in the process of breaking up. The reformed Mondays were welcomed back into the right-on fold when they appeared in the Comic Relief Debt Wish Show in June 1999 (Ryder: 'Well, I'm all for wiping debts out, man … I need help myself: wipe my debt out!')

Ryder interviewed by **Jools Holland** on the latter's

TV show was a vignette which summed up the cross-class appeal of the Mondays. There was Jools, simultaneously earnest, ironic and slightly anxious, alongside Ryder – relaxed, self-deprecating but apparently self-sufficient. Maybe at the time Ryder was inside the impenetrable wall heroin builds around you, but at that moment it was clear how much middle-class Holland was dependent, addicted even, to the rough stuff that Ryder represents (in fact, this kind of relationship has always worked both ways: the likes of Ryder really would have been small-time 'crims' without the middle-class media hanging on their every word). If the term 'underclass' was the demonisation of council estate constituents, in the Happy Mondays they were canonised as the real thing – or as near as you can get to it without being black.

After the band split in 1992, Shaun Ryder, besides writing a column for the tit-obsessed *Sport*, fronted Black Grape (Bez joined but did not stay long), while bass player Paul Ryder (Shaun's brother and a **Northern Soul** lover) was committed to mental hospital. When the Happy Mondays eventually reformed in 1999 (minus keyboard player Paul Davis and guitarist Mark Day, colloquially known as 'knobhead' and 'cowhead'), Bez (author of the autobiographical *Freaky Dancer*), was wary in case they turned themselves into 'a cabaret band'. But the money was too good to turn down.

PARENTS Sham 69, the **Krays**, Average White Band

David Hare

Running into the centre

Born in 1947, when David Hare came to the British stage he was one of a batch of controversial, left-wing playwrights which also included Edward Bond (now a recluse) and Howard Brenton. By the mid-90s Hare had become a highly respected, if somewhat staid, figure. His reputation was refreshed by his adaptation of Arthur Schnitzler's turn-of-the-century sexual merry go round, which in his hands became *The Blue Room* starring Hollywood siren Nicole Kidman.

Boyhood in Bexhill-on-Sea was a period of 'hypnotic torpor'. At Cambridge he was taught by Marxist cultural historian Raymond Williams and collaborated with the young Christopher Hampton on plays written in the Anglo-Absurdist style of NF Simpson. After Cambridge he founded the Portable Theatre Company and subsequently co-founded the more influential Joint Stock Theatre Company (1974). He says he started writing only when a play that had been commissioned for the Portable Theatre Company failed to arrive.

Slag, Hare's first play at the radical Royal Court (where Hampton was literary manager), was staged in 1970: it is a Genet-style comedy featuring three women sounding off about feminist issues. *The Great Exhibition* (1972) is a parody of a typical Royal Court play (working-class Labour MP feels alienated from public and private life). *Knuckle* (1974) is a Chandleresque thriller transposed to Surrey and an indictment of the unacceptable face

of capitalism. In *Teeth'n'Smiles* (1975), a working-class rock'n'roll band plays a Cambridge May Ball and exposes the cracks in the post-war consensus. In 1978 the National Theatre premiered *Plenty*, the first of nine Hare dramas (more than any other living playwright) to be staged there. With *Plenty*, Hare began writing stage plays thematically connected to his other television drama and film projects. *Plenty* is part of a couplet with *Licking Hitler* (1978): both dramas deal with Britain's victory in war, only to be defeated by the doubts and dilemmas of peacetime.

Hare's first full feature film, *Wetherby*, came out in 1985. After *Pravda* (1985), a successful satire on the press co-written with Howard Brenton and featuring a South African press baron who resembles Rupert Murdoch, Hare embarked upon a trilogy of plays that examine traditional British institutions: *Racing Demon* looked at the Church of England; *Murmuring Judges* dealt with the legal profession; and *Absence of War* focused on the failure of the Labour Party.

In the run-up to the general election of 1992, Hare had been granted access to the entourage of Labour leader Neil Kinnock, who was tipped to win but failed to do so on the day. Hare's play, the protagonist of which is a Labour leader not entirely unlike Kinnock, was a cause of displeasure in Labour circles; and he believes that the knighthood offered him in 1998 was partly 'about people in the Labour Party wanting to apologise for their attacks on the play's accuracy and integrity'. He accepted, even though only three years earlier he had attacked 'sycophancy in return for a shower of knighthoods'. At one point he also rejected New Labour leader **Tony Blair** as 'all things to all men', while holding a fairly high opinion of (then) Conservative prime minister John Major: 'for the first time since I became an adult,' he said of Major, 'I am ruled by a man who appears fundamentally decent and honest.'

Hare was never busier than during the last years of the 90s. He adapted Arthur Schnitzler's *La Ronde*, wrote a drama about Oscar Wilde, *Judas Kiss*, which played at the Almeida, Islington, where his production of George Bernard Shaw's *Heartbreak House* was also staged. And in 1998 he staged and starred in *Via Dolorosa*, a 90-minute monologue about his own trip to Israel. Once an outsider on the fringes of British theatre, Hare is now one of its most admired dramatists.

PARENTS George Bernard Shaw, Richard Cobbett

Tony Harrison
The worker poet

When tipped for the post of poet laureate following the death of **Ted Hughes**, Tony Harrison wrote a poem, 'Laureate's Block', in which he, a lifelong republican, not only refused the job but rubbished it too ('no, it'll be a toadie'). From his first book of poems (*The Loiners*, 1970), through his verse drama (adaptations of *Aeschylus* for the National Theatre), opera and television work, through to his

first feature film as writer/director (*Prometheus*, 1999), Harrison has combined formal structures and ancient myth with contemporary experience, told in a distilled version of ordinary speech. Pursuing excellence while polemicising against English cultural snobbery, he attempts to straddle the class divide and tries to put the people back in touch with a poetic tradition that back to Wordsworth and beyond.

Born (1937) in Beeston, Leeds, and brought up in a house that was full of love and affection but empty of books, Harrison was pulled out of working-class life (father worked long hours in a bakery for £9 a week) by Leeds Grammar School. There he learnt to love Latin and Greek, and to hate 'received pronunciation', which some staff members sought to impose upon him (later, he was amazed and relieved to find that Wordsworth was a northerner who rhymed 'water' with 'matter'). As a youth, Harrison taught himself to write in all the traditional poetic forms (the kind of apprenticeship WB Yeats described as 'sedentary toil in imitation of great masters'). Equally early on, he started to fill these 'high culture' forms with local speech and his own experience (hence the title of his first book, *The Loiners*, the local word for someone who comes from Leeds). This combination is his trademark. Harrison comes from a generation in which a handful of working-class boys were granted a gentleman's education in Classics at their local grammar school. Scholarship boys expected education to be challenging – almost as gruelling as going down the pit.

Harrison's work is often sensual: this is language

to be felt as well as read, heard aloud as well as seen silent on the printed page. His early poems are often sexual and sometimes reminiscent of DH Lawrence (when giving readings he relishes words like 'kumquat', making them sound really fruity). He never gave his parents a copy of his first book because he was embarrassed by the sexual references in it. (Shown *The Loiners* by a cousin, his mother told him he 'was not brought up to write mucky books': her disgust has stayed with him ever since.)

From the mid-80s Harrison's work took on a more political aspect. In 1985 he reworked the *York Mysteries* as a cycle of community plays. He also wrote 'V', an autobiographically inspired denunciation of Thatcher's Britain set in the graveyard overlooking Leeds where he found his parents' graves vandalised by football thugs. 'V' was subsequently televised by Channel 4. His verse-film *Prometheus* is a retelling of humanity's heroism in which the mythical figure of Prometheus arrives Up North.

PARENTS Aeschylus, Wordsworth,
Richard Hoggart
READ ON 'V'

Lenny Henry
The best of British

Born (1958) in Dudley, West Midlands (immigrants settled there, he once joked, because it was called

the Black Country), comedian Lenny Henry appeared in variety theatres and on TV from the age of 16. For *Tiswas*, the anarchic Saturday-morning children's show of the late 70s, he did impressions of bearded TV naturalist David Bellamy and ITN newscaster Trevor McDonald, renamed 'Trevor MacDoughnut'. Novelist and critic Mike Phillips has remarked that Henry's impression of McDonald was more interesting than the man himself, so that 'in a real sense' he 'invented' Trevor McDonald, the TV celebrity.

When the *Tiswas* team was invited to fill a late-night adult slot entitled *OTT* (*Tiswas* being ostensibly a children's show, all the naughtiness had to be disguised; whereas *OTT* 'started out with somebody's bottom and went on from there'), Henry felt that the programme ought to have some women writers. Scouting around, he visited a new club, **The Comic Strip**, where he met Dawn French, who went on to star in her own TV series with Jennifer Saunders. They began seeing each other and in 1985 they were married in St Paul's church, Covent Garden, with the reception afterwards at the Savoy Hotel. 'I don't think the Savoy had ever seen so many black people,' Henry later recalled.

In a BBC documentary, *The Best of British* (1998), French explained that when she first accompanied Henry to one of his live shows (at an RAF base in Wiltshire), she 'worried for him when I saw him feeling he needed to humiliate himself' to get laughs. Henry began to revise his act and started hanging out with the **alternative comedy** crowd.

In 1981 Henry co-starred in the BBC show *Three of a Kind*, also featuring Tracey Ullman and David

Copperfield. With writer Kim Fuller he developed characters such as Fred Dread and PC Ganja. His cast of characters was extended during the long-running *Lenny Henry Show* (BBC; first broadcast in September 1984), which featured probably his best-known comic *persona*, Theophilus P. Wildebeeste, an affectionate pastiche of testosterone-heavy soul singers such as Barry White.

Henry moved to Hollywood to make *True Identity* (1990), a comedy about a struggling black actor who whites up in order to escape the attentions of the Mafia. He disliked being just an actor (in all his TV shows he had contributed to the writing process), the film was unsuccessful and he was released from his Hollywood contract. On his return to Britain, Henry set up his own production company, Crucial Films, and worked with writer Peter Tilbury on *Chef!* (1994), the restaurant sitcom in which he starred as the explosive cook Gareth Blackstock.

Since its inception Henry has been centrally involved in Comic Relief, the annual TV appeal for children in need. Largely on account of his long-standing association with this charity, Henry has become known as a funny man of serious intent. In 1999 he was made a Companion of the British Empire. Charlotte Raven was one of the few critics to take exception to Henry's high status. She complained that there seems to be a BBC contract 'which states that Henry must appear in everything,' adding that 'you are not allowed to criticise Henry a) because he's black and b) because he married a fat woman, a move which made him immune to any claim that he is superficial'.

Described by his wife as either 'massive courage or utter stupidity', in 1997 Henry agreed to be left to fend for himself in the Amazon jungle for a few days. In *Lenny's Big Amazon Adventure*, the programme that resulted from this escapade, he seemed uncannily close to the man he used to take off on *Tiswas* – David Bellamy.

After reported marital problems in 1999, Henry cancelled stage shows, checked into the Priory Clinic and pulled out of a planned voyage across the Atlantic with yachtsman Tony Bullimore. In July Lenny and Dawn stayed in the official Hillsborough residence of Mo Mowlam, secretary of state for Northern Ireland, in a high-profile demonstration that they are 'still a double act'. In 1999 Henry also starred as a travel agent/wannabe singer in the one-off comedy drama *The Man*, and as the headmaster in the BBC school drama series *Hope and Glory*.

PARENTS Mike Yarwood, Dawn French, Trevor McDonald

David Hockney
Bradford blonde in America

David Hockney is the Bradford-born gay painter who found his metier in Los Angeles.

Born in 1937, Hockney's parents were radical methodists who lived in a terraced house. In 1948, by which time he already knew he wanted to be an artist, young David won a scholarship to the local grammar school. In 1952 he came second in a drawing competition run by the *Eagle* comic for boys – first prize went to future cartoonist and collaborator with Pink Floyd, Gerald Scarfe. The following year Hockney enrolled at the Bradford School of Art, where he modelled himself on the reclusive English figurative painter Stanley Spencer. A conscientious objector who refused to do national service, Hockney became a student at the Royal College of Art in London where he hated history of art and turned his hand to both abstract and figurative paintings. He is said to have failed his Diploma, but the college registrar is alleged to have altered his marks.

Materials were expensive and Hockney was poor. When he ran out of paint he learnt to make etchings. In the summer of 1960 he sold some designs to Crown Wallpapers and lived in a garden shed. Around the same time he did what was probably his first important painting: derived from a photograph of pop star Cliff Richard, *Dolly Boy*, according to biographer Peter Webb, is both an object of love and a symbol of sexual repression. Produced soon afterwards, *The Most Beautiful Boy in the World* was bought by Lord Gowrie (future chairman of the Arts Council) for the junior common room at Balliol (Oxford), where the college hearties threw tea at it.

While exhibiting in the Young Contemporaries exhibition of 1961, Hockney met art dealer John Kamsin who volunteered to act as his agent, guaranteeing him an income of £600 a year. In the summer of 1961 Hockney produced a mural for the SS *Canberra* and made his way to New York. He

also dyed his hair blond, having seen the slogan for Clairol: 'blondes have more fun'. By December 1963 and the opening of his first show at Kamsin's gallery, Hockney's student days were already receding. He was hailed as 'irresistibly fresh-faced' and the *Observer* labelled him 'top of the hips'. By 1965 Hockney had made it into *David Bailey's Pin-Ups*, the collection of black-and-white photographic portraits that catalogued the new Britain of the 60s. Camp, decorative and inventive, he fitted in well with the British pop scene – except that he was already on the point of emigrating to the USA.

Hockney had been 'utterly thrilled' by New York; but when he visited California, where the boys looked like models for *Physique Pictorial* magazine, he decided that 'Los Angeles could have its Piranesi', and he would be it. 'Chameleon-like, he has become a Californian,' said poet and critic Edward Lucie-Smith. In 1968 Hockney returned to Britain to live in Powis Square, Notting Hill, with his favourite model and partner Peter Schlesinger, who enrolled at the Slade School of Art. But the relationship with Schlesinger ended painfully, as documented in the film *A Bigger Splash* (1976; directed by Jack Hazan, cinematography by Chris Menges). Hockney returned to California, 'married to his work'.

If his 60s output had a pop feel to it, the 'pool paintings' were Hockney's trademark work of the 70s. As depicted in this series, the combination of American luxury, hot sun and cool boys made for some kind of gay idyll. But, as one commentator put it, 'Hockney's idyllic vision of carefree life in LA is unashamedly that of a foreigner.' In the LA gay ghetto Hockney is always an English northerner, and in Bradford Hockney is an Americanised queer artist. Perhaps his restless creativity is partly dependent on not quite fitting into either environment.

Stage design (Royal Court, Glyndebourne), drawings, collages, photographs and photocopies have all figured in Hockney's extensive œuvre. For a time he seemed to enjoy fiddling with technology more than painting. But in 1998, while in London for his first commercial showing in the British capital for 15 years, he declared 'the idea that painting is dead, I now see as an absolutely ridiculous notion'.

Throughout his creative life Hockney has walked a tightrope between tradition and innovation. In the 70s, along with RB Kitaj, he called for a return to figurative art and polemicised against the 'joylessness' of the abstract, while at the same time experimenting with a new type of acrylic paint that was originally designed for film animation. Combining love for traditional forms with an air of up-to-date sophistication, Hockney has been tagged 'the Cole Porter of modern art'.

Hockney has always held radical views. A one-time CND member who marched against the Vietnam War, in the 80s he spoke out against Clause 28 (Thatcherite anti-gay legislation) and 'nanny Britain'. He continues to smoke cigarettes but does 30 minutes a day on a treadmill in an effort to keep fit.

PARENTS Jean Dubuffet, *Espresso Bongo*, beefcake magazines
CHILDREN Derek Jarman, Jarvis Cocker
READ ON *A Portrait of David Hockney* by Peter Webb

Jools Holland
Singin' the blues

His passport simply says 'musician' but Jools Holland is more widely known as a TV presenter. In the 80s he co-hosted Channel 4's Friday teatime pop show *The Tube* (shot almost-live in Newcastle with co-host Paula Yates), before finally turning up on BBC2 where he has presented more than a dozen seasons of his own show, *Later With Jools Holland*. In the autumn of 1998 Holland went on to introduce a series of travelogue-cum-music documentaries in which he visited exotic places and conversed with some equally exotic local musicians. The title of the show, *The Beat Route*, harked back to the eponymous London club of the late 70s and early 80s.

Often immaculately dressed in velvet-collared suits, like some 50s dandy, Holland's success as a TV presenter is partly dependent on his parallel career as a musician. He came to prominence as keyboard player in the south-east London band Squeeze, led by songwriters Glenn Tilbrook and Chris Difford – the Deptford boys whose wry and tuneful take on the lives of their peers prompted comparisons with Ray Davies (**The Kinks**) and even Lennon and McCartney. After a string of hits in the late 70s and early 80s, beginning with 'Cool for Cats' and including the highly evocative 'Up The Junction' (taken from Nell Dunn's 60s novel), Squeeze came unstuck. As a soloist (usually backed by former Squeeze drummer Gilson Lavis), Holland is an impressive piano player (he loves to

Nick Hornby

boogie-woogie) and a poor singer whose pale voice sounds like a caricature of a white boy trying to sing the blues. But he knows a good instrumentalist when he hears one, and his 16-piece Rhythm and Blues Orchestra, sounding something like Count Basie plus amplification, is long on solos and thankfully short on singing.

In TV interviews, Holland's experience as a musician allows him to engage closely with the musical styles of his guests. Towards the audience (both live in the studio and the viewers at home), Holland behaves like a highly knowledgeable but still slightly gauche teacher. Described as 'the man who mislaid his ego', Holland's self-deprecation stems from his own recognition that he is just a white boy in awe of those who invented the blues.

The adoration of blues and the black Americans who sing them is now as British as bacon and egg. In conversation with Nigel Williamson of *The Times*, Holland noted that 'the unique sound of London … has to be British rhythm and blues'. What, then, are the roots of this 'London' sound? Holland, who still lives in south London, thinks that the 'experience' of the Blitz 'had a profound effect' which in turn had some sort of resonance with the blues. Not that it turned out the same as the African-American version: 'Keith Richards says he tries to play like Chuck Berry but he can't. It comes out different, which is what makes it great, because instead of being a straight copy it comes out sounding totally original and British.'

Holland knows that he and his ilk cannot be as cool as the idols they have always admired. But this typically British recognition is also a kind of cool; and he has it in spades.

PARENTS 'Pinetop' Smith, Count Basie, Alexis Korner

Nick Hornby
The sad lad

First he was known as the ultimate adultescent, a thirty/fortysomething who admitted to being fixated with **football** and music and stuck at the mental/emotional age of 14. For a few weeks he was castigated as Feckless, Reckless Dad, after he separated from his wife Virginia, leaving their autistic son Danny in her care. But far from being an absentee father, Nick Hornby sees wife and child every day, pays for her to have all the assistance she needs, and funds an expensive special education programme for his son ('And I thought, "Oh now I see what the money is for." I thought it was for having fun with, but it's not. It's for Danny'). He is now the perfect postmodern father: pale rather than patriarchal; doting on his not-quite-family.

Born in 1957 in the prosperous town of Maidenhead (parents divorced when he was a child; father Sir Derek was chairman of Rank Xerox then deputy to Tory minister Michael Heseltine at the Board of Trade before becoming chairman of the Channel Tunnel Consortium), Nick Hornby was a suburban youth in search of identity. Prone to depression but keen to shake off middle-to-low-brow suburban culture (*Evita* and Jeffrey Archer, as he recalls), he went looking for an urban (preferably north London) existence. After hanging around local garages learning to chain smoke, he found it in the form of soul/pop/rock music and Arsenal Football Club. In accordance with his new-found, artificially authentic sense of self, around this time his vowel sounds went downmarket, while those of his sister became noticeably posh. People used to wonder which of them was adopted.

Hornby enjoyed himself at Cambridge but never felt part of the university. He felt more kinship at Cambridge United's football ground; and he used the music and laddish image of singer **Rod Stewart** to protect himself against the varsity spirit. On coming down, like other listless Oxbridgers he drifted into teaching English (first at a comprehensive, then to executives of the Korean company Samsung); then he drifted into writing – something he had vaguely wanted to do, but which only became his profession when he realised he could not go on teaching. Recalling his early years as a self-declared writer, Hornby has said, 'I became a writer because everything else had gone out the window. At 12 I knew I wasn't going to play for Arsenal, and at 23 I knew I wasn't going to be in The Clash,' whereas with becoming a writer there is no cut-off point; you get used to a certain kind of life and meanwhile the gap in your CV gets so long you become virtually unemployable.

But Hornby was lifted from relative obscurity (writing reviews for *Time Out* and Toby Young's *The Modern Review*; reading blue-collar American fiction writers such as Anne Tyler and Raymond Carver and admiring their ability, unlike British novelists, to change gear and take in a wider spectrum of life; and writing a respectable academic volume, *Contemporary American Fiction*) by the outstanding success of *Fever Pitch* (1992; 600,000 copies sold in first five years), the memoir of a football supporter. In an amusing and imaginative fashion, *Fever Pitch* tells the story of Hornby's life through the prism of being an Arsenal fan (the film version, 1997, starring Colin Firth, turned this fan's story into a love story with football as its setting).

At the core of *Fever Pitch* is a conundrum: during the period Hornby describes in the book, football fandom was an almost exclusively working-class preserve; but it is chronicled by a middle-class, working-class wannabe. By the time his memoir came out, there were many more rootless, middle-class males looking for something rooted and authentic to identify with. Hornby flagged up a return to football as the source of just such an experience, and his book catalysed the turn to football on the part of the British middle classes ('the soccerati'). Taken together with other developments in the game, such as the fallout from the Hillsborough disaster, fanzines, new supporters' associations and academic institutions devoted to the sociology of football, *Fever Pitch* was the cue for the beautiful game to acquire a new literary respectability. Not only a personal memoir, *Fever Pitch* was a key component in a broader social trend that has even been described as 'the Hornbyisation of football'.

In his first 'novel' (it seems almost as autobiographical as *Fever Pitch*) Hornby applied the same treatment to the musical side of his life. The protagonist of *High Fidelity* (1995) is a 35-year-old record shop manager who documents his relationships with women in accordance with his taste in music and his record collection (kept in strict alphabetical order, of course). Again Hornby seemed to catch the crest of a social trend. This time it was 'the crisis of masculinity': suddenly everyone was observing that, like Hornby's anti-hero, boys cannot really handle relationships – they can only deal with statistics and pop trivia.

In 1998 Hornby published *About A Boy*, centring on a selfish, immature 36-year-old man who goes cruising for single mothers because he enjoys the combination of sex and temporary parenthood (no strings attached), until he discovers the importance of responsibility and commitment when a fatherless 12-year-old called Marcus turns to him for support. He does not feel up to being a father to the boy, but opts instead for the lesser role of elder brother. This is a Hornby hero taking two steps towards growing up and then one step back.

The film rights to *About A Boy* went to Robert De Niro's TriBeCa production company for the grown-up price of £2 million. Later that year, Hornby transferred his next two novels from Gollancz to Penguin for a further £2 million. Some critics feel that this is way over the odds. Novelist **Will Self** rubbishes Hornby (and Helen Fielding, creator of Bridget Jones – the female equivalent of Hornbyesque characters) as 'wimp fiction' – novels for the kind of boys who stayed 'in the kitchen at parties' (Self, according to himself, was always dancing, out of his bonce, and grabbing at somebody). First there were heroes (Homer), says Self, then there were kings (Shakespeare), and now there are Hornby's 'nonentities'.

Hornby does his best to live an insignificant life. He has bought a house down the road from Highbury, but he does not drive or wear expensive clothes. He smokes Silk Cut (the most self-effacing of cigarettes), enjoys computer games, and makes occasional visits to a Jungian therapist and a practitioner of the Alexander Technique for relaxation. In keeping with the protagonists of his books, he suffers regularly from pangs of self-doubt. In particular, he worries about writing 'all the time'.

PARENTS Jerome K Jerome, Richard Ford, Anne Tyler
CHILDREN Yellow Jersey Press, the lad novel
READ ON *Fever Pitch*, *High Fidelity*, *About A Boy*

Ted Hughes
Mr Sylvia Plath

Described by the Irish poet Seamus Heaney as 'a poet of the land and Eng-land', handsome Ted Hughes is still remembered by many primarily as the husband of Sylvia Plath, the brilliant American poet who committed suicide in 1963 after their marriage broke down. For more than 30 years the power of Hughes' poetry was surpassed by the magnetism of the terrible soap opera in which he co-starred. Finally, in the months before his death from cancer in 1998, the two aspects of his life were brought together by the publication of *Birthday Letters*, a best-selling, award-winning collection of epistolary poems written over three decades and addressed to Plath.

Born (1930) in the West Yorkshire mill town of Mytholmroyd and brought up in nearby Mexborough, where his parents ran a tobacconist's shop, Hughes won a scholarship to read English at Cambridge. But he felt uncomfortable with the intellectual analysis of literature, and, switching to a degree in archaeology and anthropology, embarked on a lifelong search for the primitive and elemental. Hughes was not short of animal magnetism himself. With his thick hair, large frame, piercing eyes and strong jaw, he was highly attractive to women. At a party in Cambridge to launch a small magazine, Hughes was approached by a Fullbright scholar who bit him on the cheek. This was Sylvia Plath, and four months later (January 1956) they were married. He 'went like a lamb to the slaughter,' says Germaine Greer.

Also in 1956 Hughes won an American poetry competition with the verse that was to comprise his first collection, *The Hawk In The Rain* (1957). For three years he taught in the USA, returning with a pregnant Plath to set up home near Primrose Hill in London. She had been a gifted student and short-story writer, but Hughes encouraged her to become a poet. 'He helped her get in touch with her demons,' recalls critic Al Alvarez. 'But what was in the cellar turned out to be a nightmare.' Plath's collection, *The Colossus*, was published in 1960. The following year they moved to Devon, to a house overlooking a graveyard. Plath's work took on a morbid tone as their marriage came under strain (see the autobiographical novel *The Bell Jar*, 1963, based on her nervous breakdown while an undergraduate). Hughes moved out in the autumn of 1962 after she discovered he was having an affair. Plath returned to London shortly afterwards, determined to make it as a poet. Her work improved but her life deteriorated. While London froze up during the worst winter in living memory, Plath's poetry burnt like ice. Subsequently collected in *Ariel* (1965), *Crossing The Water* (1971) and *Winter Trees* (1972), her late poems are the longest suicide note in literary history. She stuck her head in a gas oven on 11 February 1963.

For the burgeoning women's movement, Plath was a hero denied; not by history, but by heartless Hughes. He 'existed to be punished,' remembers Germaine Greer. Feminists, some of whom scratched his name off Plath's gravestone, kept up hostilities for decades. Meanwhile Hughes entered into another relationship; again his partner killed herself. In 1970 he retired to Devon where he married a local woman, farmed 95 acres and continued to write.

With *Crow* (1970), Hughes created a symbol of resilience. Like him, the Crow survives. Although the bulk of his work (*Lupercal*, 1960; *Wodwo*, 1967; *Cave Birds*, 1975; *Season Songs*, 1976; *Gaudete*, 1977; *Moortown*, 1979; *Wolfwatching*,

1989) deals primarily with nature red in tooth and claw, this is as a response to the blood and guts of human society. As a boy, Hughes was acutely aware that his father was one of less than 20 men from his First World War regiment who survived the Gallipoli campaign. In the West Yorkshire of his boyhood, nature was flooding back in as the mills closed down and the English landscape emptied itself of the first wave of industrialisation. The focus on nature in Hughes' work is a reflection of and upon the limitations of humanity.

With the death of John Betjeman in 1984, Hughes was appointed poet laureate. Although the verse he wrote for official occasions (collected in *Rain-Charm for the Duchy and Other Laureate Poems*, 1992) is negligible, Hughes was serious about the public role of poetry as a component in 'the spiritual unity'. John Carey describes him as 'patriotic', although Seamus Heaney sees in Hughes not traditional, stuffy nationalism but 'the England of Arthur Scargill: he was going to the court with the voice of that which was outside the court.' This sums up the style of his poetry and his relationship with the British establishment; but Hughes' primary reputation as the poetic equivalent of a *femme fatale* is best summed up in a message he wrote to a boyhood friend: 'before us stands yesterday'.

PARENTS Lévi-Strauss, Sylvia Plath
CHILDREN Simon Armitage
READ ON *Birthday Letters* by Ted Hughes; *Ariel* by Sylvia Plath

Ibiza

E stands for Ibiza

In the 50s and early 60s British visitors to Ibiza tended to be well-off bohemians and resting thespians who came to drink Pimm's and Martinis at Sandy Pratt's cocktail bar. In the late 60s it became a staging post along the hippie trail to the Far East. And in the 70s, after the opening of the new airport in 1967, it turned into a package holiday destination: 'Margate in the Med'.

During the 70s there were just a couple of cool clubs on the island (Amnesia and Pacha), both of which played psychedelia and then reggae. In the 80s more clubs and bars opened up in the town of San Antonio, and club owners started adding extravagant attractions: foam parties, swimming pools (Wham!'s video for 'Club Tropicana', 1983, was shot by the pool at Pike's Hotel), lasers, live bands and better dancefloors. A gay crowd started coming to Ibiza and in 1983 Amnesia began after-hours sessions opening at 5am; two years later Amnesia DJ Alfredo was playing mostly house music interspersed with **indie**, reggae and Euro disco. It was around this time that the drug **Ecstasy** was brought on to the island; its effects (empathy, energy) on how people danced and behaved were immediate. From then on, dance music, E and Ibiza were joined at the hip.

In the mid-80s Ibiza became the focal point for a new contingent of DJs. Danny Rampling and Nicky Holloway organised their first club trip to Ibiza in 1985. Having been to the Paradise Garage in the USA, Trevor Fung and Ian St Paul set up The Project in 1987. These were effectively the travel agents who brought coachloads of clubbers over to Ibiza for the time of their lives. Some of them, including City high-fliers and other assorted yuppies, did not go back for years.

Along with Paul Oakenfold, an ex-chef from Thornton Heath, Fung had already tried to bottle the Ibiza atmosphere and take it back to a new London club, Fun City. But in 1985 the timing was not right. A couple of years later, however, and the spread of E catalysed the transformation of London's clubland into an imitation Ibiza. For the next five years, the whole point of clubbing was to regain the Balearic experience – musically a mixture of the Euro-house, open-minded eclecticism and Cafe del Mar ambience first heard in the warm night air of the Mediterranean. It was a reciprocal relationship: while clubland turned itself into Ibiza, the biggest names to emerge on the club scene began putting on summer shows on the island. Within a few years, no top-tier British club could afford not to be part of Ibiza's summer line-up.

The E/Ibiza vibe proved difficult to sustain, however, and not only in London but also in Ibiza itself. More and more punters led to a messier club scene. Muso-sophistos complained of 'cheesey ravers', just as their parents had protested against the package holiday-makers who had invaded Ibiza a generation earlier. Ibiza compilation albums became the 90s equivalent of *Top of the Pops* albums in the 70s. Drunken goings-on in the West End of San Antonio featured in a host of 'shocku-mentary' TV programmes, and the British vice-consul resigned in 1998 citing the disgraceful behaviour of younger compatriots. By the end of the 90s, Ibiza had acquired a reputation for being laddish and uncomfortable for vulnerable women (explicit floor shows, ostensibly an expression of sexual diversity, added to this image). But it was still an essential showcase for British clubs. Among those who set out their stall in the 1999 season were Renaissance at Pacha (opening night by DJ Dave Morales), 'Brum glamsters' Miss Moneypenny's at El Divino, Cream at Amnesia (featuring Belgian Paul Van Dyk, together with Judge Jules and Sasha), and Manumission at Privilege (who promised to tone down the sexual content of their floor show). In competition with the commercial club scene, history repeated itself with the re-emergence of unlicensed outdoor parties advertised by word of mouth in the markets of Es Canar and Sant Carles. Some voices in the dance music press are touting Cyprus as the next, as yet unspoilt, Ibiza.

PARENTS Margate, UFO, hippie happenings, Paradise Garage, Northern Soul all-niters
READ ON *Adventures in Wonderland* by Sheryl Garratt

Indie
Are you?

'Indie' is the tag applied to the music scene orientated towards independent record labels – that is independent from 'the majors' (CBS, EMI and the like). The indie record label at its purest is the musical equivalent of a fanzine: the gathering together and promotion of like-minded musicians in a business venture that can be run out of your bedroom. The bands signed to such labels have often been described as 'alternative'. But nowadays 'the indies' are often independent in image only and are actually nesting within the major corporations; and 'alternative' is a term of doubtful value, given that the monolithic mainstream no longer exists.

In the 60s, **Rolling Stones** manager Andrew Loog Oldham set up his own label, Immediate. The **Who**'s managers (Chris Stamp and Kit Lambert) established Track (track records, geddit?), and Chris Blackwell, scion of a colonial family, got Island Records up and running in Jamaica before opening for business in Britain. All of these enterprises were seen as additions to the record industry, not as challenges to its very existence.

In the mid-70s, a new tranche of independent labels carried different connotations. The first of these were Chiswick (prompted by American interest in old records) and Stiff. When they got going in 1975, the music they put out was more like pub rock than punk. But with the advent of punk and the accompanying ethos of 'complete control' (maintaining control over your own output), being independent from the tired old industry and its overweight record companies took on a new significance.

During the rest of the 70s, as part of the DIY ethic of punk, a host of bands took the independent route: either they signed with indie labels such as Small Wonder, Postcard or Factory, or they formed their own label and arranged a distribution deal with independent distributors Rough Trade (also a record shop and label in its own right). Often they discovered that independence meant lots of ideological purity and little or no marketing clout. The ones that did best were those that made licensing arrangements with larger operations, such as **Two-Tone** with Chrysalis.

During the late 70s and early 80s major record companies used the independents as their unpaid r&d department: they would let indie labels try out new bands, then cherry pick the best and sign them to their own labels. But towards the end of the 80s, a new relationship emerged between established companies and new product. By this time 'independent labels' tended to be subsidiaries (wholly or partly owned) of majors. Seeking to disestablish their image as money-making, number-crunching, mind-numbing bureaucracies, music industry corporations hit upon the idea of reconstituting themselves as a jigsaw of smaller identities, each designed to corner a particular niche in an increasingly fragmented music market. Often schooled in subcultural theory and nowadays as horrified as anyone else at 'the commodification of music', the execs at central office rely on creative

enthusiasts to put them in touch with various sections of the record-buying public. They give them an office, a budget and a degree of autonomy; but the final say-so remains in the hands of the majors.

So much for the business arrangements, but what of the music and styles associated with 'indie'? As a musical genre, the term came into widespread use when 'alternative' music began to exceed the boundaries of punk. Joy Division set the tone in the late 70s: alienated, depressed, ill at ease with the world. The torch of mental torture was picked up by The Wedding Present and The Smiths. A sense of discomfort with the status quo can be heard in the faux naivety of 'shambling bands' such as Stump and Mighty Lemon Drops (championed by an *NME* eager to find the next big thing, and gathered as a showcase on its *C86* compilation). Indie music (and the indie look) was a deliberate stand against the silky smooth production values of the synthesised pop and the power-dressing and big hair look of the mid-80s.

Despite protestations from Radio 1 DJ Steve Lamaq, who complained when the *Guinness Book of British Hit Singles* adopted a cartoon glum face as its indie icon, black (anti-success, anti-happiness, existential angst) has always been the genre's staple colour. The indie habit of dressing down in charity-shop clothes (hooded anoraks and old cardigans) was a continuation of the Beats' (Kerouac and Co) anti-business ethic. Dressing up as children was a variation on the refusenik theme (wearing a Scooby-Doo T-shirt meant you were refusing to grow up), which prompted the terms 'indie kid' and 'cutie'. In the mid- to late 80s, there were hundreds of them on every campus, easily identifiable by the combination of black jeans, second-hand jumper/suede coat, kiddie rucksack from Camden, lanky hair and scuffed **DMs**.

Crossover killed the indie kid. First, their style crossed over the Atlantic to Seattle, and by the early 90s it was being mass produced and sold back to Britain as grunge – no longer an 'alternative' form, but the most marketed mode of pop. Meanwhile home-grown indie was meshing with the new alternative of the late 80s: dance culture. By the end of 1987, 4AD had released a dance record ('Pump Up The Volume'). Indie adopted drum machines, sportswear and E-induced good times, and its miserabilist incarnation came to an end. If it was not dead already, **Britpop** delivered the coup de grace. By adopting the guitar sound and the melancholy of indie, dressing it up in **Mod** and 70s retro, turning up the irony level and pitching the whole package as the new focus for national identity, Britpop brought down the lid down on indie's traditional position as the musical opposition.

PARENTS Beat, punk, the Student Union

Eddie Izzard
The funny man who doesn't tell jokes

Born in Aden, South Yemen, in February 1962 (father worked for British Petroleum), Eddie Izzard was schooled in English boarding schools (mother had died of bowel cancer) and attended Sheffield University (accountancy and maths) for a year before dropping out. At the **Edinburgh** Fringe **Festival** throughout the 80s, Izzard made frequent appearances as a stand-up comedian. But acclaim was a long time coming: it took him ten years to get a nomination for the Perrier award (1992). Meanwhile, in London, he spent years busking with a unicycle and fellow ex-student Russ Ballard.

Izzard is a transvestite, which he describes as 'running, jumping, climbing trees and putting on make up when you get there'. He remembers being keen on frocks since the age of four, and was caught stealing lipstick at 15. In October 1992 he came out on stage in a frock for the first time. When Tony Blair hosted a series of post-election parties at No 10 Downing Street in the summer of 1997, Labour-donor Izzard was the only man who turned up in a skirt. He sometimes sports a beard along with it.

Incongruity is the essence of Izzard's act. David Quatnick, who collaborated with Izzard in the writing of his autobiography (*Dress to Kill*, 1998), once remarked that 'he doesn't do jokes. He just comes on stage and does Eddie Izzard.' What's that, then? Well, it is never the same twice (during the course of a British tour Izzard's rate of improvisation was such that by the halfway stage he was already doing a whole new show). But it nearly always involves the unpicking of conventions and the sewing together of elements that would not normally be connected but somehow belong together in Izzard's surreal mindscape. The effect is like Noël Coward and Marcel Duchamp combined. It is also a kind of free association 'riffing' reminiscent of US iconoclast and comic Lenny Bruce (Jonathan Miller once said that *Beyond The Fringe* was a satirical pinprick whereas Bruce was a bloodbath): Eddie played Lenny in the West End production (1999) of the eponymous play about his life (first produced on Broadway in 1971).

Izzard's comments on the nature of comedy show his unique approach to it. Critical of the 'mainstream pap' that operates on the 'first level of comedy', he once declared that 'alternative comedy plays on both the first and second levels of comedy', before going on to explain that 'to appreciate the second level of comedy, you need to have been exposed to the conventions of comedy … and then you need to stand in a bucket. Then you will be ready to have these conventions undermined.' Izzard has also said that 'comedy needs to be staged like theatre and promoted like rock'n'roll,' adding, 'and now we have reached Planet Sexy, I think British comedy must set up a moonbase so others from our nation can come and visit.' He lives and dies by the *non sequitur*.

Izzard had wanted to be an actor since the age of seven. As a student he failed his audition for the National Youth Theatre but in January 1993 he packed out the Ambassador's theatre in London's West End for a 13-week solo comedy show. One of his videos sold 200,000 copies. A committed Europhile, Izzard performs in Paris in French (being dyslexic has not stopped him learning languages). He now is enjoying a measure of success in the USA, where, according to journalist Sheryl Garratt, he is seen as 'a one-man **Monty Python**'.

As a straight actor Izzard has appeared in stage productions such as *The Cryptogram* (1994) and *Edward II* (1995). His film credits include *The Secret Agent* (1997, from Joseph Conrad's novel), **The Avengers** and **Velvet Goldmine** (both 1998). In 1999 he finished work on a raft of films including *Circus*, a gangster flick set in Brighton, and *The Shadow of the Vampire* with John Malkovich and Willem Dafoe. He played a forensic scientist in *The Criminal*, and in *The Mystery Men* he was a character with a quiff called Tony Pompadour. Not all his films have been successful (*The Avengers* flopped badly) but Izzard himself has generally found favour with the critics – the one exception being the pilot episode of *The Cows*, a TV sitcom he wrote. The rest of the series was never made.

PARENTS Lenny Bruce
READ ON *Dress To Kill* by Eddie Izzard

The Jam
Left-leaning little Englanders

Led by Paul Weller (b. 1958), backed by Bruce Foxton (bass, b. 1955) and Rick Buckler (drums, b. 1955), in the late 70s and early 80s the Jam clocked up four No 1 singles and worldwide sales of more than five million. Not bad for a band that might have ended up on the cabaret circuit.

Managed by Weller's father (former featherweight boxer turned taxi-driver and builder), in

1975 The Jam were selling themselves as 'most rock and roll and maximum R&B' (a lift from the **Who** when they were the High Numbers). Their combination of suits, soul covers and a 60s-style Rickenbacker guitar sound got them gigs in the Woking area and an audition for *Opportunity Knocks* (the ITV talent show hosted by Hughie Green). Then along came punk, and The Jam's insistence on short, snappy songs stopped seeming simply retro and took on a more contemporary significance.

Their first album, *In The City*, was recorded in 11 days; and the single of the same name, marked out by a driving bass riff, reached No 40 in April 1977. But during the course of their first press interview, Weller had said that he would be voting Conservative at the next general election. This was probably meant as a wind-up; if so, it had perhaps too much of the desired effect. At a time of increasing disillusion with the Labour government and with parliamentary politics in general, while the rest of the music business was making radical noises, The Jam were tagged as selfish, suburban southerners with no empathy for the experiences that gave rise to inner city 'dole queue rock'. Jon Savage complained that there were 'too many Little Englandisms' in their make-up.

Faced with conflicting signs, the music press did not know how to classify The Jam: were they punk (the speed at which they played)? Were they **Mods** (the suits and the soul influences)? Were they post-political or politicised? The Jam were in fact a distillation of Mod through punk's amphetamine-fuelled energy and left-wing disgruntlement. Weller

might argue that the manic, auto-destructive energy and three-piece R'n'B attitude of The Who made them the first punk band, long before the Sex Pistols were a twinkle in **Malcolm McLaren**'s eye.

In many ways The Jam were far more grass-roots proletarian that the art-school posturing of many punk acts. In the dark night of the early 80s, between the demise of punk and the birth of The Smiths, The Jam ploughed an almost lone furrow as a genuine voice of disaffected suburban youth. Unlike many bands their constituency was not the urban sophisticates but the housing estate kids of overspill towns like Weller's very own Woking. As the fantasy escapism of New Romantic took hold of the nation, they still spoke the language of the streets, displayed the same angry energy and set their dissaffected tales on a recognisable English landscape: part contemporary realism, part mythologised English past (using everything in the cultural closet from **kitchen sink** to the war poets). They set themselves in a Mod tradition by acknowledging a debt to soul classics, covering the English greats (**The Beatles**, **The Kinks**, the Who and **The Small Faces**) and playing with much of Mod's existing iconography: the clothes, the hair, pop art, **scooters**. Theirs was the same working-class landscape laid out by the Who (particularly from *Quadrophenia*) of dead-end jobs, the weekend release and dreaming of an escape to a better life than the dreary 9 to 5. Their pride in Englishness was not traditionally patriotic, Weller's lyrics were deeply scathing of everything from the delusions of Empire and war-mongering, to the media and town planners. Although, lyrically, not the most sophisticated, they represented a raw commuter-belt honesty that struck a chord with millions.

Weller's interest in the English tradition increasingly showed a left-wing perspective. As its title suggests, their third album *All Mod Cons* acknowledged their Mod heritage and interleaved it with echoes of Weller's favourite writers (such as Allan Sillitoe and George Orwell). The next album *Setting Sons* continued their investigation of the defining characteristics of English life. Their fifth album *Sound Affects* had three verses of Percy Bysshe Shelley's 'Mask of Anarchy' printed on the back of the sleeve and also showed the influence of Orwell's *Homage to Catalonia* and *Road to Wigan Pier* ('That's Entertainment' was a trip through decaying working-class England). It was the end of Weller's 'sitting on the fence period' and the start of his emergence as an out-and-out left-winger (CND benefit 1981; Albert Hall benefit for the miners, 1986; association with the lobbying-for-Labour roadshow Red Wedge, 1987).

For two years running (1979 and 1980) The Jam came top in the *NME* readers' poll for best group. But Weller was already looking for a sound that was bigger and brassier than a guitar-based three-piece; in June 1982 he told the other two he was leaving, and the break-up of the band was announced at the end of October (before their farewell tour). In a commemorative gesture Polydor rereleased all their singles, and 13 of them were in the Top 100 at the same time.

Bruce Foxton went on to produce Belfast's Stiff Little Fingers. Rick Buckler had his fingers burnt when he invested in recording studios; he eventually moved into the furniture restoration business. Paul Weller has continued to make successful records, although opinions differ as to whether he is a tired old man, a seminal figure in the history of British pop, or both.

PARENTS the High Numbers,
the Flaming Groovies
CHILDREN **Blur**, **Oasis,** the **Who**
READ ON *The Jam – our story* by Bruce Foxton and Rick Buckler; *The Beat Concerto* by Paulo Hewitt

Derek Jarman
History is personal

Set designer, painter, essayist, gay activist and, above all, film-maker, Derek Jarman directed the first British homo-erotic feature film (*Sebastiane*, 1976), before documenting the decline and desperation of modern Britain in movies such as *Jubilee* (1978) and *The Last of England* (1987). He died of AIDS in 1994.

Michael Derek Elsworthy Jarman (b. 1942) was the son of a New Zealand-born RAF squadron leader, Lance Jarman. His mother Evelyn (née Puttock) was a former art student who later worked as personal assistant to the Queen's dress designer Norman Hartnell. Jarman's childhood occurred during the afterglow of war. Buoyed by the defeat of fascism, Britain temporarily regained a sense of self-worth. The Jarman family moved house along with Lance Jarman's RAF postings abroad (Rome, the shores of Lake Maggiore, Pakistan), and the family garden often ended in the barbed-wire of a military airfield. The juxtaposition of English gardens and militarism was to be a recurring feature of Derek's subsequent work. His father's fraught relationship with Britishness (a returning colonial who felt he never really fitted in) is another legacy of this period; so too was Lance Jarman's home movie-making (original footage of the Jarman family was incorporated into *The Last of England*).

At public school Jarman disliked sports and took 'refuge in the art house'. His father agreed to support him through art school (the Slade) if he first read for a degree (English History and Art) at King's College, London. In London he soon hooked up with the trendy art set centred on **David Hockney**. Although Jarman once described this period as 'the swinging decayed', he was also proud of the swinging 60s and his own small part in it: 'unsophisticated as we were, we were to be part of the change that was to revolutionise life in the next few years'. He admired Hockney ('the first English painter to declare his homosexuality in public') but later criticised him for emigrating to the USA and being taken over by 'dollar dowagers'.

Jarman's artistic interests were English and European. His set designs for Prokofiev's *Prodigal Son* were exhibited in Paris in 1967, as a result of which he was commissioned to design Frederick Ashton's *Jazz Calendar* at Covent Garden ('Licorice Allsorts dancing'). But his designs for John Gielgud's *Don Giovanni* (1969) at the Coliseum 'faced a barrage of hissing'. Although Jarman mixed with pop art people, his own paintings of the period have been described as 'cool, analytical and somewhat surreal'.

By the early 70s the gay glitterati, dubbed the 'Them' people by **Peter York**, were making the running in the pop world. Jarman designed Ken Russell's film *The Devils* (contributing to Russell's juxtaposition of modern images in historical contexts, subsequently a feature of his own work) and staged a show by US singer Alice Cooper. He was an enthusiastic spectator at performance art experiments (Living Theater, David Medalla's Exploding Galaxy) and a central participant in Andrew Logan's Alternative Miss World competitions. When the partnership with Russell came to an end, Jarman turned to making his own films with a Super-8, launched by Kodak as a home movie camera in 1967. He also moved to the first in a series of Thameside warehouse-studios. In his first film, *Studio Bankside* (1970–73), a montage of static shots of his home, Jarman described his new, more ascetic environment in a new, intensely personal medium.

Jarman's first feature film, *Sebastiane* (1976) framed sainthood and homosexuality in Latin dialogue (thus keeping away the masses and avoiding censorship). Set in a Roman military camp (echoes here of the Jarman family background), *Sebastiane* is partly about an army with no sense of purpose – a recurring theme in Jarman's work is the absence of the sense of purpose that informed his father's life and the post-war years in which he grew up;

likewise, his rendition of Shakespeare's *The Tempest* (1979), panned by some critics ('a fingernail scratched along a blackboard') but admired by many Shakespeare scholars, is concerned with the loss of community (it features a boiler-suited Ariel – 'a sight for sore gay eyes' – and a chorus of sailor boys).

Remembered as the first punk movie (the cast includes Jordan and Adam Ant), *Jubilee* (1978) timeshifted the first Queen Elizabeth into the jubilee year of Elizabeth II (1977). Devised as a 'fantasy documentary', *Jubilee* is part Swiftian satire, part Blakean poetic. At once dystopian and Romantic, according to the *Guardian*'s Nicholas de Jongh *Jubilee* is 'a personal cry of nostalgia for a time and a security this country never knew'. Named after the Ford Madox Brown painting in which an emigrating couple look back at the coastline of their native land (and the translation of it made by David Hockney in 1961 as part of his studies at the Royal College of Art), *The Last of England* (1987) employs fast editing and intense, Turner-esque colours to provide a critique of Little England in its current state of decay. But as well as criticism there is a sensitivity to Britishness, prompting critic Annette Kuhn to compare it to the superior wartime propaganda of Humphrey Jennings' *Listen to Britain* (1942).

In his most successful work, Jarman paints a picture of Britain and its history intertwined with his own strain of intimacy, as in *The Angelic Conversation* (1985) which combines gently erotic images with Shakespeare's sonnets. The combination of fractured Britain and fragile personality is also visible in his pop videos for The Smiths and the **Pet Shop Boys**. In *The Garden* (1990), shot around his house in the shadow of the power station at Dungeness, Jarman brought the 'I-movie' (personal) together with the allegorical (a rendering of the Christian myth). The film is redolent with the English landscape (the industrial in the rural) and a sense of mortality (diagnosed as HIV-positive in 1986, Jarman was already ill when the film was made). Jarman's backyard becomes the Garden of Eden and the Garden of Gethsemane, and he takes on the quasi-mythical role of the English gardener. Observations on herbalism and his garden take up a large part of *Modern Nature*, Jarman's published journal of 1989–90.

Of his adaptation of Christopher Marlowe's *Edward II* (1991), Jarman said: 'I hope it's more interesting [than the original]. *Edward II* is fairly indigestible as a play.' His version featured Tilda Swinton as a spurned Queen Isabella who also evoked Ivana Trump, Princess Diana, Margaret Thatcher, Jackie Onassis, Jean Shrimpton, Grace Kelly and Audrey Hepburn. *Caravaggio* (1986), Jarman's most commercial movie, interspersed the life and loves of the Renaissance painter with deliberate anachronisms such as the street noise of modern Italy. His last feature films were *Wittgenstein* (1992), a reworking of Terry Eagleton's script about the Austrian philosopher in Cambridge, and *Blue* (1993), a blue colour field with spoken commentary and accompanying music. *Glitterbug* (1994) is a compilation from Jarman's personal Super-8 archives.

Jarman renders history as an extension of the

self. This has the effect of bringing history alive; it may also have the unintended effect of reducing history to the level of personal preoccupations.

One of the central elements of Jarman's selfhood was his homosexuality. Interviewed by Jonathan Romney for *Blitz* magazine during the making of *Edward II*, he indicated that, for him, self-expression and the realisation of what came to be known as the gay lifestyle were akin to a sacred duty: 'I realised very early in the 60s when I met David [Hockney] that our agenda was very different to the agenda of, say, marching against the Cuban [Missile] Crisis. What we were going to do was dance every night. We were meant to be having a bad time. But we were having the best time. ... It was: "OK, we can put them back in the cage with the HIV thing. Look they *are* having a bad time." But I wasn't going to let that happen.'

HIV-positive, Jarman suffered from secondary infections such as TB, pneumonia and toxoplasmosis (which sometimes left him temporarily blind); but this did not prevent him from continuing to produce the largest body of work by a gay man in British cinema; nor did it curtail his role as a polemical essayist (see *At Your Own Risk*, 1992, subtitled 'a saint's testament' in a reference to Jarman's 'canonisation' by drag queens the Sisters of Perpetual Indulgence). He was outspoken in his opposition of the Tories' anti-gay Clause 28; and he also objected to the acceptance of a knighthood by gay thespian Ian McKellen, on the grounds that it contributed to a context in which 'everybody shuts up and says "it's not as bad as we thought".' The violence of his sexual imagery has not always found

favour with the gay community, however.

Jarman's sexual orientation and radical film-making would once have excluded him from Middle England. But his writings on gardening prompted his inclusion on BBC2's *Gardener's World* in June 1995, where he was described as a 'genius'.

PARENTS William Blake, Jonathan Swift, the Living Theater, Fellini
CHILDREN **Tracey Emin**, Tilda Swinton

Elton John
The agony and the banality

Tortured yet homely, Elton John is the non-family man who turned rock'n'roll into family entertainment.

Reginald Kenneth Dwight was born in Pinner at the heart of the English suburban world which its poet laureate John Betjeman dubbed 'metroland'. After a frustrating musical apprenticeship in the 60s **Mod** band Bluesology, Reg Dwight emerged from the lengthy shadow of lead singer Long John Baldry and started recording as a solo artist under the name of Elton John (the songs he sang were co-written with Bernie Taupin, who had just arrived in London from Sleaford, a village in Lincolnshire). After two albums that appealed mainly to **John Peel**'s radio listeners and the hippie-ish readership of *Melody Maker*, he broke into the mass market, first in Britain and then in the USA. Noting that

John notched up seven consecutive No 1 albums in the USA, that out of more than 30 albums since 1969 at least 25 have gone platinum, and that his total sales of well over 100 million have been estimated to account for 3 per cent of all record sales … ever, biographer Philip Norman tags John 'the definitive rock star of the 70s … bigger than any solo artist before or since, with the single exception of Elvis Presley'.

Elton's music has always been accessible. It combines the straightforward rhythm of rock'n'roll with the melodic lines of Tin Pan Alley: you can whistle and tap your feet to it. His singing communicates depth of feeling without being demanding. The songs he co-writes are highly personal, often poignant but never too painful. They cannot be dismissed as pap but neither are they likely to offend anyone – not even granny.

Elton's image was initially that of the introspective singer-songwriter: tinted glasses and velvet jackets. To promote his records in the mainstream market, he turned himself into a one-man pop pantomime. With monstrously high stack heels and ludicrously oversized glasses, Elton's OTT stage gear was as excessive as the decade in which he adopted it – the 70s. Nowadays his shows are less extravagant (Norman refers to a 'gargantuan modesty'), but Elton has stayed loyal to the extravagant shopping habits of the old-style rock'n'roll life: he even calls himself a 'looter'. In a confessional conversation on footballer Ian Wright's Friday-night chatshow (1999), Elton admitted to being a former 'selfish prick' who has matured since he gave up shagging, coke and booze benders towards the end of the 80s. No more sex and drugs: now there's only rock-'n'roll – and shopping.

From the early 80s Elton devoted more time to his role as chairman of Watford Football Club (childhood trips to Vicarage Road had been a rare point of contact with a somewhat distant father; in 1998 he described Premiership football as 'lazy and overpaid'). While Elton courted sportspeople (he is keen on tennis and cricket as well as football), he himself was the first rock star to be 'taken up' by royalty. In September 1997 this connection attained full realisation when Elton was invited to sing at the funeral service for Princess Diana. In her memory he rewrote his song about Marilyn Monroe, 'Candle In The Wind', retitled it 'Goodbye English Rose', and sang it for one time only. Elton was duly recommended for a knighthood by prime minister **Tony Blair**, and dubbed 'Sir Brown Nose' by the Duke of Decadence, Keith Richards.

Watched by billions, the Diana funeral was the biggest gig of Elton's life. His performance was entirely in tune with the proceedings. Like Diana, he has lived a tortured life: two suicide attempts, a shortlived marriage, problems arising from his self-confessed 'bisexuality', a predisposition to depression and outbursts of anger (as shown in a fly-on-the-wall TV documentary *Tantrums and Tiaras*). Elton once told *Paris Match* that 'the stage is about the only place where I feel safe'. But, as with Diana, the vulnerability Elton exudes (on display again in July 1999 when he went into hospital to have a pacemaker fitted) is one of the reasons why his audience identifies with him so strongly (Norman compares the solicitude expressed by Elton's audience to the public concern for Judy Garland).

Unlike Garland or Princess Diana, Elton could never be described as glamorous. His face is prone to the kind of podginess that is as English as bread pudding, and the stocky frame beneath is equally Bunteresque. Roly-poly Reg makes rock'n'roll Elton unthreatening; and this may be both the secret of his commercial success and the source of his inner turmoil.

PARENTS Little Richard, Judy Garland, Billy Bunter, Liberace
READ ON *Elton* by Philip Norman

James Kelman
Scottish lyricist of the marginal

Born in Glasgow in 1946, James Kelman was apprenticed to a typesetter at 15, left Scotland briefly in 1953 when his family emigrated to the USA, odd-jobbed around Scotland and London, spent time on the **dole** reading books, enrolled at Strathclyde University when threatened with a benefit cut, dropped out during his philosophy degree, and became a writer instead. In 1998 one of his characters summed up his philosophical outlook: 'All we can do is carry on going, trusting that we can somehow live our way out of it.'

Kelman's first book was *Not Not While The Giro* (1983), a collection of short stories featuring the fatalism and humour of west Scotland's disaffected.

His first novel, *The Busconductor Hines* (1984), introduced the writing technique that has since become his hallmark: blurring the distinction between the authorial voice and the voices of his characters. 'I don't want to tell stories about this community,' says Kelman, 'rather the stories are created within the community. Therefore, those divisions between dialogue and narrator all have to go.'

Kelman wants to make a clean sweep of the value judgements inherent in most English literature: 'There's a judgement from within the narrative, in terms of language, for instance – that this person's language isn't as good as this person's and therefore that person's culture is inferior to this culture, which is the culture of the authorial God-voice, "standard English".' He identifies strongly with Scotland ('affirming your culture is a terribly important and subversive thing to do') and opposes what he regards as the domination of his country by the English hierarchy.

Kelman's next novel was *A Chancer* (1985), the story of a 20-year-old loner and compulsive gambler who lives to bet because the rest of the world seems closed off to him. *A Disaffection* (1989) was shortlisted for the Booker Prize (protagonist Patrick Doyle, a teacher who cannot believe in what he is teaching, was compared to the original **Angry Young Man** Jimmy Porter in John Osborne's play *Look Back In Anger*, 1956), but Kelman had to wait until 1994 before winning the prize with *How Late It Was, How Late*, which was strongly criticised by Simon Jenkins of *The* (London) *Times* for reflecting the life of 'an illiterate savage'.

Kelman has written three plays, published in 1991, and has published two further short story collections: *The Burn* (1991) and *The Good Times* (1998). Of the latter, one reviewer, referred to the story 'Comic Cuts' as a spoof on *Waiting for Godot* (a spoof on life itself) featuring four part-time musicians; another critic described it as 'Beckett with a West Coast accent'.

PARENTS Samuel Selvon, JP Donleavy,
DH Lawrence, Samuel Beckett
CHILDREN **Irvine Welsh**, Jeff Torrington
READ ON *A Disaffection*; *Some Recent Attacks –
essays cultural and political*

The Kinks
Mod meets music hall

A London-based four-piece (backline: Mick Avory and Pete Quaife; the Davies brothers – Ray and Dave – up front), The Kinks' (formerly The Ravens) first hit was 'You Really Got Me' (1963) which went to joint No 1 (a rare occurrence in the British charts) with 'Have I The Right?' by The Honeycombes. It was the first in a series of hits based on the combination of Ray Davies' nasal whine and choppy, riffing power chords – a technique copied first by American garage bands and then by British punks (compare 'You Really Got Me' with '1977' by The Clash).

Early Kinks records sounded more aggressive

than anything else in the charts, and this aspect of the band's character was underlined when they hit the headlines for fighting (between themselves) on stage. But the aggression they expressed was not boorish or crude. Though not closely associated with the **Mods**, like them The Kinks were young, urban sophisticates using music and style to express their frustration and aspiration. Trained as a commercial artist, Ray Davies had walked out of an ad agency when he was asked to produce a design on toilet paper. Even when he wrote songs that were ostensibly about love and romance – such as 'You Really Got Me' – you got the feeling he was frustrated, imprisoned, by his surroundings.

Besides their aggression, the early Kinks were satirical, as in 'Well Respected Man', a jaunty but bitterly sarcastic song about British commuterland, 'Sunny Afternoon', a biting slice of melancholia about the idle rich, and the self-satirising 'Dedicated Follower of Fashion'.

If not fully fledged Mods, the early Kinks were certainly modernists. But in the second half of the decade, Davies concerned himself with what was being lost in swinging London. In songs like 'Autumn Almanac', 'Dead-End Street' and 'Waterloo Sunset' he evoked the working-class life that was fast disappearing (in *The Uses of Literacy*, 1957, Richard Hoggart had already warned that it was in danger), treating it with affection but retaining enough satirical distance to avoid sentimentality. This turn was clearly audible in the 1967 album *Something Else*: its echoes of music hall were self-consciously out of sync with the psychedelic wave that everyone else was riding at the time.

The form of Davies' writing changed alongside his subject matter: three-minute pop songs gave way to concept albums; power chords (often major sevenths) were replaced by minor ones; songs of personal complaint were superseded by narrative verses (back to the ballad) and singalong choruses reminiscent of the music hall – but written from the point of view of a 60s sophisticate whose real-life experience was of sexual freedom and social mobility rather than tradition, community and restraint. This intriguing combination reached its climax in *The Village Green Preservation Society* (1968), an evocation of old-English life by an urban cosmopolitan. With songs like 'Last of The Steam-Powered Trains' and 'Do You Remember Walter?', this was a kind of musical communitarianism, written around the same time as the first **skinheads** were making violent attempts to hold on to traditional, white working-class communities. Davies followed it with *Arthur, or the Decline and Fall of the British Empire* (1969), an elegy for the 'little men' of England. In the 70s he re-emphasised the camp and satirical aspects of The Kinks with *Lola vs Powerman and the Moneygoround* (a satire on the music biz), including the song about a transvestite which became the band's anthem. *Celluloid Heroes* (1972) is a tribute not to the English tradition but to the heritage of Hollywood.

The early Kinks' aggressive frustration with England made them palatable to punks, hence borrowings by The Clash, the cover of 'David Watts' by **The Jam**. Meanwhile the ostentatious Englishness of The Kinks had gained them a substantial cult following in the USA. In 1972 pop critic Dave Laing suggested that the lines in 'Autumn Almanac' about liking football, roast beef and Blackpool would have held 'the same kind of cross-cultural appeal that "Wichita Lineman" and "Route 66" hold for us'. And if the past really is a foreign country, then presumably The Kinks appealed to the **Britpop**pers of the mid-90s for similar reasons (**Blur** and others wanted to evoke an idea of Englishness, so they, like the Americans of the late 60s and early 70s, turned to The Kinks' evocation of the kind of Englishness that was already disappearing – if indeed it ever existed – in the days when Davies was writing about it).

While The Kinks were riding high, Dave Davies also enjoyed solo success with the melancholic *Days of a Clown*; but little was heard of him after the band broke up. After appearing in the disastrous film of *Absolute Beginners* (1986), in the mid-90s Ray Davies went on tour with a one-man show that combined songs and story-telling – another retake on the English folk tradition. After a low period in the mid-80s he emerged with *X-Ray,* an autobiography, and, in 1998, *Waterloo Sunset*, an even more confessional collection of short stories.

PARENTS Max Miller, Chuck Berry
CHILDREN The Clash, The Jam, Blur
READ ON *The Kinks – the official biography* by **Jon Savage**; *X-Ray – the unauthorised biography* by Ray Davies

Kitchen sink
Pretty gritty

'Kitchen sink' is the label applied to a particular kind of British drama that was regarded as very un-British when it first came out. The label denoted the move away from the niceties of drawing-room drama (which tended to draw a veil over working-class life), towards films and theatre that gave a far less restricted warts-and-all working-class view of British society. The two key brand names in the history of kitchen sink are Woodfall Films and *The Wednesday Play*. The films and television plays produced under both names were continuing a hard-hitting tradition that was already established in literature, beginning with novels of the Great Depression such as Walter Greenwood's *Love on the Dole* (1933) and moving on to stories of post-war, upward mobility such as John Braine's *Room at the Top* (1957).

Woodfall was the company formed in 1958 by director Tony Richardson, playwright John Osborne and producer Harry Saltzman in order to make a film of Osborne's play *Look Back In Anger* (starring Richard Burton and Mary Ure). Their model was the successful film production of *Room at the Top* (1958), starring Laurence Harvey as a sympathetic but ultimately heartless social climber. Woodfall enjoyed further success with *Saturday Night and Sunday Morning* (1960), from Alan Sillitoe's novel about a young working-class man on the make, *A Taste of Honey* (1961), with doe-eyed Rita Tushingham as Shelagh Delaney's schoolgirl in

trouble, and *The Loneliness of the Long Distance Runner* (1962) – Sillitoe again – about a borstal boy who bucks the system first by running and then by refusing to win.

Woodfall Films were innovative in that they took working-class people seriously: various commentators have noted the pleasurable experience of self-recognition on the part of working-class cinema audiences who were used to seeing people of their social station represented on screen as clowns, dupes or both. Woodfall also acknowledged both the sex and the suppressed violence underneath the surface of British life – unlike the **Ealing** Comedies that preceded them. But they were made at a time when traditional working-class communities were already under pressure, and their protagonists are often young, highly individualistic people at odds with their staid surroundings. Thus one of the iconic elements of a Woodfall production is a shot of a young man on a hill looking down at the industrial town below: the geographical distance between them reflects the estrangement between the individual and his traditional background, which, even then, was already receding away from him.

Woodfall Films also reflected the concerns of the people who made them: mainly middle-class types who came in search of authentic working-class existence. There was something of a misalignment between their idea of gritty working-class life and the real thing. Woodfall movies tend to focus on life in two-up, two-down terraces with outside lavatories at the back; but by this time council housing estates (with indoor sanitation) were the model for

real working-class life. Such disparities have prompted some critics to accuse the Woodfall team of 'complacency', of settling for a myth of the working class rather than digging into the reality. While some observers have noted the contrast between the social realism of kitchen sink and the stylisation of swinging London films, others have suggested that kitchen sink provides a depiction of the provincial working class which is as stylised as anything in Carnaby Street.

The television equivalent of Woodfall Films was the BBC's *Wednesday Play* series, of which *Cathy Come Home* (1966) is now acknowledged as the exemplar. Made by **Ken Loach** and Tony Garnett, and starring Ray Brooks and Carol White, *Cathy Come Home* follows the troubled life of a young, working-class couple who become homeless and end up losing their children. Shown when London was in full swing and there was much talk of a modern, forward-looking Britain, the play caused a stir among politicians and public alike: it was a factor in the formation of Shelter, the national campaign for the homeless.

PARENTS: Emile Zola, Walter Greenwood, Robert Tressell
CHILDREN: Terence Davies, *Coronation Street*

KLF
Doctorin' the charts

Jimmy Cauty (drew JRR Tolkien's Hobbit for the Athena poster in the 70s, co-produced the first Orb album with Alex Paterson) and Bill Drummond (former A&R man at WEA, member of Big In Japan alongside Holly Johnson and Ian Broudie, manager of Echo and the Bunnymen and The Teardrop Explodes, co-founder of Zoo Records) are old enough to remember when the letters 'LF' stood for 'liberation front' (Vietnamese, Gay, Animal etc). But what's left of liberation? The K stood for kopyright and the KLF (aka K Foundation, the JAMMS and the Timelords) wanted to take on the whole music industry.

On New Year's Day in 1987 Drummond went for a walk and decided that guitar bands and well-crafted songs were out of date. He had picked up on US hip-hop and, with Cauty as his partner in crime, set about flouting copyright and sampling from 'All You Need Is Love' (1967) by **The Beatles** and 'Kick Out The Jams' by Detroit's MC5 (1968). The original pressing of 'The Justified Ancients of Mu Mu' (JAMMS) numbered only 500, but the track was soon in demand. Relying on anonymity, the KLF used more pirated samples (Abba, Sex Pistols and the national anthem) on their first album, *What The Fuck Is Going On?* (1987; Abba caught up with them and instigated legal proceedings). Under their various names and incarnations utilising cheap sampling technology to its fullest, they built up critical acclaim and a cult following but did not sell many records (this was interrupted by the novelty record 'Doctorin' the Tardis', issued under the name of the Timelords which was a worldwide hit and stayed at No 1 in the UK for three weeks). They even wrote a DIY book about it called *The Manual – how to have a No 1 hit the easy way* (a kind of *Anarchists' Cookbook* for the music business). Their *Chill Out* **ambient** album (1989) practically started the whole 90s ambient scene. But they finally found fame in the emerging UK **rave** scene and released a string of worldwide hit dance singles in the 90s, selling more singles than any other band in 1991. They took genre-bending, eclecticism and irony to its furtherest boundary, remixing their own tracks until the originals were unrecognisable. They also collaborated with acts as far apart as thrash outfit Extreme Noise Terror and country legend Tammy Wynette.

In courting controversy, the KLF have carried on in the Situationist vein **Malcolm McLaren** brought to British pop. The 'pranks' or 'happenings' included billboard defacements and a crop circle hoax, but their most famous stunt, which may or may not have involved burning £1 million in banknotes on the Isle of Jura, brought them more than a million pounds-worth of publicity. As the K Foundation, they appointed **Rachel Whiteread** the 'worst artist' in Britain and gave her twice as much prize money as she got from winning the Turner Prize. Suffering from exhaustion and feeling they couldn't take their act much further, they retired after a final stunt (involving a dead sheep and buckets of blood) at the 1992 Brit Awards. They deleted their entire back catalogue, and burned all remaining mer-

chandise to prove they meant it. They have commercially released one single since then: the K Foundation's interstellar anthem 'K Sera Sera (War Is Over If You Want It)', which is 'Available Nowhere … No Formats' until world peace has been established. Bill Drummond has written two books in the 90s: a recent collection of short stories and *Bad Wisdom* (co-written with Zodiac Mindwarp) – an account of a journey to the North Pole to plant an icon of Elvis, and something of a homage to Hunter S Thompson's *Fear and Loathing* cycle.

In 1997 Bill Drummond wrote a caustic article for **The Face** about New Labour, and at the height of the Cool Britannia craze he attacked **Oasis** manager **Alan McGee** for signing up with the government. In 1998 the K Foundation mounted an event called Fuck the Millennium at the Barbican arts centre in London, complete with lifeboat men, a brass band, three violinists, and the two of them dressed in pyjamas and sitting in wheelchairs. When a journalist questioned the validity of this exercise, their associate Stewart Home (Neoist novelist and essayist) replied that 'blowing it is part of their act'.

The KLF are important figures in Jeremy J Beadle's study of the cannibalistic and subversive aspects of postmodern music-making, *Will Pop Eat Itself?* (1993). But in today's circumstances it is hard to see how their pranksterism could take on a broader significance. As Baudrillard has suggested, when there's no critical margin left, everything becomes just another part of the show. Sometimes it seems like a series of practical jokes from a pair of permanent students.

PARENTS Dada, Marcel Duchamp,
Malcolm McLaren, Rag Week
READ ON *Will Pop Eat Itself?* by Jeremy J Beadle;
Bad Wisdom by Bill Drummond and Mark
Manning; *Head On* by Julian Cope

The Krays
'East End Villains in a West Side Story'

Twin brothers Ronald and Reginald Kray were born
in 1933 and brought up in Vallance Road, one of
the oldest streets (a leftover from the nineteenth-
century 'rookeries', or slums) in the East End district of Bethnal Green. On leaving school they
became boxers; when called up for national service
they went on the run. After spells in the military
prisons of Colchester and Shepton Mallett, the
Krays (the name is Austrian; their antecedents
included Jews, Irish and Romanies) were dishon-
ourably discharged (like their father, a wartime
deserter) in 1954. Later that year the twins rented
a billiard hall in Mile End (a low rent was set following damage to the property) which, together with
their mother's house, they used as a base for an
increasingly wide range of criminal activities (protection, stolen goods, fraud, violence and murder).

The Krays were not just criminals. Taking advantage of the Gaming Act 1963, which turned London
into a 'European Las Vegas', they made crime
glamorous. As nightclub owners (first in Bow Road,
then up West), they mixed with slumming socialites

and a new generation of pop celebrities. They
appeared in photographer *David Bailey's Box Of
Pin-Ups*, the definitive image bank of Swinging
London, and when Reggie Kray (Ronnie was gay)
got married in 1965, **David Bailey** acted as wedding
photographer. In the *East London Gazette* they
were described as local boys made good; and for
many East Enders 'the twins' were the guardians of
a modicum of local tradition (pro-family, anti-
police) in a period of devastating social change
(terraced houses replaced by tower blocks, London
Docks in decline). Their reach even extended to the
corridors of national power: at one stage their
names were linked to Labour ministers Emmanuel
Shinwell and Lord Boothby over a scheme to build
a new model town in Nigeria.

In *The Krays: a study of a system of closure*
(1974), Dick Hebdige explained how the image of
the Krays became inseparable from their real activities. The bourgeois world, Hebdige maintained,
needs the gangster as a myth of negativity and
alienation; and the advent of 'the global village' of
televisual communications, coupled with the Krays'
own media savvy, enabled them to play an iconic
role in the broader mythology of swinging London.
Their role, said Hebdige, was to play the East End
villain in a fable made in the West End. The Krays
themselves became embroiled in this process of
myth-making: hence the out and out theatricality of
the violence and murder they orchestrated.

Eventually the Krays' melodramatic self-
aggrandisement became too much for the authorities to bear. They and their familial 'firm' were
arrested in May 1968 and in the following year they

259

were sent to Parkhurst for 30 years each. Ronnie Kray, who had been diagnosed as a paranoid schizophrenic during a previous prison term, was later transferred to Broadmoor mental hospital. He died there in 1995.

The iconic status of the Krays did not end with their incarceration, however. Films which draw on their myth include *Performance* (starring Mick Jagger) and *Villain* (starring Richard Burton), besides Peter Medak's *The Krays*, featuring impressive performances in the lead roles by Gary and Martin Kemp (of Spandau Ballet), and Billie Whitelaw as the twins' domineering mother, Violet (in an interview Whitelaw explained how frightened she was when she found she had lost one of Violet's brooches which had been loaned to her). Martin Kemp later appeared in *EastEnders* as a clubowner who kills his ex-girlfriend and in 1999 he featured in a *Time Out* cover story about East End gangsters. Even at the end of the century, the Krays were still a reference point for social observers: in the *Independent* Yasmin Alibhai Brown suggested that a letter of condolence from Reggie Kray to the mother of Stephen Lawrence (black youth murdered in a race attack in 1993) indicates the unprecedented possibilities for genuine multiculturalism in British society. As a West End idea of what the East End is like, the Krays still loom large in the British imagination.

PARENTS Al Capone, Violet Kray
CHILDREN *Lock, Stock and Two Smoking Barrels*, **gangster chic**
READ ON *The Krays – a study of a system of closure* by Dick Hebdige

'It was wet and foggy; people called you "Sunny Jim"; there was never enough to eat, and dad never took to dripping on toast. "Nose drippings more like," he'd say, pushing away the staple diet of the working class. "I thought it would be roast beef and Yorkshire pudding all the way." But rationing was still on, and the area was derelict after being bombed to rubble during the war. Dad was amazed and heartened by the sight of the British in England, though. He'd never seen the English in poverty, as roadsweepers, dustmen, shopkeepers and barmen. He'd never seen an Englishman stuffing bread into his mouth with his fingers, and no one had told him the English didn't wash regularly because the water was so cold – if they had water at all. And when dad tried to discuss Byron in local pubs no one warned him that not every Englishman could read or that they didn't necessarily want tutoring by an Indian on the poetry of a pervert and a madman.'

The Buddha of Suburbia by Hanif Kureishi

Hanif Kureishi
Man of many cultures

Born (1954) in Bromley, heartland of the south London suburbs, Hanif Kureishi remembers his Pakistani family being the only Asians in their street. In his teens the National Front was on the march and some of his classmates became **skinheads**. Nowadays he feels quite at home living in West Kensington with his new partner and their infant son. If London life seems more multicultured and less monochrome than in the 70s, this is partly because of the contribution made by writers like Kureishi.

After university (London) he wrote plays for fringe theatres (notably *Outskirts*, 1981, about two violent racists), financing himself by churning out pornography. He came to prominence in 1985 as the scriptwriter for the film *My Beautiful Launderette*, directed by **Stephen Frears**, which featured a gay relationship between men of different races and was hailed by left-leaning London listings magazine *City Limits* under the headline 'Victim Victorious'. Kureishi said of his script that he was aiming for something that was partly Godfather-gangster-epic and partly Sunday-afternoon-slushy-romance. Critics have tagged it as an early example of 'hybridity' – a way of living in which different cultures pick and mix from each other.

Not that Kureishi wanted to pick up the traditional British way of life. Around the time that he made the film *London Kills Me* (1991), he described Britain as 'an intolerant, racist, homophobic, narrow-minded, authoritarian rat-hole'. He also described the Poll Tax riot as 'terrific': his screenplay for *Sammy and Rosie Get Laid* (1987) is set in the forgotten wastes of Thatcher's Britain amid the rioting dispossessed of Ladbroke Grove.

Kureishi's first novel, *The Buddha of Suburbia*, came out in 1989 and was televised soon after. It is a coming-of-age tale set on the mid-70s fissure between the fag end of hippie and the explosion of punk. Asked if his novel was the first to give a voice to young Asians in Britain, Kureishi replied that 'lots of Asian kids have told me that *The Buddha of Suburbia* was their story. … It hasn't been told enough.' Rather than the one-dimensional Asians the English novel had traditionally manufactured, Kureishi offered a whole spectrum of truths that smashed the simple them-and-us myth: from his gay young Asian hero to his father who manipulates orientalist myths of the East to his own benefit.

One of the main characters in *Buddha* is loosely based on Kureishi's (white) Bromley schoolmate Billy Idol (singer in punk band Generation X). Kureishi places himself on the cusp between literature and pop culture. As a youth he used the world of pop as an escape from the supposedly safe world of the suburbs. '**The Beatles** weren't working in banks,' he noted. As an adult writer his proximity to pop culture prevents his work from becoming too literary. And he knows his stuff: with **Jon Savage**, a pop critic who does not suffer fools gladly, Kureishi was co-editor of the mammoth *Faber Book of Pop* (1995). In the same year he published *The Black Album*; set in 1989, it is an ambitious but only partially successful novel about cultural disintegration among Muslims in Britain dealing with sex, drugs, **rave** culture and religion along the way. Like *Sammy and Rosie Get Laid* (1987), *The Black Album*, while exhilarating and challenging, throws up so many diverse themes and so much hybridity that none leaves a real mark.

As befits a writer entering his mid-forties, Kureishi's third novel (*Intimacy*, 1998) moved away from youthful pursuits (clubs, drugs and identity) towards the terrain of domesticity. From the writer's point of view, this shift was merely a reflection of different personal priorities. 'As a young man,' he explained, 'I wouldn't go home for two days and I can't do that now. Going to Soho on a Saturday night seems like going into hell – all those people blowing smoke in your face and the noise. I don't really understand that anymore.' But Kureishi's ex-partner protested that *Intimacy* was intrusive auto-biography, not a novel at all. Kureishi maintained that, as in all his writing, 'you take the things that matter to you – marriage, race – and then you imagine around that'.

Kureishi is multi-talented: his collection of short stories *Love In A Blue Time* (1997) was well received. In 1999 his play *Sleep With Me* was staged at London's Royal National Theatre and he started work on a film version of *Intimacy*. In today's multi-faceted Britain, the man of many cultures is much in demand. In November 1999 he published another short story collection, *Midnight All Day*.

PARENTS Stuart Hall, A Sivanandan, **David Bowie**
CHILDREN Parv Bunsen, Meera Syal
READ ON *The Buddha of Suburbia*; *There Ain't No Black In The Union Jack* by Paul Gilroy

Ladettes
Blondes have more fun

If the mid-90s were dominated by the 'new lad', the late 90s were ruled by laddettes – girls who match their boys drink for drink and traded put-downs with them if not punches. It began around 1996 with *The Girlie Show*, the far-out replacement for a TV programme that had already gone too far – *The Word*. *The Girlie Show*'s mission was to 'flip the script of laddish culture' and presenter Sara Cox (brought up above a pub) boasted of her pool skills and 'filthy' sense of humour. The target audience was the 'new lass', a hybrid of good-time girl next door and 'Secret Sharon' – a Sloane who 'turned Essex after dark'. The show sank but the social type took off and soon even had its own girls-with-attitude version of *Loaded* – *Minx* magazine.

One of its main proponents was undoubtedly Swedish-born Ulrika Jonsson (b. 1967) who graduated from TV-AM weather girl to *Gladiators* compere and finally went on to be a team captain in the celebrity quizshow *Shooting Stars* hosted by Vic **Reeves and** Bob **Mortimer**. Here she is a willing stooge, described by one critic as 'perfect for the age of irony TV'. 'In this country,' Jonsson once said, 'you would be hard pressed to separate the words dumb and blonde with a crowbar. Because I am noisy in company, I also get called "bubbly", which is also pejorative.' Much more than an 'auto-cutie', she plays the sex card when it suits her. Interviewed by *Loaded*, she did a Sharon Stone and told the interviewer (and hundreds of thousands of 'men who should know better') that she wasn't wearing any knickers.

During the World Cup in the summer of 1998, Jonsson was sitting in a bar in Paris when her (then) boyfriend, Aston Villa footballer Stan Collymore, punched her. While the rest of the country wondered how she would cope with the trauma (only **Sun** columnist Richard Littlejohn was unmoved), Jonsson made a quick recovery and was to be seen interviewing the chancellor of the exchequer on BBC2 not long afterwards.

Daughter of a security guard and a teacher, Denise Van Outen (b. 1974) was also a weather girl before she got the job of co-hosting Channel 4's *The Big Breakfast* with Johnny Vaughan. After a walk-on part in *Les Miserables* when she was 12, she attended the Sylvia Young stage school where her contemporaries included Dani Behr and Baby Spice. On the breakfast show, she and Vaughan seemed to play with the possibility that there might be more between them than a TV partnership. But Van Outen, who has been described as 'the sexiest woman on TV', prefers pop stars: Andy Miller from Dodgy was replaced in her affections by Jamiroquai's Jay Kay (of his music she says she cannot listen to 'that didgeridoo business': she prefers Wham!).

No wonder women write to Van Outen inviting her to their hen nights: she always comes across as one of the girls (and one of the lads). At Buckingham Palace as a 'young achiever', she was miffed when the Queen did not know who she was, so she nicked an ashtray in retaliation. When she asked George Michael to go out with her (the request was made via the Internet), and his publicist rang to say yes, Van Outen suggested meeting at Lakeside shopping centre in Thurrock: once an Essex girl, always an Essex girl. Ignoring the poor response to her role in the sitcom *Babes In The Wood*, at the start of 1999 she left *The Big Breakfast* for pastures new.

Some would have it that the laddette is not a ballsy broadside to *Loaded* Man from the fairer sex but in fact the Frankenstein's bride (made in their own image) of lad culture, that they are a product of the proliferation of men's magazines and their need for visually appealing and publicity-hungry Barbie cover girls to please all those Ken readers 'who should know better'. From this viewpoint, they are girls who are willing to play ball with new lad culture if it will advance their celebrity; they might talk tough but are invariably ready to roll over when readers' fantasies demand it. Beyond Ulrika, Van Outen and Sara Cox, the list includes Melanie Sykes, Kelly Brook and Zoe Ball (who all proved their game feistiness and laddette credentials as co-hosts on *The Big Breakfast*).

As with the lad, the laddette wears a protective coat of irony so we are never quite sure who's pulling the strings. Are their antics part of a real self or just a ritual display demanded by the lads out there in the audience in return for cover-girl publicity? Some would have us believe that, like Madonna, though they trade on their own sexual image, they are still calling the shots and in ultimate control. Others believe that these bubbly stage-school 90s wannabes will do whatever it takes to get them on TV (dance, sing, act, host, strip, play

Lara Croft Digital Spice

The launch of Lara Croft in 1996 coincided with the rise of the Spice Girls. Computer games had been considered a male preserve ('they don't call it GameBOY for nothing'), but the Croft combination of boots, boobs, shorts, shades and an Uzi brought gaming together with Girl Power.

Croft is the heroine of the *Tomb Raider* series (the fourth game was issued in time for Christmas 1999), created by software publishers Eidos. Described by her developers as 'the first female games character who has been given a credible personality', 'Lara' is frequently interviewed online and in magazines, and represented at trade fairs and conventions by human lookalikes. Asked to comment on Girl Power, 'she' replied that 'if it means getting what you want, what you really, really want, with a pair of loaded pistols, then I'd certainly recommend it. If it means singing, then no.' In 1999 Croft was adopted as the model for Lucozade. In the USA in May 1999, Eidos was served with a writ that lists Lara as one of a number of virtual characters who allegedly encourage violent crime.

PARENTS the Spice Girls, *Doom*, Emma Peel
READ ON: *Lara's Book* by Kip Ward, featuring a short story by Douglas Coupland

dumb) and are not that far removed from the irony-free old school of Sam Fox, Linda Lusardi and the dolly-birds who caressed the prizes on gameshows.

PARENTS Mae West, Emma Peel, Barbara Windsor, Sam Fox

Mike Leigh
Life-affirming

Bearded Mike Leigh (born in Salford, Manchester, during the war), has been burrowing into the British psyche for 30 years. His work is a close-up on personal relationships; sometimes bleak, sometimes funny. Though rarely overtly political, they are always an oblique dissection of the way we live. From the open spaces of the campsite in *Nuts In May* to the street under gentrification in *High Hopes*, or Leigh's regular party-piece – the uncomfortable family get-together, he devises situations where Britons from different walks of life must face each other, and then waits for the fireworks.

Starting out in the theatre (his films still betray this discipline) Leigh's first film, *Bleak Moments* (1971) follows a young woman in her forlorn attempts to establish relationships with a teacher and a chronically shy guitarist. Harrowing and humorous, the film depicts both the boredom and the pressures of office work and family life (the protagonist is responsible for looking after her

David Thewlis in *Naked* (1994)

retarded sister), and describes the difficulties that people have with their allotted social roles. It was made for the princely budget of £13,000.

Leigh was then commissioned to devise and direct a series of plays for the BBC: *Hard Labour* (1972), *Abigail's Party* (1977), *Nuts In May* (1978), *Ecstasy* (1979), *Meantime* (1983, starring Phil Daniels, **Gary Oldman** and **Tim Roth**), and *Four Days in July* (1985), set in Belfast. This was his last piece for the BBC: questions were asked in parliament after a *Radio Times* interview in which Leigh said that his sympathies were republican. Looking back on his BBC years, Leigh said: 'I had the privilege of making a lot of films for the BBC during the period when Tony Garnett and **Ken Loach** really got going. What we were all concerned with was making films which came to terms with real lives and real issues. On the whole that has been unfashionable and now it's all about other things which are ephemeral and decorative, so in a way I'm still trying to hold on to doing that.'

Leigh returned to the cinema with *High Hopes* (1988), a story of human resilience and the search for a sense of family in the shadow of Thatcher's Britain, followed by *Life Is Sweet* (1990, featuring Jane Horrocks) – a film which was itself slightly sweeter than his previous work, and which brought him to the attention of a wider public. The tone of

Naked (1994, starring David Thewlis) was darker, but Leigh lightened up again with the award-winning *Secrets and Lies* (1996).

Now that the stresses and strains experienced by ordinary people in Britain are a fashionable subject in the USA (see also **The Full Monty**, 1996), Leigh's name attracts megabucks, and in 1999 he began working on *Topsy-Turvy*, his big-budget take on the lives of Gilbert and Sullivan.

Leigh enjoys the minutiae of ordinary existence: 'I'm instinctively and naturally fascinated by the texture and quality and detail of everyday life. There is joy for me in working from the raw seam of the way in which people talk and express themselves.' Audiences who may previously have dismissed his work as obscure now seem to be connecting with the care and attention he applies to the ordinary.

The dialogue in Leigh's films reproduces the halts and hesitations of daily conversation, leading some people to suggest that his scenes are improvised. In fact they are tightly scripted, but only after a prolonged period of character development during which Leigh works alongside his actors. As part of the process Leigh tends to use the same actors again and again: ex-wife Alison Steadman, Timothy Spall. *Meantime* co-star Tim Roth, who says he would pay to work with Leigh again, recalled the process thus: 'You build a character over weeks of rehearsal, so you know the character. Then Mike can just put you all together and something is going to happen, because you'll react genuinely. He calls it organic.'

When Leigh is happy with what's emerged, he writes it down and sticks closely to what has now become the script. 'The writing comes last' he says.

Drawn from 'the nose-picking, arse-scratching mundane world', he nevertheless hopes that the final product will be 'a celebration of people in all their detail and filigree, but also the awfulness of existence which one often talks about by sending it up'.

If he has a fault, it is that his naturalism, set mainly amid London's working and lower middle classes, can spill over into caricature. His characters that fall outside the classes to which he is sympathetic can be poorly drawn stereotypes; and occasionally his view of the working class (outside toilets and all) can appear sentimental and outdated. Though Leigh is now a Hollywood darling he struggles to keep his feet on the ground, living in the 'everyday' London suburb of Wood Green.

PARENTS: BBC, Ken Loach, **Harold Pinter**, **Galton and Simpson**

Mark Leonard
'Commissar of cool'

'I really hate all the Cool Britannia stuff, you know. I really do.' Mark Leonard (b. 1964) does not want to be pigeon-holed as the author of *Britain*™, the report published by the think-tank Demos, which called for Britain to be 'rebranded' and which became the central reference point in the debate about Cool Britannia. Nevertheless Leonard accepted a job as director of the Foreign Policy Centre (brief: rebrand the Foreign Office by serving notice on 'grey suits' and ending the tradition of 'sending Morris dancers to Oagadoogoo'), prompting journalist Quentin Letts to brand him 'the commissar of cool'.

'People still think we are a strike-ridden country full of draughty, dirty, country houses', warns Leonard. 'We are seen as white, imperialistic, arrogant and unfriendly.' Noting that 'Indian cuisine has a higher turnover than coal, steel and shipbuilding combined,' he insists that 'the vibrant street culture of Camden market' is more indicative of Britain today.

Son of MP-turned-Eurocrat Dick Leonard, Mark spent much of his childhood in Brussels. A contemporary at Caius College, Cambridge, said that the young Leonard was 'determined not to fit in' (when published in the *New Statesman* his criticisms of collegiate tradition and regimentation led to legal action by one don, and an apology published in the magazine). After gaining a 2:2 degree and a brief spell as a trainee at *The Economist*, Leonard joined Demos where besides the rebranding Britain report, he produced other papers that called for a Netherlands-style modernisation of the British monarchy (including a referendum on whether Charles or William should become king) and a revamping of the BBC World Service and its 'bowler hat image'. He once revealed that 'we're sending researchers out on the streets to talk to tramps and ask them why they feel left out of society'. Critics described him as 'an insufferable wunderkind'.

Like **Tony Blair**, Leonard thinks of himself as a man of the people. His estuary accent ('sub-EastEnders speak') is thought by some to be contrived, but he denies that his voice has been 'artificially yobified'. Of the London district where he lives, Leonard told Letts: 'All of Britain is distilled into our street. Beryl Bainbridge and Anne Diamond have lived here. And there's a bus driver two doors down from me.' Funny how the new boys of the British establishment sometimes sound like old-school, one-nation Tories.

PARENTS Michael Young, co-author of the 1945 Labour manifesto and founder of the Open University; Roy Jenkins, associated with the cultural development of the Labour Party at the end of the 50s

Ken Livingstone
Red Ken

Ken Livingstone came to prominence in the late 70s as the deputy leader of the Greater London Council (GLC), the elected all-London authority that controlled the capital's transport policy and other matters of strategic importance. At the time he lived with his mother, kept newts, wore safari suits and sported a dubious moustache. Livingstone won widespread support from Londoners with his 'fare's fair' policy of keeping public transport costs down. But when the GLC began to spend money on minority interests (committees were set up to cater for the Irish, blacks, lesbians and gays, as well as the infamous women's committee), the tabloids led an effective campaign against the alleged excesses of 'Red Ken', and Tory prime minister Margaret Thatcher was able to move in and abolish the GLC in 1986.

Livingstone bounced back from defeat in local government and into parliament. Elected MP for Brent East in 1987 (which did not stop him writing a book entitled *If Voting Changed Anything, They'd Have To Abolish It*), he also gained a seat on Labour's National Executive Committee where he has been a thorn in the side of successive Labour leaders (Neil Kinnock, John Smith and **Tony Blair**). Since the election of the New Labour government in May 1997, Livingstone has repeatedly spoken out against the influence of spin doctors such as Blair's official press spokesperson Alastair Campbell. Meanwhile New Labour's party machine reciprocated by trying to block Livingstone's right to stand for election to the new office of Mayor of London. Livingstone and New Labour are locked in a feud, but they also have much in common. The government's attitudes to the arts (celebrating difference, encouraging social inclusion through culture) might have been modelled on GLC policies during Livingstone's period of office.

Despite his much-mocked nasal whine, Livingstone is viewed with affection by many Londoners. He is one of the few MPs of recent times who has managed to make politics sound relevant to the public. He writes about food and drink in the Friday supplement of the *London Evening Standard*.

PARENTS Keir Hardie, Jason King
READ ON *If Voting Changed Anything, They'd Have To Abolish It* by Ken Livingstone

Ken Loach
The right to reply

Born in 1936, veteran film director Ken Loach grew up at a time when the British working class was organised into a labour and trade union movement with plenty of muscle.

The son of an electrician, Loach went to school in Nuneaton, Warwickshire. He won a place at Oxford, where he studied law, and wanted to act. After university he became a teacher. Then, as a substitute for acting, he accepted a job directing plays for a provincial repertory company. Taken on by the BBC, Loach found himself directing one of its most popular programmes, *Z Cars* (this in the days when programmes went out live and the vision mixer, as Loach recalls, managed to do her knitting during transmission).

Loach came to fame with *Cathy Come Home* (1968), the *Wednesday Play* about a young couple who become homeless and lose their children. It was the first ever TV drama-documentary, shot partly in the style of a Bertolt Brecht play, complete with caption cards and pieces to camera. Broadcast at a time when the whole country watched the same TV programmes (there were only a couple of channels to choose from), and prestige programmes

came with a sense of occasion, *Cathy Come Home* was the talk of the nation and is said to have prompted the formation of Shelter, the national campaign against homelessness.

By this time Loach had formed a partnership with producer and fellow-Trotskyist Tony Garnett. Their first feature film was *Kes* (1969), from the Barry Hines novel *A Kestrel For A Knave*, the story of an alienated Yorkshire boy and his relationship with a bird of prey. The cast included well-known faces (Colin Welland from *Z Cars*) with non-professional actors. Loach uses stylistic devices alongside documentary-type footage (the US distributors complained that the dialogue might as well have been in Hungarian). The film is didactic – there is a point being made in almost every scene – but not preachy. *Kes* has been described by the *NME* as 'the all-time juvenile delinquent classic'.

In the 70s Loach was frustrated by the small scale of the British film industry. With Garnett he made the harrowing film *Family Life* (1972), partly based on the ideas of left-wing, anti-psychiatrist RD Laing. Together with scriptwriter Jim Allen, Loach and Garnett also made *Days of Hope* (1975) and *The Price of Coal* for the BBC. Garnett eventually went to Hollywood and made a name for himself there before coming back to Britain to produce programmes such as the controversial 90s police series *Between The Lines*.

The tide turned against Loach when the Conservatives won the general election of 1979, and as Marxist historian Eric Hobsbawm put it, 'the forward march of Labour halted'. Loach found himself out fashion. In a moment of desperation he even made commercials for McDonald's ('the worst moment of my professional life'). In the 80s he was commissioned to make four TV programmes (*A Question of Leadership*) criticising trades union leaders for selling out their rank-and-file members; but, having scheduled it, Channel 4 came under pressure and withdrew the series. (When a union leader demanded the right to reply to one of his previous shows, Loach had replied 'I thought I was the right to reply'.)

Loach reckons that all his work has been about struggle, either in an individual sense or through a class perspective. In the late 80s he managed to recapture the lighter touch of his earlier work. His comeback film was *Riff Raff* (1990), the small-budget, award-winning, tragi-comedy about building workers. *Hidden Agenda* (1991), about the touchy subject of Ireland, remained largely unseen in Britain but was widely praised in Europe and America. At Cannes in 1990 a group of English journalists asked for it to be rejected on the grounds that it did not 'represent' British cinema; instead Loach's movie was awarded the Special Jury prize. But Loach does not take awards too seriously: he refers to his trophies as 'my Jimmy Riddle cups'.

Loach's most recent films are *Land and Freedom* (1995), a nostalgic retelling of the Spanish Civil War, *Ladybird Ladybird* (1996), a polemic against social workers, **My Name is Joe** (1998), about an unemployed Glaswegian, and a documentary in support of the striking Liverpool dockers. He has no time for **Tony Blair**'s 'repressive' New Labour, and boycotted a 'Cruel Britannia' party thrown by

Gordon Brown. Loach is the epitome of the lonely socialist (while thanking Bafta for his lifetime achievement award in 1999 he could not resist the chance to have another go at New Labour). But nowadays his socialism is so unthreatening (it counts for nothing among the working-class people for whom it is intended) that critics can marvel at the warmth and humanity of his films without paying much attention to his socialist politics. In 1999 he was domesticated to the extent that he was a guest of Sue Lawley on *Desert Island Discs*.

PARENTS Bertolt Brecht, Robert Tressell

Loaded

For not-quite-men

In February 1996 ex-*Mirror* editor turned media commentator Roy Greenslade remarked that 'Only *Esquire* has retained its former image of seriousness … *Loaded* has a lot to answer for.'

Loaded was launched by IPC in 1994 under the editorship of diminutive John Cooper Clarke lookalike and former *NME* writer James Brown (advice to budding magazine journalists: read *Pictures on a Page* by Harold Evans, look at **Neville Brody**'s typography, write intelligent letters to get noticed by editors). With the subtitle 'for men who should know better', *Loaded* waxed lyrical about tits, booze and bums. Laced with irony, this was gonzo journalism gone mainstream (but with Hunter

Thompson's subversive and political intent missing), and it stood out like an elephant's erection against the images of masculine sophistication built up by magazines like *Arena* (launched in 1986 by Nick Logan, seemingly modelled on Michael Heseltine's 60s magazine *Town*), and the recently established British editions of *Esquire* and *GQ*. Besieged by political correctness, yearning for old-fashioned lust, young British men were gagging for *Loaded* and monthly sales rocketed to 400,000.

Why did *Loaded* hit the boys' G-spot? Back in 1991, Sean O'Hagan wrote an article for *Arena* on a social phenomenon he identified as 'new lad'. The new male species, O'Hagan wrote, 'aspires to New Man status when he's with women, but reverts to Old Lad type when he's out with the boys'. What O'Hagan had identified was the unprecedented indecision among young British males about how they should behave. By the time of *Loaded*'s launch date three years later, this indecision was thickening the air – and irony was its coagulant: here was a generation who did not know how to become men, so they acted out a pantomime version of traditional masculinity, topped with a cheeky smile to let you know they were only joking. *Loaded*, with its jokey, blokey manner and continuous sampling from the pop culture tradition, was the ideal format for boys who did not know how to grow up. As *Independent* columnist John Little observed, their fathers would have had the confidence to go out and buy pornography; but the lads of the nervous 90s made do with *Loaded* – and then proceeded to boast about it.

Of course their boastfulness offended some people, and this only added to the status of *Loaded*. At various awards ceremonies Brown and his staff did their bit to fuel the mythology of lad, prompting different commentators to issue a variety of complaints. Radio DJ turned TV columnist Jaci Stephen presented a programme in Channel 4's *J'accuse* series in which she lambasted lads for being boorish and boring. In *The Sunday Times*, Cosmo Landesman argued that the lads' original line of defence – 'we were only joking' – was no defence at all, because not everyone realised it was just a joke (it was 'wrong to assume everyone else was ironically hip'). In **The Face**, editor Richard Benson thought that any 'wit and irony' had now been replaced by 'beers and leers'. He concluded that 'the joke isn't funny anymore'.

Instead of coming to an end, laddism percolated throughout British culture, diluting itself in the process, to the point where it became indistinguishable from its surroundings. Founding editor James Brown got married and left *Loaded* ('my ambition was being clouded by what was going through my body') for the upmarket offices of Conde Nast's *GQ*. *FHM* remodelled itself on *Loaded* and surpassed the sales of the original (500,000 copies per month since the first half of 1997). While full-on James Brown was 'coached' in how to deal with cool Conde Nast people (it didn't work: within a couple of years he was sacked, allegedly for including Nazi general Rommel in a line-up of style icons), his *Loaded* chair was taken by Derek Harbinson, a Silk Cut smoking 'designer baldy' who looks and sounds rather like any other men's magazine editor. At the end of the century *Loaded* was

still talking tits and arse, but we'd heard it all before.

In *Getting Away With It: the inside story of Loaded*, original deputy editor Tim Southwell describes the magazine as a 'fanzine'. What made it different, he says, is that the writers wrote only about the things that interested them, and shared their interests with like-minded readers. There is nothing new about this, however: it is the 'story' of any modern, consumer magazine at its most successful. Nevertheless his account, which includes contributions from other *Loaded* contributors who were in at the start, is a rollickin' good read. Besides revealing the considerable number of right-on women associated with the birth of the magazine (Miranda Sawyer, for instance) it also serves to correct the impression that *Loaded* was entirely the work of founding editor James Brown.

PARENTS *Men Only*, *Playboy*, fanzines, *NME*
CHILDREN *FHM and the lad mags*, *Minx*
READ ON *Getting Away With It – the inside story of Loaded* by Tim Southwell

John Lydon
Rotten to the core

Born to Irish parents living near Finsbury Park in North London, John Lydon was hospitalised with spinal meningitis at seven, and at fourteen decided he'd 'had enough' of school. After a brief spell as a youth worker, in 1975 he was spotted by ex-Situationist Bernie Rhodes wearing a T-shirt with 'I Hate Pink Floyd' written on it. Rhodes invited him to meet **Malcolm McLaren** and the band he'd been working with (which provisionally included *NME* writer Nick Kent). After a few drinks in the Roebuck on the King's Road, Lydon (soon to be Rotten) went back with the others to McLaren's shop, SEX, and mimed to a jukebox playing '18' by Alice Cooper. Three minutes later he had passed his audition for what became the Sex Pistols (and Kent was kicked out).

Their first gig was in November 1975 at St Martin's College of Art, where bassist Glen Matlock was a student. The two years that followed were a whirlwind of provocation and publicity. The Sex Pistols signed with EMI and A&M, but both companies released them from their contracts when the band's angst and deliberately provocative antics proved too much for them to handle. Eventually they were signed by Virgin, whose greatest hit up until then had been hippie-ish Mike (ex-Kevin Ayers and The Whole World) Oldfield's *Tubular Bells*. In the meantime the Sex Pistols were picked up by the *NME* (reversing an earlier editorial decision to go with pub rock rather punk), appeared alongside **Peter Cook** on **Tony Wilson**'s late-night show for Granada, *So It Goes*, and came to the attention of the nation when they riled teatime TV presenter Bill Grundy, whom Rotten/Lydon later described as 'a fat, sexist, beer monster'. Niggled by Grundy's questions, the band responded with a swear-fest which made headline news and prompted one Liverpool viewer to put his foot through his television screen.

With hindsight, it seems like an easy stunt. But, back then, the Johnny Rotten persona Lydon adopted – bug-eyed and tremulous with anger and rage – was both innovative and subversive.

To coincide with the Queen's Silver Jubilee in 1977, the Sex Pistols released their first single, the anti-anthem 'God Save the Queen' (lyrics written by Lydon while waiting for a tin of baked beans to heat up). Although the BBC has never admitted as much, everybody knows that the Sex Pistols were the real No 1 in Jubilee week. On the public holiday to mark the 25th anniversary of the Coronation, McLaren organised a boat trip up the Thames which was intercepted by police: more headlines; more outrage; soon the Sex Pistols were banned from playing half the towns in Britain.

Such notoriety increased the sales of the album *Never Mind The Bollocks* and the singles 'Pretty Vacant' and 'Holidays in the Sun'. But the pressure of being Public Enemy No 1 must have contributed to mounting frictions within the band and their entourage. Glen Matlock – the middle-class one – was ousted and replaced by Lydon's delinquent friend John (Sid Vicious) Beverley. Meanwhile Lydon was also falling out with McLaren. In Lydon's eyes McLaren was a middle-class manipulator who did not understand that punk was primarily a working-class thing. In January 1978 Lydon ended a gig in the Winterland, San Francisco, with the words 'ever get the feeling you've been cheated?'. He walked off stage and left the band. The Sex Pistols passed from the real world into the equally important realm of mythology. Their sound (distilled rock'n'roll) and their image (DIY derangement and disgust) have been an influence on live bands and record producers ever since.

Lydon was involved in a legal dispute with McLaren's management company Glitterbest for eight years, prompting **Jon Savage** to quip that 'the real beneficiaries of their legacy have been the lawyers'. Even after the legal proceedings came to an end, the two protagonists continued to clash over who created the Sex Pistols. In his 1993 autobiography, *No Irish, No Blacks, No Dogs*, Lydon claimed that the Johnny Rotten *persona* was all his – except the bits inspired by Laurence Olivier's performance as Richard III. He also suggested that bondage gear was not a McLaren/**Vivienne Westwood** creation, but arose from his own efforts to recreate the feeling of being in a straitjacket while on stage. Some commentators side with Lydon (notably Caroline Coon who described both Rhodes and McLaren as 'failed chauvinists' and credited Lydon with creating a 'theatre of rage'), while others have suggested that the explosive charge of the Pistols may have arisen from the creative tension between manager and lead singer.

After his sudden exit from the Sex Pistols, Lydon went on to form PIL (Public Image Ltd) along with guitarist Keith Levene and schoolfriend Jah Wobble on bass. Heavily influenced by reggae, the band hung out in Notting Hill, and tried to combine dub reggae recording techniques with experimental, expressionist guitar noise. The results were mixed, but high points include 'Death Disco' (1979) and 'Flowers of Romance' (1981). After the death of his mother from bowel cancer in 1979, Lydon, now married to Nora, the daughter of a German pub-

lisher, began to spend most of his time in the USA. 'This Is Not A Love Song' (1983) and 'Don't Ask Me' (1990) were hit singles in the UK. In 1996 Lydon ignored warnings about being fat and nearly 40, and fronted a reformed Sex Pistols for a one-off tour – an event which, like the **Happy Mondays**' reformation of 1999, turned a once-dangerous gang into a music hall troupe. His 1997 album *Psycho's Path* showed Lydon (who is an epileptic) continuing to plough the twin furrows of madness and creativity. He describes himself as a 'survivalist'.

PARENTS Richard III, Malcolm McLaren
READ ON *England's Dreaming – the Sex Pistols and Punk Rock* by Jon Savage

Colin MacInnes
In at the beginning

'"Those clothes you wear," he said at last, "disgust me." And I hope they did! I had on precisely my full teenage drag that would enrage him – the grey pointed alligator casuals, the pink neon pair of ankle crepe nylon-stretch, my Cambridge blue glove-fit jeans, a vertical-striped happy shirt revealing my lucky neck charm on its chain, and the Roman-cut short-arse jacket … not to mention my wrist identity jewel, and my Spartan warrior hair-do, which everyone thinks costs me 17/6d in Gerrard Street but which I, as a matter of fact, do myself with a pair of nail scissors and a three-sided mirror that Suzette's got, when I visit her flatlet up in Bayswater, W2.'

The exchange between the protagonist of Colin MacInnes' *Absolute Beginners* (1959) – budding photographer, post-political, pre-**Mod**, and his elder brother Vernon – Labourite, greaser, veteran of National Service, marks the beginning of the generation gap between those youngsters who defined themselves as consumers of pop culture and their predecessors who identified each other as producers, workers and patriots. Although much older himself (b. 1914), MacInnes was close enough to observe and record the absolute beginning of a way of life which is now so much the norm in Britain that it appears to have no beginning and no end.

Great-grandson of pre-Raphaelite painter Sir Edward Burne-Jones, cousin to erstwhile British prime minister Stanley Baldwin and Raj raconteur Rudyard Kipling, and son of once-fashionable writer Angela Thirkell, Colin MacInnes was born into the Australian branch of what his biographer Tony Gould called 'a Victorian cultural dynasty'. But MacInnes and Victoriana did not mix. As a young man he moved to London, gravitating first to the bohemian territory of Soho and then to the west London district of Notting Hill and its newly arrived population of immigrants from the Caribbean.

In his own lifetime (d. 1976), MacInnes' reputation as a writer rested largely on his non-fiction. He documented the rise of the 'classless class' of youth ('the children's crusade') for the broadsheets and for magazines such as *Encounter* and *New Society* (since collected in *England, Half English*). As a homosexual, MacInnes was opposed to the censor-ship of sexually explicit material. He campaigned to end discrimination against black people, defended the Mangrove Nine against their police accusers, and was one of the first intellectuals to put down 'the white man's burden' (the task of civilising the rest of the world) and declare that the West had a lot to learn from Africa. Such sentiments are commonplace today, and MacInnes must take some credit for their introduction into public debate. To his detractors, however, something of the colonial, cultural dynasty always remained in MacInnes, albeit in an unusual form: while foraging for sex among black men he seems to have behaved almost like a missionary in search of converts.

Nowadays, MacInnes is remembered chiefly for his trilogy of London novels, written in the run-up to the 60s and prefiguring some of the developments that would transform British society in the coming decade. *City of Spades* (1957) follows the fortunes of a Nigerian immigrant in London and is reminiscent of Samuel Selvon's seminal novel of black life in the metropolis, *The Lonely Londoners* (1956). *Mr Love and Justice* is a tale of policing and pimping. *Absolute Beginners* (1959) captures the look, sound and feel of the first London teen scene as it spilled over from Soho's jazz dives and coffee bars towards the cool black cats in Notting Hill. Featuring neat Italian styles, sex, drugs, multiculturalism and post-politics, this is pop culture before British pop music really existed.

What makes *Absolute Beginners* so attractive is that MacInnes portrays both the confidence and the nervousness of a generation that knows its time has come. Republished by Allison & Busby in

Samuel Selvon Before the beginning

A full year before *City of Spades* (1957), Samuel Selvon's *The Lonely Londoners* (1956) followed the fortunes of a group of immigrants from the Caribbean who, like their real-life counterparts on the Empire Windrush that docked in 1948, arrived in Britain with 'cardboard grips and felt hats'. Told mainly through the eyes of Moses, who like Selvon himself (b. 1923) had served in the wartime British navy before taking up residence in England, the narrative contrasts his world-weariness with the high hopes of newcomer 'Sir' Galahad.

Selvon wrote *The Lonely Londoners* in the historic present (see also Damon Runyon's tales of the criminal classes on Broadway), which accentuates the sense that his characters partake of a culture beyond the reach of British tradition. Selvon's use of dialect confirms this impression, although Caribbean linguists have shown that the dialect he uses is a fictional one, not a literal translation from the real speech of immigrants.

Selvon was not the only writer of the period dealing with the new experience of black people in London: Panamian-born Andrew Salkey, broadcaster, teacher and founder member of the Caribbean Artists' Movement, published *A Quality of Violence* in 1959 and *Escape To An Autumn Pavement* the following year. Close behind Salkey came ER Braithwaite's *To Sir With Love* (1961; later filmed with Sidney Poitier in the lead role) and its sequel *Paid Servant* (1962). Salkey's and Braithwaite's books were about educated black people who spoke better English than Cockneys; but it was the patois-patter of Selvon's blue-collar blacks that became fashionable in the late 90s.

CHILDREN the *NME*'s Penny Reel, *Q*, *X-Press*
READ ON *The Lonely Londoners*

1980, the novel became a revered icon in the new retro-style scene emerging around clubs like the Beat Route and coffee bars such as the Bar Italia in Frith Street. Starring Patsy Kensit, Julien Temple's film of the book (1986) was a disastrous attempt to capitalise on its cult status and generalise the magic of being an absolute beginner. Temple's film implied a comparison between Soho in the late 50s and the new club circuit emerging there in the 80s; but the freshness was gone and London looked stubbornly tired, unimaginative and uncool.

PARENTS Oscar Wilde, F Scott Fitzgerald
CHILDREN Adam Diment, Nicholas Blincoe
READ ON *Absolute Beginners*;
England, Half English

Madchester

'Manchester, so much to answer for'

In 1990 the industrial city of Manchester made it to the front cover of *Time* magazine; the city's one-man publicity machine, Factory records boss and *Granada Reports* presenter **Tony Wilson** said that 'everywhere else is seriously dull by comparison'; and everyone (even Liverpool fans) agreed that Manchester was 'cool as fuck'. Many of Britain's top new acts (**Happy Mondays**, **Stone Roses**, Inspiral Carpets, 808 State) hailed from Manchester, and the city boasted some of the best clubs (**The Haçienda**, Konspiracy) and record stores (Spin Inn, Eastern Bloc, Vinyl Exchange and Expansion). As well as their own youth culture sociologist, Steve Redhead, the Mancs even had their own uniform and an indoor market (Afflecks Palace) for selling it: baggy flared jeans (made by local Asian firm Joe Bloggs), hooded tops, pudding-bowl haircuts and loose, day-glo T-shirts with slogans such as 'On the seventh day God created Manchester' (alternative slogans included 'On the sixth day God created Manchester' and '061 Cock of the North'). So how come they were so full of themselves?

First, there was **Ecstasy**. The **Ibiza** combination of E and all night dancing survived the transfer to rain-swept Manchester, partly because it was underpinned by house ('obscure black American homosexual music' – Wilson), imported to The Haçienda by DJ Mike Pickering. 'E-dancing all night finds its hip music in this very obscure stuff which is being played by Mike', Wilson boasted. E and house

made for acid house, a winning combination that made it possible to ignore the grim realities of the de-industrialised north. And E was usually a manageable high. You could do it and be back at work, a bit wrecked, on a Monday morning. Instead of days of hallucinating and years of dropping out, 60s-style, this way you could take a trip and still stay plugged in to the city. The result was a city of middle-distance highs known as 'Madchester'.

Born in the Balearics and imported into Manchester, the acid feel and the baggy look were not really true to the purist spirit of the original creators of house and techno. But there may have been a genuine affinity between the toppling smokestack cities of the USA where these genres were developed (Detroit and Chicago), and Manchester – the cradle of the English industrial revolution, but increasingly empty of heavy industry.

Given that some London clubs were already dancing to the same tune (Shoom!, for example), why was it Manchester that became the Haight Ashbury of housE? Partly because a few bands, notably the Happy Mondays and the Stone Roses, made a connection (through the E experience) between dance tracks and **indie**-ish guitar music. This meant that a much wider music scene, including live venues as well as DJ-based clubs, became focused around the same ideas, and the whole thing gathered momentum. Furthermore, although Wilson admits that at first he failed to spot the new scene emerging under his nose at 'the Hac', when he did get behind it he moved quickly to establish the right setting for it to thrive. Alongside the

Haçienda, his Dry bar became a clubhouse for music people and their hangers-on. Wilson reckoned that the people who made Madchester were the 400 on the guest list at the Happy Mondays G-Mex gig in 1990, who acted as 'a community where everyone knows each other and bounces off each other'. In London the same number of people would have been too widely dispersed (this may explain why southern versions of the Mondays, such as Flowered Up, never took root); but Manchester was big enough not be incestuous and small enough to be accessible. Wilson's community theory had its dissenting voices, however. Ian Brown of the Stone Roses thought it was wrong to make out 'as if we all socialise together. I only met the Inspirals last week. Manchester is just the place we are from.'

Perhaps Madchester took off simply because Manchester is not London. Throughout the 80s there had been talk of a north-south divide, and by the end of the decade hostility to southern fashions and London music was widespread throughout the north. Just when the south was picking up negative associations to do with yuppies and Porsches, along comes a northern-based style that advertised its working-class (anti-southern) roots. 'This is the most blue-collar popular culture since 1956,' Wilson claimed.

He is surely right to remember the middle-class/art school elements in supposedly proletarian trends like the beat boom and punk. But the idea that Madchester was purely working class is equally debatable. Certainly some of the bands at the centre of Madchester were crews from council estates. But the scene they moved in was largely operated by middle-class, graduate entrepreneurs like Wilson, who once compared scouting for bands to 'the practical criticism paper of the Cambridge Tripos: you have to decide whether it's Shakespeare or doggerel'. It was not the undiluted proletarian character of Manchester that gave it a head start, but the fact that proles like the Happy Mondays got the chance to rub up against the city's expanding student population and a growing cohort of ex-student promoters and music-biz wannabes.

Noting the retro elements (flares, fractals, psychedelic graphics) in Madchester, some commentators accused it of being nostalgic. This was hotly denied. 'The best thing about the 60s is that it was 20 years ago and we weren't there,' quipped the Inspiral Carpets. Jeans might have been cut from 70s patterns but were 'worn differently, always in the context of now,' insisted Afflecks Palace stallholder Mick Anderson. The immediate precursor to the baggy look was not 70s disco but 80s casual, as adopted by football supporters in the early 80s (their style included flares and trainers which were given an 'acid' twist at the end of the decade).

In 1990 Madchester was set to be the music of tomorrow's world. Some people mourned the loss of intimacy, like Dean, manager of Expansion Records and a former Haçienda DJ: 'underground is when you only know if you go. The media have discovered clubland and taken it over.' In the spring of 1990 it was hard to find a flare-wearing Manc who had not been interviewed by the *Independent*, *i-D* or German TV. But just at the moment when Madchester went global, it ceased to be local and stopped being special. Madchester was everywhere and therefore nowhere. The force went out of Wilson's wind, new bands like Northside and Paris Angels were left in the doldrums, and 'Madchester' sank from the headlines as quickly as it had floated in. When in 1999 the Happy Mondays reformed after Shaun Ryder received 'a tax bill the size of fucking Canada' (the *NME*'s cover line was 'Madchester Reunited'), it was already an exercise in nostalgia.

PARENTS Ecstasy, casuals
READ ON *Manchester, England – the story of the pop cult city* by Dave Haslam

Manic Street Preachers
Bevan boys

Nicky Wire, Sean Moore and James Dean Bradfield are known for their integrity and their socialist roots. But they are the remaining members of a band whose original plan was to make one album and then split up. Now more than halfway through their ten-record deal with CBS, their very existence is a kind of compromise. 'We feel, personally, to ourselves, that we have spoiled it,' says Moore.

Now they are three, but the original Manic Street Preachers consisted of four boys who went to school together in the Welsh valleys, and set out to conquer the music world with a combination of Nietzschean poetry, socialist rhetoric, a look bor-

rowed from the New York Dolls (make-up, blouses and Babycham), and a sound that owed plenty to The Clash. The frontman during this phase was lyricist Richey Edwards, who made it to the cover of the *NME* by carving '4Real' on his arm.

With a debut album entitled *Generation Terrorists*, the Manics declared they would be 'the last group'. 'No one has ever sacrificed themselves,' said Edwards. 'If we become huge and just throw it away, that is a big statement. Then maybe people will see that it's all shit.' He was true to his word, but he also became imbalanced. After a year in and out of institutions, Edwards disappeared the day before a planned trip to the USA to promote the band's third LP, *The Holy Bible* (1995). His car was found abandoned by the Severn Bridge, but Edwards has never been seen since.

The Manic Street Preachers only became complete when Edwards disappeared. His absence endowed the presence of the remaining trio with a special significance. On stage the band looked more ordinary (off with the make-up, on with the Pete Townshend boilersuits), but Edwards' extraordinary story provided an invisible backdrop to their image. Their sound was more accessible without him, but their songs sounded especially heartfelt and authentic because this was a band that had survived great difficulties.

It was a winning combination. The Manics' first single without Edwards, 'Design For Life', was also their first major hit. They've been selling well ever since, and their fifth album *This Is My Truth, Tell Me Yours* (1998) was a Brit award winner in 1999.

Now pushing 30, the Manic Street Preachers

wear their ordinariness with pride. Wire lives in a terraced house in the Valleys and writes lyrics about vacuum cleaning. He attended the ceremony to commemorate the fiftieth anniversary of the National Health Service, which took place halfway up a hill in the Tredegar constituency of the late Aneurin Bevan, the firebrand left-winger associated with the establishment of the NHS.

With sheaves of leftish lyrics which aim to expose the hypocrisy of capitalist society, Wire feels able to declare that 'we've made honesty cool'. But he also identifies with multi-millionaire Howard Hughes and his legendary history of compulsive disorders. Likewise Moore has a fetish for 'things fresh out of the wrapper'. These preferences are in tune with today's post-political concerns about risk and safety, not with old-fashioned, muscular socialism. Equally out of sync with traditional socialist politics is Moore's misanthropic declaration that 'if the human race ended tomorrow, I wouldn't have any regrets about it whatsoever, because I don't think we've contributed anything whatsoever, in the entire history of the planet.'

Such hostility to humanity is Nietzschean rather than socialist, but neither of these historic world-views is significant any more: socialism cannot be expected to change the world; and Nietzschean lack of faith in society means nothing when nobody believes in it anyway. In the pick'n'mix of British culture, these two traditions, once mutually exclusive, can be sampled and mixed together by a power trio of extraordinarily ordinary blokes.

PARENTS Nye Bevan, Friedrich Nietzsche, The Clash

Patrick Marber
Gambling man

In the 90s, along with Armando Ianucci, **Chris Morris** and **Steve Coogan**, Patrick Marber wrote and starred in the spoof news show *The Day Today* – and in particular helped develop and script Coogan's best-loved characters: Alan Partridge (originally the sports journalist on *The Day Today*) and Paul Calf. He continued to co-write for these characters once they had been given shows of their own and it is this that he was primarily known for until, with the production of his plays, he stepped out of Coogan's shadow.

At Oxford, Marber was known as a drinker and gambler. As a stand-up comic he would do a show and then hit the casino, gambling 'with everything I had'. The wager finally paid off: his experiences formed the basis for his first play, *Dealer's Choice*, which opened at the Royal National Theatre in 1995. Marber's second play, *Closer* (1997), sold out at the National before transferring first to the West End and then on to Broadway (1999) in a production that starred hyper-Englishman Rupert Graves and former *Brookside* babe Anna Friel.

Featuring no-holds-barred language and a cast of sexual predators (obituary writer Dan, dermatologist Larry, photographer Anna and stripper Alice), *Closer* has been described as 'a thinking person's night of depravity, a *Who's Afraid of Virginia Woolf?* for disillusioned swingers, steeped in educated disgust and nasty one-upmanship.' Marber's characters are dissatisfied with their own Machiavellian

manoeuvres, but addicted to them all the same. What stops the play being just another example of ostentatious *ennui* is that, for all their sense of terminus (particularly the obituary writer) and personal failure, Dan, Larry, Ann and Alice are still trying to get closer to other people. In our cynical age, suggesting that there is something worth going on for might be Marber's biggest gamble so far.

PARENTS Arthur Schnitzler, Samuel Beckett

Alan McGee
Lord Rehab

Alan McGee (b. 1960; estimated personal fortune of £25 million) is co-owner of Creation Records, manager of **Oasis**, a New Labour supporter (£50,000 donation) and a rebel against New Labour (refused to attend meetings of the Creative Industries Task Force), a reformed drug addict who wants to reform the drug laws, a £250,000 shareholder in Chelsea Football Club, and a loyal Glasgow Rangers supporter. After 20 years in the music business, in 1998 he said that 'music is my job whereas football is my passion'.

Red-haired McGee was born in Glasgow within

earshot of the Hampden Park roar. His father was a panel beater ('that really grounded me') and his upbringing was 'traditional working class'. He told his careers officer he was going to be 'a pop star', and described himself as 'a Lennonist'. From 1977 he played in a succession of (post)-punk bands but at 22 realised that his talents lay elsewhere. By 1984 he had moved to a flat in Tooting, south London, from where he managed the Jesus and Mary Chain and ran Creation, his fledgling record label. McGee was the band's best booster: he constantly badgered the music press about 'the greatest rock'n'roll band in the world'. But when the pressure paid off and the Jesus and Mary Chain got noticed, they quickly became too big for an operation that involved band members and their manager folding record sleeves to send to **indie** distributors Rough Trade. They sacked McGee, who soldiered on and steadily built a roster of bands including My Bloody Valentine, **Primal Scream**, the Boo Radleys, Teenage Fanclub and the Super Furry Animals.

The late 80s and early 90s were difficult years for Creation. Often on the brink of financial disaster, it became customary for McGee to go to the States and 'sell a band for US$100,000'. But 'it got to a point where there was nothing left to sell'. In 1992 McGee and his publicity-shy partner Dick Green were forced to sell 49 per cent of their company to Sony, who 'were investing in me bumping into a superstar, recognising them and signing them up'.

In 1993, after a gig at King Tut's Wah Wah Hut in Glasgow, with '12 people' (McGee, his sister and some Japanese tourists) in attendance, he went up

to the band who had been playing and said 'I'm Alan McGee. Do you want a record deal?' Afterwards he could not wait to tell the rest of the world 'I've found the greatest rock'n'roll band in the world and they're called Oasis.'

With McGee as their manager, Oasis were steadily gaining popularity when **Blur** initiated the battle of the bands. 'It was the best thing that ever happened to us,' explains McGee. 'They had built up expectations … which on our own I don't think we could have done.' Blur lost out, Oasis were rocketed into superstardom, and McGee became known as the Brian Epstein of our age. But he was in no position to enjoy the accolades.

For years the Creation offices had been used for acid house partying at weekends. Members of staff recall that 'the first time I ever got E'ed up was at the office'. At the centre of it all was 'party boy'/'binger' McGee (it never stopped him lining people up on a Monday morning and sacking them). Then in 1994, while in Los Angeles on a business trip, his blood pressure rose to 172 and he was rushed to hospital in an oxygen mask. 'This is a bad movie,' he thought. It was the last scene in McGee's rock'n'roll fantasy life. The threat of thrombosis hung over him: 'I decided I wanted to live … it was pretty basic.' He moved back to Glasgow to recuperate and clawed his way towards health and happiness. 'Four to five months into it, I was scared to get on a bus from Renfrew to Paisley,' he recalls. He 'still wasn't there' until spring 1996. Since then McGee has been a health freak instead of a manic muso ('health is No 1 in my world'). He uses a running machine regularly, watches his diet carefully and prompts disbelieving comments from decadent old stagers like **Malcolm McLaren** who cannot understand 'the extraordinary new world of the rock entrepreneur who only drank camomile tea, didn't smoke, and was concerned with his health'.

Asked why he became a drug addict, McGee quipped 'because I enjoyed taking them'. On another occasion he cited 'the mystery, the illegality' of drugs. He believes that legalising drugs would 'remove the criminality' and take away some of their attractiveness. McGee is no libertarian. 'I only want to legalise it, to control it,' he maintains. If offered a peerage, McGee said he would take the title of 'Lord Rehab'.

McGee may eventually be offered a seat in New Labour's second chamber. Apart from arranging for **Tony Blair**'s children to see Oasis at Earl's Court (accompanied by chief spin doctor Alastair Campbell), he was one of the first appointees to the Creative Industries Task Force, established during the honeymoon summer after New Labour's election victory in May 1997. McGee, a veteran of the Tory-run Enterprise Allowance Scheme in the early 80s, said he wanted 'to make it easier for musicians and managers – small businesses – to set up labels and bands, to get them training in a largely self-taught industry'. But when the New Labour government showed no sign of loosening up on drug laws or the welfare-to-work rules concerning availability for work and the receipt of benefits, McGee walked out. Blairite stalwarts such as Mick Hucknall claimed he only did it for his street credibility. For a few weeks McGee was the top name in what

became the New Labour/Cool Britannia backlash. But he relented somewhat after employment ministers drew up plans for budding musicians to claim benefit and receive training so long as they can prove their worth. 'I'm basically very pro-Labour,' McGee says. Having shown an independent streak, he can now afford to go back into the fold.

In the summer of 1998 McGee warned that the end of the music business was nigh: rock'n'roll was no longer distinctively youthful, unlike the Internet which has the ability both to baffle parents and bamboozle the industry. Meanwhile McGee forced unofficial Oasis websites to close and launched a state-of-the-art website for Creation Records. If the empire does need to fight back, his enterprise looks like being in the vanguard.

As Oasis are compared to **The Beatles**, so McGee is compared to Brian Epstein. Like Epstein, he took an obscure bunch of northerners to the top of the heap. But whereas Epstein remodelled The Beatles (and they admired him for it), McGee is a post-punk manager who makes a point of letting bands have 'creative control … we do let musicians be themselves'. This may not always be for the best: if Primal Scream had been more directed, maybe they would have achieved more. In other respects, however, McGee is more old-fashioned than Epstein, who took a gamble on music that had never been heard before. 'Alan's taste is very traditional,' says *NME* editor Steve Sutherland, describing the Jesus and Mary Chain as a reinvention of the Stooges and Velvet Underground, Primal Scream as a traditional rock band who collided with acid house for one album (*Screamadelica*), and

283

Oasis as 'The Beatles with bits of the Pistols thrown in'. McGee has 'a great pair of ears for a certain kind of music', but like many prime movers in current British culture, he likes to hear history repeating.

In November 1999, after 17 years as boss of Creation, McGee announced he was selling his remaining stake in the company to Sony and leaving Creation for good in June 2000.

PARENTS Brian Epstein, Betty Ford
CHILDREN Oasis

Ewan McGregor
'Not drop-dead gorgeous'

Heart-throb Ewan McGregor (b. 1971) comes from Crieff, a prosperous market town in Perthshire. He made his acting debut as David in a Sunday School play based on the Bible story of David and Goliath. As a boy McGregor idolised his uncle, actor Denis Lawson (particularly his small part in *Star Wars*, and starring role in Bill Forsyth's *Local Hero*), and identified with old American movies, especially Frank Capra's *It's A Wonderful Life*.

As a teenager McGregor became increasingly dissatisfied with small-town life. At 17 he quit school (fee-paying Morrison's Academy) for an unpaid placement at Perth repertory theatre, followed by a foundation course in drama at Kirkcaldy Technical College, and, rejected by RADA, a three-

year course at London's Guildhall, which he found as stiflingly formal as his secondary school. Fortunately McGregor was talent-spotted at a Guildhall open evening, and before the end of his final year he was on the set of *Lipstick on Your Collar*, the song-based television series by **Dennis Potter**.

After *Lipstick*, McGregor was unemployed for a full four months. Since then he has always been in demand, moving from costume drama (Jane Austen's *Emma* and Julian Sorel in the televisation of Stendhal's *The Scarlet and the Black*) to a tale of northern grit (*Brassed Off*), to painterly **Peter Greenaway**'s *Pillow Book*. But it was his association with the **Boyle**-Hodge-Macdonald triumvirate that made McGregor a star. After playing the part of wise-cracking Alex in *Shallow Grave* (1994), McGregor starred as Renton in the screen version of *Trainspotting* (1996), followed by 'banana-heeled' Robert in *A Life Less Ordinary* (1997). The lead role in Boyle's film of Alex Garland's *The Beach* was expected to go to McGregor; but Boyle went with Leonardo Di Caprio instead.

At the end of the 90s McGregor starred in *Velvet Goldmine*, Todd Haynes' evocation of **glam** (McGregor's motto: 'more eyeliner, more eyeliner'), and *Rogue Trader*, the biopic of the man who broke Barings bank – Nick Leeson. Of his major role as a young Obi-Wan Kenobi in the George Lucas prequel *Star Wars: Episode One*, McGregor modestly said: 'this was more about being in the right place at the right time so the special effects match up'. After finishing work on the *Star Wars* set, in the winter of 1998 he received favourable reviews for his performance as a 60s revolutionary in a revival of David Halliwell's play *Little Malcolm and his Struggle Against the Eunuchs*, staged at the tiny Hampstead Theatre. In 1998 he formed a production company along with Jude Law, Sean Pertwee and Jonny Lee Miller.

Unlike his *Trainspotting* co-star **Robert Carlyle**, McGregor is no method actor: he harks back to an older tradition, exemplified by Jimmy Stewart and Cary Grant. *Time Out* critic Tom Charity has said of McGregor: 'you watch him for who he is, not who he is pretending to be'. However dour the part, McGregor's eyes always seem to be smiling. There is enough Scottishness in McGregor's voice to give him a local identity, but not so much as to interfere with his universal appeal. Likewise, there is sufficient quirkiness (this is the great British film star who says he really likes pigeons) in his otherwise regular features to make him interesting as well as highly presentable. Danny Boyle says of him: 'He's not one of those drop-dead gorgeous Brad Pitt types, but there's something enormously attractive about him, because he's more human.' McGregor has that star quality: in his slightly off-centre way, he reflects our common humanity while representing it to an extraordinary degree.

PARENTS Jimmy Stewart, Denis Lawson
READ ON *Choose Life – Ewan McGregor and the British Film Revival* by Xan Brooks

Malcolm McLaren
Mis-manager

The man who created the Sex Pistols and made the music industry look foolish, Malcolm McLaren combines the money-making nous of early pop managers like Larry Parnes with the revolutionary pranksterism of the Situationists. For most of the 90s, his media profile was increasingly that of a veteran commentator rather than an active producer/manager, but in 1999 he made a comeback as the creator of Jungk, a karaoke quintet of girls from the Far East.

McLaren's parents (engineer Peter McLaren, Scottish; Emily Isaacs, Jewish) split up soon after he was born, and Malcolm came under the influence of his maternal grandmother. After a brief spell as a trainee at Sandeman's wine merchants, he attended a succession of art schools: Harrow, where he met future partner (personal and professional) **Vivienne Westwood**; Croydon, where in the revolutionary year of 1968 he led a sit-in alongside Jamie Reid, who later provided the famous cut-up graphics for the Sex Pistols, and Robin Scott, subsequently leader of the post-pop group M; and **Goldsmith's**, where he met up with the British section of the Situationiste Internationale (SI) and the breakaway group King Mob. The Situationists were the first group of left-wing revolutionaries to realise that media images are now the key elements in our common existence. In 1962 their leader Guy Debord announced that this is 'the society of the spectacle'. Taking their name from a phrase used to describe the Gordon Riots of 1780, which started as an anti-Catholic pogrom and turned into an attack on the prisons and asylums of London, the tiny King Mob contingent sought to revive the repressed English tradition of utopian violence and apply it to today's media landscape. McLaren was later to pursue these ambitions through the medium which he did more than anyone else to bring about: punk.

In the first half of the 70s McLaren and Westwood ran a series of shops at 430 King's Road. Their first venture, Let It Rock, was an outlet for teddy boy clothes and accessories. For McLaren, the ted image represented the original mode of teen subversion – an image seemingly confirmed at the Albert Hall in 1969 when teds rioted in favour of rock'n'roller Chuck Berry and against the **Who**. But the Let It Rock clientele tended to be as conservative as 'meat pies and racism' (**Jon Savage**). McLaren's restless years as a shopkeeper were marred by the contradiction between his hunger for subversion and the need to shift product and make a profit.

The contradiction was partly resolved by his move into management (first with the New York Dolls) and the creation of the Sex Pistols. Here was a band designed to make money by breaking the rules. McLaren enjoyed signing them to record companies (EMI, A&M) that could not handle their explosive message. He fed the press the moral panic they were crying out for, turning first Johnny Rotten (**John Lydon**) and then Sid Vicious into the epitome of the irresponsible and undesirable. McLaren's combination of millenarianism and

media savvy was a winner (despite the radio ban on 'God Save The Queen' and the refusal of major chains to stock the record, it still made No 1 in the week of the Queen's Jubilee); it also lost him his own band.

McLaren modelled himself on Larry Parnes, the manager who ran a stable of early British pop performers (Billy Fury, Vince Eager, Johnny Quickly), manipulating them as readily as their made-up names. But times had changed and Rotten/Lydon was hardly likely to doff his cap to 'Mr McLaren'; nor would Malcolm the revolutionary have wanted him to. After years of pressure from old-fashioned moralists (sustained attack made the Pistols cutting edge, but it wounded them as well as keeping them sharp), the Sex Pistols collapsed in a heap of recriminations and, finally, litigation. McLaren claimed that the Pistols were all his own work. He seemed to regard the boys in the band, including Lydon, as mere ciphers for his original vision. Lydon saw it differently: he took McLaren to court for 'mismanagement', in particular for diverting royalties into the production of the film *The Great Rock'n'Roll Swindle* (1979; directed by **Julien Temple**; the film opens with punks as Gordon Rioters). Years later, on the Jo Whiley Show on Channel 4, McLaren turned this accusation around: he had never been a manager, he said; he had only 'mis-managed' the various bands under his control.

After the Pistols, McLaren invented Bow Wow Wow (one version of the story is that Adam Ant came to him for a makeover, but McLaren nicked his band and found a teenage starlet to front it). He borrowed 'vogueing' from the New York gay scene, combined hillbilly with 'that sporty, New York street look' for Buffalo Gals (1982). One of the first Brits to pick up on rap and hip-hop, his *Duck Rock* (1983) was remade in 1998 featuring De La Soul and KRS One. When McLaren met Afrika Bambaata in Harlem, he claims the latter was wearing a *Never Mind The Bollocks* T-shirt; 15 years later, New York's hip-hoppers made the album *Buffalo Girls – Back To Skool*, as a tribute to the man who showed them the pop potential of their own music.

McLaren has always enjoyed mixing genres. He turned hip-hop into pop, sampled the best tune in all of Gilbert and Sullivan's light opera, made a dance record in waltz time, directed a film about the violent history of Oxford Street (a remake of a student project) with the **Happy Mondays**, and dabbled with a jazz sound for the albums he made in Paris.

Camp, cutting and chain-smoking, in TV appearances McLaren has mocked the reformed teetotalism of today's Prodigal Son managers like **Alan McGee**. He belongs to a generation which believed that pop was like patricide – killing off the old society – but nowadays he knows it has lost its subversive element. Of the Sex Pistols' reunion tour, which he didn't attend, he said: 'The Pistols were mouthing the words of the group they were in. … In their original form, they were a much more chaotic and angry offspring but it was a group that promoted an attitude that can be nothing other than a karaoke attitude today.' With Jungk, McLaren's response to karaoke culture is to make the play-acting element even more explicit.

McLaren has entered in to a new business arrangement with veteran entrepreneur Chris Blackwell, founder of Island Records, but he is not convinced that the cut-and-paste techniques of today's DJ-dominated culture offer much of a future for pop: 'It's a very different way of looking at it. It's about taking the library which exists and remaking it. It's recycling which is very much part of a postmodern world but not necessarily pointing to a future. We are coming to an end, the turkey has been cooked, we've laid it all down, what else is there?'

PARENTS Larry Parnes, Guy Debord, the Gordon Riots

Alexander McQueen

'Effing and blinding his way through kissy-kissy fashion life'

With a taxi driver dad and brickie brother, Stepney-born (1969) Alexander McQueen is the crop-haired ('tres football-club de Liverpool'), plump, beercan-carrying Brit (proud of his Scottish roots, likes to dress men in kilts) with the top job at French haute couture house Givenchy. 'It is unlikely that a Briton would achieve what he has,' says his former headmaster, 'but for a pupil from an all-male comprehensive in deepest Newham it is incredible.'

Apprenticed to Savile Row tailors Anderson & Sheppard, McQueen amused himself by sewing lewd messages ('I'm a cunt') into the linings of suits (clients included Prince Charles). At St Martin's College of Art, he was the student whose designs were thought to be unwearable ('bumster' trousers, for instance, allegedly inspired by building workers' bum cleavage). But by 1996, after spells with Koji Tatsuno and Romeo Gigli in Milan, McQueen had set up shop in Hoxton Square (cheap then, but about to become highly fashionable) and was selling £700,000-worth of clothes per season to a client list including stylist Isabella Blow (soon to become 'his muse'), **David Bowie** and **Prodigy**'s Keith Flint.

Men's magazine *Arena* enthused over McQueen's spring 1996 collection: 'his zip-waisted, wide-shouldered menswear is cut in a clash of modernist plastics and traditional cottons and wools, in blue, black, white and red … his menswear is even more refined and desirable than the pared-down but still shocking womenswear offerings.' He won the Best British Designer award that year. In 1997, after producing six collections – four for Givenchy and two for his own label, he shared the award with his predecessor at Givenchy, **John Galliano**. McQueen's work is a street-style counterpoint to the debonair chic of Galliano.

Why did a traditional Paris couture house like Givenchy call in a designer known for producing 'shocking womenswear'? Perhaps because, for Givenchy and its rivals, couture is now, in terms of profitability, secondary to sales of what used to be mere accessories – perfume, tights etc. In this con-text, the main role of the couture house is as window-dressing – to provide publicity and newsworthiness for the parent company – and what could be more newsworthy than the takeover of a traditional firm by a young iconoclast described as 'effing and blinding his way through kissy-kissy fashion life'?

However, in a 1999 interview with London lifestyle magazine *Dazed and Confused* McQueen denied that his role at Givenchy is merely decorative. He maintained that although this might once have been the case, his clothes were now selling so well that even the couture house was making a decent contribution to the firm's overall turnover. Senior fashion journalist Suzy Menkes agrees that McQueen is much more than a gimmick: 'not just a fine tailor with a soaring imagination, but one of those rare designers who catches the spirit of the times'.

Before he got the call from Paris, McQueen declared that 'I never wanted to hang out with the Lagerfelds of the world and I'm not going to start acting the snob now.' He added, 'but I do know I have to be business-minded.' His impressive track record at Givenchy indicates that acting the anti-snob iconoclast can be good for business nowadays. If exiled from the fashion business to Radio 4's Desert Island, McQueen's preferred luxuries would be 'a bottle of poppers, a vibrator and a ready supply of coke'.

PARENTS **Leigh Bowery**, Zandra Rhodes, Savile Row, St Martin's

> 'Haute couture should not be a jacket so over-embroidered and beaded that it looks like someone has thrown up over it.'
>
> Alexander McQueen

George Melly
Bohemian blues

George Melly is the septuagenarian, former homo-sexual, fat, white, half-Jew pretending to be Bessie Smith, whose Christmas residency at Ronnie Scott's Soho jazz club became a British institution.

Born (1926) in Liverpool to a Swiss father and a Jewish mother, George Melly went to Stowe (public) school and into the ranks of the Royal Navy. In 1948 he began working at the Surrealist gallery owned by ELT Messens. He reckons he once scared off some yobs who were going to attack him in a London alley by reciting some of Apollinaire's poetry at the top of his voice. For 12 years Melly sang the blues in a revivalist jazz band led by trumpeter Mick Mulligan. In those days 'trad' jazz came with a tad of anarchism and rebellion, as well as duffle coats, CND badges and 'leapniks' who practised a pre-punk version of the pogo. Melly moved from music to Fleet Street (15 years co-writing the *Daily Mail*'s Flook cartoon strip with fellow jazzman Wally 'Trog' Fawkes; almost as many years as a pop, television and film critic for the *Observer*), and

back again. In 1971 he put on his loudest suits and went on the road with John Chilton's Feetwarmers, playing to young audiences as well as veterans.

Melly represents a mainly middle-class bohemia which loves sex, music, food and drink. In two autobiographical books (*Owning Up* and *Rum, Bum and Concertina*) he recounts homosexual and heterosexual experiences with equal relish. His musical tastes are catholic but as a performer he confines himself to a rendition of black women singing the blues – part pantomime, part homage. He likes full English breakfasts and has the girth to match. Like many others of his generation, Melly has always had a real appetite for life.

As a touring white, blues singer Melly lived a 50s prototype of the British pop life, which left him well placed to understand the real thing when it came along in the 60s. In 1969 he published *Revolt Into Style: the pop arts in Britain* (title based on poet Thom Gunn's line on Elvis Presley: 'he turns revolt into a style', also the title of a painting by Richard Hamilton), the first history of British pop and an account of swinging London which recognises the recurring transformation of youthful rebellion into music, fashion and what was later labelled 'lifestyle'. It was also one of the first books to identify the common ground between pop music and fine art. In one slim volume Melly prefigured British cultural studies and signposted young people's turn away from politics.

PARENTS Bessie Smith, Guillaume Apollinaire
CHILDREN Michael Bracewell, Damon Albarn
READ ON *Revolt Into Style, Owning Up*

Spike Milligan

Comic bolshevik

Spike Milligan was the chief writer of *The Goons*, the anarchic 50s radio comedy show that reflected the growing feeling that British society no longer made sense. The team that made up The Goons offered a reference point for National Servicemen, they were heroes to heir-to-the-throne Prince Charles and precursors of the counter-culture.

Terence Alan Milligan was a son of the British Army in India: his father and grandfather both served in it. His earliest memories are of soldiers in colourful uniforms at the barracks in Ahmadnagar. When his father was discharged and the Milligan family was shipped to England, his mother promised a life of 'chocolate and cream'. Instead they lived in one 'abominable' room in Catford, southeast London, and Spike's first job was washing 'shitty sheets' in the laundry of Lewisham Hospital. Drafted into the Second World War, he was sent to join the North African campaign against Rommel. Having being 'blown up' during a tank battle, he suffered from what was then described as 'battle fatigue'. Milligan recalls that 'whatever courage I had left ran out'. He became a wine waiter for the officers' mess, while also playing trumpet in a dance band for officers. When a brigadier told Milligan he was playing too loud, 'I told him to dance further away.'

Milligan came upon comedy by chance. While playing guitar in a duo with a jazz violinist, as a gimmick they began dressing up in rags and larking

about. After demobilisation, Milligan rented a room above the Grafton Arms in Victoria, a pub run by part-time scriptwriter Jimmy Grafton. Milligan, a friend of Ronnie Scott who founded the first jazz club in London, started to conceive *The Goons* as a show based on the kind of humour shared by jazz musicians. Meanwhile, Harry Secombe, another veteran of the Western Desert, introduced him to **Peter Sellers** and Michael Bentine (both ex-RAF), and Grafton joined the team in an editorial role. The first Goon shows took place in the Grafton Arms; it was three years before the BBC signed them up. The first broadcast, under the title of *The Crazy People*, went out on 28 May 1951. The original series prompted a reviewer in the *News Chronicle* to observe that 'Goon humour is obviously crazy and clever. It will either be loved or detested.'

In the nine years until *The Goons* came off air in 1960, Milligan, aided and abetted by Grafton, occasional co-writer Eric Sykes and fellow Goons Secombe and Sellers (Bentine's ideas clashed with Milligan's approach and he left after the second series), developed a host of legendary characters, such as the cowardly Major Dennis Bloodnok of the Indian Army; Bluebottle, the scoutmaster with the falsetto, and his idiotic friend Eccles; master-criminal Moriarty; and the villainous Hercules Grytpype-Thynne, modelled on silk-voiced actor George Saunders. But the success of the Goons lies not in any of these individual characters, but in the way that they combined to form an alternative world with its own internal logic.

Producer Peter Eton explained that 'unlike any other comedy programme of its time, *The Goon*

Spike Milligan

Show was less a criticism of any social system than a bold and melodramatic rearrangement of all life. It was obliged to create a nightmare landscape of its own and to people it with men, beasts and machines terribly at variance with the observable universe.'

The Goon Show was indeed a fantasy, but for millions of listeners it also served as a heightened version of the chaos of real life, and of bureaucratic confusion in particular. Peter Sellers observed that 'the public identified themselves with these charac-

ters and situations because to many of them they were more than just funny voices.' Milligan, who later described himself and Sellers as 'comic bolsheviks', insisted that it was 'critical comedy. It is against bureaucracy and on the side of human beings. Its starting-point is one man shouting gibberish in the face of authority and proving by fabricated insanity that nothing could be as mad as what passes for ordinary living.'

The exorcism of the madness of the real world by the creation of fictional madness, was something that young people in particular were quick to iden- tify with. According to Jeff Nuttall, the first chroni- cler of the British counter-culture, '*The Goon Show* was every National Serviceman's defence mecha- nism.' The Goons were at once protest and surreal- ist art, and among Nuttall's bohemian circle '*Goon Show* caricature voices spread into everybody's conversation and provided us all with schizoid sub- terfuges, vocal disguises.' A few years later, Goon voices were all the range among pop musicians. Biographer Christopher Sandford observes that Eric Clapton would 'awake from an apparent coma to engage in the kind of comic monologue character- istic of the Goons'. In his Cambridge rooms, the young Prince Charles was talking in the same crazy way.

The pressure of producing Goons scripts became too much for Milligan. He had a nervous breakdown and has suffered from manic depres- sion ever since. Years later his condition was ame- liorated by the prescription of lithium, but only after spells in psychiatric homes, a 'token' attempted suicide, and prolonged periods of feeling 'like not being alive'. In the midst of this he has conducted a complicated private life (five children from his first marriage which ended in divorce; one daughter with his second wife, who died of cancer; a son from an affair in the 70s; now married to Sheila, for- merly a typist in his office), written various books including the absurd novel *Puckoon* (1963), *Adolf Hitler: My Part In His Downfall* (1971) and another autobiographical piece, *Where Have All The Bullets Gone?* (1985). Besides cameo roles in numerous films, and a prominent part in *Curry and Chips*,

Johnny Speight's largely unsuccessful successor to *Till Death Us Do Part*, Milligan wrote and starred in his own TV shows: the *Q* series.

Milligan's work has been widely influential. TV programmes like **Monty Python's** *Flying Circus* could not have existed without him. John Lennon's comic writing (*In His Own Write*, 1965) bears the mark of Milligan. More broadly, the idea that life does not make sense, which in the 50s was articu- lated only by Milligan and a handful of others, is now common throughout British culture.

PARENTS jazz, war, Surrealism
CHILDREN **The Beatles**, Prince Charles, Monty Python, **Reeves and Mortimer**

Martin Millar
PG Wodehouse of the Brixton crusties

Apart from the real Brixton where people actually live, there are two mythical places that go by the same name: the Brixton of the media-led moral panics of the 70s and 80s, where every other inhabitant is a black mugger or rioter; and the bohemian Brixton of cheap housing and Spiv's Cafe as described by (then) Brixton Road resident Geoff Dyer in his semi-autobiographical and self-con- sciously nostalgic novel *The Colour of Memory*. Published in 1991, this was a look back with fond- ness to 'what for a while had qualities of arcadia' for the species of 'homo skiver', whom Dyer defined as 'that community of low-income radicals who moved in just after the first lot of riots'.

The arcadia went sour during the 80s: suddenly there was a yawning gap between the yuppie, glossy magazine lifestyle and the sad but crazy business of eking out a living on the **dole**. This is where Martin Millar (b. 1959) comes in.

Tattooed Millar is the godfather of British grunge fiction. His crustie characters are just not built for a regimented, workaday life: they only know who they are by virtue of their ear-ringed idiosyncrasies. Instead of working, they live in the confined space between the (real-life) Railway Hotel and the Cooltan, the DIY arts centre housed in Brixton's old dole office, scamming this and making an occasional bundle out of that, as is the way with 'the giro generation'.

The eponymous hero of *Lux The Poet* (1988) tries to do all right by his girlfriend Pearl but gets caught up in a right-wing genetic-engineering conspiracy. The central character in *Milk, Sulphate and Alby Starvation* (1987) is a sympathetic speed dealer. *Dreams of Sex and Stage Diving* (1994) focuses on a tomboy called Elfish. Millar's ribald humour has been compared to that of Tom Sharpe and even Geoffrey Chaucer. But the real star of his books is the unconventional lifestyle – except that the life which once was unconventional now seems as mannered and predicable as Bertie Wooster's (if you can imagine him as a member of the **underclass**). In this respect, Millar might well be described as the PG Wodehouse of the Brixton crusties.

In 1998 Millar published *Love and Peace with Melody Paradise*, which earned him favourable reviews as 'Brixton's answer to Kurt Vonnegut'. On his website he posted the nine rejection letters he received before finding a publisher for it. A novelist with a serious interest in theatre, his adaptation of Jane Austen's *Emma* played to packed houses at the **Edinburgh Festival**.

PARENTS Damon Runyan, Tom Sharpe, PG Wodehouse
CHILDREN Nicholas Blincoe, Jeff Noon

The Mini
Small is beautiful

The diminishing spiral of car production is typical of the decline of British manufacturing industry during the last 30 years. But the downward trajectory has been punctuated by some spectacular successes. Designed by Alec (later Sir Alec) Issigonis and advertised as 'wizardry on wheels', the Mini was launched by the British Motor Corporation (BMC) in 1959. In the following 40 years, five and a half million Minis were manufactured at the Longbridge car production plant in Birmingham.

At first, the Mini was not the Mini. Two almost identical cars were brought on to the market in 1959: the new Austin Seven and the Morris Mini Minor (a reference to the earlier Morris Minor, also designed by Issigonis). Together they became known simply as the Mini. Although it became known as the epitome of 60s motoring (quick, neat

and stylish), the Mini was a product of the 50s. And although his work was a byword for modernity and social mobility, the designer of the Mini was an unmarried man who lived with his mother, 'hated modern buildings', and loved 'the Edwardian atmosphere' of his favourite holiday resort, Monte Carlo. After retirement in 1971, Issigonis devoted more time to his model steam locomotives.

Powered originally by a 900cc engine (reduced to 848cc by BMC who feared that it was too big for young drivers), the Mini was only 10 feet long yet could comfortably carry four six-footers. Until then small cars had been a joke, but the Mini proved that small could mean sexy and powerful.

The non-phallic, pared-down, almost androgynous look of the Mini, made it the car that **Mods** dreamt about while riding their **scooters**. With rally driver Paddy Hopkirk at the wheel, the Mini Cooper seemed heroic (it was exhibited on stage at the London Palladium after the 1967 Monte Carlo rally). Stripped down like a parody of an American army jeep, the Mini Moke was daring and cosmopolitan, especially when driven on the beach during the opening credits of the *Simon Dee Show* – the hip precursor of *Parkinson* that used to go out on Saturday nights after *The Monkees*. And by the time it appeared in the film *The Italian Job* (1969), the Mini evoked a notion of the swinging 60s that was as British as Lord Kitchener.

For the fortieth anniversary of the Mini in 1999, the Design Museum mounted a Mini Design competition for which 1000 contestants entered their own custom-painted vehicle: the winner was student Mark Ward with his 'Time Machine' Mini; other participants included **David Bowie**, **Kate Moss** and **Paul Smith**, who described the car as 'the epitome of the British design classic'. Later in the year there was a Mini birthday party at Silverstone race track, attended by thousands of Minis and their owners.

In 1998, German firm BMW unveiled plans to invest £400 million in building a new Mini at the Longbridge plant in Birmingham. The great British Mini will be reborn, under German ownership.

> 'This teenage ball had had a real splendour in the days when the kids discovered that, for the first time since centuries of kingdom-come, they'd money, which hitherto had always been denied to us at the best time in life to use it, namely, when you're young and strong, and also before the newspapers and telly got hold of this teenage fable and prostituted it as conscripts seem to do to everything they touch. Yes, I tell you, it had a real savage splendour in the days when we found that no one could sit on our faces because we had loot to spend at last, and our world was to be our world, the one we wanted and not standing on the doorstep of somebody else's waiting for honey, perhaps.'
>
> From *Absolute Beginners* by Colin MacInnes

Mods
Amphetamines, existentialism and r&b

Now regarded as the quintessential swinging London stylists, the first Mods manufactured their look from elements that came from outside the 'stagnant society' that was early-60s Britain: black American music; American pop art; shades and porkpie hats, like those of the Kingston (Jamaica) rude bwoys; the violence of New York gangsters; Italian shirts, **scooters** and short Roman jackets; Left Bank existentialism, Nouvelle Vague movies and maybe a French crop. Early Mod heroes ranged from John Lee Hooker to Jean-Paul Sartre. They were buoyant, ultra-style-conscious young Britons who having 'never had it so good' were eager to accentuate their newness and cast off from the past. They assembled their favoured cosmopolitan aspects from a modern continental Europe and urban America and refashioned them in their own fetishised constellation of cool. They were the first urban working-class generation who had breathing space between beginning to earn good money and settling down with a family, and they were determined to make expressive use of this new-found leisure.

On the cusp of the 60s, London's first 'Modernists' were keen on modern jazz. They disliked rock'n'roll and the teddy boy style because of their working-class associations. In a new age of social mobility, they wanted to be classless. Not even their vandalism was lumpen: 'it was like a Magritte painting,' said a member of the East

295

London gang, The Firm. At the start of the 60s, Modernists picked up on the new urban black music that was just arriving in Britain (r&b plus sophistication = Tamla Motown), and became Mods. They also found that long hair was more suited to the non-macho androgyny to which they aspired (sex, all grunting and groaning, seemed old-fashioned). But there were still only a handful of them. In a piece about Mods and classlessness, 'Today There Are No Gentlemen' (1962), journalist Nik Cohn reported that 'there were enough converts to make them a sect, which was called Mod'.

How did Mod become more than a tiny minority of young men who shopped at John Stephens' His Clothes in Carnaby Street, took blues and purple hearts (amphetamines) in clubs (The Scene, Flamingo) and spent whole evenings posing in front of the mirror drinking whisky and coke? First there were the London-based bands who showed the rest of the country what Mod looked like: the **Rolling Stones** (in their *Aftermath* phase, under the influence of manager Andrew Loog Oldham); **The Who**; and **The Small Faces** (recording for Loog Oldham's new label, Immediate). Alongside the bands came the media reports which, as Stanley Cohen explained in *Folk Devils and Moral Panics*, presented some fairly arbitrary acts of unruliness in seaside towns – such as that in Clacton on Whitsun bank holiday 1964 – as if there were a fully fledged war between two tribes. Mods vs Rockers was a bit of a myth which served to describe the apparent volatility of youth; but after the myth was propagated across the nation it became more like reality. In a more positive sense, Mod also came to symbolise the hope that Britain could be a smarter, faster, neater society, with pedestrianised shopping precincts (Minis and scooters in rooftop car parks – Mod) in place of smoke-belching factories (union members on motorbikes – Rockers).

In *The Meaning of Mod* (1975), cultural critic Dick Hebdige noted that: 'The Mod was the first all-British White Negro of Mailer's essay, living on the pulse of the present, resurrected after work only by a fierce devotion to leisure.' Although Mods saw themselves as alienated from the rest of society, and their identification with blacks was a symbol of this, in identifying themselves primarily as consumers rather than workers ('resurrected after work'), they were dancing to a tune that the rest of British society would soon catch on to (the Consumer Association was founded in 1966, not long after the birth of Mod). It was the Mods who really began the fetishisation of the weekend – 'The Weekend Starts Here' (*Ready, Steady, Go!*). They were a hyper-stylised version of the straight world of midweek 9 to 5 and weekend leisure: working in straight jobs all week for their money then exploding at the weekend and artificially expanding that leisure time with amphetamines.

In the 40 years since the first Modernists there has been a succession of Mod revivals. In the late 70s, bands like the Merton Parkas adopted some of the outward signs of Mod but they were everything the originals weren't: local and parochial instead of urban and cosmopolitan, they wore their parkas as a badge of identity, whereas for the first Mods an ex-army parka was just an overall to keep your suit clean. The early 80s band Secret Affair was closer

Jimmy from The Who's original Quadrophenia album

in spirit to the originals; meanwhile the **Two-Tone** crowd adopted some of Mod's most-favoured heroes (Prince Buster, for example). Towards the end of the 80s bands like the James Taylor Quartet referred back to the long-lost jazz element among early Modernists. Franc Roddam's film (1979) *Quadrophenia*, based on the rock opera by former Mods the Who (1973), was reissued in 1997, sparking off a new wave of interest in Mod. But by this time Mod was either a caricature (as in soft drink adverts) or as elusive as the holy grail. Britain at the beginning of the twenty-first century seems more hooked on retro than modernism.

Many Brit bands from the **Stone Roses** to **Oasis** and **Blur** have borrowed the signifiers of 'classic' Mod, from scooters and pop art to Fred Perry shirts, to give themselves a twist of old-school cool. But if any subculture has truly inherited the spiritual mantle of mod, it is 90s club culture: its cosmopolitan eclecticism, willingness to embrace the shock of the new in style and sound, how it revels in display and has taken the fetishisation of the weekend even further – the stylised leisure-time pilgrimages to the seaside have just moved on from Brighton to the Balearics – make today's clubbers the Mods of the new millennium.

PARENTS images of New York, Detroit, Kingston, Paris, Rome
CHILDREN swinging London, **Northern Soul**, **rave** culture
READ ON *The Meaning of Mod* by Dick Hebdige

298

Monty Python
Comic Sgt Pepper's

Just as **The Beatles**' masterpiece *Sgt Pepper's Lonely Hearts Club Band* (1967) laughed at Englishness as well as venerating it, so the BBC comedy series *Monty Python's Flying Circus* (1969–73) mocked Britain's old guard from within a public school/Cambridge tradition. Known the world over as the epitome of British humour, the team that created Monty Python included an American animator (Terry Gilliam), and was regarded at the time as subversive and almost anti-British. Yet two of the original group (John Cleese and Michael Palin) did indeed go on to become quintessential Englishmen: Cleese as hotel proprietor Basil Fawlty in *Fawlty Towers* (1974–79), the series he created with his (then) wife Connie Booth; and Palin as host of travel documentaries in which he seems to play the role of the Perfect English Gent.

Cleese, Palin, Terry Jones, Graham Chapman and Eric Idle all met at Cambridge in the early 60s, where they were members of the Footlights (secretary: David Frost) revue group (the test-bed for the epochal British satire show *Beyond The Fringe*). After Cambridge, Cleese worked as a journalist in the USA, where he met Gilliam. Returning to Britain, he wrote sketches and appeared in *The Frost Report*. In 1968 all six future-Pythons met on the set of ITV's *Do Not Adjust Your Set*, ostensibly a children's programme (it went out at 5.15pm on Wednesdays) but in fact a sophisticated, witty deconstruction

of television genres and media conventions in general.

Broadcast in 1969, the first series of *Monty Python's Flying Circus* offered a surreal and sometimes cruel parody of the pretensions and traditions of British life (both aspects were directly expressed in Gilliam's animated sequences, but also clearly discernible in the comedy sketches). It was also the first television programme to subvert the medium itself. For a sketch they would take a recognisable format, the chatshow or documentary, for instance, and let insanity demolish it from the inside out. With their deconstructive mixing of genres and registers, and guerrilla raids on the conventions of film and television language, the whole programme would steadily break down, with characters from one sketch intruding on another.

When first broadcast on BBC2, *Monty Python* attracted a mainly middle-class audience which was already familiar with the grammar of absurdity (despite the show's defining catchphrase, Python was not 'something completely different', rather a distillation of existing trends in art and literature). But after the television programmes became available on video, and the series of Python films (*Holy Grail*, 1974; *Life Of Brian*, 1979; *The Meaning of Life*, 1983) proved successful, the base of Python fans widened to include council estate kids as well as campus cronies. By the early 80s, Python was part of the British vernacular – and quoted verbatim and *ad nauseam* (silly voices and all) by bores everywhere.

After the fourth TV series ended in 1974, the team continued to work together on Python films while pursuing successful solo careers: Cleese as an actor, director, anti-smoking activist and occasional campaigner for the Liberal Democrats; Gilliam as a film director (one of the first to recognise the talents of Quentin Tarantino); Palin with his *Ripping Yarns* series (which hilariously parodied the conventions and manners of the classic English 'Boy's Own' adventure stories – everything from public school bullies to giant-killing football teams) and as an actor and TV presenter; Idle as a writer, actor and musician – his spoof of The Beatles, The Rutles, originated in a parody TV series called *Rutland Weekend Television* (1975–76). Graham Chapman died of cancer in 1989.

PARENTS Donald Barthelme, the *Men From The Ministry*, Spike Milligan, Marty Feldman, Edward Albee

Morecambe and Wise
Exceptional routines

Eric Morecambe and Ernie Wise were 'the most brilliant comic duo ever' (**The Sun**). But this 40-year partnership depended on their combined portrayal of a seemingly ordinary kind of Britishness.

John Eric Bartholomew was born in Morecambe in 1926. His mother and future manager Sadie always wanted her son to go on the stage. At 10 he started dancing lessons, and by 15 he was appearing at the Liverpool Empire in a new juvenile, comedy double act, Bartholomew and Wise. Ernest Wiseman (b. 1925) was the son of a railway porter who doubled as an entertainer. At seven, Ernie and père were going out under the name of Bert Carson and his Little Wonder. Ernie's version of Al Jolson's 'Let's Have a Tiddly at the Milk Bar' was said to be a showstopper.

The Second World War put a temporary stop on the Morecambe and Wise partnership. Wise enlisted in the navy and Bartholomew/Morecambe went down the mines as a Bevin Boy. In 1947 they were reunited. Drawing on Abbott and Costello and Laurel and Hardy ('a very stupid guy who thinks he's a cut above another stupid guy'), they gradually developed an act in which Ernie's character (the one with 'short, fat hairy legs' who was 'vain, snobbish, puritanical, mean, sexually naive, magnificently smug and given to delusions of artistic grandeur') was constantly upstaged by bespectacled, gormless Eric, the fool who knew he was being stupid. This comic relationship was the core element in a lifetime's performances, first on stage in variety theatres up and down the country, on radio, on TV and, less successfully, on film (*The Intelligence Men* and *That Riviera Touch*). *Running Wild*, their first outing with the BBC, was a failure; but on Lew and Michael Grade's ATV London in the 60s they became 'the biggest attraction on television', and after head of light entertainment Bill Cotton lured them back to the BBC in 1968, their shows became national institutions: the 1976 Christmas special drew an audience of 28 million.

While comedy changed all around them, Morecambe and Wise retained many of the characteristics of a traditional, variety act: the banter in front of the curtain, the combination of songs and sketches. Likewise, while sections of the British population were drawn into the maelstrom of the swinging 60s and the sexual revolution of the 70s, Eric and Ernie remained reassuringly square – so much so that they could even go to bed together on screen (Eric smoking a pipe while pyjama-clad Ernie piped up about the 'play what I have wrote') without a hint of homosexuality. But Morecambe and Wise were not as immune to social and cultural change as they might at first have appeared. In line with the development of situation comedy, in the scripts written first by Sid Green and Dick Hills (ATV), and latterly by Eddie Braben (BBC), characterisation took precedence over jokes. Furthermore, the most memorable moments of their BBC TV shows involved the affectionate defrocking of serious public figures (siren Shirley Bassey, pianist and conductor André Previn, actress Glenda Jackson, prime minister Harold Wilson, and newsreader Angela Rippon). Beneath their besuited, Middle England exteriors, they were also lords of misrule – very much in the spirit of 60s-style disestablishmentarianism.

Their combination of familiarity and innovation bred a great deal of affection. Eric and Ernie's theme tune was 'Bring Me Sunshine', and it is generally agreed (disagreement comes only from professional controversialists such as AN Wilson) that they brought sunshine to the whole British nation.

Though an intensely private man (he loved his family, fishing and cricket), Eric's only novel, about an unhappy comedian (*Mr Lonely*, 1980), a seemingly autobiographical work, suggests a more complex and somewhat troubled persona, and offers a beguiling yet inconclusive glimpse behind the glasses and the smile. After recovering from a serious heart attack in the 70s, Morecambe suffered from recurring heart problems and finally succumbed after coming off stage on 27 May 1984. At something of a loss without his stage partner, Wise tried briefly to relaunch himself as a song and dance man before retiring to Florida. He too died of heart failure, on 21 March 1999. Morecambe and Wise produced 130 TV shows. Those that survive are often rebroadcast on British terrestrial TV.

PARENTS Laurel and Hardy, Abbott and Costello CHILDREN **Reeves and Mortimer**, **Ben Elton**

Chris Morris

Mockumentarist

Reclusive Chris Morris is the stylish media parodist and prankster who makes Michael Moore seem like Richard and Judy.

After graduating in zoology at Bristol University, Morris was taken on by veteran DJ Johnnie Walker at Radio West. He moved to London and GLR, then on to Radio 4 where, together with **Patrick Marber** and **Steve Coogan**, he wrote and performed the parody news programme *On The Hour*. In 1994 this was translated into television as *The Day Today* (BBC2), featuring spoof media archetypes such as

disaster-reporter Ted Maul, sports commentator Alan Partridge, unintelligible business correspondent Collaterly Sisters, and Morris as the show's Paxmanesque anchorman. 'Paxman was the most obvious target,' Morris later said, 'because he's the most ridiculous. But to me, [Michael] Buerke is more preposterous. It's an acting performance: "hush, hush, don't laugh, this is a cathedral, anybody who's feeling remotely unserious can leave the room now because I'm telling you this is powerful stuff".' After *The Day Today*, observed *Face* writer Simon Price, TV news programmes were permanently stripped of their 'artificial *gravitas*'.

The Day Today prompted rows about taste, and Morris' next offer came from Channel 4. *Brass Eye* was a six-part series of 'mockumentaries', designed to do for *Panorama* what *The Day Today* had done for *Newsnight*. Apart from controversial items such as a Pulp parody which took the form of a love song to child-killer Myra Hindley, and the fake doctor who claimed that the disabled were just lazy, the pivotal points of the show were the hoaxes: real-life worthies duped into denouncing a fictional drug called Cake; and concerned stars (Jilly Cooper, Carla Lane) conned into campaigning for an elephant with its trunk stuck up its arse. 'People just walk along with an air of "hi, take me",' Morris claimed. Meanwhile *The Sunday Times* complained that he 'does not just want to ridicule his soft targets, but to stamp them into the ground.' Bemoaning his intention to 'wound' Noel Edmonds, the *Radio Times* called Morris 'crass, tasteless'. The *Daily Mail* dubbed him 'the most loathed man on television.'

Channel 4 boss Michael Grade had backed the show, but on the day the last episode was due to go out, he phoned from Los Angeles and cut an item about the Yorkshire Ripper called 'Sutcliffe: the musical'. Morris retaliated by inserting a flash-frame caption, 'Michael Grade is a cunt'. It might never have been noticed, except that someone (guess who?) told *The Sun* it was there. In the furore that ensued, Morris was supported by the novelist and (then) *Observer* critic **Will Self**, who called him 'God'.

After the glare of television, Morris went back to radio. In 1998 he made a series of late-night pro-grammes for Radio 1. *Blue Jam* combined Dadaesque monologues with trippy music. Mixing comedy with fear, Morris described it as 'a show for when you've reached a stage of evolution where stumbling is more advanced than walking'. He added: 'it's not laundry-endangeringly funny, but it's not meant to be taken seriously. It's a floppy pro-gramme.'

On-air, Morris veers between extreme naughti-ness and kamikaze social criticism. Off-air, he is a normal family man, and determined to stay that way. He has so far avoided becoming one of the roster of self-perpetuating British media personali-ties. Just as well, or he'd end up having to satirise himself.

PARENTS Michael Moore, *Do Not Adjust Your Set*
CHILDREN Ali G

Morrissey
Who's miserable now?

The Smiths were an antidote to the 80s. Fronted by avowed celibate Morrissey, their cadences made you think of solitary melancholy and a nostalgic yearning for lost times rather than shoulder pads and serious money. On the other hand, Morrissey's self-absorption could be seen as endorsing the dic-tum of that decade, Thatcher's 'there is no such thing as society'. Always an outsider, never opening up (except in his songs), he has walked the line between **indie** (jangling guitars) and yuppie (tight hold on royalties), left (associated with feminism and vegetarianism; once said he wished Thatcher had been blown up in Brighton) and right (repeat-edly accused of racism), sowing seeds of contro-versy as he goes.

The cover for the first Smiths' single, 'Hand In Glove' (1983), was taken from a gay porn maga-zine. Performances of their early hit 'This Charming Man' were accompanied by Morrissey throwing gladioli into the audience. On stage he cultivated an air of angst-ridden vulnerability, halfway between James Dean and **Derek Jarman**'s *Sebastiane*. Sometimes compared to Oscar Wilde (he self-con-sciously developed this, quoting Wilde, posing like him for press shots and developing his own line in barbed aphorisms) he has always loathed the boor-ish element in rock'n'roll (in 1990 he described the **Stone Roses** and the **Happy Mondays** as 'the revenge of the daft'). Taken together with his obvi-ous interest in male physicality – the poster of a young Charlie Richardson (East End gangster) on the solo album *Your Arsenal*, the boxing imagery for *Southpaw Grammar*, his friendship with former boxer Jake Walters – Morrissey's combination of feyness and barbed wit has been interpreted as a sign of homosexuality (the tour programme that listed close friend Peter Hogg as 'rent-a-chap' gave credence to this impression). But Morrissey will not say he's gay, and some gays have been offended by his apparent failure to come out (journalists Kris Kirk and Richard Smith were the first to level this accusation in the mid-80s). The controversy is compounded by Morrissey's insistence that he, an intellectual, is simply curious about men who live physically rather than intellectually; and that his interest is anthropological rather than sexual: 'I am quite fascinated by people who – quite happily – steam through life with an astonishing lack of thought. But I know it's just me prodding with a stick again and saying "how fascinating".'

The work of Dublin-born Steven Patrick Morrissey is 'peculiarly English, its concerns ranging from the grimy backstreets of provincial cities to the over-excited hairdressers of Sloane Square'. Interviewed by Tony Parsons, Morrissey explained that to him Englishness means 'the village atmosphere, the small-mindedness, which is still very much part of me. I can't shake it off.' He reported walking round the East End in what seemed like an attempt to find Englishness: 'I walk to Wapping for absolutely no reason. I walk to Bethnal Green for absolutely no reason … I find that the working-class areas of London are more English than any of the more affluent areas.' Morrissey worked a seam of

Englishness, à la Ray Davies and Damon Albarn. Visually The Smiths celebrated a mythical lost England. Situated in a grim and smokey post-war northern metropolis that really never was, it was the tough anti-glamour of working-class **kitchen sink**. Like some sentimental grieving widow, Morrissey has always been the curator of a dead past he never really knew. Shut away from a problematic present, its protagonists and places become an immaculate and unsullied cosmology.

Some critics have accused him of wallowing in chauvinism. *The Queen Is Dead* (1986) was interpreted as an attempt to crawl inside an exclusively English heritage. A *Melody Maker* journalist accused the single 'Panic' of being 'an attack on black pop'. The lyrics to 'Bengali In Platforms' were repeatedly derided as racist. Supporting Madness at an open-air concert at Finsbury Park in 1992, Morrissey was canned off stage after he appeared draped in a Union Jack. The following week the *NME* ran a four-page article headlined 'This Alarming Man'. Morrissey insists he is not racist: the single 'Suedehead' was a homage to the Richard Allen books; and, anyway, he did a gig for Artists Against Apartheid. 'There is a hate campaign against me,' he claims. 'There have been many other groups with Union Jacks and nobody has commented on them. But of course I do it and I'm Hitler'. Then he blows it by saying 'there has been a complete invasion' of Englishness – a turn of phrase which sounds a lot like Margaret Thatcher's infamous comment that Britain was being 'swamped' by aliens. Perhaps Morrissey secretly craves an elegantly inelegant fall from

Smith stars

The Smith's cover art featured the odd Warhol or Cocteau star but was largely a discerning history of post-war British working-class cool. Cover stars included:

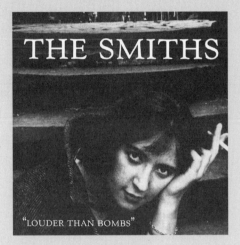

THE SMITHS

"LOUDER THAN BOMBS"

Terence Stamp from *The Collector* (1965)
Rita Tushingham from *A Taste of Honey* (1961)
Viv Nicholson, Pools winner (twice)
Billie Whitelaw from *Charlie Bubbles* (1967)
Colin Campbell from *The Leather Boys* (1963)
Sean Barrett from *Dunkirk* (1958)
Pat Phoenix from *Coronation Street*
Richard Bradford from *Man in a Suitcase* (1967)
Yootha Joyce on the set of *Catch Us If You Can* (1965)
Shelagh Delaney in 1961
Avril Angers from *The Family Way* (1966)
Murray Head from *The Family Way* (1966)
Vanessa Redgrave from *Blow Up* (1966)
David Hemmings from *Blow Up* (1966)
Diana Dors from *Yield to the Night* (1956)
Billy Fury
Sandie Shaw

social grace on a par with his idol's Oscar Wilde in order to complete his self-image.

At the height of The Smiths' popularity, Morrissey was regarded by the faithful as something of a saint and martyr – an image he himself cultivated and encouraged: a lone voice of independent, intelligent pop sanity amid the chart wastes of Stock, Aitken and Waterman. Every school had its melancholic Morrissey imitator, bedecked in beads, quiff,

blouse and hearing aid. For some (probably those who also took the Morrissey tour of Manchester) the break-up of The Smiths was as difficult as the break up of **The Beatles** – an unbearable watershed in English music. Though Morrissey soldiered on post-Smiths, his time centre stage had come and gone: the **Ecstasy** generation, who would have no time for his morbid nostalgia, was waiting in the wings. His solo projects have continued but never quite reached the heights he achieved when his lyrical guile was matched note for note by Johnny Marr's robust guitar play. His largest fan base is now in the States where teenagers cherish his quaint English world and are still charmed by his safe and comforting brand of angst. The English themselves are now less convinced.

Morrissey's dubious sexuality and doubts about multiculturalism have both given offence to different sets of people. But there were few complaints about the title of his first solo album, *Viva Hate* (1988). Equally uncontroversial was the press release for the LP *Maladjusted* (1997), announcing that Morrissey 'prefers the company of animals to humans' and has 'no interest whatsoever in modern life'. For a time, perhaps, the most famous celibate in the world, Morrissey was the first pop star who was a hero-worshipper himself, preferring a portrait of Wilde or James Dean to the warm embrace of a groupie any day of the week. Where other pop stars require girls, boys and other stimulants for their après-gig, the ascetic Morrissey demands 'just pure silence'. He says he lives above and beyond 'the slimy, unstoppable urges. ... I think I was meant to have other things.' Morrissey is a confirmed misanthrope. But in today's British culture, involuntary distrust of other people does not cause offence. Instead Morrissey is revered as 'the king of bedsit of angst' and 'spokesman for the Miserabilists.' Yet strangely, for a man perennially labelled as miserable, his lyrics have always demonstrated great wit and irony.

What of the real Morrissey behind the public persona? The judge who presided over the 1996 court battle over royalties between Morrissey and the other ex-Smiths, concluded that he is 'devious, truculent and unreliable'. But not talentless: with highly accomplished solo albums like *Your Arsenal*, Morrissey made fools of those who said he was finished without the jangling guitar and songwriting skills of Marr. Writer, critic and Morrissey's mate Michael Bracewell has compared him to Andy Warhol. But like Warhol, says Bracewell, 'there is really nothing there … his power stems from a concentrated emptiness'. Perhaps Morrissey would agree. In 1997 he declared 'Artists aren't real people. I am 40 per cent papier mâché.'

PARENTS Oscar Wilde, James Dean, **Alan Bennett**
CHILDREN indie angst, Jarvis Cocker

Kate Moss
The waif

'Do I feel beautiful? It depends. If I've been hanging out with Christy and **Naomi**, I feel like a piece of shit.' In her own words Kate Moss summed up the combination of (mainly) beauty and (a touch of) ugliness which made her the most talked-about model of the mid-90s.

Croydon-born Moss (b. 1970) was 14 and on her way home from a New York holiday with her father when she was spotted at JFK airport by Sarah Doukas, head of Storm model agency. Her first job was for *Mizz* magazine (fee: £150). Then a young photographer called Corinne Day saw a polaroid in Storm's files and decided to use Moss in her first shoot for **The Face**. The Kate/Corinne partnership first appeared in that magazine in March 1990, and art director Phil Bicker decided to continue with it. In 1990–91, Kate Moss was the face of *The Face*. This work was unpaid, but Moss got noticed by the big money. She went on to work for the most prestigious designers (Versace, Yves St Laurent), and has now been photographed by the greatest living lensmen, including Bruce Weber, Herb Ritts, Helmut Newton, Steven Meisel and Richard Avedon. The adverts she did with Marky Mark (New Kids On The Block) to launch Calvin Klein's CK underwear made her name in the USA and caused a storm in Middle America (especially the one with topless Moss sitting on Mark's lap, which was not even shown on British TV).

At five foot seven inches, Moss is of average height, but she is dwarfed by supermodels like Christy Turlington and Elle Macpherson. In her early pictures she looked particularly skinny, prompting repeated descriptions of her as 'waif-like'; her breasts are undersized too, and she has a famously 'lazy' eye which confirms the impression of a not-quite-healthy street urchin. The look that made Moss famous was described by Calvin Klein's advertising executive as 'young but knowledgeable'. But British writer William Leith saw something more downbeat in her 'pinched and poor' demeanour. Of a photo published in *Harper's Bazaar*, he wrote: 'here is an image in which all optimistic, old-fashioned ideas have taken a beating. You see gender confusion, fear, stains on the sidewalk; a world of cheapness and discomfort. It's a picture that makes you realise you have got a lot to think about. And here's another of the qualities of Moss – just as her extraordinary not-quite-beauty can be seen in all this rattiness, the reverse is also true. Even at her most glamorous, something of the other side always shows through.' The pull-out quote in Leith's *Arena* article makes the point even more forcefully: 'This is the face of the 90s, the face that reminds you your optimism was misplaced.'

To many, Moss – who once said she 'might've been a bank manager' – was a refreshing contrast to the perfect specimens who dominated the runways in the power-dressing days of the 80s and early 90s. To others, she was a one-woman-moral-panic: encouraging anorexia among young girls; promoting 'heroin chic' and cigarette smoking. But as she grew older, Moss stopped looking so exceptional compared to other models (a whole crop of 'waifs' wafted into the limelight), and the controversy surrounding her started to fade. By the end of the 90s, she was briefly associated with the kind of glamour from which she once seemed so distant. But in November 1998 she checked into the exclusive Priory Clinic for a spot of rehabilitation: someone from her office cited too much work and too much partying. In the March 1999 edition of *The Face* she confessed that, for a while, 'I lost the plot'. The purplish photos accompanying the interview showed Moss back at being almost-bruised.

PARENTS Twiggy, Isabel Rossellini
READ ON *The Face*, March 1999

New age travellers

Nearly new

Also known as crusties, drongos, hedge monkeys, brew crew and giro gypsies, new age travellers are the combined result of radicalism, recession and retrenchment. Once vilified as 'new age vermin' (Paul Morland MP), they have now become an accepted part of the British landscape.

Towards the end of the 60s, the forces of law and order went on the offensive against youthful radicalism. 'Far out' hippies found themselves locked out of mainstream society. Forced into a mobile lifestyle, they initiated 'the heady politics of disappearance' which entailed living in 'communes on wheels' and establishing their own temporary, focal points around the country. Among the first of these was the hippie camp at Cinnamon Lane, Glastonbury (1971), followed by the Windsor Free Festival (1972), the first Stonehenge Free Festival, organised by legendary activist Wally Hope in the summer of 1974, and the New Age Gypsy Fair at Inglestone Common (1980). By the late 70s, hippie convoys could be seen threading their way between an established circuit of DIY venues and campsites.

New age travellers saw themselves as witnesses to the dawn of a new Aquarian age of anti-materialist spirituality; but they were brought into being by the increasingly repressive policies of successive Tory and Labour governments. With the formation of Margaret Thatcher's right-wing administration after the general election of 1979, British society was polarised still further, and new age travellers were politicised even more. In 1982, the year of Britain's war with Argentina over the Falkland Islands in the South Atlantic, a group of vehicles calling itself the 'Peace Convoy' left the Stonehenge Free Festival to join the feminist anti-nuke camp at Greenham Common. By then the original hippie ethos had been augmented by a new age of the new ager, born out of the anarchistic tendencies within punk and epitomised in bands like Crass, the post-punk outfit formed in 1978.

In the decade between 1982 and 1992, new age travellers were thought of as longhairs (hippie) who spat (punk) in the mouths of authority. In fact it was usually the authorities that went on the offensive: the eviction of the Rainbow Fields Village at RAF Molesworth (1985); the Battle of the Beanfield (1985), when police attacked travellers; the blockade of the Peace Convoy at Stoney Cross in Hampshire (1986); and the heavy-handed treatment of anti-M3 protesters at Twyford Down (1992). Like the miners and other strikers, new age travellers were an 'enemy within' whose function was to provide an anti-British image that the Tories and others could identify themselves against.

Not surprisingly, the travellers saw themselves differently. As the 80s wore on and the Lawson boom was followed by economic slump, a new cohort turned their backs on job insecurity and opted for the 'permanent recession' of life on the road. This group saw itself as 'economic refugees' whose DIY lifestyle was largely a matter of necessity. Continuing in the vein of hippie radicalism but also making reference to the longer tradition of mainly middle-class Arcadianism, other travellers insisted that theirs was an authentically English way of life in contrast to the falsehoods of Thatcherite jingoism, 'popular capitalism' and yuppiedom. For example, Jeremy of the post-punk band The Levellers, who took their name from the most radical section of the Roundhead army in the English Civil War, declared that travelling is 'the English dream, really … all those images of *Tess of the D'Urbervilles*'.

Various commentators have emphasised the differences between new age travellers and the rest of the British population. Pat Kane writes of 'an alternative politics of the individual' and George McKay observes 'conscious actions of self-marginalisation' while including new age communities in Hakim Bey's category of Temporary Autonomous Zones – 'cracks in the map, "outside the cartography of control".' Although these notions might once have been appropriate to new age travellers, they seem less so now. When *The Archers*, the radio soap opera closest to the heart of Middle England, includes a sympathetic treatment of a young character (Kate) who joins a convoy, it can no longer be assumed that new age travellers are beyond the pale of British identity.

At a time when all our relationships (at work and in the home) are less permanent – transient, even – it seems more appropriate to suggest that, in some respects, we are all travellers now. Hence the increasing readiness to sympathise with new age travellers and to see them no longer as alien outsiders but as the epitome of our increasingly impermanent existence.

PARENTS the Merry Pranksters, 60s communal living
CHILDREN squat punks
READ ON *Senseless Acts of Beauty* by George McKay

New Order
sad/happy/sad/happy

The trio described as 'a band decapitated' after the suicide of lead singer **Ian Curtis**, added a female keyboard/guitarist who could not play and became 'the most culturally significant British band of the past 20 years'. The group that began as a byword for Mancunian austerity, 'weren't serious people' (singer/synth/guitarist Bernard Sumner), and took 'more drugs than the Grateful Dead', according to PIL's **John Lydon**. The musicians most associated with the introduction of automated electronica into British pop, they made music that is 'pure emotion' (**Primal Scream**'s Bobby Gillespie). Ensconced in Manchester and largely isolated from the London-based music industry, New Order anticipated trends like no other British band of their generation. Factory Records boss **Tony Wilson** believes that 'the fact that a group who were so significant in creating post-punk, and the next big thing with 'Blue Monday', should be so alive and so much a part of the next explosion – is a phenomenal achievement'. In 1998 New Order's Peter Hook (whose name was plastered across the tabloids when he separated

Bernard Sumner

from his wife, Caroline 'Mrs Merton' Aherne) was endearingly modest about their achievements: 'In the USA they are now saying we invented electronic music. Of course, mate. They seem to have forgotten that Kraftwerk were before us. We haven't done anything for five years and people still gag for it.'

They might have been called the Witchdoctors of Zimbabwe, instead they settled on New Order: as in 'the new order of Kampuchean liberation' (taken from an article in the *Guardian*), or perhaps from a book of Situationist essays that belonged to manager Rob Gretton; the press found an echo of the Nazis' Thousand Year Reich and sinister continuity with the name Joy Division). Having drafted in Gillian Gilbert (intelligent girl next door) from her graphics course at Stockport Tech and her all-girl group The Inadequates, Bernard Sumner (guitar; pretty and sharp), Peter Hook (bass; bluff but emotional) and Stephen Morris (drums; tall and laconic) set about teaching her what to play.

The first New Order release, complete with ecclesiastical typography from Factory designer Peter Saville, consisted of two songs, 'Ceremony' and 'In A Lonely Place' (March 1981), with lyrics written by Curtis (one verse about a hangman) shortly before he died. Sumner was nervous about writing and they were all nervous about playing live (Hook took to standing with his back to the audience), but they got through an American tour (in New York they had all their gear nicked but tried poppers, came out of mourning and re-learnt to party), and produced an album *Movement* (1981) that was stark (as in Joy Division) but also prefigured the electro-pop sound and the combination of acoustic and synthesised instrumentation that became their trademark. One track in particular, 'Chosen Time', contains an upfront bassline (played near the top of the instrument's register) and 'shards of synth'. The overall feel was closer to new disco, but it retained some of the old post-punk elements.

Sumner (who made his first synthesiser from a kit and showed it to Stephen Morris who recalls 'I'd always wanted to be a bit of a drum machine myself') was setting the pace of change, resisted by Hook. For Sumner the move to incorporate more electronic music was about drug-enhanced self-expression not regimentation: 'Various substances

opened my eyes and ears to the beauties of precise, strict rhythm.'

By the end of 1981 Sumner still did not own any sequencers but had employed hippie boffin Martin Usher (rewarded with acid tabs) to rig up tape loops and other devices. The combination of hallucinogens (Morris kept off them because he had done it all before) and electro-precision was a major factor in the B-side 'Everybody's Gone Green', and the influential single 'Temptation' (1982), capped the following year by the biggest selling 12-inch single of all time, 'Blue Monday' (reached No 12 in charts, March 1983; rose to No 9 in August the same year; remixed by Quincy Jones, got to No 3 in 1988; reworked and reached No 17 in 1995, used as soundtrack for American Express advert in 1998). While 'club culture' was being talked about in media circles and experienced by trendy young people, 'Blue Monday' has been described as its 'first point of access for the general public'. On the grounds that, just as the Sex Pistols made punk popular, 'Blue Monday' brought electronic music to a wide audience, it has been described as 'the first crossover record since "Anarchy In The UK"'.

According to Morris the next album, *Power Corruption and Lies* (1983) shows 'the influence of a certain Mr AM Phetamine', while Sumner describes his favourite (Kraftwerk-influenced) track as 'rhythmic, abstract, aesthetic, arty, fucked up and with a sense of humour'. Again New Order combined the automatic with the acoustic, austerity with joy – even if white-coated Sumner was acting like a mad scientist at the time.

Moving to New York to record with producer

Arthur Baker, they finally shed the image of dour Mancunians by skipping from one danceteria to another dressed in shorts, T-shirts and sneakers. In 1986 they over-produced *Brotherhood* (too much overdubbing) and the following year issued 'True Faith', which signposted the E-experience just as it was unfolding. In 1987 Factory issued a New Order compilation (it's said that Wilson wanted to play all his favourite tracks on a single tape in his car) which has sold six million copies out of their total sales to date of 20 million. *Technique* (1989) was their first No 1 album (John Denver sued them over the alleged similarity between 'Run' and his 'Leaving on a Jet Plane'), and it seemed to be infused with the smiley vibe of **Ibiza**. In fact they came back from the island with just a few drum tracks and the realisation that they did not operate like a band any more. From 1989–93 the various members of New Order concentrated on solo projects: Sumner/Electronica; Hook/Revenge and Monaco; Gilbert and Morris/The Other Two and music for American and British TV. In 1990 they came together briefly to record the football anthem 'World in Motion', alongside comic **Keith Allen** and the England football team. In 1993 they were the subject of a documentary (*neworderstory*) made by old friend Paul Morley. They released another album, *Republic* (issued by London Records after Factory went into receivership) and headlined the Reading Festival that summer. But after putting down their instruments they did not speak to each other for another five years – until they got back together again in 1998. Says Hook 'I think people have come to realise that the whole is greater than the sum of its parts.' Others have observed that underneath all their individual projects is a note of 'fun-loving electro-melancholia' which no one can do better than the four people who invented it – New Order. That's why in 1999 they started work on their seventh album.

When *Power, Corruption and Lies* was issued in a facsimile of a floppy disk cover, Neil Tennant broke down in tears. He had intended to make the **Pet Shop Boys** the first digi-pop band, combining computer culture with warmth, romance and humour, and was horrified to discover that New Order had got there first. Five years later New Order premiered something like acid house on national TV. Their performance of 'Fine Time' on *Top of the Pops* in 1988 was nearly a full year before the legendary appearances of the **Stone Roses** and the **Happy Mondays**. Bobby Gillespie reckons they could have been the biggest band in the world, and that U2 are a poor copy of their template. Perhaps they were held back by Factory's financial problems and relative lack of weight in the global music industry. On the other hand the independent development of New Order seems to have been partly based on the splendid provincialism afforded by Wilson's Factory set-up. From Manchester they could survey the world and take what they needed to reinvent British pop music.

PARENTS Joy Division, Kraftwerk, Giorgio Moroder
CHILDREN U2, Primal Scream

New Romantics

Conspicuous consumption

Luxury is especially highly prized during periods of poverty. Cinemas became People's Palaces during the Great Depression; likewise, during the early 80s recession, punk ('**dole** queue rock') and its aftermath were replaced by a style of escapist conspicuous consumption.

They weren't called New Romantics at first. Buoyed by the success of their **Bowie** Nights at Billy's in Soho, Steve Strange (doorman and daytime shop assistant) and Rusty Egan (DJ) moved upmarket to Blitz in Covent Garden, where Boy George was the cloakroom attendant and Marilyn the cigarette girl. Their club night was soon on the must-see list of style editors like **Peter York** (*Harper's*), and they themselves received invites to London's most fashionable parties. Press attention followed, along with a media label: 'Blitz Kids'. Insider Robert Elms (starting out as a journalist with new magazine **The Face**) preferred 'the cult with no name'.

Elms described the Blitz clientele as 'still a very small, closed world of 300 young devotees, among them clothes designers, artists, hairdressers and musicians. The looks there ranged from shoulder-padded futurism to fringed outlaw revivalism, ideas later to be taken up and exploited by fashion moguls, destined to end up on the racks of the mass marketeers.'

The 'devotees' of Blitz were committed to a new extravagance. No more social conscience; no more gobbing and swallowing the grottiness of Britain. The idea was to reinvent yourself as the most outrageous object in the room. Dismissed as posers by the *NME* ('the enemy'), Blitz Kids replied that posing is everything. Egalitarianism ('the kids are united') was out, and elitism (Steve Strange hand-picking who could come through the red rope and into Blitz) was fashionable again. Not that Blitz Kids came from elite backgrounds. Writing in the American magazine *Mother Jones*, British critic Simon Frith described them as 'Fops, but working-class fops, whose response to Thatcherism certainly doesn't make left-wing sense, but which isn't simply escapist either.'

Less than two years elapsed between the first Bowie Night at Blitz (6 February 1979) and the publication of Elms' retrospective article in *The Face* (November 1980). During that time, the Blitz Kid mentality stopped being the preserve of a 'very small number' and percolated through to a wider public. Elms reported that 'the idea of commandeering a local club for one night of fashion and fun has already spread to Cardiff (the Tanschau) and Birmingham (at the Rum Runner). Embryonic scenes are also happening in Liverpool and Southend.' By May 1981, DJ Rusty Egan was taking 'Blitz to the sticks' (touring the provinces with a set that was '50/50 soul and electronic dance cuts'), and he himself was described as a 'New Romantic' (*The Face*, May 1981: 'New Romantic goes to the country').

As with **Mod** 15 years earlier, the main distribution agents for the new sensibility were the bands associated with it. Apart from **Culture Club**, Blitz spawned Steve Strange's short-lived Visage (remembered for taking the video promo to a new level) and Spandau Ballet, who began as electro-funk experimentalists ('To Cut A Long Story Short', 1980) before resorting to traditional white soul with 'Gold' and 'True' (both 1983). The owners of Birmingham's Rum Runner became managers of local band Duran Duran (name taken from a character in Roger Vadim's *Barbarella*, 1967), fronted by London art student Simon Le Bon. Though Duran Duran (bland enough to appeal to Princess Diana) lacked the exoticism of the Blitz scene (swiftly caricatured as make-up, kilts and berets), they shared its sense of fun and extravagance, as did Wham!, the hugely successful duo (George Michael and Andrew Ridgeley) who met in 1979 as members of The Executives.

North of Watford, New Romanticism took on a more serious tone. From the city of Sheffield (gripped in 1980–81 by a steelworkers' strike) came ABC (Manchester-born frontman Martin Fry studied English at Sheffield University) and The Human League, two groups who played with the idea of electro-pop while retaining a self-critical stance. In its original line-up, The Human League was a band of neurotic boy outsiders, until Ian Craig Marsh and Martyn Ware departed to form Heaven 17 and vocalist Philip Oakey was left to find two girl singers at a local disco. In a winning combination, Susan Sulley and Joanne Catherall played the straight men to Oakey's far-out fool.

The music they produced ranged from pop/soul of many of the aforementioned bands to the early experimental futurist sounds of the likes of Depeche Mode, Soft Cell, Blancmange (all show-cased on the *Some Bizarre* sampler album). Though their fledgling brand of electronica may sound weak and dated today, they were the first bands to embrace the technological innovations that laid the foundations later in the decade for dance music to bloom. (In some ways 80s bands like The Human League were as much an influence on the Chicago house sound as Kraftwerk.) In the futurist tradition, both in sound and look, they rejected the back-to-basics, 'no future', DIY ethos of punk, preferring to put their faith in and celebrate technology and tomorrow.

The New Romantics are often regarded as youthful counterparts to Thatcherism. In his retrospective on the 80s, Peter York likened them ('posers') to the think-tanks of the New Right such as the Institute of Economic Affairs and the Adam Smith Institute ('plotters'): in their different ways they were harbingers of a new, anti-welfare state of mind. Although there are flaws in this thesis (the bands from the 'socialist republic of Sheffield', the fact that Spandau Ballet's Gary Kemp played a solo spot on the pro-Labour Red Wedge tour of 1986), both camps are clearly post-post-war consensus. Punk was a scream of disappointment at the failure of consensus Britain, but with Thatcher and the New Romantics you realised it was all over.

In the USA, the New Romantics comprised the most successful British invasion force since the beat boom of the 60s. As well as providing the soundtrack to influential films such as *The Breakfast Club*, 80s Brit-bands loomed large in the lives of young upwardly mobile Americans as documented by Jay McInerney and Bret Easton Ellis. On both sides of the Atlantic, excess was the key to success.

PARENTS the 'new look' during the post-war age of austerity
READ ON *Like Punk Never Happened* by Dave Rimmer; *The Crypto-Amnesia Club* by Michael Bracewell

Jeff Noon
Kids' stuff

Having studied fine art and drama at Manchester University, Jeff Noon was appointed writer in residence at the city's Royal Exchange Theatre. But the British realist tradition of theatre did not mesh with the fantastic worlds he was itching to invent. While doing an upmarket McJob behind the counter of the local Waterstone's, a colleague suggested he write a novel. The result was *Vurt* (1993), a sci-fi story that reflected the concerns of crusties and cyberculturists, who reciprocated by making it the hippest British sci-fi novel since the heady days of Michael Moorcock in the 60s. Noon's reputation was confirmed with the publication of *Pollen* (1995), *Nymphomation* (1997), set in a near-future Manchester enthralled by a lottery-based game called Domino Bones, and *Pixel Juice* (1998), a short story collection.

Like Moorcock, Noon is not preoccupied with technology *per se*, but incorporates technological developments into worlds of magic and fantasy. Clearly influenced by Lewis Carroll, Noon cites his re-reading of the Alice books as the defining moment of his artistic career, and in *Automated Alice* (1996) he updated Carroll's character to make her into a gun-toting robot (shades of **Lara Croft** in the *Tomb Raider* series of computer games). Besides Lewis Carroll, as a teenager Noon was addicted to American comic heroes and still turns to them for inspiration. Like a number of new British novelists, he has said that music is more of an influence on his writing than the literary tradition of the novel. He 'usually writes to music' and his collection ranges from classical to **drum'n'bass**.

Noon does not like being bracketed with the middle-class **Martin Amis** school of soul-searching; nor does he fit in with the E-scene writers, although he did contribute a story to *Disco Biscuits* (1997), Sarah Champion's anthology for 'the chemical generation'. He describes his output as 'like kids' stories … but with weird sex and drugs thrown in', and he says he wants to be thought of as the man who reintroduced 'whimsy' into British fiction (echoes here of **Syd Barrett** and the Incredible String Band). Critics might say that Noon's predilection for the childlike and the naive is itself a cynical abdication from the task of developing an adult worldview.

PARENTS Lewis Carroll, Michael Moorcock, the Silver Surfer

Northern Soul

Post-Mod, pre-punk, proto-rave

Northern Soul was so-named because of its audience: white working-class northerners (all points above the line from the Wirral to the Wash) who did not follow when London went hippie, but stayed true to the Motown-influenced soul music beloved by **Mods**. Their pill-filled 70s scene (advertised only in specialist publications such as *Blues & Soul* and *Black Echoes*) was a test-bed for breakdancing, for the kind of camaraderie associated with **rave** culture in the 80s, and for the authoritarian response to clubbers that peaked with the Criminal Justice Act 1994.

It all started at the Twisted Wheel in Whitworth Street, Manchester (yards away from the future **Haçienda**), where a well-informed Mod crowd came to hear DJ Les Cockell play the best in soul. At the end of the 60s, when the rest of Britain was dividing into **prog rock**ers and teenyboppers, the Twisted Wheel crowd carried on listening to the same sort of music ('keep the faith!'), while developing a more sophisticated dance style. The term 'Northern Soul' was invented by *Blues & Soul* reporter Dave Godin, who visited the Twisted Wheel in 1970 and was impressed by its clientele: 'the dancing is without doubt the finest I have ever seen outside the USA. Everybody there was an expert in soul clapping.'

When the Twisted Wheel closed after a series of police raids, the focus shifted to the Highland Room above Blackpool's Mecca Ballroom, where the star DJs were Colin Curtis and Ian Levine (lat-

terly the man behind post-disco Hi-NRG and producer of Take That). Taken on holiday to the USA by his rich parents (mum and dad owned a casino), Levine had amassed a considerable collection of black American records on a host of obscure labels modelled on Motown. His personal collection, identified by 'swirling strings and lots of girl vocals', became the definitive canon of Northern Soul.

The Highland Room was outclassed only by the Saturday/Sunday 'all-niters' (2am to 8am; the last records, the legendary 'three before eight', were the same every week) at Wigan Casino, hosted by 60s soul-revivalists Russ Winstanley and Richard Searling (Willie Mitchell's 'The Champion' and the World Column's 'So is the Sun' were particular favourites). It was here that dancing became less narcissistic (Mods) and more athletic (breakdancing). Sports brands like Adidas were seen on the floor for the first time.

The Casino was a members-only venue. Critics claim that Northern Soul was cliquey. Adherents maintain that membership rules were necessitated by licensing laws, and that the Northern Soul scene was friendly and open-ended (not hostile to gays, for example).

Northern Soul club nights also occurred at the Golden Torch in Tunstall, Samantha's in Sheffield and the Catacombs in Wolverhampton. But apart from these commercial venues, Northern Soul fans also organised their own all-dayers and all-niters in church halls and rugby clubs. The DIY aspect of these gigs, and the almost exclusively working-class background of the punters, did not endear them to the police, who sometimes used roadblocks to stop people attending.

Northern Soul carried on the 'white negro' tradition of elevating black styles and copying black performers. DJ Jon Le Saint was not alone in claiming that 'I might be white outside but inside I'm all black.' In this respect Northern Soul carried on where Mod, the first British wiggas, left off. But in their preference for old black music rather than the latest releases, Northern Soulies turned away from modernism and helped to initiate retrospection. Living off a finite era of music, the only way to inject fresh blood into the scene was the discovery of new record rarities, which obviously became harder and harder to find. (For this reason, more than any other subculture, Northern Soulers are fanatical vinyl junkies.) Though there is still an underground scene out there keeping the faith alive, and new generations discovering its emotional power all the time, its enjoyment is now largely an act of immaculately sealed nostalgia.

PARENTS Mod, soul
CHILDREN jazz-funk, rave, retro

Oasis
Definitely definitive

According to *Select*, Noel Gallagher 'rescued rock-'n'roll'. There is no doubt that Oasis, the band Gallagher fronts with his younger brother Liam, are *the* British rock'n'roll band of the 90s. Ironic, then, that the Gallaghers are of Irish stock and that Oasis draw on cultural references far beyond the scope of rock'n'roll.

The Gallagher brothers hail from Burnage, Manchester, where their Irish-born mother, Peggy, brought them up after escaping the clutches of their abusive, violent father, Thomas Gallagher. But the place where young Noel acquired a taste for freedom was not Manchester but County Mayo, his mother's family home and the setting for successive summer holidays. When Noel returned to school in Burnage each autumn, he brought a touch of the Irish rebel back with him. Years later, the Irish-born desire to live without reference to rules or regulations would find expression in songs like 'Live Forever' which became the epitome of **Britpop**.

The Gallaghers' musical parentage includes the **Stone Roses**, The Smiths, The Faces and, above all, **The Beatles**. Liam and Noel were following the path carved out by The Beatles and the **Rolling Stones** when they transplanted elements of black soul singing into what is now the traditional vehicle for white rock music – the guitar band. But they also incorporated other musical ingredients. Noel was a bemused participant in '**Madchester**', in which **indie** guitar music crossed over with house and other forms of electro-dance. Liam was dismissive of this 'student' scene, but equally grounded in electronic sounds: whereas Noel's first musical passion was punk, teenage Liam, five years his junior, listened to hip-hop and Mantronix. Both these early experiences affected the brothers' later work. Although Oasis are well within the guitar band tradition, they have also updated it by absorbing dance-based elements and reapplying them – just listen to Liam's phrasing and the self-sufficient character of Oasis rhythm tracks. Written by Noel, sung by Liam, Oasis make song-based records that take account of today's sound-orientated listening culture.

Summer visits to Peggy Gallagher's family home in rural County Mayo were like a breath of fresh air, but by his early teens Noel was already into traditional urban pastimes like glue sniffing, burglary and, most of all, football. While most Mancunians of Irish Catholic extraction tend to support United, the Gallaghers backed the blue team – Manchester City. The brothers carried their footballing passion into their music: Liam, complete with V-signs and thousand-yard stare, incorporated the uncompromising attitude of the football hooligan into his stage and off-stage persona. Noel brought the sound of the terraces – big-hearted and super-confident – into his choruses. For Oasis, the transformation from Britpoppers to stadium rockers came easily, because their sound is part derived from football stadia and the crowds that sing in them.

Irish-inspired City fans with a feel for dance records and football chants – these are some of the ingredients that helped make Oasis the top British pop group of the 90s and Noel possibly the most successful English songwriter since Lennon and McCartney.

The other factor in the hegemony of Oasis is the charisma of frontman Liam Gallagher. On and off stage, his full-on persona is readily identifiable (arrogant, ostentatious, courageous, obstinate, swaggering) while flexible enough to allow a wide range of people to identify with it for various different reasons. Thus for James Brown (founding editor of **Loaded**) 'he works as an icon because he's a composite; because he's stylish, but he can also be a hard bastard'. While wary of icons, novelist **Irvine Welsh** explains that 'despite all the fame, Liam has really remained an ordinary geezer. And that is a key reason why ordinary people like him so much.' Meanwhile for pop critic **Jon Savage**, Liam is interesting because his masculinity is far more ambiguous than is usually allowed for: 'he seemed androgynous. Obviously there is a hard side, with the audience-baiting and all that stuff. But there were moments – many moments – when Liam would actually look very beautiful. Like a spoiled Greek god.' Writing in *Select*, Savage went on to explain that he 'always had a problem with the way Oasis were framed within lad culture. They've gone along with that, but it's not the only side to them. … Liam is what gives them their edge, and androgyny is part of the edge.'

At face value, Oasis are easily pigeon-holed as the working-class, northern alternative to the rich kids of the south. But, as with Princess Diana, their deeper significance is derived from the extent to which various audiences can bring their own meanings to them.

PARENTS The Beatles, The Faces,
the Stone Roses, Manchester City, Ireland
READ ON *Getting High: the adventures of Oasis* by Paolo Hewitt

Gary Oldman
Prodigal sonofabitch

Deptford-born Gary Oldman was in danger of being typecast as a Hollywood villain and off-screen hell-raiser, until he broke the mould as director of the hard-hitting and semi-autobiographical *Nil By Mouth* (1997).

His alcoholic father left Oldman and his mum when the boy was seven. At fifteen, Gary was already into drinking and looked like repeating the pattern of his dad's life. But he became an actor with attitude, made a name for himself at the Royal Court Theatre, and co-starred in Alex Cox's punk love story, *Sid and Nancy* (1986). After starring as **Joe Orton** in **Stephen Frears**' *Prick Up Your Ears* (1987), and appearing in Nic Roeg's *Track 29* (1987), Oldman headed out to Hollywood. Afterwards he explained that the small scale of the British film industry left him no choice: with only a couple of decent parts each year, if Daniel Day-Lewis got one and **Tim Roth** took the other, there would be nothing left for him.

Hollywood has drawn good and bad performances out of Oldman. He excelled as Lee Harvey Oswald in Oliver Stone's *JFK* (1991), and as the prince of darkness in *Dracula* (1992). His white rasta pimp in *True Romance* (1993) was enjoyably over the top, as was his murderous New York cop in Luc Bresson's *Leon*. But Oldman's villainy soon became formulaic (*Airforce One*, *The Fifth Element*, *Lost in Space*); and his occasional serious roles (football hooligan Bex in *The Firm* for British

TV; slow-witted Rosencrantz opposite Tim Roth in Tom Stoppard's *Rosencrantz and Guildenstern Are Dead*) were offset by laughable performances as Beethoven (*Immortal Behaviour*) and the puritan minister in *The Scarlet Letter*. For a while it seemed as if Oldman would go down as an under-achiever, besides being a boozer (two bottles of vodka a day) and a womaniser (married to actress Lesley Manville; married to Uma Thurman; engaged to Isabella Rossellini, now married to model Donya Fiorentino). He always resisted this image, claiming that 'there's a class issue. There is a certain perception that people like Ralph Fiennes can earn money and have great careers because they talk like that, don't they?'

Oldman met his third wife while in rehab. Not long afterwards he wrote the first draft of *Nil By Mouth*, a film about a dysfunctional family in Deptford, south-east London – his home turf. The main characters are larger-than-life versions of Oldman's parents: a father (Ray Winstone) who brutalises his long-suffering wife (Kathy Burke, winner of the Cannes prize for best actress, 1997).

Nil By Mouth has been compared to the films of Roberto Rossellini (Italian neo-realist) and John Cassavetes (like Oldman he was a respected mainstream actor as well as a director, and funded his films by taking on undemanding Hollywood acting assignments). Oldman says he wanted to achieve 'a visual sense of being trapped in these small council flats'. The dialogue is foul-mouthed and funny: loose enough to sound real but still pacey. Critics agreed that the prodigal Oldman had redeemed himself by writing, directing and investing US$2 million in his own film. He felt able to excuse his roles in the 'conveyor-belt, multiplex, popcorn stuff' which 'I wouldn't go to see', on the grounds that he needed the money and the exposure 'so I can make another film like *Nil By Mouth*'. Having sorted out his own demons an emboldened Oldman declared 'we all need therapy'. Only a handful of critics dared disagree.

PARENTS: **Alan Clarke, Michael Caine, Steven Berkoff**

Joe Orton
What a way to go!

Stocky, cheeky-faced Joe Orton took British theatre beyond John Osborne's Angry Young Man towards the concerns which characterised 60s pop culture: sending up the old guard, celebrating sex, and thinking out loud about how to live in a society where tradition had already fallen from grace.

Orton was born in Leicester in 1933. His parents worked in hosiery and shoe factories. Joe (christened John) was always at odds with his family's drab existence. As a teenager he sought glamour in acting lessons and amateur dramatics, and in November 1950 RADA accepted him as a student.

'O bliss' was Orton's diary entry on the day he started at RADA. By the fifth term he was highly cynical of the RADA manner and the overblown acting style he was expected to adopt. On graduat-

ing he went into repertory theatre in Ipswich, but was disillusionned by this experience (uncreative, routine, mechanical) also.

Orton was rescued by Kenneth Halliwell. They had been fellow-students at RADA but at 27 Halliwell was considerably older than Orton and already inclined to be morose. Together they set up home in an Islington bedsit (purchased with Halliwell's inheritance). They became lovers as well as professional partners. When their attempts to enter the West End stage came to nothing, they worked together on a series of unpublished novels and other literary projects (*The Silver Bucket, The Last Days of Sodom, The Boy Hairdresser*).

For the rest of the fifties and into the early sixties, Orton and Halliwell lived a hermetically-sealed existence in their tiny bedsit. In life as in art, Halliwell took his stylistic clues from camp novelist Ronald Firbank. Along with David Hockney, Orton would later come to embody the gay side of Swinging London, but as yet there was no young scene for him to personify. In 1962, more than a decade after Orton arrived in London with such great expectations, their names had appeared in the tabloids only once - when they were convicted of defacing library books (replacing original book covers with their own satirical versions which were often intricately produced and sexually explicit). They were both sent to prison.

In jail Orton was freed of Halliwell's overbearing presence. In the four years following his release (1963-7), he found a new range of dramatic voices and produced a body of work which established him as one of Britain's leading playwrights: The

Ruffian On The Stair (1963); *Entertaining Mr Sloane* (1963); *The Good and Faithful Servant* (1964); *Loot* (1964-6); *The Erpingham Camp* (1965); *Funeral Games* (1966); and *What The Butler Saw* (1967). Orton's style was spare and direct; he used established theatrical forms (farce, the well-made play) in a subversive manner; and he demonstrated an awareness of ancient literature while creating characters that were as modern as the Beatles. It was Orton that the Fab Four turned to for the script of what was to have been their third film, *Up Against It.*

As Orton's star went into the ascendant, so Halliwell's failures and insecurities came into even sharper relief. When Orton looked like moving out of the Islington bedsit which had been their shared place of refuge a decade earlier, Halliwell bashed out his lover's brains and then killed himself by taking 22 Nembutals. Like a scene in one of Orton's own plays, the manner of their death was both macabre and laughable in its absurdity.

Played by Gary Oldman (Orton) and Alfred Molina (Halliwell), the paths of these star-crossed lovers were described in *Prick Up Your Ears* (1987), Stephen Frears' biopic in which the confines of their Islington bedsit seem like a metaphor for the pressures and restrictions of Thatcher's Britain.

PARENTS RADA, rock'n'roll
READ ON *Prick Up Your Ears* by John Lahr

Tony Parsons
Mr Sharp

On BBC2's *The Late Review*, ferret-faced Tony Parsons is the one with the barrow-boy accent, sharp tongue and matching suit. It is a role he plays as if to the manner born; in fact he's had to work bloody hard at it.

Born in Romford in 1955 (mother a dinner lady from the East End, father a Second World War hero from the Old Kent Road who died of lung cancer in the 80s but never said he had it until his final collapse), Tony Parsons always wanted to be a writer. His first published piece (on why Leeds play dirty) appeared in Jimmy Hill's football magazine when Parsons was 10. As a youth he wrote to *Daily Mail* columnist Keith Waterhouse asking how to become a writer (get an agent, was the reply). He left grammar school at 16, and worked nights in the Gordon's gin distillery in Islington while writing a novel of teeming teen life, *The Kids.*

When, at the height of its influence in 1976, the *NME* advertised for 'young gunslingers', Parsons was one of two writers selected out of an estimated 5,000 applicants. Under the editorship of Nick Logan, future proprietor of **The Face** and *Arena*, he worked on the *NME* for three years (1976–79), which he remembers as 'the perfect time to work for a weekly music paper. You could go out seven nights a week in London and see a different great unsigned band every night – and still have change for a pair of bondage trousers.' And if the hack could not be bothered to go out, he could sit at his desk and wait for the sex, drugs and rock'n'roll to come to him: 'Good times, bad times, hard liquor, soft women, weird sex, exotic cocktails, good friends, bitter enemies, creative fulfilment – you could get absolutely everything you wanted without ever stepping out of the office.'

No wonder Parsons always 'walked into the office with a shiver of excitement, wondering what was going to happen that day'. What was happening at that time was punk, and with stories like 'Blank Generation Out On The Road' (on the Sex Pistols tour, December 1976) and 'Sten Guns in Knightsbridge' (about The Clash and their 'commitment', April 1977), Parsons became one of its leading chroniclers: he was as pale, fast and spikey as the subjects he wrote about.

The other *NME* appointee of 1976 was the 16-year-old **Julie Burchill**. Together she and Parsons terrorised the paper's old guard, did a bucketload of drugs (except heroin) and produced a sharp critique of rock'n'roll, *The Boy Looked At Johnny*. They also got married (1978; Burchill claims that their first coupling was 'a nasty, brutish, short shag') and had a son, Bobby; but Burchill left when Bobby was five, after she was informed of her husband's one-night stand with a student at the University of East Anglia. Parsons now regrets 'that we didn't stay friends for the benefit of our son, but we didn't'. She took pot-shots at him in her autobiography (*I Knew I Was Right*, 1998); and he could not resist sniping at her ample figure: 'hell hath no fury like an ex-wife run to fat'.

In the early 80s, while the ex-wife's career went into the ascendant, Parsons' professional life entered the doldrums. During his twenties he wrote four more novels (the best one is *Platinum Logic* about the corrupt record industry), but did not find a niche until he started working for Nick Logan's *Arena*, launched in 1986. Branching out from music, Parsons did interviews (notably with Muhammad Ali), travel writing and polemics. His infamous 'Tattooed Jungle', about the degradation of the British working class ('the salt of the earth have become the scum of the earth, a huge tribe of tattooed white trash. Today the working class are peasants.'), began as an *Arena* article (1989) and was then translated into a Channel 4 programme (*J'accuse*, 1990). Since then Parsons has fronted a series on class for BBC2 ('class isn't about who you are now. It's about where you have come from.'), hosted the magazine show *Big Mouth* for Channel 4, and presented the sex-war documentary *Equal But Different*. He blames middle-class reviewers for the fairly negative response most of these programmes received.

Although his broadcasting career has failed to lift off, Parsons is now a highly successful writer. He received £250,000 for writing the definitive biography of George Michael (*Bare*, 1990). In 1992 he was invited to write a weekly pop music column for the *Daily Telegraph*, and in the second half of the 90s he was given a much wider brief at the *Daily Mirror* (as a *Mirror* columnist, he joined his ex-wife in the ostentatious mourning of Diana).

'Fit-looking' Parsons gave up drugs at 23 so as to avoid 'being a pathetic old git'. He recalls getting 'rat-faced with experts in my youth' but claims 'there is nothing magical or glorious about it'. Instead he practises martial arts and works out on a Nordic Ski machine. Expensively dressed (**Paul Smith**, Tag Heuer watch), Parsons clearly enjoys the trappings of success, but insists 'I earned it. I never thought I had a right to it.'

Moral responsibility is an important theme in *Man and Boy* (1999), Parsons' novel (he insists it is not autobiographical but concedes it is 'grounded in real emotions') about the changing priorities of a 30-year-old media man who takes sole responsibility for bringing up his son. Critics who had, wrongly, bracketed Parsons with laddism were surprised by its tenderness. Parsons ('I'm the least laddish person I know') describes it as his 'first grown-up book', far removed from laddism's juvenile mimicking of masculinity. Whereas **Nick Hornby**'s protagonist in *About A Boy* (1999) is afraid to be a father, Parsons' Harry strives to be a fully fledged father and a full-on adult. Of his own role as a parent, Parsons observes that: 'My son and I like a lot of the same things, especially the same music, but we've had a traditional father and son relationship, we've never been just friends.'

Parsons' motto is 'stay close to the things you love. And take a baseball bat to the rest.' He has lived by the pen for 25 years, and, on occasion, his career has come close to dying. But he has pulled himself up by his bootstraps, and now occupies a senior position in the media meritocracy.

PARENTS Keith Waterhouse, Nick Logan
READ ON *Man and Boy*; *Dispatches From the Front-Line of Popular Culture*

Jeremy Paxman
Paxo'ed

'Having read HL Mencken's opinion that the correct relationship of a journalist to a politician was that of a dog to a lamp post, there was really only one career open to me.' Jeremy Paxman is the television journalist who, most single-handedly, has kept alive the art of the hard interview. In 1998, when BBC director-general John Birt ordered 'sneering' interviewers to be brought under control, Paxman was taken to be the one he had in mind. He is the neatly dressed, well-coiffed *Newsnight* anchorman whose off-the-cuff jibes have stung senior ministers (Paxman to ailing chancellor of the exchequer Norman Lamont: 'Do you enjoy being chancellor?' Lamont: 'Yes'. Paxman: 'Will you miss it, then?') and brought pleasure to millions, many of whom now consider him 'the *de facto* official opposition'.

Paxman, or 'Paxo' as he is known in *Private Eye*, famously asked Tory home secretary Michael Howard whether he had over-ruled the director of the Prison Service, and repeated the question 13 times while Howard tried to avoid answering it. His approach to New Labour politicians is equally dogged. So much so that when **Tony Blair**'s spin doctor Alistair Campbell redirected senior ministers away from *Newsnight* towards daytime TV, Paxman's performances were reckoned to be a significant factor in the move. *Newsnight* is 'on late with a dwindling audience', Campbell claimed in a letter to *The Times*. Pointing out that the programme's viewing figures had risen by 7 per cent since 1992, Paxman countered that the government is 'obsessed with public relations'.

All good knockabout stuff. But there is more at stake here than point-scoring and personal pride. Paxman's professional authority stems from his belief that airing difficult questions is an important public role. As a private individual he is said to be 'prone to doubt, depression and a yearning for religious faith'. Angling (he writes about it for *Esquire* and has edited a fishing anthology) is his spiritual salve. His first book, *Friends in High Places*, exposed as a myth the much purveyed idea that the Britain of the 1990s is a meritocracy, a place where he believes gender, race and the old school tie still dominate political life.

Paxman was mooted as a potential anchor for ITN's early-evening news programme, eventually launched in 1999 with Trevor McDonald in the chair. Instead he has confirmed his position at the BBC by taking on Melvyn Bragg's old role as host of *Start The Week* (Radio 4) and becoming the new Bamber Gascoigne on *University Challenge*. Popular with the punters (*Sun* readers voted Paxman the best possible chair of a debate between party political leaders), he has made enemies among the establishment. He was blackballed when he applied to join the Garrick Club some years ago. In 1998 he published *The English*: partly investigative, part-cultural commentary, it is a timely book which discusses how 'being English used to be easy', but 'it is all so much more complicated now'.

John Peel
OBE

Once the leading DJ in the British counter-culture, John Ravenscroft aka Peel is now a member of the Order of the British Empire and a programme presenter on Radio 4 (formerly the Home Service) who has been described as 'the new John Betjeman'. Meanwhile he's still a reference point in music. REM asked to be allowed to record for his radio show (three nights a week, still broadcasting on Radio 1 after more than 32 years), and in 1999 he introduced *Sounds of the Suburbs* for Channel 4, a series of documentaries about music-making in out-of-the-way British towns. Starting with **Elton John** and **Marc Bolan**, Peel has had most of Britain's major recording stars on his programmes at some time – not bad for a sixtysomething who describes himself as looking 'like a minicab driver'. He also says, 'I don't really know much about pop music. If you asked me to name the **Spice Girls** I frankly couldn't do it.'

Born in Heswell near Liverpool in 1939, Peel went away to prep school aged seven (by the time his father got back from the war, it was too late to get to know him). After National Service, he moved to the USA where he cut out his cut-glass accent and sold insurance. Finding work as a radio DJ in Texas, he emphasised his Merseyside connections, and became known locally as 'the fifth **Beatle**'. Back in Blighty, after a stint on Radio London, a **pirate radio** station, Peel was one of 22 DJs recruited by the BBC for the opening of Radio 1 in September 1967.

Peel's first show for Radio 1 (*Top Gear*) filled the 'Underground' slot, featuring records and specially recorded tracks from new stars such as Jimi Hendrix and nearly-made-its like Birmingham's The Idle Race. His delivery stood out against the rest: whereas other DJs were talking fast, enthusiastic and pseudo-American (Emperor Rosko, for example), Peel's microphone voice coupled scouse vowels with a tone of droll disdain (his apparent lack of 'side' is somewhat misleading; Peel's colleagues recognise the 'passive aggressive' in him).

In the early 70s Peel went folkie: under the wing of CBS he ran a record label (Dandelion) whose roster included singer-songwriter Bridget St John. On his radio show he promoted Arcadian bands like Forest. In 1976 he caught on to punk, and whereas most pop figures of his generation were despised by the new cohort, Peel became a sponsor of punk (which he maintains was a form of liberation that also 'liberated itself from the entrepreneurs who sought to control it'), and its fans came to regard him as an admirable uncle – too old to be a threat but still cool and supremely knowledgeable. This is a position he has maintained ever since, though his avuncular role is now largely directed towards dance music ('it's generally the dance records that are the most exciting').

Peel introduced Captain Beefheart to the record buying public and has been a consistent supporter of **The Fall**, perhaps the most uncompromising band in the history of British pop. He has championed some great music, and, with producer John

John Peel

Walters (who says he cannot understand why Peel does *Home Truths*), developed a working method that allowed bands to use the sessions they recorded for his show as a stepping stone to making an album. In some cases the legendary 'Peel Sessions' were retrospectively released as albums in their own right. Peel has also showcased a fair amount of dross (you're better off if you don't remember Wild Man Fischer from the 70s). Unlike the other Radio 1 DJs Peel's late night slot was never governed by the heavy rotation playlist. He could play absolutely anything. This included the record's label when he wasn't concentrating and, more interestingly, tapes sent in by bands without recording contracts: a precursor of what is now happening on the internet.

Over the years Peel has come to play the role of cultural catalyst to the British nation, introducing new sounds and sometimes nudging the listening public into accepting them. His eclectic taste includes just about everything except what he terms 'pop shite'. In 1999 he extended this role with a new gig at the South Bank. Having served the previous year as director of the Meltdown Festival, an annual event which seeks to meld various forms of music in a distinctive summer programme, he agreed to host the Peel Sessions Live, an ongoing series of concerts at the Queen Elizabeth Hall.

As well as *Home Truths*, the triple Sony award-winning Saturday-morning programme about domestic problems and personal triumphs, in the late 90s Peel also hosted a TV series about the trials and tribulations of moving house. His own house (referred to as Peel Acres because there is a smallholding attached) is in Suffolk where he lives with his wife Sheila (known as 'The Pig' because she snorts when she laughs), three grown-up children (who were consulted before he accepted the OBE, which he then received from Prince Charles during an 'immensely glum' ceremony at Buckingham Palace) and an enormous record collection.

In addition to his OBE, Peel was *Melody Maker*'s top DJ for 11 years in a row. He was Sony Broadcaster of the Year (1993) and *NME* Godlike Genius (1994). His critics are few but vociferous. World music DJ Andy Kershaw reckons *Home*

Truths is 'piffle'; radio critic Gillian Reynolds compares it to swimming in condensed milk. Journalists Jim Shelley and **Julie Burchill** claim he operates a 'whites-only music box' (have they forgotten the hours of dub reggae he played in the 70s?). Burchill has also resurrected the sad story of Peel's first wife (married at 15 having lied about her age, divorced in 1969, did time in Holloway Prison and died in the late 80s), and pointed out that, during the 70s, he used to 'drool on' about schoolgirls. I can recall that Peel did talk about girls 'with a dangerously high nubility quotient' (this was the lusty 70s not the nervous 90s). But no sooner had Burchill referred to Peel's under-age interests than a self-confessed 'schoolgirl groupie' wrote to the *Guardian* to say that throughout 'a two-year friendship' which she had instigated, he 'never once tried it on'. The reputation of Uncle John Peel, eclectic tastemaker to the British public, remains unsullied.

PARENTS John Betjeman, **The Beatles**
CHILDREN Andy Kershaw, X-FM, people-sound.com

Reginald Perrin
No escape

The total running time of all the original episodes of *The Fall and Rise of Reginald Perrin* (1976–78) is less than 11 hours. But the comedy series, written by David Nobbs and starring Leonard Rossiter as Perrin, has been a recurring feature on British television screens for 25 years.

In the first episode, Reggie Perrin is introduced as a hapless middle manager at Sunshine Desserts, who is bored by the routine nature of his work and scared by his authoritarian boss, CJ (catchphrase: 'I didn't get where I am today by …'). He fakes his own suicide on a Dorset beach (a fictional event not unlike the real-life disappearance of Labour minister John Stonehouse), returns to remarry his wife, and ends up as the unwilling boss of his own chain of shops, Grot. In the very attempt to escape the corporate machine he is once again embroiled in it.

Although first-time audiences for *Perrin* were not exceptional (approximately 10 million), he was soon acknowledged as the leading symbol of disillusionment with business and distrust of corporate culture. Not a new theme in British culture: it had already been explored by novelists George Orwell (*Coming Up For Air*) and John Wain (*The Smaller Sky*). But *Perrin* brought this current into the mainstream and added comic genius.

As a boy, *Perrin*'s creator David Nobbs (b. 1935) travelled by train (the 8.14 from Orpington) every day to his prep school. 'My train was always teeming with commuters,' he recalls. 'I spent the whole journey watching everyone with their briefcases, rolled umbrellas and bowler hats heading for the office. Even at that young age I hoped I would never end up like them.' Nobbs avoided being a commuter himself by inventing Reggie Perrin, the clown of the commuter belt. Educated at Marlborough College and St John's, Cambridge, he had been a

local journalist, a scriptwriter for *That Was The Week That Was* (the first satire show on British TV), and the author of three novels. Since *Perrin* was first broadcast he has written a further nine novels and 'a myriad of TV scripts', including *A Bit Of A Do*, the comedy of family rivalry screened by Yorkshire TV in 1989.

Ronnie Barker (*Porridge*, *Open All Hours*, *The Two Ronnies*) was slated to appear as Perrin but there was not enough room in his schedule. He later wrote to Nobbs saying he was sorry to have missed the opportunity, but also pleased that the chance went to Leonard Rossiter. Born in Liverpool in 1926, Rossiter's early ambition to become a teacher was thwarted when his father was killed in an air raid in 1942. Rossiter worked in an insurance office to support his mother, and took up amateur dramatics after boasting to a girlfriend that he could do it better than the group of actors they had just seen. Blessed with 'a false nose that isn't and a mouth like the grin on a Halloween pumpkin', Rossiter found plenty of work in repertory theatre, notably at the Bristol Old Vic and the Belgrade Theatre in Coventry, where he met his future wife Gillian Raine. By the mid-60s he had played supporting roles in film (*A Kind of Loving*, *This Sporting Life* and *Billy Liar*) and on TV (**The Avengers** and *Z Cars*). His big break came in 1969 when he took on the lead role in the West End revival of Bertolt Brecht's *The Resistible Rise of Arturo Ui*. As Rigsby, the seedy landlord in the sitcom *Rising Damp* (1974) he became a household name. Apart from his *Perrin* role he is best known as the clumsy oaf who appeared in the Cinzano ads with Joan Collins.

He died in 1984 from a congenital heart defect.

Rossiter was a prickly performer, noted for perfectionism and a high-speed delivery (in his first-ever notice this was described as a problem; instead it became his trademark). Fellow actor Richard Briers (*The Good Life*) observed Rossiter's 'extraordinary' energy in the role of Arturo Ui, and summed him up as 'one of the great eccentric actors'. The great eccentric actor went on to play one of the greatest eccentrics in British TV comedy.

Reggie Perrin lives on. In 1996 a fourth series was broadcast, in which Reggie's friends and enemies respond to his death (real this time, not faked). But the prolonged life of *Perrin* is guaranteed not by new episodes but by the frequent repetition of the originals. Today's audiences love Perrin as a period piece; but the freshness of a comedic rebellion against corporate culture must have worn off, now that everyone says they are against it – even the corporations themselves.

PARENTS George Orwell, John Wain
READ ON *The Life and Legacy of Reginald Perrin* by Richard Webber, David Nobb's Perrin novels

Pet Shop Boys
Seriously camp

The Pet Shop Boys (Neil Tennant and Chris Lowe) are an ultra-intelligent pop group – an oxymoron they are wise to. Indeed they have been living and working off this contradiction-in-terms since their first hit single ('West End Girls') in 1985. As Tennant says, 'we are of pop music and we attack it at the same time'.

Although **Tony Parsons** has said that their work is comparable to the songs Lennon and McCartney wrote for **The Beatles**, the two Pet Shop Boys could not be further removed from the traditional pop model of three guitarists and a drummer. Their style, as Tennant once said, is defined 'by what we don't do'. They do not do 'gigs'. After a live debut at the ICA in 1986, the PSBs did not tour (a proposed tour that year was cancelled) until 1988 when they did 14 dates in a show directed by artist and film director **Derek Jarman**. In 1991 their Performance tour was even more theatrical. Designed by David Alden and David Fielding who work mainly with the English National Opera, the show incorporated other singers, dancers and an impressive array of scene and costume changes. There were no musicians on stage and the PSBs themselves were not on stage for the whole show. The operatic element in their stage work derives from Tennant's love of classical music. His instinctive references to the latter (the chord sequence of 'A Red Letter Day', for example, is taken from Beethoven's setting of Schiller's poem 'Ode to Joy') combines with Chris Lowe's love of dance music to produce 'dance music with strings'. Jon Wilde and Michael Bracewell have called it 'dance music for people who can't or won't dance'.

Besides classical music, Tennant is also steeped in pop culture. Formerly a journalist on *Smash Hits* (the 'poppiest' of music magazines), he monitors the charts avidly, loves the idea of pop celebrity, and often sings the praises of the pop song as a musical form. Wilde and Bracewell summed up the PSBs' modus operandi as how 'to be in a pop group without being in a pop group'.

'Camp has a type of sincerity,' Tennant once said – a phrase that sums up the PSBs' contradictory combination of irony and seriousness. Examples of their camp side include: that they met in an electronics shop while Tennant was editing books on tropical fish and Lowe was designing staircases; their knowingly indifferent debut on *Top of the Pops*; their 1987 show at the London Palladium introduced by Jimmy Tarbuck (Lowe was born in the home of tacky showbiz, Blackpool); Tennant's yawn on the cover of *Actually*; Lowe's statement that 'the less effort we put in the better it goes'; Lowe's stage presence which Tennant has dubbed 'that style of keyboard playing where you just stand there in a pair of shades doing nothing'; their ironisation of U2's rock anthem 'Where The Streets Have No Name' (achieved by seguing into Andy Williams' 'Can't Take My Eyes Off You' and setting the whole thing against a trashy disco track); their habit of using the deliberately inarticulate throb of disco and mixing it with urbane, intelligent lyrics. They also have an ironic take on the whole business of pop stardom. Tennant has said that if it all ended tomorrow he might 'open a launderette' or 'settle down with a good bottle of wine and a book'.

But irony is only half of the PSBs' sensibility. They describe themselves as 'serious and comic' and hate to be seen simply as ironists who are just playing with the pop process. One of the 'misun-derstandings' Tennant vehemently objects to is that 'we strive to make pop records about pop records. I don't think we do and, in fact, I really don't like that sort of thing. Most of what we do is meant totally sincerely.' The sincerity and seriousness even in their irony is clearly demonstrated on *Very* (which accounted for 4 million of the 24 million album sales clocked up by the PSBs in their first decade). This album is less bleak than its predecessor *Behaviour* (critically acclaimed but among the poorest sales in the PSB catalogue), but there is sadness even in its humour. 'Dreaming of the Queen' is a comic song about the break-up of the marriage between Prince Charles and Princess Diana, but it is also an 'anxiety dream' containing lines like 'there are no lovers left alive' which refer to the devastating effects of AIDS on the gay community. Similarly, The PSBs' reworking of 'Go West', originally recorded by the Village People as an invitation to join in the free and easy sex life of the San Francisco bath-houses, becomes a lament for the man who wrote it, AIDS victim Jacques Morales.

Like their ironism, Chris Lowe's declaration that their paradoxical work reflects 'how you don't have a single message, and how difficult it is to live in a complex, difficult world', would seem to put the PSBs in the camp of postmodernism. But Tennant insists that 'we come from a modernist tradition, believing that music progresses through technology and innovation'. Although they have recorded with pop divas from the 60s, such as **Dusty Springfield**, the retro aspect of po-mo is largely absent from their work. Comparing the PSBs to the self-conscious revivalists of **Britpop**, Andrew Smith of *The Sunday Times* wrote: 'They have faith. The postmodern Britpoppers don't.'

The PSBs have been hostile to laddish, parochial Britpop (with some exceptions). Tennant despises the 'cult of the lad', cannot stand the work of the 'godfather of Britpop' – Paul Weller, and dislikes football (unlike Lowe who supports Arsenal). In 1996, with Britpop at its height, they released an album, *Bilingual*, which Tennant described as 'cosmopolitan … an international album', and which was sold in a deliberately 'sophisticated, international piece of packaging' put together by designer Mark Farrow. In the accompanying press release, the record was described as 'aggressively non-British … not at all parochial, when so much British music is.' When so much was being said about British music, the PSBs chose to present themselves as cosmopolitans. But their most cosmopolitan album was released on perhaps the most British of record labels – Parlophone, home of The Goons and The Beatles; and on other occasions their singularly British aspects have been more to the fore. Tennant has situated the PSBs in 'the cultural tradition of Joe Orton and Noël Coward', two gay playwrights who played around with British identities. Their video for 'Go West' was partly a homage to *A Matter of Life and Death* (1946), the lyrical film by Michael **Powell** and **Emeric Pressburger** about a British air force pilot (David Niven) in the no-man's land between heaven and earth. In 1991 they toured the USA with what their biographer Chris Heath described as a sense of 'mission and disdain': they feared America but also wanted to convert it to their sensibility. Earlier that year, Wilde and Bracewell suggested that the atmosphere in the PSBs' dressing room was such that the quintessentially British comedian Eric Morecambe might start 'suddenly peeking through the curtain' at any moment. Perhaps it takes a quirky Brit to enjoy both Noël Coward and Noel Gallagher, as Tennant is known to do.

Although born into the lower middle classes (the same social band as the PSBs – both their fathers were sales reps), Noël Coward became the archetypal upper-class British homosexual. Tennant was a central figure in the media coverage of Coward's centenary in 1998. This seems particularly appropriate because, just as Coward's sexual orientation was rarely referred to openly, so the PSBs have been unwilling to define themselves as Gay with a capital 'G'. On occasion they have come close: Tennant's self-outing in an interview with *Attitude* magazine around the time of his 40th birthday in 1994; their participation in **Jon Savage**'s history of gay disco in the TV programme *Out on Tuesday* (1988); their involvement in AIDS benefits and public declarations against Clause 28 (anti-gay legislation, now repealed); male nudity in the video for 'Domino Dancing'; Lowe's sex rap and striptease during the Performance tour of 1991; songs like 'The Truck Driver and His Mate', a deliberately homo-erotic take on the adverts for Yorkie chocolate bars. On the other hand, the PSBs were said to be 'climbing the walls' when *Time Out* reviewer John Gill praised the 'gay subtext' of their ICA debut and first album, *Please*. In his book *Queer Noises*, Gill castigates the PSBs for complying with 'the bourgeois tradition of discreet perversion and collusion with the establishment'. He clearly thinks they are cowards for not being out and proud like Erasure.

In 1999 the right-wing philosopher Roger Scruton made a foolish attack on the PSBs in his book *An Intelligent Person's Guide to Culture*: 'As with the **Spice Girls** or the Pet Shop Boys,' wrote Scruton, 'serious doubts arise as to whether the performers made more than a minimal contribution to the recording, which owes its trademark to subsequent sound engineering, designed precisely to make it unrepeatable.' Threatened with libel action, Scruton retreated. 'It's over-sensitive to think this is in any way a criticism,' he told *The Sunday Times*. 'Actually, I quite like the Pet Shop Boys – certainly the early stuff.'

PARENTS Noël Coward, Derek Jarman, Lennon and McCartney
READ ON *The Pet Shop Boys versus America* by Chris Heath

Harold Pinter
No longer Pinteresque

Born (1930) in Hackney, East London, the only child of Jewish parents (name derived from the Portuguese da Pinta), Harold Pinter was encour-

aged to write by Joseph Brierley, his English teacher at Hackney Downs school. At 18 he refused to do National Service and was listed as a conscientious objector. In the 50s he trained and worked as an actor, using the stage name David Barron. He was inspired to write plays by Samuel Beckett.

His debut (*The Birthday Party*, 1958) was rubbished by critics and taken off after a few nights; 40 years on, Pinter was described by Melvyn Bragg as 'Britain's leading playwright'.

Pinter's early plays are oblique and mysterious. In *The Birthday Party* a middle-aged married couple hardly communicate; then their lodger is visited by two menacing men. *Old Times* (1975) begins with a man and a woman in a room, together with the ghostly presence of another woman. They speak their minds, but the underlying connections between their thoughts are not always apparent. Even Pinter himself says 'I can't tell you exactly what happens.' Along with other works such as *The Dumb Waiter* (1959), *The Caretaker* (1958; filmed 1963), *The Homecoming* (1965), *The Basement* (1967), *No Man's Land* (1975) and *Betrayal* (1978), these are the plays that prompted the epithet 'Pinteresque', defined by the *Chambers English Dictionary* as 'a world of halting dialogue with an air of menace'. As a director of his own work, Pinter is precise about his silences. It's been said that he once told a bewildered actor: 'You're playing two dots when the text says three.'

With regard to the 'halting dialogue', Pinter has explained that in his plays 'characters use words not to express but to disguise what they feel'. He

Harold Pinter

also declared that 'speech is a constant stratagem to cover nakedness'. But in recent years Pinter has moved away from the dictionary definition of his early work.

Plays such as *One For The Road* (1984), *Mountain Language* (1988) and *A New World Order* are political dramas rather than existential ones. Pinter now says that even his early works had political connotations: the menacing visitors in *The Birthday Party*, for example, are representatives of the traditional structures of society and its guardian, the state. These plays, he suggests, were 'metaphors', whereas his newer work is more explicitly political. *Mountain Language*, for exam-

ple, was inspired by the situation of the Kurds, particularly the ban on the Kurdish language imposed by the Turkish state.

Pinter dates the change in his work to the 80s – the age of Thatcherism – when 'I had a sense of suffocation as a social being.' Although he and his circle of associates (including his second wife Lady Antonia Fraser; he was divorced from actress Vivien Merchant in 1980) have been derided as 'champagne socialists' and 'claret comrades', his writing has maintained a campaigning aspect. Whereas in the 60s he wrote screenplays for Joseph Losey films such *The Servant* (1963; elliptically describing class conflict), in the 80s and 90s he has written polemical poems and political essays (many of which are directly opposed to American foreign policy). In 1991–92 he was involved in a campaign against the quinquecentennial celebrations of the 'discovery' of America by Columbus. Pinter's poem about the execution-by-burial of Iraqi conscripts during the Gulf War of 1991 was refused publication by the *Observer* even though the reports on which it was based were published in the self-same newspaper. Keen on cricket, a complete set of *Wisden* lives in his study alongside mementos of political protests since the 60s.

PARENTS Samuel Beckett, Bertolt Brecht
READ ON *Harold Pinter – you never heard such silence* edited by Alan Bold

Pirate radio
Outlaws no more

On two occasions in the past 40 years, pirate stations have navigated the way forwards for British music radio, only to be overtaken by events.

In the 60s, when the BBC Light Programme was less likely to play hit records than a live concert by a Glen Miller-style dance band, teenagers turned to the fleet of pirates (Radio London, Radio Caroline, Radio City) moored just outside British territorial waters. Perched, sometimes precariously, on the ocean waves, pirate disc jockeys pumped out a steady stream of soul and pop. Tuning into the

pirates meant turning away from the British tradition of radio broadcasting which had been developed as a medium of shared national experience during the Second World War. But in August 1967 the pirates closed after the Labour government enacted the Marine Broadcasting Offences Act which made it illegal to even to 'aid' an unlicensed station ('the future does not exist for them', telecommunications minister Tony Benn had warned in 1965). A month later, the BBC modified its own tradition with the launch of Radio 1, an all-record pop music station staffed mainly by ex-pirate DJs.

Despite the spread of regional radio throughout the 70s, by the late 80s a gap had emerged once again between mainstream broadcasters and the developing tastes of young people. Black music was particularly under-represented. Led by Horizon, JFM, Dread Broadcasting Corporation, LWR and Kiss FM, by the end of the decade a new generation of 600 (non-nautical – now operating from tower blocks) pirate radio stations served the new dance music just as the previous generation had spread the gospel of **Mod**. Listening to the pirates was once more part of a package of anti-establishment activities that also included **Ecstasy**, warehouse parties, and driving round the M25 looking and listening for the next illegal **rave**.

During an amnesty under the terms of the Broadcasting Act 1990, Kiss FM went legit, opting to pay an annual licence fee of more than £250,000 (LWR also applied but was refused). The emergence of Kiss from the underground coincided with the demise of the rave scene as a focus for anti-government attitudes. Apart from a brief flurry (1991–92) of anti-establishment activity associated with fundamentalist, hardcore ravers, the next generation of dancers and DJs would take a more pragmatic, less confrontational attitude to the music business and the social order associated with it.

Pirate radio stations continue to operate out of tower blocks and empty houses, albeit on a smaller scale than before. Today's pirate DJs are as frustrated as their predecessors by the conservatism of the music business (the refusal to promote jungle; the predictability of 'alternative' licensed stations like Xfm). But their activities no longer connote a clash of ideologies. Following the Kiss model, many in 'the pirate community' are keen to compromise with the Radio Authority: they would like to rent time from licensed stations, or purchase weekend-only licenses, or arrange to function as highly localised stations. These attitudes are sometimes reciprocated by those commissioned to close down the pirates. 'I honestly like to feel there is no great animosity,' explains Barry Maxwell, chief of Branch Five of the Radio Communications Agency. 'I keep saying we are not policemen, we are radio engineers, and I hope the pirates see us as that.'

Prosecutions continue (the founder of one reggae station was fined more than £11,000 in a 12-month period and warned that he could face a jail term); but the thrill is gone. In among the diversity of today's officially recognised British culture, the pirates' lack of legal status seems more like a technicality than a symbol of essential difference.

Planet 24
New Labour TV

Planet 24 was the independent television production company that set the tone for young people's programming in the 90s. Bankrolled by Irish-born pop star Bob Geldof (Boomtown Rats, Live Aid, ex-partner of Paula Yates) and headed by ex-public schoolboy Charlie Parsons (creativity) and Waheed Alli ('piranha-like' business acumen), Planet 24 produced the programmes politicians watched in order to find out about young people. These same qualities attracted the attention of the corporate sector, and in March 1999 Planet 24 became a not-so-independent production company when it was bought for £15 million by the Carlton Group, an entertainment conglomerate whose interests include ITV's London franchise holder, Carlton TV.

Independent production companies came to the fore in 1982 when Channel 4 was set up with a remit to commission its programmes from them. Before this, the bulk of British TV was made in-house by the BBC or by one of the ITV companies. Among those commissioned to produce young people's programmes were Janet Street-Porter and her second in command, Charlie Parsons. Partly inspired by punk, Street-Porter and Parsons made shows such as the ground-breaking *Network 7*. With hand-held, wobbly cameras and ad-libbing presenters, their programmes were raw, garish and anarchic. This was TV for young people, by (mainly) young people, and became known as 'yoof TV'.

Neither Street-Porter nor Parsons came from a

business background. Street-Porter went on to struggle with the finances at L!VE TV, before being ousted by hard-nosed former **Sun** editor Kelvin Mackenzie. After a stint as a producer at TV-AM, Parsons hooked up first with Geldof and then also with Alli, whose head for business is the perfect complement to his partner's creative flurries. When Alli came on board, Planet 24 was already making *The Word*, the Friday-night music/chat/grotesque show with a fairground feel (repeated on Channel 4 in 1999). After his arrival the operation became more businesslike: this was 'yoof TV' produced to make money (often from selling formats abroad) as well as waves.

Planet 24 put in the wackiest bid – wrapped in a cornflake packet – for Channel 4's breakfast slot – and won. *The Big Breakfast* was initially ruled out by the selection board, whose members used it as a reference point so many times that network boss Michael Grade realised there must be something in it. The show gained 1.5 million viewers within weeks, and when Channel 4 was rumoured to be axing it, Parsons (previous signings include Gaby Roslin, **Chris Evans**, Mark Lamarr and Zoe Ball) put together the winning combination of Johnny Vaughan and Denise Van Outen, and called it *The Bigger Breakfast*.

Now a New Labour sympathiser, while at Oxford Parsons set up the Happy Party as a response to po-faced student activism. Alli, on the other hand, has been a Labour Party member since his teens. Having left school (a south London comprehensive) at 16, he rejected the recommendation of his careers tutor (bus conductor) and found work as a researcher at a magazine called *Planned Savings*. Within a few years he was a publisher and a grand-a-day financial consultant. He is credited with turning Planet 24 from a bunch of programme makers into a £20 million-a-year business.

Planet 24 has thrived on its reputation as a company that knows how to splash out on a party (free flavoured vodka, Prada presents for staff) and make economies (young, relatively low-paid staff hungry for experience).

The combination of business sense, new money, creativity and youth made Planet 24 into the kind of company New Labour dreamed about. The affection was mutual. During the run-up to the 1997 general election, Alli made regular visits to Labour's campaign HQ at Millbank. After winning the election, a host of New Labour ministers asked him for advice. Chris Smith, secretary of state for media, culture and sport, requested an inside view of broadcasting. Foreign secretary Robin Cook enlisted Alli in Panel 2000, the committee set up to redesign Britain's image abroad. Alli helped to organise the Belfast Peace Concert starring **Elton John**, and when Northern Ireland secretary Mo Mowlam flew back to England after signing the Good Friday agreement, it was in his Kent country house that she took refuge (Alli also has a Georgian house in Islington, where he lives with his male partner). In June 1998, aged 34, Alli was included in the honours list and made a life peer. His maiden speech in the House of Lords was expected to be on the age of consent (Planet 24 is the maker of Gaytime TV) … he spoke on a financial matter instead.

PARENTS *Ready, Steady, Go*, Janet Street-Porter
CHILDREN *Bizarre!*

Dennis Potter
Sex please, we're British

Playwright Dennis (Christopher George) Potter is not a single icon but a triptych. In his first incarnation, he described the doubts and insecurities thrown up by post-Second World War social mobility, but did this in so vigorous a way as to suggest that these problems might yet be overcome. Crippled by an arthritic condition, in his second phase Potter represented a twisted Britain flailing in repression and desire, and failing to find satisfaction. In the months before he died of throat cancer in 1996 (he called the cancer 'Rupert'), Potter found peace and rekindled his creativity. His final television interview – an hour-long conversation with Melvyn Bragg – was an event of national significance. 'The only thing you know for sure is the present tense,' he told Bragg. 'I'm almost serene … things are both more important than they ever were and more trivial.' In this last incarnation Potter symbolises serenity through suffering, not unlike the mythical Greek figures of Philoctetes and Oedipus at Colonus.

Born (1935) in the village of Jolyford Hill in the Forest of Dean, Potter was the son of a miner. His family went to chapel. At the village primary school he was considered 'very withdrawn' and 'namby-pamby'. At ten, he went to London to live with his mother's family in Hammersmith, sharing a bedroom with a bachelor uncle who is said to have performed oral sex on him. Potter attended St Clement Dane's grammar school nearby, and won a place at New College, Oxford (Politics, Philosophy and Economics), where he edited *Isis* magazine, befriended Kenith Trodd, the undergraduate who would produce many of his television plays, and appeared in a TV documentary (1958) in which he explained that he felt caught between two worlds: his rural, working-class background and the Oxford world of privilege and sophistication.

Potter continued to live in two dimensions: on graduating he married Margaret Morgan, a girl from the Forest of Dean, and together they raised a country family (one son and two daughters); but he also established and maintained a major media profile, kept a London flat and once told Trodd that he had been with hundreds of prostitutes.

The gap between Potter's two worlds provided him with the subject matter for his early television plays. *Stand Up, Nigel Barton* and *Vote, Vote, Vote for Nigel Barton* (both 1965) followed a bright working-class boy to Oxford and into politics (Potter was an unsuccessful Labour candidate in the general election of 1964). Barton is shown as doubly alienated, from his background and from the system which would absorb him; but in the final scenes a sense of humanity is restored.

These were days of hope for British television drama, and Potter's career was developing fast. Besides writing for the stage and small screen, he was, successively, a member of the BBC current

Dennis Potter

affairs staff, feature writer and then TV critic for the left-wing *Daily Herald*, leader writer for **The Sun** (in its earliest, Labour days), feature writer for *New Society* and TV critic for the *New Statesman*. As a journalist he was a bit of a show-off. In *New Society* he described the Aberfan slag heap, which slipped and crushed a primary school and many of the pupils in it, as 'a reclining female monster, a wanton negress shifting awkwardly on smelly hams'.

Aged 27 Potter was beset by psoriatic arthropa-

thy, a painful and potentially fatal affliction. In just one week his hands buckled and his joints knotted up. To prevent his skin from flaking off, he had to wear pyjamas under his clothes and tucked into his socks. His writing reflected isolation and the yearning to connect (sexually or otherwise) with other people: *Double Dare* (1976) likened a tart and her client to the relationship between an actress and a playwright. *Pennies From Heaven* (1978, starring Bob Hoskins as the travelling music salesman) demonstrated fascination with sex and a horror of it. Director Piers Haggard believes that Potter's 'early life' was 'in a British sense moderately repressed … sexual liberation is a major theme'. In *The Singing Detective* (1987), which Potter described as 'a detective story about how you find out about yourself and how an event has lodged in you', a diseased writer, played by Michael Gambon, confronts his loathing of sex as described in his own fiction. Also in 1987, the BBC finally screened Potter's *Brimstone and Treacle*. Written a decade before, it is the story of a comatose young woman who regains consciousness after being sexually assaulted by a Satanic young man – the underbelly of the Sleeping Beauty myth.

Although Potter's work became a cry of anguish against his affliction and the physical isolation it imposed on him, he also observed correspondences between his illness and his personality: '[there are] characteristics in this condition which match up with my deeper impulses. Reclusive … tense, I prefer to live in tension and at the point of tension … [this] illness is almost an ally of certain things in me.'

In the 80s a new generation of drugs gave Potter more freedom. He enjoyed drunken dinners in London, and in his personal and professional relationships gave vent to a combination of sarcasm, spurious innocence and hypersensitivity. His work seems to have suffered. Kenith Trodd started producing *Blackeyes* but felt unable to finish it: 'I was in awe of him and he was contemptuous of me.' Potter persuaded the BBC to let him direct. Claiming the play would 'show the way men shape the culture to demand these things of women', he insisted that leading actress Gina Bellingham 'could demonstrate exploitation without being exploited'. Most critics felt differently: *Blackeyes* was just a middle-aged man's fantasies about a young woman. Bellingham has explained that 'he was very verbal about being obsessed with me. I was his muse, and he was my mentor … I had been reduced to the Blank Page'. Potter's previous work had dealt with obsessions, but this time he seems merely to have indulged his own. He retired, hurt, to Ross-on-Wye, emerging only to involve himself in *Lipstick On Your Collar* (featuring a young **Ewan McGregor**), a pale re-run of the themes in *Pennies From Heaven*.

Then, with only months to live, Potter wrote two linked dramas, *Karaoke* and *Cold Lazarus*. He once said of his protagonists 'they're all me', but these television plays had to be the final retelling of his life, and he put everything into this, his last and possibly his best work. *Karaoke* follows the final days of a writer and his passion for a waitress in a karaoke bar. In *Cold Lazarus*, future scientists probe the remains of the author's brain, releasing his memories. The two plays have been described as 'Dennis releasing himself'.

Reviewing the authorised biography by Humphrey Carpenter, Craig Brown noted that Potter was 'a dramatist who was also an adroit self-dramatist'. Brown also believes that Potter's work is too repetitive. The trademark use of Tin Pan Alley songs, he notes, 'is a device Potter first pioneered aged 23', and the plays rely on 'rebarbative sex and valedictory violence'. Potter's naughtiness was contrived: 'portraying himself as a sinner struggling to be a saint, he was perhaps rather closer to a saint struggling to be a sinner'. A case of 'Jeffrey Archer in reverse,' concludes Brown. But this dismissive account of Potter's work is at odds with most British critics, who have come close to canonising a writer who once explained that 'the great bulk' of his work 'is about the victim … someone who cannot explain'.

PARENTS John Knox, DH Lawrence
READ ON biographies of Potter by Humphrey Carpenter (personal) and John Cook (literary)

Powell and Pressburger
Arch-British

Known collectively as 'The Archers', director Michael Powell and screenwriter Emeric Pressburger brought visual splendour to parsimonious British cinema. Sometimes denounced as extravagant and vulgar, their work influenced American directors such as Martin Scorsese and Brian De Palma as well as the triumvirate of 90s British film – **Danny Boyle**, John Macdonald (Pressburger's grandson) and John Hodge, jointly responsible for *Shallow Grave*, *Trainspotting* and *A Life Less Ordinary*.

Born (1905) in the Kent village of Bekesbourne, Michael Powell got into the film business in France in 1925, before returning to Britain to direct a clutch of 'quota quickies' (cheap, domestically produced flicks, mistakenly intended to limit the power and influence of Hollywood). His work with Pressburger (see below) is now regarded as a national treasure. After their partnership came to an end, Powell continued to make movies. But his solo masterpiece *Peeping Tom* (1960; a psychotic voyeur committing crimes of rage against his stepmother and father, fleetingly portrayed by Powell) was too strong for British critics, and he was effectively shut out of the film industry here. Aged 75, Powell crossed over to the old enemy, Hollywood. But the opportunity to work with Francis Ford Coppola foundered with the collapse of Zoetrope studios. He died in 1988.

In his autobiography, *A Life In Movies* (1986), Powell declared himself 'a truculent and dreamy small boy who is determined to impose his views on any audience he can get'. In The Archers, he played the part of maverick genius to Pressburger's steady hand.

Like many of the best chroniclers of British life, screenwriter Emeric Pressburger was born (1902) outside the British Isles. He came from Miskoic in Hungary and worked in the world-renowned UFA studios in Germany (also the workplace of Fritz Lang) before fleeing to Britain after the rise of Hitler. Pressburger first worked with Powell on the London Films production *The Spy In Black* (1939), a First World War story with gloomy premonitions of the Second World War. When The Archers split up in 1956 he tried directing and producing before returning to writing. Pressburger died in 1988, the same year as his ex-partner.

Deborah Kerr in *The Life and Death of Colonel Blimp* (1943)

Powell and Pressburger are revered for 'welding Hollywood spectacle to European arthouse sensibilities to create a cinema that was as British as any Ealing comedy, but infinitely more ambitious'.

The Life and Death of Colonel Blimp (1943), based on David Low's cartoon character, follows a dashing young Edwardian officer on his way to becoming a fuddy-duddy old colonel. Made at a time when 'Blimpishness' (the inefficiency and complacency of the old guard) was regarded as a major problem for the British war effort, *Blimp* reveals the romantic sensibility behind the British stiff upper lip. The War Office refused to co-operate and the lead character's lifelong friendship with a German officer prompted complaints that Powell and Pressburger were 'pro-German'.

A Canterbury Tale (1944) is the story of three wartime travellers through Kent, the garden of England. The film begins with shots of medieval pilgrims on their way to Canterbury Cathedral, and includes scenes of rural life and a sequence in which a falcon is transformed into a military aircraft. After one of the three travellers is attacked by 'the glueman', the latter is revealed as Thomas Colpepper, a magistrate and local historian who believes that British girls ought not to consort with American GIs while their boyfriends are serving abroad. His missionary zeal for national heritage is clearly misguided, but England's noble identity is restored when Sergeant Peter Gibbs (Dennis Price) gets the chance to play the organ in Canterbury Cathedral during a service for departing troops. While revealing tensions in a decaying social order, *A Canterbury Tale* is also redolent with historical continuity.

A Matter of Life and Death (1946, known in the USA as *Stairway To Heaven*) stars David Niven as Squadron Leader Peter Carter, an RAF pilot in limbo between life and death. While doctors try to save his life, Carter dreams he is being judged before God in a heavenly courtroom (5,000 extras in front of a 350-foot backcloth). Commissioned by the Ministry of Information in an effort to encourage Anglo-American co-operation, *A Matter of Life and Death* joshes at British and American identities while promoting romance and international harmony. In the USA the main selling-point was the eponymous stairway, a prop built by London Underground engineers who called it 'Ethel'.

Adapted from a Rumer Godden novel, *Black Narcissus* (1947) follows five Anglican nuns as they set up a school and hospital in a former brothel in the foothills of the Himalayas. Their attempts to establish order are upset by a flamboyant Indian army officer and his Black Narcissus perfume. Powell preferred to shoot at Pinewood Studios rather than travel to the Himalayas. India 'emerges as a state of mind', and the hysterical and erotically charged atmosphere of the film arises from the poetic tension between sensuality and repression.

Released during the grey deprivations of postwar rationing, *The Red Shoes* (1948) is a splash of splendid melodrama about a young ballerina torn between love for a composer and her obsession with dancing. Based on a Hans Andersen story of a dancing girl possessed by a pair of red shoes, the Powell/Pressburger film was condemned at the time as extravagant and indulgent.

Although Archers films were frequently acclaimed by international critics, the initial British reception of their work was often mixed, if not hostile. In the 1940s the opulence of the Powell/Pressburger vision seems to have been regarded as un-British. Nowadays the Archers' œuvre is seen as proof positive that British films do not have to be drab and cheap: they have become not the anomaly but the epitome of the British filmmaking tradition.

PARENTS British tradition, Hollywood scale, European poetics
READ ON *A Life In Movies* by Michael Powell

Primal Scream

Radical funk

One of the attractions of the **rave** scene was the absence of rock stars. Top DJs were valued as facilitators rather than performers, E'ed-up punters were joint headliners at their own show and, for a moment, it seemed that stardom was as outdated as Marshall stacks and the guitar heroes who once plugged into them. But the egalitarian moment did not last, and the contradictory connections between mythical rock'n'roll stars and the idea of an ecstatic community of equals, are summed up in the story of one band: Primal Scream.

Musically, Primal Scream bridged the gap between dance beats and rock'n'roll ('they grooved from rock to beats and back again'; 'a musical voyage, from shambling **indie** through to assured, dubbed-out rock'). Signed to **Alan McGee**'s Creation label, their first record release ('Come Together', 1990) pointed towards *Screamadelica* (1991, winner of the first annual Mercury Music Prize), the album that mapped the common ground between two musical genres which until then were thought to be mutually exclusive: on the one hand, a singer who plays maracas like the early Mick Jagger fronting a band that sounds like the **Rolling Stones** circa *Exile On Main Street* (1972); on the other hand, rhythm tracks produced by DJ Andrew Weatherall and a spacey feel that harmonises with the buzz of **Ecstasy**.

In the early 90s much of the dance music scene existed on the fringes of the law. It saw itself as the sworn enemy of yuppies and other social climbers. Some people regarded it as a challenge to the social inequalities fomented by Margaret Thatcher and her gospel of grasping individualism. Participants in the rave scene had no time for Spandau Ballet, Duran Duran and all the other pouting rock stars who seemed to flaunt their sense of superiority. But Scream singer Bobby Gillespie was clearly one of us. Brought up in 'a Catholic socialist household' (his father a Glasgow trades unionist), the youthful Gillespie likened Che Guevara to Jesus Christ. He described the **royal family** as 'incompetent, in-bred fuckers', and declared himself a man of the people. His drugged-up radicalism showed that you could be lead vocalist in a rock band and still be part of the new community of ravers. Looking back at the period, he remembers that 'Thatcher said there is no such thing as society and a lot of people wanted to believe her. I'm completely opposed to that, we should all stick together. I think that's what music should do – it should be soulful and uplifting and reinforce beliefs that you've got, make you feel strong.'

While preaching egalitarianism, Primal Scream lived the life of the decadent rock'n'roll star more assiduously than anyone since 'Keef' Richards in the early 70s (or Mick Jagger in the role of Turner, 'the acid-fuelled Miss Havisham' in Nicholas Roeg's 1970 film *Performance*). They wore Keef-shades, talked in a Keef-drawl and seemed to be copying Keef-cool. Their guitar sound was even derived from what the *NME* used to call 'Keef-raunch'. In the early 90s they were famous for the kind of

Priority people

The following over-stressed celebrities have all done time at the £3,000-a-week Priory Clinic, Roehampton:

- Caroline Aherne (aka Mrs Merton)
- Michael Barrymore
- Stan Collymore
- Derek Draper, disgraced New Labour spin doctor
- Paul Gascoigne
- Jane Goldman, wife of Jonathan Ross
- Lenny Henry, quoted as saying 'I'm fighting for my life in here'
- Kate Moss
- Paula Yates
- Ruby Wax

Inmates can choose between therapy sessions and a light regime of yoga, swimming and flower arranging. Disappointed guest Alexandra Audley told the *Observer*: 'It's like a three-star hotel really. Most of the people were just there to bask in their celebrity.'

hotel-trashing 'rock'n'roll mayhem' associated with ancient 'rock royals' such as Keith Moon. Perhaps it was pastiche, but at the time it had serious connotations.

This was a period when even the most adventurous young people had resigned themselves to living only at weekends and merely existing – vegetating – through the rest of the week; but here was a group of cocksure, working-class Glaswegians who seemed to be living for the moment *all the time*. The hedonistic mythology of rock'n'roll proved as attractive as ever, and Primal Scream were set to play the important role that all major stars are required to perform: to dramatise our lives by being

like the rest of us, only much, much more so.

Superstardom beckoned, then closed the door on them. From being 'the greatest rock'n'roll band in the world', Primal Scream became just another mid-range act. Some people put their failure down to 'near-mythic debauchery', which in turn contributed to an unstable line-up (Gillespie, Innes and 'the Throb' are the only permanent band members), and a two-year lay-off (1995–97) from live work. But maybe they just missed their moment. Around the time of *Screamadelica*, the authorities were cracking down on raves. A lifestyle based on permanent raving seemed doubly attractive, and radicalism came over as relevant. But the moment of confrontation has passed. In 1997, when Primal Scream put pictures of gun-toting Black Panthers on their EP 'Star', it seemed like another instance of white wannabes poncing off black people, while Gillespie's apparent preference for Cuba rather than Britain, where 'people shit on each other', now comes across as trite and unconvincing. The fact of the matter is that radical, danceable rock'n'roll – even with 'such a hard rock sound' that 'real metal kids' come to the gigs – is out of time.

PARENTS: Rolling Stones, rave, Tony Benn

The Prisoner

His own man

The Prisoner, the 17-part mid-60s TV series that has been compared to Aldous Huxley's *Brave New World* and George Orwell's *1984*, was mainly the work of Patrick McGoohan, who conceived the idea, obtained funds for its production, wrote many of the scripts, starred in all the episodes and directed some of them too. McGoohan is something of a loner, just like the character he played in **The Prisoner** and the show from which it originated, *Danger Man*. For such a collaborative and popular medium as TV, with *The Prisoner*, McGoohan became something of a subversive auteur.

McGoohan was born (1928) in New York of Irish parents but brought up in Sheffield (except for the wartime years when he was evacuated). He is said to have passed Oxford entrance exams but 'didn't want to go there'. While working in steel mills and a bank (suffering from bronchial asthma), he was keen on amateur dramatics and eventually signed on at Sheffield Playhouse as an assistant stage manager. Within a few years he was a leading actor on the West End stage (winner of the *Evening Standard* drama critics' best actor award in 1959 for his rendition of Brand in Ibsen's eponymous play) and a contract player with the Rank Organisation. In 1961 he starred in two films: Brendan Behan's *The Quare Fellow* and *All Night Long* (based on the story of Othello), in which he played a neurotic jazz drummer.

In 1960 McGoohan appeared in the first series of *Danger Man* as NATO special agent John Drake, who preferred to outwit his opponents rather than out-hit them. McGoohan refused to do sex scenes in *Danger Man* and is said to have turned down the roles of James Bond and Simon Templar for the same reason. Another *Danger Man* series (complete with groovy theme tune played on a harpsichord) was made in 1961 and production of a third series began in 1964, by which time McGoohan was fed up with the special agent formula. He went to see ATV's Lew Grade early on a Saturday morning and told him about his idea for *The Prisoner*. Grade said he did not understand it but promised that the funds to produce the series would be in McGoohan's business bank account by Monday morning.

In *The Prisoner*, McGoohan played No 6 ('I am not a number, I am a free man'), a former special agent who tried to get out of the system but is exiled

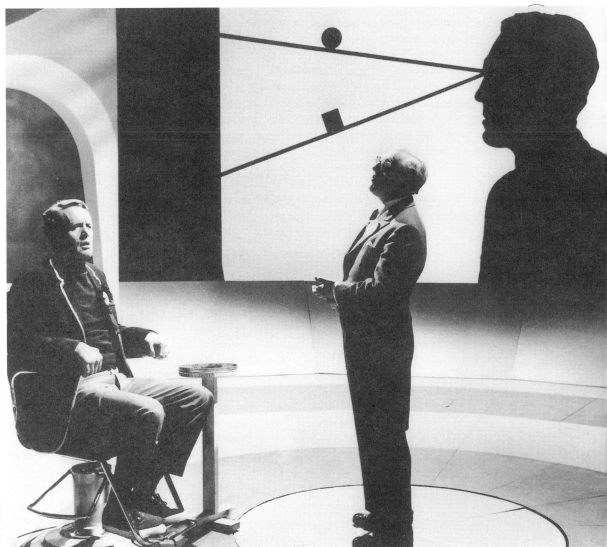

to The Village instead. Shot in the picturesque setting of Portmeirion, The Village is pretty but sinister; 'a place,' as McGoohan later explained, 'that is trying to destroy the individual'. By his own admission *The Prisoner* is overlong; it is also a prophetic parable of a world where authority takes on an innocent-looking, insidious form. Clearly a product of the psychedelic era (the look of *The Prisoner* shares The Beatles *Sgt Pepper*/Yellow Submarine era obsession with a lost village England, filtered through a 60s sensibility), the most startling thing about The Prisoner is the weight of interest that still surrounds it. Like *Star Trek* it is a cult of cults and thirty years on its fans still eat, sleep, drink and continually reinterpret the frame-breaking enigma that is *The Prisoner*.

Fleeing from complaints about the ending of *The Prisoner*, McGoohan fled first to Switzerland and then to the USA, where he worked for many years as a writer/director on the *Columbo* series, with occasional appearances in offbeat films such as David Cronenberg's *Scanners* (1981). There are frequent rumours of a film of *The Prisoner*. Having seen what happened to *The Avengers*, maybe it should be left to rest in peace rather than made a prisoner of tinseltown.

PARENTS *1984, The Trial, Brave New World*
READ ON *Be Seeing You: Decoding The Prisoner* by Chris Gregory

The Prodigy
Electronic Essex Man

At the end of the 80s, when the term Essex Man was frequently used to sum up the presumed boorishness, acquisitiveness and conservatism of the southern, working-class male, the radical, anti-materialist, sometimes spiritually uplifting **rave** scene got going around the new perimeter fence formed by the M25. Out of this scene came the combination of techno, hip-hop and Essex chutzpah known as the Prodigy. They are Thatcher's children, but they do not take after their parents.

Liam Howlett is the Prodigy's composer, programmer and producer. The first record he ever purchased, around the time of **Two-Tone**, was a compilation of ska hits. He bought his first turntable after working all summer long on a building site, and got into rave when frozen out of the all-black hip-hop scene. Leeroy Thornhill, former electrician, was an athletic E-buzzing breakdancer, going into clubs with a sheet of lino and a bottle of Mr Sheen. Frontman Keith Flint, early 80s casual, was introduced to bikers' music (Led Zep, Jimi Hendrix) by his step-brother, and travelled through the Middle East and North Africa after he was thrown out of his father's house. Maxim Reality, aka Keith Palmer, was a Peterborough-based reggae MC. Together they became the Prodigy.

After a PA at the Labyrinth in Dalston, East London, the Prodigy's first record came out on XL, the dance-orientated subsidiary of Beggar's Banquet. Released in February 1991, 'Android'/

'Everybody In The Place'/'We're Gonna Rock'/'What Evil Lurks?' sold 7,000 copies, each of which would now fetch in excess of £120. Produced on Howlett's Roland W30, these tracks brought hip-hop breakbeats together with techno in what XL described as 'a uniquely British perspective'. Fronted by gurning Keith Flint, their videos and live performances combined an element of Hammer horror films and a comic touch, offset by hi-speed dancing and MC-ing from Thornhill and Palmer.

With 'Charly' (1991), another four-track EP with its title track built around a sample from a children's information advert – 'Charly says never go out without telling your mummy first' – the Prodigy outsold and overtook new British dance acts like NJoi and Altern8. Their third release was a reworking of 'Everybody In The Place' using Howlett's newly purchased U220 Roland sound module. For the second time they refused to go on *Top of the Pops*. Nevertheless they were out of favour with dance purists. In the August 1992 edition of *Mixmag*, the Prodigy were accused of killing rave by introducing mindless kiddie samples. Essex style was said to mean 'simple, obvious and always over the top'. The band retaliated in the video for their next single, 'Fire' (based around a sample from the 1969 single by Arthur Brown), during which Howlett takes a copy of *Mixmag* from his jacket and throws it on to a bonfire.

The Prodigy's first album, *Experience*, came out in time for Christmas 1992 and stayed in the charts for six months. Including frenetic breakbeats (most tracks are in excess of 145 beats per minute), ragga, and a speed metal version of 'Everybody In The House', it was cut over two pieces of vinyl so as to deliver maximum clarity and volume. Their second LP, *Music For The Jilted Generation*, came to symbolise ravers under siege from the police and the oncoming Criminal Justice Bill, enacted in 1994. Forget the authorities, the Prodigy advised, the dance scene is too strong to disappear. Soon afterwards the 'real and normal yet weird' video for 'No Good' (directed by Walter Stern) was played repeatedly on MTV and won them a wider audience. Meanwhile **Chris Evans** refused to play the single 'Firestarter' on Radio 1 because he did not like the accompanying video, featuring Flint as a 'pierced homunculus'.

For nearly a decade, the Prodigy have championed the stubborn spirit of youth against politicians and moral entrepreneurs. Sometimes described as 'electronic punks', like the Sex Pistols they over-act ('pantomime evil rock band' fronted by 'a gargoyle arsonist in a shell suit') but their performance is genuine nonetheless. The controversy over the 1997 single/video 'Smack My Bitch Up' reinforced their reputation as rebels. The single was released without the original cover which showed a car wrapped round a lamp-post (this was not long after the funeral of Princess Diana), but the accompanying video and just the title of the track was enough to prompt horrified outbursts from MPs and others.

The Prodigy did not set out to be political. Howlett once explained that 'our music works on a really basic level … it's just direct. We're not trying to think of a deep message for what we are doing.' But seeking to address the senses directly tends to offend those in authority, and, at certain times dur-

347

ing the 90s, the Prodigy were seen as a post-political opposition to the British powers that be.

PARENTS Jimi Hendrix, Public Enemy, the Sex Pistols, *The Young Ones*
READ ON *Electronic Punks* by Martin Roach

Progressive rock

Aspirational, not always inspirational

In the late 60s pop was upwardly mobile. It was no longer a trivial business but deeply serious. Hailed by critics (**George Melly**) and academics (Wilfrid Mellers), it aspired to art (*Sgt Pepper*) rather than entertainment (*With The Beatles*). Songs got longer, drum breaks turned into solos and guitar solos became Indian-style ragas. The LP (which usually came complete with gatefold sleeve and a laboured 'concept') took over from the single. Pop groups transformed themselves into rock bands ('pop' came to mean pap for teenyboppers). Existing record stores devoted floorspace to a new category of music, labelled 'progressive', and a new breed of record shop (Virgin) stocked little else. Having grown out of the aspirational and mind-expanding culture of psychedelia, progressive as a genre loved virtuosic instrumental solos, new technology, weird old instruments and gargantuan stage shows à la Spinal Tap. It was influenced by classical, jazz and folk (anything but pop in fact) and its main performers were upper middle class.

Only half a decade later, the ballooning self-importance of progressive (prog) rock was punctured by the back-to-basics puritans of punk; and prog rock has been dismissed as snobbish, decadent self-indulgence ever since. But this is to ignore the positive aspects of progressive: the attempt to extend the pop format, to develop music that people could grow up to. In this age of 'middle youth', 'adultescents' and 'kidults', at a time when adulthood is in short supply, prog rock might even be worth a revisit.

Prominent progressives

Arthur Brown

The 'god of hellfire', famous for his flaming head-dress (made out of a colander), Brown mixed a soulful voice (his version of 'I Put A Spell On You' is more compelling than the Screamin' Jay Hawkins original) and jazzy keyboards (Vincent Crane) with elements of traditional English theatre, as observed by Charles Fox in the *New Statesman*: 'His face concealed inside a glistening helmet and visor, a saffron robe floating from his shoulders … he belongs to a tradition which goes beyond music hall, right back to mummers' plays. … He's disconcerting, even faintly perverse, but distinctly original and very, very English.' Brown's debut album appeared on Track, the **Who**'s label, and Pete Townshend is credited as 'associate producer' – an indication that what became progressive came partly out of the **Mod** scene of the mid-60s.

Colosseum

Jazz-leaning prog rockers, the high-point of their set was the drum solo by band leader Jon Hiseman. First LP title was in Latin.

Cream

Cream was composed of Eric 'God' Clapton (lead guitar), Jack Bruce (bass) and Ginger Baker (drums). Clapton (ex-John Mayall and The Yardbirds) supplied the blues, Jack Bruce (cellist and classical musical student) provided depth and respectability, and Baker (ex-Graham Bond Organisation) was the wild jazzman. Together they took blues chord progressions and pop vocal lines, and jazzed them up into 20-minute epics. Their farewell concert at the Albert Hall was the subject of a BBC documentary.

Curved Air

Famous for including a classically trained violinist (Darryl Way) and releasing the first-ever single on coloured vinyl.

Emerson, Lake and Palmer

A 'supergroup' composed of keyboardist Keith Emerson (with the Nice, Emerson wrote the pseudo-classical *Five Bridges Suite* and produced 'the world's first instrumental protest song' – a version of Leonard Bernstein's 'America' in which the band vented their anger on the song and sometimes accompanied their rendition by burning the Stars

and Stripes), bassist and singer Greg Lake (ex-King Crimson), and drummer Carl Palmer (previously in The Crazy World of **Arthur Brown**). They shared a love of classical music and jazz, and set about incorporating elements of these into a rock format. In the process their work became corpulent in the extreme: Palmer played specially designed steel drums weighing half a ton. Their gear filled three articulated trucks – one each. ELP became a byword for pomposity and a prominent DJ dismissed them as 'a waste of electricity'.

Soft Machine

With a name borrowed from William Burroughs' book, this Canterbury-based quartet did not include a guitarist. The line-up of sax, keyboards, bass and drums/vocals absorbed influences from electronic music, jazz and folk. They were the first rock group to take part in the Proms (the prestigious series of summer concerts inaugurated by conductor Henry Wood). Their Albert Hall concert was televised by the BBC and introduced by old-style broadcaster Richard Baker.

Yes

The most talented and the most tiresome of all **prog rock** bands. Fiercely proficient musicians, they were innovative (extending the range of keyboards to provide 'mini-symphonies on stage'; acoustically produced polyrhythms bear comparison with the digital fabrications of today's drum'n'bass) and obscurantist (Jon Anderson's lyrics made sense to

349

Harvest The most English record label?

In 1969, Manchester University graduate Michael Jones persuaded EMI to set up a distinctively English record label with Arcadian undertones. The result was Harvest, and the rustic performers who signed to it included: The Albion Dance Band, Kevin Ayers, Syd Barrett, Barclay James Harvest, Martin Carthy, Shirley and Dolly Collins, Forest, Roy Harper, Ashley Hutchings (formerly of Fairport Convention), Southern Comfort.

But Harvest was not all swains and maidens. It also hosted the sub-Beefheart Edgar Broughton Band, black country Mods The Move, and the urban noise of Deep Purple.

no one but himself). In the mid-70s the music press turned against 'the people's band', dubbing them 'rock dinosaurs' and even 'corpse rock': the writing was on the wall for progressive music.

PARENTS classical, jazz, folk, anything but pop
CHILDREN most performers would rather be seen as orphans than acknowledge their prog parents

Queen
OK to be gay?

In the 70s Queen were the height of heterosexism. In the 80s lead singer Freddie Mercury's image became ambiguous; and when he died of AIDS-related illness in 1991, his memorial concert catalysed the change in the British image of gay men from social lepers to super-victims.

Freddie Mercury and lead guitarist Brian May found college boys John Deacon (bass) and Roger Taylor (drums), and formed Queen. Live, they were a rock band with pop overtones. On record, the ratio was reversed. Their first single, 'Seven Seas of Rye', was a pop song (pseudo-mythical lyrics were popular then) with a heavy sound. Likewise, their first major hit, 'Killer Queen' (1974) combined singalong pop with pomp rock. With May as guitar hero, and a solid but sophisticated rhythm section in Deacon and Taylor, Queen could be heavy like Uriah Heep while remaining fairly melodic: hard rock you could hum to.

On stage and screen, Freddie favoured furs and a peculiarly camp way of holding the microphone, but these were the **glam** days when some of Britain's biggest womanisers wore eye make-up and sequins. Neither the band's name nor their climactic cover-version of Shirley Bassey's 'Hey, Big Spender' was interpreted as a deviation from the heterosexual norm.

Until the end of 1975 Queen were just another rock band. It was then that they released a single, 'Bohemian Rhapsody', that included too many time changes to qualify as a pop song, yet it turned out to be their most popular release so far. 'Bohemian Rhapsody' was remarkable neither lyrically (pretentious) nor instrumentally (technically proficient rock), but because of the video that accompanied it. Major bands had used promotional films before (**The Beatles** and **T Rex** among them), but these were little more than footage of live performances interspersed with short, melodramatic scenes. The promo for 'Bohemian Rhapsody', on the other hand, used images of the band in a far more abstract and innovative way. The video made such an impression that the punters kept the record at No 1 for weeks. In the record industry it set a new standard; and a few years later when major companies were looking for a way to differentiate their acts from bands on the small labels that mushroomed after punk, they poured money into expensive video promos, safe in the knowledge that the indies could only afford a couple of photos and maybe a black and white ad in an inkie music paper like the *NME*. It was never Queen's intention, but their technical innovation became a stick for major record companies to beat the minors with.

'Bohemian Rhapsody' was pompous, but it worked. In the decade that followed, Queen worked their own pomposity in an intelligent way. With songs like 'We Will Rock You' and the riff-based 'Another One Bites The Dust', they played rock and played with the idea of it. The result was a sound and an image that was huge yet approachable. It went over well in stadiums all across the world. At the end of the 80s, after 16 consecutive hit singles, their total record sales topped 100 million.

Queen played their last major tour in 1986 (the itinerary included the first major stadium show behind the Iron Curtain). For this tour, Freddie Mercury dressed in the gay style known as the 'clone'. But the 'clone' look was itself an exaggeration of straight masculinity, and Freddie's appearance could be interpreted either way. In the mind's eye of the British public, the image started to come into focus when news of his illness emerged in 1989, but only became conclusive after he admitted he was suffering from AIDS shortly before his death in November 1991. This was less than five years after chief police constable James Anderton had consigned gay men to hell, but the expected backlash failed to develop. Instead of rejecting Freddie and the manner of his death, the people of Britain seemed to take him to their bosom.

Compered by Elizabeth Taylor and telecast to an estimated one billion viewers, the Freddie Mercury Memorial Concert was the biggest rock event of 1992. Performers included **David Bowie**, who talked of 'an explosion of awareness' about AIDS, George Michael, who described it as 'the proudest moment of my career', and Axl Rose and Slash from Guns'n'Roses, an American rock band with a reputation for homophobia: 'It really brought us together,' Slash declared.

Freddie's death, and the response of his peers and the public, pointed the way to the shared experience of mourning that followed the death of Princess Diana in 1997. If some British people

Freddie Mercury

might have frowned at his gay sex life, in death he became a victim first and a gay man second. Moreover, on this as on other recent occasions (the death of film-maker **Derek Jarman**, for example), the proximity of victimhood to gayness has helped to remove the image of the predatory pederast from British culture and lessen the stigma attached to homosexuality. Everybody knows that Freddie was a poof, but it does not prevent football fans from singing Queen songs like 'We Are The Champions'.

In the quarter of a century since Queen first entered a recording studio, British society has changed so much that, if he were starting out now, Freddie could afford to be open about one of his secrets. But homosexuality was not the only skeleton he kept hanging in the closet. Faroukh 'Freddie' Bulsara was born in Zanzibar of Indian (Parsee) parents, and attended an English-style school in Bombay before becoming Britain's first Asian pop star. At the start of his career he was sometimes described as 'Armenian', and his real ethnicity is still not widely acknowledged. In the 70s you might just get away with playing at gay (David Bowie), but being an openly Indian rock star was out of the question. Nowadays it need not be prohibitive (**Talvin Singh**, Jyoti Mishra), but there are still no 'out' Asians in the British big league.

PARENTS Jeff Beck, Shirley Bassey
CHILDREN Skunk Anansie

Rastafarian
Made in Babylon

For many black people in Britain, probably the first sighting of a rastaman came in 1973 when Perry Henzell's film *The Harder They Come* opened here. Henzell depicts rude boy Jimmy Cliff on the run from the Jamaican music industry, traditional Christianity and the organised church, and the Kingston police. He finds temporary sanctuary in a rural settlement of ganja-smoking rastas. In the years that followed, with ex-rude boy Bob Marley as their role model, thousands of second-generation, inner-city British blacks turned their backs on both the idea of integration (the ambition of their West Indian parents; in the 60s it would have been absurd to call them 'African') and the modernity of the Americanised rude boy image (before being transposed from Jamaica to Britain, tonic suits had been transposed to Jamaica from the US corporate culture of the 50s). Like Jimmy Cliff, they sought sanctuary in the religious, anti-western tradition of Rastafarianism. With their self-assured separation from respectable British society, they themselves were something of a role model for rebellious young whites. But for those in authority, rasta came to symbolise the transition from 'evasion to truculence' – aka foreign gentleman to bad black youth – on the part of the black British population.

The belief system of Rastafari was a kind of African Arcadianism, born in 1930s Jamaica. It combines the black nationalist politics of Marcus Garvey, who wanted Africa for Africans, with a mythological framework in which blacks are the lost tribe of Israel and Ethiopia's Hailie Selassie (aka Ras Tafari Makonnen – crowned Emperor of Ethiopia in the 1930s) is the Lion of Judah. Rastafarians look to ancient Africa (Zion) for spiritual inspiration in order to insulate themselves from the white culture of the modern West (Babylon). In Garvey's day the political element was dominant. But by the 1970s, when rasta became influential in Britain, the mythology was what counted; hence its medium of expression was the quasi-Biblical Bob Marley lyric, rather than political speeches or organised activism. Let down by British society, failed by the Labour Party, ripped off by the music industry, alienated from the white working class, a cohort of young blacks inverted their exclusion and used the mythology of rasta to create an exclusive lifestyle that allowed some whites to enter, but only on their say-so.

The move from rude boy to rasta did little to alter the position of blacks in Britain, nor did it change the positioning of young black men towards each other: group affiliations ('black gangs' in the tabloid press) remained paramount. But at a time when British society was identifying itself in opposition to black youth, as in the 'mugging' panics of the mid-70s, it provided black youth with an oppositional identity against British society, now known only as 'Babylon'.

Rasta was seen as something exclusive to blacks. The rastaman (to the horror of feminists, rastawomen were little more than menstruators, babymakers and backing singers) took pride in his black dreadlocks (usually kept covered; uncovering them, as in the Brixton riots of the early 80s, was a sign of righteous anger); he had his own sacrament (ganja), his own dress code (the red, gold and green of the Ethiopian flag), his own music (reggae), and his own language (patois); he kept contact with the agents of Babylon, especially the police, down to a minimum. It all added up to an alternative reality, which could be entered by willing himself into it ('the faith is the strength to overcome oppression'). But, far from being specific to black Britons, the trends that underpinned rasta were discernible throughout British society: growing disillusionment with Labour Party politics; alienation from official religion (the decline of the Church of England) and the turn towards (new age) spirituality; distrust of modernism and re-enchantment with nature (from Mod to hippie). In the second half of the 60s, **Mods** stepped out of their suits, stopped having French cuts and started growing their hair. Ten years later, young blacks started doing similar things. Seen in this light, perhaps rasta should be

seen as the last stand of the 60s British counter-culture.

Nowadays rasta is almost irrelevant. Back in the 70s the British establishment had an identifiable belief system, that prompted alienated young blacks to devise an alternative belief system of their own. At the start of the twenty-first century the established worldviews have all been disestablished, and there is as yet no demand for a coherent alternative. Pragmatism and pick'n'mix are the only co-ordinates in our (non)-ideological landscape, and rasta is reduced to one of many sources from which individual identities can, provisionally, be patched together.

READ ON   *Rastaman* by Ernest Cashmore; *Policing the Crisis* edited by Stuart Hall

Rave
Divided unity

World Dance, One Nation, One Family, Harmony, Infinity: the names of dance music promoters reflected the desire for togetherness that found expression in rave culture. During the late 80s there was a sense that E-fuelled, house-driven young people could come together to transcend the narrow individualism of Margaret Thatcher's there-is-no-such-thing-as-society. But by the early 90s rave was riven by rivalry between, for example, hardcore and 'intelligent techno'. Even at 100,000 watts, the sound of music was not loud enough to obliterate social divisions.

It started with warehouse parties and in a handful of clubs like Shoom! With the arrival of **Ecstasy** and the advent of house, the cool vibe and the showing off associated with early 80s clubbing (such as the Wag and the Culture Club crowd, described by Robert Elms in his *Face* feature 'The Cult With No Name'), were superseded by a new ethos of empathy and egalitarianism. By 1988 the E-house trend was becoming too big to be contained indoors. Working from opposite ends of the social spectrum, public schoolboys and working-class lads organised unlicensed, outdoor events – raves. According to former *Face* editor Sheryl Garratt, author of *Adventures in Wonderland: a decade of club culture*, it all came together in the summer of 1989: 'the raves gathered up all the separate strands of 80s youth culture and knitted them together. Black and white, male and female, **indie** rockers and dedicated soul boys, crusties and Sloanes all met in the fields that summer. It was a cliché often repeated but generally true that bankers were dancing next to barrow boys, Sharons and Selinas. There were no elitist door policies here. Anyone could go on an adventure to wonderland: all they needed was a ticket, some transport and perhaps a pill.'

The 'adventure' sometimes involved dodging police roadblocks in order to get to an unlicensed event; riding the M25, tuned in to a pirate radio station, waiting for a call on your mobile phone and looking for lights and lasers in the surrounding fields. If the route to the rave was blocked, some-

times the party would continue in the nearest motorway services station (a raver by the name of Timmi Magic claims that on one occasion a man drove off from a petrol station and discovered when he arrived home that he had been tailed by a convoy of ravers, all desperate for a party: he invited them all in and the party lasted for two days). Outwitting the police seemed like a major achievement then: they were Maggie's boys in blue, the guarantors of Tory individualism; and just being together, a community of ravers dancing to the repetitive beats of loud music in a field, took on a subversive significance.

As a counter-culture, rave did not last long. Gangsters moved in on the promoters. So did the music industry. By September 1989, dance tracks accounted for 25 per cent of the UK Top 30: the music was spreading across society but also being absorbed by it. Meanwhile the police set up a special Pay Party Unit based in Kent, led by an inspector with previous experience of keeping flying pickets out of the Kent coalfields during the 1984–85 miners' strike. Police tactics included broadcasting invitations to phantom raves and then surrounding the ravers for the rest of the night. Under police pressure, the rave scene shifted ground from the south-east to the north of England; but raves were further curtailed by new anti-pay party legislation enacted in July 1990, and subsequently by the Criminal Justice Act 1994. Various campaigns (such as that by the Freedom Party) tried to resist the new laws, but the full force of Tory repression came at ravers like the tanks on Tiananmen Square.

Perhaps the government need not have bothered, for the rave scene was already collapsing under the weight of its own internal conflicts. The proliferation of dance-derived genres (hardcore, intelligent techno, laddish big beat, over-the-top gabba, 'filthy acid techno', the nostalgia of 'old skool') reflects the recurring tension between the hordes of sweaty youths who use dance as 'a culture of consolation', and a more discerning in-crowd who, in the manner of 60s Mods, adopt certain forms of dance music and develop particular fashion accessories as the means to demonstrate their cultural superiority. From the earliest days, with the operation of a strict door policy at Shoom!, there were dividing lines between the *cognoscenti* and the common people. But back then, there was a striving for togetherness that, ironically, was given added impetus by the authorities' attempts to isolate ravers and unite the nation against them. Without the sense of community arising from government attacks on rave culture, the trends toward fragmentation might have surfaced more rapidly.

It would be wrong, however, to conclude that rave had no lasting effect on British society. Garratt notes that even on New Year's Eve 1989, 'only one London venue was granted an all-night licence', and Manchester's prestigious **Haçienda** had to choose between a late licence on either Christmas Eve or New Year's Eve – but not both. Only a decade ago, British licensing laws were still in tune with the Protestant Work Ethic. Nowadays it seems as if our whole society is organised around the pleasure principle. Clubbing is seen as a vital aspect of urban regeneration, and superclubs like London's Ministry of Sound are touted as part of official British culture. Rave and what happened to it are essential elements in this transformation.

During the 90s unlicensed, uncontrolled raves were shut down by the authorities; meanwhile a new generation of people in authority responded warmly to some aspects of rave culture – such as the search for shared experience – and facilitated the development of a licensed, controlled version which is now as British as bowler hats. Welcome to the government-backed, corporate funded British Wonderland!

Today's post-ravers take a pragmatic attitude to such developments. They still exhibit an instinctive desire to rebel against authority, as shown by the backlash against Cool Britannia when Blair and Co were felt to be cashing in on the kudos of clubbing and **Britpop**. But these instincts no longer take on an ideological significance: that is, post-rave does not think of itself as the alternative to society. Whereas back in the late 80s some music promoters thought that what they were doing was anti-capitalist, nowadays obtaining sponsorship from capitalist corporations is often their first consideration. Everybody agrees that 'there is no alternative'.

PARENTS **Northern Soul**, hippie festivals, **Ecstasy**
READ ON *Night Fever – club writing in* The Face *from 1980 to 1997* edited by Richard Benson; *Adventures in Wonderland* by Sheryl Garratt; *Energy Flash* by Simon Reynolds

Vic Reeves and Bob Mortimer

Reeves and Mortimer

Postmodern Eric and Ernie

Vic Reeves and Bob Mortimer have moved from late night on Channel 4 to Saturday teatime on BBC1, occupying the slot formerly taken by Bruce Forsyth's *Generation Game* and Noel Edmonds' *House Party*. What they do has stayed essentially the same; what has changed is the readiness of the British public to accept TV that deconstructs itself.

Born in Darlington in the north-east of England, Vic Reeves (real name Jim Moir) is a punk-rocker who transformed himself into a stand-up comedian/performance artist. When Bob Mortimer first clapped eyes on him in a London pub called the Green Dragon, he was wearing a leather jacket with the names of classical composers (Vaughan

Williams, Debussy and Grieg) in studs on the back. He is now known as something of a dandy – a **Mod** with an extra helping of camp.

Born in the industrial city of Middlesbrough, Robert Renwick Mortimer met Reeves when they were both in their late twenties, by which time Mortimer was a qualified if unenthusiastic solicitor. Seeing Reeves was 'the road to Damascus' for him: he realised he wanted to be a performer, and that it was possible to make a performance out of a mixture of physical clowning and intellectual absurdism. The two of them started working together and were soon compared both to conceptual artists like Joseph Beuys and **Gilbert and George**, as well as to mainstream comedians such as Eric **Morecambe** (according to TV critic Charlotte Raven, Vic is a 'coked-up Eric Morecambe') **and** Ernie **Wise**. They themselves have cited **Spike Milligan**, particularly the *Q* TV series made in the 70s, as a primary influence.

With **Paul Whitehouse** as script editor and Charlie Higson as producer, their breakthrough came with *Vic Reeves' Big Night Out* for Channel 4 – a two-hour programme halfway between performance art and a variety show. They switched to BBC2 for *The Smell of Reeves and Mortimer*, a shorter show which emphasised their connections with Eric and Ernie. In 1996 they began hosting a new quiz programme, *Shooting Stars*, which 'gently eroded the dignity of its participants, mocking the idea of celebrity'. *Shooting Stars* was also the first quiz show in which the questions were contrived to appear arbitrary and answers were expected to be irrelevant. Whereas the origins of the TV quiz pro-gramme lay with the positivist preoccupation with facts, *Shooting Stars* reflected the postmodernist rejection of right and wrong.

In 1999, Vic and Bob introduced *Families At War*, a tongue-in cheek retake of programmes like the *Generation Game*, *Telly Addicts* and *Ask The Family*. Participants were ordinary people, not celebrities, so they were spared the barbed wit of Vic and Bob. Shortly before the show made its debut, Bob Mortimer announced that the comedy duo would separate for a while after finishing their remake of the cult 60s TV show *Randall and Hopkirk Deceased*. Perhaps there is only so much deconstruction you can do before you end up with nothing.

In the early 90s Vic and Bob were the British act most likely to appear on the front cover of fashionable lifestyle magazines such as **The Face**. By the end of the decade they were more likely to appear on the front of the *Radio Times*. The solo work of their mentor Spike Milligan has remained a minority interest, but by the time Reeves and Mortimer came along the British public were ready for TV shows that are mainly about TV itself.

PARENTS Punk, Spike Milligan, Morecambe and Wise
CHILDREN Austin Powers, Mike Flowers
READ ON *sunboiledonions* by Vic Reeves

Bridget Riley

Op-ortunist

Born in 1931, Bridget Riley came to fame in the 60s and is highly respected by the Young British Artists (**YBAs**) of the 90s. Her education (Cheltenham Ladies' College) and training (**Goldsmith's** and the Royal College of Art) were stamped with 'English provincialism'. After a breakdown and a stint at advertising agency J Walter Thompson, she was inspired by Jackson Pollock and Paul Klee to shift from figurative art to black-and-white abstractions in which she aimed for 'this essential quality of precipitating itself as "surprise"'.

She surprised the British art world, and shattered the traditional image of the 'gentle' female artist, with a series of dazzling, eye-bending 'Op Art' (based on the idea of the optical illusion) black-and-whites. Riley was taken up by the 60s media – her monochrome work could have been made for black-and-white TV, and heralded as a new British woman alongside Mary Quant and Jean Shrimpton. Her canvases became a backdrop for a new modern Britain.

Commenting on her appearance in *Private View*, Lord Snowdon's photographic celebration of London culture, John Russell wrote that 'nothing in British art prepared people for the impact, now deservedly famous, of Bridget Riley's paintings. Not only do they exemplify an armoured professionalism of a kind that has always been thought to be rather bad form in this country, but the experience which they offer runs contrary to all ordinary ways of looking at a picture.'

Riley herself was unprepared for the sampling of her work by the fashion world. Arriving at the opening of The Responsive Eye (1965), a prestigious New York show featuring her work, she was shocked to see guests wearing dresses plagiarised from her paintings. Riley retreated from medialand and remains wary of interviews to this day – unlike today's YBAs, who always aimed to be accessories of the fashion world and would only complain if they didn't get their cut.

PARENTS Jackson Pollock, Paul Klee, Piet Mondrian, Igor Stravinsky, James Joyce

Bruce Robinson
Doubting Thomas lensman

A writer who never puts pen to paper without a glass of red wine to hand, Bruce Robinson lived the life of *Withnail and I* (1986) before scripting and directing what turned out to be the most important British cult movie ever.

Born in 1946, Robinson enrolled at London's Central School of Speech and Drama in 1965. Living, along with a score of other reprobates, at the **Camden Town** house of fellow-student David Dundas, Robinson was a good-looking, impressionable young man who fell under the spell of a charismatic student named Vivian MacKerrell (on the first day of term MacKerrell turned up looking like Marlon Brando in sunglasses and a blue suit). Described as 'seedy, dopey, Gothic and dusty', the Dundas household was a shrine to bohemian squalour and under-achievement. A typical day consisted of a lunchtime session at the nearby Spread Eagle followed by a few joints and bottles of wine to wile away the afternoon, with another marathon drink-and-dope session every evening. When funds ran out, Robinson and MacKerrell took desperate measures: joining the Tories in search of free sherry; being refused entry to Sotheby's wine tastings; stealing a neighbour's whisky supply and getting his electricity cut off instead of theirs.

MacKerrell was an apparently magnificent talent who never applied himself to anything. Robinson recalls him as 'smart but sad', fond of making grandiose declarations: 'if I was a writer I'd be better than you'; 'if I was a photographer I'd be better than **David Bailey**'. At the time, Robinson felt that his later years with MacKerrell were 'the most depressing period of my life'. But he later saw the humour in it ('the predicament of a thespian in crisis'), and started to write it down. The result was the script of *Withnail and I*: years of MacKerrell's and his own real life distilled into the story of two out of work actors holidaying in the Lake District. At the end of the tale, the 'I' character has the prospect of a job to go to, whereas Withnail is at a dead end. Likewise, the real-life Robinson made it to Hollywood where he wrote the script for Roland Joffe's *The Killing Fields* (1982); but MacKerrell never found work in theatre, films or TV.

Attracted by the 'controlled mania' of actor Richard E Grant, Robinson cast him as Withnail and then discovered that Grant was a teetotaller with an allergy to alcohol. Like Dean Martin, his performance as a drunk is exactly that – a performance. Nevertheless it has been a role model for hundreds of aspiring young boozers.

Sunday Times film critic Tom Shone talks of the 'slightly obnoxious cult' of friends in pubs quoting Withnail dialogue at each other. Other than the perennial attractions of drink and drugs, Robinson believes that one of the main attractions of the film lies in the precarious but aspirational position of its protagonists: 'it touches that moment we've all had when we're broke and all aspiring, knowing that it might not work in our lives'. *Withnail and I* is also about the last blast of never having it so good. The Swinging Sixties are being demolished around them and the two are on the last puff at the fag end

Withnail and I (1986)

of their wild years forced to consider the road ahead. It is a road movie: a rare thing in Britain because there is nowhere to go. And that's exactly where they go – in a stylish barrage of excess and expletives. The silver-spooned Withnail is another classic comic misanthrope, a gentleman prince from a dying class without a throne to inherit who rages for all he is worth against the inevitable.

Grant was again the perfect mouthpiece for Robinson's next broadside agaainst British life. After his meditation on the 60s, in *How to Get Ahead in Advertising* (1989), Robinson turns his scalpel on the greed of 80s Britain in a satirical comedy about a yuppie whose disgust at his own grasping profession (advertising) finds expression in a huge growth on his neck. The final scene turns William Blake's Jerusalem into a wild rant about Britain becoming 'one big fucking shop'. Robinson is far from dewy eyed about his own line of work. He describes Hollywood as a 'jungle' in which the animals are divided between 'those who do the screwing and those who get screwed'. He himself has tried to tread a path between the two, choosing projects carefully (co-writer for *Shadowmakers*, 1989, about the race to make the A-bomb) and maintaining his independence.

Most recently Robinson has become a successful novelist. His first effort *The Secret Life of Thomas Penman*, is a slightly surreal child's tale of his parent's disintegrating marriage , his first crush and his obsession with sex, shitting and Charles Dickens. Set in the austere years of Britain in the 1950s it is a wonderful evocation of what smalltown English life was like for a bored teenager.

READ ON: *Withnail and I – the script* by Bruce Robinson; *With Nails – the memoir* by Richard E Grant

Rolling Stones
Long players

In existence now for nearly 40 years, the Rolling Stones have been white negroes, dandified droogs, failed hippies, blues revivalists and pseudo-soul boys, stadium rockers and, in Mick Jagger's case, rebels-turned-patriots. Although some people mock them for their age (in the *Observer* in 1998, Barbara Ellen said they had 'faces like month-old cat litter'), mostly they are respected for having lasted so long. From being the ones that our parents used to love to hate, they have become the ones for whom everyone has a sneaking admiration.

Mick Jagger (said by Joan Rivers to have 'child-bearing lips'), Keith Richards, Brian Jones, Bill Wyman and Charlie Watts came together as fans and imitators of black bluesmen. Richards also liked Chuck Berry, and this gave the Rolling Stones a rock'n'roll element that annoyed purists like harmonica-player Cyril Davies, who dominated the blues revival scene, but made them more contemporary and accessible to the fans of the new British beat groups. The Stones' first single (they were signed in a hurry by Decca who had let **The Beatles** go), 'Come On' (No 28, March 1963) was a Chuck Berry song. Their second, 'I Wanna Be Your Man', was written for them by The Beatles. In the Stones' rendition of it, there was enough pop for the mass market and enough r&b for the 'serious' music fan. In the years that followed, they were held up against The Beatles (suits and smart haircuts) as the outlaws who had not sold out. This image was encouraged by **Mod** manager Andrew Loog Oldham, who likened the Stones to Alex and his gang in the novel *A Clockwork Orange* by Anthony Burgess, in order to market them as dandified droogs. It was confirmed by their infamous appearance on David Jacobs' Saturday teatime record show *Juke Box Jury* – in which they grunted but refused to speak properly – and finalised by Keith Richards' response to the charge they faced for urinating on a garage wall: 'We'll piss anywhere, man.'

In classrooms and coffee bars up and down the country, there were feuds between Stones fans and Beatles supporters. Stones fans held that their champions were the real thing: rebels from the wrong side of the tracks. Whereas in fact Jagger had been to the LSE, Richards went to art college, Jones came from the upper-middle-class town of Cheltenham, Watts was a commercial artist and Wyman was already an old man. The real working-class rebels were the ones in suits: The Beatles.

When The Beatles stopped touring, the Stones became the No 1 live act in Britain. They needed constant protection from the 'screamers' (there is film footage of them playing behind a steel cage with teenage girls crawling all over it), and pop writer Nik Cohn reported going back into a hall after the Stones had finished playing and the audience had left, and discovering that the auditorium smelt of 'piss': the screaming young girls had wet themselves.

In 1968 Jagger and Richards (along with Jagger's then girlfriend Marianne Faithfull and art dealer Robert Fraser) were busted for drugs and both received jail sentences (Pop artist Richard Hamilton painted a picture from a photo of Jagger and Fraser handcuffed together). The liberal section of the establishment was outraged. In *The Times*, editor William Rees-Mogg famously wrote that you 'do not break a butterfly on a wheel': the Stones were colourful adornments to British culture, and even if they were in the wrong they should not have been punished in this heavy-handed way. The sentences were commuted and on his release Mick Jagger was flown by helicopter to an unofficial summit where he talked about the state of the nation's youth with the Archbishop of Canterbury. He spoke then about a spiritual revolution but a few years later said that we had a sexual revolution instead. In 1970 his marriage to Bianca, a Nicaraguan aristocrat (they divorced at the end of the decade), was seen as a symbol of sexual and social mobility.

The Stones' songwriting partnership (Jagger–

Richards) was never as sophisticated as that of Lennon and McCartney, but it did produce mid-60s classics such as the anthem to frustration '(I can't get no) Satisfaction'. The emergence of this duo (later known as the Glimmer Twins) within the five-piece group left Brian Jones in a weaker position (in the early days it had sometimes seemed like his band). He finally left early in 1969, only to be found dead in his swimming pool some months later. Meanwhile The Beatles had moved pop music on with *Sgt Pepper's Lonely Hearts Club Band* (1967), and the Stones (with and without Jones) were struggling to catch up. Their attempt at a *Sgt Pepper* was the largely unsuccessful *Their Satanic Majesties Request*. Later in 1969 they went back to basics with the raunchy riff-based 'Jumpin' Jack Flash'. This time around The Beatles seemed to be copying them by issuing the retro-rocking single 'Lady Madonna'.

In the early 70s the Stones gained greater substance. After delving too far into the past (*Let It Bleed*), they found a formula that combined guitar-driven rock with brassy-sounding soul (*Sticky Fingers*), a hot sound and a cool attitude (*Exile on Main Street*, 1972; the model for 90s bands such as **Primal Scream**). In France in the 60s they had been the epitome of English pop-rebel chic (as featured in the Jean-Luc Godard film *One Plus One/Sympathy for the Devil*, 1968); in the USA in the 70s they became the embodiment of the rock-'n'roll lifestyle. The awful experience of Altamont (1970; Woodstock in reverse), the Stones' free concert outside Los Angeles during which the Hell's Angels ran riot and a black man was shot and

killed, was recorded on film by the Mayles Brothers but was largely forgotten. (Years afterwards Altamont was held up as the moment when the counter-culture went sour, but the response at the time was low key.) Their tours (the live album *Get Your Ya Yas Out* captures them in action) were reported as continuous orgies of sex and drugs (a reaction against this followed later in the decade when feminists objected to records such as 'Brown Sugar' and 'Midnight Rambler'). There was a widespread urban myth about a man and a woman making love and both of them fantasising about the same sex symbol: Mick Jagger. By the mid-70s, guitarists 'setting their amps to give maximum Keefraunch' were fast becoming a cliché in the *NME*. Their reputations far exceeded the actual music they made. Seeing them live at Earl's Court in 1976 was a major disappointment: they looked like mere impersonations of their own legends.

The Stones were just the kind of decadents that puritan punks wanted to do away with. Refusing to move aside, they reacted to the new wave by emphasising their role as patrons and elder statesmen, taking a supportive interest in jazz (Charlie Watts' speciality) and various black artists such as New Orleans piano player Professor Longhair and the acerbic reggae star Peter Tosh.

Now down to a trio (Jagger, Richards and Watts, plus the salaried musicians of their choice), the Stones have come to symbolise the generation that will not give way: still playing (and touring) after all these years. Such staying power is today regarded as an example of true Brit grit, and even the *Daily Telegraph* was only half-joking when it said they

should be knighted. Jagger has prepared the ground by supporting national non-events like British Music Day (although he blotted his copybook by claiming that he had never been legally married to Jerry Hall), leaving it to Keith Richards to keep alive the rebel image. It was Richards who, after finally coming off heroin himself, said he could not interfere with Charlie Watts' alleged decision to go on it; and when asked to play on a commemorative album for Princess Diana, his refusal was as sharp, terse and unreconstructed as one of his own guitar breaks: 'I never knew the chick.'

PARENTS Chuck Berry, Muddy Waters,
The Beatles
READ ON *The Rolling Stones: the greatest rock-'n'roll band in the world* edited by David Dalton

Tim Roth
'Ballistic leftie'

While **Gary Oldman**'s readiness to play 'popcorn' parts prompted comparisons with **Michael Caine**, his fellow south Londoner Tim Roth (b. 1962) is a latter-day Michael Redgrave whose left-wing scruples have frequently prevented him from taking 'roles that you really shouldn't do politically'.

Roth grew up in a socialist household (father a Fleet Street journalist turned freelance; mother a teacher turned painter). 'We were always going on demonstrations when we were kids,' he recalls. He was first praised in the early 80s for his 'tour de bovver' as the right-wing **skinhead** in **Alan Clarke**'s *Made In Britain* (1983). In Mike Leigh's *Meantime* he was dozy Colin in thrall to Gary Oldman's Coxy. After a year on the dole for lack of a good part, he appeared in **Peter Greenaway**'s *The Cook, the Thief, his Wife and her Lover* (1989), before starring as an alternately morose and violently intense Van Gogh in Robert Altman's *Vincent and Theo* (1990). 'I avoided America for nine or ten years,' Roth recalls, 'saying that I'd never come until I was invited and till I had a project I really wanted to do.' His first major pay cheque was the 'lavender' role of Archibald Cunningham in the MGM/UA production of *Rob Roy*. Immediately afterwards he worked on a low-budget independent film directed by Buddy Giovinazzo.

While in Hollywood, Roth has tried to stick to his principles: 'You get offered a lot of films which have very, very high budgets and so on, but they are things that you really shouldn't do politically. These movies tend to be very right wing. … The films I do tend to have some political content. Those are the type of scripts I tend to get sent. Maybe they just think of me as a ballistic leftie.'

In 1991 Roth appeared as the injured Mr Orange in a low-budget flick that went ballistic: Quentin Tarantino's *Reservoir Dogs*. In 1994 he was back with Tarantino, playing one of the hapless restaurant robbers in the opening and closing scenes of the episodic *Pulp Fiction*. Both roles rely on Roth's legendary intensity and his generosity in allowing his role to become comic. After years at odds with Hollywood and its preference for one-dimensional characters, Roth finally found his metier as a new kind of actor – a tragi-comedian.

Roth's reputation is that of 'a visceral actor'. Jessica Lange, who starred in *Rob Roy*, said of him: 'He's like raw nerves. And this is what makes him great. There something so absolutely truthful about what he does.' Indeed, Roth is absolutely dedicated to arriving at something truthful in his performances; but the truth he is seeking to communicate is more complex than 'raw'. Like Tarantino's direction, his acting can swing from humour to violence at an accelerated rate. Roth is a postmodern British actor in that his performances are ambiguous, contradictory and complex.

At Cannes in 1999 Roth made his directorial debut with *The War Zone*, a harrowing film about incest and family violence starring Ray Winstone and Tilda Swinton. The themes and the setting of the film are oddly similar to those of *Nil By Mouth* (1997), Gary Oldman's debut as a director. The two films even have the same actor playing the male lead.

PARENTS Michael Redgrave, the old-style *Daily Mirror*, Alan Clarke, Robert De Niro

Princess Diana

The Royal family
Unstable firm

The House of Windsor (née Hanover) has reigned in Britain (but not necessarily ruled over us) for nearly 300 years: it is a fixed entity in British culture. During that time, however, the role of the monarchy has changed repeatedly. The Windsors are fluid as well as firmly established.

With her plummy voice, reserved manner and penchant for dogs and horses, Queen Elizabeth II epitomises all that is apparently unchanging about the manners and mores of the British ruling class. But she also represents the extent to which chang-ing popular tastes percolate through to the monarchy. In the 60s, the Queen gave permission for an intimate television documentary series on the royals. Their unofficial lives – that is, the way they live above and beyond official engagements – became public property for the first time. Three decades later, the Queen bowed to public pressure when she flew the Royal Standard at half-mast and appeared to revise her opinion of the late Princess Diana. Initially the Windsors responded to Diana's death in the manner to which they are accustomed: suppressing private feelings on the altar of public duty. But since this frame of mind was widely held to be partly responsible for Diana's bulimia, her divorce from the Prince of Wales and, ultimately, her demise, in the midst of the wave of emotion following her death in a car crash in 1997 it became something of a liability. In acknowledging Diana's contribution to the life of the country, and subsequently adopting a less formal style in some of her official engagements, the Queen publicly acknowledged the need for the monarchy to move on.

Prince Charles also embodies the combination of tradition and innovation that characterises both the monarchy and British culture in general. But in his case the mix has been harder to manage. According to Beatrix Campbell (in *Diana, Princess of Wales: how sexual politics shook the monarchy*), Charles' marital and extra-marital affairs were orchestrated on traditional lines (experienced mistresses and a virgin bride, both procured by the patriarchal 'firm'). But Charles the polo player and sower of wild oats is offset by Charles the new age mystic, with interests in alternative medicine and a variety of religious beliefs (the pluralist prince once said he wanted to be 'defender of faiths', rather than 'defender of the faith', the singular title granted to Henry VIII by the Pope). The traditionalist in architecture is also the Green-tinged opponent of genetically modified foods. Whereas in his mother's public profile the combination of old and new is usually held in high regard, Charles stands accused of hesitation and doubt. He is often seen as a man who does not know whether to be of his own generation or of timeless tradition.

The unchanging aspects of the monarchy are represented in pure form by Prince Philip, an unreconstructed man's man whose insensitivity to the demands of political correctness is as legendary as

Greek gaffes

Prince Philip's habit of saying the wrong thing is well-documented.

- Touring a hi-tech factory in Scotland, he said that a fusebox looked 'as though it was put in by an Indian'.
- At the opening of the Welsh Parliament he noticed a group of deaf people standing by a steel band: 'if you are near there, no wonder you are deaf,' he quipped.
- He once asked a Scottish driving instructor: 'How do you keep the natives off the booze long enough to pass the test?'
- On a visit to China he informed British students that 'if you stay here much longer you'll all be slitty-eyed'.

his aristocratic sexual appetite. At the other end of the scale, the complicated personal and financial affairs of loose cannon Sarah Ferguson, ex-wife but still close friend of Prince Andrew, indicate that the grip of the firm is not as strong as it used to be.

The royal family's attempts to reinvent itself have sometimes invited mockery. Commenting on Prince Edward's new title, the Earl of Wessex, a columnist in *The Times* described it as 'an honorific that owes more to the first series of *Blackadder* than to Debrett's Peerage … [it] combines sepia-tinted Victoriana with New Labour **Britpop**pery'; the attempt to invoke Thomas Hardy and a moral universe both pastoral and medieval, belonged instead to the '***Carry On*** *Camping* school of chivalry which he [Edward] inaugurated' when in 1987 he persuaded a cohort of younger royals to appear in the TV show *It's a Knockout*. But for all that, the ceremony in which Prince Edward married Sophie Rhys-Jones was widely regarded as a popular success. British people, it seems, do not mind if their royals are slightly ridiculous.

Noting the problems involved in negotiating the old and the new, some commentators have predicted the imminent demise of the royal family; but such predictions do not fit the British pattern. During the last two centuries, the Royal Family has 'died' on several occasions, only to be reincarnated in a modified form. At present, there is nothing that prohibits the remodelling of the royals in line with ongoing changes in British culture. The making of a multicultural monarchy came a step closer in 1999 with reports that the royal veins run with black blood (from a relative of Queen Caroline's) as well as blue.

READ ON *Charles* by Jonathan Dimbleby; *Diana, Princess of Wales – how sexual politics shook the monarchy* by Beatrix Campbell

The Royle family
ladies (and gentlemen)-in-waiting

Much more representative as a national institution than the Royals are the Royles. Co-written by and starring Caroline 'Mrs Merton' Aherne, The Royles are a Manchester council estate family, who stay together by watching telly together – Coronation Street, The Bill, Wish You Were Here, anything that's on really. Shot in static real time in the Royle's front room, it was described in the Guardian as 'the nearest mainstream television will ever get to the work of Samuel Beckett'.

Apart from TV, it is pretty basic anthropology: eating, gossiping and going to the loo. The most you can expect in terms of drama is someone leaving on a trip to the cornershop for booze or fags and the odd visitor (family, neighbours and other freeloaders) to get in the way of their viewing habits.

The show's punch is largely provided by the father Jim (catchphrase: 'my arse') Royle, played by Ricky Tomlinson in a reprisal of his husband-wife partnership with Sue Johnson in Brookie. Jim's misanthropic pearls of wisdom (spat at both the TV and other family members) are aimed at anyone foolish enough to champion the world outside the safe confines of his beloved throne room. Full of know-it-all patriarchal bravado, Jim is quietly wary of the modern world outside and to be on the safe side castigates everyone and everything from Chris Evans, '[he's] everywhere … he's like shit in a field,' to the shoddy workmanship of his crack-riding undies, 'they only cost a quid and I've got 50p's-worth up my arse.'

You would think the dramatic possibilities of the programme would be limited, but rumour has it there's even a feature film in the offing.

PARENTS Samuel Beckett, Jim Jarmusch, Steptoe Senior (for Jim), Paul and Pauline Calf, Mrs Merton

Salman Rushdie
Reprieved

When Ayatollah Khomeini of Iran issued a *fatwa* (decree) calling for his death, Bombay-born novelist Salman Rushdie was offered the protection of the British Secret Service. He went into hiding and was hardly seen in public for the best part of a decade; meanwhile his photo became an unlikely symbol of British free speech and fair play. In September 1998 the Iranians let it be known that the *fatwa* would be withdrawn, and Rushdie came out into the full glare of publicity. He revealed himself as one of a minority of figures on the British cultural scene who still speaks in the upper-middle-class manner known as 'received pronunciation'. Born (1947) a Muslim during the last months of the Raj (India and Pakistan were granted independence in 1948), he sounds more old-style British than most Brits.

Rushdie went to an English public school (Rugby), and from there to Cambridge (1965–68). Although he has said that 'the 60s happened to 30

Salman Rushdie

people and I wasn't one of them', Rushdie was a frequent visitor to the 'locations' of swinging London (clubs/happenings such as UFO and Middle Earth), where it was 'advantageous in many ways to be Indian'. This was the period when **The Beatles** went meditating with the Mahareshi and George Harrison hooked up with sitarist Ravi Shankar. But the fashion, says Rushdie, was for 'an India that didn't exist' – an India of mysticism, of exoticism. Meanwhile he thought of himself as the offspring of an altogether different, modern India.

While working as an advertising copywriter in

371

London, Rushdie began his first novel, in the style of James Joyce, Gunter Grass and the magic realists of Latin America. *Grimus* (1975) has been described as 'a confused fable'; it was a commercial and artistic failure. *Midnight's Children* (1981) brings the same stylistic influences to India on the brink of independence; but by this time Rushdie had found his own voice also. Awarded the Booker Prize when first published, and subsequently named 'the Booker of Bookers', *Midnight's Children* is dense but illuminating. *Shame* (1983), a political satire, raised eyebrows in Pakistan; but it was Rushdie's next book that was to change his life.

Published in 1988 by Viking Penguin, *The Satanic Verses* contains a 'blasphemous' portrayal of the prophet Mohammed. It was banned almost immediately in India, where relations between Muslims and Hindus are often volatile. In January 1989 British Muslims marched to Hyde Park in protest; in Bradford they burnt copies of the book. On Valentine's Day the Ayatollah Khomeini issued the *fatwa*: Rushdie, born a Muslim, had committed blasphemy and killing him was a religious duty (there was also a US$2-million reward). Rushdie became one of the first 'western' fiction writers since Dostoevsky to live under an official death threat.

In September 1989 small bombs were found in four Penguin bookshops; Penguin's Norwegian publisher was later shot and wounded. Rushdie lived in hiding, with an armed guard in permanent attendance. Visitors were subject to intimate searches which he described as 'dry cleaning'. Months after the *fatwa* was issued, his wife Marianne Wiggins left him, claiming 'he would do anything to save his life'. Rushdie has married again, but the identity of his second wife has been kept secret.

The *fatwa* caused ructions in Britain. It coincided with a turn away from the Labour Party and a general disillusionment with British society on the part of many Asians in Britain, many of whom moved towards Islam as an alternative form of self-definition. For some of this group, the fact that the *fatwa* was hostile to the British tradition (in English law it constituted incitement to murder) made it, and the belief system under which it was issued, doubly attractive. Meanwhile most of the British intelligentsia rallied to Rushdie, although a minority talked of cultural difference and noted that he might have chosen his words more carefully.

In the hands of some politicians and pundits, the affair became a test case for 'British civilisation' versus the Mad Mullahs and their fanatical supporters. But in 1990 when the friends of Rushdie suggested that the government could do more on the diplomatic front, Tory backbenchers condemned Rushdie for exploiting the situation. Some people began to wonder whether it was worth providing £1 million per year of taxpayers' money for round-the-clock protection, particularly for an author who was far from complimentary about Britain's record in India. At one stage former Conservative cabinet minister Lord Tebbit said Rushdie was 'despicable'.

In February 1998, nine years after the *fatwa* was first issued, New Labour foreign secretary Robin Cook vowed to put more pressure on Iran. Shortly afterwards, Rushdie met **Tony Blair**, and in

September the *fatwa* was effectively (though not formally) withdrawn. Rushdie emerged from hiding, saying how glad he was that his work would no longer be a matter for the news pages.

During the years of forced seclusion Rushdie published a book of children's stories (*Haroun and the Sea of Stories*, 1990) and a collection of essays (*Imaginary Homelands*, 1991) – both minor works. But the publication of *The Ground Beneath Her Feet*, a novel set in the rock'n'roll world, was a significant development in Rushdie's œuvre and the British literary event of 1999. **Julie Burchill** was one of only a handful to complain that Rushdie (a balding, fiftysomething with a professorial beard) should leave pop music to the kids.

Told from the point of view of a journalist, *The Ground Beneath Her Feet* is a reworking of the Orpheus and Eurydice myth which follows the lives of two Indian pop stars from their roots in Bombay to swinging London and 70s New York. For the narrator, and surely for the novelist also, the book is a way of saying goodbye to his 'home country', India (Professor John Sutherland observed that it is about 'disorientation – literally the loss of the East'), and a means of moving into the global terrain of rock'n'roll.

The story covers three decades of the music scene, a bold sweep that Rushdie feels entitled to make because 'this is the music I grew up with'. Interviewed by Francine Stock for BBC2's *Arena*, he explained that ever since he first heard it in the late 50s, rock'n'roll has seemed like 'one of the links between eastern and western worlds. It didn't feel alien, it felt like our music too.'

The music scene provides the context for *The Ground Beneath Her Feet*, but the themes of the book are celebrity and 'provisionality'. Rushdie is adamant that it is not a metaphor for his own experience (even though the climax takes place on Valentine's Day 1989, the day the *fatwa* was issued against him). Nevertheless his own life story makes him well qualified to write about these phenomena. His secluded life, complete with bodyguards, was not unlike that of a pop star; and the death threat he lived under must have been a constant reminder that life is impermanent and relationships provisional.

Rushdie's life as an unwilling celebrity, and his professional interest in the subject, have brought him into contact with the Irish band U2, whose ninth album *Zooropa* (1992) and world tour, Zoo TV, comprised a pop opera on life in medialand. Rushdie appeared on stage at Wembley with U2, and subsequently worked with singer Bono on a song also entitled 'The Ground Beneath Her Feet'.

Rushdie's reprieve closes an awkward moment in British cultural history. As long as the *fatwa* hung over him, there was always the possibility that people in Britain would be forced to choose between imported religion and the home-grown tradition of relative artistic freedom. But the suspension of the *fatwa* demonstrates that religious absolutism is as provisional as everything else. Relativism rules, and Rushdie can now co-exist with the Muslims of Bradford in the pick'n'mix of British culture.

PARENTS Dostoevsky, James Joyce, magic realism, Islam, swinging London

373

The Saatchis

Ambition

Charles and Maurice Saatchi changed the face of political advertising in Britain, and created the biggest advertising agency in the world before being booted out of their own company. According to Adrian Kelmsley, one of their former creative directors, they 'put England on the map as a global player' in the US-led advertising business.

Born in Baghdad, the brothers Saatchi grew up in 50s Finchley among a family of Sephardic Jews. In 1970, after Charles (creative) resigned as an associate director of Collett Dickenson Pearce, he and Maurice (implementation) started their own agency, Saatchi & Saatchi, with a small client list consisting mainly of charities. They made their name with hard-hitting anti-smoking ads and the infamous 'pregnant man' for the Health Education Council ('Would you be more careful if it was you that got pregnant?'). When they later lost the HEC account, they switched to advertising cigarettes, creating the equally memorable 'purple' series of ads for Silk Cut.

British advertising in the 50s had been staid and slightly tweedy. The Saatchi's working methods were a long way from the previous generation of 'gin and tonic, wood panelling' admen. Extremely competitive ('it is not enough for one to succeed, others must fail'), they hustled their creative people into producing fine work at a fast pace ('two ads a day keeps the sack away'). Successful employees were generously rewarded (the first £100,000-a-year copywriter, cash bonuses in brown envelopes).

Known as the agency's 'mad father', Charles had a violent temper from which even his brother was not immune – he once threw an office chair at him. Not that Maurice is self-effacing either: according to close colleagues they would both 'fail the waiter test'.

From the earliest days the Saatchis courted the press. They wined and dined journalists, showering them with champagne and smoked salmon. Industry trade paper *Campaign* soon became known in some circles as a pro-Saatchi publication; the brothers even made the front page of *The Sunday Times* with a hyped-up story about charging other agencies 'transfer fees' if they dared to poach Saatchi creatives. But neither Charles nor Maurice ever spoke on the record – that would have destroyed the mystique that already surrounded them.

In some circles the Saatchis are credited with having altered the course of British political history. Hired by the Conservative Party in the summer of 1978, they produced an ad consisting of a photo of a **dole** queue and the slogan 'Labour isn't working'. At a time of rising unemployment, the ad became a news item in its own right. Labour prime minister James Callaghan ruled out an October election and found himself embroiled in 'the winter of discontent' – a difficult season the Saatchis made much of in the forthcoming general election campaign.

Not long before the Tories were elected, party chairman Lord McAlpine came to see the Saatchis and asked for more time to pay the brothers' bills. They agreed, and were granted access to an inner circle of powerful figures after the Conservative Party came into office.

Former Saatchi copywriter John Hegarty, now a principal in his own agency, reckons you can be either the best or the biggest – and the Saatchis chose the latter. That meant breaking into the USA, which they set about doing in the mid-80s. In one day in 1985, Saatchi & Saatchi bought three different US agencies. Their biggest acquisition overall was the Ted Bates agency, for which Saatchi shareholders shelled out US$500 million. Then they tried diversifying into business consultancy (bidding unsuccessfully for consultancy giant Arthur Andersen) and banking (the Saatchi bid for the Midland Bank was described by the *Financial Times* as 'an idle daydream by a firm that has got carried away with its own self-importance'). The parent company was still growing by 30 per cent a year, but it was all done by debt and creative accounting; and when at the end of the decade the casino economy was hit by stockmarket crashes signalling recession, Saatchi stock lost a third of its value. After four years on the brink of bankruptcy, the value of Saatchi shares was only 10 per cent of its 80s peak.

Ensconced in their luxurious headquarters in London's Berkeley Square, the brothers Saatchi were still living the life of Riley (in 1988 their salaries, expenses and the wages of their assistants came to £6 million). In 1993 Charles was forced off the board; Maurice was invited to stay if he accepted demotion (and an increased salary), but he elected to leave. A few weeks later the brothers set up the New Saatchi Agency, subsequently renamed M & C Saatchi, and, beginning with British Airways, won four accounts back from Saatchi & Saatchi. The ad they produced for the *Mirror* ('tells it like it is') retells the story of their own expulsion.

Maurice Saatchi was ennobled by Tory prime minister John Major and now sits in the House of Lords. In a rare television interview, Maurice came close to admitting that he and his brother had committed hubris – the Ancient Greek word for fatal, Oedipal ambition. Nearly a decade after the collapse of their great ambitions, the Saatchis have gone down in British cultural history as the personification of the 'greed is good' hubris of the 80s.

PARENTS Margaret Thatcher, Gordon Gekko
READ ON *Masters of Illusion*, Channel 4 (1999)

Satire
British bile

In the early sixties the great British tradition of oppositional satire – William Hogarth, Alexander Pope, Jonathan Swift – became the favoured form of expression for a country seeking the 'white heat' of modernisation. In the eighties satire was in use again as the unofficial opposition as Thatcher's monetarist modernisers dragged Britain beyond post-war consensus. Nowadays, under a New Labour government whose defining characteristics are so indefinite, satire, with nothing to sink its teeth into, is at a loose end.

In the eighteenth century Jonathan Swift lambasted the Enlightenment doctrine of the infallibility of man. Siding with the Tories against the progressive Whigs, he presented a comic picture of humankind as essentially venal and irrational. In the nineteenth century WS Gilbert (playwright and professional partner of composer Arthur Sullivan) satirised modern manners and the goings-on at the court of Queen Victoria. In those days, satirical depictions of royalty and other top-ranking personages had to be coded (*The Mikado* was a coded reference to the Palace of Windsor). This remained largely the case until the early 60s, when a new generation started to define itself against the old guard.

In October 1961, after the satirical revue *Beyond The Fringe* became the hit of the year at the official **Edinburgh Festival**, **Peter Cook** set up The Establishment ('London's first satirical nightclub'; the name was taken from the title of historian Hugh Thomas's book of polemical essays against what he termed 'the establishment'). Cook's club enjoyed what Christopher Booker called 'a torrent of publicity'. Booker was himself editor of another project Cook was involved in, the satirical magazine *Private Eye*, 'the first amateurish copies … [of which] … were beginning to circulate in the bistros of Kensington and Chelsea'. Meanwhile the BBC commissioned a topical, satirical TV show, *That Was The Week That Was* featuring David Frost, Willie Rushton and singer Millicent Martin. Suddenly Britain was in the midst of 'the satire boom'.

The targets of 60s satire were the old men who'd fought the last war (and the one before that), and reckoned they still had a right to run the country. When one doddery old Etonian (Harold Macmillan) was replaced by another (Sir Alec Douglas Home) as Conservative prime minister, Rushton went so far as to stand against the latter in the Kinross by-election (45 votes received out of 20, 000). Not that he had a political programme to speak of ('I didn't have then, and I don't have now, any serious political beliefs'), but simply because he – and the rest of the Establishment crowd – wanted, in the words of his election slogan, to 'debag flannel pants' and embarrass the real British establishment.

Talk of 'flannel' and 'debagging' was typical of 'the satire boom'. Many of its participants were ex-public school (Winchester, Shrewsbury) and those born outside this charmed circle had become insiders by going up to Oxbridge (grammar-school boys Dudley Moore and **Alan Bennett** were both at Oxford). This meant that Britain's upper echelons could afford to look upon the 60s satirists as their own naughty children. In *The Neophiliacs* Christopher Booker records that *Private Eye*'s first readership also read fashionable magazines such as *Town and Queen*, and satire was 'the rage of progressive young upper-middle-class London'. In *The Young Meteors*, Jonathan Aitken observed that 'the satirists, who expected to find themselves society's outcasts, in reality became society's darlings. … Indeed, both the Queen and Harold Macmillan attended *Beyond The Fringe* and were reported as having loved every minute of it.' The BBC suspended *That Was The Week That Was* during the run-up to the general election of 1964, and satire was never the same again. Those of the wider public who had been interested in satire shifted their interest to the incoming Labour government, which was expected to be much more effective than the satirists in geeing up a tired old country (Michael Shanks, another Oxford alumnus, dubbed Tory Britain 'the stagnant society').

The satire of the 60s was cheeky and increasingly frantic, whereas the satire of the 80s was usually pessimistic and frequently violent. In the puppets of Luck and Flaw's *Spitting Image* (Sunday nights on ITV), politicians and public figures were presented as out-of-control . While railing against monstrous Tory modernisers and their coercive methods, the show reflected the new level of class confrontation occurring in British society. The formula for *Not The Nine O'Clock News*, featuring Mel Smith, Griff Rhys Jones, Rowan Atkinson and Pamela Stephenson, was more like *That Was The Week That Was*, but lacked the relative confidence underlying the latter (back in the 60s it was possible to believe that Britain could undergo a collective transformation, in the 80s everybody knew it was dog eat dog). For a time, after 'the longest suicide note in history' (Labour's 1983 election manifesto) and during the first years of Neil Kinnock's windy opposition, these shows sometimes seemed like the only available expression of anti-Thatcher sentiment.

Satire limps on. *Stop The Week*, a radio show with a format akin to *That Was The Week That Was*, lasted until the mid-90s. *Private Eye* continues to publish and to require the occasional services of libel lawyers. *Scallywag* disappeared after a writ issued by John Major. *Punch*, which is in a permanent state of relaunch, seems punch-drunk and ineffective. In Britain today there are plenty of would-be satirists who would like to have a go, but they don't know who to have a go at – or how.

Have I Got News For You, the Hat Trick produced quiz show was the most popular satirical bastion of the 90s. With Ian Hislop (*Private Eye*) and the more surreal Paul Merton as the team captains, weekly guests were often the very politicians and media figures they would be satirising in other weeks. This gave the show a sense of being a laddish post-politics pantomime rather than one of the truly biting satirical beasts of old.

PARENTS Hogarth, Jonathan Swift
CHILDREN *Have I Got News For You*

Jon Savage
Out and proud to be a pop intellectual

'People used to come up to me during the punk period and say "You can't write about punk because you went to Cambridge", and I used to say "fuck off", and at that point it was either fisticuffs or spitting at one another.' So says Jon Savage, author of the definitive account of punk, *England's Dreaming* (1991) which, as novelist and critic Michael Bracewell noted in the *Independent*, 'brought him more or less equal praise and condemnation for being perceived as an intellectual at work on popular culture'.

Jon Savage

Classics; No 1 is Oxford where they call it 'Greats') and finished his Law Society exams in 1979 (he never practised as a solicitor because he did not like lawyers). In 1976 he started a fanzine, *London's Outrage*, and went on to be the most prominent punk writer for *Sounds* (weekly music paper, now defunct). In 1980 he began writing for **The Face**, Nick Logan's new monthly magazine – an association that lasted seven years.

In the late 80s Savage contributed to *The Media Show* and *Out On Tuesday* (both for BBC2); in the 90s he worked on Channel 4's history of disco, *The Rhythm Divine*. *England's Dreaming* won the Ralph J Gleason music award in 1992. Savage's articles were collected in *Time Travel*, published by Faber in 1996. He still lives in West London but is spending more time in North Wales, partly because 'I find myself almost unemployable in Fleet Street.' He has been working on a history of twentieth-century youth culture.

Like **Julie Burchill** and **Tony Parsons**, Savage was there at the start of punk: for their respective weekly music papers (*Sounds* and *NME*), he and Parsons both wrote accounts of the Sex Pistols' abortive boat trip (stopped by the Thames River Police) on the day of the Queen's Silver Jubilee. But whereas 'the young gunslingers' were afraid of intellectualism, Savage was more anxious to avoid stupidity. From straightforward interview pieces (in search of authenticity, *Sounds* used to print interviews as straight Q&A sessions), he graduated to more discursive pieces in which he not only interviewed and reviewed major pop performers (**Morrissey**, Kurt Cobain) but also sought to locate

Savage confirmed his reputation as a pop intellectual by co-editing the *Faber Book of Pop* (1995), the 862-page collection of pop music criticism issued by the publishing house that was for a long time associated with the anti-popular views of its erstwhile director, cultural elitist (and modernist poet) TS Eliot. In an interview to promote the collection, Savage declared: 'Hello, I've been educated. Sorry, I can't uneducate myself.'

Born (1953) and brought up in West London, Savage (after attending Rugby, the school of *Tom Brown's Schooldays*) read Classics (Latin and Greek) at Cambridge (the No 2 place to do them within broader ideological and cultural traditions. Moving on from music papers, he contributed to style magazines (the early, experimental days of *The Face* were especially conducive), political weeklies (*New Society* and *New Statesman*), and cultural journals (*Artforum* and *Frieze*). He brought a sophisticated sensibility to pop criticism, without losing sight of pop's raw edge.

Pop criticism and legal training seem like strange bedfellows, but Savage insists that for him they were a perfect match: 'If you have a legal training you are trained to see things as they are, because if you see things as you wish them to be you end up in a hell of a mess in court.' On entering the world of the music press in 1977, he found that 'the whole Gonzo – Me, Me, Me approach was already in full effect'. After 'experimenting with doing drugs and writing' for a while, Savage 'stopped doing that' and started to 'try to get some craft in what I was doing'. He was helped in this by the working methods at *Sounds*: 'the great advantage was that you didn't have the star syndrome. You weren't encouraged to become fixed as a star rock journalist at 21–23, as happened, disastrously, to contemporaries on the *NME*.'

Savage thinks that writers should maintain a critical distance: 'People who write about pop think they should be pop as well … but that often militates against improving as a writer, which takes time and effort and discipline and all those boring things.' In the 80s, while working towards *England's Dreaming*, his legal training became even more useful, 'when I was trying to build up some structure to something which I'd begun with great enthu-

siasm, but after that enthusiasm had gone'. His work also benefited from 'a certain kind of academic discipline which means quoting your sources and finding out what the facts are, which a lot of my contemporaries don't seem to be bothered with'. Bracewell says that Savage 'combines the classic, Cambridge erudition of a Leavis or an AJP Taylor with the belief in pop as an ever reinventing pageant of protest theatre'. This puts him on a par with American pop intellectuals such as Dan Graham and Greil Marcus.

Savage recalls 'growing up in the mid-60s saturated in pop music by **The Kinks**, the **Who** and the **Rolling Stones** – very smart, very intelligent, very violent, very mediated records'. He despairs that in the laddish England of the 90s it was not 'considered sexy to be intelligent, which to me is a national disease'. Although conceding that 'there is something very exciting about going into the earthiness of pop music when you have been over-educated', he has no time for what he calls 'bad class faith', as when an erstwhile editor of the *NME* would never admit having been to Cambridge, but 'would hide it behind a primitive mask'. The Savage response to such immaturity is: 'grow up'.

Contempt for dumbing down is matched by Savage's distaste for 'the faux chumminess of **Nick Hornby**'. And although he wrote the definitive account of it, he has become wary of the fact that 'everybody's obsessing on punk rock' for all the wrong reasons. Savage is insistent that his hostility to 'people who are intelligent pretending not to be' is not just a personal prejudice on his part: 'it seems like a wilful failure of nerve, especially since if there is one thing that's going to get us through all this stuff it's our brains'.

In *England's Dreaming*, Savage depicted punk as the hope of the nation. He recalls the Sex Pistols as 'incredibly brave throughout 1976 and 1977. … They were the only people who had the balls to say something organised about the Queen's Jubilee.' Punk was a moment of great significance, a culture of resistance that more than merits a highly detailed account running to more than 600 pages including diary entries, exhaustive bibliography and discriminating discography. But now he looks askance at the epigones of punk and pop – those who emphasise dumb insolence while forgetting the intelligence and sophistication that form an equally essential part of the British pop tradition.

PARENTS Richard Hoggart, Stuart Hall, Greil Marcus
READ ON *England's Dreaming*; *Time Travel – from the Sex Pistols to Nirvana: pop, media and sexuality (1977–96)*

Scooters
Roman holiday

It all began with Gregory Peck and Audrey Hepburn in William Wyler's *Roman Holiday* (1953). Hepburn is a princess on the run, Peck the American journalist who finds her. They fall in love on the seat of a Vespa. Here was American panache in a European setting, and the vehicle for this magical combination was an Italian scooter.

In the 60s Italian-made goods were a constant feature of Britain's most-wanted list (also including Olivetti typewriters, espresso coffee machines as used by **Michael Caine** in *The Ipcress File*). This is partly because of the long tradition of Italian craftsmanship, and partly because from the 50s onwards Italian craftsmen were setting out to make a new generation of artefacts that would distance them from their country's fascist past. By the time these goods arrived in the UK, a new generation of Britons was trying to distance itself from their own country's imperial past, and wanting to reinvent themselves as discerning, European, individual consumers rather than an undifferentiated mass of workers. For the front-runners of this cohort, the **Mods**, Italian-made scooters (Vespas and Lambrettas) were the perfect, affordable symbol of their aspirations.

Scooters were originally advertised in Britain as 'the sports car on two wheels'. They came to be thought of as a highly respectable form of transport ('social scootering' was more like the Boy Scouts on wheels), but the Mods overrode this part of the scooter's image and invested it with their own set of connotations (which in any case were closer to the original Italian motivation). In *The Meaning of Mod*, cultural critic Dick Hebdige explains that 'the scooter, a formerly ultra-respectable means of transport was appropriated and converted into a weapon and a symbol of solidarity'. Italian style was a weapon against British backwardness; sharing a mode of transport identified Mod stylists against the drabness of the traditional British way of life. This much (if not the violence and pills among scooter-riding Mods) was in line with manufacturers' adverts which showed the scooter as a symbol of cosmopolitanism; it was also in sync with the Italian tradition of the *pavoneggiarsi* (peacock male) and with the enjoyably estranged way of living depicted in Federico Fellini's film, *La Dolce Vita* (1960).

Lambrettas and Vespas were originally a sign of social superiority: Mods were more sophisticated than anyone else, and owning one was a way of showing it. When scooters came back with the Mod revival (one band even called themselves The Lambrettas) of the late, post-punk 70s, they were more a sign of having been excluded: scooter-riders were left-behinds, more like the Rockers of the 60s than the snob Mods who first rode them. Throughout the 80s the scooter continued to drift downmarket: scooter clubs were largely made up of white, lower-working-class youths who were often closer to **skinheads** than Mods.

In the late 90s the scooter was rehabilitated as a fashion accessory. Although sales of scooters did not really take off again, a new range of associated clothing did become briefly fashionable. The Gallaghers and design guru Graham Wood (Tomato) were spotted wearing Vespa's £190 Teflon-coated 'technical jacket'; and various members of Ocean Colour Scene, The Verve and The Charlatans wore Lambretta's suede bowling shoe.

Afficionados were shocked in September 1998 when the pollution-conscious Italian government looked set to ban scooters from city centres. After howls of protest, the Ministry of the Environment backed down, leaving local authorities to decide the fate of the *motorini*.

After 40 years here Italian scooters have become absorbed into the British heritage museum: a foreign-made machine symbolising progress for all is now an icon of Britain's nostalgia for the future we used to look forward to.

READ ON *Hiding in the Light* and *The Meaning of Mod* by Dick Hebdige; *Scooter* and *Scootermania* magazines

ScotLit
Magnetic north

Beginning in the 80s and coming to full power in the 90s the wealth of good literature being produced by writers north of the border began to outshine the traditional middle-class English sources. As has been the case in the past (demonstrated by the wealth of Irish and Indian writing talent) it seems that those who get the best out of the

English language at the cusp of a new millennium are from cultures where English is, to a greater or lesser extent, an alien tongue recrafted by the host culture.

The issue of nationalism has always been a romantic ideal rather than a militant passion in Scotland. Even in an age of fracturing ethnicities all across Europe, devolution raised little interest. But organised politics' loss is culture's gain and it is in the new voices of Scottish fiction that a sense of Scottish identity can be witnessed.

Of even greater importance is the fact that these writers (Jeff Torrington, **James Kelman**, **Irvine Welsh**, Janice Galloway, AL Kennedy, Duncan MacLean) offer not just a regional variation (writing in varying degrees of dialect) but, crucially, different class perspectives rarely on view in the traditional English novel. They write, from experience, about working-class life on the margins: the **dole**, dead-end jobs, drink and drugs, domestic violence, petty crime – and the disenfranchised who live there, giving a voice to this experience not just in Scotland but across the whole of Britain.

Will Self

Risking himself

With 'a constitution like an ox' (criminal-turned-writer John McVicar) and a sensibility that 'finds it hard to write an uneuphonious sentence' (novelist **Martin Amis**), Will Self is a writer who takes baroque

but visceral metaphors to the limits of endurance (ours as well as his own).

Born (1962) in North London, 'nouveau Jew' Will Self was diagnosed 'borderline personality (schizoid)' as an adolescent. His youth was marked by trips to casualty, 'taking drugs which derange the senses', and scraping a third in PPE at Oxford. Of his years of excess he says he 'finds it hard to be totally negative about it'. In 1986 he was featured in a TV documentary about a home for recovering addicts. Heroin withdrawal, he recalls, gives rise to 'an obscene image hunger'. Much of his fiction might be seen as an attempt to satisfy such a craving.

Self's first collection of short stories, *The Quantity Theory of Insanity*, appeared in 1991. The following year he published *Cock* and *Bull*, two novellas of the grotesque in which a woman sprouts a prick and a man grows a cunt. *My Idea of Fun* (1993) is a full-length novel of grotesquerie and a satire on money and psychosis, described by a reviewer in the *London Evening Standard* as 'the most loathsome novel I have ever read'. To **Salman Rushdie**, Self was 'already a cult figure'. Martin Amis described him as 'thrillingly heartless, terrifyingly brainy'. In 1994 Self published another short story collection, *Grey Area*, and in 1995 he issued *Junk Mail*, a collection of essays and journalism. As restaurant critic (one of the various journo roles to which he has been assigned) he chose to review McDonald's and its like rather than swish gastrodomes. In 1996 he produced *The Sweet Smell of Psychosis*, followed by *Great Apes*, a Swiftian satire in which a middle-aged London painter awakes to

Will Self

find first his girlfriend and then the rest of the world transformed into chimps. Another short story collection, *Tough Tough Toys for Tough Tough Boys* (1998), was set in a world of crack dealers, fast cars, quickie sex and long drink binges, but critic Melanie McDonald remarked that, nonetheless, 'Mr Self … strikes me as a rather moral writer.' In 1998 Self was the victim of a spoof magazine, *Self*, which seemed to have come from his satirical pen, whereas in fact he had nothing to do with it.

Self says he was 'in many ways trained to be a writer' by his parents' recognition of 'a good turn of phrase'. He regrets that his mother died before he was professionally published (in *Tough Tough Toys* he included the 1991 story 'North London Book of the Dead' in which dying means moving to another part of London and the narrator gets to meet his dead mother). But what finally drove him to writing was 'my fear that I couldn't'. He now approaches writing '*con brio*', and aims to obtain 'a fingerprint of the psyche'. His favourite device is what he terms the 'exploded metaphor': pursuing a metaphor to the extreme. He takes off in various directions and ends up in the thematic/stylistic

383

Magnetic North Ten of the best modern Scottish writers

Alasdair Gray (b. 1934, Glasgow), painter, novelist and author of the polemical essay 'Why Scots Should Rule Scotland'. Typical sentence: 'McAlpin studied the page of a glossy magazine, then said, "does she smell of the bakery, the brewery, or the brothel?".' *Lanark*

James Kelman (b. 1946, Glasgow), polemical essayist and author of 15 works of fiction including the 1994 Booker Prize winner *How Late It Was, How Late*. Typical statement: 'There is simply no question that by the criteria of the ruling elite of Great Britain so-called Scottish culture, for example, is inferior, just as *ipso facto* the Scottish people are also inferior.' *Oppression and Solidarity*

Douglas Dunn (b. 1942, Renfrewshire), poet and editor of the *Oxford Book of Scottish Short Stories*. Opening sentence: 'The countryside of the Scottish Borders was wearing its winter tweeds.' *The Political Piano*

AL Kennedy (b. 1965, Dundee), novelist and short story writer. Typical observation: 'Margaret, like many others, will take the rest of her life to recover from a process we may summarise thus: THE SCOTTISH METHOD (for the perfection of children): 1) Guilt is good 2) The history, language and culture of Scotland do not exist. If they did, they would be of no importance and might as well not 3) Masturbation is an abuse of one's self: sexual intercourse, the abuse of one's self by others.' *Looking For The Possible Dance*

Gordon Legge (b. 1961, Grangemouth), novelist and short story writer. Typical opening: '… and I'm playing some records and dancing about and generally enjoying myself when there's a knock at the door. It's Wee Harry and his problems. He tells me Wendy's chucked him so I let him in and make him a coffee and prepare to hear his life story for the millionth time.' *Life on a Scottish Council Estate*, Vol 1

Liz Lochead (b. 1947, Motherwell), painter and art teacher turned poet, prose writer and playwright. Typical situation: 'Five minutes later found me flinching and clenching, biting into the black vinyl of the couch as cold steel penetrated. I spat out a curse. Ten minutes after that — I sat in triumph, six precious months' supply of the pill in my grasp.' *Phyllis Marlowe: Only Diamonds Are Forever*

William McIlvanney (b. 1936, Kilmarnock), novelist, crime writer and essayist. Typical opening: 'The pub was quiet. When the big man with the ill-fitting suit came in, the barman noticed him more than he normally would have done. The suit was slightly out of fashion yet looked quite new and it was too big for him. He could have come back to it after a long illness. Yet it wasn't that either. Whatever had happened to him had tightened him but not diminished him. The charcoal grey cloth sat on him loosely but that looked like the suit's problem. You wouldn't have fancied whoever the suit might fit to come against the man who wore it.' *At The Bar*

Agnes Owens (b. 1926, Milngavie), published her first novel at the age of 58. In the highly influential collection *Lean Tales* (1985), her stories appeared with Gray's and Kelman's. Typical opening: 'It was a raw March morning when Ivy came into the village hotel where she was employed as a cleaner'. *When Shankland Comes*

Jeff Torrington (b. 1935, the Gorbals). A former shop steward at the Talbot/Chrysler plant in Linwood, his *Swing Hammer Swing!* won the Whitbread Prize in 1992. Typical opening: 'McQuirr, scarcely half-awake, trudged to the clocking on point.' *The Fade*

Irvine Welsh (b. 1958, Edinburgh), novelist by appointment to the E-generation, in some respects a follower in the footsteps of Alexander Trocchi whom he once described as 'a Scottish George Best of literature'.

ballpark of such diverse writers such as Jonathan Swift, William Burroughs and JG Ballard.

Like Burroughs, Self says that writing sometimes come to him in the manner of dictation. Ballard he regards as 'a great mentor', and recalls going to interview him for a short article and staying to talk for four hours. Swift he describes as 'the satirist's Shakespeare', adding that 'a modern satire has to have the message, think for yourself'. As the *enfant terrible* of 90s English fiction, Self was often compared to his predecessor Martin Amis. His prose has the same fizz and sparkle, and he has a wonderful ability to concoct off-key descriptions that match his out-of-kilter worlds. As with Ballard and Burroughs, Self's protagonists are often the helpless inhabitants of warped realities where an explanation is always one more Kafkaesque step away. Perhaps this is how Self feels about the real world, although he insists that he is 'far more negative as a writer than I am as a person'.

Self is supremely sensitive to the inflated character of contemporary British medialand, so it is only appropriate that he himself should have become embroiled in a scandalous news story during the run-up to the 1997 general election. Barred from **Tony Blair**'s battlebus by spin doctors wary of his 'reputation and possible behaviour' (Self later said 'there are no words to describe my contempt for Tony Blair and what he represents'), he was nevertheless allowed on prime minister John Major's plane – until caught snorting heroin in the lavatory. Expelled from Major's hack pack, Self was sacked by the 'liberal' *Observer*: the paper that had 'marketed me as a drugs influenced, counter-cultural writer ... these same people summarily fired me'.

So far Self has managed to mix media punditry with serious fiction, the one role lending credibility/accessibility to the other. In literary terms he is a bad boy, but in publishing terms bad is now good for marketing. The one aspect of Self that does not sit well with current cultural trends is his willingness to show that he is highly educated. It may be a cause for carping criticism in the short term, but in the long term it could be the making of him as a fully mature writer.

PARENTS Jonathan Swift, William S Burroughs, JG Ballard
READ ON *My Idea of Fun*, *Great Apes*

Peter Sellers
Light and dark

In the USA Peter Sellers is best known as the light comedy actor who starred as Inspector Clouseau in the *Pink Panther* series that began in 1963. In Britain his reputation as a heavyweight is based on key roles in *The Goon Show* (1951–60) and Stanley Kubrick's *Dr Strangelove: Or How I Learned To Stop Worrying and Love the Bomb* (1963). The combination of laughter and darkness in his work has given rise to contrasting assessments of Sellers: was he simply the most brilliant comic actor of his generation, or a schizophrenic who relied on his comedy roles the way a junkie needs his stuff?

There's a Girl In My Soup (1970)

Skinheads

Perhaps the complexity of Sellers' image has something to do with the way he spanned different generations (old enough to be a war veteran, young enough to be part of the swinging 60s), without quite fitting into either.

Sellers was born (as Richard Henry Sellers, 1925) into a theatrical family. His father led a four-

piece band, while his mother and grandmother featured in an underwater review entitled Splash Me! He made his first stage appearance at the age of two weeks, during one of his parents' music hall shows. During the Second World War Sellers appeared with Michael Bentine in the RAF Gangshow. Demobbed, they met up with ex-Desert

Rats **Spike Milligan** and Harry Secombe. Under the guidance of publican and producer Jimmy Grafton, this quartet began to work together as The Crazy People. By the time of their second **BBC** radio series, they had become *The Goon Show*.

Throughout the 50s Sellers made a big screen name for himself in a series of show-stealing Ealing and Ealing-esque roles in *The Ladykillers* (1956), *I'm Alright Jack* (1959, for which he won a British Academy Award, defeating Laurence Olivier and Richard Burton) and his multiple roles in *The Mouse That Roared* (1959) that brought him to the attention of Hollywood. The Goons also brought recognition and a recording contract. Sellers' recordings were admired by Kubrick, who noted his talent for mimicry and cast him in the louche role of Quilty in the film (1962) of Vladimir Nabokov's *Lolita* (the cover of *The Best of Sellers* LP hangs on the wall of Lolita's bedroom). The following year (1963), Sellers starred in Blake Edwards' *Pink Panther* (he was asked to play the shrewd but accident-prone Inspector Clouseau after Peter Ustinov turned down the part) and in Kubrick's *Dr Strangelove* where he played three different roles and improvised a great deal of Dr Strangelove's mad antics and murmurings. In a single year he made mainstream film unusually artful and brought mass appeal to arthouse cinema.

Not all Sellers' roles were up to this standard. He played the lead (suave TV personality meets young girl and is swept off his feet) in the film of Terence Frisby's swinging 60s sex comedy *There's A Girl In My Soup* (1970), described by one critic as 'suet pudding' rather than 'soufflé'. Sellers' own marriage to Britt Ekland, 19 years his junior, was marred by jealousy. During the 70s he consulted psychics, took drugs and suffered a series of heart attacks. His penultimate film role, as the empty-headed citizen-turned-political figure in Hal Ashby's satirical *Being There* (1979), marked a return to form. Sellers was back at the top of his profession, but died of heart failure in 1980.

Behind the multifaceted comedy mask he was obviously a troubled man. Sellers once said: 'As far as I'm aware, I have no personality of my own whatsoever.' And yet he was cherished by so many for the very reason that his insane comedy took so much of himself. His antics were a 24-hour-a-day habit rather than a display for the camera. It can be summed up by an anecdote Spike Milligan once told about hearing a knock at his front door in the middle of the night, only to find a naked Sellers on the doorstep asking him if he could 'recommend a good tailor'.

PARENTS Alec Guinness
CHILDREN Keith Moon

Skinheads
Boot boys

Daytime wear: Harrington jacket, bleached Levi's, steel-capped boots, clip-on braces; plain white work shirts or Ben Shermans. Evenings: Trevira tonic suits, Crombie coats with football club badges. And the No 1 crop to make you 'feel nasty whether you are or not'. These were the outward signs of a cult which, according to its adherents, stood for 'self-belief, pride in yourself … the only cult that's ever been true'. To some people, however, skinheads were the ugly face of British bigotry; while others have suggested that, for all their macho posturing, in their grossly exaggerated masculinity the skinheads were really camp all the time.

The first gig I ever went to, aged 11, accompanied by my elder sister, was in the spring of 1968. Topping the bill was Jimi Hendrix (it was what used to be called a 'package tour' with half a dozen other bands on the bill including Pink Floyd, Amen Corner, The Nice and The Move). In the seat next to me, screaming her head off, was a girl with a haircut that was short on top and straggly at the back. She was a Hard **Mod**. A year or so later and my hair would have been longer than hers; but it would have been difficult to compare, because she wouldn't have been seen dead at a Jimi Hendrix gig; and the boys she knew would have chased me (the grammar-school boy) down the street. She was about to become a skinhead girl, but she didn't know it yet.

At Hyde Park in July 1969, they showed their strength. According to Geoffrey Cannon's report on the event, a free concert given by the **Rolling Stones**, it was 'A Nice Day In The Park'. It was things 'nice' that the skins objected to. **John Peel** and the other beautiful people saw everything as being 'really nice' – the skins wanted others to see them as really horrible.

In 'The Emergence of the Skinheads', which

appeared in the 1972 edition of *Rock File* edited by Charlie Gillett, Pete Fowler explained how the skins grew out of disillusionment with pop and where it was heading. A gap between performer and punter had opened up; and there could be no more pretending that they were near-equal participants in a teenage revolution. The skins were still stuck where their sort always had been, at the bottom of the pile; and their exaggeratedly hard image – particularly the exposed boots and the close-cropped hair – were a dramatic turn-away from the trends within pop culture towards middle-class softness. As Mod hair flowed longer and Carnaby Street drifted into embryonic hippiedom, the skinheads cut back to the basics of Mod: sharp, cool and working-class tough.

So skinheads rejected their pop parents, but they were the sons of pop all the same. Their No 1 crop was a hardline version of the French crop worn by Jamaican bluebeat singers who were much admired by the Mods. When the No 1 became associated with hooliganism, some skins went back to something like the original French crop – as 'suedeheads' they regained their social mobility and went after 'a better class of bird'. Two-tone Trevira suits and Crombie overcoats were a continuation of Mod-ish concern for neat, classy clothes. In their love of Motown, the skins carried on where Mod left off. Even the form of writing (straight lines only) which they often used for their graffiti was a DIY imitation of modernist typography.

But if the skinheads were part-modernist, they were also trying to recover a sense of tradition in a fast-changing Britain. In his essay 'The Skinheads and the Magical Recovery of Community' (1975), sociologist John Clarke concluded that 'the Skinhead style represents an attempt to recreate through the "mob" the traditional working-class community, as a substitution for the REAL decline of the latter'. According to Clarke the 'lower working class' had experienced a 'rapidly worsening situation' during the second half of the 60s and this, combined with the end of consensus in youth subcultures, produced 'an intensified "Us–Them" consciousness' which was personified in the skins and their burning desire for aggravation.

The relationship between skinheads and blacks was always complicated. As defenders of the traditional, they wanted to keep out black people whose presence seemed to be a serious threat to old-style white, working-class communities. Meanwhile they loved black music, and some black musicians reciprocated by dedicating records to skinheads (Symarip's 'Skinhead Moonstomp' and 'Skinhead Girl', for example). But a love of black and racism have managed to go hand in hand since the 'nigger minstrels' of nineteenth-century America. In the early 70s most skinhead gangs seemed to tolerate those of West Indian descent while taking out their frustrations on 'Pakis'. In the mid-to-late 70s skinheads were courted by the National Front and the British Movement, and some of them did join or identify with neo-fascist parties. In the early 80s skinhead was revitalised by punk and then the rebirth of Mod; 'white noise'/oi bands such as No Remorse tried to reinforce this connection but were not always successful.

In the 90s new constituencies – even those whose very existence is entirely contrary to the skins' original ethos – got the chance to don the skinhead uniform. In a book about gays who adopted the skinhead look, Murray Healy observed that gays and skins had always shared 'a propensity for stripping to the waist, all-male environments and hard lads', and wondered whether 'all skinheads [were] always just a touch queer'. Meanwhile Asian skinhead girls appeared on the front cover of *2nd Generation*, the magazine for the sons and daughters of 'Paki' immigrants. In days like these when the definition of 'British' is far from clear, styles and subcultures originally associated with holding on to traditional Britishness can now be appropriated by erstwhile 'aliens'. Nowadays the middle classes can be skinheads too. Skinhead/suedehead novels written in the 70s by 'Richard Allen' (one of the pen names used by Irish-Canadian pulp writer Jim Moffat) stand next to **Nick Hornby** on many a middle-class bookshelf, and medialand is bristling with successful young-ish men who favour the skinhead crop.

PARENTS Mods, manual labour
CHILDREN designer baldies
READ ON 'The Skinheads and the Magical Recovery of Community' by John Clarke in *Resistance Through Rituals* edited by Stuart Hall and Tony Jefferson

Slade
Illiterati

Slade were a band of ex-**skinheads** from Wolverhampton who grew their hair but kept the attitude of working-class aggro. Their first hit (1970) combined minor chords, a violin riff, deliberately basic beat and the gruff vocals of Noddy Holder (b. 1947, but his deliberately old-fashioned sideburns made him look something like John Bull). Equally important was the deliberate mis-spelling of the song's title: 'Coz I Luv You'. At a time when British pop music was turning into rock and the domination of the art-college/grammar-school boys was becoming obvious to everyone, Slade affected illiteracy as a way of pinning their working-class credentials to every record and every advert placed in their name. By keeping up their downmarket image with titles such as 'Cum On Feel The Noize' (1972), they became standard-bearers of working-class masculinity in every comprehensive (as a concession to the girls, guitarist Dave Hill was allowed to wear make-up and a silly fringe).

Slade were even big enough to make a feature film in 1974 (*Flame*) but their career as working-class heroes was finally interrupted when their drummer was involved in a serious car accident. Frontman Noddy Holder has since become a quiz show panellist and a cuddly pantomime version of his former, scary self. In ITV's comedy drama series *The Grimleys* (1999) he played kindly music teacher Neville Holder.

Looking back at the 70s, Holder maintains that pop provided remission from class conflict: 'The 70s were very tongue-in-cheek. The music was an antidote to the politics of the time, which was all strikes and power cuts ... you can't take rock'n'roll too seriously. If you do, you're missing the point.' Slade always were a good laugh – besides being a tight rock band. But by undermining the new seriousness of **prog rock**, they were also striking back and making a point on behalf of those who felt increasingly excluded from it.

PARENTS Little Richard, *Crossroads*

The Small Faces
'The authentic Mod band'

'They were **Mods** who formed a band,' says their biographer Paolo Hewitt. 'They taught everybody else how to be Mods. They were the authentic Mod band,' says veteran rock scribe Charles Shaar Murray, who has also said that first they were soul boys, then they were soul boys on acid, but 'they never lost sight of being East End herberts'.

The Small Faces consisted of Kenny Jones (drums), Ian McLagan (keyboards), Ronnie 'Plonk' Lane (bass vocals) and former child actor (played the Artful Dodger on stage in *Oliver* aged 12) Steve Marriott (lead vocals and guitar). They were East End soul boys (Tamla Motown, Stax) who dressed sharp and released some of the neatest British singles of the mid-60s. Everything about them spelt Mod: up to date, up to speed, up to the mark.

The Small Faces ('faces' from the Mod term for a fashion leader; 'small' because they were short – and perhaps they originally became Mods because this was a style that short men could look good in) first charted with 'Whatcha Gonna Do About It?' (1965), followed by their first No 1, 'Sha La La La Lee' (1966). The hits kept coming (as they used to say in 60s pop annuals): 'Hey Girl' (1966), 'All or Nothing' (1966), 'Get Yourself Together' (1967), 'Talk To You' (1967), 'Here Come The Nice' (1967), 'Itchycoo Park' (1967), 'Tin Soldier' (1967), and 'Lazy Sunday' (1968). Their early records were white soul sieved through early 60s British beat, with McLagan's Booker T-style organ almost as prominent as Marriott's Wilson Pickett-style voice.

In their middle period The Small Faces summed up the impact of drugs on the Mod scene. The 'Nice' in the eponymous record of 1967 referred to a drug dealer who was 'always there if I need some speed'. But during the summer of love (1967), the amphetamine-driven, besuited Mod started to be overtaken by the combination of cannabis, LSD and hippie kaftans. For their next appearance on *Top of the Pops*, Marriott wore a silk tunic to sing 'Itchycoo Park', a song about an East End park favoured by canoodling couples, which in his imagination became the setting for hallucinogenic visions that were 'all too beautiful'. The track concluded with a stereophonic, panoramic (from one speaker to the other and back again) recording of a Kenny Jones drum break (sounds too naff even to be a cliché now; sounded disorientating and subversive back

then). For their last big hit, 'Lazy Sunday', taken from their concept album *Ogden's Nut Gone Flake*, The Small Faces drew on their East End roots and presented a sound-picture of London life with echoes from the music hall ('Max Wall with pop songs' – Paolo Hewitt), complete with ex-Artful Dodger Marriott singing in a mock-Cockney voice. The effect was completed by a film which they had specially produced for *Top of the Pops* (a pre-video promo).

In a Channel 4 documentary show in 1997, McLagan looked back at 'Lazy Sunday' with regret: 'It was a hit and it killed us, because now we were a joke band.' But showing their roots need not have diminished The Small Faces. On *The White Album* and *Sgt Pepper*, **The Beatles** had already moved in this direction; and **The Kinks** were set to go deeply into Britain's heritage with their *Village Green Preservation Society*. The demise of The Small Faces came about because of internal pressures, not because Englishness was a musical cul de sac.

Marriott did try to shake off his background (both Mod and music hall) in the American-style boogie band Humble Pie (he was killed in a fire in his Essex home in 1991). Meanwhile the other Faces teamed up with a north London ex-Mod lead singer called **Rod Stewart** who brought with him the pineapple-haired guitarist Ronnie Wood. In the early 70s The Faces played the part of sharp London wide boys making whoopee in a rock world that had gone sluggish and soft. In their distance and disdain for adult oriented rock (AOR), and their determination to have a white soul version of 'a real good time', they were a breath of fresh air. But in

1976 they themselves were blown away by punk. Stewart had already crossed over to the USA. Wood became a **Rolling Stone** (foolishly, he opted for a wage rather than royalties). Jones half-joined the **Who** after the death of drummer Keith Moon. Lane, who suffered from multiple sclerosis for 20 years, died at home in Colorado in 1997. McLagan has retired.

In the late 90s, partly because of Paolo Hewitt's biography, The Small Faces have been re-appraised. *Ogden's Nut Gone Flake* is referred to as a forgotten masterpiece, and **Blur** have picked up and run with the combination of Mod and music hall The Small Faces helped to develop more than 30 years ago.

PARENTS Wilson Pickett, Lionel Bart
CHILDREN Blur
READ ON *The Small Faces* by Paolo Hewitt

Paul Smith
Big in Japan

Paul Smith shops take British history and give it a twist. His clothes (from suits to shirts to shoes) are successful because they combine both the witty artificiality of fashion and the organic tradition of tailoring. Visiting Washington for the first time as prime minister, **Tony Blair** wore a Paul Smith suit. When the Design Museum devoted an exhibition to his work, to mark his silver jubilee in fashion, they called it 'Paul Smith True Brit'. Throughout Britain and the rest of the world, Smith is associated with the mix of tradition and innovation that is now the nation's preferred image.

Born in Nottingham in 1946, Paul Smith left school at 15 to be a runner (£3 5s a week) in the city's lace district. Early ambitions as a competitive cyclist (350 miles training a week) were thwarted by a collision with a speeding car that put him in traction for seven months. After helping out in a friend's boutique, on 9 October 1971 Smith opened his own (Vêtement) in a tiny shop (12 square feet) in Byard Lane. He took evening classes in tailoring and by the end of 1976 was acting as a consultant to the International Wool Secretariat and an Italian shirt manufacturer. Two decades later, the Smith empire has spawned 225 shops – 200 outlets in Japan alone, eight shops in London, and premises in Paris, New York, Manila, Singapore and Hong Kong. Apart from menswear, he now offers womenswear, childrenswear, jeans, spectacles, toiletries, bags and watches. Awarded a CBE in 1994 and holder of the Queen's Award For Export (1995), Smith is a member of the Creative Industries Task Force and a recipient of the British Design for Industry award.

In May 1998 Smith opened his flagship London store in Westbourne House, Kensington Park Road, Notting Hill – a three-storey Victorian (built 1858) former dwelling and, latterly, restaurant. Restored by Sophie Hicks (brief: 'spare no expense'), who previously designed the Sensation exhibition at the Royal Academy, the shop is Smith's rejoinder to 'clone retailing'. He believes that 'someone has got to speak out against this cloning of style. Someone once said we were a nation of shopkeepers. They never specified that all the shops had to look the same.'

Entering through the Victorian garden, customers experience 'something with the Englishness of the old corner shop'. Wherever possible, salesrooms echo their original function, childrenswear in the playroom, for example. Upstairs the bespoke tailoring service ('classic made to measure with self-expression if you want it') strives to maintain the atmosphere of a gentlemen's club. In the womenswear room there might be a Dior couture dress on the rack next to something from the Paul Smith range (launched in 1992), alongside a beaded jacket from 60s boutique Granny Takes A Trip.

Westbourne House is the fullest expression yet of Smith's *persona*. He is a child of the 60s who was born into a city that puts a high premium on craftsmanship. Through the 70s and 80s he moulded himself into a retailer who combines love of tradition with playfulness and experimentation. His takeover (1991) and remake of Newbold, a century-old Derbyshire factory workwear manufacturer, is another example of this mix.

Smith opened his first London store in 1979 in a former banana warehouse in Floral Street, Covent Garden (previously the home of London's main fruit and veg market, just then coming into its own as a cultural quarter). Style journalist Dylan Jones points out that 'the 80s made Smith – his flair for idiosyncratic yet traditional menswear coinciding with a boom in men's retailing'. Surprisingly, for a decade associated with overstatement, the 80s revered Smith's combination of reserve and quirkiness: his suits (especially the Prince of Wales check) acquired talisman status alongside Porsches, Tag Heuer watches and Philippe Starcke furniture.

Smith the employer could not be less like the 80s image of highly strung, contemptuous creatives. Staff report that he does not ask them to do anything he would not do himself. Accessible, not aloof, Smith believes that 'the reason I'm successful is because I'm available'. This aspect of his personality is also reflected in his shops. Whereas some designer stores seem to operate an exclusive door policy, Paul Smith shops have always been non-threatening environments. Perhaps the open-door atmosphere has its origins in Smith's working-class roots, and in the craftsman's creed that everyone should be entitled to high-quality goods.

Smith is probably most successful in Japan, where 'the John Cleese of British fashion' is admired as a bit of a joker. A frequent visitor to Japan since 1982, on an early trip Smith dished out red noses instead of business cards and tapped into the frivolity that lies under the formality of Japanese life. His combination of British eccentricity and tradition (the floors of his flagship store in Shibuya are made of British oak) is revered in Japan even more than it is at home. In Tokyo Smith is frequently stopped in the street by adoring fans, and mobbed after public appearances.

PARENTS Savile Row, Raleigh bicycles, Nottingham lace, 60s Carnaby Street, Edward VII

Soap Operas
Virtual Britain

The soaps grew up in an age when the media was replacing real communities as a place where Britons discovered and acted out their communality. The 'Big Two' soaps on TV now are both set in communities that really don't exist anymore: the cobbled Northern terraces of *Coronation Street* (the street itself had to be rebuilt as a set during the 80s) and the fictitious cockney market square of *EastEnders*. For better or worse, these days, geographically at least, we live alone. Instead of gossiping about our own neighbours we exchange views on the lives and loves of Albert Square, Coronation Street and Brookside Close.

Britain's first soap, *The Archers* (subtitle: an everyday story of country folk), started life on the BBC's Midland Regional radio in the spring of 1950. The first national broadcast occurred in December the same year, and the first omnibus edition (introduced by Tom Forrest, who was still summarising the week's events four decades later) was transmitted in 1952. The Archers originally had a didactic purpose: patched into the storyline was useful information for farmers and other food-growers (food in Britain was still rationed and many householders maintained allotments), and the foot and mouth outbreak of 1956 featured prominently in the programme. It has already enjoyed twice the lifespan of *Mrs Dale's Diary*, the other BBC radio soap created in 1950.

The first TV soap, *Coronation Street* (devised by Tony Warren), aired in December 1960. It soon became a firm national favourite and for years it had little to challenge it (neither *Crossroads* nor *Emmerdale Farm* were of the same standard). Granada Studio's now offer Hollywood-style tours of the set and sound stages, while characters like Jack and Vera Duckworth are more readily recognisable to the public than some recent prime ministers.

The idea for *Brookside* was sold to Channel 4 controller Jeremy Isaacs two years before the network's launch in November 1982 (the first episode of *Brookside* was broadcast on Channel 4's opening night). Producer Phil Redmond took over six houses as a permanent set, and fostered local actors and writers (Jimmy McGovern, Frank Cottrell-Boyce) in a new production company, Mersey TV. As pitched to Isaacs by Redmond (ex-quantity surveyor, mature student at Liverpool University, writer for ATV, creator of children's soap *Grange Hill*), *Brookside* would push the boundaries of what was acceptable on British TV. After years of controversy (from child abuse to rape and the infamous lesbian kiss), it is known as an issue-led soap. Set, more realistically than the Big Two, on an anonymous modern close, the writers have, as a result, found it harder and harder to generate plausible excuses for communal life to wrap their stories around. Several key actors have left Brookie – most notably Ricky Tomlinson – when they felt the original integrity of their characters had been compromised for plot motives.

Launched in April 1985, *EastEnders* was the BBC's in-house response to 'Brookie'. *Coronation Street* had become more comic, but like *Brookside*,

EastEnders sought serious issues and topicality. it was initially as didactic as the early Archers. It has gone on to hold its own in the ratings war with 'Corrie' and become an indispensable part of our TV culture.

As a forum, all these soaps help reflect and shape our social outllook and landscape. Having the first black, gay, lesbian, eco-warrior character on a soap opera can have a pioneering effect on how acceptable these things are to the nation. The fate of soap characters is important enough to be the subject of frequent national debate. It can make front page news for the tabloids and be the subject of questions in parliament.

If the sitcom has been largely dominated by male characters, then the soap with its predominantly female audience has produced some of the strongest female role models of the post-war era: Elsie Tanner, sixties siren of the street, and Angie Watts, at the helm in the Queen Vic doing battle with Dirty Den, and their ilk are independent women not afraid to make mistakes in life and strong enough to bounce back from anything.

Parents **Kitchen Sink**, Peyton Place

Soho
Sex, sleaze and style

Named after 'So-ho', the huntsman's cry that he had sighted a hare, Soho is the one-square-mile district of central London bordered by Oxford Street to the north, Shaftesbury Avenue to the south, Charing Cross Road to the east, and Regent Street to the west. Originally an area colonised by a succession of recently arrived immigrants – Jews, Italians, West Indians – it has always, by this token, been a slightly exotic and un-English demi-monde that has acted as both stage to and catalyst in several English cultural transformations. Traditionally associated with sex and vice, in the late 50s and 60s it was also the launch pad for the young modernists as described by **Colin MacInnes** in *Absolute Beginners* (1959) and portrayed in the film *Beat Girl* (1960). From the 80s onwards it took on a more openly gay aspect. It now combines all three elements of gay ghetto, style showcase and sex parlour. Not forgetting the 5,000 folk who live there too.

'Soho was lined with tarts,' says singer and Surrealist **George Melly**. Mostly congregated in Great Windmill Street and Brewer Street, in the 50s 300 or so prostitutes were controlled by mainly Maltese pimps. In the 60s the street-corner prostitute began to go elsewhere, and Soho was the setting for new sex games such as 'clipping': getting the punter's money, sending him to a fictitious address and then disappearing. The number of drinking clubs and strip clubs increased rapidly: the world-famous Raymond Revuebar opened in

1959. But by the late 90s there were far fewer strip clubs left in Soho, and some of those that remained were patronised mainly by pensioners.

The late 60s and early 70s were Soho's porn years: pornographic magazines were shipped over in Danish Bacon lorries while the Obscene Publications Squad (OPS) was bribed to turn a blind eye or even to make phone calls warning of police raids. But in April 1972 Robert Mark was appointed Metropolitan Police commissioner with a brief to clean up Soho. The OPS was suspended and senior officer Keith Drury (previously seen on holiday with porn king James Humphries) was forced to resign. In the early 80s new legislation came into effect that required all sex shops to be licensed. Responsibility for policing such outlets now falls to the Clubs and Vice Unit of the Metropolitan Police.

Originally regarded as only marginally less suspect than the sex industry, the British film industry also maintains a strong presence in the area (on behalf of the music industry, Denmark Street, the miniature British equivalent of Tin Pan Alley, is just on the other side of the Charing Cross Road). Major film companies have their offices along Wardour Street, there are preview theatres and post-production houses nearby, and so too is the British Board of Film Classification (formerly the British Board of Film Censorship) which occupies an early-Victorian building in the north-west corner of Soho Square. For more than a quarter of a century, film (and latterly video) censorship in Britain was largely controlled by American-born BBFC official James Ferman, but he retired at the beginning of 1999.

In the 50s Soho was one of the few places (even in London) where you could buy foreign food (food that was not part of the traditional British diet). Berwick Street market was surrounded by Italian and French delicatessens, and Soho restaurants were legendary (Wheeler's in Old Compton Street, Gennaro's on the site now occupied by the Groucho Club, among others). Now that every supermarket has a deli counter, and every provincial high street contains enough restaurants for a gastronomic world tour, Soho's role as the food capital of Britain has been largely superseded.

Its drinking haunts are still as famous as the people who once populated them: Francis Bacon and friends in **The Colony Room**, or in the pub known as the French House (meeting place for the exiled members of the French Resistance during the Second World War; one of whom, Gaston, stayed on to run what was originally the York Minster pub); and Jeffrey Bernard in the Coach and Horses just a few doors down the road. These temples of dypsomania have been joined by newer, members' only clubs such as the Groucho (associated with 80s-style excess), Soho House (associated with 90s-style moderation), and Black's (partly populated by younger members who will one day move on to either Groucho's or Soho House).

Soho's musical landmarks include Ronnie Scott's (tenor saxophone player, committed suicide Christmas 1997), founded in 1959 because the owner needed a place to play modern jazz in London; and the Marquee (originally in Wardour Street, moved to Charing Cross Road, now closed), where seminal 60s bands such as the **Rolling Stones**, the **Who** and The Yardbirds (featured in

Michelangelo Antonioni's definitive swinging London film *Blow Up*, 1966) all had residences. Soho was also the setting for late 70s/80s music clubs such as the Beat Route and The Wag. Its late-night coffee bars, such as the Bar Italia in Frith Street, continue to provide essential early-morning refreshment for homeward-bound clubbers, many of whom get an extra heritage hit from being in a 'legendary Soho coffee bar'.

In the early 80s, when lesbians and gays were coming out of the closet but not yet into the full glare of mainstream society, the seedier side of Soho became a gay ghetto. In the following decade, during which homosexuals gained more confidence and 'the pink economy' grew equally rapidly, Soho's gay ghetto expanded and smartened up. Now the main drag through the district, Old Compton Street, is often referred to as 'the gay street'. George Melly recalls that Soho, with its ethnically mixed population, 'always was a tolerant place', so it is hardly surprising that London's gay community should have made Soho its base camp. The open gayification of Old Compton Street is an indication of how much more tolerant Britain has become (the bomb that exploded there in 1999 was planted by an isolated loner; but the continuing tendency for gays to huddle together in Soho also shows that there is still some distance to go.

On a smaller scale, the bohemian atmosphere of Soho has been reproduced in bars and cafés all over Britain. But the generalisation of the Soho-Boho could never have occurred without the original to copy from. Neither London nor the rest of Britain would be the same without it.

PARENTS Left Bank, Greenwich Village
CHILDREN The small-scale Sohos that now exist in every sizeable city in Britain
READ ON *Adrift in Soho* by Colin Wilson; *Soho in the Fifties* by Daniel Farson; *Low Life* by Jeffrey Bernard

Soul II Soul
Funki Dreds

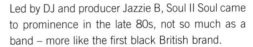

Led by DJ and producer Jazzie B, Soul II Soul came to prominence in the late 80s, not so much as a band – more like the first black British brand.

Jazzie B (b. Beresford Romeo, 26 January 1963, London, England; rapper), and Daddae (Philip Harvey; multi-instrumentalist) started a sound system in the early 80s: 'an organisation [which] came together to build upon making careers for people who had been less fortunate within the musical and artistic realms'. They built up a reputation by playing blues parties, street parties, youth clubs and regularly at the Paddington Dome, near King's Cross, London where they met subsequent collaborator Nellee Hooper, formerly of the Wild Bunch. By the end of the decade, their new residence at the Africa Centre, Covent Garden, was attracting a large and loyal crowd. Jazzie B had a regular DJ'ing spot on then **pirate radio** station Kiss FM and Soul II Soul were signed to Virgin subsidiary Ten Records.

As well as their sound, Jazzie and Daddae were

Jazzy B

known for their look, which combined the rootsiness of **rasta** (dreadlocks) with the cool modernism of American funk and Philly. The two influences came together in a figurative logo, the Funki Dred, which in turn became a T-shirt design and a motif for a range of clothes (and ultimately a record label). Soul II Soul were a clothes shop in **Camden Town** before they became a chart-topping band: the merchandising came first, then they developed a musical outlet for it.

Debut single 'Fairplay', featuring singer Rosie Windross, gained a hearing in London clubs and attracted the attention of the music press. 'Feel Free', with Do'Reen as lead vocalist, topped the dance charts. The slinky sound of 'Keep On Movin'' (vocals by Caron Wheeler) peaked at No 5 in the national charts (1989). Follow-up single 'Back To Life' reached No 1 (1989), and the debut album *Club Classics Volume One* (1989) went double platinum. They were also the first real sound of black Britain to be taken seriously and to gain commercial success in the States.

Mounting successes allowed Jazzie B to establish a recording complex in a converted warehouse in Camden. The early part of 1990 saw Soul II Soul diversify into various ventures: a film company, a talent agency and an embryonic record label. There was talk of Soul II Soul as Britain's answer to Tamla Motown (Jazzie B's ill-fated record label Funki Dred was backed by Motown money). But the group's creative impetus seemed to dissipate after the departure of Wheeler and co-producer Nellee Hooper (to **Massive Attack**). In addition, the British music scene moved swiftly on, leaving Soul II Soul as something of a period piece. Subsequent releases have been critically panned as being too conservative and the band were dropped by Virgin in 1996 (they resigned to Island).

With their slogo, 'a happy face a thumpin' bass for a lovin' race', Soul II Soul signposted the communal high of rave and the multiculturalism of **drum'n'bass**. But they themselves were unable to provide the soundtrack to the popular realisation of these experiences. Although the soft funk style of their music is not entirely out of place today, subsequent producers have tended to apply it as a quote or sample rather than work within it as a full-blown genre. Perhaps Jazzie B was too rooted in the musical styles associated with analogue recording to exploit the potential of digitisation. As one of the first black Britons to combine creativity with entrepreneurship, his most lasting contribution is business-based rather than purely musical. Before Soul II Soul, black music was either radical and rootsy or commercial and safe. Since they came on the scene, commercialism and cultural identity have become much more closely integrated.

PARENTS the Sigma Sound of Philadelphia, Prince, Misty in Roots, Eddy Grant

Johnny Speight
Creator of Britain's biggest bigot

Son of a London docker (born 1920), would-be jazz musician and successful scriptwriter Johnny Speight was turned on to drama by the witty journalism of George Bernard Shaw. He assumed that Shaw was a comedian, and was surprised to see a row of his published plays on the shelf of his local library in Canning Town. 'Reading Shaw was to me at that time as near as one could get to a divine revelation,' he recalled.

Speight began his writing career in the 50s, working on sketches for Frankie Howerd, Eric Sykes and **Spike Milligan**. By the end of the decade he was writing plays for TV: his play *The Compartment* (1962) provided **Michael Caine** with his first starring role. But it was not until 1967 when he came up with the character of Alf Garnett (originally Alf Ramsey but that was also the name of England's football manager, so it had to be changed) that Speight himself came to the attention of the British viewing public. What began as a one-off play turned into the long-running BBC series *Till Death Us Do Part*.

Bald-headed Alf, played with just the right combination of malice and vulnerability by Warren Mitchell (Speight had wanted **Peter Sellers**), was a West Ham supporter and a working-class Tory of the old school: contemptuous of blacks, Jews, 'long-haired gits' like his son-in-law (played by **Tony Blair**'s father-in-law, Tony Booth) and 'silly moos' (women), such as his sensible but deadpan wife

Elsie (Dandy Nichols in her finest role). Alf dominated the programme, just as he tried to be a legend in his own front room; but all his schemes came to nothing and Speight meant for his prejudices to be mocked and discredited accordingly.

That was not how some people saw it, however. Apart from complaints about swearing from fuddy-duddy Mary Whitehouse of the newly formed National Viewers' and Listeners' Association, some leftish critics thought that Alf's prejudices might be taken at face value. Their concerns increased the following year when Enoch Powell made his 'rivers of blood' anti-immigration speech (a bit rich from the man who, as a Tory employment minister during the early 50s, had mounted a recruitment drive in the West Indies), and dockers from Alf's home ground were demanding 'Enoch for Prime Minister'. In 1968 Speight was asked by 'BBC liberals' to tone down some of Alf's opinions. He was unwilling to do so, on the grounds that 'I didn't create Alf Garnett, society did.'

The focus on Alf's bigotry has detracted attention from the real basis of the comedy in *Till Death Us Do Part*: the generation gap. Alf's opinions are as old as his homburg hat and muffler; he is constantly beaten down by the younger generation – long-haired Mike and his wife/Alf's daughter, played by Una Stubbs. Elsie is clever enough to see that they are the future, but Alf won't budge from his old ways. This was a comedy derived from Britain's attempt at modernisation (Alf was conceived while prime minister Harold Wilson's talk of 'the white heat of technology' still resonated throughout the land), and all the stuff about blacks and Jews was initially included to substantiate Alf's old-fashioned character. But gradually his prejudices took centre stage, and the comedy became less sharp as a result.

Speight himself seems to have been carried away with the hateful aspects of Alf. Featuring Spike Milligan as a blacked-up Pakistani, his next work was the largely unsuccessful sitcom *Curry and Chips* (1969), which was taken off air after a short run. In 1985 Alf, now a pensioner, came back with an equally elderly Elsie for *In Sickness and in Health*. But in the 90s this too was pulled following complaints about Alf's attitudes to lesbians and AIDS. If censorship was not really the question of the day in the 60s when the rows between old Alf and young Mike represented the real conflict in British society, a quarter of a century later when Alf was buried by political correctness, censorship had become the burning issue. Speight hated working in that kind of atmosphere: 'There is terrible censorship now. So many subjects are taboo. It seems to me that if you want to write the truth you have to be careful not to be too truthful.' Lifelong socialist and radical, he died in 1998.

PARENTS George Bernard Shaw
CHILDREN Ian Chappell

Spice Girls

Are you really, really real?

On their way up the Spice Girls were celebrated as the real thing: yer actual young British women, feisty, sassy and smarter than their menfolk. After a couple of years of Spicemania, the backlash kicked in and they were reviled as a manufactured act with no street cred (unlike the upcoming All Saints). Among people who take pop music seriously the hostility continues; meanwhile the Spice Girls still sell millions of records to people who, like them, are game for a laugh.

In 1994 managers Bob and Chris Herbert auditioned dozens of candidates for an all-girl group. The hopefuls they chose were Melanie Chisholm from Cheshire, former child actress and model (girlfriend of the Milky Bar Kid) Emma Bunton, Melanie Brown from Leeds, Victoria Adams from Hertfordshire, and (the oldest of the troupe) Geraldine Estelle Halliwell, Watford-born daughter of a Jehovah's witness whose showbiz CV included 'glamour modelling' and a stint as a gameshow hostess on Turkish TV. The chosen five were put through a course of singing and dancing lessons, and assigned nicknames (Mel C/Sporty, Baby, Mel B/Scary, Posh and Geri/Ginger) which suggested a gang of girls-next-door (in yer face but not violent; they knew how to rap but wouldn't mug you). Their spectrum of regional accents and different styles of dress (tracksuits and trainers for Sporty, designer dresses and Emma Peel catsuits for Posh) signalled both variety and togetherness (they could all have fitted in at any young people's party anywhere in Britain). They were not uniform, but they shared a common attitude which came to be known as Girl Power ('we don't only talk about Girl Power, we live it,' said the blurb on the back of their first video compilation).

'Tell me what you want, what you really, really want'. The intro-chant of the Spice Girls' first single, 'Wannabe', was a not so much a request as a declaration that these girls were upfront, rebellious (the accompanying video shows them running riot, in a friendly fashion, through a posh gents' joint) and sometimes sexually aggressive – a recurring stance that was reprised in the title of their fourth No 1 single, 'Who Do You Think You Are?'. Far from being intimidated by new lads, the Spice Girls could out-party the lot of 'em, as an intrepid reporter from **Loaded** found out when he tried to keep pace. Showing off her tattoo for the first time, Ginger Spice explained that she did not cry when it was done because 'women are stronger than men'. She said this while in the Mojave Desert to shoot the video for 'Say You'll Be There' (their second No 1), which echoes Russ Meyer's girl-gang movie *Supervixens*. Girl Power was not about spikey dykes and dungarees; but about glamorous girls having fun on their own terms. Some commentators dubbed them post-feminists; others, like the American critic Camille Paglia, suggested that they harked back to the 60s and the days of 'sorority girls'. As with other **laddettes** it's ultimately unclear whether they are an empowered step forward or an enserfed step back, puppets on a string or self-made icon entrepreneurs.

The Spice Girls were young, energetic and diverse, yet they acknowledged British national traditions (Ginger's Union Jack mini-dress with a ban-the-bomb logo on the back; the V-for-Victory sign that became as much theirs as Winston Churchill's). When they pinched Prince Charles' bottom and pronounced it 'wobbly', you knew their irreverence was mixed with affection. Above all they seemed to genuinely get off on the pleasure they gave their audiences (mainly teen or pre-teen, predominantly female: the audience response to their concerts consisted of girls screaming at girls). It was a winning combination. Their first six singles went to No 1, and their debut album (*Spice*) sold 16 million copies. For a while the credibility of national politicians hung on how many Spice Girls they could name (**Tony Blair**, 3; John Major, 2); and when the Girls seemed to say, in an article in the *Spectator*, that they would be voting Tory in the 1997 general election, this became headline news (they maintained that their comments had been misconstrued).

Late in 1997, while one or two of the Spice Girls seemed to be battling with the bulge (pregnancy for Mel B and Posh), their whole reputation went pear-shaped. Manager Simon Fuller (the Girls had sacked the Herberts) had concluded a series of lucrative sponsorship deals with Pepsi, Sony, Benetton, BT and Asda. Suddenly they looked like just another packaged, supermarket product. Although they got rid of Fuller in November 1997, the image of the Spice Girls as street-real girls next door was irretrievably damaged. In May 1998 the image of a tight-knit girl gang took another batter-ing when Ginger, now known only as Geri, walked out just as the Girls were about to appear on the National Lottery TV show (the video accompanying the Spice Girls/England football team World Cup anthem 'How Does It Feel To Be On Top Of The World?' was outdated overnight – long before England were knocked out). In the wake of Geri's exit a former chauffeur reported that the others (especially Mel B) had teased and taunted her about her limitations as a singer and performer. For an uncomfortable moment the four that were left were dubbed 'The Spite Girls'.

While the Samaritans offered counselling to those traumatised by the prospect of Ginger-less Spice, various pundits suggested that the remaining Girls would be unable to cope without the media savvy of their elder sister ('four will become none, and probably sooner rather than later,' according to the *Guardian*'s Caroline Sullivan). In fact their first post-Geri single, 'Viva Forever', went straight in at No 1. The days of Spicemania were over, but the photographs of Victoria 'Posh' Adams, football millionaire David Beckham and their new-born son Brooklyn, still filled the front pages nearly a year after Geri's departure (she did lots of charity work and at Prince Charles' 50th sang a breathy version of 'Happy Birthday To You' in imitation of Marilyn Monroe's serenading of birthday boy John F Kennedy).

Slammed as a second-rate copy of **The Beatles**' *A Hard Day's Night* (in 1999 Radio 1 listeners voted it the worst film ever made), *Spiceworld: the Movie* grossed US$70 million, topped in the States only by *Titanic*. In 1996 the Spice Girls won three awards in the poll run by *Smash Hits* magazine; in 1998 they were voted Worst Group (Geri was also voted Worst Dressed and Least Fanciable). But the Spice Girls' grit and gumption has turned out to be more than just an image. Despite their lowly position in the hierarchy of British culture, these plucky girls have shown the Blitz spirit and carried on regardless.

PARENTS the Andrews Sisters, Pan's People, the Nolans, Margaret Thatcher

Dusty Springfield
White soul

With her backcombed blonde hair and heavy black 'panda' eyeshadow, Dusty Springfield (b. Mary Isabel Catherine Bernadette O'Brien, 1939) was a monochrome madonna for the black-and-white 60s. She was also the blackest-sounding white woman singer ever to emerge from Britain.

After a few hits with her brother's folk-tinged trio, The Springfields, late in 1963 Dusty Springfield embarked on a solo career. Her string of chart-toppers include 'I Only Want To Be With You', 'I Just Don't Know What To Do With Myself', 'In The Middle Of Nowhere' and 'I Close My Eyes And Count To Ten' – all between 1964 and 1968. Other British singers (Lulu, Sandie Shaw, Cilla Black) were juvenile by comparison. With a voice both breathy and mellifluous, Dusty was an adult who had soul – the kind of older woman that most **Mod**

teenagers could only dream of.

As the host of her own BBC TV show in the late 60s, Dusty introduced a succession of sophisticated performers to British audiences – Jimi Hendrix, Tina Turner, Scott Walker. In 1968 she dared to work with the cream of American sessions musicians in Memphis, recording a celebrated album, *Dusty in Memphis*, which also provided the last of her big solo hits, 'Son Of A Preacher Man' (1968).

With backing musicians Dusty was demanding, with waiters and officials she could be stroppy. Deported from South Africa for refusing to perform in front of segregated audiences, she rejected comedy actor Derek Nimmo's criticisms of her conduct. 'Prat,' she retorted. She also whacked drummer Buddy Rich after a row about top billing in a New York theatre.

In the early 70s Dusty moved to LA but did not fit in there ('it was sort of *nouveau riche*, the trouble was I was not very *nouvelle* and not very *riche*'). Between 1974 and 1977 she did plenty of drinking but no recording. In 1975 she gave an interview to the *London Evening Standard* which hinted at her sexuality (lesbian). It did her no favours at the time, but in 1987 she was asked to record with the **Pet Shop Boys**. Her guest vocal on their single 'What Have I Done To Deserve This?' was her first chart action in more than a decade and 'a watershed in my life'.

Fêted in a BBC documentary, receiving good reviews for her 1995 LP *A Very Fine Love* – it seemed like the lean years were over for Dusty. But in 1995 she was diagnosed with breast cancer, and in 1998 it recurred. She died in March 1999.

Dusty Springfield belonged to a generation of singers who were not expected to write songs. Her interpretation of other people's work was as distinctive and original as the songs themselves. She broadened the emotional range of pop, turning it – like jazz – into the kind of music you don't have to grow out of. She also proved that white British singers could sound as hurt as blacks and almost as sophisticated as Sinatra.

PARENTS Aretha Franklin, Julie London

Rod Stewart
Ur-lad

'My passions are soccer, drinking and women – in that order,' says Rod Stewart. In *Rock Dreams* (1972), the book of iconic images co-produced by Nik Cohn and Guy Peelaert, he is depicted as a hooligan in the grip of arresting officers, but still with an impish grin on his face: he's having a real good time. Nearly 30 years later ('I treat my body like a machine and look after it. It's like an old Austin 70'), Rod's image is much the same. Older, sure, but still up for a spot of non-malicious mayhem.

Born (1945) in Highgate, North London, Stewart's early career shows the connections between British beatnik and the London-led **Mod** scene. Apart from a short stint as a gravedigger, young Rod went on CND marches and busked his

way around France (influences: blues, r'n'b and folkies like Ramblin' Jack Elliott) before becoming Rod the Mod and singing, alongside Long John Baldry, in Steampacket, the nearest any British band ever came to the soul music revues of mid-60s Stax and Tamla Motown. Stewart's early solo albums, *An Old Raincoat Won't Ever Let You Down* and *Gasoline Alley*, combine beat-up folk and soul brought together by his distinctive, rasping voice.

For the sleeve of *Gasoline Alley*, Rod sports his trademark feather cut ('the pineapple'): too long for Mod, too modern for hippie. Together with his overgrown nose and twinkling, boyish eyes (the eyes of a boy who knows Mama will give him what he wants), this was the look he brought to The Faces, the remnants of **The** (ex-Mod) **Small Faces** after singer Steve Marriott's exit. While many of their contemporaries went from psychedelia to **progressive**, Rod and the lads deliberately regressed to good-time rock'n'roll: they were the original men who should know better. Their ostentatious unseriousness (playing football on *Top of the Pops* when they should have been miming, with **John Peel** sitting in on mandolin) masked a high degree of musicianship. This combination made them the best British live band of the early 70s – the live tracks on *Long Player* (an LP called *Long Player* – geddit?) bear this out.

Rod was living it up large, but he still had an eye for the main chance. He kept his solo career on the boil, and the songs he wrote with acoustic guitarist Martin Quittenton (including the big hits 'Maggie May' and 'You Wear It Well') were far superior to The Faces' studio work. Rod and The Faces drifted

Rod Stewart

apart when the single 'Sailing', written by Scottish folk duo the Sutherland Brothers, and the solo album he made in the USA, *Atlantic Crossing*, crossed over into the mainstream American market.

Rod followed the big money and moved to LA (in 1999 his personal fortune was estimated at £62 million). Critics claim that he lost his integrity when he emigrated. They make unfavourable comparisons between 'cheesy' disco-rock tracks, epitomised by 'Do You Think I'm Sexy?' (1982), and the high moral tone of 'The Killing Of Georgie', the epic protest against gay-bashing that appeared on *A Night On The Town* (1976). They also maintain that when Rod dyed his hair (blonds have more fun, right?) and swapped tartan for leopardskin, he lost his roots. But Rod's roots were always artificial. His father was Scottish, but he was a north-London boy who chose to idolise Manchester United's Caledonian striker Denis Law. In any case, a life of blonde women (Joanna Lumley, Britt Ekland, Alana Hamilton, Kelly Emberg, Kelly LeBrock, Teri Copley, Rachel Hunter), sports cars and nose candy was entirely consistent with Rod's Mod heritage. This is just what the boys in parkas always wanted.

When Rod settled in the USA, his British fan base changed. **Nick Hornby** has described the experience of buying *Every Picture Tells A Story*, the 1971 album that contains 'Maggie May' and a scorching version of Jimmy Ruffin's '(I Know) I'm Losing You': 'Rod wasn't a mere recording artiste,' he notes, 'he was a lifestyle.' The lifestyle Rod represented ('all you needed to do to acquire Rodness was drink, sing, pick up girls and like football') was particularly attractive to teenage middle-class males who liked football but were not of it, hadn't mastered picking up girls yet, were too shy to sing, but were learning fast how to drink. A host of Hornbys latched on to Rod as the epitome of the working-class lad they wanted to be. Hornby goes on to say how, at Cambridge, he used Rod as an emblematic defence ('a talisman') against 'the Athena prints of Renoir and Matisse paintings that hung on my neighbours' walls, and the classical music I occasionally heard coming from their stereos'.

To his credit, Hornby stayed loyal ('an ironic devotion') when Rod made his Atlantic crossing. But as soon as Stewart became a fixture in the heartland of the blue-collar masses, he was dumped by most of the British, middle-class proto-lads who had previously adored him. Only in the late 90s did it become OK to like him again. When James Brown, founder of **Loaded**, turned up at the LWT studios for the making of *An Audience With Rod Stewart*, his Americanisation was forgotten and Rod was re-admitted into the gallery of great British rogues. His reputation was re-affirmed by a photo on the front page of **The Sun** showing Rod drinking Gazza under the table. But he nearly blew it by declaring 'I've got more in common with Liam Gallagher than Eric Clapton. **Oasis** are like The Faces were in the 70s', and by releasing an album (*When We Were The New Boys*, 1998) of songs by the likes of Oasis and **Primal Scream**. This was all a bit too obvious. The latter-day Hornbys like to think that they alone have discovered that Rod Stewart is really all right, and it spoils their fun if everyone's in on the rehabilitation of Rod.

PARENTS: Ramblin' Jack Elliott, Chuck Berry, the Artful Dodger
READ ON *Rod Stewart: the biography* by Ray Coleman

St Luke's
Advertising ethics

No boss. No board of directors. Every employee an equal shareholder after six months with the company. St Luke's (named after the former hospital in which it is based) is a new advertising agency (b. 1991) that sounds like an old dream come true.

Co-founded by chairman Andy Law, St Luke's was set up to provide 'fun, happiness and profitability'. Within the working day, employee/shareholders are allowed time to socialise, so as to encourage 'thinking together'. Decisions are taken by an elected group called The Quest. One of their decisions was to set up a training budget, known as 'Make Yourself More Interesting', of which anyone can claim their share. The women in this feminised workplace also get to choose a Man of the Month from among their y-chromosome colleagues.

St Luke's is known for its ethical stance. When it pitched to GM food manufacturers Monsanto, it advised the client to pay for anti-GM campaigners to take out equal advertising space (St Luke's didn't get the job but Monsanto did include links to Greenpeace sites in its adverts). Impressed by its reputation as *the* agency of the 90s, New Labour's Department for Education and Employment awarded St Luke's an £11-million contract (out of a total budget of £3.5 billion) to provide the ads for the New Deal benefits-to-work programme. Senior government adviser Geoff Mulgan has also identified St Luke's as the kind of agency New Labour can do business with.

From the 50s, when American critic Vance Packard exposed the men of Madison Avenue as 'the hidden persuaders', to the 80s when the Saatchi brothers were renowned as 'masters of illusion', the advertising industry has been associated with artifice and, on occasion, dishonesty. St Luke's, on the other hand, identifies itself by not being like other agencies and is associated with authenticity and ethical correctness. At times, it comes close to a cult, as when a member of The Quest complained that employee/shareholders giving flowers to others was establishing a pecking order contrary to the egalitarian ethos of the jointly owned, non-hierarchichal company.

Chairman Andy Law believes that the St Luke's egalitarian approach is 'changing business'. But within this changing environment, familiar patterns seem to re-emerge. Some employees have said that there is 'a hidden hierarchy' at St Luke's, and others have noted that the 'right-on-ness' of the company engenders a sense of commitment that prompts shareholders (who do not receive a dividend) to work longer hours and more weekends for salaries that are slightly below the market rate. Now that's what used to be called 'man management'.

PARENTS Utopian socialists, William Morris

READ ON: *The Empty Raincoat* by Charles Handy; *Connexity* by Geoff Mulgan

Stone Roses
Waiting for the resurrection

Second albums are often a trial. After the slow-burning success of their first LP, the Stone Roses turned the making of their second into a five-year saga that almost overshadows their actual music. Their legendary failure to deliver has become a mighty monument to the fragile and momentary character of pop music.

Singer Ian Brown (b. 1963, the mouthy one) and guitarist John Squire (b. 1962, the quiet one) both went to Altrincham grammar school (south of Manchester). They first played together in The Patrol (modelled on The Clash). When The Patrol went nowhere they quit music and took up **scooter**ing (Brown's scooter was emblazoned with the motto: 'cranked up really high'), while working in a **dole** office (Brown) and an animation studio (Squire; he made the models for *Wind in the Willows* and *Dangermouse*). Meanwhile bass player Gary 'Mani' Mounfield (b. 1962) had attended Xaverin College, a Catholic grammar school on the north side of the city, before becoming one of Manchester's Perrys, the post-punk, pre-**Madchester** equivalent to Liverpool's scallies with a modish taste for Fred Perry sportswear and European 'gear' such as Tachini, Ellesse and Lacoste jeans. Born (1964) and brought up in the Ardwick-Gorton area (to the north of the city centre), Alan 'Reni' Wren learnt to play drums in his parents' pub.

The Stone Roses were a collection of contradictions. Two of them came from south Manchester (softer), where the city becomes suburban and more middle class. The other two were from the north side (harder), where council estates and terraced houses pan out into Lancashire mill towns. The band was conscious of its contrasts. Explaining the origins of the Stone Roses, Squire said that 'the idea was to include art and wild sounds with attractive melodies. We chose the name because it reflected this contradiction.'

This was a band that behaved like a street gang while painting their guitars (Gretsch, Gibson Les Paul and Rickenbacker bass) and album sleeves in the style of American Abstract-Expressionist Jackson Pollock. *Melody Maker* cranked up the contradictions still higher by describing them as 'four blokes from the Stretford End (Manchester United's home fans' terrace) and four teenage Jesus Christs' (they were all in their twenties at the time).

The Stone Roses came together in 1985. In their early days (playing Manchester's first warehouse parties and hooking up with manager Gareth Evans, owner of important local live venues International 1 and International 2), they looked and sounded something like the Jesus and Mary Chain, the doomy, feedback-obsessed outfit who signed with **Alan McGee**'s Creation Records and later sacked him. Brown's on-stage presence was wired rather than relaxed (he would come down from the stage and walk through the audience winding people up), and the sound behind him was essentially rock music sieved through post-punk (the 1985 tracks they recorded with Martin Hannett, released years later as Garage Flowers). **Ecstasy** changed all that. From 1987 onwards their sound became groovier, the drums loosened up (Reni had spent years playing along with jazz records; Brown later said that 'the reason I loved the Roses was because we had a great beat'), and Squire made more of his wah-wah guitar (via Jimi Hendrix and psychedelia/blaxploitation as in 'Psychedelic Shack' by the Temptations), interspersed with shards of pared-down James Brown funk. Although Ian Brown continued to hero-worship boxers and maintained an arrogant Muhammad Ali-style patter (demonstrated in his dealings with the press and when he turned down the support slot on a **Rolling Stones** tour), like Ali he also learnt to relax and roll with it.

The end of the 80s was the high point of **rave** culture and the new dance music. Although by no means all their songs were now dance tracks, the E-driven Stone Roses became a rock band infused with a dance sensibility. With a foot in both camps, they swore allegiance to neither. Squire said that some of the new dance music seemed to have been written by a 'computer virus', while Brown rejected the rock'n'roll ethos as 'redneck'. Produced by John Leckie, who learnt his trade as tape operator for the Pink Floyd, their first album (*The Stone Roses*, 1989) was a triumph that transcended both sides (Brown always resisted the idea

that there were sides, insisting that the soul/dance and pop/rock constituencies had never been that far apart). Opening with the chugging bass and crystal guitar of 'I Wanna Be Adored', riffing through 'This Is The One', matching the traditional tune to 'Scarborough Fair' with anti-monarchy lyrics ('Elizabeth, My Dear'), and evoking the spirit of the student revolt of 1968 ('Bye, Bye Badman'), the album received mixed reviews (*Billboard*: 'gloom-rock derived … old-time psychedelia'), but has since come to be recognised as the best of its generation, and an all-time classic to boot (voted No 1 in the *Q* magazine poll of great albums). A few weeks later the Stone Roses capped it with the 12-inch version (just under 10 minutes) of 'Fool's Gold', complete with catchy bassline, wah-wah overlaid by fluid lead guitar and Brown's husky voice. There was enough pop and sufficient sinister funk in the mix to warrant the description 'macabre Monkees'.

1990 was the year when 'Madchester' was made in **Tony Wilson**'s Factory. The Stone Roses stood aside from it, and Brown once said that Manchester-ism was as small-minded as patriotism. Their contribution to 1990 was the big gig at Spike Island, an attempt to celebrate the new found E-friendship between young people from Manchester and Liverpool, which was marred by uncongenial surroundings in the midst of a rust-belt industrial landscape.

The Stone Roses may not have considered themselves part of Wilson's 'community' but when its star began to wane, theirs did too, although a contentious interview with veteran rock writer Nick

Kent (*The Face*) and a fractious performance on BBC2's *The Late Show* (complete with power failure) kept them in the headlines for a while.

By this time the Stone Roses had already embarked upon their second album, which proved almost as elusive as the Holy Grail. First there were contractual difficulties. At their lowest ebb, manager Gareth Evans had signed the band to a poor deal with Silvertone, a small subsidiary of the South African publishing giant Zomba, run by veteran talent-spotter Andrew Lauder. Attempts to renegotiate the deal proved unsuccessful, and in the process the band fell out with Evans (a previous conflict with another record company, FM Revolver, had led to its offices and the managing director's car being sprayed, and convictions for wilful damage). They were snapped up by the US label Geffen, run by David Geffen formerly of Bread, which inadvertently found itself funding a further four years of virtual inactivity by the band that came to be called the Stoned Roses ('we were in cosmic intellectual retirement' – Brown). Squire got into cocaine and Reni followed the Reds (Manchester United) everywhere. After trying a succession of studios and finally settling on Rockfield in Monmouth, they stayed there so long that Mani married a local girl and set up home in the town.

Eventually there was an album, knowingly entitled *The Second Coming*, complete with loops and multiple edits (they recorded about as much tape as Terence Malick shot feet of film for *The Thin Red Line*, 1999). According to Mancunian music journalist John Robb, it also combined 'hard rock and English folksiness' in the manner of Led Zeppelin.

Accompanied by a deliberately grainy video, the single 'Love Spreads' went straight in at No 2. But after so many expectations over such a long period of time, it was bound to be something of a let-down. While fans and reviewers wondered what to make of it, the Stone Roses themselves drifted further apart. Drummer Reni upped sticks and left in 1995. The long-awaited comeback gig (with new drummer) at Glastonbury had to be cancelled when Squire broke his shoulder while mountain-biking (Pulp stole the show). In 1996 Squire left to form The Seahorses (they split early in 1999 and there were rumours that the Stone Roses would reform). Brown and Mani played the Reading Festival in 1996 (decried as 'a travesty') before Mani went further north to join Glasgow's **Primal Scream**.

Jailed in October 1998 having been convicted of 'air rage', Brown was released on Christmas Eve (he had already released a solo album, *Unfinished Monkey Business*) and went on to record with James Lavelle's UNKLE project. He remains a compelling mixture of arrogance and cool self-deprecation: 'The Stone Roses at their height were capable of going places Oasis can only dream about … **Oasis** are okay but they are like *The Sun*: base … I'm the only singer that will never be copied on *Stars In Their Eyes*. There's no one to do me, because they're all in bands making a living from my act. … People confuse my confidence with arrogance. All we were ever saying was "we're beautiful and so are you".'

Brown had a point when he said that he is the model for many of today's frontmen. From Liam Gallagher downwards (saw the Stone Roses at 16 and felt inspired) those influenced by him (and his thousand-yard stare) are legion. Above and beyond Brown's personal magnetism, the Stone Roses are important because they managed to reinvest rock with a cool mystique – something they achieved partly by their playing and partly by their protracted silence.

PARENTS 60s west coast psychedelia,
Led Zeppelin
CHILDREN Oasis
READ ON *The Stone Roses and the Resurrection of British Pop* by John Robb

Suede
Miss-hit

'We did instigate the blueprint that later became known as **Britpop**,' claims lead singer Brett Anderson. But in *The Sunday Times* Robert Sandall once dismissed Suede as 'the most hyped band in the history of rock' and despaired of their 'humourlessness'. Are they under-rated innovators or over-sold imitators? Or perhaps the real problem with Suede is that they chose to play-act the Jim Stark-role of Alienated Originators at a time when the hyper-ordinary (as in **Oasis**) was just coming into fashion?

Asthmatic Anderson was born in Hayward's Heath, a town that doesn't know whether it is inside or outside the commuter belt. His parents were not

well off, but well into art and music. He remembers 'hanging around 7–11s' as an 'aimless youth', buying records by the Sex Pistols, The Smiths and the Pet Shop Boys. 'There is a real punkish aspect to Suede,' Anderson later said. He lasted two weeks at Manchester University before trying his hand at architecture at University College, London: he never qualified. With high cheekbones and an expression reminiscent of the young **David Bowie** (when he wasn't hiding it behind lank long hair), he practised the look that **Peter York** calls the Neurotic Boy Outsider. **Tony Parsons** suggested that 'in his photographs he can make Oscar Wilde seem like Mike Tyson'.

In the late 80s and early 90s Suede spent 'three years hanging around London on the **dole**, wearing suits and singing in English accents'. The accents were also reminiscent of Bowie, and the guitar sound carried on where Johnny Marr left off. As one of the protégés of **Camden**-based publicists Savage and Best, Suede started to get noticed: in 1992–93 they were on 20 front covers and John Best won the *Music Week* award for best press campaign. When *Select* launched Britpop with the infamous 'Yanks Go Home' feature in April 1993, Suede (winners of the second annual Mercury Music Prize) were at the centre of the new in-crowd. Patriots of pop, they dared to tour the USA at the height of Seattle-based grunge.

Maybe Anderson took himself too seriously. He got embroiled in a needless row with *The Face*. Personal friction pushed Bernard Butler, guitarist and co-songwriter, out of the band. Anderson liked to make faux-controversial comments such as 'I

Brett Anderson

see myself as a bisexual man who's never had a homosexual experience.' This was like Bowie without the balls. It annoyed many people in the gay community, who thought he had no right to play with their identity, and it was famously mocked by comedians David Baddiel and Chris Newman. Rejecting the accusation that he was just using gay imagery (gay iconography was an identifiable aspect of the minor-hit singles 'My Insatiable One' and 'Animal Nitrate'), Anderson later insisted, 'I'm involved in it [the gay world] through my friends.'

From being the golden boy of the pop press, Anderson became its whipping boy. By 1994 he had acquired an unhelpful reputation as a superficial, super-sensitive dilettante. Pop is all about posing, but this – the years of **Oasis**, *Loaded* and pseudo-macho-masculinity – was not the time to look fey, quasi-gay and virtually neurotic. Britpop ran off without him, Suede missed their own bandwagon and, for a brief moment, Anderson really was an

Outsider. Afterwards he could only claim that 'we were instrumental in there being a renaissance in British music but we didn't care about it and went our own way'.

The years 1995–97 were spent 'regrouping' and trying to offset the negative image of 'bombast'. In 1996 Suede's third album, *Coming Up*, went straight in to the charts at No 1. According to bass player Matt Osman, *Head Music* (1999) contained 'a lot more tracks that work on the level of a groove', possibly the influence of producer Steve Osborne (part of the Perfecto remix team). Having missed the chance to be kings of guitar-based Britpop, Suede were moving on and moving up: in the summer of 1999 this album also went to the top of the charts.

In interviews given in 1999, Anderson sought to distance himself from his previous persona as a Neurotic Boy Outsider: 'Before, I was really into the idea of a life as a very difficult, complex thing. I wanted Suede to be this isolated little being, on its own, in its bedroom. Now, I want it to be more connected. … Bollocks to unhappiness, really. There's nothing better than feeling at peace with yourself.' Having visited his 'civilised residence in Notting Hill' and looked inside his 'peculiarly level head', *London Evening Standard* interviewer Zoe Williams credited Anderson with having 'conquered pop iconography'.

PARENTS David Bowie, The Smiths, Brinsley Schwarz

The Sun
Bastard tabloid

Owned by the Mirror Group and launched in 1964 as a Labour paper (successor to the trade union paper the *Daily Herald*; market research carried out by the first sociologist to identify the teenage consumer, Dr Mark Abrams), *The Sun* was smaller than a broadsheet and bigger than a tabloid: known in the print world as a bastard tabloid. For five years it was 'pale and watery': kept open only because to have closed it would have prompted the print unions, at the height of their power, to bring the rest of the parent company to a halt.

In 1969 new owner Rupert Murdoch (Australian-born, son of Sir Keith Murdoch who broke the First World War story about Allied inefficiency at Gallipoli and became a newspaper owner, kept a bust of Lenin in his rooms at Oxford, already a veteran of circulation wars down under) told staff that, henceforth, *The Sun* would be based on 'sex, sport and contests'. He appointed bluff Yorkshireman (same hometown as Geoffrey Boycott) Larry Lamb as editor. The first page-three girl appeared in 1973; but *The Sun* (now the 'soaraway *Sun*' as advertised on TV by Christopher Timothy) did not turn Tory until 1979. Far from it. When Margaret Thatcher, as education secretary in Tory Ted Heath's government, stopped free milk for schoolkids, *The Sun* coined the phrase 'Maggie Thatcher – milk snatcher'. However, during the 'winter of discontent' in the run-up to the general election of 1979, Lamb summed up Labour prime minister Jim Callaghan's

rebuttal of reporters' questions about 'mounting chaos' in the influential headline 'Crisis – what crisis?' Not a direct quote, but close enough to make Callaghan look complacent and a fool. He lost the election.

In the months prior to the 1979 election, Margaret Thatcher had been coming in for whisky and chats with Larry Lamb. He was knighted the following year. The year after that he made way for new editor Kelvin Mackenzie – educated at Alleyn's School, Dulwich, former editor of Murdoch's *New York Post*, and perhaps the most abusive man in Fleet Street (news editor Tom Petrie was once found banging his head against the wall – according to press historian Matthew Engel he said he was saving Mackenzie the trouble of giving him a bollocking). On 4 May 1982, the day after the Argentinian warship the *General Belgrano* was sunk by British missiles, Mackenzie went down in the history of journalism with the headline 'Gotcha' (when reports came in of the fatalities he toned down later editions with the replacement headline 'Did 1,200 Argies die?'). This was war reporting at its most aggressive.

Like Thatcher, Mackenzie helped identify and demonise the enemies within, such as Winston Silcott (convicted of killing PC Keith Blakelock at Broadwater Farm, 1985; conviction later overturned) and 'loonie lefties' like **Ken Livingstone** (Red Ken's call for troops out of Ireland made him *The Sun*'s 'most odious man in Britain'; only a few years previously proprietor Murdoch had suggested to editor Lamb that the paper should take this very line); and there were enemies without – 'Frogs', 'Krauts', and EC commissioner Jacques Delors (as in 'Up Yours, Delors!').

During Mackenzie's reign, *The Sun* also became known for blurring fact and fantasy (for example, the front-page headline 'Freddie Starr Ate My Hamster', 13 March 1986). *The Sun* was the first paper to develop a harmonious relationship with TV (previously newspapers had seen TV as a deadly rival), and there were times when TV actors and their characters seemed to merge into one (Dirty Den/Leslie Grantham, for instance). Mackenzie also oversaw *The Sun*'s move from Fleet Street to Wapping. Printers were locked out and replaced, and the unions never regained their power.

Mackenzie rejoiced that 'they haven't got us by the balls anymore'.

The Sun was credited with helping the Tories back into power in 1992 ('It's *The Sun* wot won it') and a Labour supporter wrote to the *Guardian* saying she did not like to sit next to *Sun* readers on the tube. But Mackenzie experienced famous reversals as well as victories: he lost a libel action brought by **Elton John**; he was forced to make a charitable donation for having nicked a family picture from the royals' Christmas card; and he eventually apologised to the city of Liverpool for saying that the fans in the Hillsborough disaster brought it upon themselves (sales of *The Sun* in Liverpool never recovered). Early in 1994 Mackenzie was eased out of the editor's chair to become managing director of Murdoch's Sky-TV (telling a parliamentary select committee they were 'nuts' may have accelerated his 'promotion'). His successors (Stuart Higgins and, latterly, Coventry Polytechnic graduate/ex-*New York Post* editor David Yelland) have not made anything like the same impression.

In the 80s *The Sun* seemed to carry almost as much authority as the Thatcher government. If previous governments, especially Labour ones, had spoken and listened to the masses via trades unions, in the Thatcher decade it was *The Sun* that seemed to play the role of liaising between government and working-class people. In those days the influence of *The Sun* was strong enough to provoke concern about the 'tabloidisation' of the broadsheets. But now *The Sun* no longer speaks with such authority, and with Yelland trying to take it upmarket to keep up with the success of the mid-

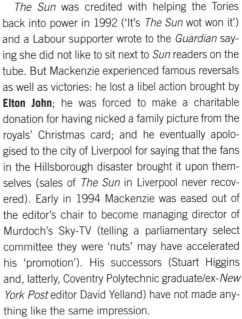

dlebrow *Mail*, it seems more appropriate to talk about the 'broadsheetisation' of the tabloids.

PARENTS *Daily Mirror*, *New York Post*, *Titbits*
READ ON *Tickling the Public* by Matthew Engel

Chris Tarrant
Not the man he Tiswas

In the late 1970s there was only one way to wake up after a hard-drinking Friday night: paracetamol washed down with mugs of tea, toast if you could stomach it, cigarettes (smoking was as compulsory then as non-smoking is now) and *Tiswas*, the anarchic Saturday-morning ITV programme made for children but watched in their dressing gowns by legions of lazy twentysomethings.

Tiswas was an amalgam of interviews, quizzes, comedy sketches and music. It had its roots in *Crackerjack!*, the 60s Friday-teatime kids' show made by the BBC and presented first by Eamonn Andrews and then by Leslie Crowther; but this was a *Crackerjack!* infused with the spirit of the Marx Brothers and laced with something rebellious, if not illegal. There were buckets of gunk to be thrown over unsuspecting members of the juvenile audience, John Gorman (late of Liverpool performance art/gallows humour group and occasional popsters The Scaffold) as the Masked Poet and Smello the Incredible Stinking Man, Spit the Dog – Brummie ventriloquist Bob Carolgee's dummy who did noth-ing but spit, **Lenny Henry** performing high-speed impersonations of TV naturalist David Bellamy, and the Phantom Flan Flinger – the missing link between Mr Pastry (of *Crackerjack!*) and Les Entractes – the hit squad who made the front pages in 1997 when they creamed Bill Gates full in the face. Presiding over this Saturday-morning mayhem were co-presenters Sally James and the lord of misrule himself, Chris Tarrant.

Blond, clean-shaven with regular features, Tarrant (b. 1946) could have been a straight man but chose television anarchy instead. Born in Reading, he attended the King's School, Worcester. After Birmingham University ('bluffer's degree' in English), he was a lorry driver and a schoolmaster in the East End. At 28 he joined ATV as a trainee. *Tiswas*, which he also produced, was his big break. As with all comedy, the timing was all: the Sex Pistols were still fresh in the collective memory, Tarrant was the Johnny Rotten of children's programming, and post-punks loved him for it.

After *Tiswas*, Tarrant moved on to a late-night grown-up version of the same thing, *OTT*. But *OTT* was on at the wrong time (Saturday night) and the fact that it was supposed to be anarchic – and that's official – made it less interesting. *Tiswas*, by contrast, was meant for kids and you felt that the adult anarchism (which in fact consisted of grown-ups behaving like kids) had been smuggled in illic-itly.

Tarrant was never as good again. He moved to Capital Radio where his pranksterish tone became just another ruse to cheer us up on a workaday morning. After a series of quiz shows (*Lose A*

Million, *The Main Event*, *Pop Quiz*, *Man O Man*), he moved on to present *Tarrant On TV*, which seemed to duplicate the formula for *The Clive James Show* (without an Australian accent but with the same readiness to poke fun at the Japanese). In 1999 he began hosting *Who Wants To Be A Millionaire?*, the riveting (because somebody might win a million) but ultimately mundane (everything except the prize money is formulaic) quiz show, for which he is said to have been paid £2.5 million.

Meanwhile the rest of medialand has caught up. Zaniness is now ubiquitous and nauseatingly de rigueur, as Nick Curtis pointed out in the *London Evening Standard*. Even Noel '*Swapshop*' Edmonds (Tarrant's Saturday-morning rival in the old days) has been hosting a House Party for Middle England that became as anarchic as only *Tiswas* once was.

PARENTS the Marx Brothers, *Crackerjack!*, *Do Not Adjust Your Set*
CHILDREN **Chris Evans**, *The Word*, L!VE TV

Peter Tatchell
Outraged

Born (1952) in Melbourne, Australia, Peter Tatchell was a keen surfer and athlete before emigrating to Britain in 1971 and becoming a leading campaigner for gay rights. As frontman for the campaign group Outrage! ('we want to achieve an end to homophobic prejudice, discrimination and vio-

lence'), Tatchell is associated with 'outing' closet gays in public life. His official line is more reticent: he recommends coming out on the basis that 'it removes the stress of leading a secret, double life', and because 'hiding your homosexuality reinforces the idea that it is shameful to be gay'; but insists that public figures should only be forcibly 'outed' if they are 'acting in a way that is hypocritical or homophobic' (not Peter Mandelson).

Tatchell has been attacked with iron bars, bottles and knives, and his home has been subject to arson attempts. He reports that 'the police tell me I am lucky to be alive. Doctors say that most people in my situation would have committed suicide.' But the winds of change have been blowing Tatchell's way. In 1983, as a parliamentary candidate in the south London constituency of Bermondsey, he lost a previously safe Labour seat to the Liberals after his sexual orientation became an issue in the press. In 1998, when Tatchell was threatened with imprisonment under a little-known ecclesiastical law after interrupting the Archbishop of Canterbury's Easter Sunday sermon (he was protesting about Archbishop Carey's voting record on the age of consent, but has also said that 'the Bible is to gays what *Mein Kampf* is to Jews'), most of the middle-class media rose to his defence. The Outrage! mission to 'transform cultural attitudes towards homosexuality' continues apace, whether this means quizing Michael Portillo on his double standards concerning gay rights or knobbling Robert Mugabe about Zimbabwe's anti-gay policies.

PARENTS the Suffragettes, Gay Liberation Front

Julien Temple

Well connected

Cambridge-educated Julien (his pipe-smoking mother preferred St Julien tobacco) Temple (b. 1955) summed up the punk side of the 70s when he directed *The Great Rock'n'Roll Swindle* (1978). He tried to set the tone for the 80s with *Absolute Beginners* (1986), a celluloid musical based on **Colin MacInnes**' novel of the same name (1959, the curtain raiser to swinging London). But the freshness of the original did not travel well into the stylisation of the 'designer decade'. Exiled to Hollywood, Temple directed *Earth Girls Are Easy* (1988; sci-fi as satirical sex comedy) before returning to Britain to make *Vigo: Passion For Life*, a biopic of the French film director Jean Vigo (1999). During 1999 he started work on *Pandemonium*, a film about William Wordsworth and Samuel Taylor Coleridge in the year (1798) they published the Ur-text of English Romanticism, *Lyrical Ballads*.

Temple now lives in Somerset, where his neighbour is Joe Strummer, formerly of The Clash (**Julian Cope** also lives nearby). Like Strummer (Westminster), Temple (Hampstead) was an upper-middle-class boy who turned his back on his family's social milieu (Strummer's dad was a diplomat, Temple's sister became the secretary of the Democratic Left). Equally alienated from his architecture degree, he played sax in a jazz band, The Bombers, before studying at the National Film School, buying a Bolex camera and making a Bosch-like short about drunkenness. By chance he heard the Sex Pistols rehearsing in Rotherhithe, followed them to their gigs and became their celluloid chronicler.

More than 20 years later, Temple is seeking to reconnect the Romanticism he encountered during his privileged education (Coleridge and co) with the **dole** queue dystopia of punk – hence his description of Coleridge as 'the first rock'n'roll casualty'. Like his near-neighbour Julian Cope, who has written extensively about Neolithic Britain, Temple is patching pop culture's recent past back into a much longer tradition.

PARENTS Jean Vigo, the Sex Pistols, Samuel Taylor Coleridge
READ ON *England Is Mine: pop life in Albion from Wilde to Goldie* by Michael Bracewell

Terry-Thomas

Male pygmalion

With his carnation, cigarette holder, trademark gap-toothed caddish grin and exaggerated diction ('absolute shaaaar' – shower), on stage and screen Terry-Thomas (not 'Terry Thomas') was the epitome of the English upper crust (comic actor Lionel Jefferies said he 'would have asked for a wine list in McDonald's'). But in life and in theatre this was a role he had to learn. For Terry-Thomas was really Thomas Terry Stevens, born (1911) in Finchley, North London: his father was a butcher and he first

worked as meat porter in Smithfield market (where he stood out from the rest by wearing suede shoes).

In the 30s Terry-Thomas found work as a film extra and dance teacher. He said he had little knowledge of dance but 'if you have confidence you can fool anybody', a comment that might also have been his philosophy of life. By the 40s he was appearing as a comedian on the variety circuit, where his upper-class *persona* contrasted with the wide-boy image of contemporaries such as Max Miller, and in films such as *The Brass Monkey* (1947). Adopted by the Boulting Brothers (the most important British film producers of the 50s), he played the role of the upper-class cad/bounder in many of their films, such as *Lucky Jim* (1957, from the novel by Kingsley Amis), in which Terry-Thomas tries to steal junior lecturer Jim Dixon's girl. He introduced his catchphrase 'absolute shower' as an army officer in John Boulting's *Private's Progress* (1956). The phrase was repeated by personnel officer Major Hitchcock in *I'm All Right Jack* (1959), where Terry-Thomas was pitted against **Peter Sellers** as a shop steward with Stalinist ambitions. He also appeared in *School for Scoundrels* in 1960 and, in *The Naked Truth* (1957), he played another cad Lord Henry Mayley, a peer caught with his pants down, set on masterminding revenge. By the 60s a brief look at the characters he played, both here and in the States, shows that this stereotype had stuck: Cadogan de Vere, Carlton-Browne (*Carlton-Browne of the FO*, 1959), Sir Harry Washington-Smythe (*Rocket to the Moon*, 1967), Sir Percy Ware-Armitage (*Those Magnificent Men In Their Flying Machines*, 1965).

Terry-Thomas was well known for forgetting his lines on set: the sherry-drinking scene in *I'm All Right Jack* needed 87 takes. But after 107 takes for a scene in *Brothers In Law* (1959; Terry-Thomas in the uncharacteristic role of a Cockney criminal), he never again appeared on set without knowing the script.

In order to develop his craft as a comic character actor, Terry-Thomas had to drop some of the theatrical mannerisms that had been his stock-in-trade in variety. But some of them came in useful for his TV shows, which, especially in the early days, were essentially a broadcast version of a music hall package. In 1956 Terry-Thomas was the first comedian to have his own TV show. In 1968 he was host of *The Big Show*, one of the last in a succession of brash variety programmes, of which the BBC's *Billy Cotton Band Show* was probably the best known. The following year he appeared in the first series of *The Old Time Music Hall*, which, along with *The Forsyte Saga* (the dramatisation of John Galsworthy's epic series of novels about a British bourgeois family), introduced the fashion for nostalgia on British television.

By this time the Terry-Thomas *persona* was a quaint anachronism, whereas originally it had been a larger-than-life rendition of a real-life social type. The cultural shift of the late 60s had left him without a role to play and on the big screen he was forced to subsist on small parts in low-budget shlock.

During the Second World War Terry-Thomas was had up for impersonating an officer with intent to 'purloin' carpets from the US Army in the hope of selling them on to a British officers' mess. In one sense he was impersonating a British gentleman all his life; but it was a role he was born to play. He relished having a fresh carnation delivered to his home every morning. When he became successful in the USA, he clearly enjoyed flying the Union Jack outside the place where he was staying. A man of 'enormous charm', who in 1974 told TV interviewer Michael Parkinson that his motto was 'I shall not be cowed', Terry-Thomas played his chosen role for as long as he could.

Sadly, he suffered from Parkinson's disease for many years and died, impoverished, in a church charity flat in Surrey in 1990. Less than a decade later the National Film Theatre hosted a season of his films at the South Bank.

PARENTS the British ruling class
CHILDREN Dick Dastardly, Vic Reeves

Mark Thomas
Thomas the Prank

Mark Thomas is the 80s alternative comedian who became an investigative TV prankster in the manner of America's Michael Moore (*Roger and Me*, 1989). In 1999 *The Mark Thomas Comedy Product* and the imported *Michael Moore Show* ran back to back on Channel 4.

Son of a builder, Thomas (b. 1963) won a scholarship to a public school and became 'middle class. Once you go to a public school you're no longer working class, no matter what you say. You change.' Not that he went into a traditional middle-class occupation. A drama student during the miners' strike of 1984–85, he became a left-wing political activist ('kicked out for nicking the paper money') and an alternative comedian, playing a packed schedule of miners' benefits in Labour clubs and the like. Of the 80s **alternative comedy** scene, he says it was never as big or as right-on as it's been made out to be: 'for every **Ben Elton** or Alexei Sayle there was a Rik Mayall dangling his goolies out'.

When alternative comedy became the mainstream, Thomas reconfigured himself into a new kind of investigative journalist – out to expose politicians and corporations, and laugh at them at the same time. Apart from Michael Moore, his models are hip American comedian Lenny Bruce and old-style campaigning journalist John Pilger. BNFL (nuclear waste) and McDonald's are among the prominent companies that have been embarrassed by him. Home secretary Jack Straw (refusal to legalise cannabis) was also a memorable target of Thomas the Prank.

An admirer of Noam Chomsky's neo-Marxist writings on the insidious power of the media, Thomas has no illusions about the political impact of his recent television work. 'The last thing I'm doing is infiltrating the system from the inside,' he says. 'The system is accommodating me so that they can show how liberal they are, simple as that. I'm Channel 4's pet rebel in the way that **John Peel** used to be Radio 1's pet rebel.'

Like his theoretical mentor, Thomas seems to over-estimate the conspiratorial capacity of media moguls. Rather than calculating that audiences will be deceived and pacified by the incorporation of radicals such as Thomas, perhaps the 'organisation men' in today's media are genuinely outraged by the activities of the wider social 'matrix', hence their willingness to commission his show and others of its ilk.

PARENTS Michael Moore, Lenny Bruce, John Pilger, Noam Chomsky

Emma Thompson
More famous than the male

Once the junior partner to husband **Kenneth Branagh**, since their break-up in 1995 it is Emma Thompson who has gone on to become the senior ex-partner.

Daughter (b. 1959) of Eric Thompson, writer of the British version of children's TV series *The Magic Roundabout*, and actress Phillida Law, Emma Thompson went to Edinburgh and Australia with the Cambridge Footlights, starring soon afterwards in ITV's comedy series *Alfresco* (1983) along with **Ben Elton** and Stephen Fry. She won two Bafta awards for best actress (the first for *Tutti Frutti* with Robbie Coltrane, the second for the epic series *Fortunes of War*, co-starring with her husband-to-be). Since then she has won Oscars (kept in the lavatory of her house in Hampstead) for acting in EM Forster's *Howard's End* (1993) and for her adaptation of Jane Austen's *Sense and Sensibility* (1996; also Oscar-nominated for her acting role). Her part as campaigning solicitor Gareth Pierce was one of the highlights of *In The Name Of The Father*, the big-screen dramatisation of the miscarriage of (British) justice against the (Irish) Guildford Four. Hollywood thought highly of her comedy performance opposite Arnold Schwarzenegger in *Junior*.

Touted in the early 90s as the dynamic duo of British film, in the tradition of Laurence Olivier and Vivien Leigh, Richard Burton and Elizabeth Taylor, 'Ken and Em' were pulled apart by their punishing schedules. According to Compton Miller (one-time 'William Hickey' for the *Daily Express*), he moaned that 'I have to make an appointment to see Emma, she's so busy' and, asked about whether they were planning to have children, she quipped that 'Ken is so tired his sperm are on crutches.' In December 1999, at the age of 40, Emma gave birth to her first child with her new partner, actor Greg Wise.

Cambridge-educated Emma is a bit of a bluestocking, whose intelligence and wit befit the sophisticated female leads of Austen and Forster. She has left-wing leanings (attended anti-Gulf War rallies). Hampstead (long-established as the place where lefties and luvvies meet) is her ideal home.

PARENTS Mary Shelley, Judi Dench

Two-Tone

The other side of the 80s

Two-Tone records was the brainchild of Jerry Dammers, keyboard player, arranger and chief songwriter for The Specials, a multi-racial band from Coventry. The name of the label evoked both the tonic suits beloved of Jamaican rude bwoys and latterly donned by their Coventrian imitators, and the aim of multiracial harmony at a time when the National Front was winning council seats, the leader of the incoming Conservative government spoke of Britain being 'swamped' by aliens, and Specials guitarist Lynval Goulding was attacked and hospitalised by racists. While the New Right was on the march through Britain, The Specials offered liberalism with style.

The musical origins of The Specials (previously known as The Automatics) lay in the mix of punk, soul and reggae that became fashionable in the mid- to late 70s. But, when maestro Dammers tried to turn the punky reggae party into a coherent musical format, he found that the elements did not mix: the punk passages were just too fast for the reggae bits (and the beats didn't match either). As a last resort, he turned back the musical clock to the days of blue beat and ska, and grafted the up-tempo sound of early Studio One on to a Steve Jones-ish lead guitar combined with Terry Hall's little-boy-lost vocals and the proto-rapping of a Jamaican-style MC.

Born in India, Dammers was an art school graduate and the son of a Church of England missionary who returned home to be a vicar in Sheffield, south Yorkshire, and then a canon (senior cleric) in the cathedral city of Coventry, where the young Jeremy went to secondary school. His formative experience was of a boomtown (based on the car industry) going into decline, later crystallised in the 1981 hit 'Ghost Town'.

In the late 70s The Specials supported The Clash and entered talks with manager Bernie Rhodes, before opting for a different manager (Rick Rodgers) and negotiating a good deal for their own label (identified by a Two-Tone cartoon man called Walt Jabsco) with Chrysalis Records. Soon they had a roadshow and a roster of ska-based artists including Madness from north London, fellow Coventrians the Selecter and The Beat from Birmingham. There were also new acts being groomed for the Two-Tone showcase, including the kitsch Swinging Cats whose repertoire combined ska with TV theme tunes. When Dammers' gap-toothed grin (the result of a cycling accident in his early teens) appeared on the front of the first issue of **The Face**, it looked for a moment as if Britain's motor city would produce a record label to rival Detroit's Tamla Motown.

But it was a case of too much, too young. First the other bands went their separate ways. After a functional but fairly primitive first album produced in London by Elvis Costello, The Specials returned to Coventry whence they delivered a much more sophisticated platter, *More Specials*. But by this time there were tensions within the band. Three members left to form a less demanding act, The Fun Boy Three; and guitarist Roddy Radiation went back to his rockabilly roots. Under the name of The

Special AKA, Dammers released a controversial single about rape ('The Boiler') before involving himself in Artists Against Apartheid and recording the anthem 'Free Nelson Mandela'. After an accident left him with tinnitus he spent more time as a DJ with only occasional forays into playing and producing. In the 90s the other Specials reformed as a ska/80s nostalgia act but Dammers wanted nothing to do with them.

At their best, The Specials combined missionary zeal with a humorous and rhythmically sophisticated realisation of late 70s/early 80s Britain – a combination so powerful that even their sworn enemies – right-wing **skinheads** – could not help dancing to it. If British history had turned out differently, Two-Tone might have become a powerhouse for a funky kind of liberalism. In the event, the fledgling label was swamped by a social and political shift towards the New Right.

PARENTS Tamla Motown, Coventry Cathedral, Bernie Rhodes, Frederick 'Toots' Hibbert and the Maytals

The underclass
The beast within

'Millions', warned shadow home secretary Gerald Kaufman in the run-up to the 1997 general election, 'are excluded from society's benefits and they now amount to an underclass. Bitter, resentful and angry, Mrs Thatcher has created a divided nation.'

Although the term 'underclass' originated among right-wingers in the USA (notably Charles Murray, whose 1990 essay 'The Emerging British Underclass' was taken up by The Sunday Times), in Britain it was adopted by the centre-left and used to describe a new group of people who were effectively excluded from society as a consequence of rising unemployment and decreasing welfare benefits during the Thatcher years.

When Kaufman talked of Thatcher's divided nation, he was suggesting that the Labour Party could overcome social divisions and reconnect the underclass with the rest of us. But Kaufman failed to convince the British electorate, who voted the Tories back in again a few days later. They must have sensed that even the Labour Party and its theorists no longer believed they could socialise the anti-social.

The idea of groups of people impervious to wider social influences had radical roots. During the 70s various academics in fields ranging from cultural studies to criminology developed notions of culture, particularly youth culture and ethnic culture, as locations in which people could defend themselves against the homogenising pressures of mainstream society. Commentators talked of 'cultures of resistance' and praised them as places where full-on capitalist ideology could not penetrate.

By the end of the 80s, however, the same notions were acquiring a different political gloss. Alongside enthusiasm for 'cultures of resistance', apprehension arose about cultures that were resistant to moral values and civilised lifestyles. The 'underclass' entered pub talk as a tag for people who appeared to be locked into a lifetime of unemployment and – no matter what their radical social worker told them – fixed into a council estate lifestyle of video nasties, tamazepam, shellsuits, 'devil dogs', Embassy No 1 cigarettes and Tennent's Superlager. In Britain, the theoretical underpinning for the idea of the underclass was not Charles Murray's biological determinism, but a new fatalism that drew upon left-liberal traditions such as subcultural theory.

By the early 90s a cartoon version of the underclass became a convenient figure for politicians to rally British society against. In September 1994 prime minister John Major 'declared war on Britain's yob culture' and called for 'a national anti-yob culture' to combat it. With their 'back to basics' message, the Conservatives aimed to hold on to the rest of society by uniting us against the underclass. But it was their turn to sound unconvincing.

As soon as he took up office in May 1997, **Tony Blair** established the Social Exclusion Unit to ensure that everyone in Britain is fully included in British society (we have ways of making you participate). The underclass is to be abolished – official. Fatalistic ideas about uncivilised human beings are proliferating, however. Only a decade ago the uncivilised were identified as a separate group excluded from society. Nowadays the underclass is no longer out there; rather it is assumed that there is a bit of the beast – the residue of the residuum – living in each and every one of us. Compared to the idea of rational human beings that characterised the eighteenth-century Enlightenment, current definitions of human subjectivity suggest that we are all underclass now.

PARENTS residuum, reserve army of labour, lumpen proletariat

READ ON *The Making Of An English 'Underclass'?* by Kirk Mann; *Dark Heart* by Nick Davies

Wallpaper
Post-national

Founded in 1996 by American-born Tyler Brulé, *Wallpaper* is a London-based magazine (bought after a few issues by Time Warner) that appeals to urban professionals who think globally rather than nationally.

Freelance photographer Brulé was shot twice in Afghanistan. While in hospital he wondered what to do with the rest of his life, and settled on starting a magazine about interiors and travel. *Wallpaper* is about 'the stuff that surrounds you' – 'you' being 'young urban modernists'. It is an extension of fashion magazines and the style press, designed for a readership whose incomes have shot up along with their age. It is also an extension of Brulé's personality: the 'real' sets and computer-generated fantasy spaces in *Wallpaper* are derived from his personal preferences and the 'ultimate *Wallpaper* bachelor pad' in which he lives. 'It wouldn't really work,' says Brulé, 'if I was living in a trailer in Staines.'

The dominant style in *Wallpaper* is 60s corporate

Fay Weldon

American, and in some respects it is a retro-homage to what would then have been called 'the jet set'. Celebrating the idea of global travel segues into proselytising for a globalist lifestyle, in which money and taste are stronger sources of identity than nation or locality. As Brulé says of himself (and the same goes for his putative readership): 'I have more in common with someone in lower Manhattan than someone in Newcastle.'

PARENTS *Vogue, Esquire, **The Face***

Fay Weldon
Maverick among the sisters

In 1998 when novelist and scriptwriter Fay Weldon declared that rape 'isn't the worst thing that can happen to a woman', she was shouted down by feminists for whom it symbolises all the evils of patriarchy. Weldon's reputation as 'a traitor to feminism' was confirmed by the televisation (1998) of her comic novel *Big Women*, a 70s period-piece set in the offices and orifices of a women-only publishing house (based, but not too closely, on Carmen Cahil's Virago). The satirical tone was seen as almost sacrilegious.

Like Erin Pizzey, who opened the first safe house for battered women in the 70s, Weldon now believes that the attempt to raise the status of women has led to the degradation of men: 'the point of feminism was not to win, not to put men down, but to achieve equality, to be allowed to be a person first and a certain gender second. Now women diminish men in the same way that men used to diminish women.' But she denies walking out on the sisterhood: 'I can't have deserted because I was never there.'

Born Franklin Birkinshaw in Alvechurch, Worcestershire, in 1931, Fay Weldon graduated in economics and philosophy from St Andrew's University, and took a job at the Foreign Office writing 'propaganda' for the Polish desk. At 23 she became a single mother. Soon afterwards she married a headmaster 25 years her senior, then left him and hooked up with antiques dealer and jazz musician Ron Weldon. They married in 1962 and stayed together for 30 years (most of them spent in the 'airhead' county of Somerset) until he left her on the advice of a new age therapist who pronounced them 'incompatible' (he died of a stroke the day after their divorce was finalised in 1994). She considered founding Therapy Anonymous for the victims of quack counselling, but instead wrote a caustic novel, *Affliction* (1996), in which a psychotherapist steals the protagonist's husband.

In the early 60s Weldon was an advertising copywriter: she coined the phrase 'Go to work on an egg' and gave Swoop birdseed its name. From the mid-60s she wrote television plays, which she later described as 'rather like writing a long commercial, selling an idea'. Her debut novel, *The Fat Woman's Joke*, was published in 1967, the first in a darkly humorous series chronicling the sex war, of which the most widely known is *The Life And Loves Of A She-Devil* (1983; televised in Britain and then made into a Hollywood film starring Roseanne Barr as the ugly, vengeful heroine). Weldon may never have been a fully paid-up feminist (she had made a name for herself as a writer before the women's movement got going in Britain), but with its poor-quality males and superior women, during the 70s and 80s her writing fitted fairly naturally into feminist canon.

Feminists and therapists are not the only ones Weldon has offended. When the *fatwa* was issued against novelist **Salman Rushdie**, her vehement support for him prompted the anti-racist Runnymede Trust to accuse her of 'Islamophobia'. While rejecting the charge, she is certainly impatient with any form of political correctness. Asked if it is legitimate for a person coming from one culture to criticise somebody else's, her reply was straightforward: 'Yes, it fucking is.'

PARENTS Henry Fielding, Jane Austen, Aphra Behn, Evelyn Waugh
READ ON *The Life And Loves Of A She-Devil*; *Big Women*

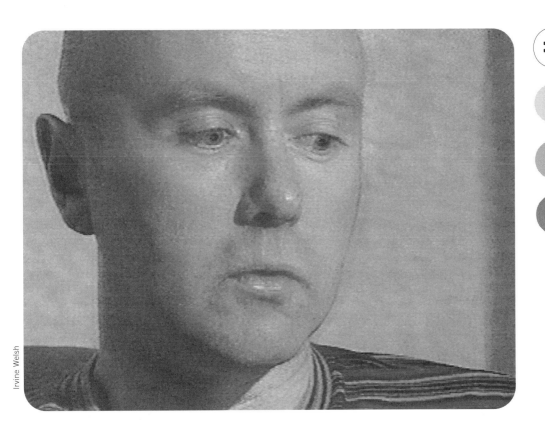

Irvine Welsh

Irvine Welsh
Laureate of the chemical generation

For many years Irvine Welsh kept mum about his family background, but it is now known that he was born in 1958 (father a docker, mother a waitress) and grew up in Muirhouse, a council housing development on the outskirts of Leith, near Edinburgh. Aged eight, he was up in court for playing football in the streets. His qualifications include a City and Guilds certificate in electrical engineering, a degree from the University of Essex and an MBA from Heriot-Watt University. Welsh made it to London just in time to be in on the punk scene. He is rumoured to have moved from punk into property, entering the 'enterprise culture' of the 80s and anticipating the boom in house prices. He now owns a flat in Edinburgh's New Town (the setting for *Shallow Grave*) and another residence in Stoke Newington.

In the late 80s Welsh returned to Muirhouse, where he worked for the local authority housing/parks department while writing short pieces that were published by Kevin Williamson in his Edinburgh imprint Rebel Inc. Some of these early fragments were subsequently incorporated into *Trainspotting* (1993) and the short stories in *The Acid House* (1994).

Welsh has described his work as a fictionalised version of the impact of drugs such as **Ecstasy** on British society, and he maintains that 'ecky culture' has provided one of the few ways to behave like co-operative human beings in an otherwise atomised society dominated by the individualism associated with prime minister Margaret Thatcher and successive Conservative governments.

Trainspotting offers a bleakly humorous take on the lowlife drug culture of Scotland's east-coast housing schemes. It is written largely in the local vernacular, but Welsh is not trying to make a point about Scottish identity – unlike James Kelman in his use of dialect. *Trainspotting* contains many descriptions of degradation without being degrading itself, and it set Welsh on the road to recognition as the literary voice of a generation. Stage and film (directed by **Danny Boyle**) versions soon appeared (with Welsh playing a bit-part in the film of his own book). The soundtrack and film poster were popular too, and in 1998 the T-shirt was said to be 'every undergraduate's favourite'.

Although *Trainspotting* centres on heroin rather than E, Welsh was bracketed with E-culture because he was clearly knowledgeable about drugs and because he seemed more in touch with contemporary dance music than with literary traditions. 'Thank fuck, along came house music,' he once said. His second novel confirmed this impression. *Marabou Stork Nightmare* (1995) explores the mind of ex-raver and former football hooligan Ray Strang while he lies in a coma tracking back to all the abuse he has given and received throughout his violent life.

Launched in a fashionable nightclub, *Ecstasy* (1997) is a collection of three tales that sold 100,000 copies in three weeks. The first story follows a Thalidomide victim (the early 60s drug that prompted deformities in the foetuses of pregnant women who were prescribed it) and her lover in their vendetta against the marketing director of the firm who manufactured it. The second instalment, 'Lorraine Goes To Hollywood', features a TV personality with a Somerset accent and a penchant for necrophilia in a relationship with an obese romantic novelist who suffers a stroke and is under the care of two nurses who are only interested in the next gig by the junglist **Goldie**. In 'The Undefeated', Welsh returns to the first-person monologue (effectively employed in *Trainspotting*) as the format in which to tell the story of Heather, a suburban housewife who swaps home and husband for the **rave** scene.

Filth (1998) follows bigoted, sadistic 'bad bastard' Edinburgh policeman Bruce Robertson who pretends to investigate the murder of a Ghanian journalist while sleeping with every woman he meets, dosing himself with cocaine and malt whisky, listening to heavy metal (Welsh says he hopes *Filth* never gets filmed because the soundtrack would be unlistenable), wanking, scratching his itchy prick and farting (he refers to his anal emissions as 'Dame Judi Denches' – Welsh always likes to *épater* the arts crowd). In *The Times*, reviewer Scott Bradfield dubbed it 'a touch too scotological', and observed that Welsh 'often works so hard at shocking his readers that he puts himself in the unenviable position of having to beat himself at his own game'. The *London Evening Standard* review of Welsh's play *You'll Have Had Your Hole* (opened in London in February 1999) adopted a similar stance: 'this calculatingly nasty stage play … comes to London brandishing its infamy like a victory banner'. Welsh replied to criticism by saying that the established theatre is moribund; but the play closed after a few weeks, ostensibly because one of the main actors had slipped a disc.

Behind all the violence and bodily fluids, Welsh's work usually exhibits a strong sense of tightening guilt and the imminent judgement of crimes past (in 'The Granton Star Cause', one of *The Acid House* stories, God himself does the judging). This is fully in accordance with a Scottish literary tradition that goes back to RL Stevenson and James Hogg.

Welsh has denied that the degenerate protagonist of *Filth* constitutes an attack on the police, who are 'in the impossible situation of having to police antiquated laws … the social fabric has been ripped up and the police are not the appropriate organisation to try and hold all that together'.

Opposed to Thatcher and now **Tony Blair**, he believes that Britain is awash with 'negative energy' and that's what fuels his writing. But he has also said that 'I don't give a toss about writing, really. It's a bit ironic that the things I'm into are music and football [he supports Hibernian, Edinburgh's Catholic team], and I have never really been good at either.' He did, however, make a single with **Primal Scream** which went to No 17, even though it was barred from the airwaves. Of his dalliance with music and his career as a lad-mag columnist, Welsh has said: 'It's not so much a delayed adolescence as a prolonged one, because I've never really grown up beyond a certain point.'

It remains uncertain whether Welsh has ever used heroin himself (some accounts have him as a former junkie), but his descriptions of heroin use are generally regarded as accurate by those who do. His reputation rests, however, not so much on factual accuracy (although this never goes amiss) as on his ability to mix and match voices and genres in a manner he himself has compared to a DJ mixing music.

Welsh's success ('the novel went supernova', he says of *Trainspotting*) prompted a wave of imitators and a whole new style of bookselling. Realising that Welsh held the key to a demographic cohort of potential readers whom they had so far failed to connect with, publishers began to package books as if they were post-E CDs, and instead of Aga-sagas started to offer an expanding range of street-sharp tales of sex, drugs and rock'n'roll. But in producing and marketing a cash'n'carry version of Welsh's world, they may have made it as formulaic and ultimately as safe as the traditional Aga-tale of adultery in Barbour-land. The brand name of Irvine Welsh is now so bankable that his launch parties are featured in society pages.

PARENTS RL Stevenson, James Hogg,
Alexander Trocchi, Hibs, Rave,
CHILDREN the new wannabe-streetwise BritLit

Vivienne Westwood
Glam Gran

Fashion designer Vivienne Westwood (b. 1941) is the pensioner (nearly) who does not wear knickers; the OBE (1992) who impersonated Margaret Thatcher for a picture in the *Tatler* and put bare bottoms on the catwalk; the 'major English artist' who was laughed at on *Wogan* (BBC1); 'one of the six most influential designers ever' who was twice passed over for the top job at Dior – on the second occasion she lost out to a designer (**Galliano**) 23 years her junior. An instinctive rebel, in the mid-70s Westwood, along with her (then) partner **Malcolm McLaren**, invented the look that became punk. But she has also stayed true to the glam and glitter her ballroom-dancing parents loved so much (her father died in 1985 while on the dancefloor with her mother).

Vivienne Isabel Swire was born in the Derbyshire village of Tintwistle, near Glossop, where her parents ran the post office. She won a place at Glossop Grammar School and made her own Suzy Wong-style dresses for school dances on Friday nights. When her parents moved south to Stanmore, on the west side of London, Vivienne went too. She soon became friends with one Malcolm Edwards (McLaren), a contemporary at Harrow Art School of her brother, Gordon. Although Vivienne was already married (Derek Westwood, July 1962), she soon became involved – professionally as well as romantically – with McLaren.

Westwood's first merchandise was the jewellery she made and sold on the Portobello Road at the end of the 60s. Sales were poor and sometimes she and McLaren ate dandelion salad. In 1971 they hired the back part of a shop at 430 King's Road, and called it Let it Rock. Here they sold second-hand ted clothes (repaired by Westwood), and started to make new outfits (jackets were contracted out to East End tailor Sid Green). Westwood's first big break was the commission to make costumes for the film *That'll Be The Day* (1973).

Two years later they switched to a biker look and renamed the shop Too Fast To Live, Too Young To Die; but this came to a swift end. It was replaced by SEX – a crossbreed of biker and fetishwear with the slogo 'rubberwear for the office'. The idea was 'to do the *Rocky Horror Show* [Richard O'Brien's Gothic sex musical] for real'. Future-Sex Pistol Glenn Matlock and future-punk Jordan were SEX workers. Westwood was prosecuted for a T-shirt featuring two, trouserless cowboys whose dicks were nearly touching.

In 1976 the King's Road shop changed again, from SEX to Seditionaries (slogo: 'seduce people

Weird TV

The fairground freak show has returned to British culture in the form of TV slots and whole programmes dedicated to the weird, freakish and bizarre:

- *The Word* didn't look for new talent, only for people prepared to do grotesque things to themselves in order to get two minutes on TV.
- **Chris Evans'** Freak or Unique?, ditto.
- Clive James and **Chris Tarrant** prefer foreign weirdness, preferably Japanese.
- *Eurotrash* shows that Britons are not the only eccentrics.
- Louis Theroux tours the world playing the British straight man confronted by foreign weirdos.
- Jon Ronson introduced a weirdos' chatshow, *For The Love Of*.
- Jarvis Cocker introduced a weirdos' art show, Outsider Art.
- *Mysteries With Carol Vorderman* packaged weirdness as investigation.
- *Dave Courtney and his Con-Men Friends*, Channel 5's gangster chic chatshow.
- *The Graham Norton Show* takes a peek at the freak show on the Internet.

into revolt'). Westwood was using lots of tartan accessorised with safety pins, razors and silver phalluses. Minus phalluses (punks never cared that much for sex) and plus bondage gear, which **John**(ny Rotten) **Lydon** insists he invented after he enjoyed being photographed in a straitjacket, this was the look that launched a thousand pogos.

When the Sex Pistols fell apart and McLaren went off to Paris to recuperate, Westwood travelled in a different direction. Her new method was to disregard what was going on around her and trawl through the history of fashion for inspiration. In the two decades since then Westwood has sampled from half a dozen centuries. Depending on how you look at it, hers is either an impressively broad approach or a bad case of history-lite.

In 1979 Westwood unveiled the eighteenth-century pirate look made famous by Adam Ant (another of McLaren's protégés). In 1981 she experimented with ethnic dress and produced the Savage collection, following this up in 1982 with the Buffalo look, featuring Bolivian women's dresses with bras worn on the outside. Her London shop, Nostalgia of Mud, was decorated with wooden maps of Africa. She also opened for business in Milan. She based her 1983 Witches collection on Haitian Voodoo. After it was featured in *Vogue*, Westwood was asked to design a collection for the

Italian couture house Fiorucci (**Rod Stewart**'s favourite fashion label). Her next collection, Hypnosis, featured sportswear fabrics. In October 1984 she introduced the Mini Crini (crinoline), an idea that was taken up by Lacroix and Versace. In 1987 she declared that 'Britain must go pagan': her new collection featured clothes slashed in the style of the Middle Ages. In 1989, as part of Pagan 5, she designed a body suit with a gold fig leaf.

In the meantime she had experimented with a classic tailored look (Time Machine, spring 1988) and the rococo style of Civilizade (autumn 1998). In the 1990 Portrait collection she tried cross-dressing, and in 1991 she won the British designer of the year award for the second time running. In 1992 her collection included six-inch platform shoes, and **Naomi Campbell** was wearing nine-inch Westwood heels when, in March the following year, she slipped and fell down on the catwalk. Westwood's 1994 collection, Erotic Zones, brought back the bustle. After some financial difficulties in the 80s, she opened a shop in Mayfair in 1990, simply entitled Vivienne Westwood. She now has three shops in London and several abroad selling her Gold Label and Red Label clothes. Annual turnover (overseen by husband Andreas Kronthaler, 'opposite to Malcolm') is more than £10 million.

Like a child, Westwood rifles through the drawers of fashion history. Yet she also has a mature, traditional side, reflected in her preference for wool, tweed, tartan and linen. She is both the *grande dame* and the *enfant terrible* of the British clothing industry. The fact that this same nearly-sixtysome-thing can play both roles indicates that there is no longer a generation gap in British culture.

PARENTS *Come Dancing*, costume drama
READ ON *Fashion+Perversity* by Fred Vermorel

Marco Pierre White
First among British superchefs

In Britain before the late 80s there was no such thing a 'foodie'. Eating was just something you had to do occasionally, like going to the lavatory. And a chef was a lowly figure who did women's work for money. Large (6ft 3ins) and loud, macho Marco Pierre White changed all that.

Born (1962) on a council estate in Leeds, Marco Pierre White (his hybrid name reflects the Italian, French and English roots of his family) left school at 16 to be a kitchen boy at the St George hotel in Harrogate, preparing 130 breakfasts every day. His big break came when Albert Roux invited him to work at the famous London restaurant, La Gavroche. In 1987 White opened his own place, Harvey's in Wandsworth. The timing was right (Labour lost another election that year; yuppiedom was still in the ascendant) and so was the location (Wandsworth was the south-London borough that turned Tory and went upwardly mobile). Harvey's acquired two Michelin stars and White got a reputation for ostentatious behaviour on both sides of the kitchen door: flirting with customers' girlfriends in the dining room and throwing pans in the kitchen. He was also known for showing customers the door if they asked for a well-done steak. Later in his career he was famous for bust-ups with business partners, including **Michael Caine** and **Damien Hirst**. Of his tantrums White has said: 'I was like a serial killer. Once I got the taste for it I couldn't stop.'

But White's supernova public persona would have been a flash in the pan without the culinary skills to match. At the Forte-owned Hyde Park Hotel he won his third Michelin star (afterwards he felt depressed, like there was nothing left to do). White takes classic dishes (beef in red wine, tuna with tomato and basil) and does them better than anyone else. His cooking is unostentatious: it is meant to taste good rather than look good; and he says his mother taught him to 'keep it simple'. White-the-showman is appropriately immodest in his contempt for fancy, fusion food – 'for people who are confused'. An enemy of middlebrow cooking, he avers that 'Harry Ramsden, Pizza Hut and Kentucky Fried Chicken serve better food than most restaurants in London.'

In partnership with Granada, White part-owns the Cafe Royal, The Criterion, Quo Vadis (originally bedecked with the work of Damien Hirst, White replaced Hirst's pieces with his own daubs and planned to put a plaque on the wall next to the one that says Karl Marx lived there), MPW at Canary Wharf, and the Oak Room at Le Meridien. The Mirabelle and Titanic (a venture repeatedly troubled by litigation) are also his. A man of passion (two divorces, now living in Chelsea with his girlfriend and two sons), he walks the line: never drank (father 'an alcoholic'), gave up coffee and smoking after collapsing with high blood pressure, drinks mineral water to keep on the right side of his stomach ulcer. In 1999 he also announced his retirement from cooking in order to concentrate on the tricky job of managing his restaurant empire.

According to *The Sunday Times*, White is worth £30 million. Both his rages and his finesse helped make eating a credible, contemporary British activity – not just something for people who are too old to drink and take drugs.

PARENTS Albert Roux, Peter Langan
CHILDREN Gordon Ramsay

Paul Whitehouse

'full-on prole from the Rhondda Valley'

Born in Wales in 1959, Paul Whitehouse was working as a plasterer when he co-wrote the Stavros sketches for **Harry Enfield**. The Greek kebab cook was one of the hits of the **Ben Elton**-hosted mid-80s variety show *Saturday Night Live*. Whitehouse also helped develop Enfield's Loadsamoney character and went on to write for Vic **Reeves** before going front-of-camera for the first time as one of *Harry Enfield and Chums*, in which his most famous persona is DJ Dave 'Nicey' Nice.

After a decade in Enfield's shadow, Whitehouse took top billing, along with novelist and former pop musician Charlie Higson, in *The Fast Show* (BBC2).

Renowned for the 'Suits You, Sir' gentlemen's out-fitters (Enfield had turned them down), and for the 'theatrical depth' of characters such as Ron Manager and Rowley Birkin QC, this was a sketch show with a different pattern of editing. Inspired by a compilation tape put together for the press launch of the second Harry Enfield series, Whitehouse and Higson decided to do a whole show in quick bursts: 'We didn't want to do anything revolutionary. We were just fed up with sketches taking too long.' Furthermore, instead of showing four sections of a sketch in the course of a single programme, Whitehouse and Higson ran their sketches in six parts over a whole series, thus requiring the audience to keep watching each week. The unusual combination of quick-fire, continuity and characterisation made *The Fast Show* into the TV comedy hit of the late 90s. Like Enfield he creates well-observed social types that need little more than a catchphrase to announce everything you need to know about them ('Brilliant!', 'Hardest game in the world' and so on). And like all great comic creations, their simplicity is deceptive, making them as popular in the office as they are in the school playground.

PARENTS George Grossmith, the Ramones

Richard Whiteley
The schoolmaster with no authority

Richard Whiteley is the host of Yorkshire TV's word-and-sums game *Countdown*, the only non-news show to have been broadcast continually since the launch of Channel 4 in November 1982. With his ill-chosen ties, puppy-dog expression and ineffectual banter, Whiteley resembles a bumbling schoolmaster – the sort who only makes it to the end of the lesson because his students allow him to. But his show is compulsory – and compulsive – viewing for thousands of students, who watch it more often than they attend lectures. The timing is crucial: *Countdown* comes on at that teatime moment when everyone wants to feel cosy and comfortable – the television equivalent of nursery food.

Born (1944) into a mill-owning family (sold in the 60s), Whiteley was an unathletic boy ('my mother never had to wash my shorts') and a shy teenager who never had a partner for the last waltz at his mum's charity balls. After attending Giggleswick boarding school (English teacher: Russell Harty) in the Yorkshire Dales (his father went there in the 20s), in 1962 he went up to Cambridge (Christ's) where he edited *Varsity* magazine but gained only a third-class degree. This was enough to get him into ITN as a trainee. Aged 29 he moved back to home territory with the fledgling Yorkshire TV, where he co-hosted a local news show (*Calendar*) with future MP Austin Mitchell.

Apart from Whiteley's atrocious choice of clothes, his face 'like a cartoonist's suicide note' and his hair that looks like a wig but isn't (or is it?), one of *Countdown*'s key elements is his relationship with Carol Vorderman, the 'dominatrix' of the scoreboard. Where he is bumbling ('There is no script, I make it all up as I go along. … I go hot and cold when I watch'), Vorderman is precise and in control. When Whiteley appeared on *The Mrs Merton Show*, she asked him whether his marriage to Carol had been consummated yet. But the bond between them is as much like mother and son as husband and wife. The imbalance between the two of them fits in perfectly with the perceived immaturity of today's men and the proficiency of post-feminist women: it is *Men Behaving Badly* without the rag-mag jokes.

Not all *Countdown* fans are students. 'I love *Countdown*', Stephen Fry told Whiteley. 'I go home at half-four, put my feet on a little pouf, and switch it on.' Dickie Bird discovered *Countdown* on Indian TV while umpiring test matches out there. Football managers ring each other up to compare scores. Even Matthew Parris' revelation that the celebrity guests are given the answers, has failed to reduce its following. This is not so surprising when you consider that *Countdown* is a quiz show in name only: it hinges on Whiteley's cuddly character, with just a tangy hint of discipline from Ms Vorderman.

PARENTS Scrabble, maths tests
CHILDREN *Never Mind The Buzzcocks*

Who
Violent, narcissistic, comic, clever

An early edition of the *Observer* colour supplement carried a cover feature on the Who and a picture of Pete Townshend (guitar, backing vocals, songwriter) with rows of smashed guitars hung like paintings on the wall behind him. Amp-bashing, guitar-smashing, on-stage violence was Townshend's transposition of 'autodestruction', the attempt by his art teacher Gustav Metzger to make creative use of destructive tendencies. The Who's violent displays were always arty, never boorish.

Townshend was the pale Ealing Art School boy who felt embarrassed about his big nose and who needed lead singer Roger Daltrey's working-class narcissism. It was Daltrey, the Face with the golden hair, who put the High Numbers (as they were originally known) in touch with the emerging west-London **Mod** scene. He made the Who's violence into something dangerous, not effete. Just when Daltrey's self-regard bordered on bathos, super-clown Keith Moon was there to upstage and undercut him. Moon's manic visage was as important to the Who as Daltrey-the-Face; and his antics, such as driving a Cadillac into a swimming pool on his 21st birthday, made him a media legend (a legend that culminated in his death-by-overdose on 28 August 1978, his 31st birthday). Incidentally, his crazed-but-crisp playing turned the drums into a lead instrument.

The Who were hyper-smart. Managers Kit Lambert and Chris Stamp were men-about-town who knew that pop had to be clever and that the Who could make it so. Even their name was a play on words ('Have you heard this new band, the Who?' 'The Who?' 'Yeah, the Who.'), and a pop-art abstraction. The same goes for their record label, Track (record track/track record). *The Who Sell Out* (1967) was the earliest 'concept' album, and the first pop record to satirise the media business (complete with cover shots of Daltrey in a bath of baked beans and Townshend with a giant can of deodorant under his arm) of music (**Bowie**'s *Ziggy Stardust* followed on from this). Just when the whole thing started to look clever-clever, there was bass player John Entwhistle, known as 'the Ox': expressionless, motionless, emotionless; seemingly as stupid as his nickname suggested, but making the smartest move by acting dumb.

For **Jon Savage**, the 'foppish violence' of the Who 'defined the paradox of British pop'. In their earliest incarnation, playing 'maximum r'n'b' as the High Numbers, they delved inside the mindset of Mod and came up with the industrial-strength braggadaccio of 'I'm The Face' and, latterly, 'My Generation' (banned by the BBC for being 'detrimental to stutterers'). By this time (1965) they were camping it up in Union Jack jackets (simultaneously rejecting and repackaging patriotism), and Townshend's new songs put self-deprecation on a par with self-aggrandisement ('Substitute', 'Pictures of Lily' – surely the first top 5 single about masturbation).

During the dopey, hippie years at the end of the 60s, the Who's amphetamine-driven sharpness seemed out of kilter. With the 'rock opera' *Tommy*

(1971, filmed by Ken Russell in 1975), Townshend tried to grow up and only partially succeeded. He combined spiritual leanings (his guru was Meher Baba) with the back-to-basics rock of *Live at Leeds*. In 1973 the Who issued *Quadrophenia*, an older man's evocation of the life of an adolescent Mod. It was an attempt both to recapture and to understand what had created youth culture. But the new youth culture of the mid-70s – punk – did not want to know. The fact that Townshend had never played solos (right-arm revolving like a windmill, his rhythm playing was the benchmark for 'power chords') did not stop him being dismissed along with all the other fallen guitar heroes and 'rock dinosaurs'. But the vituperative spirit of punk had run out of bad breath by 1978 and, soon afterwards, the Who were welcomed back as the Ur-band of the burgeoning Mod revival. The 1979 release of documentary film-maker Franc Roddam's version of *Quadrophenia* (starring the 19-year-old Phil Daniels), hailed by then *NME* editor Neil Spencer as 'the best British rock film ever', confirmed their position as one of the essential templates in the recurrent recycling that characterises British culture during the last 25 years.

PARENTS James Brown, Jackson Pollock, **The Beatles**
CHILDREN **The Jam**, **Blur**

Robbie Williams

F Scott Fitzgerald meets George Formby

Distracted by drink (favourite tipple – vodka; party trick – four pints of Guinness down in one) and charlie (he asked **Elton John** how to give up), and damaged by his own demons (he talks about 'protecting myself from myself'), chain-smoking singer Robbie Williams recalls fallen heroes of the Lost Generation such as F Scott Fitzgerald. But this Romantic *persona* is offset by a cheeky grin and the self-assigned role of 'an entertainer' (signature tune: 'Let Me Entertain You'). Robbie Williams does not play a ukelele, but this other side of him points towards a latter-day George Formby.

When the archetypal boy band Take That broke up, 'joker' Robbie Williams was tipped for trouble. The tabloid headlines kept coming: 'Robbie in drink and drug crisis'; 'Ruin of a teen idol'; 'Robbie: I'm so scared and confused'. 'I was going to the opening of a letter,' the singer later recalled. His period as a party animal was really a cry for help. After a spell in rehab, Williams got down to work (a substantial schedule of recording and touring: 'he's got work muscles', observes co-writer and musical director Guy Chambers), bought and furnished a house, and found himself a fiancée (Nicole Appleton of All Saints, the sub-**Spice Girls**). But a few months later Williams was once more 'drinking a lot – and it's not working'. His name was back in the gossip columns and, after one lapse too many, Appleton walked out. Alone again. So alone he had to blab about it to 22,000 fans at the Newcastle Arena (February 1999): 'I want to talk about Nikki,' he told the crowd. 'I had drinks, fags and women but it wasn't enough. But she still told me to get lost.'

In British pop culture, getting 'lost' is associated with the Neurotic Boy Outsider, **Peter York**'s descriptor of the rake-thin rebel figure whose customary alienation from society is symbolised in his personal pain and suffering. But Robbie is rotund ('I felt like a fat bastard'), not emaciated, nor does he show signs of feeling alienated from society. In his personal life he likes to be 'dead comfy', and on stage he just wants to clown around. 'I really don't see myself as a singer,' he once said. With that impish grin, a slightly goofy look and an undisguised provincial accent (Stoke-on-Trent), Williams really is as much like Formby as Fitzgerald. 'I know I'm incredibly naff but very cool at the same time,' he says. Nor, observes journalist and author Chris Heath, is this a temporary state of affairs: 'Generally, if people are in this kind of predicament, somewhere between cool and naff, it is because they are in the process of crossing the bridge between cool and naff. Most people are quite happy to swap the magnetic allure of the born entertainer for the poetic soul of the true artist. But it's different with Robbie. As deep as you go, and however long you study those half-sad, half-glinting eyes, it's the same. He's cool to the very core and he's naff to the very core.'

'I'm not Leonard Cohen, I'm an entertainer,' Williams declares, and in this capacity his role model seems to be his father, a publican and comedian who won the ITV talent show *New Faces*.

Another role model might be Elton John, but the latter spent a few years hanging out with **John Peel** and assorted hippies before entering the world of family entertainment. Williams, on the other hand, has been in showbiz all along (from the age of 15 when he landed a job in the manufactured Take That); and no amount of drugs and personal pain can make him into a rebel figure.

On the one hand Williams symbolises the end of the generation gap and the demise of British pop music as something symbolising rebellion. On the other hand, the sense of being pained by the world, once a characteristic exclusive to Romantics and the counter-culture, is now over-the-counter-culture and as mainstream as … Robbie Williams. The lyrics to his hit 'Angels' (about being 'really fucked up' but knowing 'there's something with me') are so widely known that at live concerts he lets the audience sing the whole song. *The Face* made him its 'man of the year: no contest' (1998), *Company* magazine asked whether he is 'the most loved man in the world'; and at the Brits in February 1999, Williams picked up a bucketload of awards. The resonance for Robbie shows that cool/naff, Fitzgerald/Formby is a combination that millions of people are currently keen to identify with.

PARENTS Take That, Elton John
READ ON *The Face*, January 1999, September 1999, October 1995

443

Tony Wilson
Motivated motormouth

The fiftysomething man whose day job was co-presenter of *Granada Reports* (local news programme in the north-west), who was the first person to introduce the Sex Pistols on TV (*So It Goes*, 1976), who founded Factory Records (a music factory, geddit?), in the heart of industrial Manchester, the city Fredrick Engels chronicled in his book *The Condition Of The Working Class*; a record company complete with radical, libertarian/egalitarian manifesto) and fronted **The Haçienda**, who sold **Madchester** to the world, who held the **Happy Mondays** together for as long as he could, who missed The Smiths (they played the Haçienda while still unsigned) and turned down **Oasis** (too baggy), Anthony H Wilson describes himself as 'a typical Charles Dickens hero, an irrelevant cipher in the middle, with energy', and as 'a groovy entrepreneur and heterosexual Brian Epstein'. A Cambridge graduate with a radical past (Situationism), Wilson courts controversy and once said that the students in Tiananmen Square 'were an example of youth culture, but I actually have a lot of sympathy for the Chinese leadership. … I would have shot them.' A smoothie himself (smart clothes, glossy hair, fast car, confident manner), he loves a bit of rough, working-class stuff – as demonstrated by his affection for the Happy Mondays.

Wilson compared the end of the 90s to the beginning of the 70s: a period in pop where nothing much was happening. But his faith in the eventual arrival of the Next Big Thing remains unshakeable. Although keen to distinguish himself from 'a bleeding liberal like Kate Adie' (hence his remarks about Tiananmen Square), like many liberal baby-boomers he has always believed that pop really matters; as self-expression and, above all, as a form of rebellion. Compared to the lower expectations of subsequent generations, Wilson's belief in music and its significance (as well as himself) is enjoyably over the top.

PARENTS Brian Epstein, Guy Débord

Barbara Windsor
Britain's landlady

Born (1938) in Stoke Newington, London (about 50 years before it became fashionable), diminutive (4ft 10ins) Barbara 'Babs' Windsor is famous for her boobs, bottom (winner of the first British Bottom of the Year award in 1976) and brassiness. After decades as the real-life version of a saucy, seaside postcard by Donald McGill, she now presides over the Queen Vic pub in *EastEnders*.

Windsor describes her own life as 'a cross between a **Carry On** and **Joe Orton**': born Barbara-Anee Deeks, she changed her name at the time of Elizabeth Windsor's coronation. Rejected by her bus conductor father, she attended a convent school before making her West End debut aged 15. In the 50s she divided her time between cabaret singing and clubs (appearing with Victor Spinetti; frequently booked into El Toro's on the Finchley Road, some gigs at Ronnie Scott's new jazz club), and Joan Littlewood's Theatre Workshop in Stratford, London E15 (Littlewood directed and devised plays primarily for a local, working-class audience; Windsor played the lead in Littlewood's film comedy about working-class life in London, *Sparrows Can't Sing*, 1962). She went on to become a fixture in the Carry On films (Babs in nurse's uniform with her bottom in the air, Babs in bra and pants …) and a regular in panto before landing the part (1995) of landlady Peggy Mitchell in *EastEnders*.

Peggy soon became romantically involved with a gangster. For Windsor, this was familiar territory. Having been engaged to a succession of suitors (Bing Crosby's son, Gary; a stallholder from Leather Lane; a jazz musician), she married Ronnie Knight, a well known face among the criminal fraternity, who first approached her by driving slowly past in a flash car as she walked up the street. Their marriage lasted 20 years. In a scene more from Joe Orton than a Carry On, shortly after Knight was acquitted on a murder charge, all Windsor's jewellery (except for some worry beads) was stolen from her house by robbers who left 'a pair of my drawers laid out on the bed. Ugh'. A veteran of five abortions, Windsor had affairs with Charlie Kray and Sid James, married an actor 20 years her junior (Stephen Hollings, now divorced) and currently lives alone in a mews house in Marylebone while dating a 50-year-old restaurateur. Kenneth Williams once asked her to marry him but she turned him down flat ('bugger you, then') when the repressed gay Carry On actor told her 'there'd be no sex'.

Windsor endows the breast cancer-sufferer character of Peggy Mitchell with her reputation as a former sex symbol (still the top-selling icon on Ann Summers underwear) who was never taken seriously. Her baby eyes (even with bags under them) and small but shapely frame represent Britain's giggly attitude to sex (you can only talk about sex if you make a joke out of it). This approach is almost an anachronism now – and so, in this particular respect, is Windsor herself. But in another aspect she is only now coming into her moment. Back in the early 60s, when *Sparrows Can't Sing* was being made, the pub scenes were a comic reflection of traditional, social life. Today's East End pubs are all but deserted, and the punters who might once have filled them are more likely to be having a drink at home while watching Landlady Barbara Windsor on TV. The set of the Queen Vic is more of a common focus than any number of real pubs, and Windsor's role is no longer merely to reflect our lives but also to act as a form of mediation between atomised individuals.

PARENTS Nell Gwynne, Jean Harlow, Gracie Fields
CHILDREN Sarah Cox, Denise Van Outen

Jeanette Winterson

The Hemingway of lesbianism

Jeanette Winterson's biological parents are unknown to her; she says she feels no urge to find out who they are. In 1959, at the age of six weeks, she was adopted by the couple whose surname she bears. Her adoptive father worked in a television factory. Jeanette grew up in a terraced house in Accrington, Lancashire, but her upbringing was hardly run of the mill. The Wintersons were Elim Pentecostalists, members of a religious sect which holds that every single word in the Bible is absolutely true. Did this make her a believer or an atheist? 'God,' she says, 'is so tattooed on me that I can't but believe in him.'

At 16, Winterson was found in bed with another woman, a fish-filleter, and denounced by her local church. Forced to leave home, she did A-levels at the nearby technical college and kept herself by working in an ice cream parlour and an undertaker's. Refused a place at Oxford, she herself refused to believe it. 'You must let me in,' she told the dons, and they found room for her at St Catherine's where she read English.

After taking an undistinguished degree, Winterson did a series of jobs in London: editorial assistant for Brilliant Books; a few weeks as a trainee stockbroker; odd-jobber at the feminist publishing house Pandora Press, where her first major book was published. Around this time she took payment for sex (not in money but in Le Creuset saucepans). With the help of literary agent

Pat Kavanagh, who became her lover, Winterson found a quiet place in which to write – the shed at the bottom of crime writer Ruth Rendell's garden. Less than two decades later, having published half a dozen mostly well received books, Winterson now has a 'hovel' of her own, standing in the field behind the Gloucestershire house she shares with academic and broadcaster Peggy Reynolds. Winterson also owns a property in the recently revamped district of Spitalfields, just over the road from Liverpool Street station on the east side of the City of London. In 1992 she informed readers of the *Guardian*: 'Unless I take to gambling in Las Vegas, it's very unlikely I'll be poor again.' She is intensely proud of having made it to centre stage of the British literary scene, all the way from a background she regards as materially, intellectually and culturally deprived.

In the 80s Winterson was prolific. Her juvenilia are the comic novel *Boating for Beginners* (1985; secondhand copies now fetch £100) and a fitness manual *Fit For The Future* (1986). The novel that made her name was *Oranges Are Not The Only Fruit* (winner of the Whitbread Award for first novel in 1985, televised by the BBC in 1989), which Winterson has insisted is not autobiographical but which most reviewers interpreted as a thinly veiled account of her own formative years.

The protagonist of *The Passion* (1987; awarded the John Llewellyn Rhys Prize) is the bisexual, web-footed daughter of a nineteenth-century gondolier. *Sexing The Cherry* (1989), another novel of lesbian love, won the EM Forster Award. The explicitly erotic *Written On The Body* (1992) features a narrator whose gender is 'ambiguous' (but without a penis), and was widely assumed to be a disguised account of Winterson's own amorous adventures. In 1995 Winterson published a non-fiction collection, *Art Objects*: essays on ecstasy and effrontery. *Gut Symmetries* (1997), a love triangle between two women and a man on the QE2 passenger liner, was the first Winterson novel to receive a bad press. In 1998 she worked on a film script of *The Passion* and completed a collection of short stories, *The World And Other Places*. This too was panned by some critics. In *The Sunday Times*, under the heading 'a large helping of baloney', Peter Kemp compared her current 'pantomime presence' with the first story she ever wrote: 'It stands here, in its quirky vitality, as a reminder that she was once an author to reckon with. The reminder is sadly needed.'

Winterson has been criticised for writing almost exclusively about her own milieu. 'Her true understanding of the human heart is confined to passionate love between women – spirited, beautiful women at that,' complained one reviewer. Her extraordinary self-confidence has also prompted criticism. When asked to name the living writer she liked best, Winterson replied: 'No one working in the English language now comes close to my exuberance, my passion and fidelity to words.' Modest she ain't, but her numerous supporters believe that she has talent enough to warrant her arrogance. Gore Vidal, the grandaddy of modern gay writing, dubbed her 'the most interesting young writer I have read in 20 years'. BBC broadcaster Joan Bakewell reckons that even when Winterson makes

a 'mess of a book', as with *Gut Symmetries*, she is sill 'scintillating … a real writer'. On the other hand the conservative critic Allan Massie holds that Winterson-the-persona gets in the way of Winterson-the-writer. Besides being saddened by the burial of 'her talent beneath the froth of pretentious verbiage', Massie compared her to Hemingway in that during 'the past few years she has become more famous for what she is, and is taken to represent, than for what she writes'. But, as with Hemingway, it is hard to see how Winterson the woman, the myth and the writer could ever be separated.

PARENTS Ernest Hemingway, Radclyffe Hall, Virginia Woolf
READ ON *Oranges Are Not The Only Fruit*

Peter York
Wide ranger

Peter York is the *nom de plume* of Peter Wallis (b. 1946), head honcho of top-notch marketing and management consultancy SRU (clients include Levi's, EMI, Kingfisher and WHSmith; former employees include Peter Mandelson). Brought up in a leftish, Hampstead household, he speaks with an accent that could cut marble, never mind glass. His handsome face is topped off with thick, dark hair; and his suits are so classic that he leaves the **royal family** looking like *nouveaux riches* (he used to wear zoot suits and winkle-pickers, but adopted a more sober style in his early forties). York's detractors claim that he is too formal (when he dances he is 'stiff in all the wrong places') and that his cultural commentary is as over-written as his elegant frame is over-dressed.

York's first collection of essays was *Style Wars* (1980), largely drawn from pieces previously published in *Harper's & Queen* (without ever learning to type, he spent ten years there as 'style editor'). It told the story of the transition from punk to Thatcher, exposing the class alliances and antagonisms beneath the dressing up. These articles also showed that York was a close observer (if not quite an active participant) in the low-life of punk. He followed it with the *Official Sloane Ranger Handbook* (1981), co-written with Ann Barr, which demonstrated the other side of York's/Wallis' double life: his intimate knowledge of the kind of people who were so well off and so well established that they did not have to pay attention to fashion.

If *Style Wars* was an account of the changes in British society as reflected in pop culture, the *Official Sloane Ranger Handbook* was a tourist's guide to the continuities in British upper-class life: 'Sloane Rangerhood is a state of mind that's eternal. You might believe it's all different now, that nobody's like that anymore. You'd be wrong.' Barr and York summed up their collaborative effort as 'the handbook of … the eternal stream of English life'.

It might have been 'eternal' then; but it is doubtful whether even the environs of SW3 and SW7 are safe from the further transformation of British society that occurred in the 90s.

During the 80s York was something of a mentor to **Julie Burchill** and her (then) husband Cosmo Landesman. In the mid-90s he made a six-part documentary series, *The 80s*, which was widely disliked because it failed to abide by the 90s etiquette which insists that ambition is a deadly sin. The series might have been York's finest hour, but it was buried under a weight of fashionable prejudice. Meanwhile York is biding his time and writing an intelligent weekly column on advertising for the *Independent on Sunday*. He is adamant that the 90s in Britain were a straightforward 'continuation of the 80s'.

PARENTS Tom Wolfe, Terence Conran, Dorothy Parker
READ ON *Style Wars*, *The 80s*